Silver Burdett Ginn

Mathematics

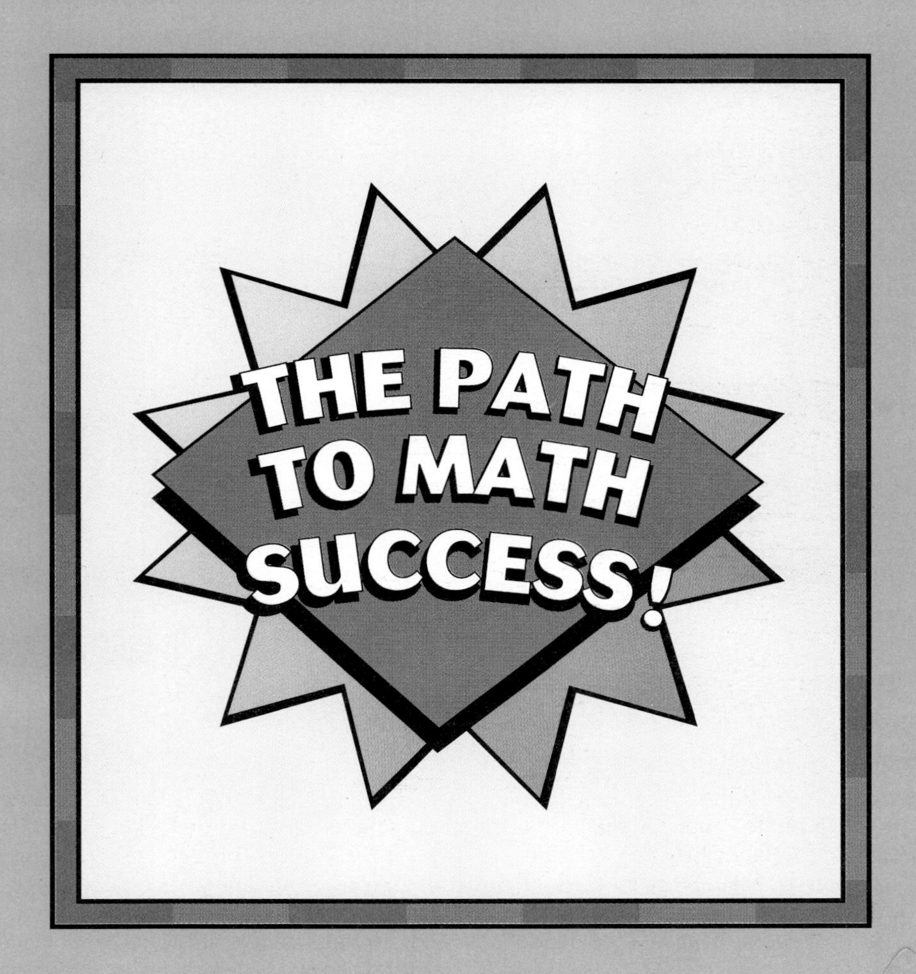

Silver Burdett G
Parsippany, NJ • Nee
Atlanta, GA • Deerfield, IL • Irvin

Program Authors

Francis (Skip) Fennell, Ph.D.
Professor of Education and
Chair, Education Department
Western Maryland College
Westminster, Maryland

Joan Ferrini-Mundy, Ph.D.
Professor of Mathematics
University of New Hampshire
Durham, New Hampshire

Herbert P. Ginsburg, Ph.D.
Professor of Psychology and
Mathematics Education
Teachers College, Columbia University
New York, New York

Carole Greenes, Ed.D.
Professor of Mathematics Education and
Associate Dean, School of Education
Boston University
Boston, Massachusetts

Stuart J. Murphy
Visual Learning Specialist
Evanston, Illinois

William Tate, Ph.D.
Associate Professor of
Mathematics Education
University of Wisconsin-Madison
Madison, Wisconsin

CREDITS

Photographs

All photographs by Silver Burdett Ginn (SBG) unless otherwise noted.

Front cover: Silver Burdett Ginn.

xii: Ken Karp for Silver Burdett Ginn. xiii: Uniphoto. 53: *m.r., b.r.* National Museum of the American Indian. 54: *t.r.* National Museum of the American Indian. 140: Ann Summa for Silver Burdett Ginn. 245: *t.* Darren Maybury/Corbis; *b.l.* Randall Hyman; *b.r.* Paul Souders/Corbis. 246: *t.* Tom McCarthy/The Stockhouse, Inc.; *b.l.* Jan Reynolds. Chapter 10 Math Storybook: B: *t.l.* Bob Torrez/Tony Stone Images; *t.r.* Superstock; *b.* Ken Karp for Silver Burdett Ginn. 308: © Tim Davis/Photo Researchers, Inc. 322: Jon Reis/The Stock Market. 331: Uniphoto. 339: *t.l.* Fred George/Tony Stone Images; *t.r.* © Rafael Macia/Photo Researchers, Inc.; *m.* Chuck Place; *b.* © Adam Jones/Photo Researchers, Inc. 340: *t.* © David R. Frazier/Photo Researchers, Inc.; *b.* © Scott Berner/The Stockhouse, Inc. 343: © Chromosohm/Joe Sohm/Photo Researchers, Inc.

Illustrations

Chapter 1 Sharon Hawkins Vargo. Chapter 2 Teresa Flavin. Chapter 3 Lehner & Whyte. Chapter 4 Brian Karas. Chapter 5 Nathan Young Jarvis. Chapter 6 Susan Lexa. Chapter 7 Jackie Urbanovic. Chapter 8 Chi Chung. 245–246: Art Thompson. 248–249: Art Thompson. Chapter 9 Amy Wummer. Chapter 10 295–298: Jerry Zimmerman. 310: Jerry Zimmerman. 312–313: Jerry Zimmerman. 315: Jerry Zimmerman. Chapter 11 Darcia Labrosse. Chapter 12 Paul Yalowitz.

ISBN 0-382-37003-1

9 10 WC 05 04 03 02 01

Senior Author

Mary Cavanagh, M.S.
Principal Investigator, Math, Science, and Beyond
Solana Beach School District
Solana Beach, California

Grade Level Authors

Mary Behr Altieri, M.S.
Mathematics Teacher
1993 Presidential Awardee
Lakeland Central School District
Shrub Oak, New York

Jennie Bennett, Ed.D.
Instructional Mathematics Supervisor
Houston Independent School District
Houston, Texas

Charles Calhoun, Ph.D.
Associate Professor of Elementary Education Mathematics
University of Alabama at Birmingham
Birmingham, Alabama

Lucille Croom, Ph.D.
Professor of Mathematics
Hunter College of the City University of New York
New York, New York

Robert A. Laing, Ph.D.
Professor of Mathematics Education
Western Michigan University
Kalamazoo, Michigan

Kay B. Sammons, M.S.
Supervisor of Elementary Mathematics
Howard County Public Schools
Ellicott City, Maryland

Marian Small, Ed.D.
Professor of Mathematics Education
University of New Brunswick
Fredericton, New Brunswick, Canada

Contributing Authors

Stephen Krulik, Ed.D.
Professor of Mathematics Education
Temple University
Philadelphia, Pennsylvania

Donna J. Long
Mathematics/Title 1 Coordinator
Metropolitan School District of Wayne Township
Indianapolis, Indiana

Jesse A. Rudnick, Ed.D.
Professor Emeritus of Mathematics Education
Temple University
Philadelphia, Pennsylvania

Clementine Sherman
Director, USI Math and Science
Dade County Public Schools
Miami, Florida

Bruce R. Vogeli, Ph.D.
Clifford Brewster Upton Professor of Mathematics
Teachers College, Columbia University
New York, New York

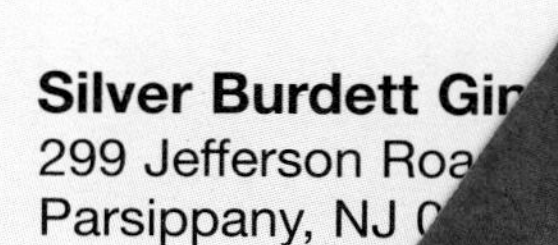

Silver Burdett Gin
299 Jefferson Roa
Parsippany, NJ 0

Contents

Using Addition Strategies

Chapter Theme: Deep Down Underground

Math Storybook: *Carrot Stew*

Chapter Resources

Using Subtraction Strategies

Chapter Theme: Polar Land

Math Storybook: *Outside Eva's Window*

Chapter Resources

Patterns and Numbers to 100

Chapter Theme: The Rain Forest

Math Storybook: *Who Lives in the Rain Forest?*

Chapter Resources

Money

Chapter Theme: Little Business

Math Storybook: *Big Jobs, Small Jobs, Odd Jobs, All Jobs*

Chapter Resources

Adding Two-Digit Numbers

Chapter Theme: Don't Throw It Away!

Math Storybook: *The Life of a Can*

Chapter Resources

Each person in the United States creates about 4 pounds of trash every day.
4
pounds
Wow! That's a lot!

Subtracting Two-Digit Numbers

Chapter Theme: By the Sea

Math Storybook: *The Missing Seashells Mystery*

Chapter Resources

Chapter 7 Time

Chapter Theme: Ready, Set, Go!

Math Storybook: *Larry Wins at Last*

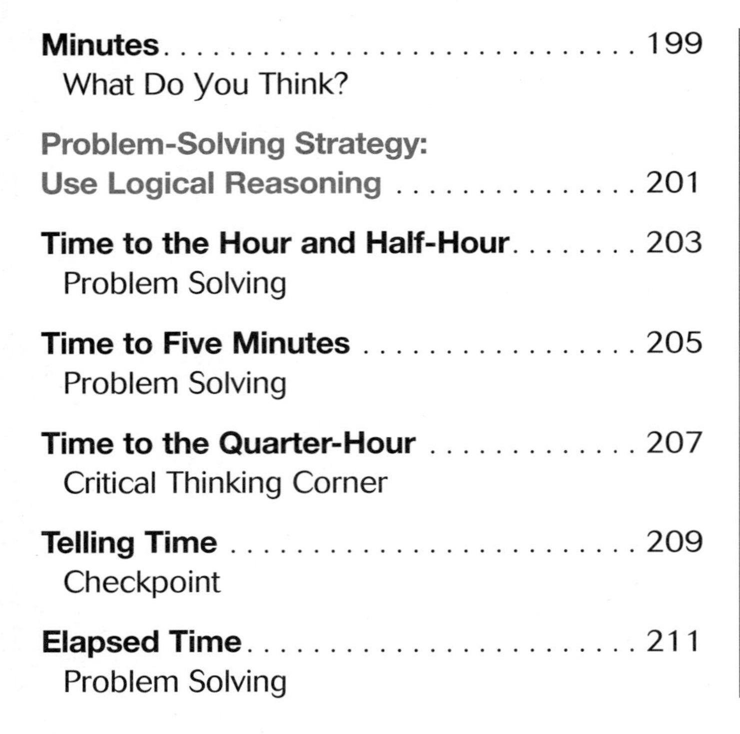

Measurement

Chapter Theme: Measure and Make

Math Storybook: *Chen's Dragon*

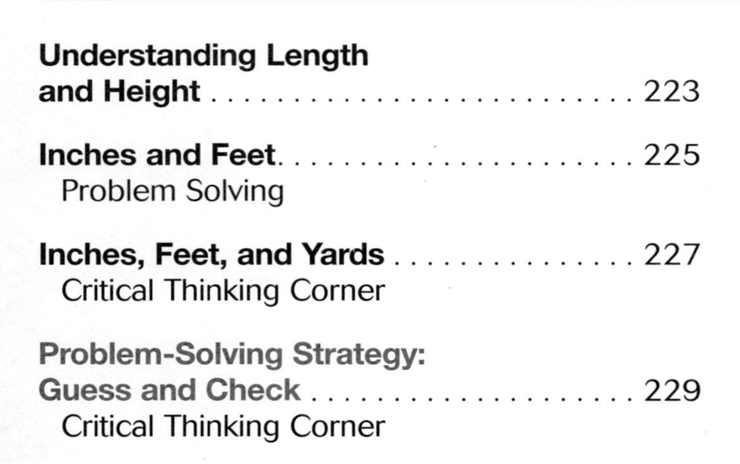

Patterns and Numbers to 1,000

Chapter Theme: My Stuff

Math Storybook: *Carl's Collections*

Geometry, Fractions, and Probability

Chapter Theme: Everyday Shapes

Math Storybook: *Shapes Around Us*

Chapter Resources

Adding and Subtracting Three-Digit Numbers

Chapter Theme: Here, There, and Everywhere

Math Storybook: *The Great Bicycle Race*

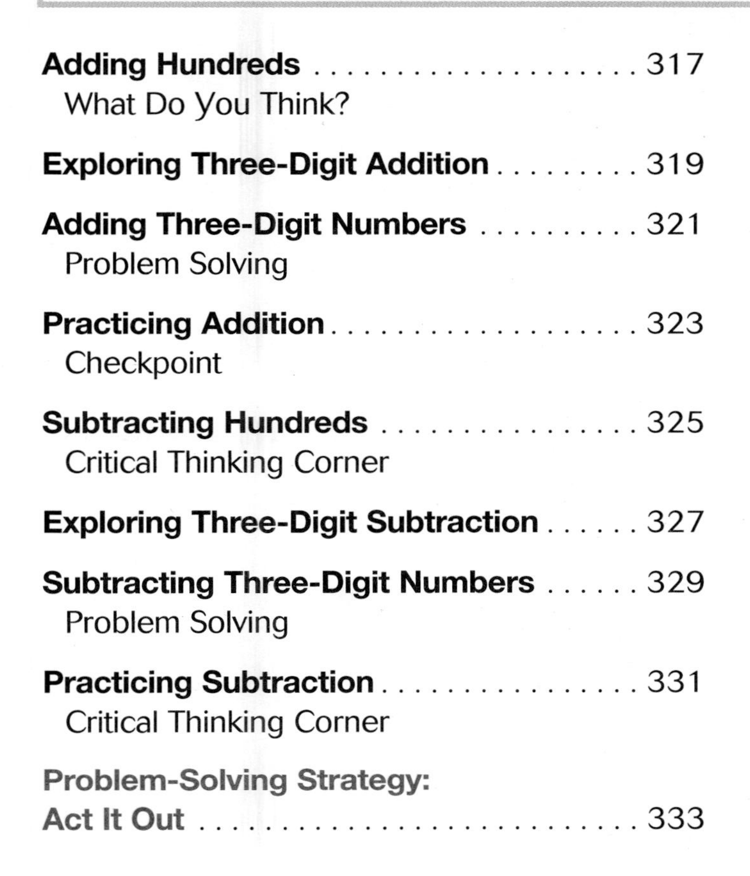

Chapter Resources

Chapter 12

Exploring Multiplication and Division

Chapter Theme: Wings and Things

Math Storybook: *Pepper's Problem*

Chapter Resources

CHAPTER 1
Using Addition Strategies
Carrot Stew
written by Janice Richardson
illustrated by Sharon Vargo
This Math Storybook
belongs to
A

"I'm hungry," said Rosie Rabbit.
"Let's make carrot stew."
"I have 3 potatoes," said Rory.
"Here are 5 more. That makes 8 in all," said Rod.
"But we have no carrots," said Rosie.
B

"Here are 6 onions," said Rod.
"Here are 6 more. That makes 12 in all," said Rory.
"But we still have no carrots," said Rosie.
c

"Here are 5 turnips," said Rory.
"I have 9 more. That makes
14 in all," said Rod.
"But we still have no carrots,"
said Rosie.
D

"Here are 8 tomatoes,"
said Rosie.
"8 plus 7 more makes
15 in all," said Rod.
"But we still have no carrots,"
said Rory.
"We can't make carrot stew
without carrots!" said Rosie.
E

"Look, I see 9 carrots,"
said Rod.
"I see 9 more," said Rory.
"That makes 18 carrots in all,"
said Rosie.
"Let's have carrot stew!"
everyone shouted.
F

Draw 3 more bowls.
How many are there in all?_______
Draw 5 more plates.
How many are there in all?_______
Draw 5 more cups.
How many are there in all?_______
Draw 6 more glasses.
How many are there in all?_______
www.sbgmath.com
G

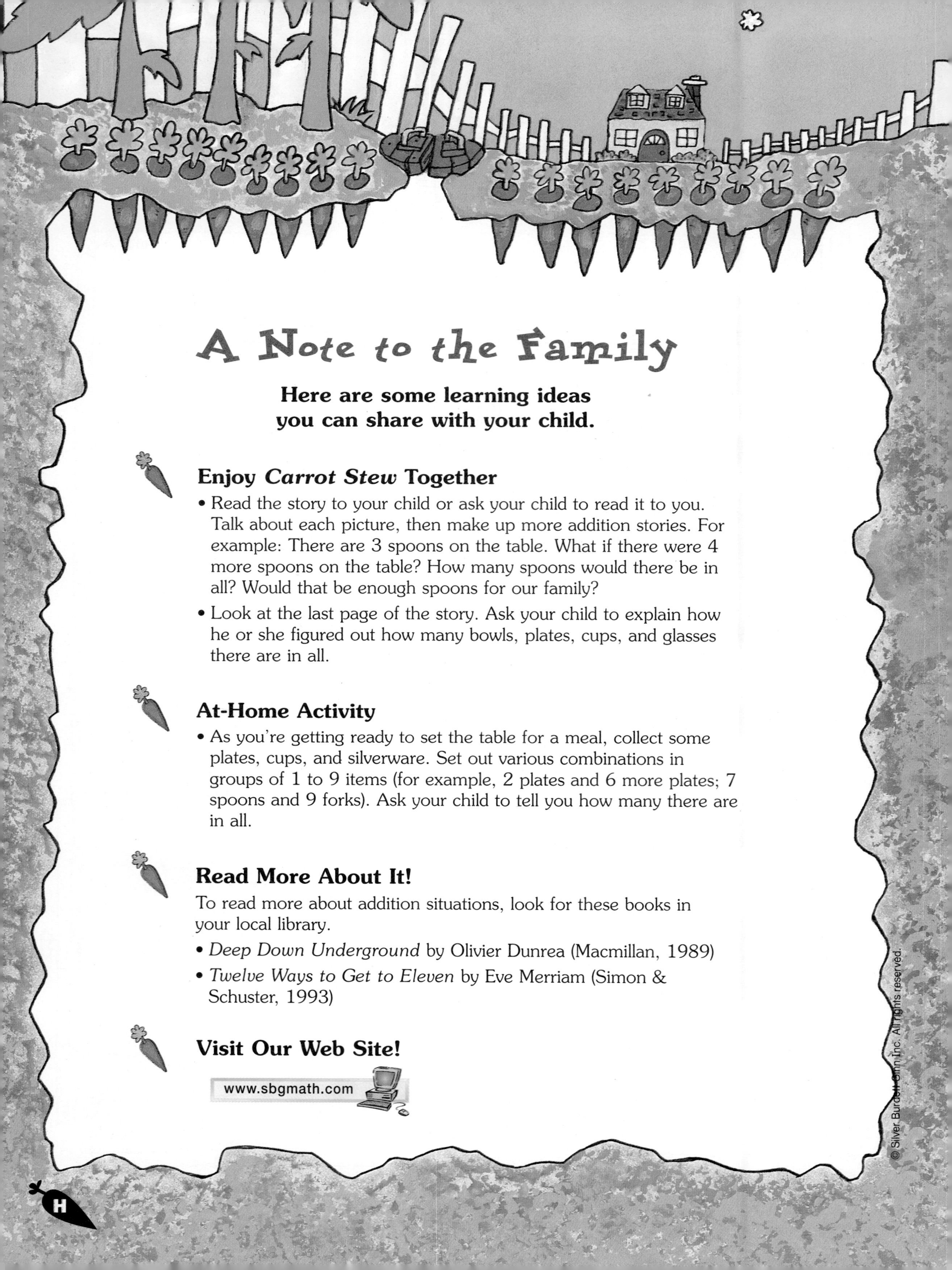

A Note to the Family

Here are some learning ideas you can share with your child.

Enjoy *Carrot Stew* Together

- Read the story to your child or ask your child to read it to you. Talk about each picture, then make up more addition stories. For example: There are 3 spoons on the table. What if there were 4 more spoons on the table? How many spoons would there be in all? Would that be enough spoons for our family?
- Look at the last page of the story. Ask your child to explain how he or she figured out how many bowls, plates, cups, and glasses there are in all.

At-Home Activity

- As you're getting ready to set the table for a meal, collect some plates, cups, and silverware. Set out various combinations in groups of 1 to 9 items (for example, 2 plates and 6 more plates; 7 spoons and 9 forks). Ask your child to tell you how many there are in all.

Read More About It!

To read more about addition situations, look for these books in your local library.

- *Deep Down Underground* by Olivier Dunrea (Macmillan, 1989)
- *Twelve Ways to Get to Eleven* by Eve Merriam (Simon & Schuster, 1993)

Visit Our Web Site!

www.sbgmath.com

Name____ **Understanding Addition**

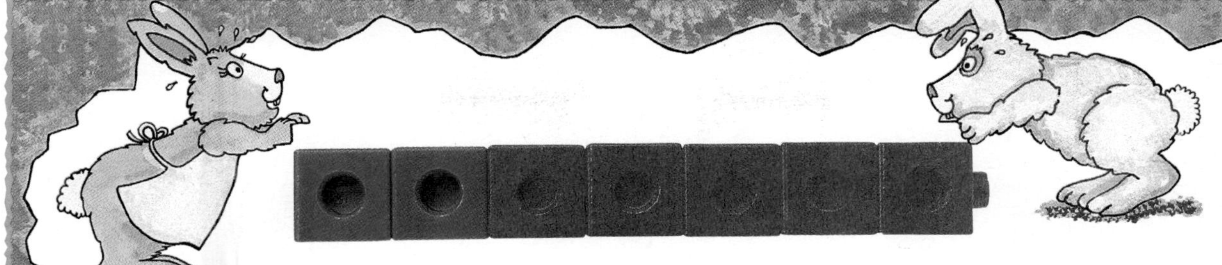

$2 + 5 = \underline{7}$

addend addend sum

$$\begin{array}{rl} 2 & \text{addend} \\ +5 & \text{addend} \\ \hline 7 & \text{sum} \end{array}$$

Word Bank

add
addend
sum

Add. Use cubes if you like.

1. $2 + 3 = \_\_\_\_$ $6 + 1 = \_\_\_\_$

2. $5 + 3 = \_\_\_\_$ $1 + 3 = \_\_\_\_$ $2 + 6 = \_\_\_\_$

3. $2 + 8 = \_\_\_\_$ $4 + 3 = \_\_\_\_$ $5 + 4 = \_\_\_\_$

4. $0 + 3 = \_\_\_\_$ $5 + 5 = \_\_\_\_$ $9 + 1 = \_\_\_\_$

5. $4 + 6 = \_\_\_\_$ $3 + 2 = \_\_\_\_$ $6 + 0 = \_\_\_\_$

6. $\begin{array}{r} 3 \\ +6 \\ \hline \end{array}$ $\begin{array}{r} 0 \\ +1 \\ \hline \end{array}$ $\begin{array}{r} 8 \\ +2 \\ \hline \end{array}$ $\begin{array}{r} 1 \\ +5 \\ \hline \end{array}$ $\begin{array}{r} 2 \\ +7 \\ \hline \end{array}$ $\begin{array}{r} 3 \\ +4 \\ \hline \end{array}$

7. $\begin{array}{r} 6 \\ +2 \\ \hline \end{array}$ $\begin{array}{r} 1 \\ +8 \\ \hline \end{array}$ $\begin{array}{r} 7 \\ +3 \\ \hline \end{array}$ $\begin{array}{r} 4 \\ +5 \\ \hline \end{array}$ $\begin{array}{r} 0 \\ +9 \\ \hline \end{array}$ $\begin{array}{r} 6 \\ +4 \\ \hline \end{array}$

Home Connection Counters can help children learn to add. Use common household items such as dried beans, noodles, or pennies to help your child find sums to ten.

Look at each picture.
Write the addition sentence.

1\.

2 + 4 = 6

2\.

___ + ___ = ___

3\.

___ + ___ = ___

4\.

___ + ___ = ___

5\.

___ + ___ = ___

6\.

___ + ___ = ___

7\.

___ + ___ = ___

8\.

___ + ___ = ___

Name______________________________ **Number Combinations**

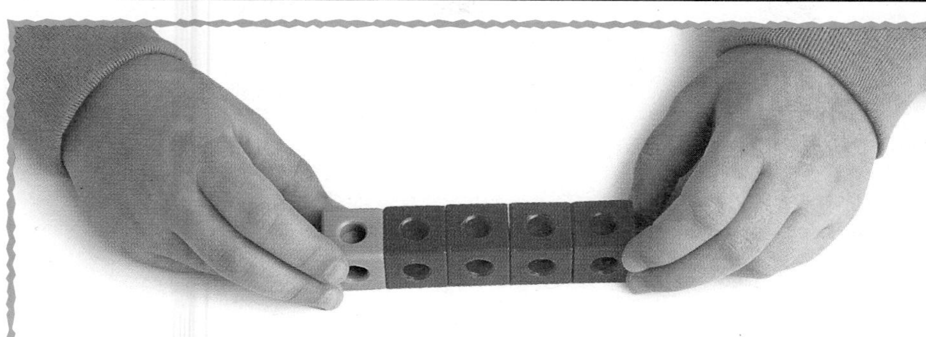

Word Bank
addition sentence
plus
equals

Use two colors of cubes to make sums.
Color to show each way.
Write each addition sentence.

1. Sums of 5

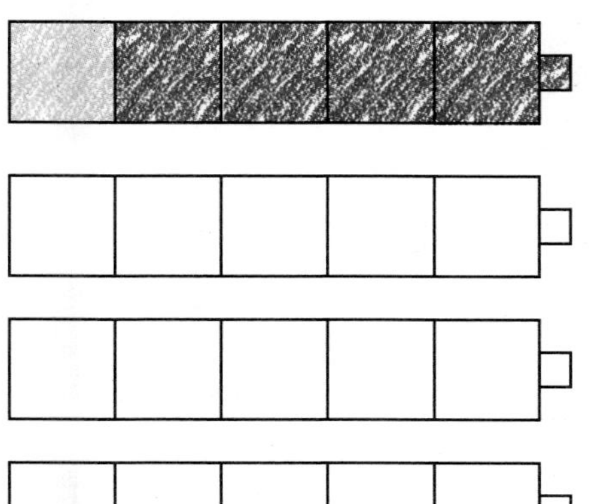

1 + 4 = 5

___ + ___ = ___

___ + ___ = ___

___ + ___ = ___

___ + ___ = ___

2. Sums of 6

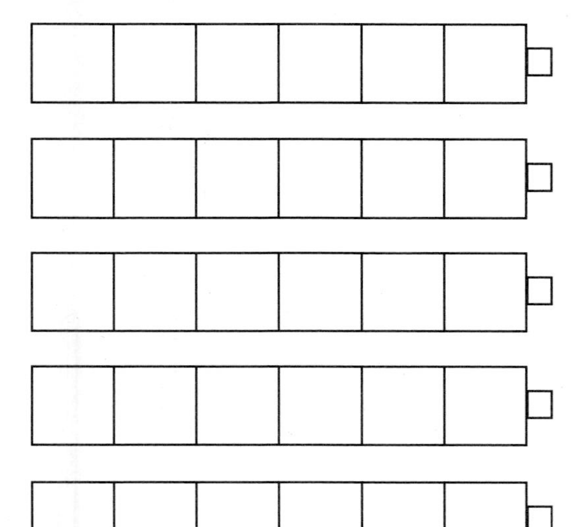

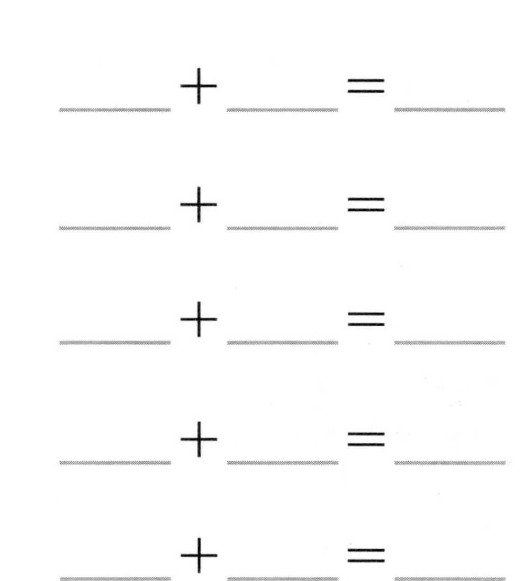

___ + ___ = ___

___ + ___ = ___

___ + ___ = ___

___ + ___ = ___

___ + ___ = ___

Home Connection Use counters such as beans or pennies to review sums of 10 with your child. Encourage him or her to write a number sentence for each sum.

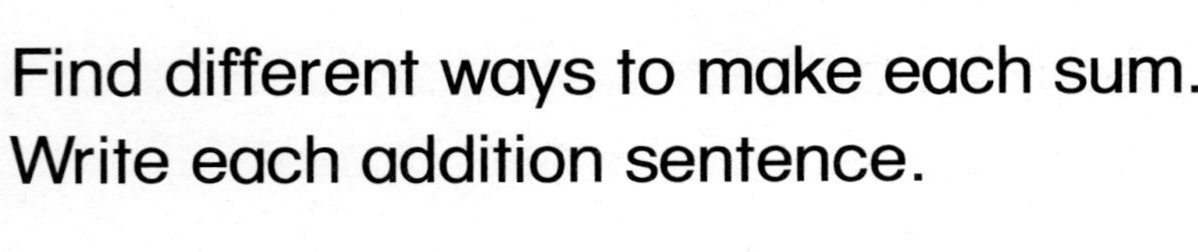
Find different ways to make each sum.
Write each addition sentence.

1. Sums of 7

___ + ___ = ___

___ + ___ = ___

___ + ___ = ___

___ + ___ = ___

___ + ___ = ___

2. Sums of 8

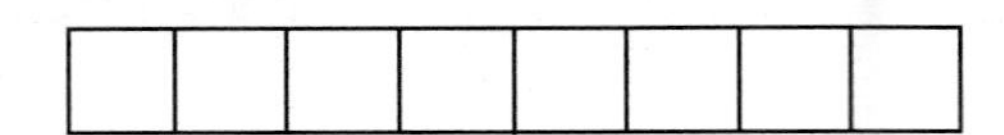

___ + ___ = ___

___ + ___ = ___

___ + ___ = ___

___ + ___ = ___

___ + ___ = ___

3. Sums of 9

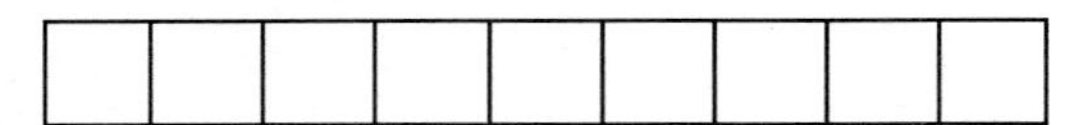

___ + ___ = ___

___ + ___ = ___

___ + ___ = ___

___ + ___ = ___

___ + ___ = ___

4. Sums of 10

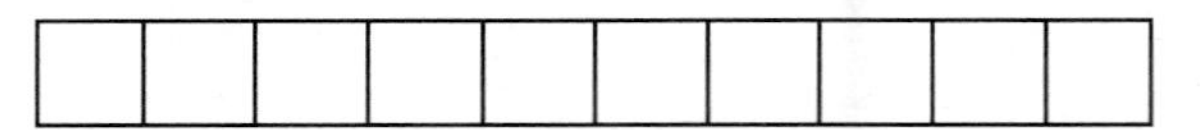

___ + ___ = ___

___ + ___ = ___

___ + ___ = ___

___ + ___ = ___

___ + ___ = ___

Name________________________ **Adding in Any Order**

When I turn
the addends around the
sums are the same.

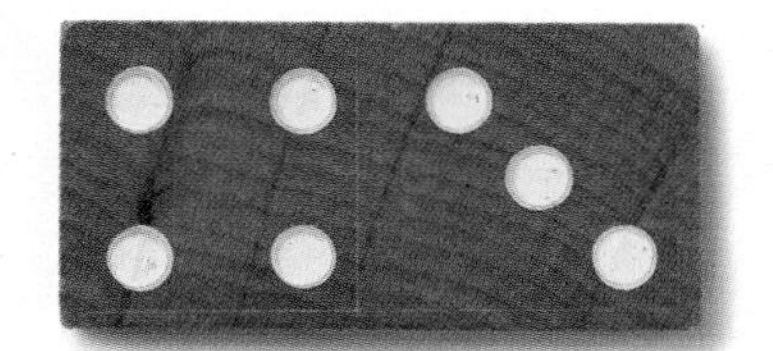

3 + 4 = 7

4 + 3 = 7

Find each sum.

1. 5 + 6 = ____

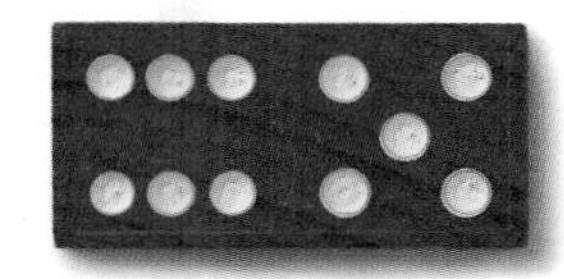

6 + 5 = ____

2. 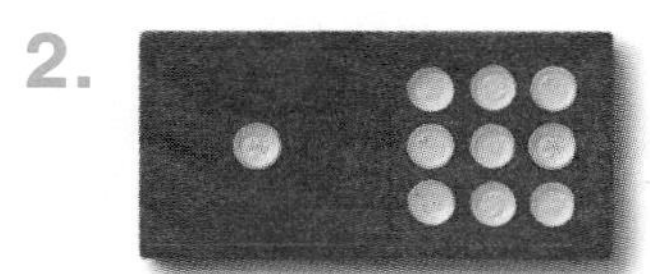

1 + 9 = ____

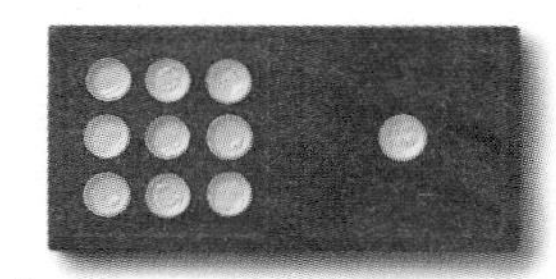

9 + 1 = ____

3. 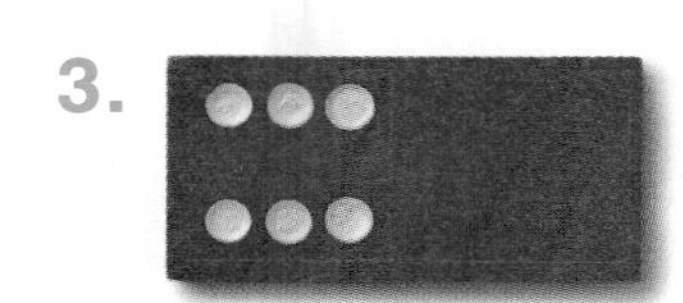

6 + 0 = ____

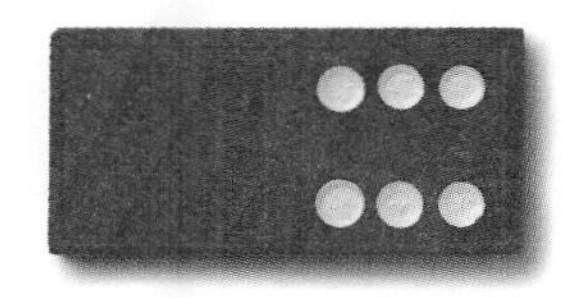

0 + 6 = ____

4. 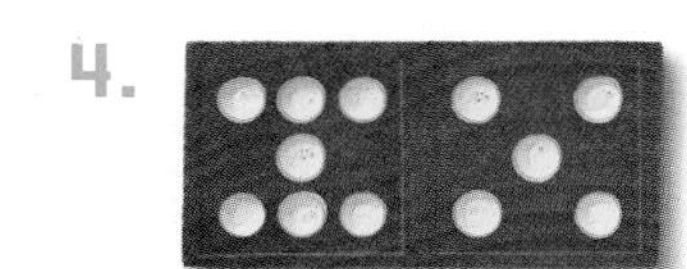

7 + 5 = ____

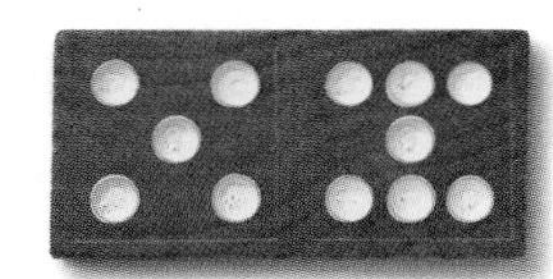

5 + 7 = ____

5. 4 + 8 = ____

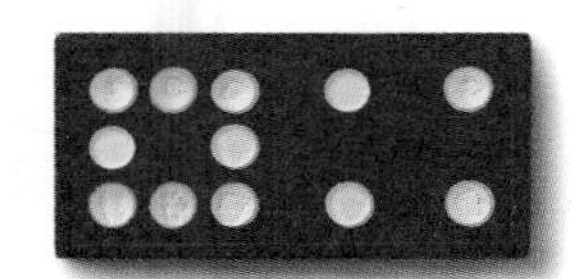

8 + 4 = ____

6. 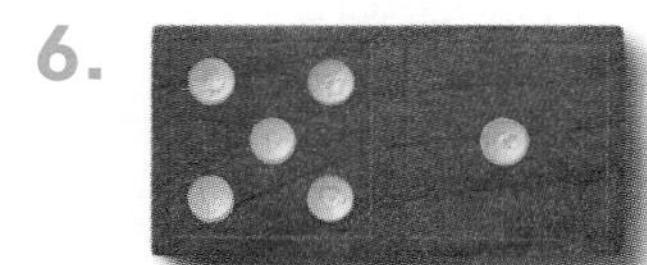

5 + 1 = ____

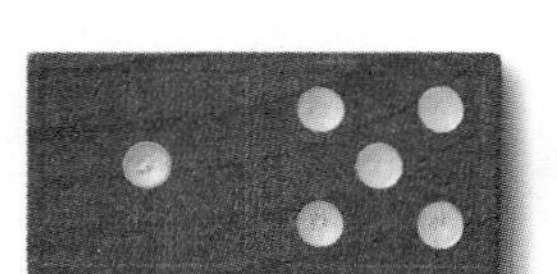

1 + 5 = ____

Home Connection Children need to understand that the order in which you add does not change the sum. Have your child use beans or pennies to show that 8+4 is the same as 4+8. Ask him or her why that happens. Repeat with other sums to 12.

Find each sum. Use counters if you like.

1. 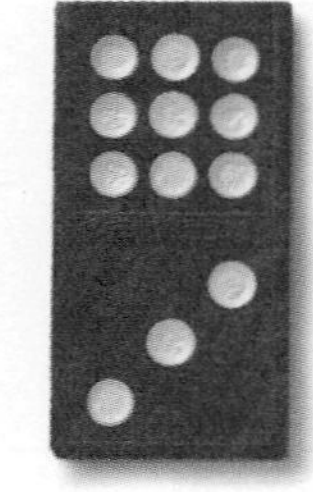
$\begin{array}{r} 9 \\ +\ 3 \\ \hline 12 \end{array}$
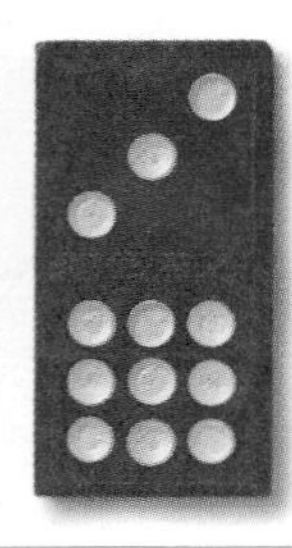
$\begin{array}{r} 3 \\ +\ 9 \\ \hline 12 \end{array}$

2. 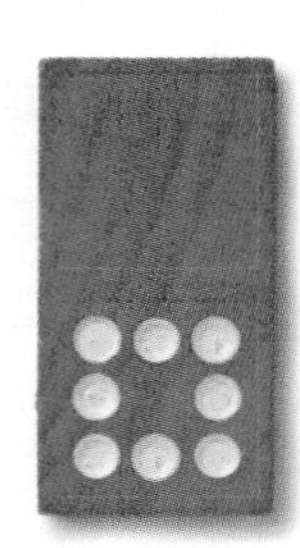
$\begin{array}{r} 0 \\ +\ 8 \\ \hline \end{array}$
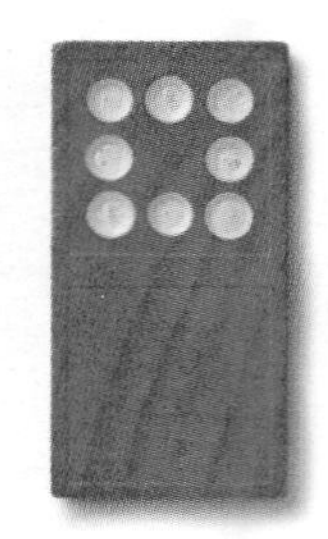
$\begin{array}{r} 8 \\ +\ 0 \\ \hline \end{array}$

3. $\begin{array}{r} 9 \\ +\ 2 \\ \hline \end{array}$ $\begin{array}{r} 2 \\ +\ 9 \\ \hline \end{array}$ $\begin{array}{r} 1 \\ +\ 2 \\ \hline \end{array}$ $\begin{array}{r} 2 \\ +\ 1 \\ \hline \end{array}$ $\begin{array}{r} 4 \\ +\ 5 \\ \hline \end{array}$ $\begin{array}{r} 5 \\ +\ 4 \\ \hline \end{array}$

4. $\begin{array}{r} 7 \\ +\ 1 \\ \hline \end{array}$ $\begin{array}{r} 1 \\ +\ 7 \\ \hline \end{array}$ $\begin{array}{r} 3 \\ +\ 6 \\ \hline \end{array}$ $\begin{array}{r} 6 \\ +\ 3 \\ \hline \end{array}$ $\begin{array}{r} 2 \\ +\ 8 \\ \hline \end{array}$ $\begin{array}{r} 8 \\ +\ 2 \\ \hline \end{array}$

5. $\begin{array}{r} 4 \\ +\ 3 \\ \hline \end{array}$ $\begin{array}{r} 3 \\ +\ 4 \\ \hline \end{array}$ $\begin{array}{r} 8 \\ +\ 4 \\ \hline \end{array}$ $\begin{array}{r} 4 \\ +\ 8 \\ \hline \end{array}$ $\begin{array}{r} 6 \\ +\ 5 \\ \hline \end{array}$ $\begin{array}{r} 5 \\ +\ 6 \\ \hline \end{array}$

6. $\begin{array}{r} 5 \\ +\ 3 \\ \hline \end{array}$ $\begin{array}{r} 3 \\ +\ 5 \\ \hline \end{array}$ $\begin{array}{r} 3 \\ +\ 8 \\ \hline \end{array}$ $\begin{array}{r} 8 \\ +\ 3 \\ \hline \end{array}$ $\begin{array}{r} 7 \\ +\ 5 \\ \hline \end{array}$ $\begin{array}{r} 5 \\ +\ 7 \\ \hline \end{array}$

7. Write your own facts.
Then change the order.

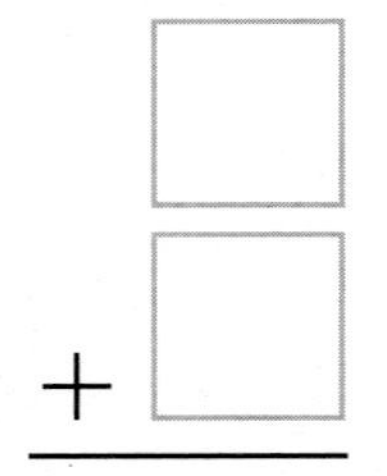
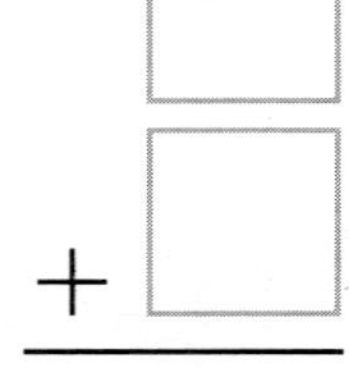
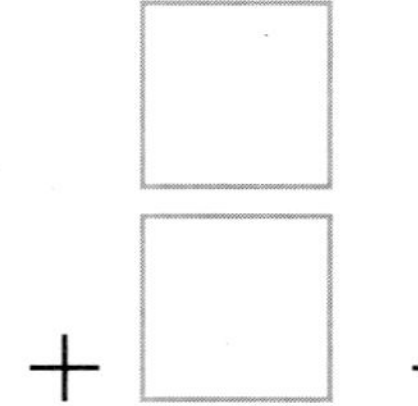
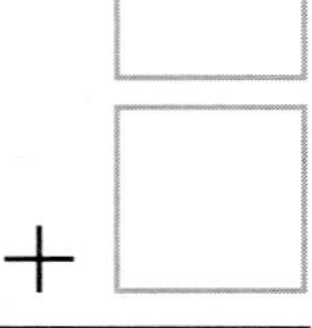
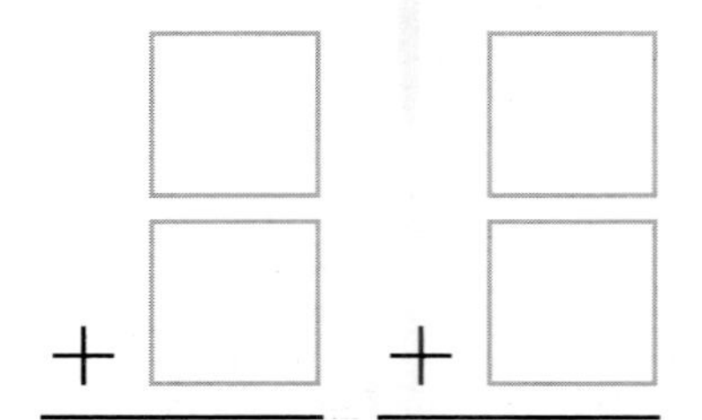

Name______________________________

To count on, start with the greater number.

Word Bank
count on

Think 4, say 5, 6, 7

$4 + 3 = \underline{7}$

Add by counting on. Use counters if you like.

1\.

$6 + 2 = \_\_\_$

2\.

$9 + 3 = \_\_\_$

3\. $8 + 1 = \_\_\_$ $7 + 2 = \_\_\_$ $2 + 5 = \_\_\_$

4\. $3 + 6 = \_\_\_$ $9 + 1 = \_\_\_$ $3 + 9 = \_\_\_$

5\. $2 + 9 = \_\_\_$ $8 + 3 = \_\_\_$ $1 + 6 = \_\_\_$

6\. $7 + 3 = \_\_\_$ $1 + 7 = \_\_\_$ $8 + 2 = \_\_\_$

Home Connection Counting on can help your child to add. Ask your child to count on from the greater number to add facts like 8 + 2.

Count on to add.

1. $\begin{array}{r} 7 \\ +1 \\ \hline 8 \end{array}$ $\begin{array}{r} 9 \\ +2 \\ \hline \end{array}$ $\begin{array}{r} 0 \\ +4 \\ \hline \end{array}$ $\begin{array}{r} 5 \\ +2 \\ \hline \end{array}$ $\begin{array}{r} 3 \\ +7 \\ \hline \end{array}$ $\begin{array}{r} 6 \\ +1 \\ \hline \end{array}$

2. $\begin{array}{r} 3 \\ +4 \\ \hline \end{array}$ $\begin{array}{r} 1 \\ +9 \\ \hline \end{array}$ $\begin{array}{r} 8 \\ +3 \\ \hline \end{array}$ $\begin{array}{r} 6 \\ +0 \\ \hline \end{array}$ $\begin{array}{r} 5 \\ +1 \\ \hline \end{array}$ $\begin{array}{r} 0 \\ +1 \\ \hline \end{array}$

3. $\begin{array}{r} 0 \\ +5 \\ \hline \end{array}$ $\begin{array}{r} 2 \\ +4 \\ \hline \end{array}$ $\begin{array}{r} 3 \\ +5 \\ \hline \end{array}$ $\begin{array}{r} 9 \\ +3 \\ \hline \end{array}$ $\begin{array}{r} 2 \\ +7 \\ \hline \end{array}$ $\begin{array}{r} 1 \\ +8 \\ \hline \end{array}$

4. $\begin{array}{r} 3 \\ +9 \\ \hline \end{array}$ $\begin{array}{r} 4 \\ +1 \\ \hline \end{array}$ $\begin{array}{r} 0 \\ +7 \\ \hline \end{array}$ $\begin{array}{r} 2 \\ +3 \\ \hline \end{array}$ $\begin{array}{r} 9 \\ +1 \\ \hline \end{array}$ $\begin{array}{r} 3 \\ +8 \\ \hline \end{array}$

5. $0 + 3 =$ ____ $2 + 9 =$ ____ $7 + 3 =$ ____

What Do You Think?

Journal Idea

I can use a number line to add 5 + 3.
I start at 5 and count on 6, 7, 8.
Tell how you would use a number line to add 2 + 7.

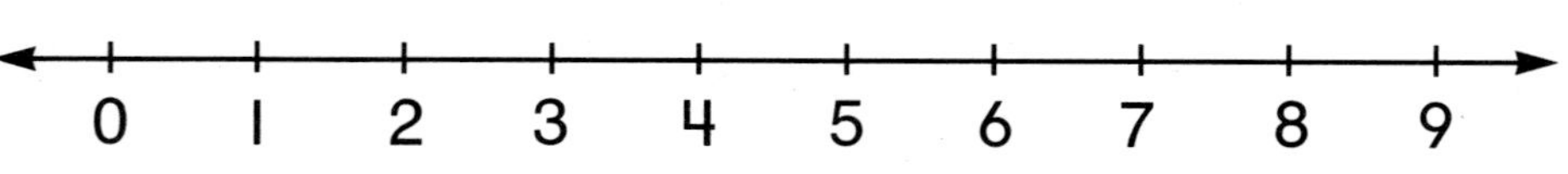

Name____

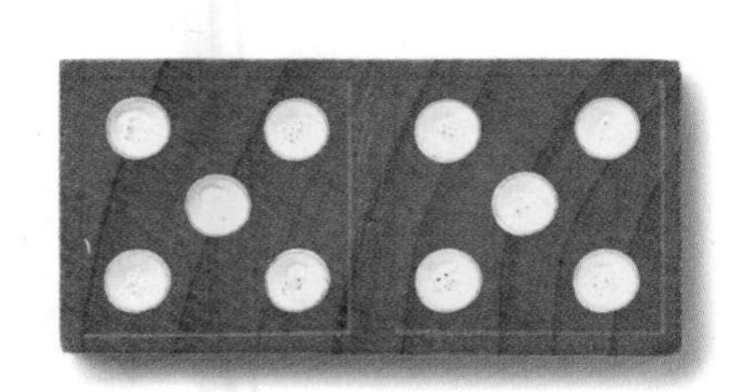

5 + 5 = 10

Draw to show the double.
Write each addition sentence.

1. 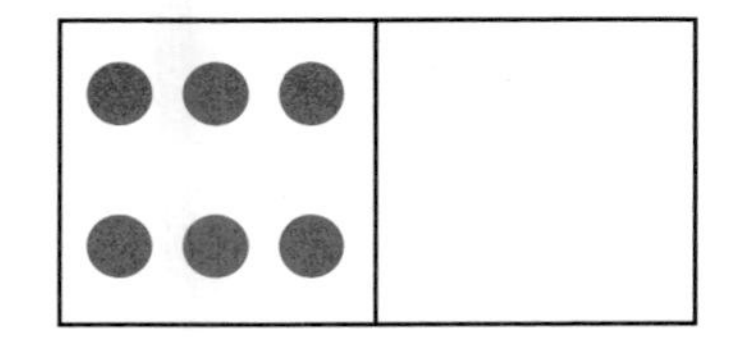

____ + ____ = ____

2. 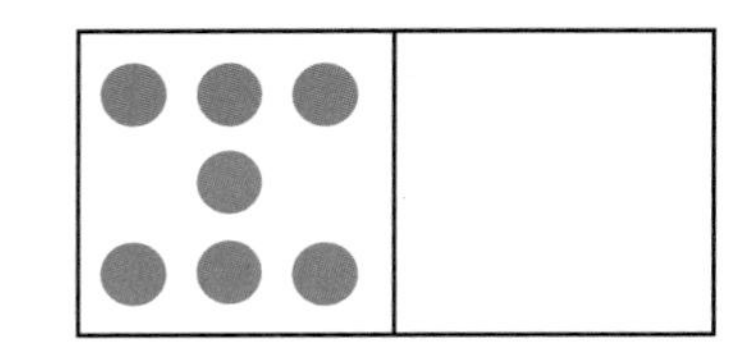

____ + ____ = ____

3. 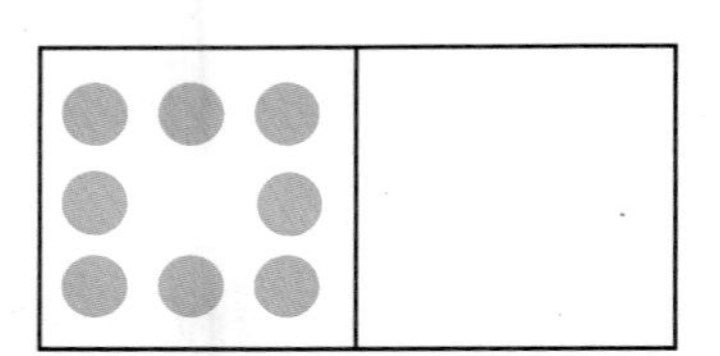

____ + ____ = ____

4. 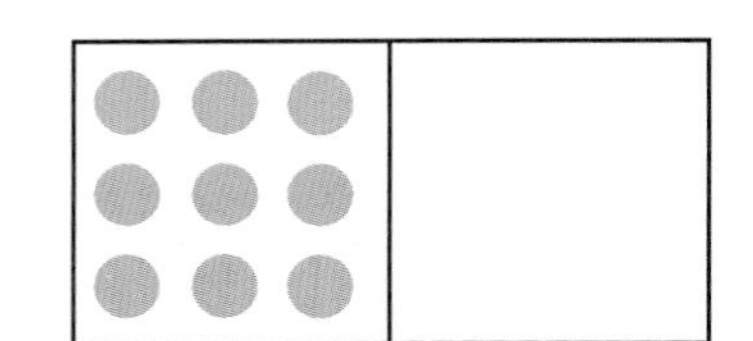

____ + ____ = ____

Find each sum.

5. 4 + 4 = ____ 7 + 7 = ____ 1 + 1 = ____

6. 3 + 3 = ____ 9 + 9 = ____ 2 + 2 = ____

7. 6 + 6 = ____ 5 + 5 = ____ 8 + 8 = ____

Home Connection Children often find it easy to remember doubles facts. Ask your child to say the doubles facts he or she knows.

Find each sum. Look for doubles.

1.
$$\begin{array}{r} 4 \\ +4 \\ \hline 8 \end{array} \quad \begin{array}{r} 9 \\ +1 \\ \hline \end{array} \quad \begin{array}{r} 2 \\ +2 \\ \hline \end{array} \quad \begin{array}{r} 8 \\ +3 \\ \hline \end{array} \quad \begin{array}{r} 3 \\ +6 \\ \hline \end{array} \quad \begin{array}{r} 9 \\ +9 \\ \hline \end{array}$$

2.
$$\begin{array}{r} 5 \\ +3 \\ \hline \end{array} \quad \begin{array}{r} 2 \\ +6 \\ \hline \end{array} \quad \begin{array}{r} 0 \\ +0 \\ \hline \end{array} \quad \begin{array}{r} 5 \\ +5 \\ \hline \end{array} \quad \begin{array}{r} 7 \\ +2 \\ \hline \end{array} \quad \begin{array}{r} 3 \\ +4 \\ \hline \end{array}$$

3.
$$\begin{array}{r} 1 \\ +1 \\ \hline \end{array} \quad \begin{array}{r} 8 \\ +8 \\ \hline \end{array} \quad \begin{array}{r} 9 \\ +3 \\ \hline \end{array} \quad \begin{array}{r} 3 \\ +3 \\ \hline \end{array} \quad \begin{array}{r} 2 \\ +8 \\ \hline \end{array} \quad \begin{array}{r} 4 \\ +4 \\ \hline \end{array}$$

4.
$$\begin{array}{r} 7 \\ +3 \\ \hline \end{array} \quad \begin{array}{r} 6 \\ +6 \\ \hline \end{array} \quad \begin{array}{r} 1 \\ +8 \\ \hline \end{array} \quad \begin{array}{r} 7 \\ +7 \\ \hline \end{array} \quad \begin{array}{r} 5 \\ +2 \\ \hline \end{array} \quad \begin{array}{r} 3 \\ +8 \\ \hline \end{array}$$

PROBLEM SOLVING

Problem Solving

Using Algebra

Solve.

5. Matt has the same number of apples as Holly. How many apples do they have in all?

_____ apples

Name ______________________ **Using Doubles to Add**

Doubles help you add other facts.

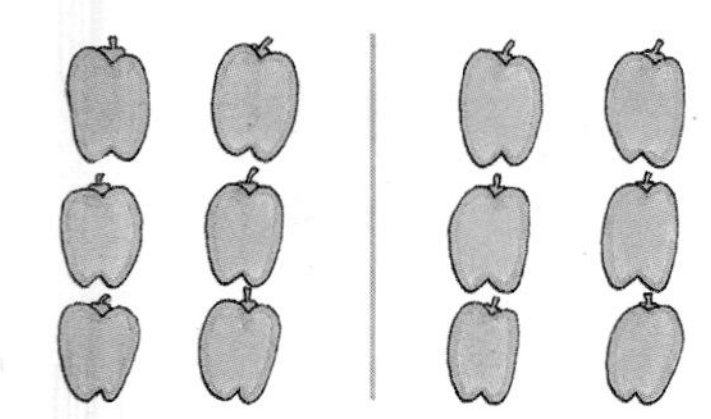

6 + 6 = 12

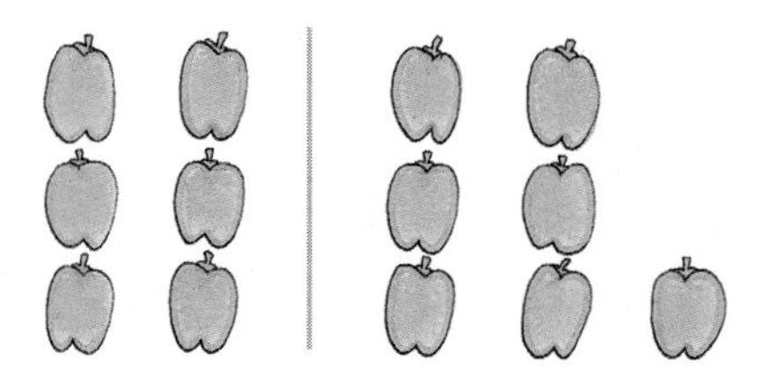

6 + 7 = 13

Write the doubles fact.
Then draw one more ●. Write the new fact.

1\.

8 + 8 = 16

8 + 9 = ____

2\.

____ + ____ = ____

____ + ____ = ____

3\.

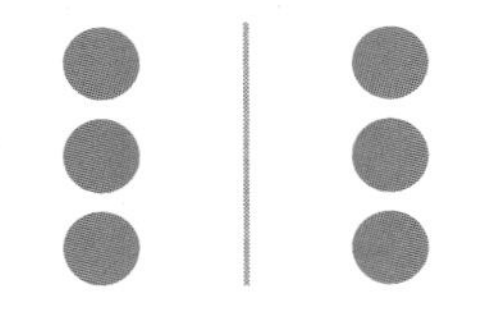

____ + ____ = ____

____ + ____ = ____

4\.

____ + ____ = ____

____ + ____ = ____

5\.

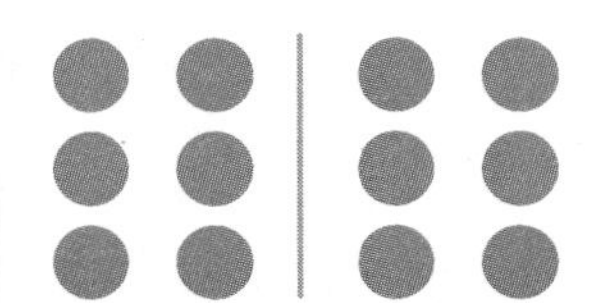

____ + ____ = ____

____ + ____ = ____

6\.

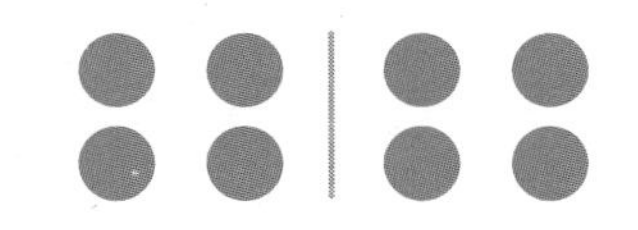

____ + ____ = ____

____ + ____ = ____

Home Connection Children can use doubles to help them add. Ask your child to solve near-doubles facts like 7 + 8.

Add.

1.	$7 + 7 = 14$	$7 + 8 = 15$	$4 + 4$	$4 + 5$	$8 + 8$	$9 + 8$
2.	$6 + 6$	$7 + 6$	$5 + 5$	$5 + 6$	$7 + 7$	$8 + 7$
3.	$3 + 5$	$7 + 8$	$0 + 0$	$6 + 5$	$8 + 9$	$2 + 2$
4.	$5 + 4$	$6 + 7$	$8 + 8$	$3 + 2$	$4 + 3$	$8 + 7$
5.	$8 + 6$	$9 + 9$	$5 + 7$	$3 + 3$	$4 + 6$	$8 + 5$

Critical Thinking Corner

Number Sense

6. Write the double that you would use to solve 5 + 6.

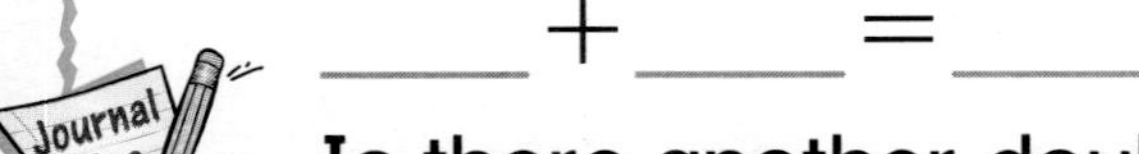

____ + ____ = ____

Journal Idea

Is there another double you could use? Explain.

Name________________________________ **Practicing Addition Strategies**

You can count on to add.

Think 9.
Say 10, 11, 12.

9

9 + 3 = 12

You can use doubles to add.

Think 6 + 6
and 1 more.

6 + 7 = 13

Count on or use doubles to add.

1. 5 + 3 = ____ 2 + 8 = ____ 9 + 3 = ____
2. 2 + 9 = ____ 5 + 6 = ____ 7 + 8 = ____
3. 3 + 8 = ____ 5 + 2 = ____ 6 + 1 = ____
4. 7 + 1 = ____ 8 + 9 = ____ 3 + 7 = ____
5. 4 + 5 = ____ 2 + 6 = ____ 6 + 7 = ____
6. 9 + 2 = ____ 4 + 3 = ____ 6 + 3 = ____

Home Connection Your child has been counting on and using doubles as strategies to find sums. Have your child tell you which strategy he or she used to solve the problems on this page.

Find each sum.

1.	7 + 8 15	9 + 3	4 + 5	8 + 8	2 + 7	7 + 7
2.	8 + 1	6 + 5	4 + 4	3 + 8	5 + 5	9 + 8
3.	6 + 6	7 + 0	2 + 9	1 + 8	7 + 6	6 + 3

Checkpoint

1. Write each sum.

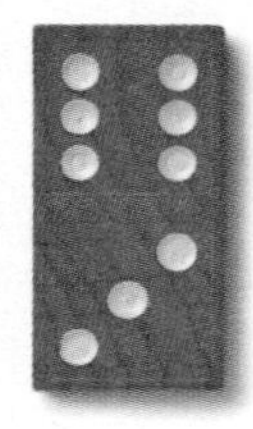

6 + 3

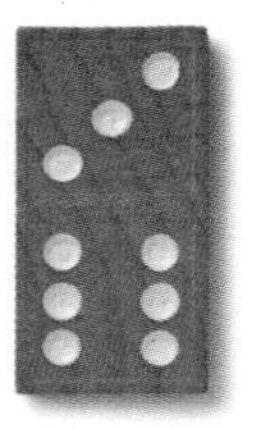

3 + 6

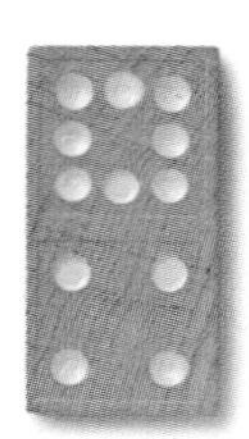

8 + 4

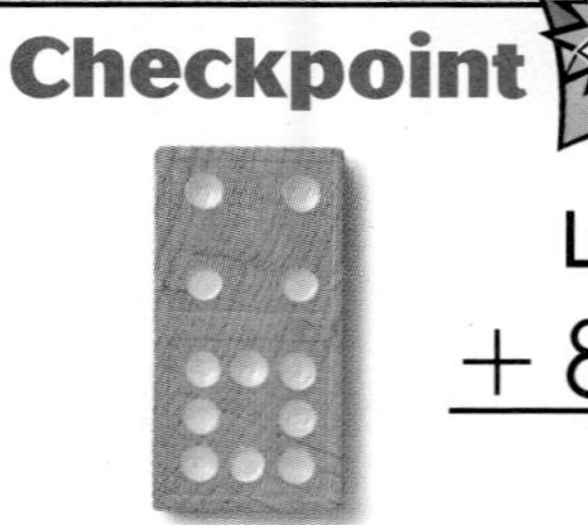

4 + 8

2. Add by counting on.

7 + 1	4 + 2	3 + 9	2 + 6	8 + 1	5 + 3

3. Use doubles to find each sum.

6 + 7 = ____	7 + 8 = ____	5 + 4 = ____
9 + 8 = ____	7 + 6 = ____	6 + 5 = ____

Name______________________________

Problem-Solving Strategy
Write a Number Sentence

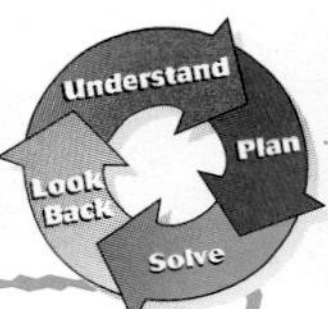

Write each addition sentence.

1\.

5 + 8 = 13

2\.

___ + ___ = ___

3\.

___ + ___ = ___

4\.

___ + ___ = ___

5\.

___ + ___ = ___

6\.

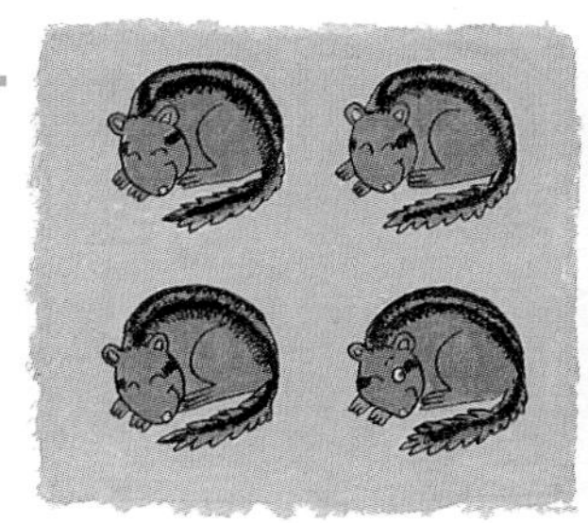

___ + ___ = ___

7\.

___ + ___ = ___

8\.

___ + ___ = ___

Home Connection Children need to describe addition by writing number sentences. Have your child write addition sentences for stories you tell or pictures they see.

Solve. Write the numbers.

1. 7 ants are digging. 3 more ants help them. How many ants are digging ?

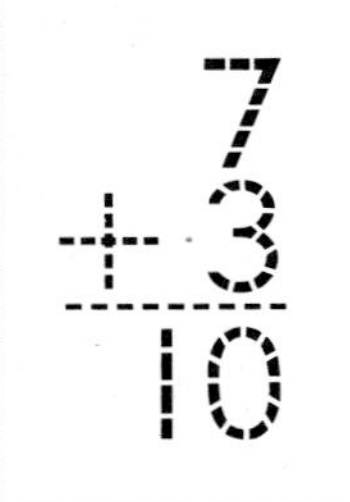

10 ants

2. 8 squirrels each have a pine cone. They each get one more. How many pine cones are there altogether?

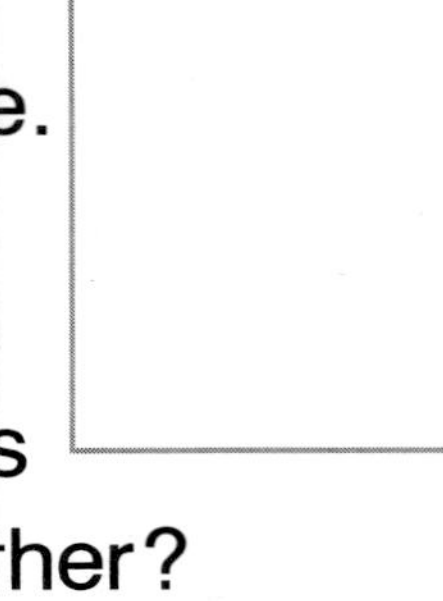

_____ pine cones

3. A mouse finds 5 acorns on the ground. It finds 1 more. How many acorns did it find?

_____ acorns

4. 6 rabbits are eating. 8 more join them. How many rabbits are eating now?

_____ rabbits

5. 3 foxes are playing. 4 more come to play. How many are playing now?

_____ foxes

6. The moles dig 9 tunnels. They dig 3 more. How many tunnels did they dig?

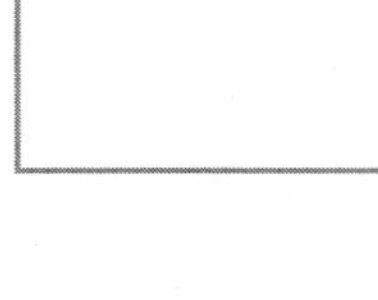

_____ tunnels

Critical Thinking Corner

Number Sense

7. Tell a story for this number sentence. $4 + 5 = 9$

Name ______________________________

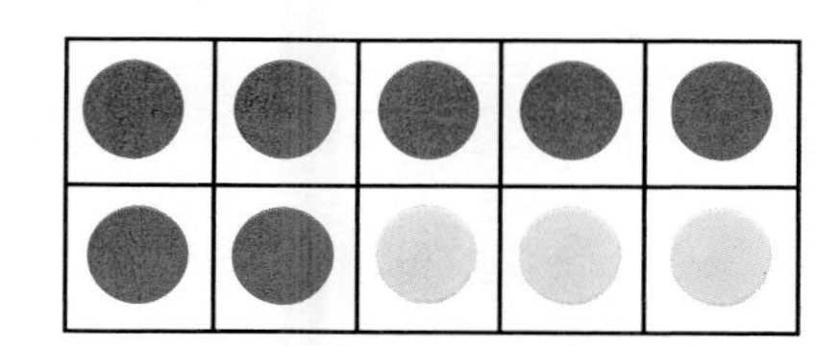

7 + 3 = 10

Word Bank
ten frame

Use Workmat 1 and two-color counters.
Find different ways to make 10. Color to record.
Write the number sentence.

1\.

___ + ___ = ___

2\.

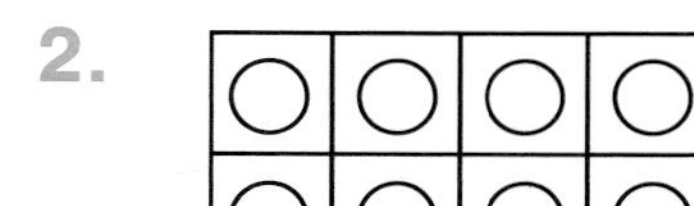

___ + ___ = ___

3\.

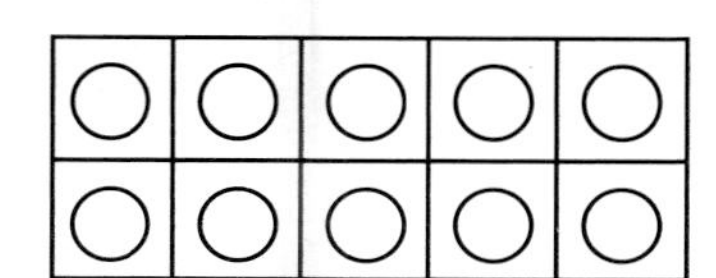

___ + ___ = ___

4\.

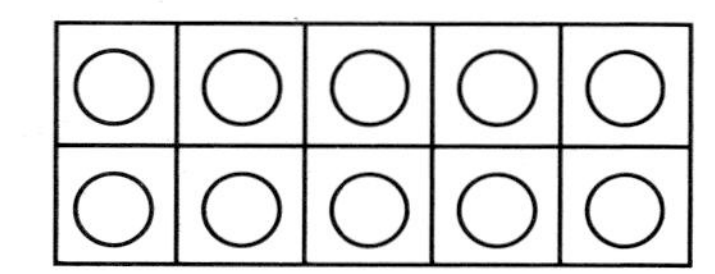

___ + ___ = ___

5\.

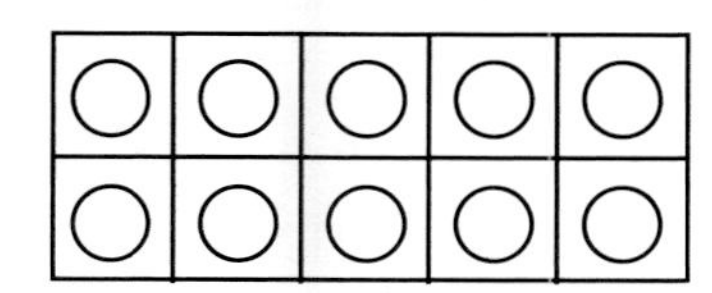

___ + ___ = ___

6\.

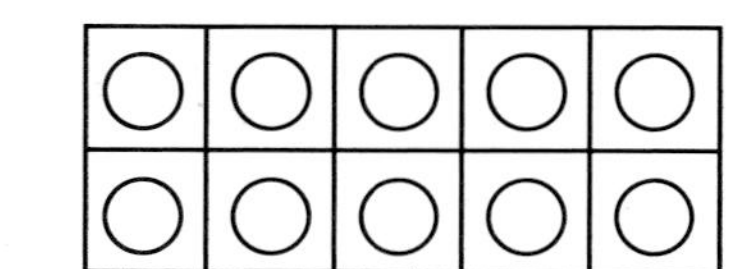

___ + ___ = ___

7\.

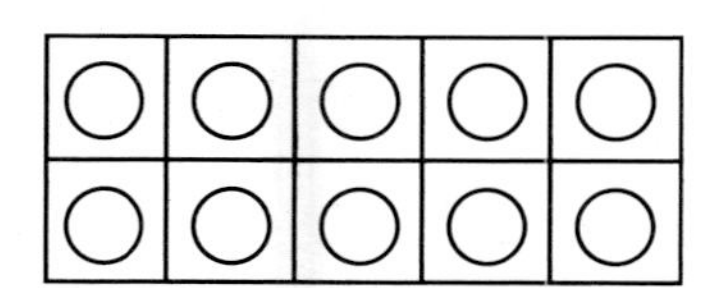

___ + ___ = ___

8\.

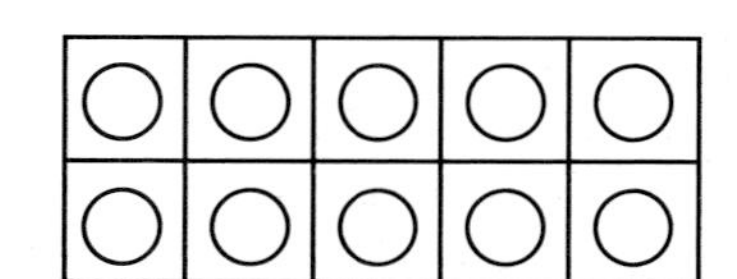

___ + ___ = ___

Home Connection Learning number combinations for 10 will help children learn more difficult facts. Have your child describe the combinations of 10 on this page.

Find each sum.

1.

$\begin{array}{r} 8 \\ +2 \\ \hline 10 \end{array}$	$\begin{array}{r} 9 \\ +9 \\ \hline \end{array}$	$\begin{array}{r} 3 \\ +7 \\ \hline \end{array}$	$\begin{array}{r} 2 \\ +6 \\ \hline \end{array}$	$\begin{array}{r} 7 \\ +8 \\ \hline \end{array}$	$\begin{array}{r} 3 \\ +3 \\ \hline \end{array}$

2.

$\begin{array}{r} 3 \\ +9 \\ \hline \end{array}$	$\begin{array}{r} 6 \\ +7 \\ \hline \end{array}$	$\begin{array}{r} 4 \\ +6 \\ \hline \end{array}$	$\begin{array}{r} 5 \\ +5 \\ \hline \end{array}$	$\begin{array}{r} 4 \\ +5 \\ \hline \end{array}$	$\begin{array}{r} 8 \\ +9 \\ \hline \end{array}$

3.

$\begin{array}{r} 9 \\ +1 \\ \hline \end{array}$	$\begin{array}{r} 5 \\ +6 \\ \hline \end{array}$	$\begin{array}{r} 2 \\ +8 \\ \hline \end{array}$	$\begin{array}{r} 4 \\ +0 \\ \hline \end{array}$	$\begin{array}{r} 7 \\ +3 \\ \hline \end{array}$	$\begin{array}{r} 6 \\ +6 \\ \hline \end{array}$

4.

$\begin{array}{r} 2 \\ +7 \\ \hline \end{array}$	$\begin{array}{r} 6 \\ +4 \\ \hline \end{array}$	$\begin{array}{r} 7 \\ +1 \\ \hline \end{array}$	$\begin{array}{r} 8 \\ +7 \\ \hline \end{array}$	$\begin{array}{r} 3 \\ +4 \\ \hline \end{array}$	$\begin{array}{r} 1 \\ +9 \\ \hline \end{array}$

Problem Solving

5. You have 10 two-color counters. Write all the ways to show 10.

yellow	0	1									
red	10	9									

I see a pattern when I add a number to 10.

14

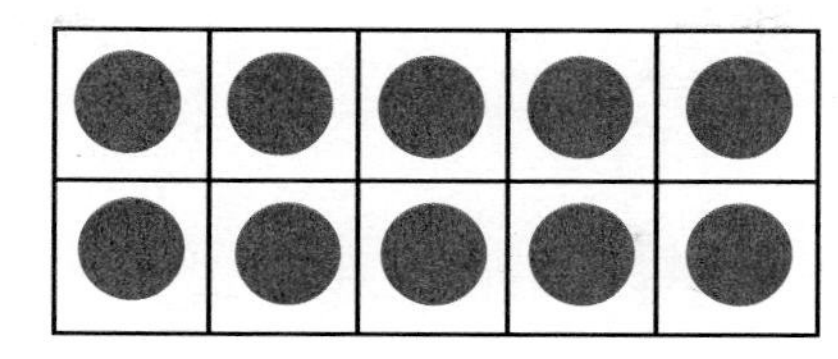

10 + 4 = 14

15

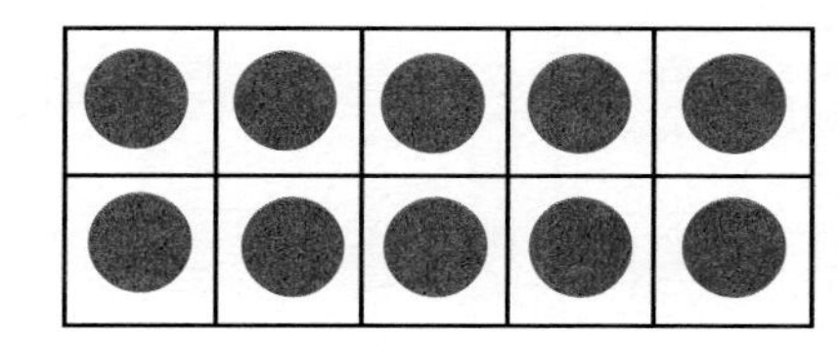

10 + 5 = 15

Draw more ◯ to show each number.
Complete the number sentence.

1. 13

10 + ____ = ____

2. 16

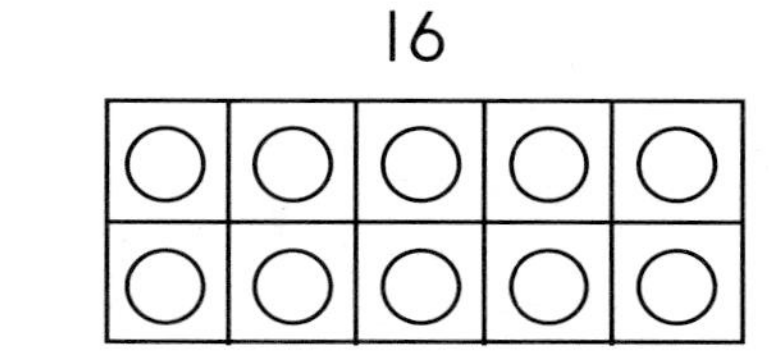

10 + ____ = ____

3. 11

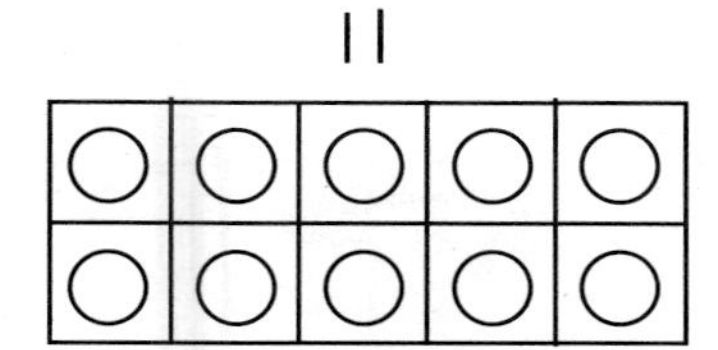

10 + ____ = ____

4. 14

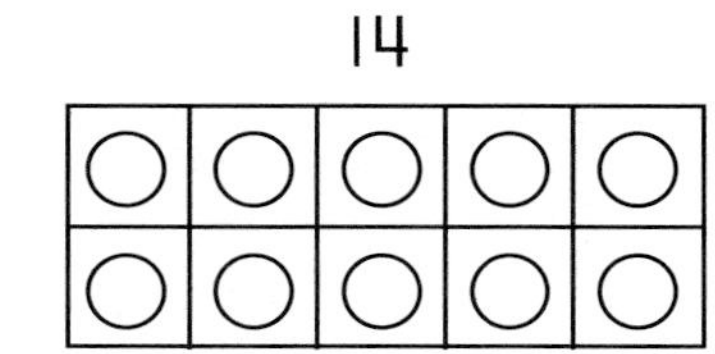

10 + ____ = ____

5. 17

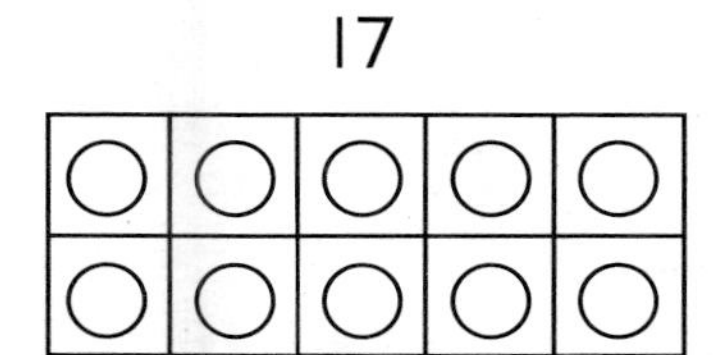

10 + ____ = ____

6. 15

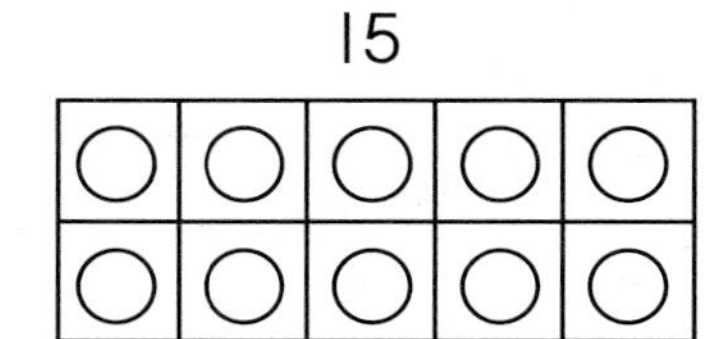

10 + ____ = ____

Home Connection Adding numbers to 10 is easy and important. Ask your child to explain what happens when numbers are added to 10.

Add.

1.	$\begin{array}{r} 10 \\ +\ 2 \\ \hline 12 \end{array}$	$\begin{array}{r} 7 \\ +\ 3 \\ \hline \end{array}$	$\begin{array}{r} 10 \\ +\ 1 \\ \hline \end{array}$	$\begin{array}{r} 4 \\ +\ 5 \\ \hline \end{array}$	$\begin{array}{r} 1 \\ +\ 6 \\ \hline \end{array}$	$\begin{array}{r} 2 \\ +\ 3 \\ \hline \end{array}$
2.	$\begin{array}{r} 9 \\ +\ 2 \\ \hline \end{array}$	$\begin{array}{r} 10 \\ +\ 7 \\ \hline \end{array}$	$\begin{array}{r} 6 \\ +\ 5 \\ \hline \end{array}$	$\begin{array}{r} 8 \\ +\ 8 \\ \hline \end{array}$	$\begin{array}{r} 6 \\ +\ 7 \\ \hline \end{array}$	$\begin{array}{r} 10 \\ +\ 8 \\ \hline \end{array}$
3.	$\begin{array}{r} 7 \\ +\ 7 \\ \hline \end{array}$	$\begin{array}{r} 4 \\ +\ 8 \\ \hline \end{array}$	$\begin{array}{r} 8 \\ +10 \\ \hline \end{array}$	$\begin{array}{r} 10 \\ +\ 5 \\ \hline \end{array}$	$\begin{array}{r} 1 \\ +\ 8 \\ \hline \end{array}$	$\begin{array}{r} 6 \\ +\ 6 \\ \hline \end{array}$
4.	$\begin{array}{r} 9 \\ +10 \\ \hline \end{array}$	$\begin{array}{r} 8 \\ +\ 7 \\ \hline \end{array}$	$\begin{array}{r} 3 \\ +\ 0 \\ \hline \end{array}$	$\begin{array}{r} 6 \\ +10 \\ \hline \end{array}$	$\begin{array}{r} 5 \\ +\ 5 \\ \hline \end{array}$	$\begin{array}{r} 10 \\ +\ 4 \\ \hline \end{array}$

Problem Solving

5. Add. Look for patterns.
Write the missing numbers.

$10 + 1 = \square$

$10 + 2 = \square$

$10 + 3 = \square$

$10 + \square = \square$

$10 + \square = \square$

Name________________________

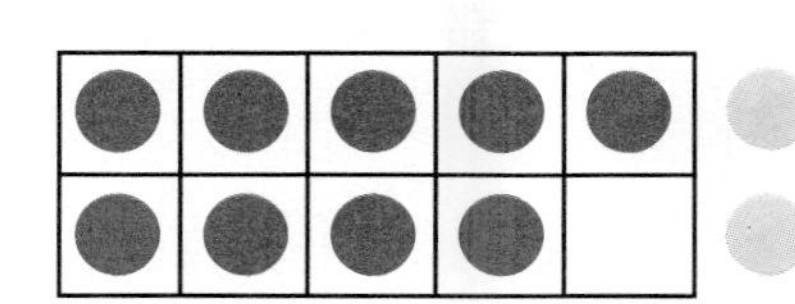

$9 + 6$ Think $10+5$

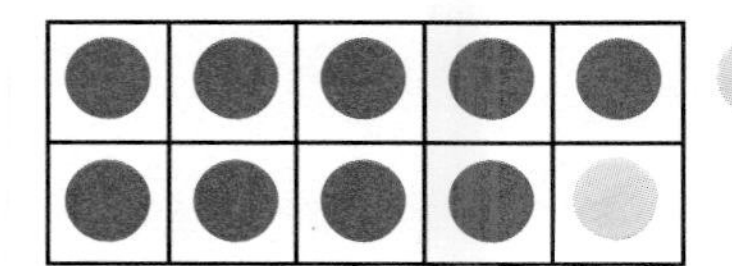

$10 + 5 =$ 15

$9 + 6 =$ 15

Making 10
can help you
add 9.

Use counters and Workmat 1.
Find each sum.

1. $9 + 7$ Think $10+6$
   $10 + 6 =$ 16
   $9 + 7 =$ 16

2. $3 + 9$ Think $2+10$
   $2 + 10 =$ ____
   $3 + 9 =$ ____

3. $9 + 4$ Think $10+3$
   $10 + 3 =$ ____
   $9 + 4 =$ ____

4. $9 + 8$ Think $10+7$
   $10 + 7 =$ ____
   $9 + 8 =$ ____

5. $5 + 9$ Think $4+10$
   $4 + 10 =$ ____
   $5 + 9 =$ ____

6. $9 + 2$ Think $10+1$
   $10 + 1 =$ ____
   $9 + 2 =$ ____

7. $9 + 9$ Think $10+8$
   $10 + 8 =$ ____
   $9 + 9 =$ ____

8. $6 + 9$ Think $5+10$
   $5 + 10 =$ ____
   $6 + 9 =$ ____

Home Connection Children can add 9 to a number by first adding 10 to that number and then subtracting 1. Ask your child to tell how to use 10 to add facts like 9 + 6.

Find each sum.

1. $\begin{array}{r} 9 \\ +\ 6 \\ \hline 15 \end{array}$ $\begin{array}{r} 5 \\ +\ 6 \\ \hline \end{array}$ $\begin{array}{r} 1 \\ +\ 9 \\ \hline \end{array}$ $\begin{array}{r} 8 \\ +\ 3 \\ \hline \end{array}$ $\begin{array}{r} 3 \\ +\ 5 \\ \hline \end{array}$ $\begin{array}{r} 7 \\ +\ 3 \\ \hline \end{array}$

2. $\begin{array}{r} 9 \\ +\ 7 \\ \hline \end{array}$ $\begin{array}{r} 2 \\ +\ 7 \\ \hline \end{array}$ $\begin{array}{r} 9 \\ +\ 4 \\ \hline \end{array}$ $\begin{array}{r} 4 \\ +\ 8 \\ \hline \end{array}$ $\begin{array}{r} 8 \\ +\ 8 \\ \hline \end{array}$ $\begin{array}{r} 4 \\ +\ 5 \\ \hline \end{array}$

3. $\begin{array}{r} 9 \\ +\ 3 \\ \hline \end{array}$ $\begin{array}{r} 0 \\ +\ 9 \\ \hline \end{array}$ $\begin{array}{r} 6 \\ +\ 1 \\ \hline \end{array}$ $\begin{array}{r} 8 \\ +\ 2 \\ \hline \end{array}$ $\begin{array}{r} 9 \\ +\ 1 \\ \hline \end{array}$ $\begin{array}{r} 9 \\ +\ 2 \\ \hline \end{array}$

4. $\begin{array}{r} 9 \\ +\ 4 \\ \hline \end{array}$ $\begin{array}{r} 5 \\ +\ 7 \\ \hline \end{array}$ $\begin{array}{r} 4 \\ +\ 6 \\ \hline \end{array}$ $\begin{array}{r} 6 \\ +\ 9 \\ \hline \end{array}$ $\begin{array}{r} 8 \\ +\ 9 \\ \hline \end{array}$ $\begin{array}{r} 4 \\ +\ 9 \\ \hline \end{array}$

5. $3 + 9 =$ ____ $9 + 5 =$ ____ $7 + 4 =$ ____

6. $7 + 5 =$ ____ $3 + 8 =$ ____ $1 + 8 =$ ____

Critical Thinking Corner

Mental Math

7. Tell how making a ten can help you add 9 + 5 in your head.

Making 10 can help you add 7, 8, and 9.

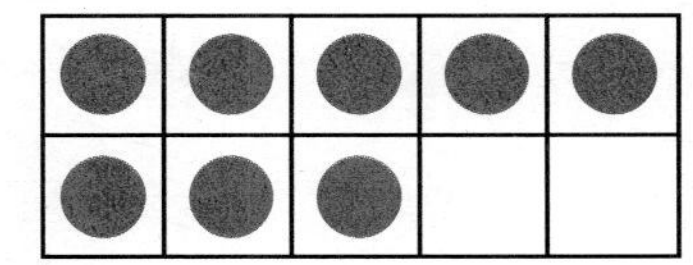

8 + 5 Think 10 + 3

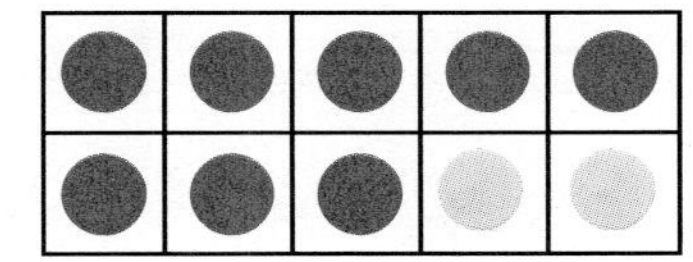

10 + 3 = 13

8 + 5 = 13

Use counters and Workmat 1.
Find each sum.

1.	7 + 5	3 + 8	6 + 7	8 + 6	5 + 7	4 + 8
2.	3 + 7	2 + 9	8 + 3	4 + 7	8 + 4	6 + 8
3.	7 + 4	8 + 7	2 + 8	9 + 3	9 + 6	7 + 9
4.	9 + 5	7 + 6	8 + 4	9 + 8	2 + 7	7 + 8

Home Connection Making 10 can help children add 7, 8, and 9. Ask your child to use 10 to explain how to add facts like 8 + 5.

Add. Color each sum.
10 and 11 red
12 and 13 purple
14 and 15 green
16 and 17 yellow
9 + 5
8 + 4
9 + 3
2 + 8
9 + 8
7 + 4
8 + 8
2 + 9
6 + 8
8 + 9
7 + 7
3 + 8
7 + 8
8 + 7
6 + 7
7 + 3

Name____ **Three Addends**

There are many ways to add 3 numbers.

$$\begin{array}{r} 3 \\ 3 \\ +7 \\ \hline \end{array} \quad \begin{array}{r} 6 \\ 7 \\ \hline 13 \end{array} \qquad \begin{array}{r} 3 \\ 3 \\ +7 \\ \hline \end{array} \quad \begin{array}{r} 3 \\ +10 \\ \hline 13 \end{array}$$

You can add in any order.

You can look for sums of 10.

You can look for doubles.

Add.

1.

$2 + 8 + 3 = 13$	$5 + 5 + 3$	$6 + 0 + 4$	$2 + 2 + 8$	$4 + 6 + 5$	$2 + 7 + 1$

2.

$2 + 8 + 5$	$5 + 2 + 2$	$7 + 3 + 2$	$4 + 2 + 4$	$5 + 3 + 3$	$7 + 3 + 1$

3.

$3 + 5 + 4$	$1 + 2 + 8$	$6 + 4 + 4$	$8 + 4 + 1$	$4 + 4 + 4$	$2 + 5 + 4$

Home Connection Children can add 3 numbers in a variety of ways. Write an addition problem with 3 numbers. Have your child tell you different ways to solve the problem.

Add. Try different ways.

1. $\begin{array}{r}1\\8\\+5\\\hline 14\end{array}$ $\begin{array}{r}5\\4\\+2\\\hline\end{array}$ $\begin{array}{r}6\\3\\+2\\\hline\end{array}$ $\begin{array}{r}4\\2\\+4\\\hline\end{array}$ $\begin{array}{r}5\\3\\+3\\\hline\end{array}$ $\begin{array}{r}7\\3\\+2\\\hline\end{array}$

2. $\begin{array}{r}3\\5\\+4\\\hline\end{array}$ $\begin{array}{r}1\\2\\+8\\\hline\end{array}$ $\begin{array}{r}6\\4\\+4\\\hline\end{array}$ $\begin{array}{r}8\\4\\+1\\\hline\end{array}$ $\begin{array}{r}4\\4\\+4\\\hline\end{array}$ $\begin{array}{r}2\\5\\+4\\\hline\end{array}$

3. $\begin{array}{r}5\\5\\+5\\\hline\end{array}$ $\begin{array}{r}1\\3\\+7\\\hline\end{array}$ $\begin{array}{r}6\\1\\+3\\\hline\end{array}$ $\begin{array}{r}4\\0\\+1\\\hline\end{array}$ $\begin{array}{r}2\\8\\+2\\\hline\end{array}$ $\begin{array}{r}3\\3\\+3\\\hline\end{array}$

4. $6 + 5 + 4 =$ ____ $2 + 4 + 6 =$ ____ $2 + 3 + 3 =$ ____

5. $8 + 0 + 2 =$ ____ $5 + 3 + 1 =$ ____ $5 + 4 + 7 =$ ____

Critical Thinking Corner

Number Sense

6. Write your own number sentence.
Tell which numbers you would add first. Explain.

____ + ____ + ____ = ____

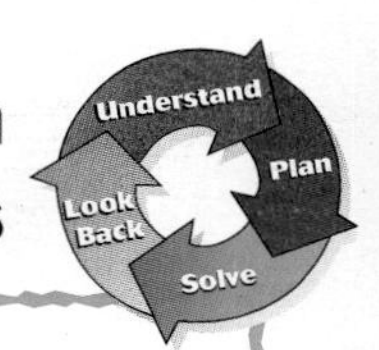

Name________________________

Using Algebra Use counters to find how many are in each basket.

1. 9 in all

 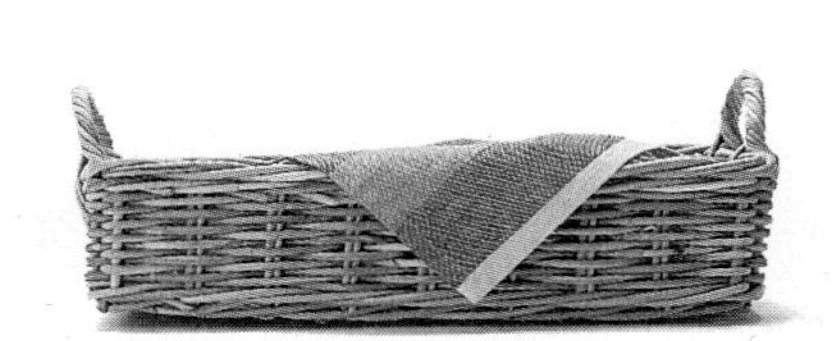

4 + 5 = 9

5 are in the basket.

2. 15 in all

 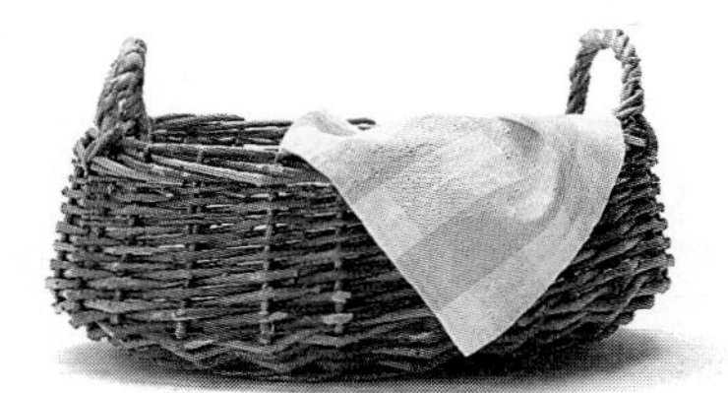

6 + ____ = 15

____ are in the basket.

3. 14 in all

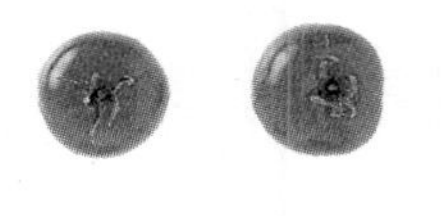 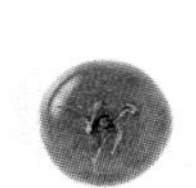 

6 + ____ = 14

____ are in the basket.

4. 12 in all

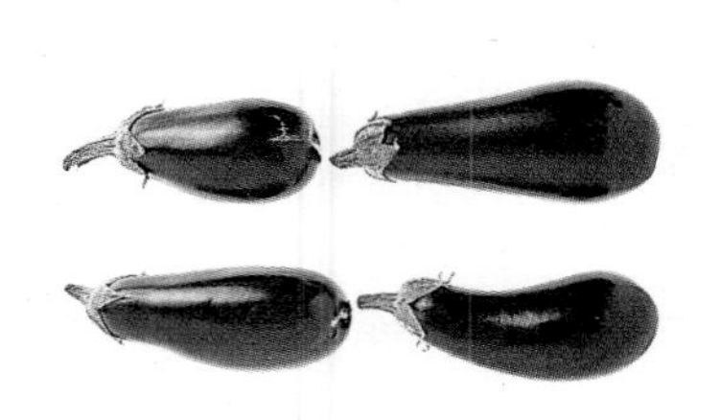 

4 + ____ = 12

____ are in the basket.

Home Connection Have your child watch you place 7 pennies under a bowl. Remove 3 pennies. Ask how many are still under the bowl.

Use counters to find each missing addend.
Write the numbers.

1. 13 in all

5 + ____ = 13

____ are in the basket.

2. 8 in all

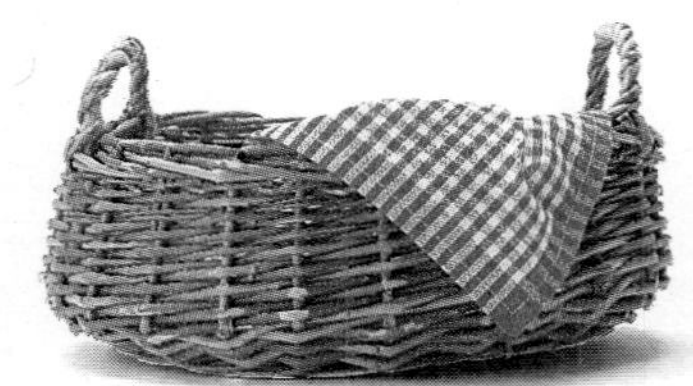

8 + ____ = 8

____ are in the basket.

3. 7 in all

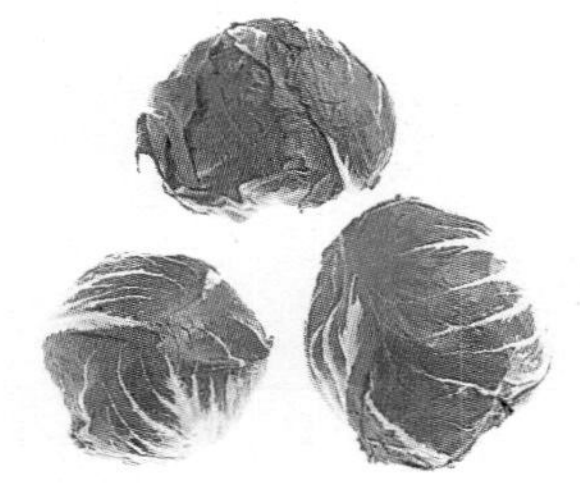
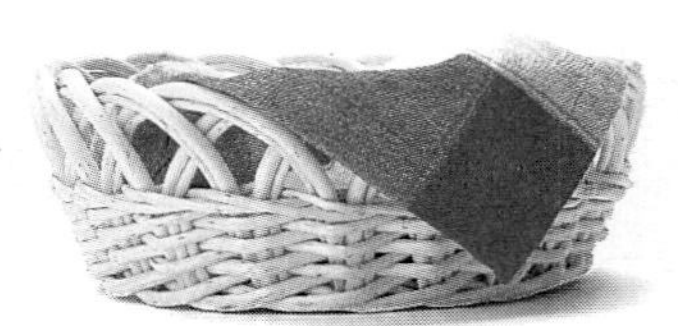

3 + ____ = 7

____ are in the basket.

4. 11 in all

6 + ____ = 11

____ are in the basket.

Name ______________________________ **Checkpoint** 

1. Write different sums for 10.

___ + ___ = 10　　___ + ___ = 10

___ + ___ = 10　　___ + ___ = 10

2. Add.

$\begin{array}{r} 10 \\ +\ 3 \\ \hline \end{array}$　$\begin{array}{r} 4 \\ +10 \\ \hline \end{array}$　$\begin{array}{r} 10 \\ +\ 2 \\ \hline \end{array}$　$\begin{array}{r} 10 \\ +\ 9 \\ \hline \end{array}$　$\begin{array}{r} 5 \\ +10 \\ \hline \end{array}$　$\begin{array}{r} 1 \\ +10 \\ \hline \end{array}$

3. Add. Make 10 when you can.

$\begin{array}{r} 9 \\ +\ 7 \\ \hline \end{array}$　$\begin{array}{r} 4 \\ +\ 9 \\ \hline \end{array}$　$\begin{array}{r} 7 \\ +\ 5 \\ \hline \end{array}$　$\begin{array}{r} 8 \\ +\ 3 \\ \hline \end{array}$　$\begin{array}{r} 6 \\ +\ 8 \\ \hline \end{array}$　$\begin{array}{r} 4 \\ +\ 7 \\ \hline \end{array}$

4. Add. Try different ways.

$\begin{array}{r} 5 \\ 4 \\ +6 \\ \hline \end{array}$　$\begin{array}{r} 4 \\ 2 \\ +4 \\ \hline \end{array}$　$\begin{array}{r} 5 \\ 5 \\ +5 \\ \hline \end{array}$　$\begin{array}{r} 2 \\ 5 \\ +4 \\ \hline \end{array}$　$\begin{array}{r} 3 \\ 7 \\ +3 \\ \hline \end{array}$　$\begin{array}{r} 6 \\ 5 \\ +6 \\ \hline \end{array}$

5. Write each addition sentence.

___ + ___ = ___

___ + ___ = ___

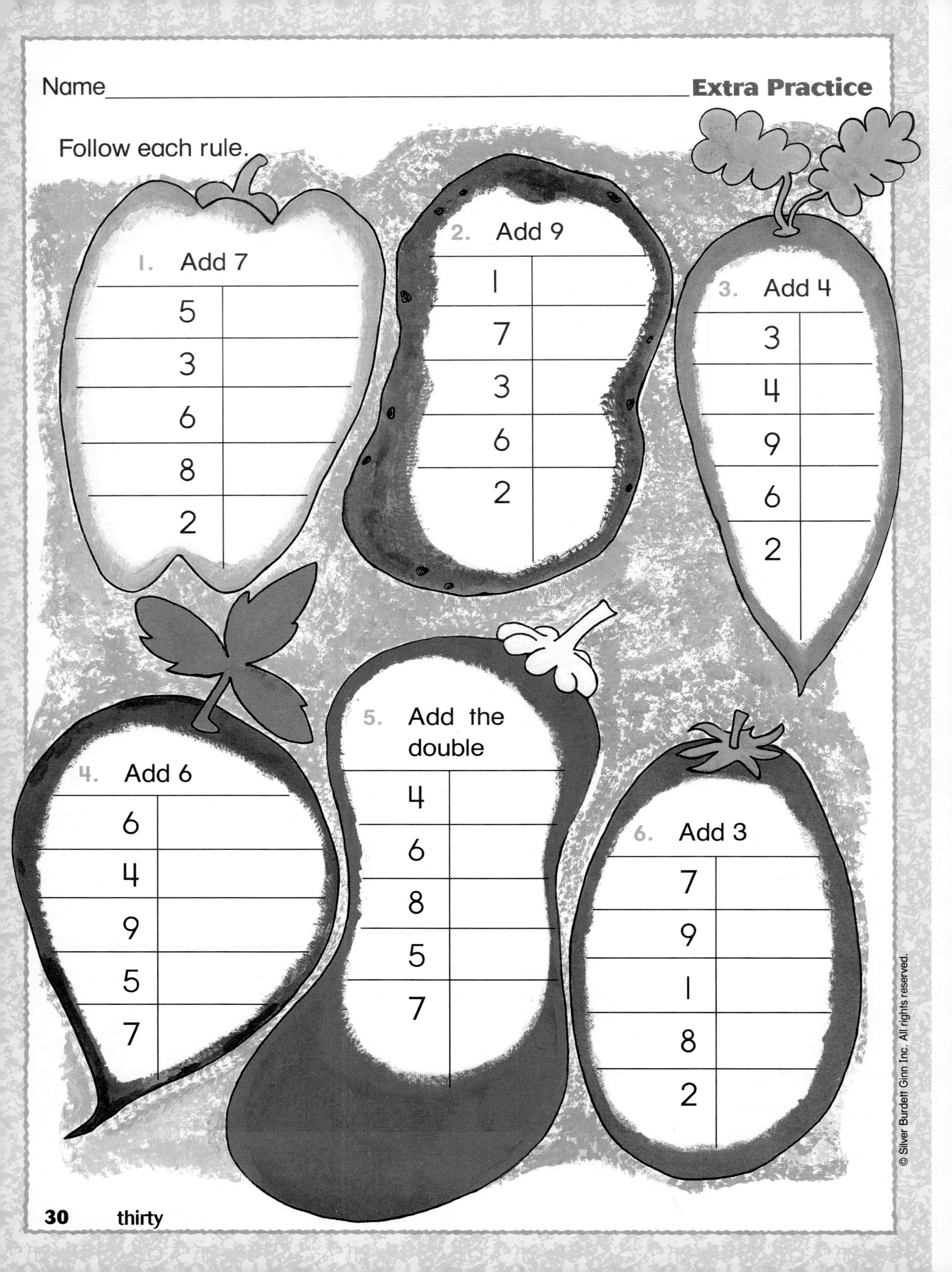

Name ______________________ **Extra Practice**

Follow each rule.

1. Add 7

5	
3	
6	
8	
2	

2. Add 9

1	
7	
3	
6	
2	

3. Add 4

3	
4	
9	
6	
2	

4. Add 6

6	
4	
9	
5	
7	

5. Add the double

4	
6	
8	
5	
7	

6. Add 3

7	
9	
1	
8	
2	

Name______________________________ **Chapter Test** 

Find each sum.

1. $4 + 8 =$ ____

$8 + 4 =$ ____

2. $7 + 3 =$ ____

$3 + 7 =$ ____

3. Add. Count on or use doubles.

$8 + 1$ $7 + 6$ $9 + 2$ $6 + 5$ $3 + 7$ $8 + 9$

4. Make 10 to add.

$8 + 3$ $5 + 7$ $9 + 7$ $7 + 4$ $3 + 9$ $5 + 8$

5. Find the sum. Try different ways.

$5 + 4 + 6 =$ ____ $3 + 7 + 3 =$ ____

Find the missing addends.

6. 9 in all

$5 +$ ____ $= 9$

____ are in the basket.

7. 14 in all

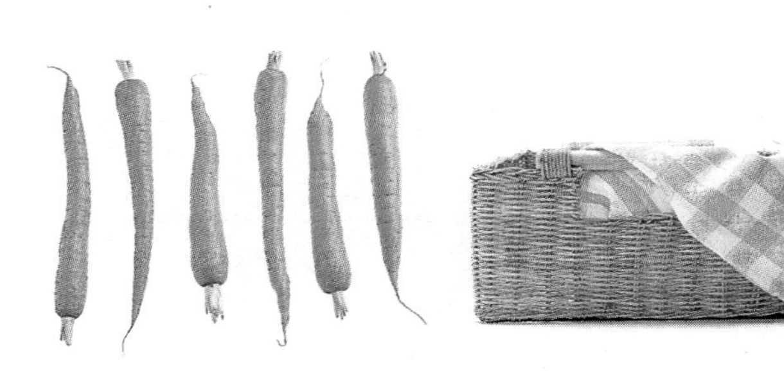

$6 +$ ____ $= 14$

____ are in the basket.

Name________________________________ **Performance Assessment**

What You Need

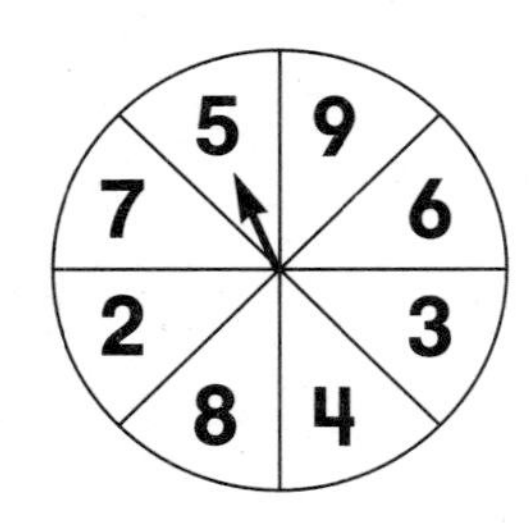

spinner

1. Spin the spinner two times. Record each spin.
2. Use the numbers to write an addition sentence.
3. Tell the strategy you used to find each sum. Tell why.

First Spin	Second Spin	Addition Sentence
1.		___ + ___ = ___
2.		___ + ___ = ___
3.		___ + ___ = ___
4.		___ + ___ = ___
5.		___ + ___ = ___
6.		___ + ___ = ___
7.		___ + ___ = ___

Name____

Complete the addition table.

+	0	1	2	3	4	5	6	7	8	9
0						5				
1										
2										
3										
4										
5										
6										
7										
8								15		
9										

Name________________________________

Time for Technology
Adding With a Calculator

Use a calculator to add 5 + 9.

Press ON/C 5 + 9 =

What number do you see? 14

Use a calculator to add.
Record the keys you press.
Write the sum.

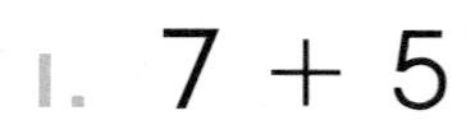

1. 7 + 5      

ON/C 7 + 5 = 12

2. 3 + 8 ON/C     

3. 7 + 9 ON/C   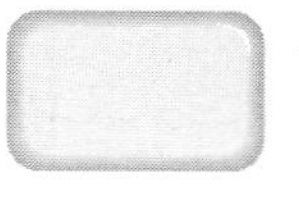  

4. 6 + 5 ON/C     

5. 8 + 8 ON/C     

6. 9 + 1 ON/C     

7. 9 + 4 ON/C     

8. 8 + 6 ON/C   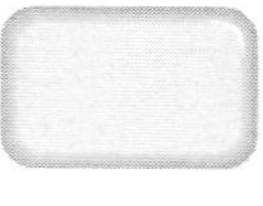  

9. 7 + 8 ON/C   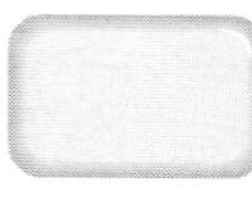  

Make your own.

10. ____ + ____ ON/C   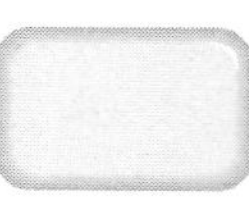  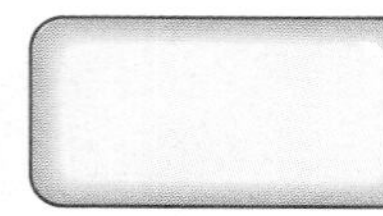

Using Subtraction Strategies

Outside Eva's Window

written by Barbara Reeves
illustrated by Teresa Flavin

This Math Storybook belongs to

____

A

Outside Eva's window the day is cool and bright.
Snowbirds fly in the morning.
They stop at Eva's window to sing.
10 birds sing. Then 5 of them take wing.
5 birds are left outside Eva's window.
B

Outside Eva's window the hares play.
They jump and wiggle in the snow.
11 hares play. Then 7 of them run away.
4 hares are left outside Eva's window.
c

Outside Eva's window, caribou roam.
They nibble on grass for a snack.
9 caribou snack. Then 8 of them walk back.
1 caribou is left outside Eva's window.
D

Outside Eva's window, fox pups climb a hill.
They roll down the hill like snowballs.
10 pups slide. Then 2 of them hide.
8 pups are left outside Eva's window.

Outside Eva's window the night is filled with stars.
Owls fly in the cold night air.
9 owls say goodnight, then all of them fly out of sight.
None are left outside Eva's window.
F

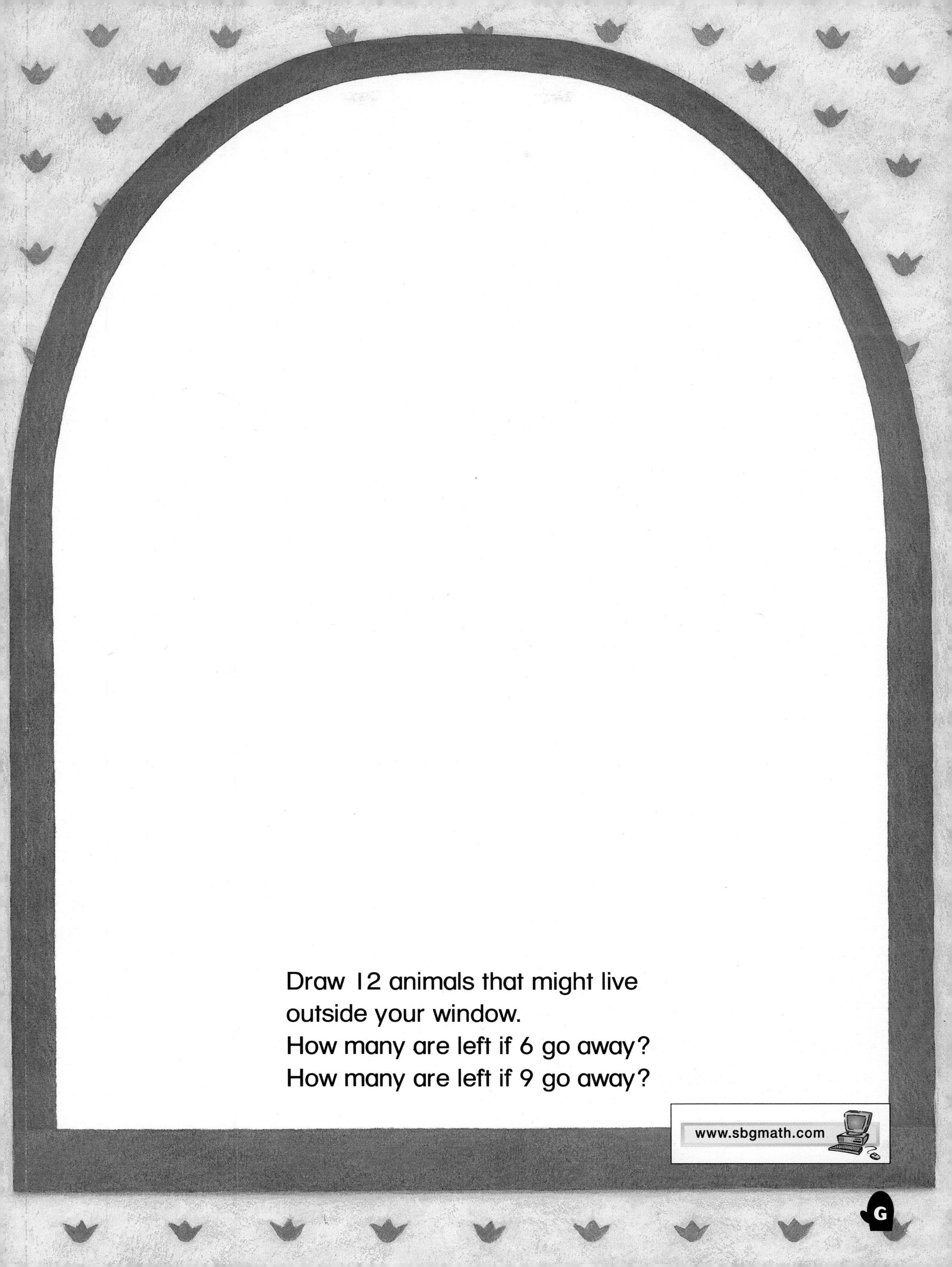
Draw 12 animals that might live
outside your window.
How many are left if 6 go away?
How many are left if 9 go away?
www.sbgmath.com
G

A Note to the Family

Here are some learning ideas you can share with your child.

Enjoy *Outside Eva's Window* Together

- Read the story to your child, and encourage your child to listen for the rhyming words. For each page ask your child to count the number of animals in each group, the number of animals that go away, and the number of animals that stay. Use simple objects such as beans or paper clips to represent the animals. Work with your child to demonstrate each subtraction problem.
- Encourage your child to share what he or she has drawn on the last page of *Outside Eva's Window*. Then help your child write subtraction sentences to answer each question. (12−6=6; 12−9=3)

At-Home Activity

- Play subtraction games with your child while doing household tasks such as cleaning a room or putting away groceries. Count out a group of objects to be put away. Make sure the group is no larger than 18. Have your child help you put away a certain number of objects from the group, such as nine toys or six cans of vegetables. Then ask how many are left. Your child can check his or her subtraction by counting the objects that have not yet been put away.

Read More About It!

For more stories about subtraction, look for these books in your local library.

- *Ten in a Bed* by Mary Rees (Little, Brown, 1988)
- *Take Away Monsters* by Colin Hawkins (Putnam, 1984)
- *Pop-Up Numbers: #2 Subtraction* by Ray Marshall and Paul Korky (Dutton, 1984)

Visit Our Web Site!

www.sbgmath.com

Name______________________________ **Understanding Subtraction**

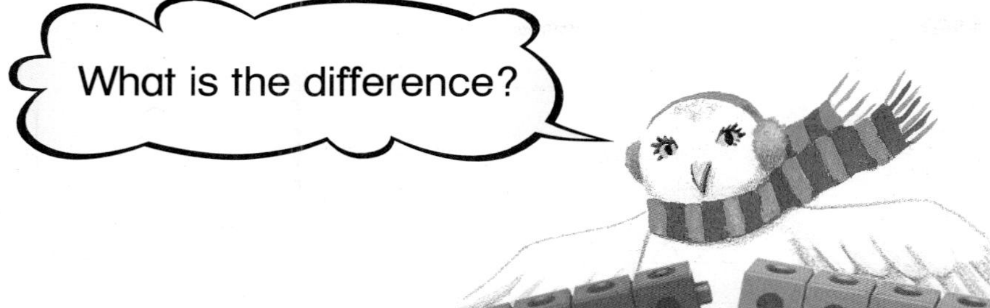

Word Bank

- subtract
- difference
- minus
- subtraction sentence

$9 - 5 =$ 4

$9 - 4 =$ 5

Subtract. Use cubes if you like.

1. $6 - 4 =$ ___ $8 - 3 =$ ___ $10 - 4 =$ ___

   $6 - 2 =$ ___ $8 - 5 =$ ___ $10 - 6 =$ ___

2. $5 - 2 =$ ___ $9 - 7 =$ ___ $7 - 3 =$ ___

   $5 - 3 =$ ___ $9 - 2 =$ ___ $7 - 4 =$ ___

3. $\begin{array}{r} 6 \\ -0 \\ \hline \end{array}$ $\begin{array}{r} 10 \\ -1 \\ \hline \end{array}$ $\begin{array}{r} 8 \\ -1 \\ \hline \end{array}$ $\begin{array}{r} 6 \\ -5 \\ \hline \end{array}$ $\begin{array}{r} 8 \\ -6 \\ \hline \end{array}$ $\begin{array}{r} 7 \\ -7 \\ \hline \end{array}$

4. $\begin{array}{r} 10 \\ -6 \\ \hline \end{array}$ $\begin{array}{r} 5 \\ -4 \\ \hline \end{array}$ $\begin{array}{r} 7 \\ -0 \\ \hline \end{array}$ $\begin{array}{r} 8 \\ -2 \\ \hline \end{array}$ $\begin{array}{r} 5 \\ -5 \\ \hline \end{array}$ $\begin{array}{r} 9 \\ -8 \\ \hline \end{array}$

5. $\begin{array}{r} 3 \\ -2 \\ \hline \end{array}$ $\begin{array}{r} 6 \\ -1 \\ \hline \end{array}$ $\begin{array}{r} 7 \\ -2 \\ \hline \end{array}$ $\begin{array}{r} 8 \\ -8 \\ \hline \end{array}$ $\begin{array}{r} 9 \\ -4 \\ \hline \end{array}$ $\begin{array}{r} 10 \\ -8 \\ \hline \end{array}$

Home Connection Your child is reviewing the meaning of subtraction. Ask your child how he or she solves subtraction problems like those on this page.

Look at each picture.
Write the subtraction sentence.

1.

6 − 4 = 2

2.

3.

___ − ___ = ___

4.

5.

___ − ___ = ___

6.

Critical Thinking Corner

Visual Thinking

7. Are there more green or orange? ______
Write a subtraction sentence to show how many more.

___ − ___ = ___

Name____

You can count back to subtract.

To subtract 10 − 2, start with 10. Count back 2.

Word Bank
number line
count back

$10 - 2 = $ 8

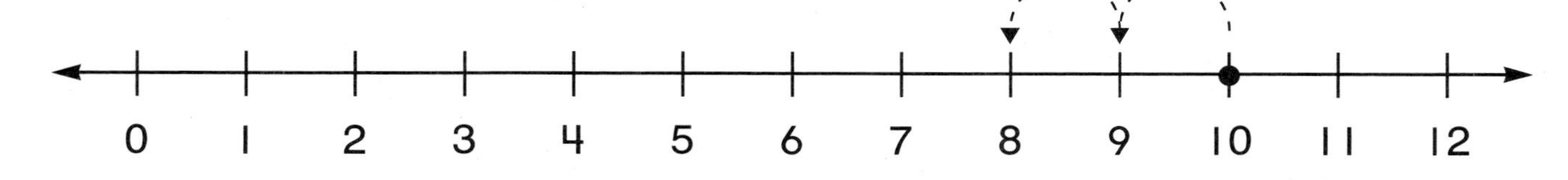

Use the number line to subtract.
Draw ⤺. Write each difference.

1. $8 - 1 = $ ____

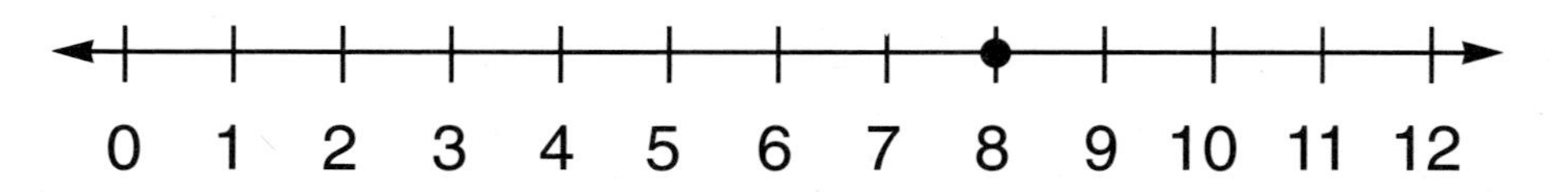

2. $9 - 2 = $ ____

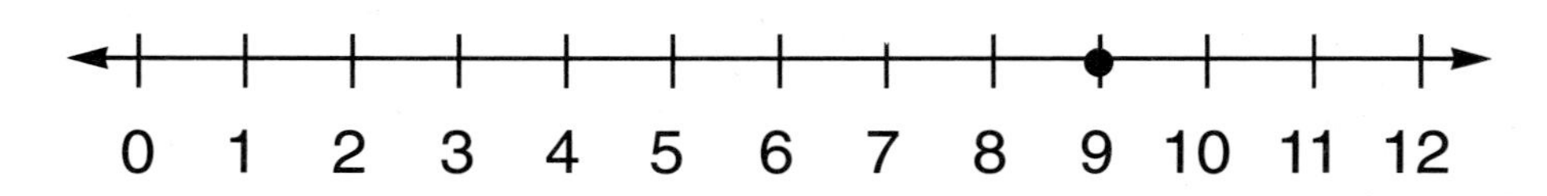

3. $11 - 2 = $ ____

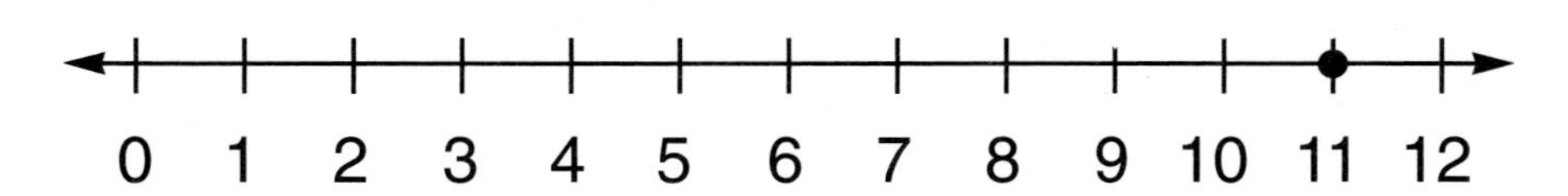

4. $12 - 3 = $ ____

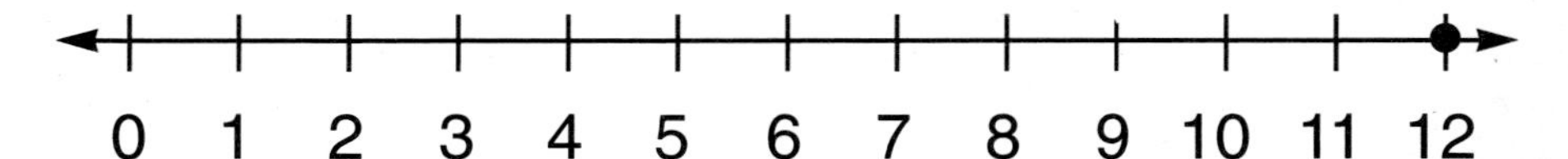

5. $10 - 1 = $ ____

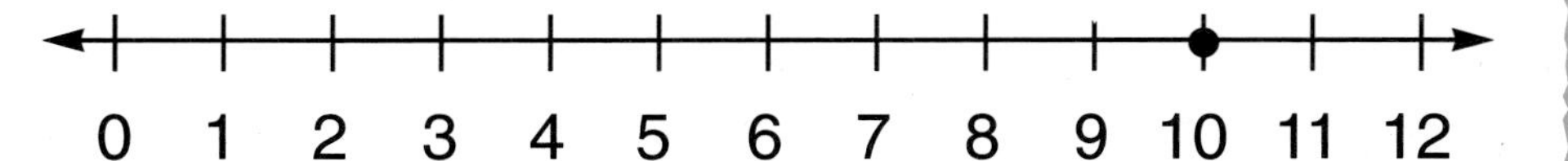

6. $11 - 3 = $ ____

0 1 2 3 4 5 6 7 8 9 10 11 12

Home Connection Some children find counting back a useful strategy. Have your child count back to subtract 1, 2, or 3 from a number.

Use the number line. Count back to subtract.

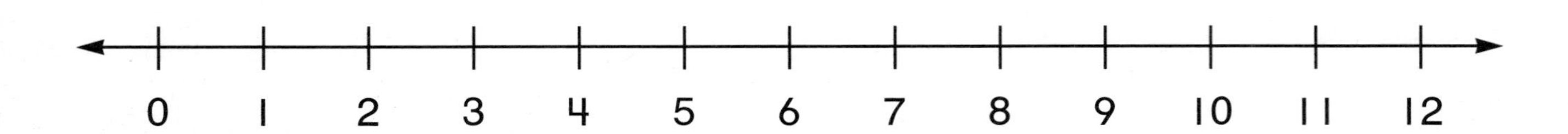

1.	$6 - 1 = 5$	$7 - 2$	$3 - 3$	$10 - 3$	$5 - 2$	$7 - 0$
2.	$11 - 3$	$6 - 0$	$9 - 2$	$8 - 0$	$7 - 3$	$4 - 3$
3.	$5 - 1$	$8 - 2$	$10 - 2$	$12 - 3$	$4 - 2$	$9 - 0$
4.	$8 - 1$	$7 - 3$	$9 - 3$	$11 - 2$	$6 - 2$	$7 - 0$
5.	$10 - 1$	$6 - 3$	$7 - 1$	$5 - 3$	$8 - 3$	$9 - 1$

Problem Solving

6,7,8

Mental Math

8,7,6

6. Think when you might count back.
Think when you might count on.
Write a problem for each.

Name ______________________

Word Bank
related facts

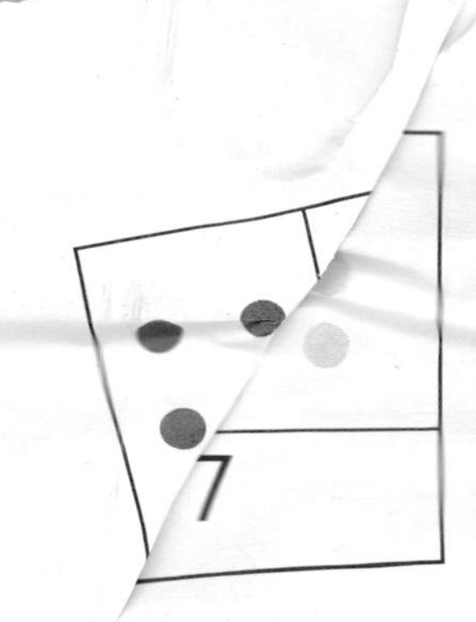
7

Subtraction is the opposite of addition.

_ + 3 = 7

7 − 3 = 4

Use counters and Workmat 2.
Add. Write a related subtraction fact.

1. 5 + 3 = ___

___ − ___ = ___

2. 3 + 6 = ___

___ − ___ = ___

3. 7 + 5 = ___

___ − ___ = ___

4. 6 + 4 = ___

___ − ___ = ___

5. 2 + 8 = ___

___ − ___ = ___

6. 6 + 5 = ___

___ − ___ = ___

Home Connection Knowing addition facts will help your child find related subtraction facts. Ask your child how knowing 4+3=7 helps find 7−3.

Find each sum and difference.

1. 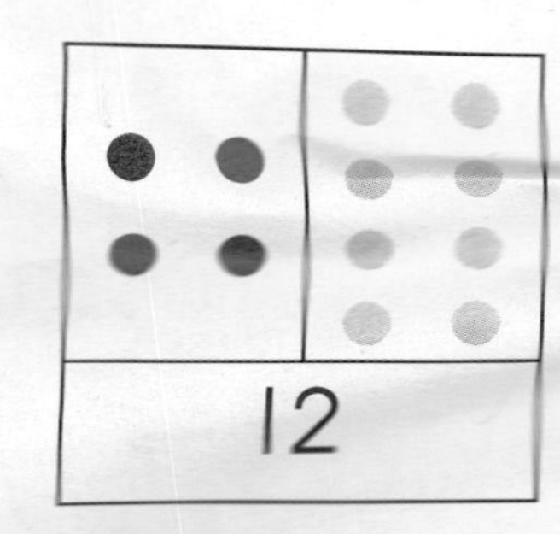

$4 + 8 = 12$ $12 - 8 = 4$

2. 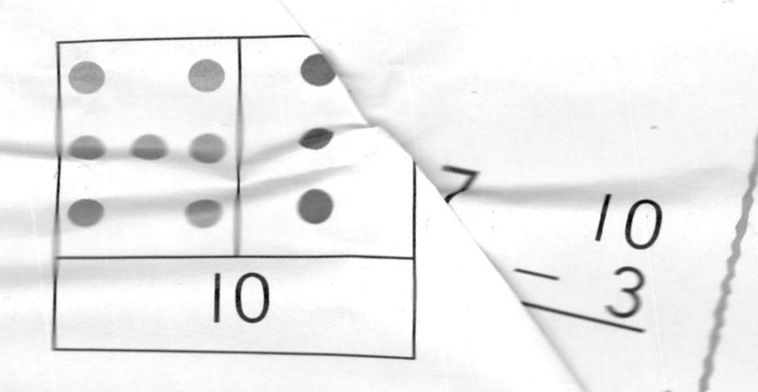

7 … $10 - 3$

3. $3 + 1$ $4 - 1$ $2 + 4$ $6 - 4$ $8 + 2$ $-$

4. $3 + 4$ $7 - 4$ $9 + 3$ $12 - 3$ $7 + 2$ $9 - 2$

5. $2 + 1$ $3 - 1$ $3 + 8$ $11 - 8$ $1 + 7$ $8 - 7$

6. $5 + 7$ $12 - 7$ $3 + 4$ $7 - 4$ $2 + 6$ $8 - 6$

Critical Thinking Corner

Mental Math

7. Subtract. Write a related addition fact.

$5 - 1$ $1 + 4 = 5$

$8 - 6$ $+$ ___

$9 - 4$ $+$ ___

Name ______________________

Word Bank
related facts

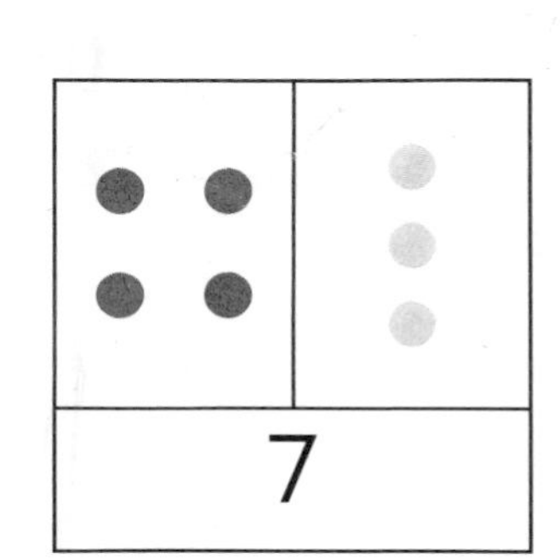
7

Subtraction is the opposite of addition.

4 + 3 = 7

7 − 3 = 4

Use counters and Workmat 2.
Add. Write a related subtraction fact.

1. 5 + 3 = ____

____ − ____ = ____

2. 3 + 6 = ____

____ − ____ = ____

3. 7 + 5 = ____

____ − ____ = ____

4. 6 + 4 = ____

____ − ____ = ____

5. 2 + 8 = ____

____ − ____ = ____

6. 6 + 5 = ____

____ − ____ = ____

Home Connection Knowing addition facts will help your child find related subtraction facts. Ask your child how knowing 4+3=7 helps find 7−3.

Find each sum and difference.

1. 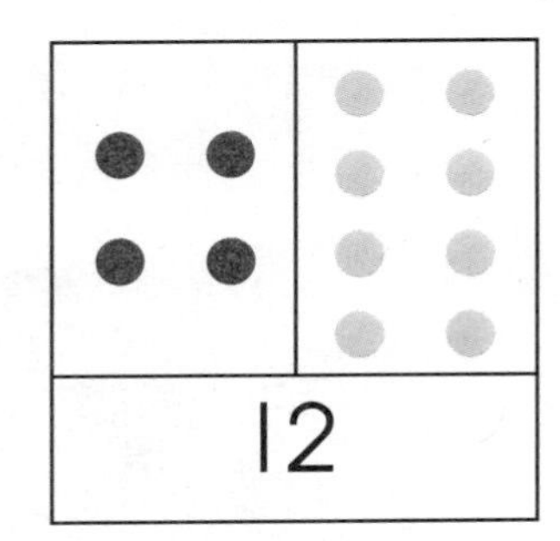

$$\begin{array}{r} 4 \\ +\ 8 \\ \hline 12 \end{array} \qquad \begin{array}{r} 12 \\ -\ 8 \\ \hline 4 \end{array}$$

2. 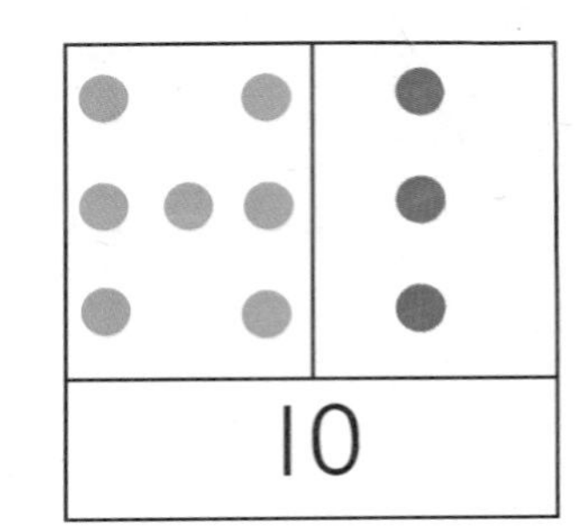

$$\begin{array}{r} 7 \\ +\ 3 \\ \hline \end{array} \qquad \begin{array}{r} 10 \\ -\ 3 \\ \hline \end{array}$$

3. $\begin{array}{r} 3 \\ +\ 1 \\ \hline \end{array}$ $\begin{array}{r} 4 \\ -\ 1 \\ \hline \end{array}$ $\begin{array}{r} 2 \\ +\ 4 \\ \hline \end{array}$ $\begin{array}{r} 6 \\ -\ 4 \\ \hline \end{array}$ $\begin{array}{r} 8 \\ +\ 2 \\ \hline \end{array}$ $\begin{array}{r} 10 \\ -\ 2 \\ \hline \end{array}$

4. $\begin{array}{r} 3 \\ +\ 4 \\ \hline \end{array}$ $\begin{array}{r} 7 \\ -\ 4 \\ \hline \end{array}$ $\begin{array}{r} 9 \\ +\ 3 \\ \hline \end{array}$ $\begin{array}{r} 12 \\ -\ 3 \\ \hline \end{array}$ $\begin{array}{r} 7 \\ +\ 2 \\ \hline \end{array}$ $\begin{array}{r} 9 \\ -\ 2 \\ \hline \end{array}$

5. $\begin{array}{r} 2 \\ +\ 1 \\ \hline \end{array}$ $\begin{array}{r} 3 \\ -\ 1 \\ \hline \end{array}$ $\begin{array}{r} 3 \\ +\ 8 \\ \hline \end{array}$ $\begin{array}{r} 11 \\ -\ 8 \\ \hline \end{array}$ $\begin{array}{r} 1 \\ +\ 7 \\ \hline \end{array}$ $\begin{array}{r} 8 \\ -\ 7 \\ \hline \end{array}$

6. $\begin{array}{r} 5 \\ +\ 7 \\ \hline \end{array}$ $\begin{array}{r} 12 \\ -\ 7 \\ \hline \end{array}$ $\begin{array}{r} 3 \\ +\ 4 \\ \hline \end{array}$ $\begin{array}{r} 7 \\ -\ 4 \\ \hline \end{array}$ $\begin{array}{r} 2 \\ +\ 6 \\ \hline \end{array}$ $\begin{array}{r} 8 \\ -\ 6 \\ \hline \end{array}$

Critical Thinking Corner

Mental Math

7. Subtract. Write a related addition fact.

$\begin{array}{r} 5 \\ -\ 1 \\ \hline \end{array}$ $\begin{array}{r} 1 \\ +\ 4 \\ \hline 5 \end{array}$ $\qquad$ $\begin{array}{r} 8 \\ -\ 6 \\ \hline \end{array}$ $\begin{array}{r} \\ +\ \\ \hline \end{array}$ $\qquad$ $\begin{array}{r} 9 \\ -\ 4 \\ \hline \end{array}$ $\begin{array}{r} \\ +\ \\ \hline \end{array}$

Name________________________________

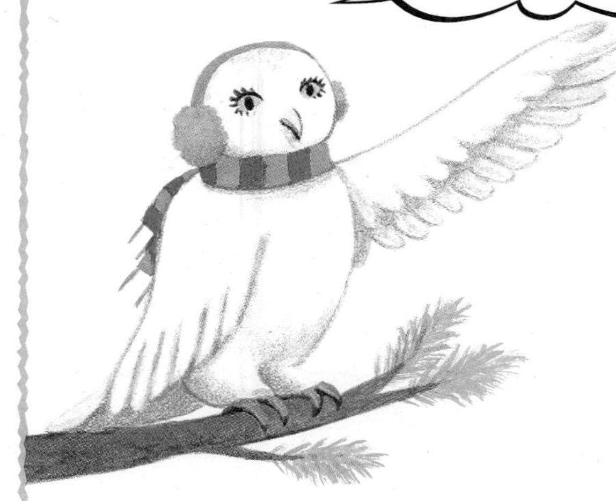

Use the doubles fact to help you subtract.

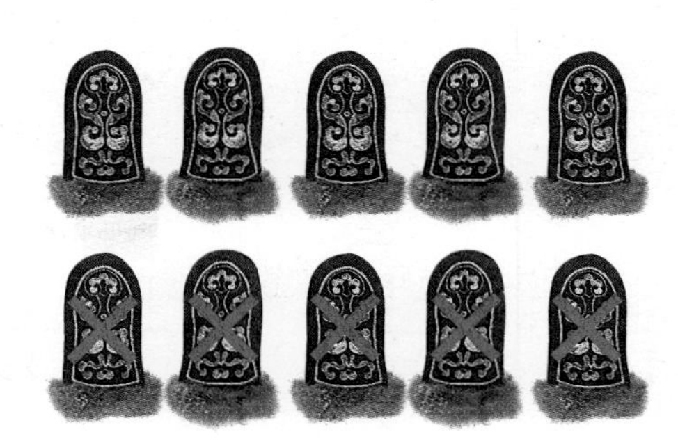

$5 + 5 =$ 10

$10 - 5 =$ 5

Complete each number sentence.

1. $7 + 7 =$ 14 $\quad 3 + 3 =$ ___ $\quad 8 + 8 =$ ___

   $14 - 7 =$ 7 $\quad 6 - 3 =$ ___ $\quad 16 - 8 =$ ___

2. $2 + 2 =$ ___ $\quad 9 + 9 =$ ___ $\quad 6 + 6 =$ ___

   $4 - 2 =$ ___ $\quad 18 - 9 =$ ___ $\quad 12 - 6 =$ ___

3. $5 + 5 =$ ___ $\quad 4 + 4 =$ ___ $\quad 7 + 7 =$ ___

   $10 - 5 =$ ___ $\quad 8 - 4 =$ ___ $\quad 14 - 7 =$ ___

4. $\begin{array}{r} 8 \\ +8 \\ \hline \end{array}$ $\quad \begin{array}{r} 16 \\ -8 \\ \hline \end{array}$ $\quad \begin{array}{r} 6 \\ +6 \\ \hline \end{array}$ $\quad \begin{array}{r} 12 \\ -6 \\ \hline \end{array}$ $\quad \begin{array}{r} 9 \\ +9 \\ \hline \end{array}$ $\quad \begin{array}{r} 18 \\ -9 \\ \hline \end{array}$

Home Connection Children often find it easy to remember doubles facts. Ask your child how knowing $5+5=10$ helps find $10-5$.

Complete the doubles fact.
Use the double to help you subtract.

1. $6 + \boxed{6} = 12$, $12 - 6 = 6$ | $4 + \square = 8$, $8 - 4$ | $3 + \square = 6$, $6 - 3$

2. $9 + \square = 18$, $18 - 9$ | $7 + \square = 14$, $14 - 7$ | $2 + \square = 4$, $4 - 2$

3. $8 + \square = 16$, $16 - 8$ | $5 + \square = 10$, $10 - 5$ | $6 + \square = 12$, $12 - 6$

Problem Solving

Write a number sentence to solve.

4. What if there were 4 fewer dolls?
How many would there be?

___ ◯ ___ = ___

5. What if there were double the number of dolls?
How many would there be?

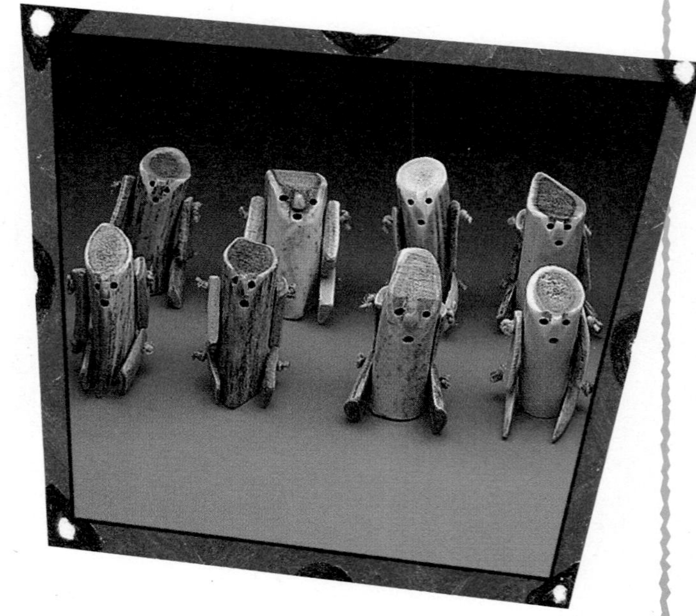

Addition facts can help you subtract.

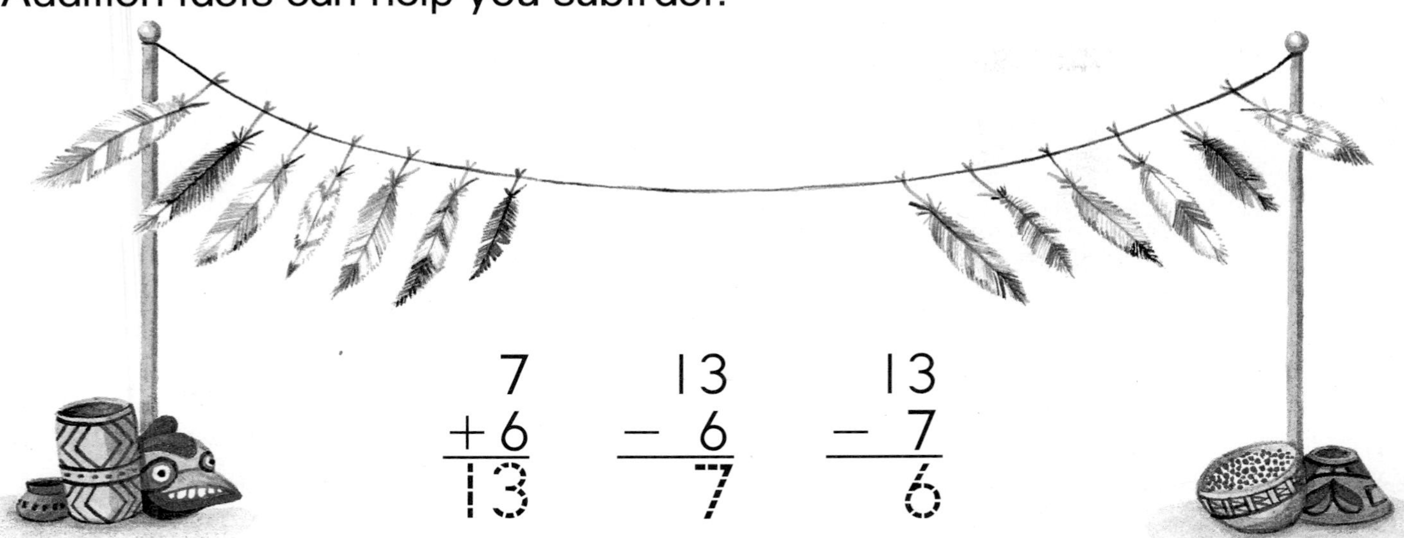

Find each sum or difference.

1. $5 + 6 = 11$ | $11 - 6$ | $11 - 5$

2. $8 + 9$ | $17 - 9$ | $17 - 8$

3. $9 + 4$ | $13 - 4$ | $13 - 9$

4. $4 + 5$ | $9 - 5$ | $9 - 4$

5. $8 + 7$ | $15 - 7$ | $15 - 8$

6. $4 + 6$ | $10 - 6$ | $10 - 4$

7. $6 + 8$ | $14 - 8$ | $14 - 6$

8. $7 + 5$ | $12 - 5$ | $12 - 7$

Home Connection Tell your child an addition fact. Then ask him or her to tell you two related subtraction facts.

Add. Write the related subtraction facts.

1. $6 + 7 = 13$

$13 - 7 =$ ____

$13 - 6 =$ ____

2. $9 + 8 =$ ____

____ − ____ = ____

____ − ____ = ____

3. $5 + 9 =$ ____

____ − ____ = ____

____ − ____ = ____

4. $7 + 9 =$ ____

____ − ____ = ____

____ − ____ = ____

5. $9 + 6 =$ ____

____ − ____ = ____

____ − ____ = ____

6. $7 + 4 =$ ____

____ − ____ = ____

____ − ____ = ____

7. $9 + 3 =$ ____

____ − ____ = ____

____ − ____ = ____

8. $4 + 5 =$ ____

____ − ____ = ____

____ − ____ = ____

Name_______________________________________

Problem-Solving Strategy
Make a Graph

Use the picture to make a graph.
Color a box for each animal.

Polar Animals

	Polar Bears	Fish	Puffins	Seals
8				
7				
6				
5				
4				
3				
2				
1				
0				

1. How many more fish are there than seals?

   _____ more fish

2. How many fewer polar bears are there than fish?

   _____ fewer polar bears

3. What if there were 2 more puffins?

   How many would there be? _____ puffins

Home Connection Children can use information from a picture to make a graph. Ask your child to explain how he or she used the graph to answer each question.

Ask 8 classmates which animal they like best.
Color a box for each answer.

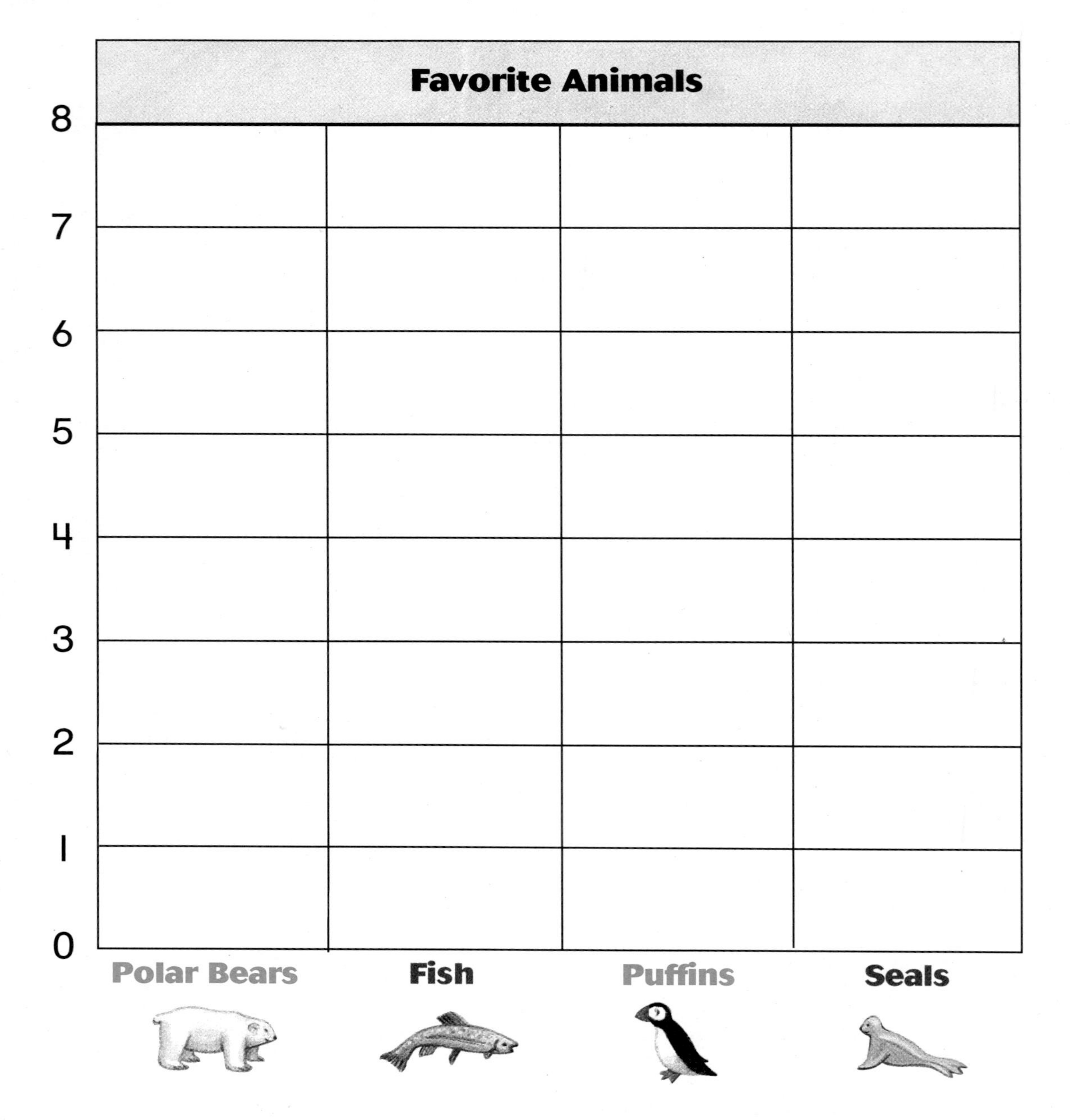

1. How many classmates in all like fish and seals? ____________
2. Which animal is the favorite? ____________
3. Which animal is the least favorite? ____________
4. How many classmates like the favorite animal more than the least favorite animal? ____________

Name________________________________

13
− 9
4
How can you use a ten-frame to subtract?

Use Workmat 1 and counters.
Write how many are left.

1. $\begin{array}{r} 15 \\ -\ 9 \\ \hline 6 \end{array}$ $\begin{array}{r} 9 \\ -9 \\ \hline \end{array}$ $\begin{array}{r} 11 \\ -\ 9 \\ \hline \end{array}$ $\begin{array}{r} 13 \\ -\ 9 \\ \hline \end{array}$ $\begin{array}{r} 18 \\ -\ 9 \\ \hline \end{array}$

2. $\begin{array}{r} 10 \\ -\ 9 \\ \hline \end{array}$ $\begin{array}{r} 12 \\ -\ 9 \\ \hline \end{array}$ $\begin{array}{r} 17 \\ -\ 9 \\ \hline \end{array}$ $\begin{array}{r} 16 \\ -\ 9 \\ \hline \end{array}$ $\begin{array}{r} 14 \\ -\ 9 \\ \hline \end{array}$

3. $18 - 9 =$ ____ $11 - 9 =$ ____ $17 - 9 =$ ____

4. $9 - 9 =$ ____ $13 - 9 =$ ____ $15 - 9 =$ ____

Home Connection Ask your child to show you how he or she used the ten-frame to subtract 9.

Cross out 9 to subtract.

1. $16 - 9 = 7$

2. $12 - 9 =$ ___

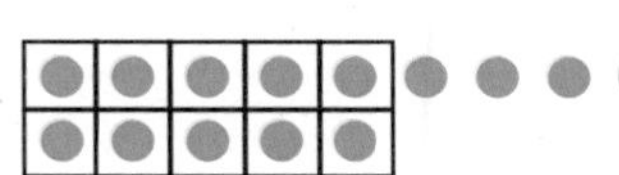

3. $17 - 9 =$ ___

4. $14 - 9 =$ ___

5. $11 - 9 =$ ___

6. $15 - 9 =$ ___

Checkpoint

Count back to subtract.

1. $12 - 3 =$ ___ $8 - 2 =$ ___ $4 - 1 =$ ___ $6 - 3 =$ ___ $10 - 1 =$ ___ $9 - 2 =$ ___

Complete the doubles fact.
Use the double to help you subtract.

2. $4 + \square = 8$ $8 - 4 =$ ___
   $5 + \square = 10$ $10 - 5 =$ ___
   $7 + \square = 14$ $14 - 7 =$ ___

Name____________________

$$\begin{array}{r} 12 \\ -\ 7 \\ \hline 5 \end{array}$$

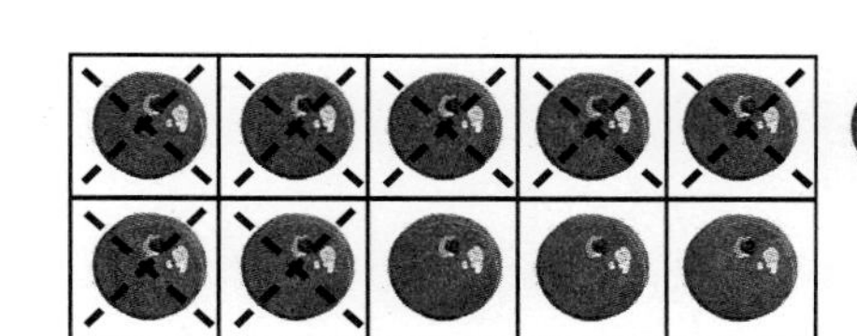

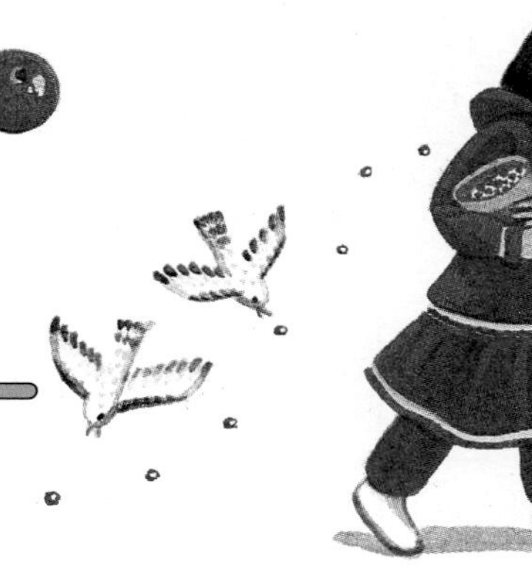

Cross out 7, 8, or 9 to subtract.
Write how many are left.

1. $\begin{array}{r} 14 \\ -\ 8 \\ \hline \end{array}$

2. $\begin{array}{r} 13 \\ -\ 8 \\ \hline \end{array}$

3. $\begin{array}{r} 15 \\ -\ 7 \\ \hline \end{array}$

4. $\begin{array}{r} 12 \\ -\ 8 \\ \hline \end{array}$

5. $\begin{array}{r} 11 \\ -\ 7 \\ \hline \end{array}$

6. $\begin{array}{r} 14 \\ -\ 9 \\ \hline \end{array}$

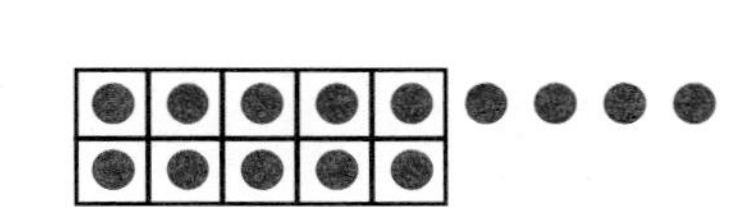

7. $\begin{array}{r} 12 \\ -\ 9 \\ \hline \end{array}$

8. $\begin{array}{r} 15 \\ -\ 8 \\ \hline \end{array}$

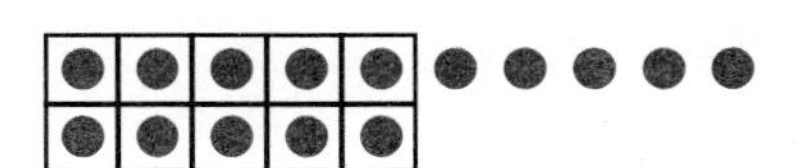

9. $\begin{array}{r} 16 \\ -\ 7 \\ \hline \end{array}$

10. $\begin{array}{r} 11 \\ -\ 8 \\ \hline \end{array}$

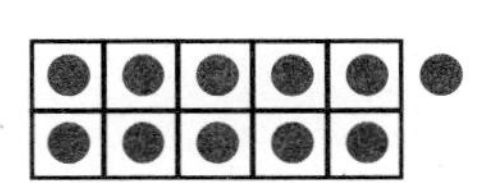

Home Connection Draw a ten-frame, like the ones illustrated on this page, for your child to use. Have your child subtract 7, 8, and 9 from teen numbers, for example, 13−7, 15−8, 14−9.

Using Algebra

Follow the rule.

1.

Add 9	
3	12
6	
8	
5	

2.

Add 8	
5	
7	
4	
6	

3.

Add 7	
5	
7	
4	
6	

4.

Subtract 9	
14	5
11	
17	
13	

5.

Subtract 8	
17	
15	
12	
14	

6.

Subtract 7	
11	
13	
15	
16	

Problem Solving

Write the number sentence.

7. 14 birds are sitting on the fence. 8 fly away. How many are left?

____ ◯ ____ = ____

8. There are 12 penguins and 9 geese. How many fewer geese are there?

____ ◯ ____ = ____

THERE'S ALWAYS A WAY!

There are many ways to subtract.

$16 - 7 = \underline{9}$

You can think of an addition fact.
9+7=16
You can use 10.
9+7=16

Can you think of another way?

Subtract.

1.	$11 - 2 = 9$	$15 - 9$	$12 - 5$	$10 - 2$	$13 - 9$	$11 - 8$
2.	$12 - 7$	$8 - 3$	$16 - 8$	$15 - 7$	$9 - 5$	$15 - 6$
3.	$11 - 4$	$14 - 7$	$9 - 2$	$13 - 8$	$7 - 0$	$18 - 9$
4.	$16 - 9$	$11 - 6$	$14 - 8$	$17 - 8$	$12 - 7$	$13 - 4$

Home Connection Children can subtract in a variety of ways. Have your child explain different ways to solve a subtraction problem from each row.

Count back 1, 2, or 3.

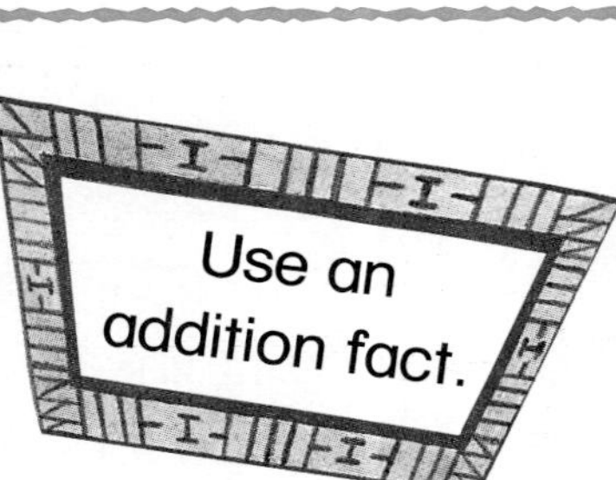

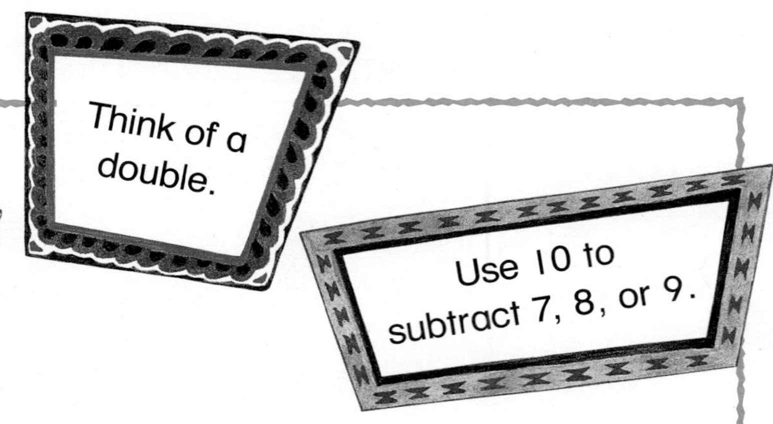

Find each difference.
Write the strategy you used.

1. $12 - 6 =$ ______ ______

2. $11 - 3 =$ ______ ______

3. $15 - 9 =$ ______ ______

4. $14 - 5 =$ ______ ______

5. $16 - 8 =$ ______ ______

6. $17 - 9 =$ ______ ______

Problem Solving

Find the secret number.

7. Subtract 8 from the number to get 8. What is the number? ______

8. Add 9 to the number to get 18. What is the number? ______

Name______________________________ **Fact Families to 12**

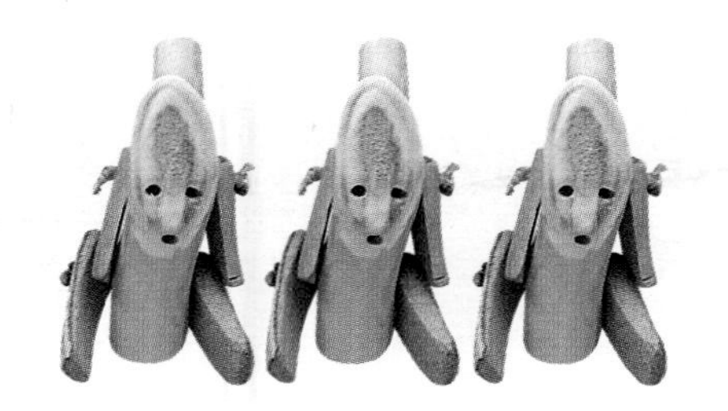

Word Bank
fact family

3 + 5 = 8
5 + 3 = 8

8 − 5 = 3
8 − 3 = 5

Complete each fact family.

1.

5 + 7 = ____
7 + 5 = ____
12 − 5 = ____
12 − 7 = ____

2.

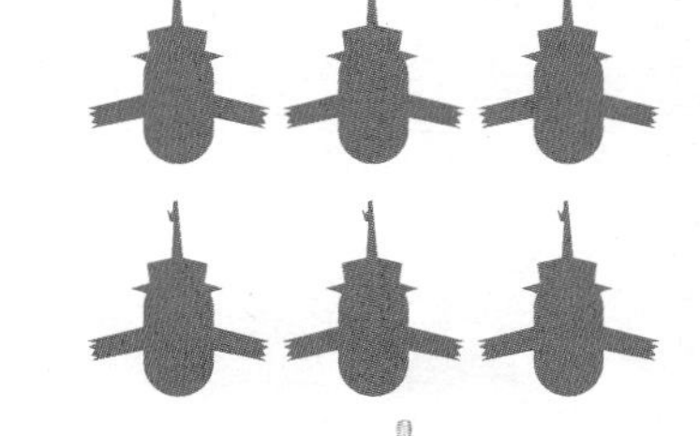

3 + 6 = ____
6 + 3 = ____
9 − 3 = ____
9 − 6 = ____

3.

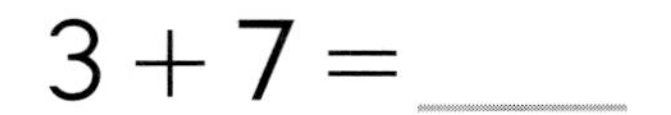

3 + 7 = ____
7 + 3 = ____
10 − 3 = ____
10 − 7 = ____

4.

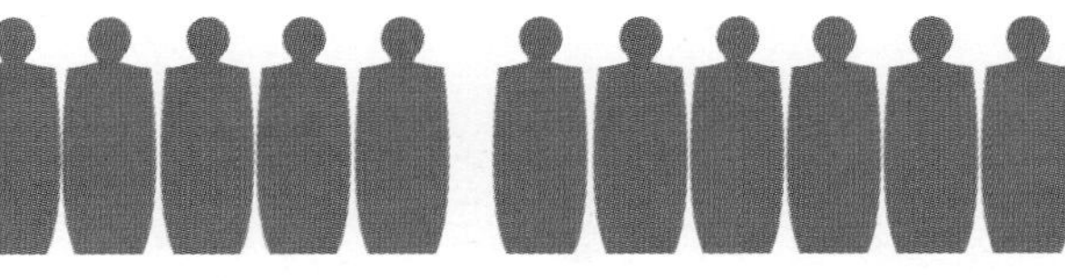

5 + 6 = ____
6 + 5 = ____
11 − 5 = ____
11 − 6 = ____

Home Connection Have your child use household objects such as beans or pennies to show fact families.

Add and subtract.

1.   

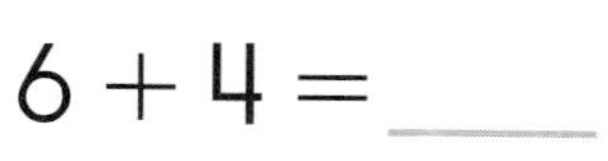
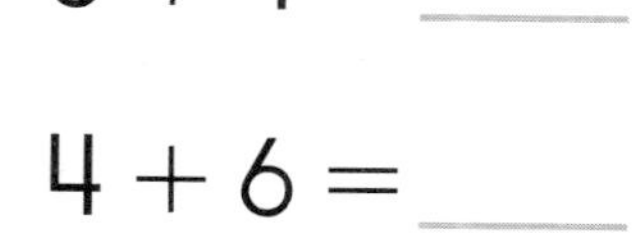

$6 + 4 =$ ____

$4 + 6 =$ ____

$10 - 6 =$ ____

$10 - 4 =$ ____

2. 

$9 + 3 =$ ____

$3 + 9 =$ ____

$12 - 9 =$ ____

$12 - 3 =$ ____

3.  

$6 + 2 =$ ____

$2 + 6 =$ ____

$8 - 6 =$ ____

$8 - 2 =$ ____

4. 

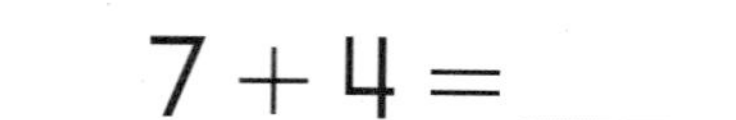

$7 + 4 =$ ____

$4 + 7 =$ ____

$11 - 7 =$ ____

$11 - 4 =$ ____

What Do You Think?

When you add, you can turn the numbers around.

$2 + 4 = 6 \qquad 4 + 2 = 6$

Can you turn the numbers around when you subtract? Tell why or why not.

Journal Idea

Name______________________________ **Fact Families to 18**

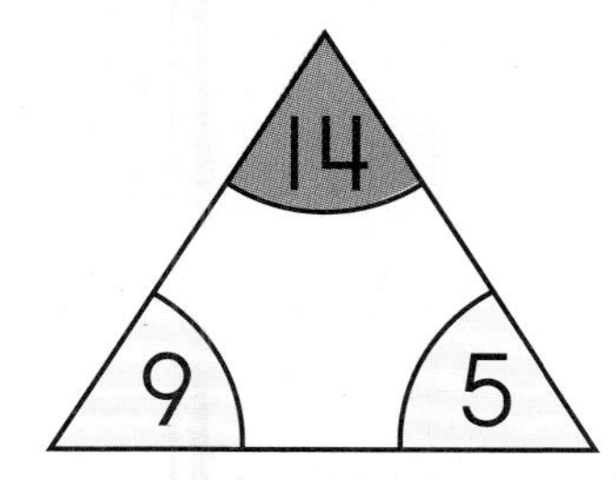

$9 + 5 = 14$ $5 + 9 = 14$ $14 - 5 = 9$ $14 - 9 = 5$

Add and subtract. Use counters if you like.

1.

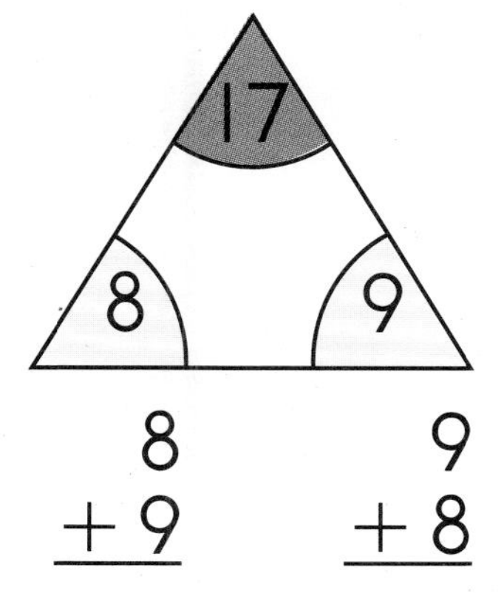

$8 + 9 =$ ___ $9 + 8 =$ ___

$17 - 9 =$ ___ $17 - 8 =$ ___

2.

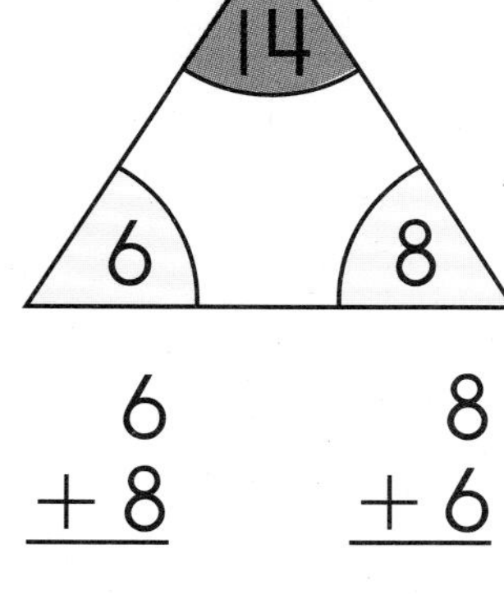

$6 + 8 =$ ___ $8 + 6 =$ ___

$14 - 8 =$ ___ $14 - 6 =$ ___

3.

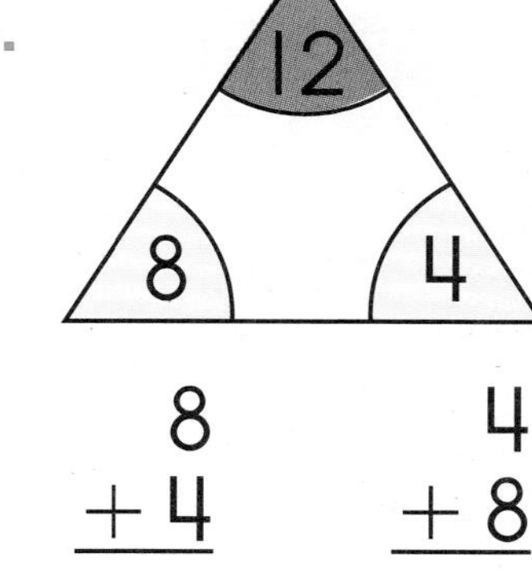

$8 + 4 =$ ___ $4 + 8 =$ ___

$12 - 4 =$ ___ $12 - 8 =$ ___

4.

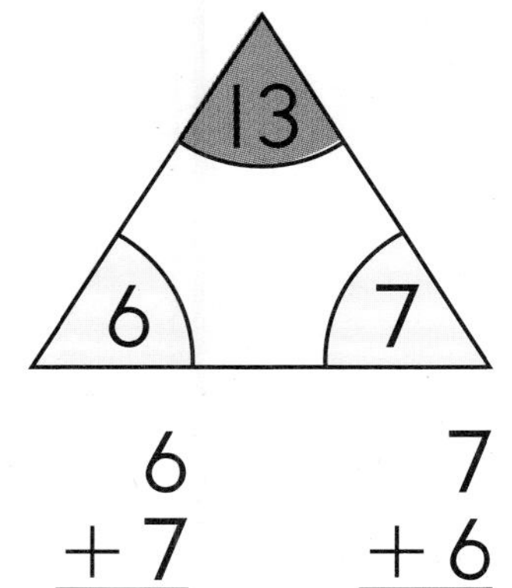

$6 + 7 =$ ___ $7 + 6 =$ ___

$13 - 7 =$ ___ $13 - 6 =$ ___

5.

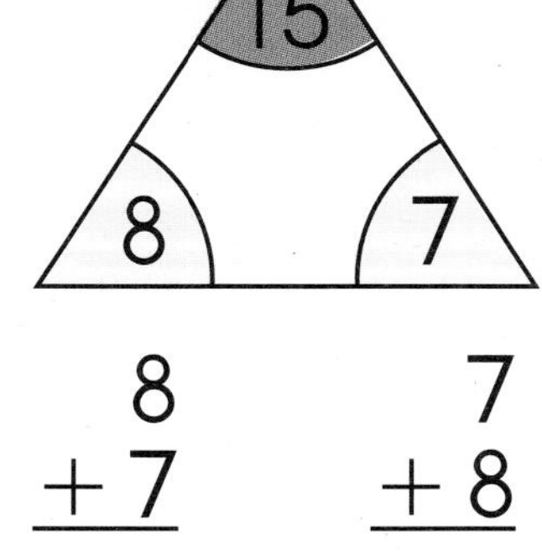

$8 + 7 =$ ___ $7 + 8 =$ ___

$15 - 7 =$ ___ $15 - 8 =$ ___

6.

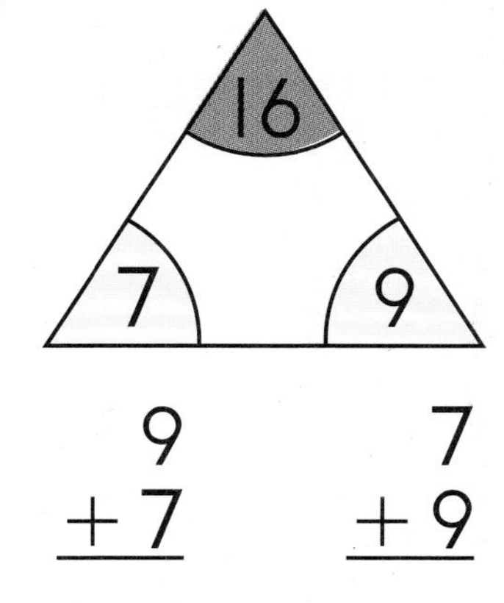

$9 + 7 =$ ___ $7 + 9 =$ ___

$16 - 7 =$ ___ $16 - 9 =$ ___

Home Connection Ask your child to tell you the fact family for 7, 8, and 15.

Write each fact family.

1.

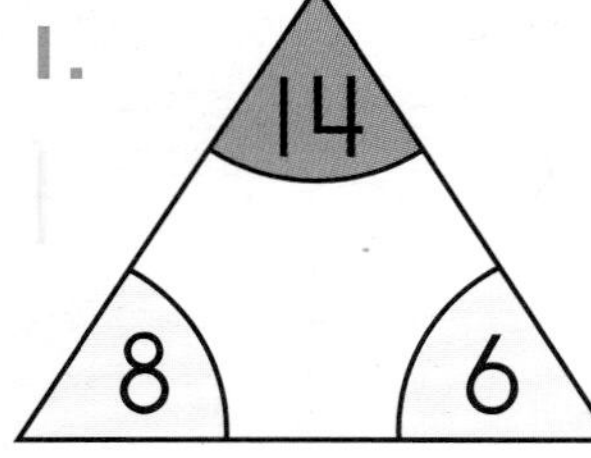

$8 + 6 = 14$ $14 - 6 = 8$

$6 + 8 = 14$ $14 - 8 = 6$

2.

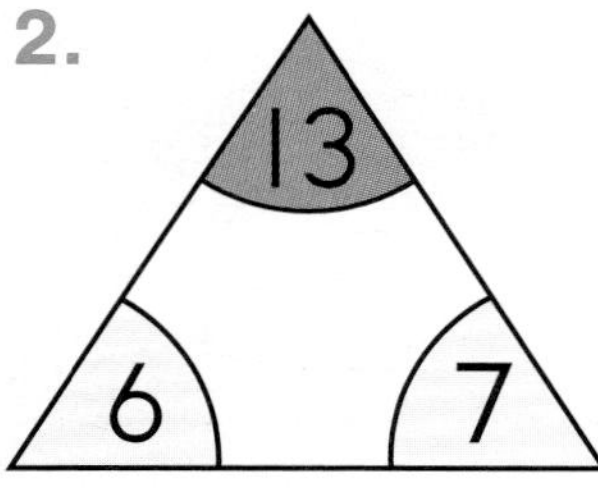

___ + ___ = ___ ___ − ___ = ___

___ + ___ = ___ ___ − ___ = ___

3.

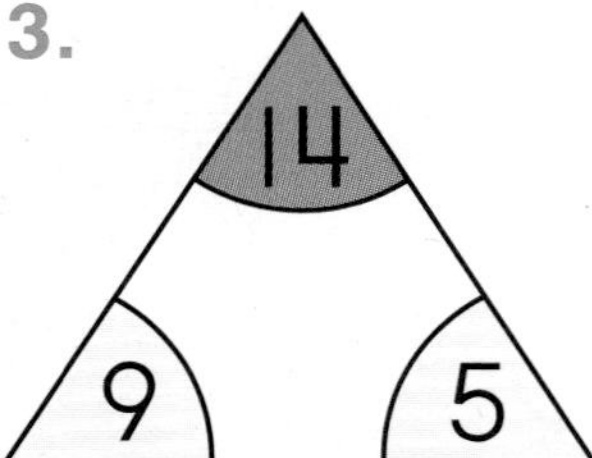

___ + ___ = ___ ___ − ___ = ___

___ + ___ = ___ ___ − ___ = ___

4.

___ + ___ = ___ ___ − ___ = ___

___ + ___ = ___ ___ − ___ = ___

5.

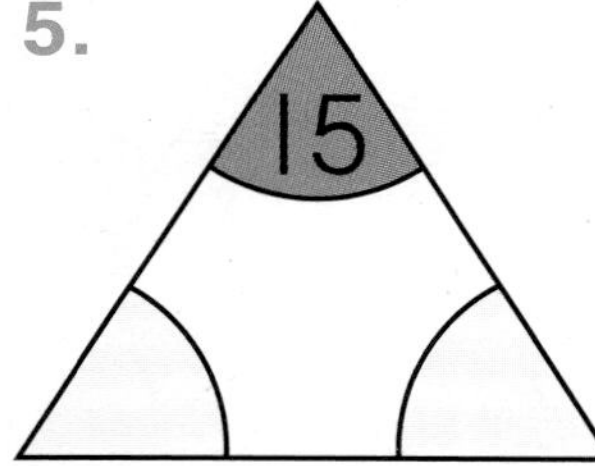

___ + ___ = ___ ___ − ___ = ___

___ + ___ = ___ ___ − ___ = ___

6.

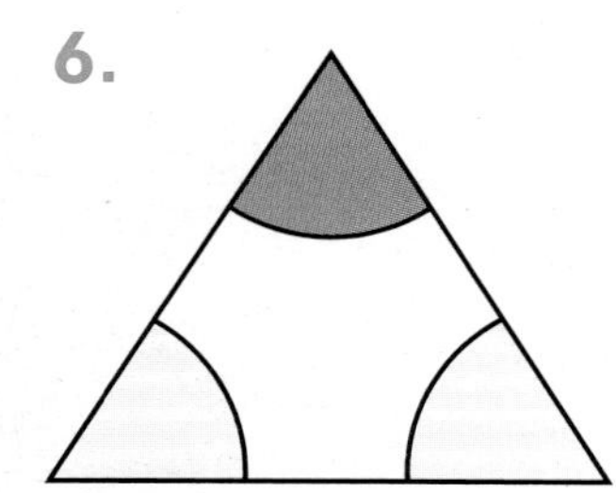

___ + ___ = ___ ___ − ___ = ___

___ + ___ = ___ ___ − ___ = ___

Name ____________________ **Names for Numbers**

Which facts are names for 8?

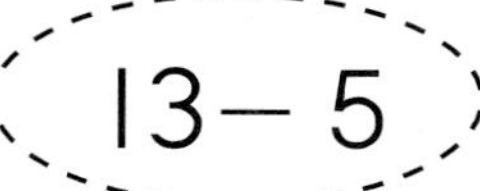
13 − 5 | 7 + 2 | 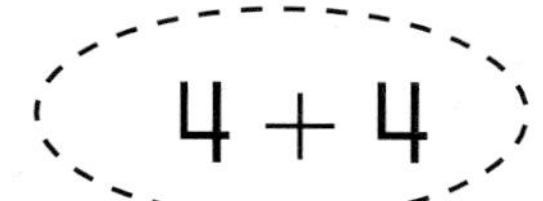 4 + 4 | 12 − 4

Circle the names for each number.

1. 

8 + 1 | 17 − 8 | 12 − 5 | 15 − 6

2. 

15 − 8 | 12 − 4 | 4 + 3 | 11 − 4

3. 

17 − 8 | 5 + 5 | 3 + 7 | 6 + 4

4. 

13 − 9 | 14 − 8 | 12 − 8 | 11 − 7

5. 

5 + 2 | 14 − 6 | 13 − 7 | 16 − 8

6. 

17 − 9 | 12 − 6 | 14 − 8 | 15 − 9

7. 

5 + 7 | 18 − 9 | 6 + 6 | 13 − 8

Home Connection Give your child 18 small objects, such as dried beans. Ask your child to show 3 ways to get a sum of 8 and 3 ways to show a difference of 8.

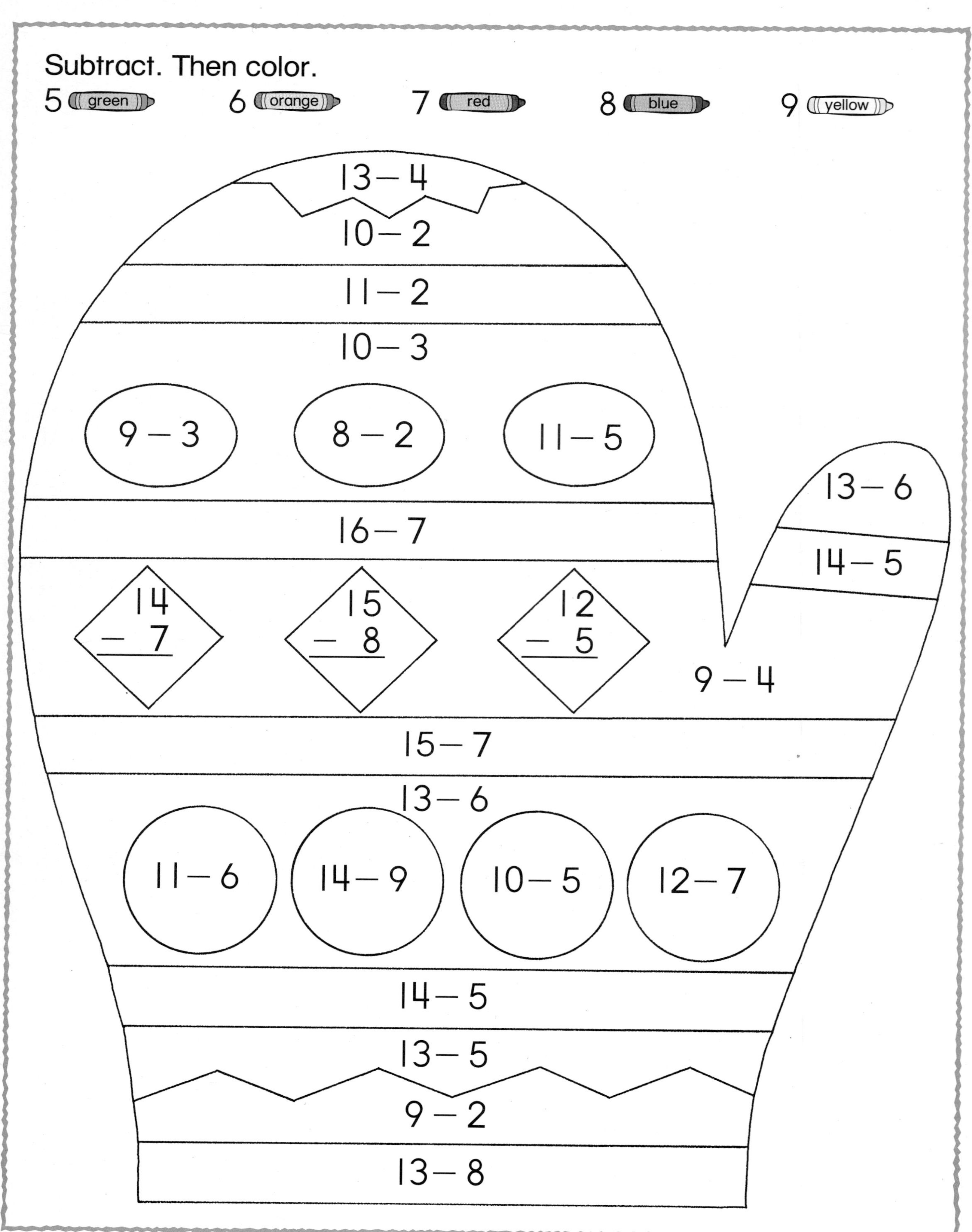
Subtract. Then color.
5 green
6 orange
7 red
8 blue
9 yellow
13 − 4
10 − 2
11 − 2
10 − 3
9 − 3
8 − 2
11 − 5
13 − 6
14 − 5
16 − 7
14 − 7
15 − 8
12 − 5
9 − 4
15 − 7
13 − 6
11 − 6
14 − 9
10 − 5
12 − 7
14 − 5
13 − 5
9 − 2
13 − 8

Name 

Do you add or subtract?

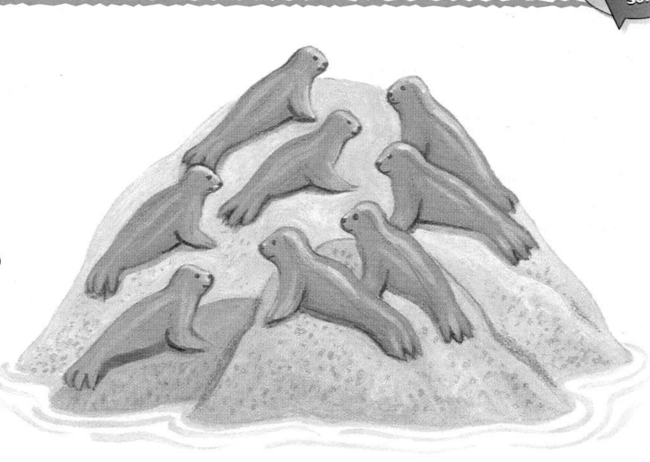

8 fur seals are resting.
6 jump into the water.
Now how many seals are resting?

add subtract

8  6 = 2 seals

Circle **add** or **subtract.**
Write the number sentence.

1. You see 6 geese flying above.
7 more geese join them.
How many geese do you see now?

add subtract

 geese

2. 9 fox pups are playing.
7 more come to play.
How many fox pups are playing?

add subtract

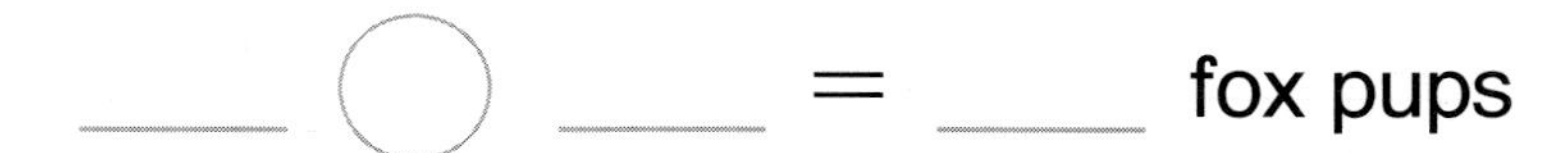 fox pups

3. There are 7 penguins sliding on the ice.
2 fall in the water.
Now how many are sliding on the ice?

add subtract

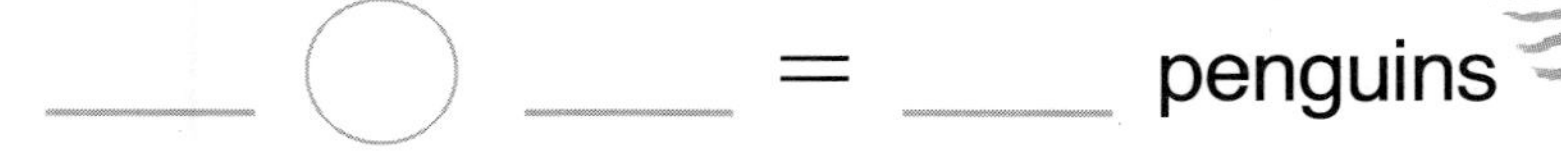 penguins

Home Connection Make up addition and subtraction stories for your child to solve. Encourage your child to write an original addition or subtraction story.

Circle **add** or **subtract**.
Write the number sentence.

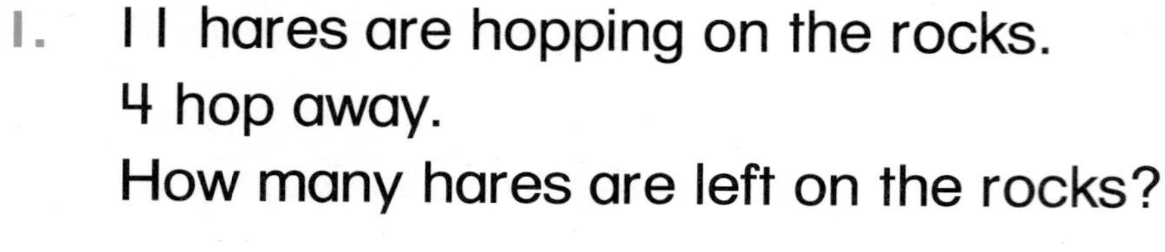

1. 11 hares are hopping on the rocks.
   4 hop away.
   How many hares are left on the rocks?

add subtract

 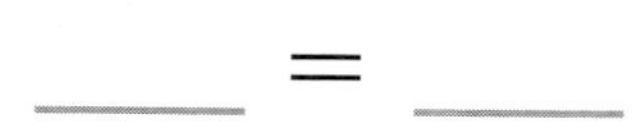 

___ ◯ ___ = ___ hares

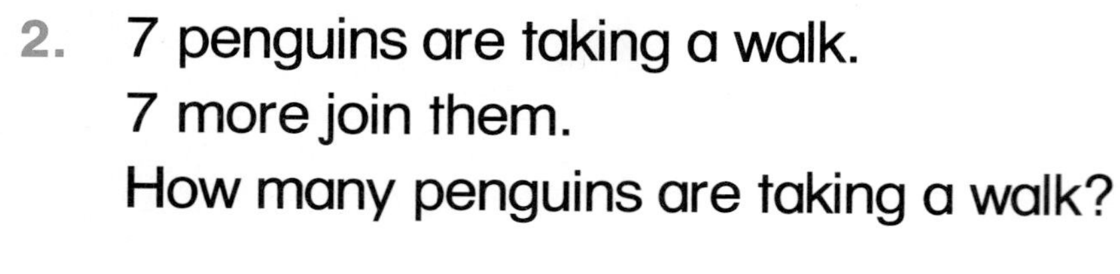

2. 7 penguins are taking a walk.
   7 more join them.
   How many penguins are taking a walk?

add subtract

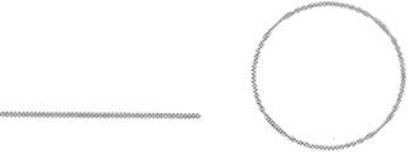  

___ ◯ ___ = ___ penguins

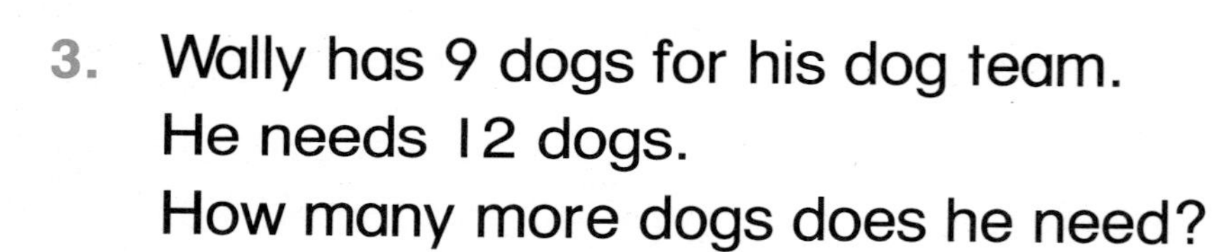

3. Wally has 9 dogs for his dog team.
   He needs 12 dogs.
   How many more dogs does he need?

add subtract

 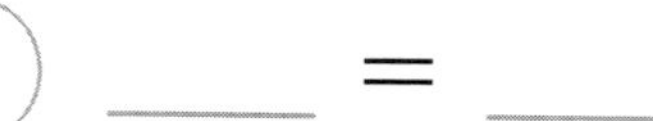

___ ◯ ___ = ___ dogs

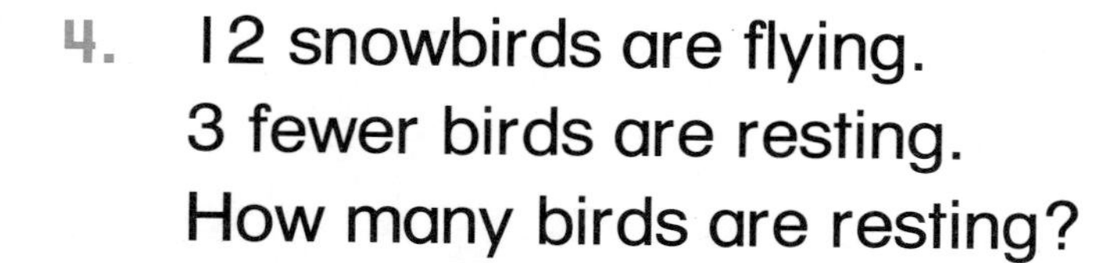

4. 12 snowbirds are flying.
   3 fewer birds are resting.
   How many birds are resting?

add subtract

   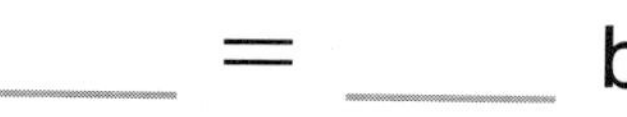

___ ◯ ___ = ___ birds

Name________________________________ **Checkpoint** 

Subtract.

1.

14	15	12	11	13	14
− 8	− 7	− 9	− 7	− 8	− 9

Complete each fact family.

2. $5 + 9 =$ ____

____ + ____ = ____

____ − ____ = ____

____ − ____ = ____

3. $7 + 6 =$ ____

____ + ____ = ____

____ − ____ = ____

____ − ____ = ____

Circle names for each number.

4.

6	14 − 8	15 − 9	10 − 4	13 − 8
8	15 − 7	13 − 6	14 − 6	18 − 9
7	11 − 4	15 − 8	12 − 8	14 − 7

Circle **add** or **subtract**. Write the number sentence.

5. There are 9 masks.
You make 7 more.
How many masks will there be?

add subtract

  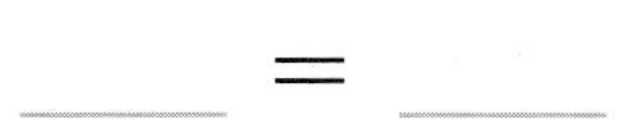

6. There are 12 dolls.
You pick 4.
How many dolls are left?

add subtract

  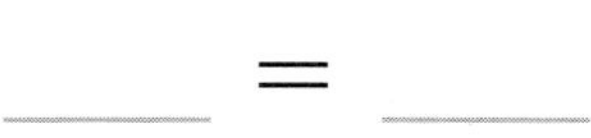

Name________________________________ **Extra Practice**

Code

4	0	10	3	2	5	7	9	1	6	8
A	D	E	I	H	L	C	O	P	S	T

Subtract. Use the code.
Find the letter that matches each difference.
Read the secret message.

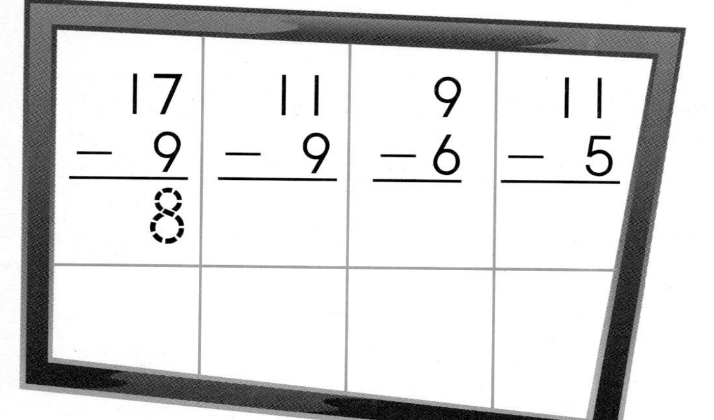

$17 - 9 = 8$	$11 - 9$	$9 - 6$	$11 - 5$

$5 - 4$	$11 - 6$	$13 - 9$	$14 - 7$	$10 - 0$

$5 - 2$	$13 - 7$

$13 - 6$	$9 - 0$	$10 - 1$	$8 - 3$

Name____________________ **Chapter Test** 

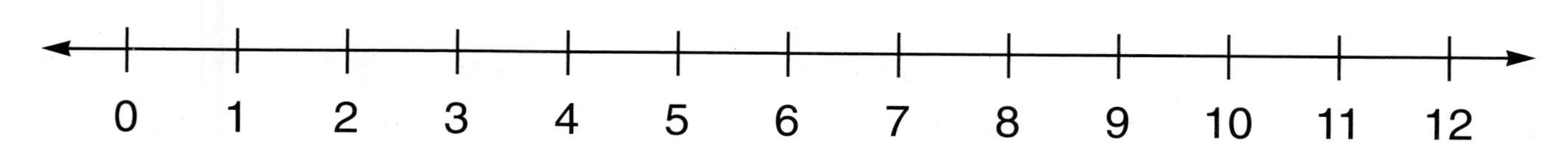

Use the number line to count back.

1. $6 - 3$ = ___ $8 - 2$ = ___ $5 - 1$ = ___ $9 - 3$ = ___ $7 - 2$ = ___ $11 - 3$ = ___

Add. Write a related subtraction fact.

2. $4 + 3 =$ ____

____ $-$ ____ $=$ ____

3. $5 + 4 =$ ____

____ $-$ ____ $=$ ____

Use the ten-frame. Cross out to subtract.

4. $12 - 8$ = ___

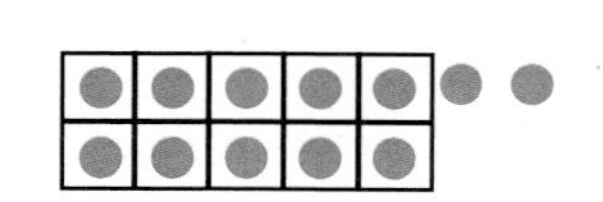

5. $15 - 7$ = ___

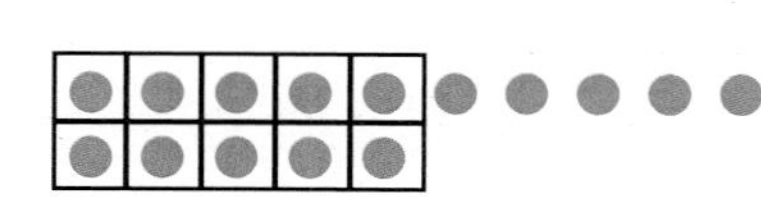

Add or subtract.

6. $5 + 6 =$ ____ $11 - 6 =$ ____

$6 + 5 =$ ____ $11 - 5 =$ ____

Circle names for 9.

7. $15 - 7$ $6 + 3$ $18 - 9$ $12 - 4$

Use the picture to make a graph.

8.

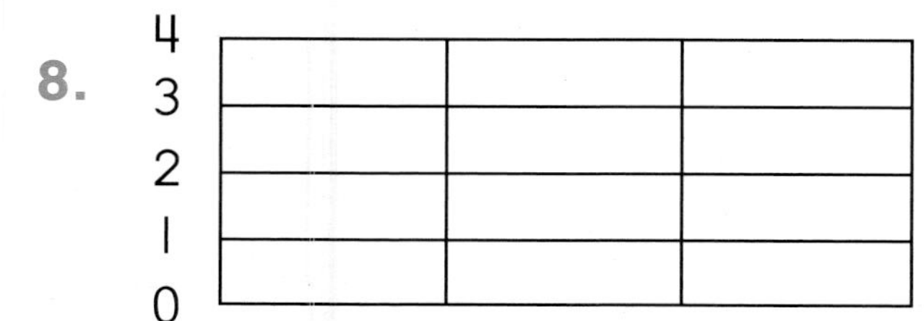

How many more fish are there than puffins? ____ more fish

Name________________________________ **Performance Assessment**

What You Need

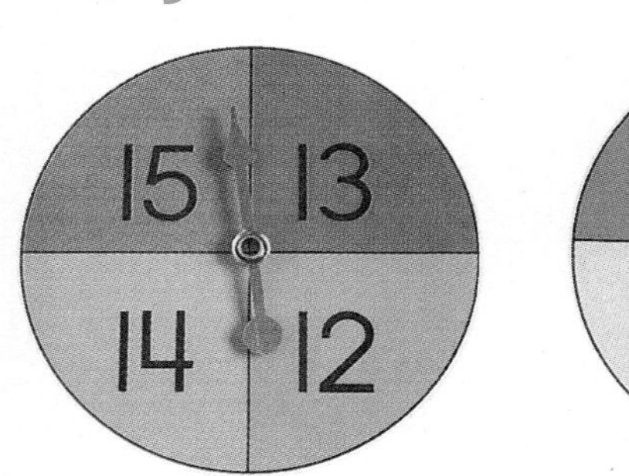

2 spinners

1. Spin each spinner. Record the numbers.
   Use the numbers to write a subtraction sentence.
2. Tell the strategy you used to find each difference.
   Explain your thinking.

First Number	Second Number	Subtraction Sentence
1.		___ − ___ = ___
2.		___ − ___ = ___
3.		___ − ___ = ___
4.		___ − ___ = ___
5.		___ − ___ = ___
6.		___ − ___ = ___
7.		___ − ___ = ___
8.		___ − ___ = ___

Name____

Counting up can help you subtract.

Start at 9. Count up to 12.

$$\begin{array}{r} 12 \\ -\ 9 \\ \hline 3 \end{array}$$

12
11
10
9
8
7
6
5
4
3
2
1

3

Count up to subtract.

1. 8 − 5   9 − 8   10 − 7   11 − 9   6 − 4

2. 7 − 5   10 − 8   11 − 8   5 − 3   7 − 4

3. 12 − 9   9 − 7   8 − 6   9 − 6   6 − 5

4. 8 − 7   6 − 3   11 − 9   10 − 9   5 − 2

5. 10 − 8   9 − 6   5 − 3   12 − 9   7 − 6

Name ______________________________

Use a calculator to subtract 14 − 6.

Press ON/C 1 4 − 6 =

What number do you see?

____

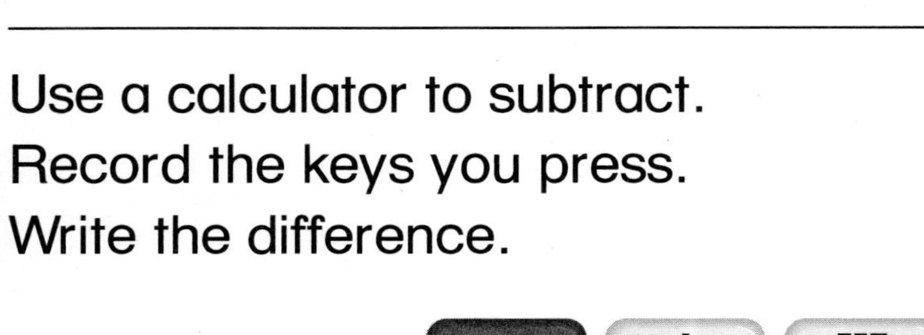

Use a calculator to subtract.
Record the keys you press.
Write the difference.

1. 17 − 8 ON/C 1 7 − 8 = 9

2. 13 − 5 ON/C ___ ___ − ___ = ___

   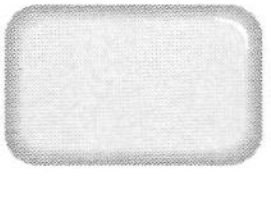 

3. 12 − 4 ON/C ___ ___ − ___ = ___

     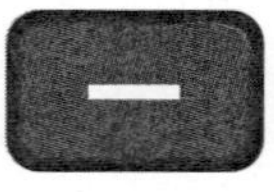   

4. 15 − 8 ON/C ___ ___ − ___ = ___

5. 14 − 9 ON/C ___ ___ − ___ = ___

6. 16 − 9 ON/C ___ ___ − ___ = ___

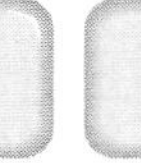    

7. 17 − 8 ON/C ___ ___ − ___ = ___

8. 13 − 9 ON/C ___ ___ − ___ = ___

9. 13 − 6 ON/C ___ ___ − ___ = ___

Make your own.

10. ____ − ____ ON/C ___ ___ − ___ = ___

    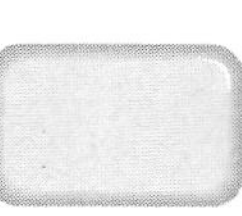  

Patterns and Numbers to 100

Who Lives in the Rain Forest?

written by Janice Richardson
illustrated by Lehner & Whyte

This Math Storybook
belongs to

____

Who lives in the rain forest?
Little tree frogs do.
Here are 10 frogs and 2 more.
How many climb for you?

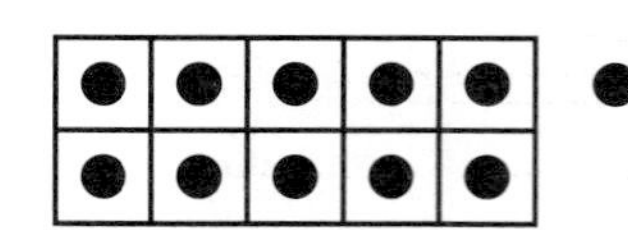

Who lives in the rain forest?
Lots of toucans do.
Here are 23 toucans with long beaks.
How many call to you?

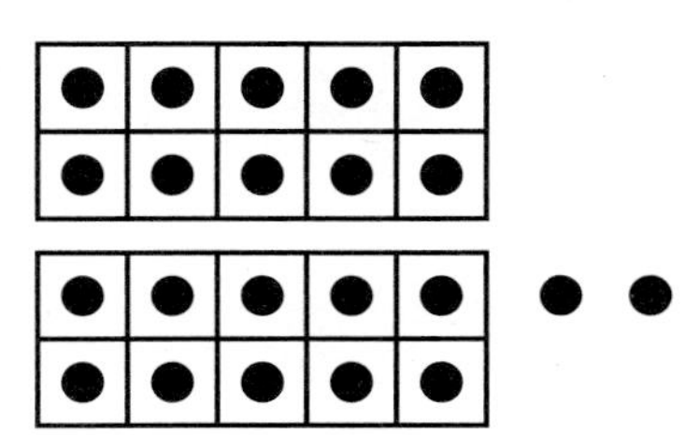

Who lives in the rain forest?
Many kinds of monkeys do.
Here are 10 night monkeys, 10 howler monkeys, and 10 spider monkeys.
How many swing for you?

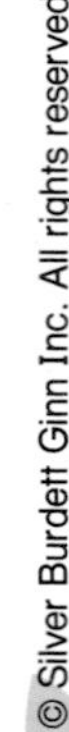

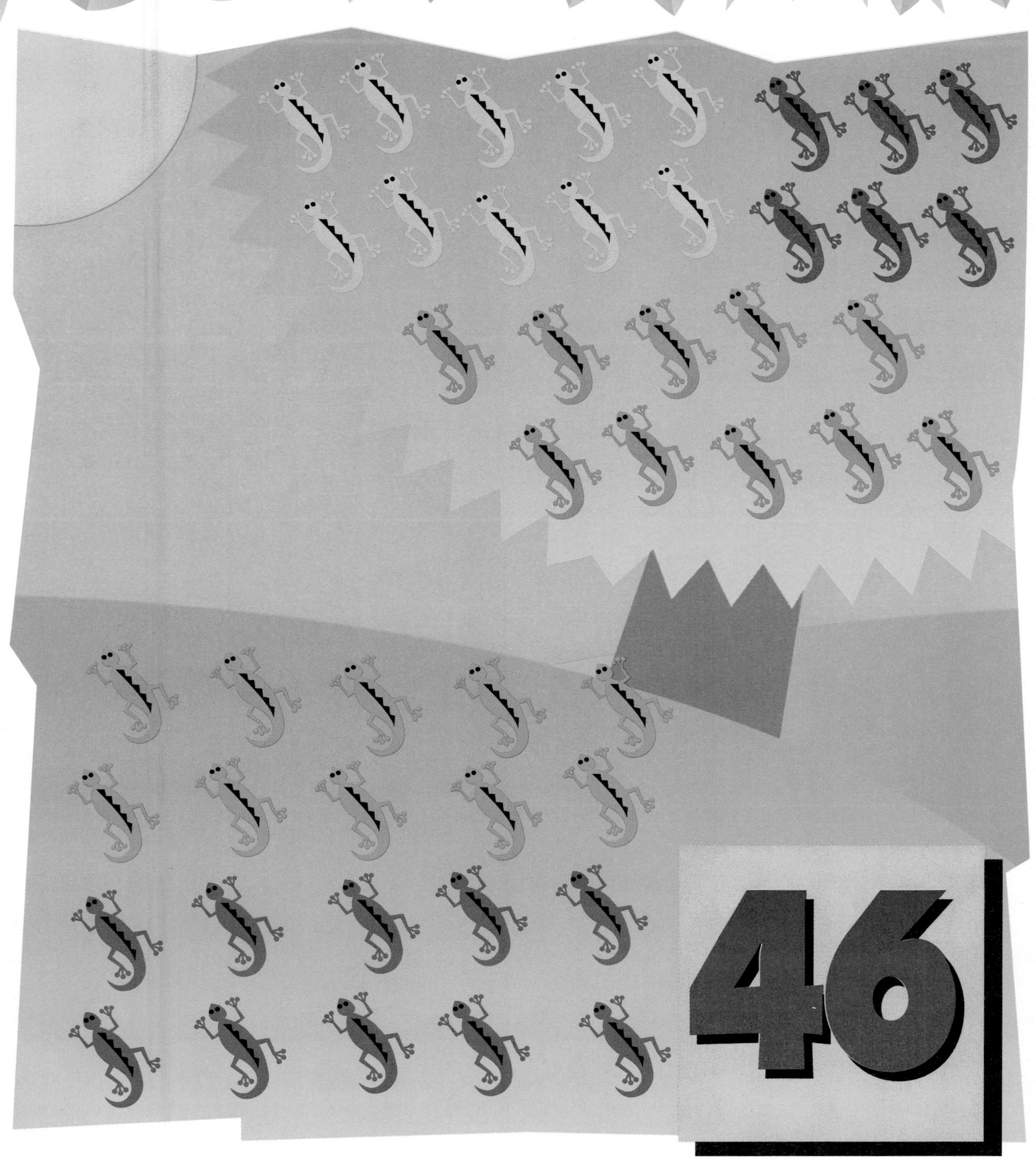

Who lives in the rain forest?
Lots of lizards do.
Here are 20 lizards on the ground
and 26 in a tree.
How many crawl for you?

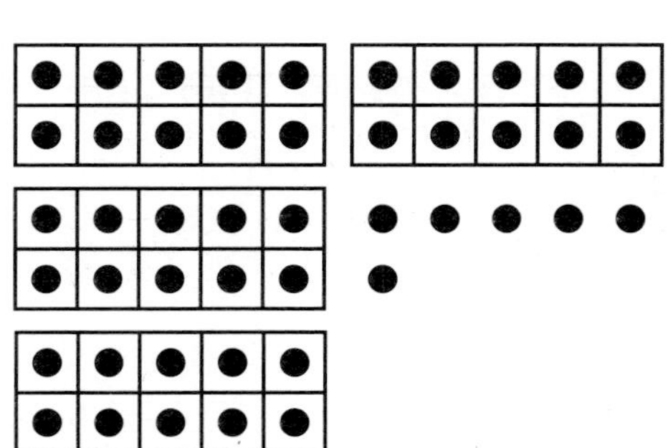

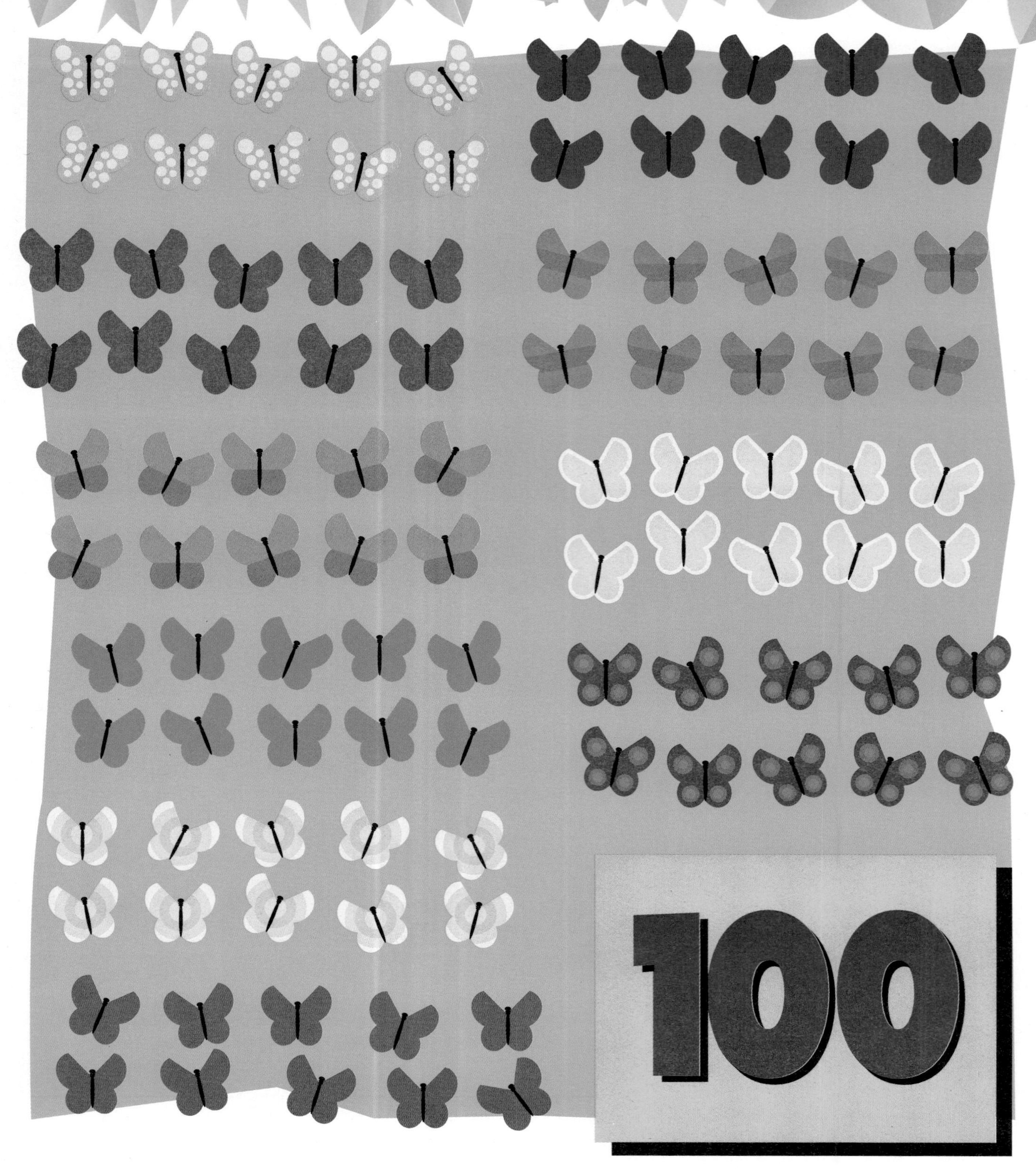

Who lives in the rain forest?
Bright butterflies do.
Here are many butterflies.
How many fly for you?

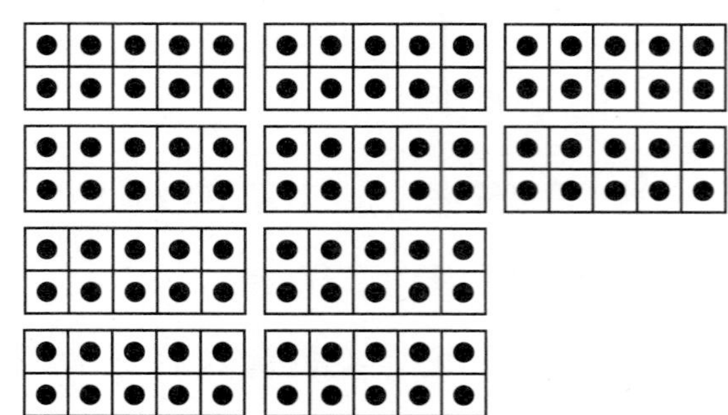

Who lives in the rain forest?
Many kinds of animals do.
Draw more than 10 animals.
How many are looking at you?

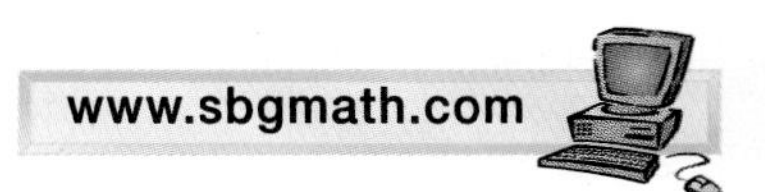

A Note to the Family

Here are some learning ideas you can share with your child.

Enjoy *Who Lives in the Rain Forest?* Together

- Read the story aloud to your child. Read it again together, or ask your child to read aloud to you. Talk about the number of animals on each page and how to show greater numbers as groups of tens and ones.
- Look at the last page of the story. Talk about the different kinds of animals your child drew. Count the number of each kind of animal. Have your child compare the numbers of different kinds of animals by asking questions like "Did you draw more monkeys or more lizards?"

At-Home Activity

- Make a collection of 100 things. It might be pennies, toothpicks, paper clips, or straws. Count the objects with your child. Then help your child make groups or piles of 10. See if your child knows some quick ways to count to 100, for example by 5s or 10s.

Read More About It!

To read more about numbers to 100, look for these books in your local library.

- *Count and Find 100 Cats and 10 Mice* (McClanahan Book Company, 1992)
- *From One to One Hundred* by Teri Sloat (Scholastic, 1991)
- *The King's Commissioners* by Aileen Friedman (Scholastic, 1994)

Visit Our Web Site!

www.sbgmath.com

Name________________________________

1 ten is 10.
2 tens are 20.
3 tens are 30.

I see a pattern.

Word Bank

tens
ones
pattern

Use tens models. Count by tens.
Write the numbers.

1. 1 ten

Tens	Ones
1	0

10
ten

2. 2 tens

Tens	Ones

____
twenty

3. 3 tens

Tens	Ones

____
thirty

4. 4 tens

Tens	Ones

____
forty

5. 5 tens

Tens	Ones

____
fifty

6. 6 tens

Tens	Ones

____
sixty

7. 7 tens

Tens	Ones

____
seventy

8. 8 tens

Tens	Ones

____
eighty

9. 9 tens

Tens	Ones

____
ninety

10. 10 tens

Tens	Ones

____
one hundred

Home Connection Counting by tens helps children to understand two-digit numbers. Have your child count by tens to 100.

Count by tens.
Write the numbers.

1.

Tens	Ones
2	0

20 in all

2.

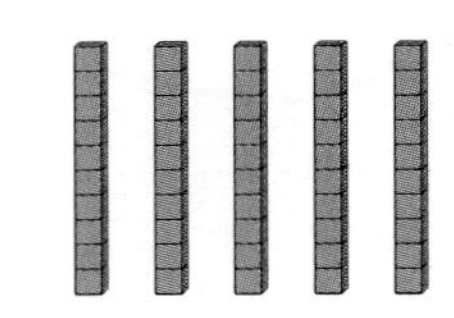

Tens	Ones

_____ in all

3.

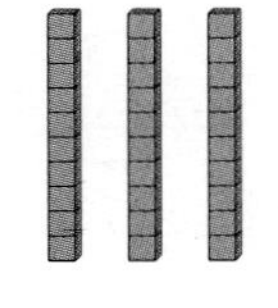

Tens	Ones

_____ in all

4.

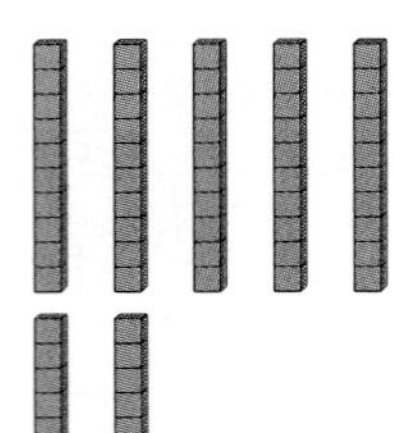

Tens	Ones

_____ in all

5.

Tens	Ones

_____ in all

6.

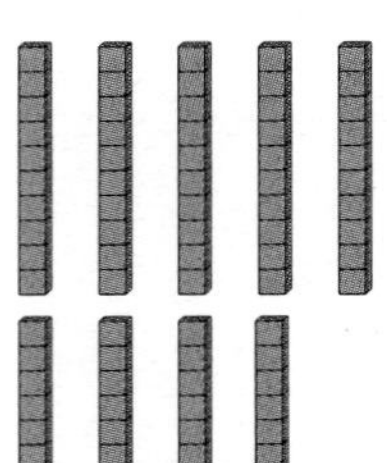

Tens	Ones

_____ in all

7.

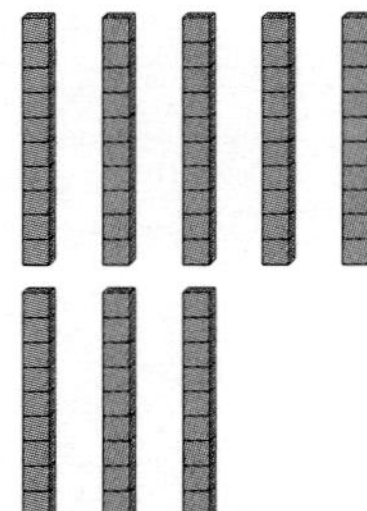

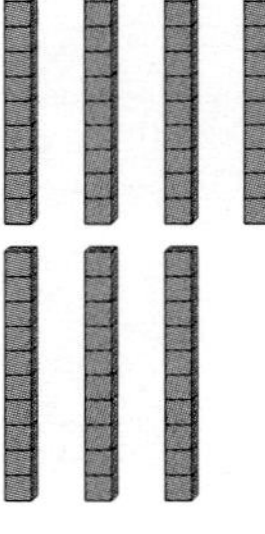

Tens	Ones

_____ in all

8.

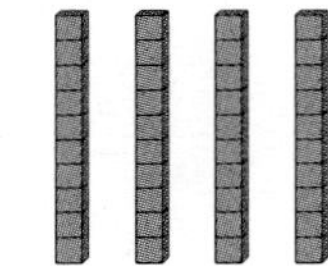

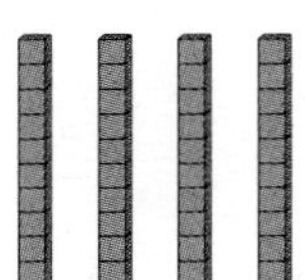

Tens	Ones

_____ in all

9.

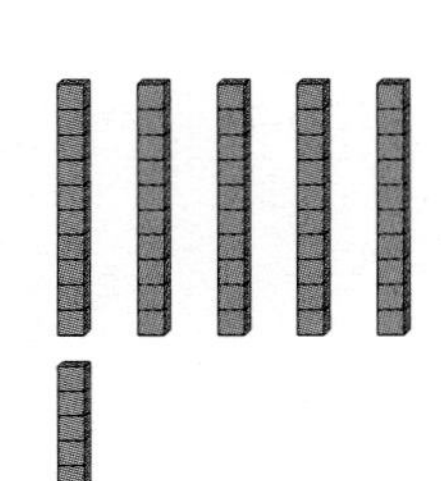

Tens	Ones

_____ in all

10.

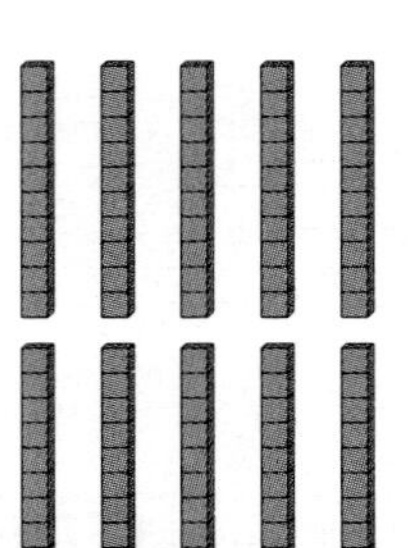

Tens	Ones

_____ in all

Name ____________________ **Understanding Tens and Ones**

How many tens and ones are there?

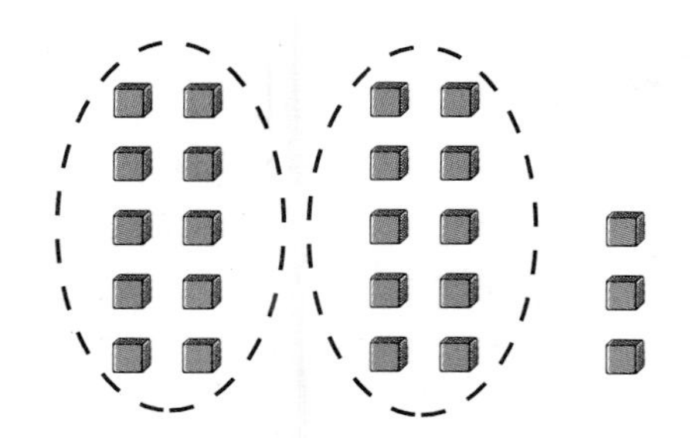

2 tens 3 ones 23 in all

Circle groups of ten.
Write how many tens and ones.
Write how many in all.

1.

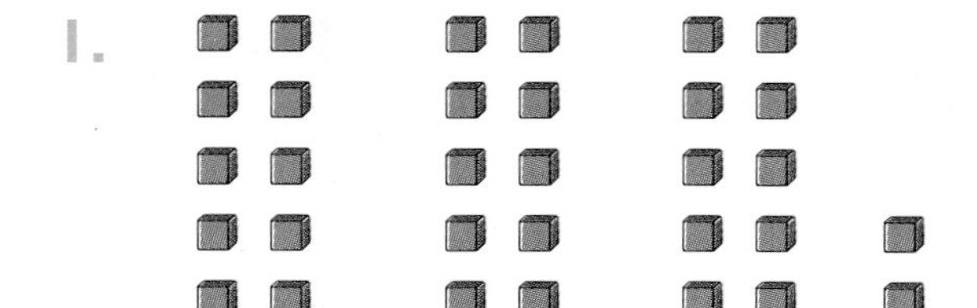

____ tens ____ ones ____ in all

2.

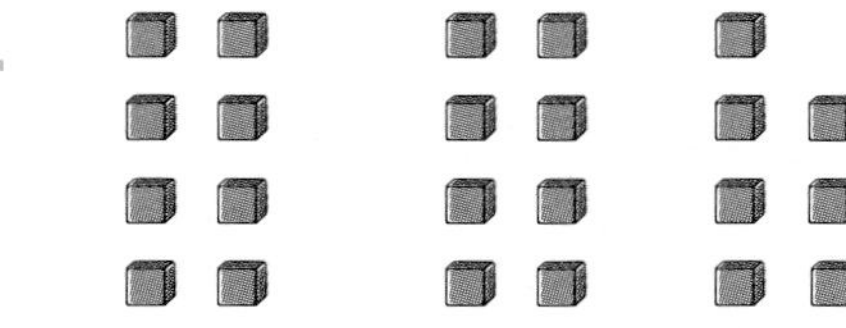

____ tens ____ ones ____ in all

3.

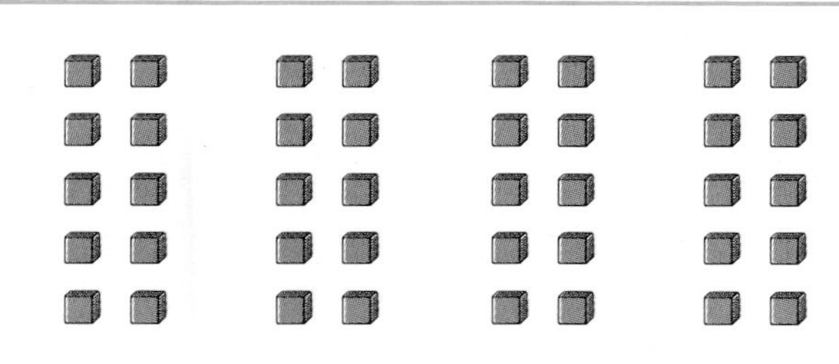

____ tens ____ ones ____ in all

4.

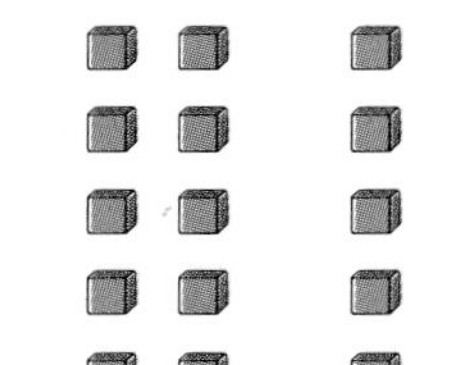

____ ten ____ ones ____ in all

5.

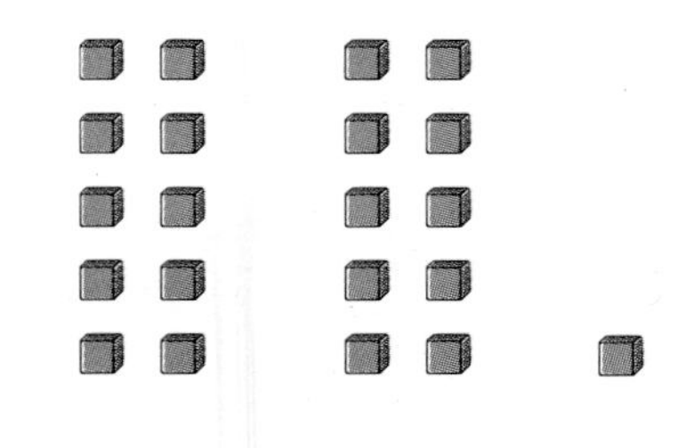

____ tens ____ one ____ in all

6.

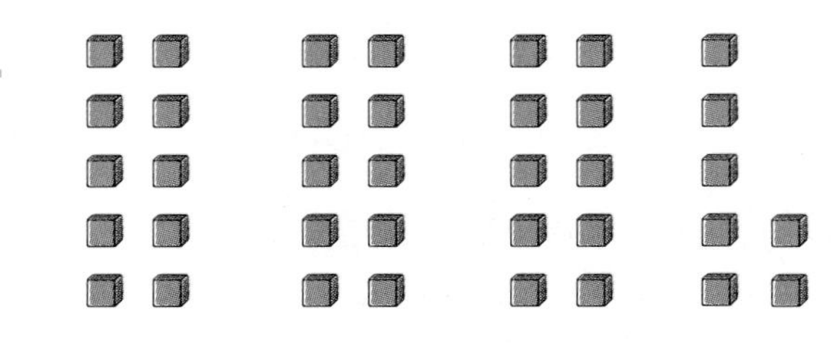

____ tens ____ ones ____ in all

Home Connection Your child has sorted objects into groups of tens and ones. Ask him or her to find the picture that shows 4 tens and 0 ones.

Circle groups of ten.
Write how many in all.

1\. 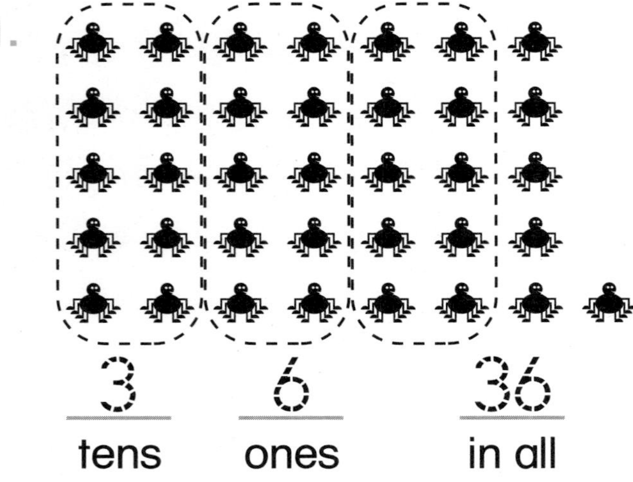

3 tens 6 ones 36 in all

2\. ___ tens ___ ones ___ in all

3\. ___ tens ___ ones ___ in all

4\. ___ tens ___ ones ___ in all

Critical Thinking Corner

Visual Thinking

5\. Does each picture show the same number? ___
Circle tens to show how you know.

Name________________________________ **Understanding Two-Digit Numbers**

2 tens 7 ones 27

Write how many tens and ones.
Write the numbers.

1.

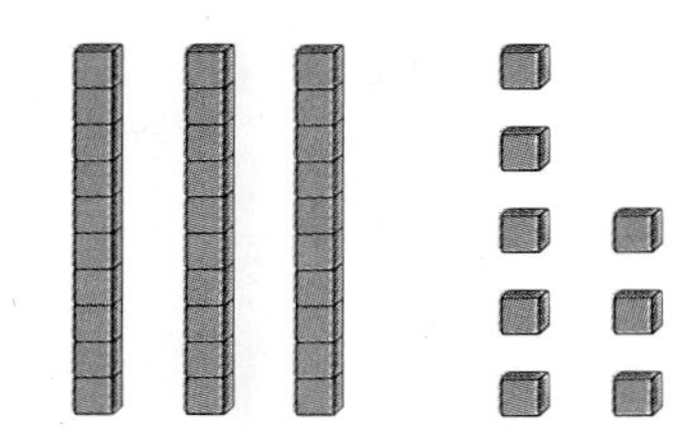

_____ tens _____ ones _____

2.

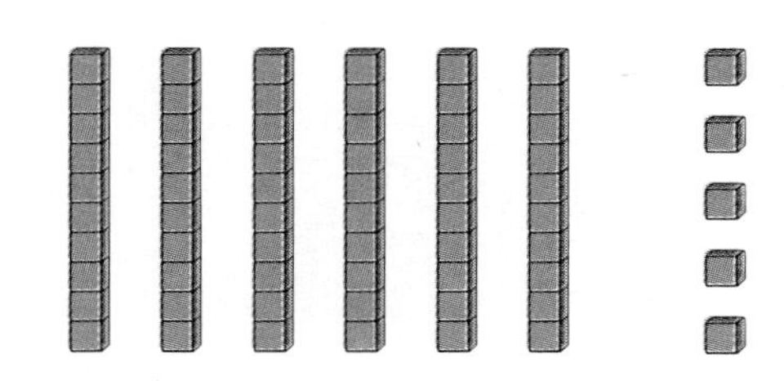

_____ tens _____ ones _____

3.

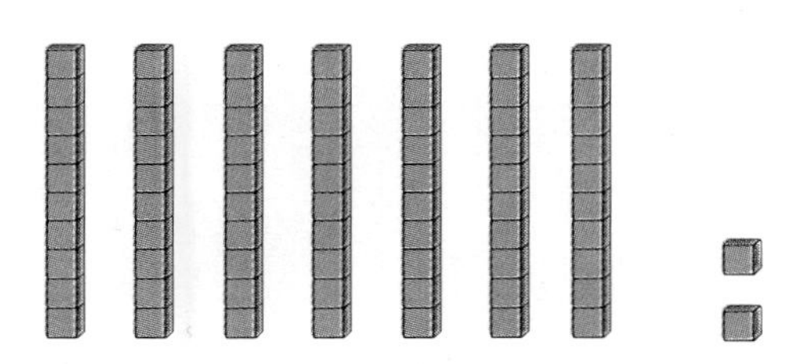

_____ tens _____ ones _____

4.

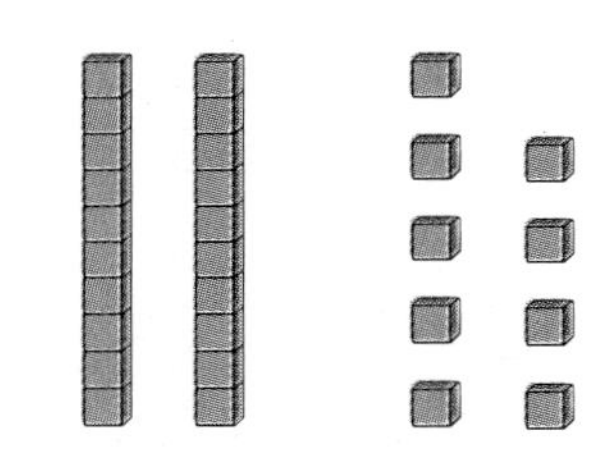

_____ tens _____ ones _____

5.

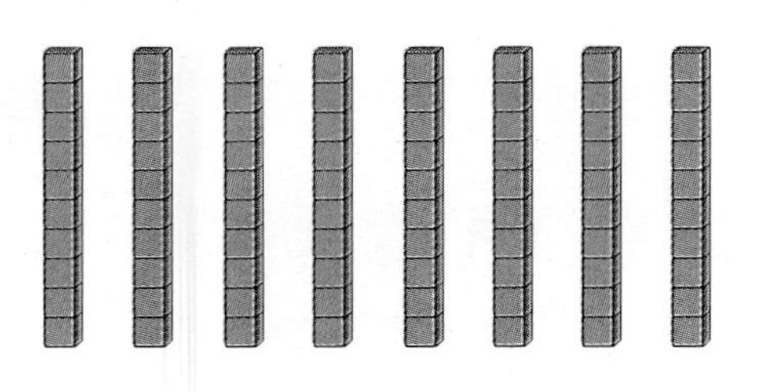

_____ tens _____ ones _____

6.

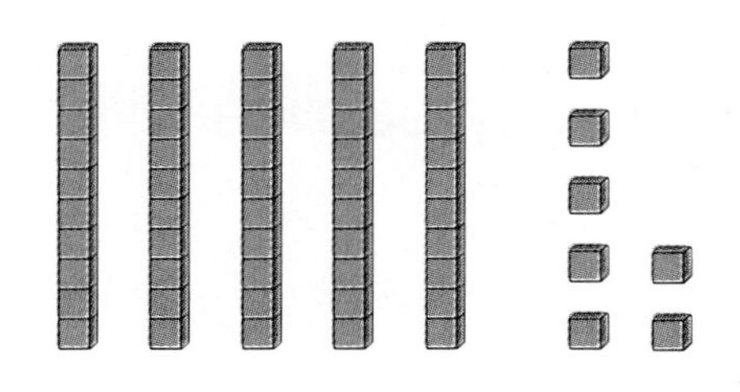

_____ tens _____ ones _____

Home Connection Children learn that groups of tens and ones make two-digit numbers. Ask your child to tell you how many tens and ones are in numbers like 24 and 63.

Write how many tens and ones.
Write the numbers.

1.

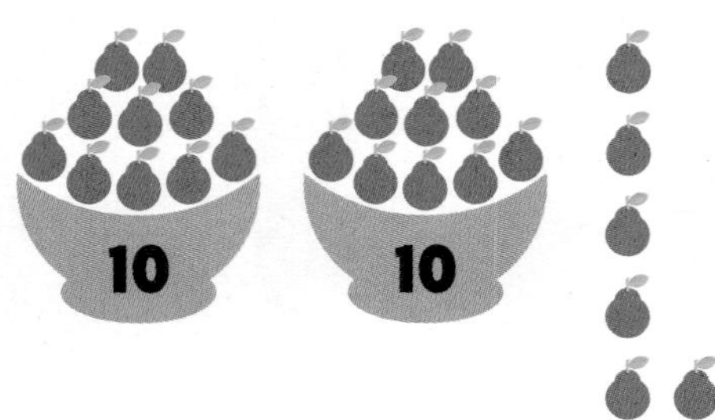

2 tens 6 ones 26

2.

_____ tens _____ ones _____

3.

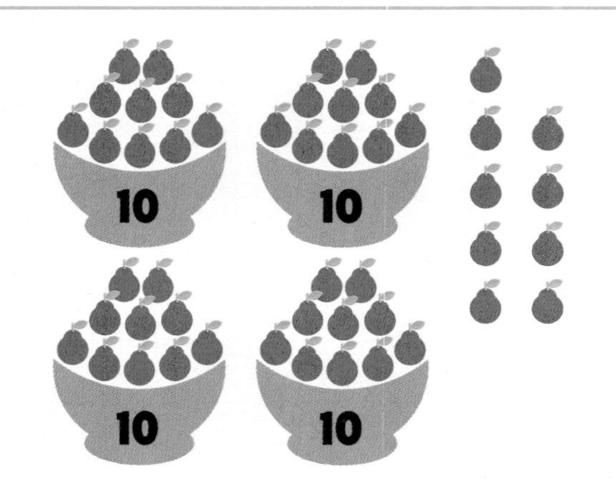

_____ tens _____ ones _____

4.

_____ tens _____ ones _____

Problem Solving

Solve.

5. What if the bird eats one of the berries?
How many tens and ones will there be?
How many berries will be left?

_____ tens _____ ones

_____ berries left

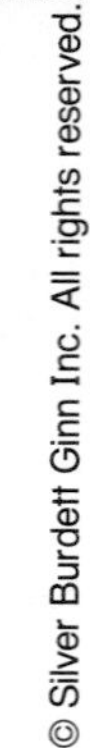

Name________________________________ **Building Two-Digit Numbers**

What You Need

tens

ones

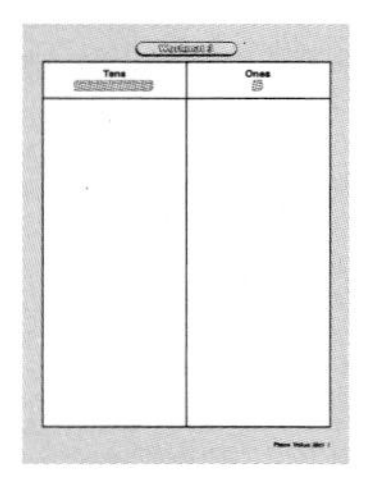

Workmat 3

Word Bank

regroup

1. Take two handfuls of ones.
2. Regroup as tens when you can.
3. Write how many tens and ones.
4. Write the number in all.

1.

Tens	Ones

_____ in all

2.

Tens	Ones

_____ in all

3.

Tens	Ones

_____ in all

4.

Tens	Ones

_____ in all

5.

Tens	Ones

_____ in all

6.

Tens	Ones

_____ in all

7.

Tens	Ones

_____ in all

8.

Tens	Ones

_____ in all

Home Connection Ask your child to explain how regrouping works. How many ones are needed to regroup as a ten? What happens when you regroup?

Use tens and ones models to show the top number.
Add 1 each time. Regroup if you can.
Write how many tens and ones.

1.

Tens	Ones
1	2
1	3

2.

Tens	Ones
2	7

3.

Tens	Ones
3	6

4.

Tens	Ones
3	0

5.

Tens	Ones
4	7

6.

Tens	Ones
5	5

Name________________________ **Ways to Show Numbers**

You can show 36 in different ways.

You can use models.

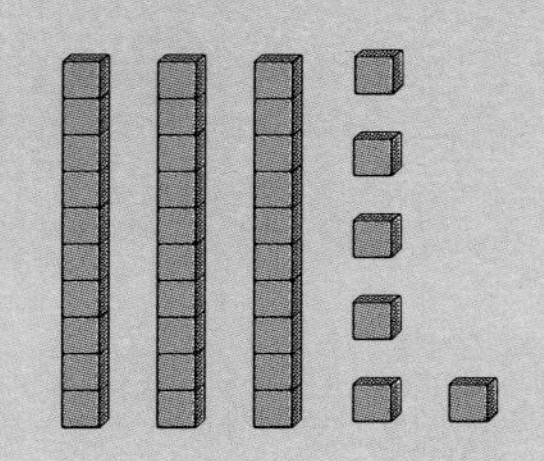

You can use pictures.

You can write tens and ones.

3 tens 6 ones

You can write the number.

36

Write tens and ones.

1. ____ tens ____ one

2.

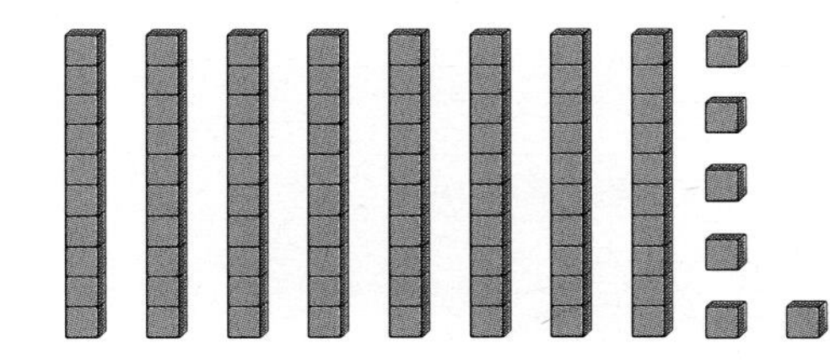

____ tens ____ ones

3. 29 ____ tens ____ ones

4. 55 ____ tens ____ ones

Write the number.

5.

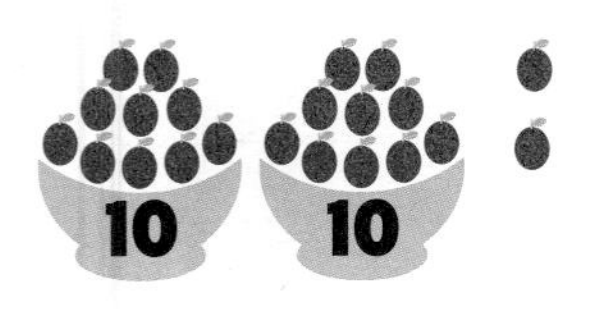

____

6.

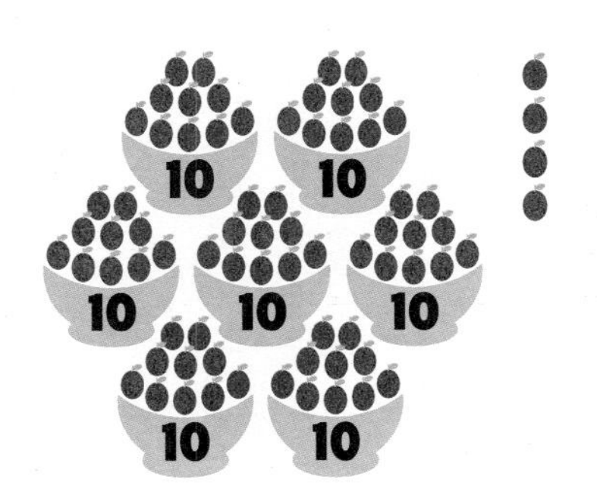

____

Home Connection Children show numbers in different ways. Ask your child to show two-digit numbers like 35 by writing tens and ones.

Match.

1.	24	4 tens 7 ones
2.	47	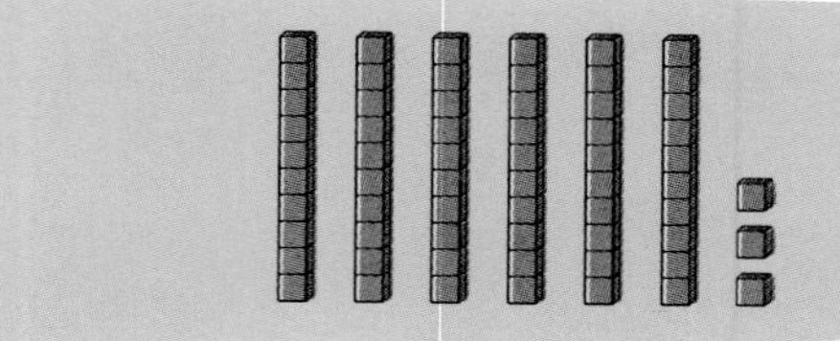
3.	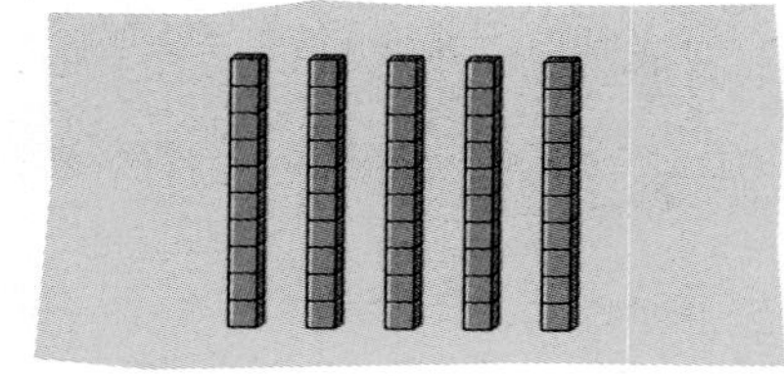	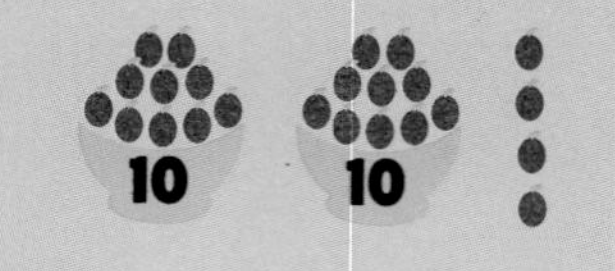
4.	6 tens 3 ones	8 ones 3 tens
5.	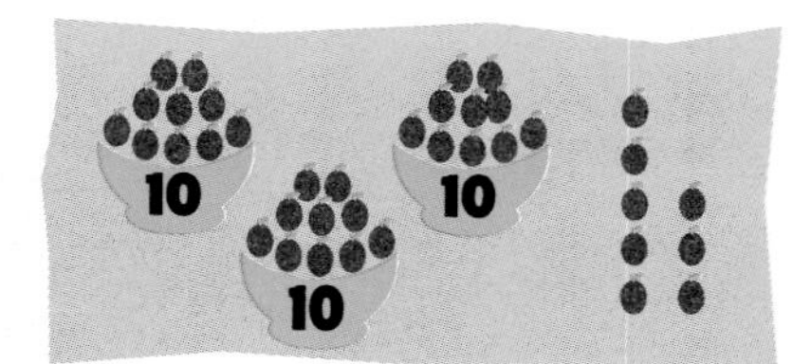	50

Critical Thinking Corner

Number Sense

6. Cross out the one that does not show 28.

8 ones 2 tens

 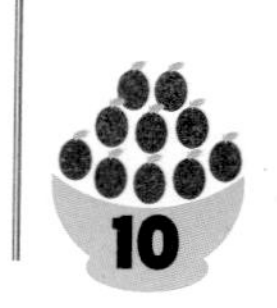 

28

Name________________________ **Understanding Place Value**

Tens	Ones
3 tens	7 ones

37

3 tens are 30.
The 3 means 30.
7 ones are 7.

Circle the value of the number in blue.

1. 61 60 or 6	2. 83 30 or 3	3. 47 7 or 70
4. 50 5 or 50	5. 39 30 or 3	6. 28 8 or 80
7. 25 twenty or two	8. 94 ninety or nine	9. 77 seventy or seven
10. 18 ten or one	11. 56 sixty or six	12. 44 forty or four

Home Connection Write some two-digit numbers, such as 37 and 82. Ask your child to tell you the value of each digit.

Circle the number.
Use tens and ones models if you like.

1. 6 tens 2 ones 26 (62)	2. 4 tens 3 ones 43 34	3. 7 tens 0 ones 7 70
4. 1 ten 5 ones 15 51	5. 3 tens 1 one 13 31	6. 8 tens 6 ones 68 86
7. 4 ones 9 tens 94 49	8. 2 tens 7 ones 72 27	9. 8 ones 5 tens 58 85
10. 1 ten 9 ones 91 19	11. 1 one 8 tens 18 81	12. 6 tens 7 ones 67 76

Critical Thinking Corner

Estimation

13. About how many mangoes are in the basket?
Circle the best guess.

10 mangoes

about 15 about 30 about 100

Name____

We can show 24 in different ways.
2 tens 4 ones
1 ten 14 ones
0 tens 24 ones

Use tens and ones models to show each number.
Then regroup to show the number another way. Record.

1. 17 ___1___ tens ___7___ ones
___0___ tens ___17___ ones

2. 13 _____ tens _____ ones
_____ tens _____ ones

3. 12 _____ tens _____ ones
_____ tens _____ ones

4. 19 _____ tens _____ ones
_____ tens _____ ones

5. 28 _____ tens _____ ones
_____ tens _____ ones
_____ tens _____ ones

6. 26 _____ tens _____ ones
_____ tens _____ ones
_____ tens _____ ones

Home Connection Your child is learning to show numbers in different ways. Ask him or her to show two-digit numbers like 12 or 24 in two different ways.

Use tens and ones.
Write different ways to show each number.

1. 25 2 tens 5 ones
1 tens 15 ones
0 tens 25 ones

2. 31 ____ tens ____ ones
____ tens ____ ones
____ tens ____ ones
____ tens ____ ones

3. 38 ____ tens ____ ones
____ tens ____ ones
____ tens ____ ones
____ tens ____ ones

4. 27 ____ tens ____ ones
____ tens ____ ones
____ tens ____ ones

5. 35 ____ tens ____ ones
____ tens ____ ones
____ tens ____ ones
____ tens ____ ones

6. 33 ____ tens ____ ones
____ tens ____ ones
____ tens ____ ones
____ tens ____ ones

Problem Solving

Solve. Use tens and ones models.

7. Tom has 2 tens and 5 ones.
Emma has 1 ten and 18 ones.
Who has more? ________

8. Lisa has 37 ones.
Filipe has 2 tens and 16 ones.
Who has more? ________

Name________________________________

Trading Pennies for Dimes

You can trade ten pennies for one dime.

Word Bank

pennies
dimes

=

Use coins. Trade pennies for dimes.
Write how many tens and ones.
Write each amount.

1. 21 pennies

Tens	Ones
2	1

21¢

2. 14 pennies

Tens	Ones

____¢

3. 26 pennies

Tens	Ones

____¢

4. 30 pennies

Tens	Ones

____¢

5. 2 dimes and 11 pennies

Tens	Ones

____¢

6. 3 dimes and 17 pennies

Tens	Ones

____¢

7. 4 dimes and 15 pennies

Tens	Ones

____¢

8. 5 dimes and 23 pennies

Tens	Ones

____¢

Home Connection Give your child more than ten pennies. Ask him or her to show how many pennies can be traded for dimes.

Trade pennies for dimes.
Write the number of dimes and pennies.
Use coins if you like.

= 10¢

1.

Tens	Ones

____ ¢

2.

Tens	Ones

____ ¢

3.

Tens	Ones

____ ¢

4.

Tens	Ones

____ ¢

Checkpoint

Write how many tens and ones.
Write the number.

1.

____ tens ____ ones ____

Circle the number.

2. 9 tens 5 ones

95 59

6 ones 7 tens

67 76

4 tens 7 ones

74 47

Name ____________________

When I estimate, I make a careful guess. First, I look at a group of 10. Then I estimate how many in all.

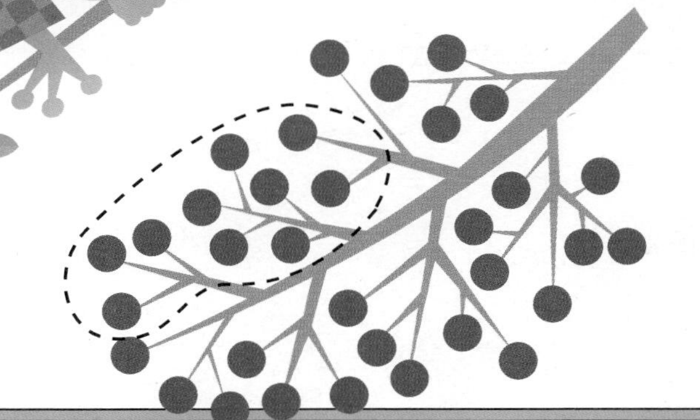

Word Bank
estimate

My estimate is 3 tens or 30.

I count 33.

Circle a group of 10. Estimate.
Circle more groups of 10 if you can.
Then count.

1.

estimate ____ count ____

2.

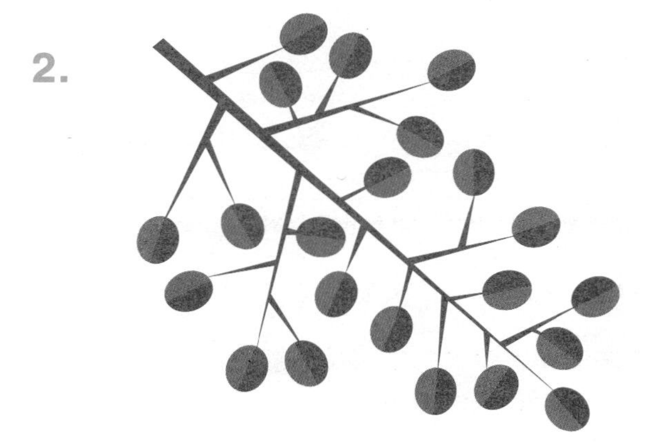

estimate ____ count ____

3.

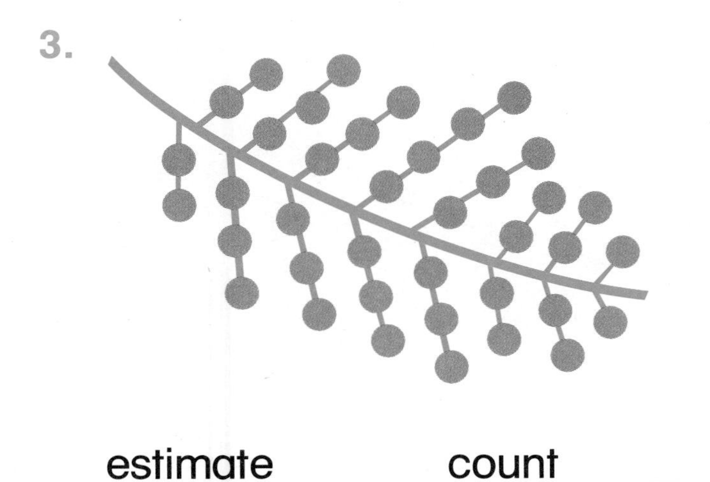

estimate ____ count ____

4.

estimate ____ count ____

Home Connection Looking for a group of 10 can help children estimate large quantities. Show your child a picture from a magazine that shows 20 or more objects. Ask your child to circle a group of 10, estimate, and then count.

Circle a group of 10. Estimate.
Circle more groups of 10. Then count.

1.

estimate _____ count 28

2.

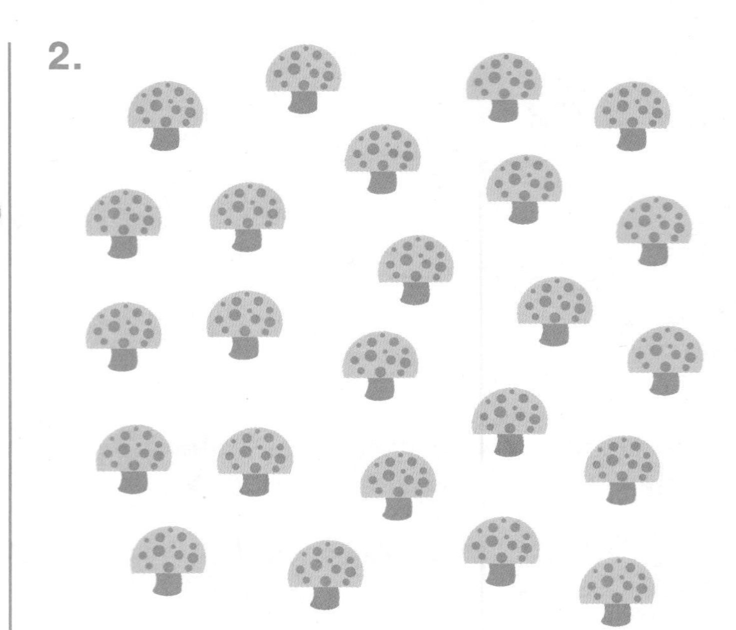

estimate _____ count _____

3.

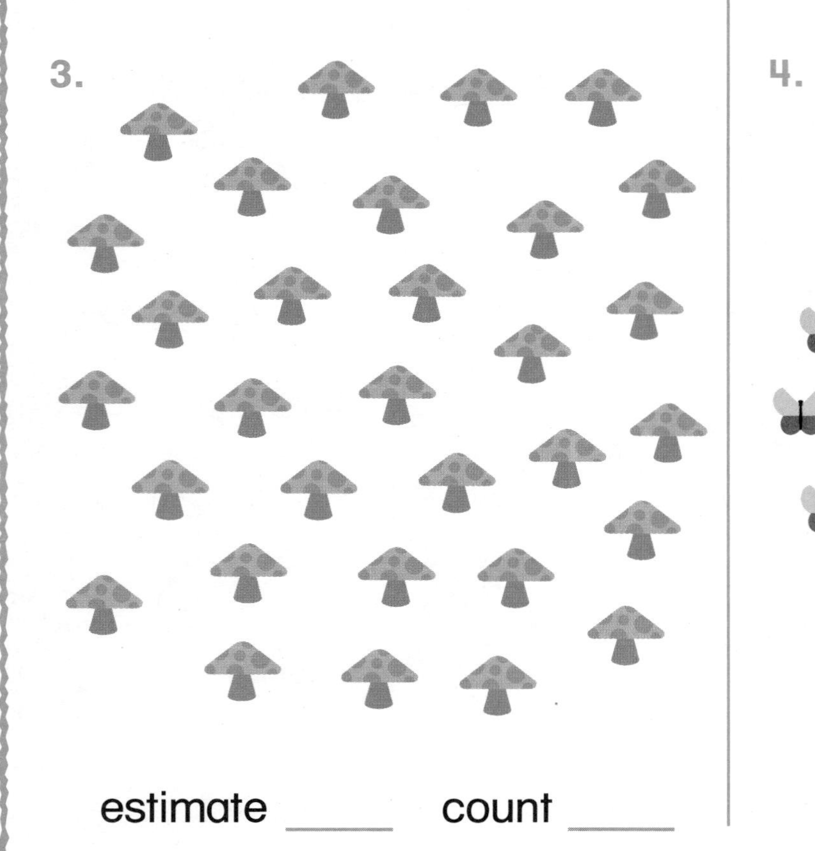

estimate _____ count _____

4.

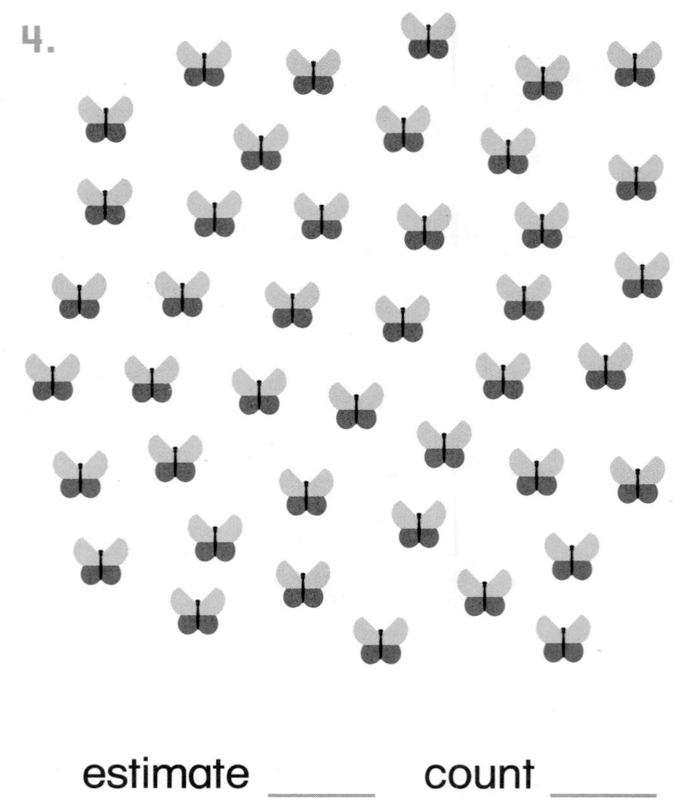

estimate _____ count _____

Name______________________________ **Number Patterns to 99**

1. Write the missing numbers.

0	1	2		4	5	6	7	8	
	11	12	13	14	15		17	18	19
20	21		23	24	25	26	27		29
30	31	32	33		35	36		38	39
40	41	42	43	44		46		48	49
50		52	53	54	55	56	57	58	
	61	62	63	64	65		67	68	69
70	71	72		74	75	76	77	78	
	81	82	83		85	86	87	88	89
90	91		93	94	95	96	97		99

2. Color the squares that have 5 in the ones place. Tell about the pattern you see.

3. Circle the numbers that have 5 in the tens place. Tell about the pattern you see.

4. Which number is circled **and** colored? ____

Home Connection Writing numbers in a chart helps children to see number patterns. Ask your child to look at the numbers in the chart and tell about different patterns he or she sees.

1. Write the missing numbers.

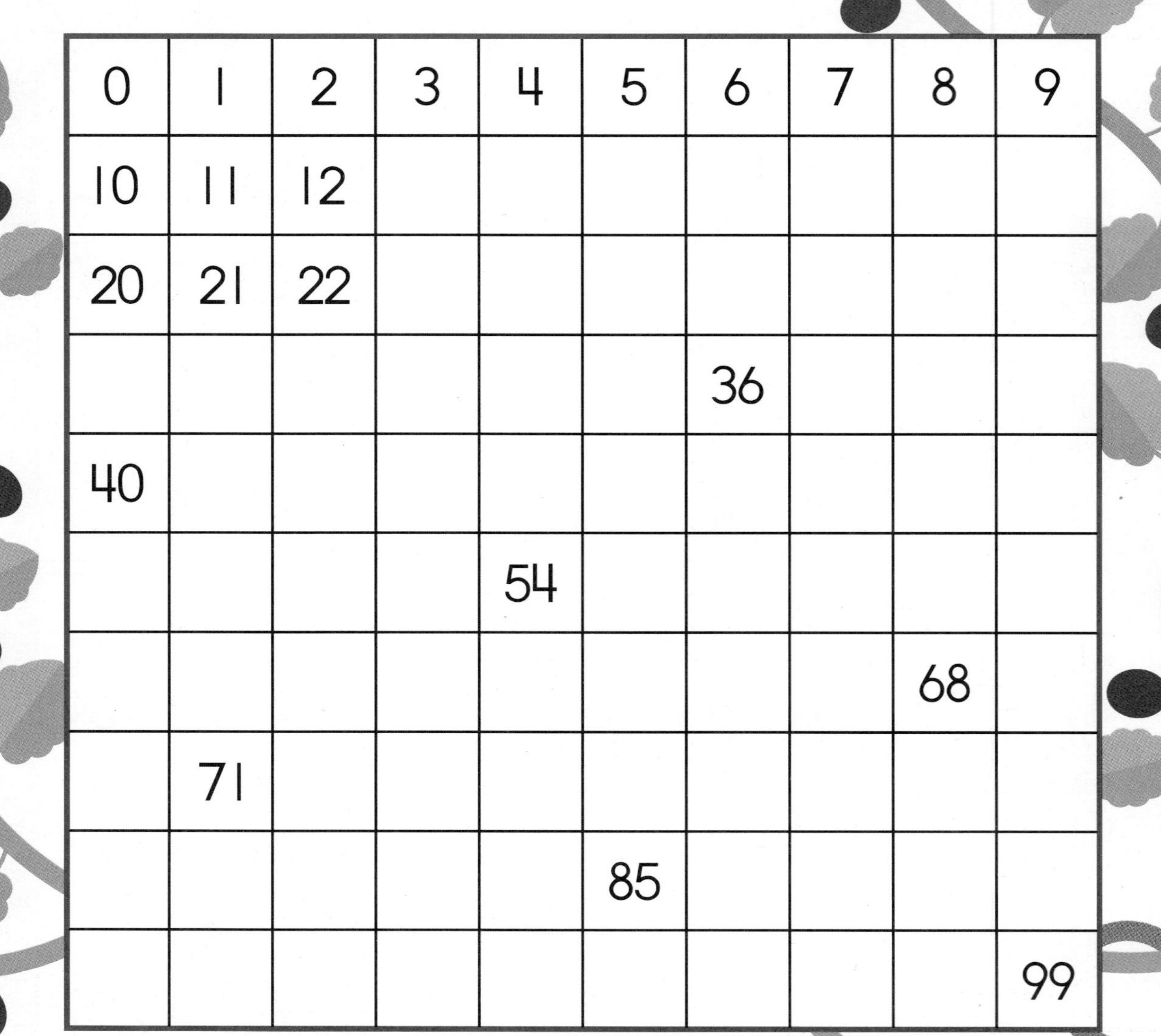

0	1	2	3	4	5	6	7	8	9
10	11	12							
20	21	22							
						36			
40									
				54					
								68	
	71								
					85				
									99

2. Color the squares that have 7 in the tens place. Tell about the pattern you see.

3. Circle the numbers that have two more ones than they have tens. Tell about the pattern you see.

4. Which number is circled **and** colored? ____

Name____

You can skip count by 10s.

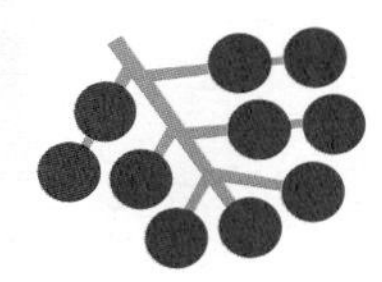 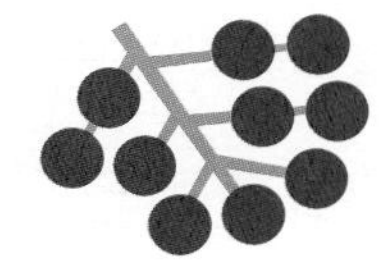 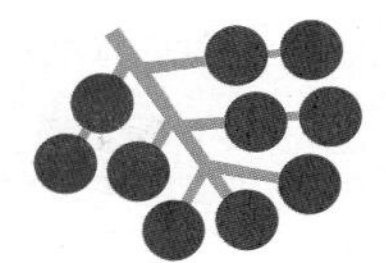

10, 20, 30

Word Bank
skip count

1. Skip count by 2s.

2, ____, ____, ____, ____, ____

2. Skip count by 3s.

____, ____, ____, ____, ____, ____

3. Skip count by 4s.

____, ____, ____, ____, ____, ____

4. Skip count by 5s.

____, ____, ____, ____, ____, ____

Home Connection Your child is learning to skip count by 2, 3, 4, 5, and 10. Ask him or her to skip count with these numbers.

1. Skip count by 10s. Circle the numbers.
Skip count by 5s. Color the squares yellow.

0	1	2	3	4	5	6	7	8	9
10	11	12	13	14	15	16	17	18	19
20	21	22	23	24	25	26	27	28	29
30	31	32	33	34	35	36	37	38	39
40	41	42	43	44	45	46	47	48	49
50	51	52	53	54	55	56	57	58	59
60	61	62	63	64	65	66	67	68	69
70	71	72	73	74	75	76	77	78	79
80	81	82	83	84	85	86	87	88	89
90	91	92	93	94	95	96	97	98	99

Problem Solving

Skip count by 10s.
Use the chart above if you like.

2. 14, ____, ____, ____, ____, ____, ____, ____

3. 17, ____, ____, ____, ____, ____, ____, ____

4. 19, ____, ____, ____, ____, ____, ____, ____

Name________________________

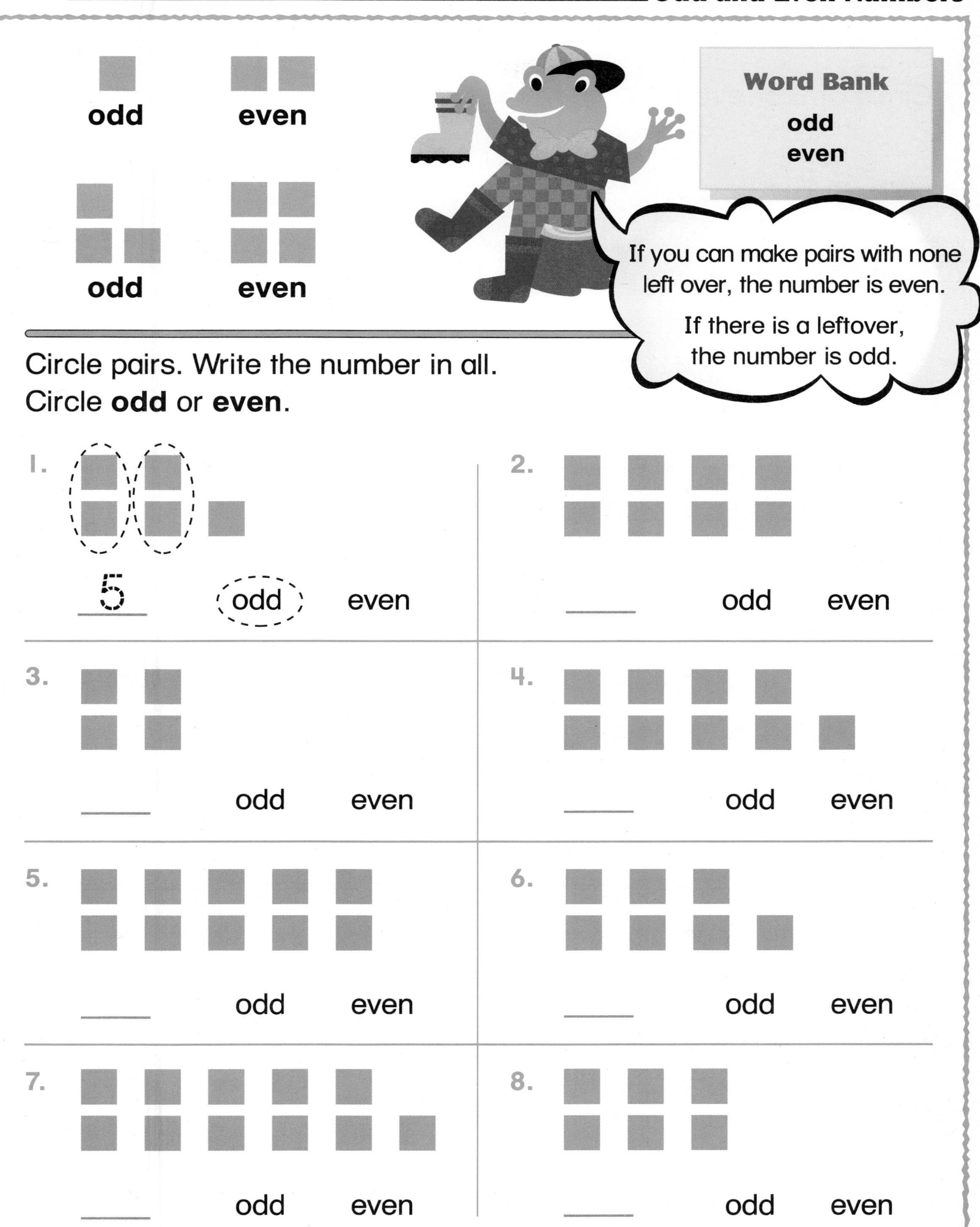

Home Connection Your child is learning about odd and even numbers. Pick a number from 1 to 15. Have your child use pennies to tell if the number is odd or even.

Circle pairs. Write the number in all.
Circle **odd** or **even**.

1. 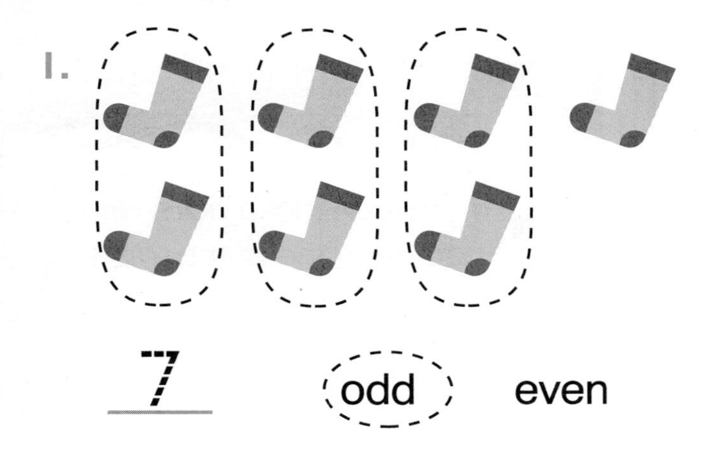

7 odd even

2. 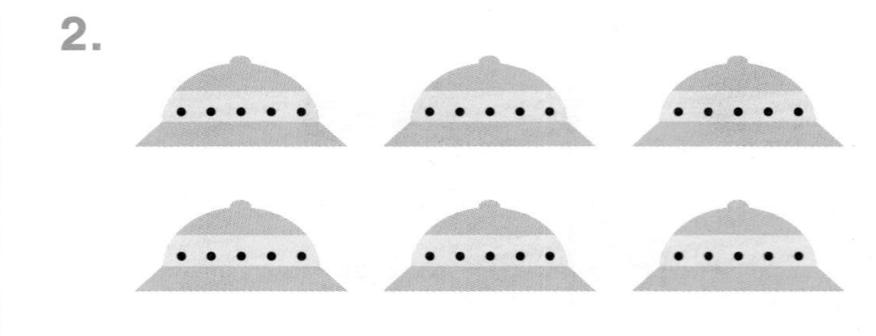

____ odd even

3.

____ odd even

4.

____ odd even

5. 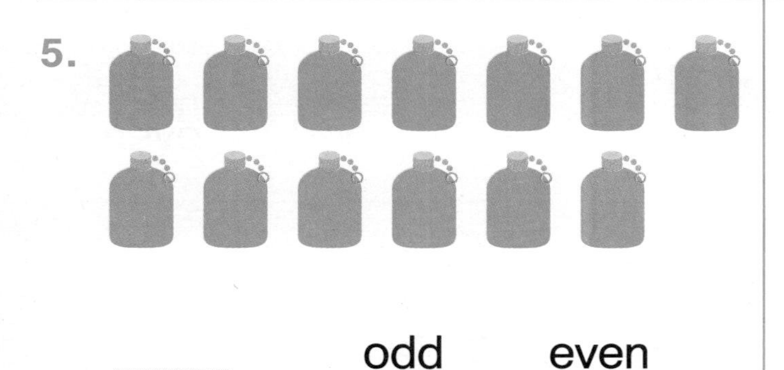

____ odd even

6. 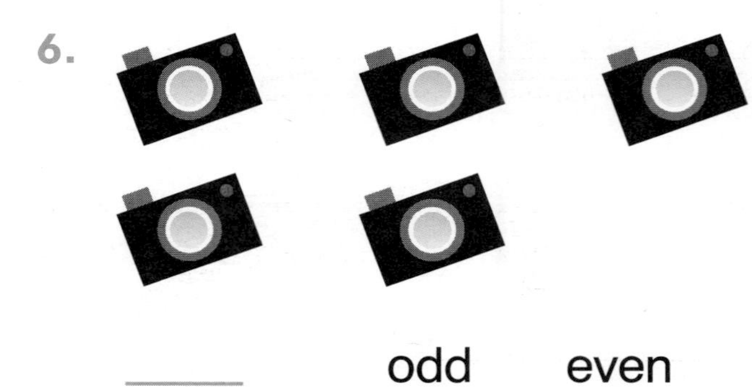

____ odd even

Critical Thinking Corner

Number Sense

7. Is 29 an odd number or an even number?
How do you know?

Name ______________________ **Comparing Numbers**

First compare the tens.
If the tens are the same,
compare the ones.

Word Bank
greater than
less than

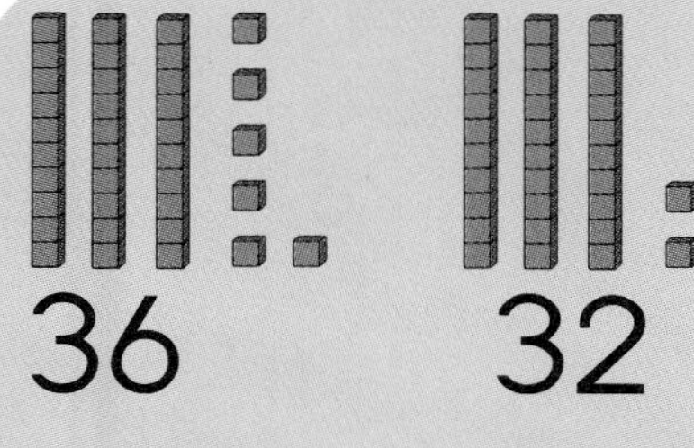

36 32

36 is **greater than** 32.

$36 > 32$

32 36

32 is **less than** 36.

$32 < 36$

Write the numbers.
Circle **greater than** or **less than**.
Write < or >.

1. 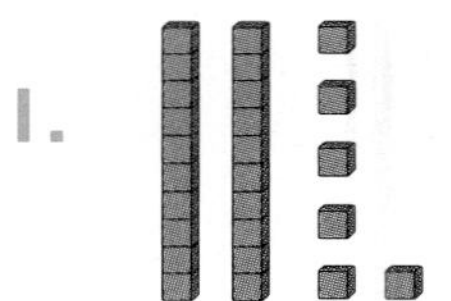

26 is greater than / (less than) 29

26 ◯ 29

2. ____ is greater than / less than ____

____ ◯ ____

3. 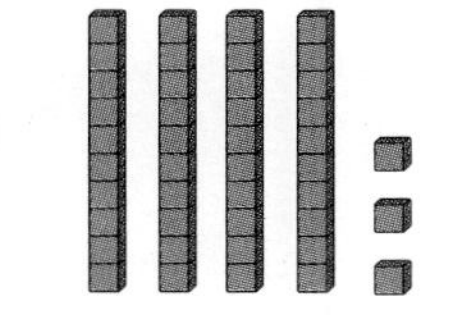

____ is greater than / less than ____

____ ◯ ____

4. 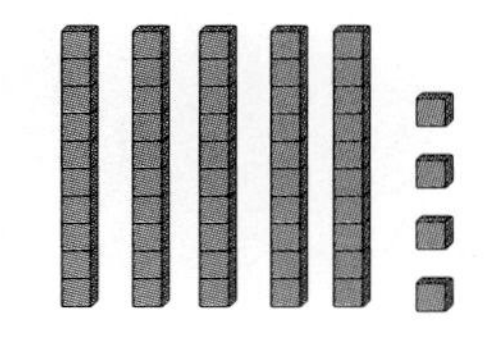 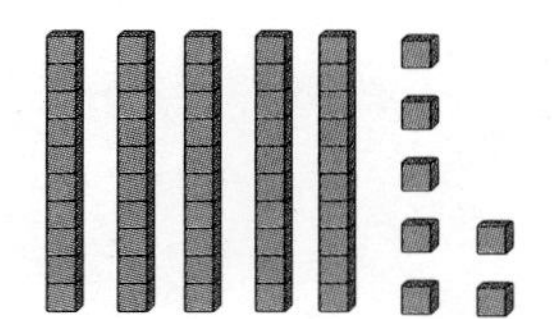

____ is greater than / less than ____

____ ◯ ____

Home Connection Children learn to compare numbers by examining tens and ones. Give your child two-digit numbers to compare. For example, ask your child if 22 is greater than or less than 24.

Compare. Use models if you like.
Write > or <.

Remember . . .
> means **greater than**.
< means **less than**.

1. 17 (>) 14   46 ◯ 42   78 ◯ 79

2. 53 ◯ 55   69 ◯ 70   28 ◯ 25

3. 96 ◯ 98   32 ◯ 37   87 ◯ 82

4. 66 ◯ 61   40 ◯ 44   90 ◯ 88

Write a number that makes each sentence true.

5. ___ > 52   ___ < 39   26 > ___

6. 85 < ___   77 > ___   ___ < 48

7. ___ > 14   62 < ___   80 < ___

What Do You Think?

I have a way to remember when to write > or <. I remember that > and < always point toward the lesser number. Does my way help you?

Name________________________

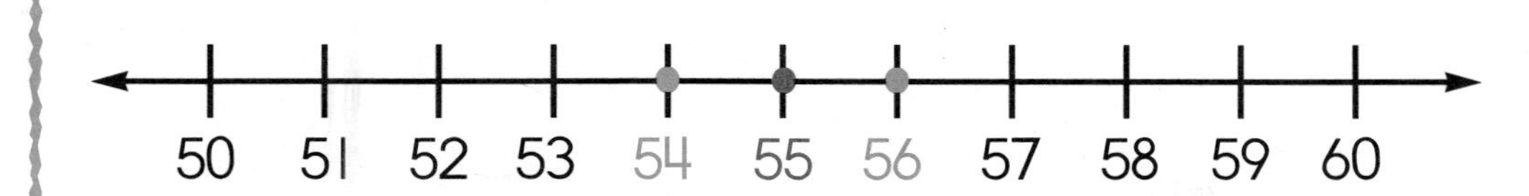

Word Bank

after
before
between

54 is **after** 53.
55 is **before** 56.
56 is **between** 55 and 57.

Write the number that comes **after**.

1. 36, 37 81, ____ 45, ____ 70, ____
2. 27, ____ 98, ____ 63, ____ 68, ____
3. 13, ____ 52, ____ 89, ____ 94, ____

Write the number that comes **before**.

4. ____, 25 ____, 57 ____, 78 ____, 40
5. ____, 33 ____, 69 ____, 20 ____, 89
6. ____, 91 ____, 47 ____, 84 ____, 66

Write the number that comes **between**.

7. 85, ____, 87 40, ____, 42 79, ____, 81
8. 65, ____, 67 37, ____, 39 91, ____, 93
9. 17, ____, 19 43, ____, 45 25, ____, 27

Home Connection Your child is learning to identify numbers that are after, before, and between other numbers. Ask him or her to tell the numbers that come before and after a two-digit number such as 49.

Write the numbers.

	Before	Between	After
1.	32, 33	34, ____, 36	37, ____
2.	____, 80	81, ____, 83	84, ____
3.	____, 28	29, ____, 31	32, ____
4.	____, 65	66, ____, 68	69, ____
5.	____, 51	52, ____, 54	55, ____
6.	____, 94	95, ____, 97	98, ____
7.	____, 49	50, ____, 52	53, ____

Problem Solving

Solve.

8. Jake has more than 46 pennies but fewer than 48 in his bank. How many pennies does he have?

____ pennies

9. Felice found 1 penny today. Now she has 27 pennies. How many did she have before today?

____ pennies

Name________________________________

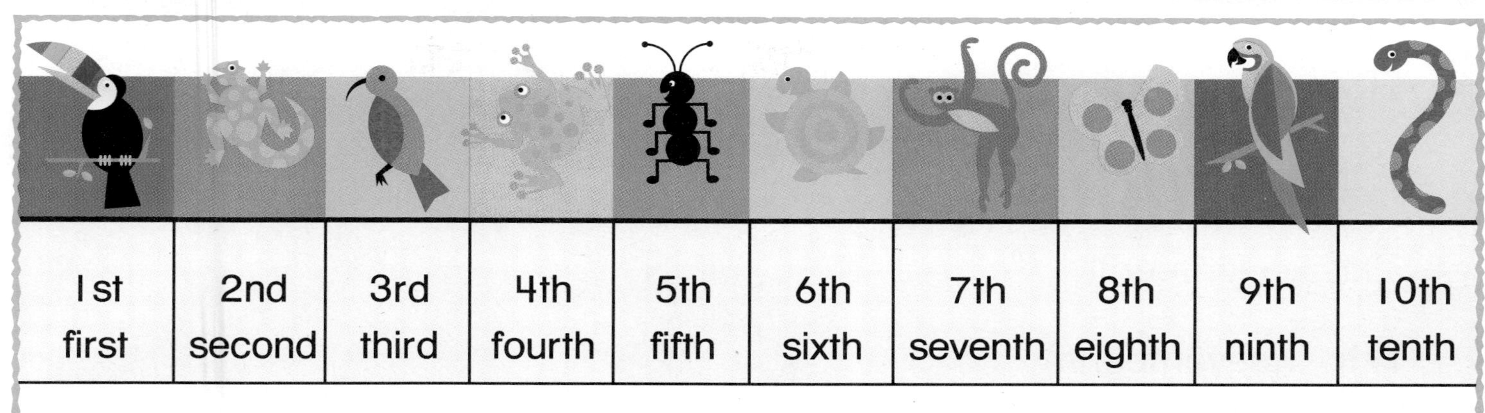

1st	2nd	3rd	4th	5th	6th	7th	8th	9th	10th
first	second	third	fourth	fifth	sixth	seventh	eighth	ninth	tenth

Write the word to show the order of each animal.

1.

third

2.

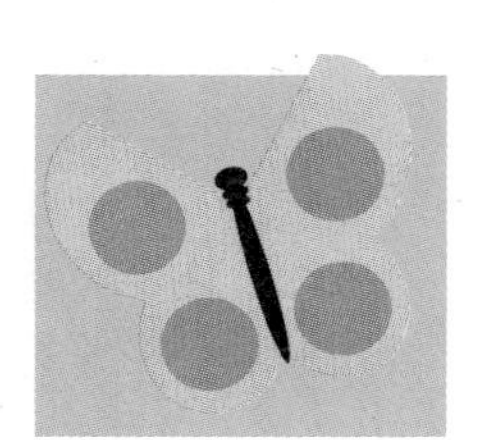

______

3.

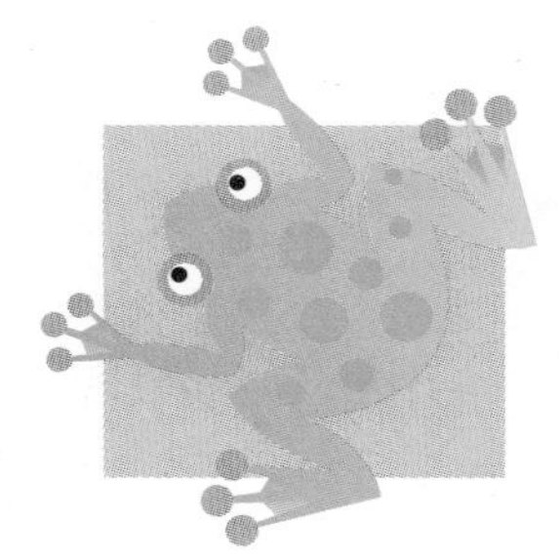

______

4.

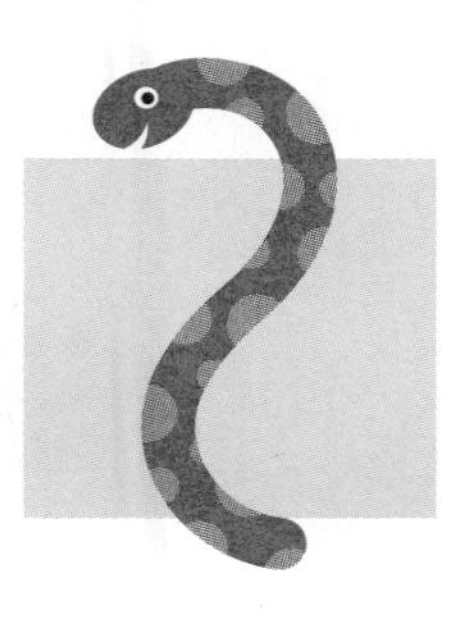

______

5.

______

6.

______

7.

______

8.

______

9.

______

Home Connection Ordinal numbers show numerical order. Show your child 10 objects arranged in a row. Ask him or her to identify the ordinal number for each object.

20th	twentieth
19th	nineteenth
18th	eighteenth
17th	seventeenth
16th	sixteenth
15th	fifteenth
14th	fourteenth
13th	thirteenth
12th	twelfth
11th	eleventh
10th	tenth
9th	ninth
8th	eighth
7th	seventh
6th	sixth
5th	fifth
4th	fourth
3rd	third
2nd	second
1st	first

Draw a line to show each bird's home.

1. 18th floor

2. 10th floor

3. 15th floor

4. 1st floor

5. 5th floor

20th

16th

12th

8th

4th

Name________________________________

Problem-Solving Application
Choosing Logical Answers

What is the secret number?

Cross out numbers when they don't fit a clue.

Clues

- It is greater than 12.
- It is less than 16.
- It is even.

0	1	2	3	4	5	6	7	8	9
10	11	12	13	14	15	16	17	18	19

The secret number is 14.

Use the clues to find each secret number.
Cross out numbers when they don't fit a clue.

1. • It is less than 60.
   • It is more than 51.
   • It has a 3 in the ones place.

50	51	52	53	54	55	56	57	58	59
60	61	62	63	64	65	66	67	68	69

The secret number is _____.

2. • It is greater than 87.
   • It is less than 90.
   • It is odd.

80	81	82	83	84	85	86	87	88	89
90	91	92	93	94	95	96	97	98	99

The secret number is _____.

3. • It has a 4 in the tens place.
   • It is less than 43.
   • It is odd.

30	31	32	33	34	35	36	37	38	39
40	41	42	43	44	45	46	47	48	49

The secret number is _____.

Home Connection Children use the process of elimination and their understanding of numbers to identify unknown numbers. Ask your child to explain how he or she found one of the "secret" numbers on this page.

Use clues to find each secret number.
Cross out numbers if you like.

1. • It is greater than 40.
   • It has a 7 in the tens place.
   • It is not odd.

   The secret number is ____.

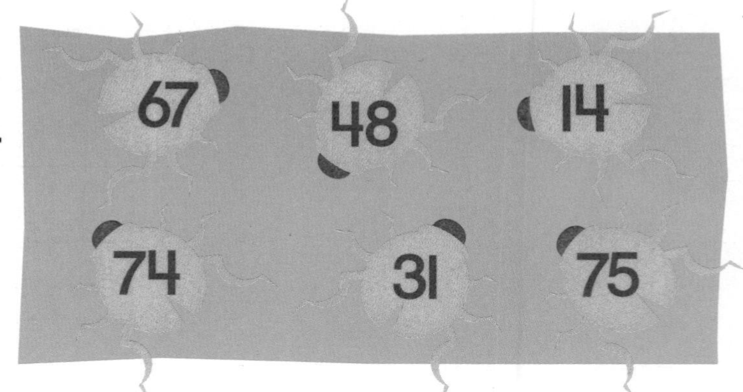

2. • It is greater than 50.
   • It is less than 90.
   • It is even.

   The secret number is ____.

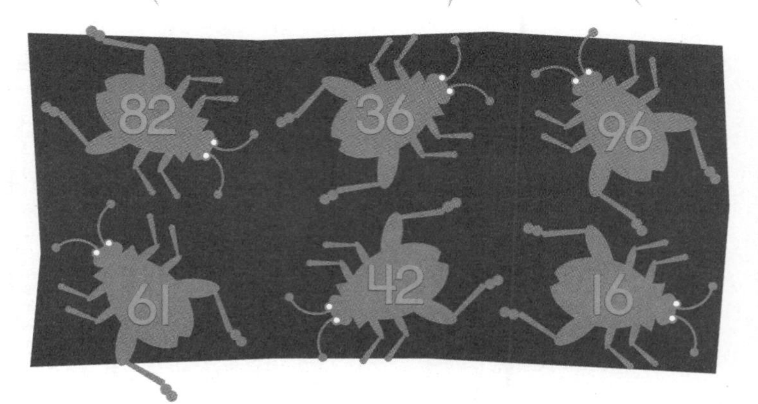

3. Choose a secret number from the chart. Write 3 clues. Ask a classmate to find your secret number.

Make Your Own

70	71	72	73	74	75	76	77	78	79
80	81	82	83	84	85	86	87	88	89
90	91	92	93	94	95	96	97	98	99

Clues

• ____________________

• ____________________

• ____________________

Name______________________________ **Checkpoint** 

1. Skip count by 2s.

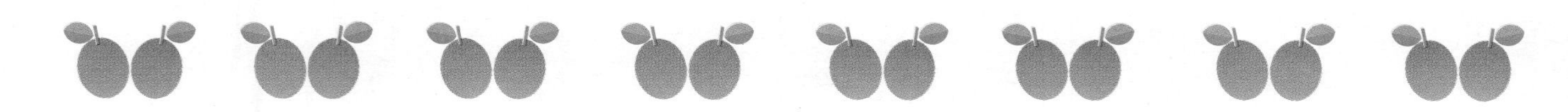

2, ____, ____, ____, ____, ____, ____, ____

Circle pairs. Write the number in all.
Circle **odd** or **even**.

2. 

____ odd even

3. ____ odd even

4. Write > or <.

26 ◯ 29 48 ◯ 50 34 ◯ 31 77 ◯ 75

5. Write the number that comes before.

____, 66 ____, 49 ____, 21 ____, 70

6. Circle a group of 10. Estimate the total.
Circle more groups of 10. Then count.

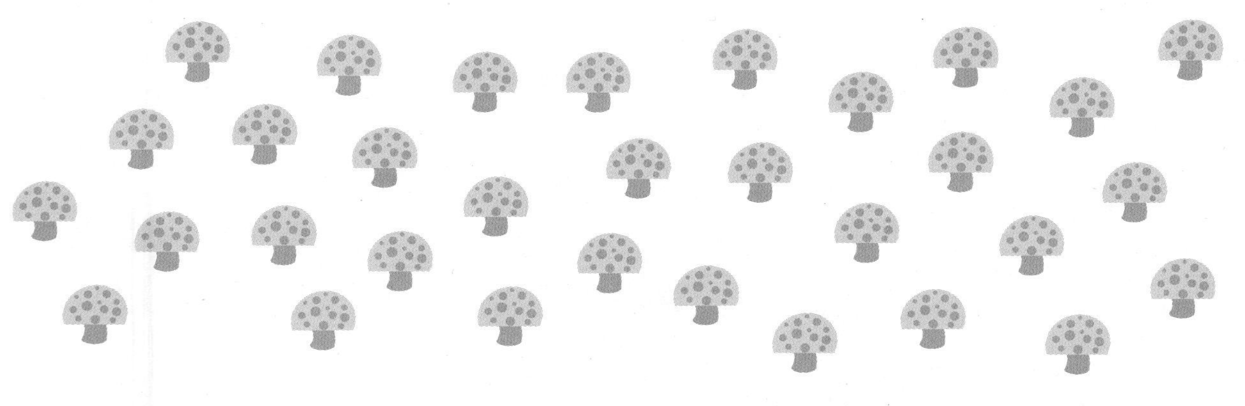

estimate ____ count ____

Name______________________________ **Extra Practice**

Color numbers less than 30 yellow.
Color numbers between 30 and 60 green.
Color numbers greater than 60 red.

89 23 52 76 9 96 92 59 73 15 34 47 26 68 29 41 12 31 22 19 84 62

Name______________________________ **Chapter Test** 

Write how many tens and ones.

1. 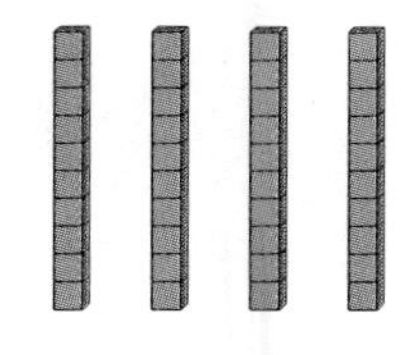

_____ tens _____ ones

2. 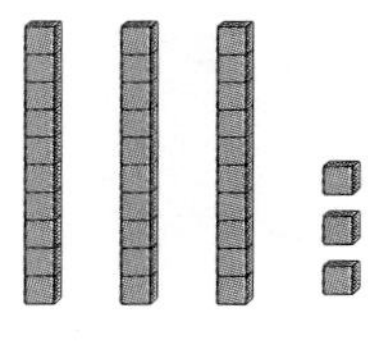

_____ tens _____ ones

Count by 5s.

3.       

5, _____, _____, _____, _____, _____, _____, _____

Write > or <.

4. 46  47 51 ◯ 39  29 ◯ 42 63  66

Write the number that comes **after**.

5. 56, _____ 89, _____ 36, _____ 90, _____ 45, _____

Match.

6.      

3rd 1st 5th 2nd 4th

Use the clues to name the secret number.

7.
- It is less than 72.
- It is greater than 67.
- It is even.

The secret number is _____.

72 69 92 81 68 67

Name________________________________ **Performance Assessment**

What You Need

tens ones

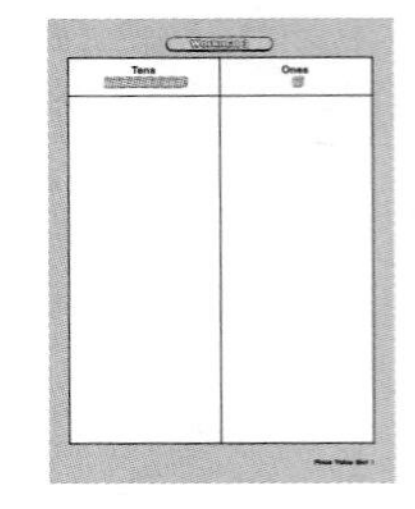

Workmat 3

2 number cubes

Try to make 50!

1. Roll the number cubes. Add. Take that many ones.
2. Regroup as tens if you can.
3. Write how many tens and ones. Write the number in all.
4. Repeat nine times. Each time, add to the tens and ones you have.

1. _____tens _____ones _____
2. _____tens _____ones _____
3. _____tens _____ones _____
4. _____tens _____ones _____
5. _____tens _____ones _____
6. _____tens _____ones _____
7. _____tens _____ones _____
8. _____tens _____ones _____
9. _____tens _____ones _____
10. _____tens _____ones _____

Is your last number greater than or less than 50? __________

Name________________________________

You can use a number line to skip count from any number.

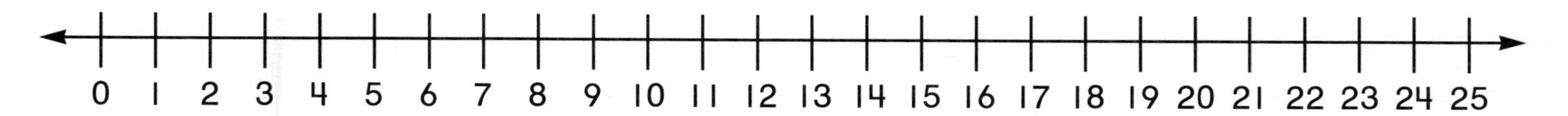

Use the number line.

1. Skip count by 2s.

   1, 3, ____, ____, ____, ____, ____

2. Skip count by 3s.

   2, ____, ____, ____, ____, ____, ____

3. Skip count by 3s.

   4, ____, ____, ____, ____, ____, ____

4. Skip count by 4s.

   2, ____, ____, ____, ____, ____, ____

5. Skip count by 5s.

   1, ____, ____, ____, ____

6. Skip count by 5s.

   3, ____, ____, ____, ____

Name________________________

Skip Counting With a Calculator

Use a calculator to skip count.

Press ON/C each time you begin.

Press the keys.

Write the numbers you see.

1. Skip count by 4s.

     4   8  ____  ____

2. Skip count by 3s.

     ____  ____  ____ ____

3. Skip count by 5s.

    ____  ____  ____ ____

4. Skip count by 10s.

    ____  ____  ____

5. Skip count by ____.

   ____   ____  ____

Name ____________________

Fill in the ⬭ for the correct answer.

Add.

1. $9 + 4$
   - ⬭ 13
   - ⬭ 14
   - ⬭ 15
   - ⬭ 16

2. $6 + 6$
   - ⬭ 12
   - ⬭ 11
   - ⬭ 15
   - ⬭ 16

3. $8 + 7$
   - ⬭ 13
   - ⬭ 14
   - ⬭ 15
   - ⬭ 16

4. $8 + 8$
   - ⬭ 13
   - ⬭ 14
   - ⬭ 15
   - ⬭ 16

5. $2 + 8$
   - ⬭ 10
   - ⬭ 11
   - ⬭ 15
   - ⬭ 16

6. $9 + 6$
   - ⬭ 10
   - ⬭ 11
   - ⬭ 15
   - ⬭ 16

7. $6 + 4 + 4 =$ ____

   ⬭ 10 ⬭ 12 ⬭ 14 ⬭ 16

8. $2 + 7 + 3 =$ ____

   ⬭ 10 ⬭ 12 ⬭ 14 ⬭ 16

Find the missing numbers.

9. $3 +$ ____ $= 12$

   ⬭ 8 ⬭ 9 ⬭ 10 ⬭ 11

10. $8 +$ ____ $= 16$

   ⬭ 8 ⬭ 9 ⬭ 10 ⬭ 11

Subtract.

11. $11 - 3$
   - ⬭ 7
   - ⬭ 8
   - ⬭ 9
   - ⬭ 1

12. $14 - 7$
   - ⬭ 4
   - ⬭ 5
   - ⬭ 6
   - ⬭ 7

13. $12 - 7$
   - ⬭ 5
   - ⬭ 6
   - ⬭ 7
   - ⬭ 8

Subtract.

14. $17 - 8 =$ ____

8　9　10　11

15. $18 - 9 =$ ____

6　7　8　9

16. $14 - 9 =$ ____

4　5　6　7

Find the related addition fact.

17. $\begin{array}{r} 13 \\ -\ 7 \\ \hline \end{array}$

- $7 + 5 = 12$
- $9 + 4 = 13$
- $7 + 6 = 13$

18. $\begin{array}{r} 15 \\ -\ 6 \\ \hline \end{array}$

- $6 + 7 = 13$
- $6 + 9 = 15$
- $8 + 7 = 15$

Match the number shown.

19. 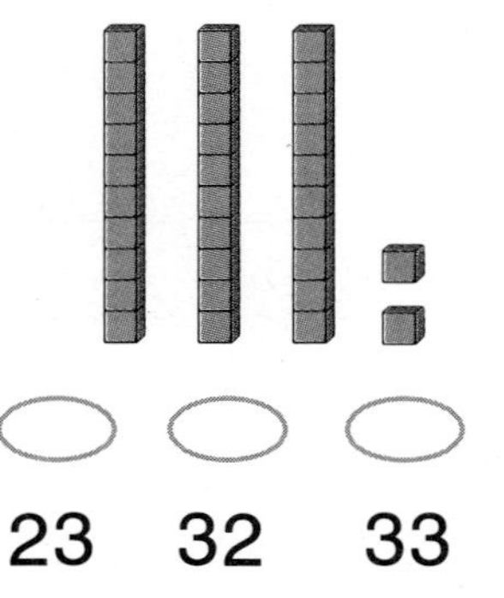

23　32　33

20. 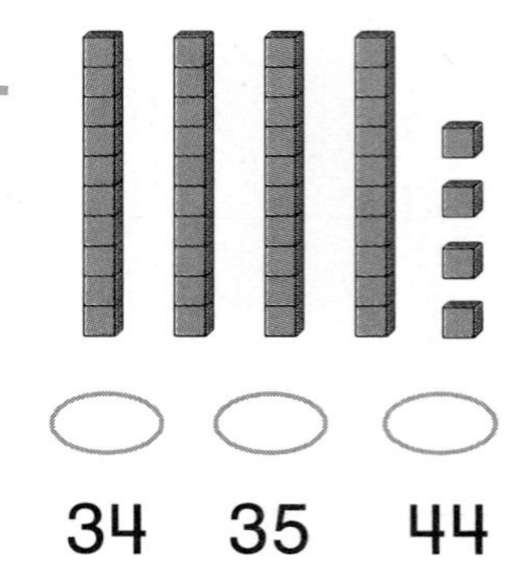

34　35　44

21. 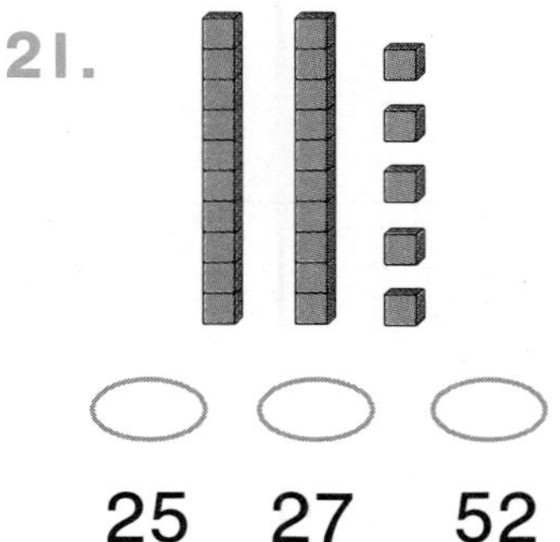

25　27　52

Find the number that is greater.

22. 55

- 54
- 47
- 74
- 39

23. 79

- 68
- 91
- 77
- 52

24. 80

- 89
- 71
- 79
- 65

25. Use the clues to find the number.

- It is greater than 40.
- It is even.
- It is less than 60.

51　62　24　58

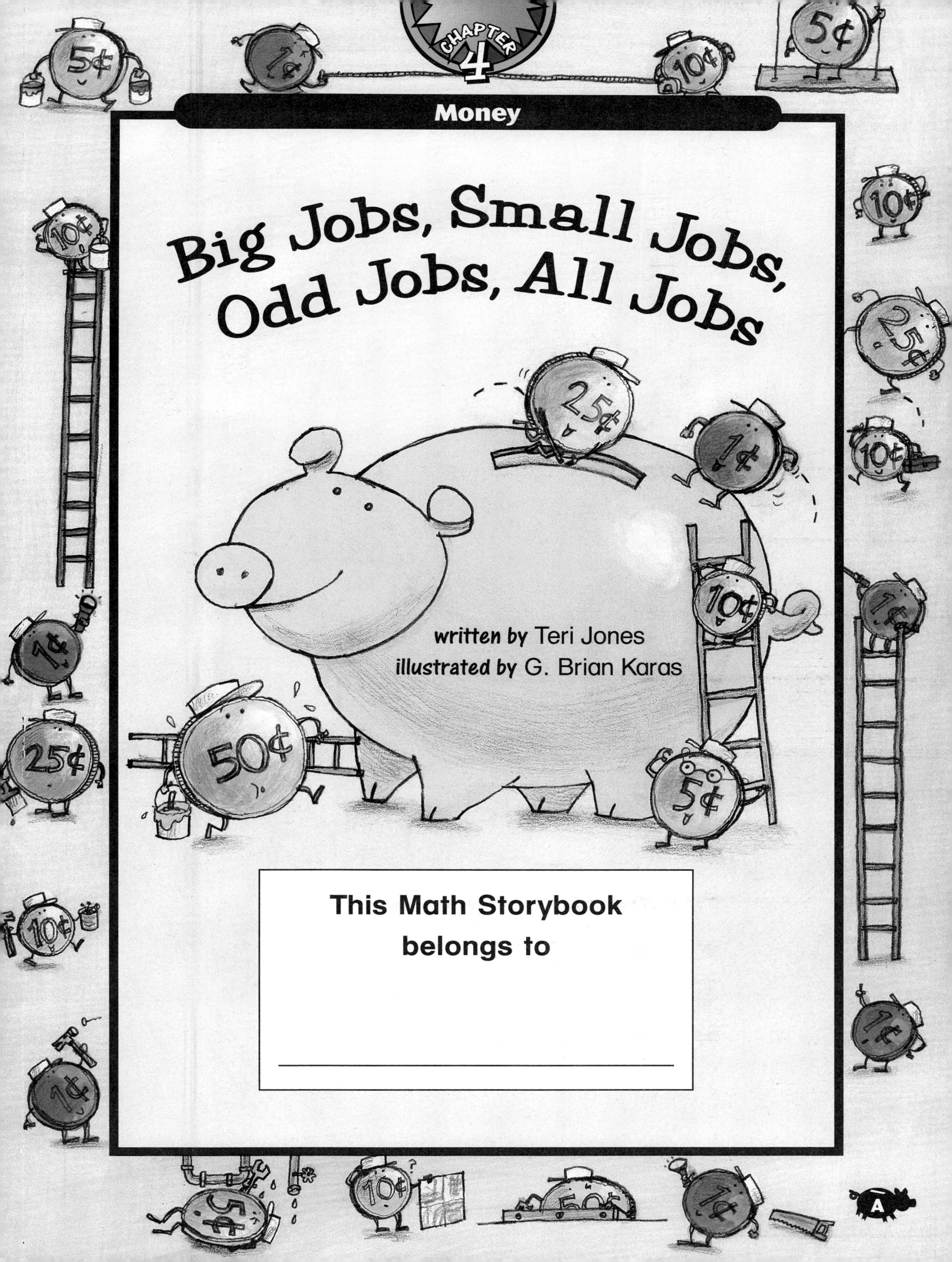
CHAPTER 4
Money
Big Jobs, Small Jobs, Odd Jobs, All Jobs
written by Teri Jones
illustrated by G. Brian Karas
This Math Storybook belongs to
A

The whole neighborhood loves Jamal's lemonade.
He charges 25 cents a glass.
What will he do with his money?

Making cards is what Rosa likes to do.
She charges 50 cents a card.
What will she do with her money?

All the dogs in the neighborhood love Janie.
She charges 75 cents to walk each dog.
What will she do with her money?

Thirsty plants love Gregg when their owners go away.
He charges one dollar a day.
What will he do with his money?

So THIS is what they're doing with their money!

What job would you like to do to earn money?
Draw or trace coins to show what you might earn.
Write the total amount.

_______ total

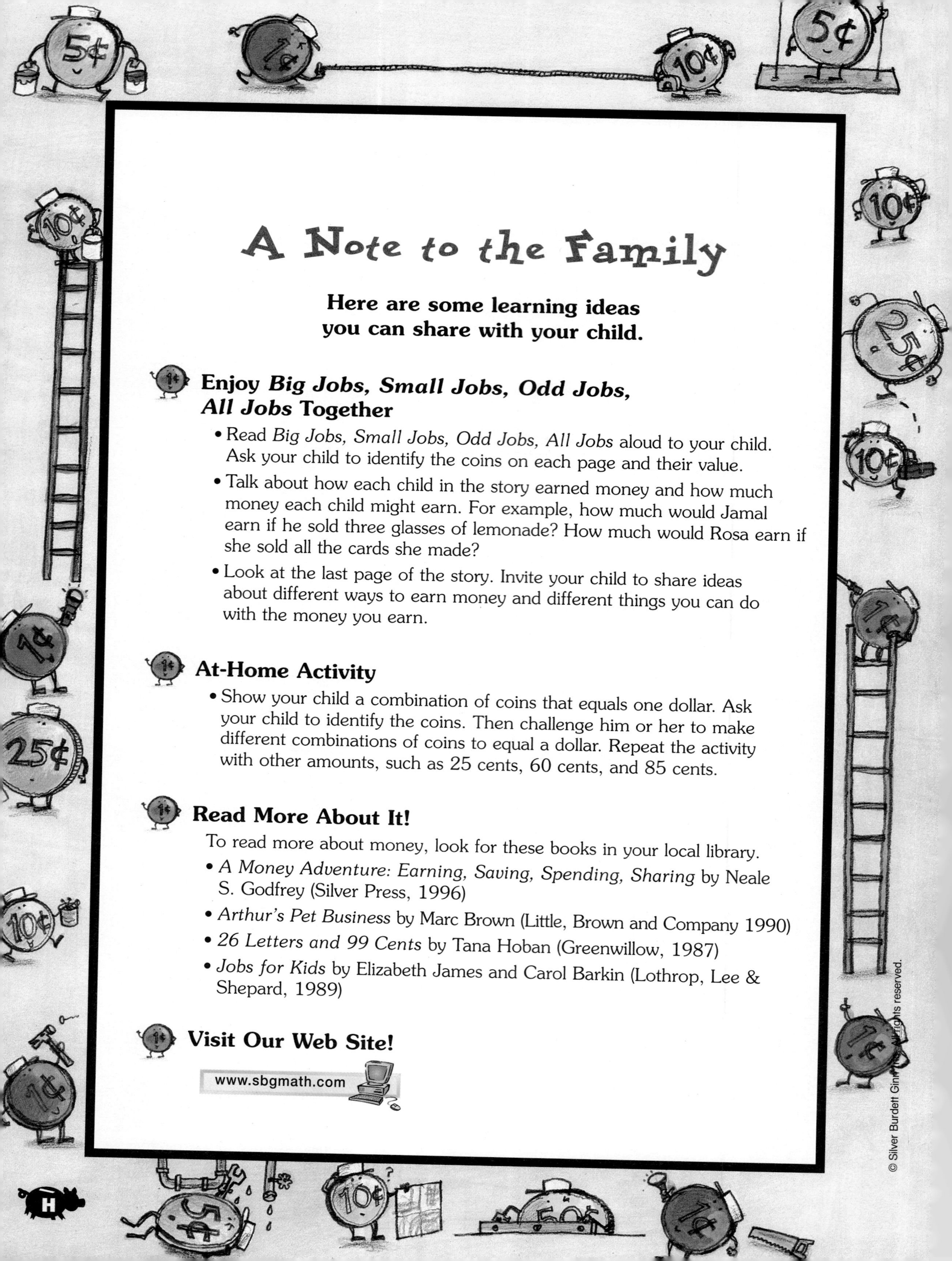

A Note to the Family

Here are some learning ideas you can share with your child.

Enjoy *Big Jobs, Small Jobs, Odd Jobs, All Jobs* Together

- Read *Big Jobs, Small Jobs, Odd Jobs, All Jobs* aloud to your child. Ask your child to identify the coins on each page and their value.
- Talk about how each child in the story earned money and how much money each child might earn. For example, how much would Jamal earn if he sold three glasses of lemonade? How much would Rosa earn if she sold all the cards she made?
- Look at the last page of the story. Invite your child to share ideas about different ways to earn money and different things you can do with the money you earn.

At-Home Activity

- Show your child a combination of coins that equals one dollar. Ask your child to identify the coins. Then challenge him or her to make different combinations of coins to equal a dollar. Repeat the activity with other amounts, such as 25 cents, 60 cents, and 85 cents.

Read More About It!

To read more about money, look for these books in your local library.

- *A Money Adventure: Earning, Saving, Spending, Sharing* by Neale S. Godfrey (Silver Press, 1996)
- *Arthur's Pet Business* by Marc Brown (Little, Brown and Company 1990)
- *26 Letters and 99 Cents* by Tana Hoban (Greenwillow, 1987)
- *Jobs for Kids* by Elizabeth James and Carol Barkin (Lothrop, Lee & Shepard, 1989)

Visit Our Web Site!

www.sbgmath.com

Name________________________________ **Pennies, Nickels, and Dimes**

penny	nickel	dime
 or 	 or   	or 
1¢	5¢	10¢
one cent	five cents	ten cents

Count on to find the total amount.

Word Bank
- cent
- penny
- nickel
- dime

1\.     

10¢ 20¢ 25¢ 26¢ 27¢ 27¢ total

2\.      

____¢ ____¢ ____¢ ____¢ ____¢ ____¢ ____¢ total

3\.      

____¢ ____¢ ____¢ ____¢ ____¢ ____¢ ____¢ total

4\.   

____¢ ____¢ ____¢ ____¢ ____¢ ____¢ ____¢ total

Home Connection Your child has been counting sets of coins. Give your child some pennies, nickels, and dimes. Ask him or her to find the total value.

Write each amount.

1.    41¢

2.    ____¢

3.    ____¢

4.    ____¢

5.   ____¢

Problem Solving

Solve.

6. You have seven coins that total 28¢. How many of each coin do you have?

____ ____ ____

Name____________________

There are 3 coins in the bank.
No coin is greater than 5¢.
How much money could there be?

You can make a list to find out.
1¢

Use coins to show what could be in the bank.
Make a list to record.
Write each amount.

Nickels	Pennies	Amount
3	0	15¢
		¢
		¢
		¢

1. What is the greatest amount you could have? ____¢

2. What is the least amount you could have? ____¢

Home Connection Your child is learning to make a list to solve problems. Ask your child to show you how he or she solved the problem above.

You have 3 coins.
No coin is greater than 10¢.
How much money could you have?

Use coins to show different ways.
Make a list to record.
Write each amount.

Dimes	Nickels	Pennies	Amount
3	0	0	30¢
2	1	0	25¢
			¢
			¢
			¢
			¢
			¢
			¢
			¢
			¢

1. What is the greatest amount you could have? ____ ¢

2. What is the least amount you could have? ____ ¢

Name______________________________ **Quarters**

Draw or trace more coins to make 25¢.

1.   

= 

2.      = 

3.  = 

4.   = 

Home Connection Your child is learning the value of a quarter. Ask your child to show you different ways to make 25¢, using dimes, nickels, and pennies.

Write each amount.
Circle the amounts that are the same as a quarter.

1. 25¢

2. ____¢

3. ____¢

4. ____¢

5.

____¢

6.

____¢

Problem Solving

Solve.

7. You have 2 dimes and 1 penny in your pocket. How many more pennies do you need to make 25¢?

____ more pennies

8. Dan has 1 dime and 2 nickels. Jill has 2 dimes and 5 pennies. Who has the same as a quarter?

____

Name________________________________

Count on to find each amount.

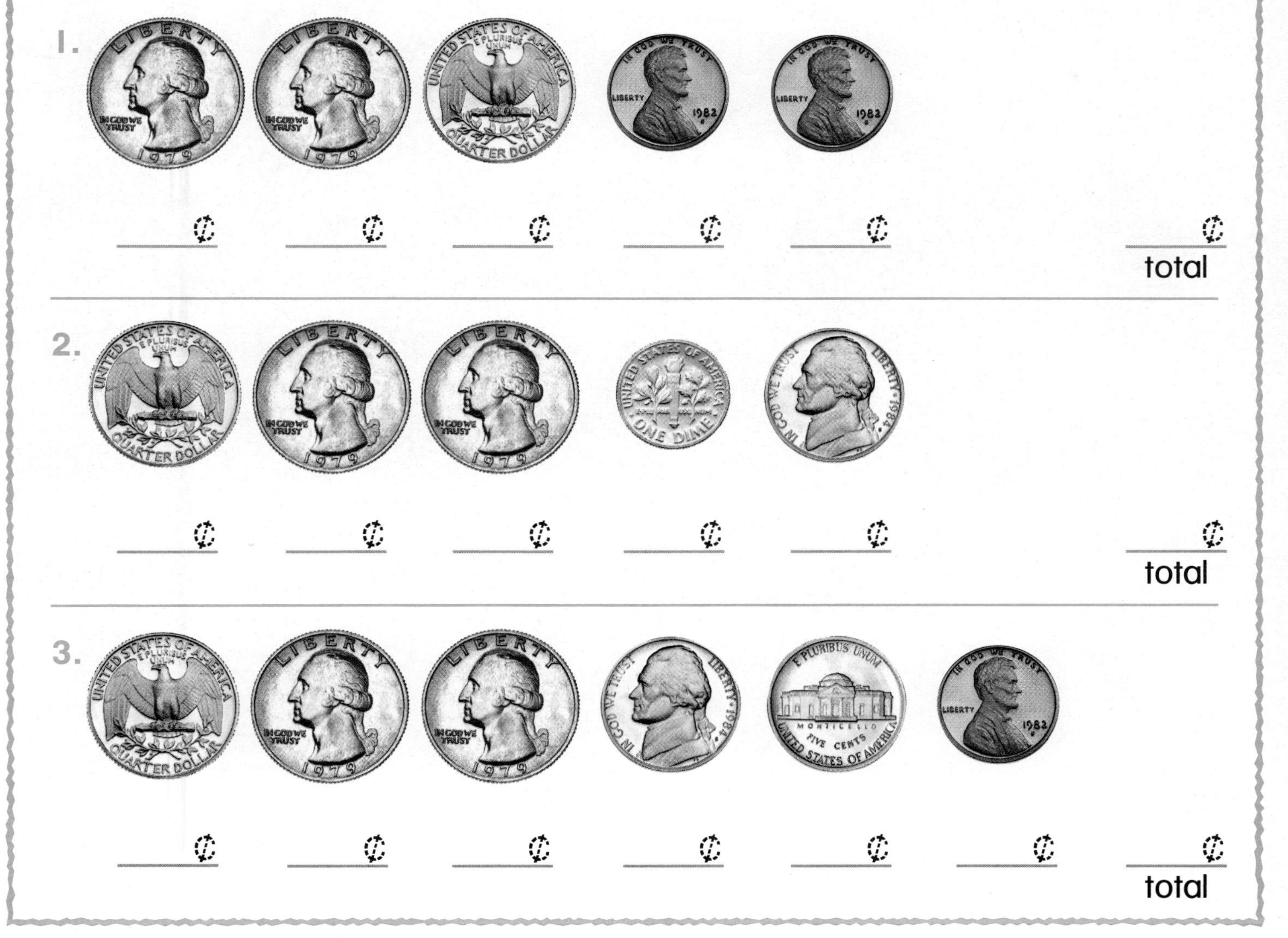

Home Connection Your child is counting sets of pennies, nickels, dimes, and quarters to 99¢. Give your child some coins to count. Remind your child to count the coins of greatest value first.

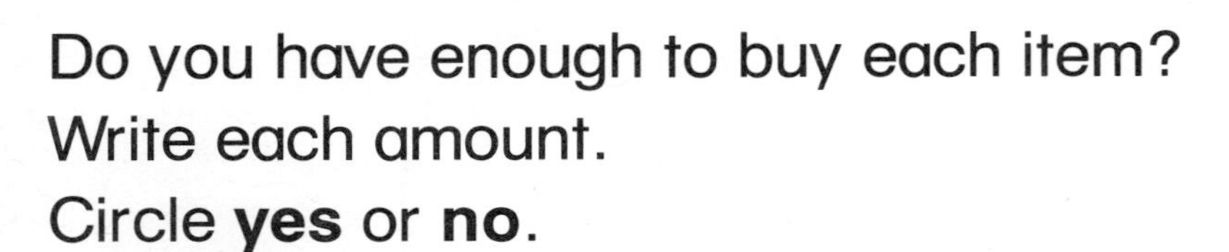

Do you have enough to buy each item?
Write each amount.
Circle **yes** or **no**.

It helps to count coins of greatest value first.

1.

51¢ (yes) no

2.

____¢ yes no

3.

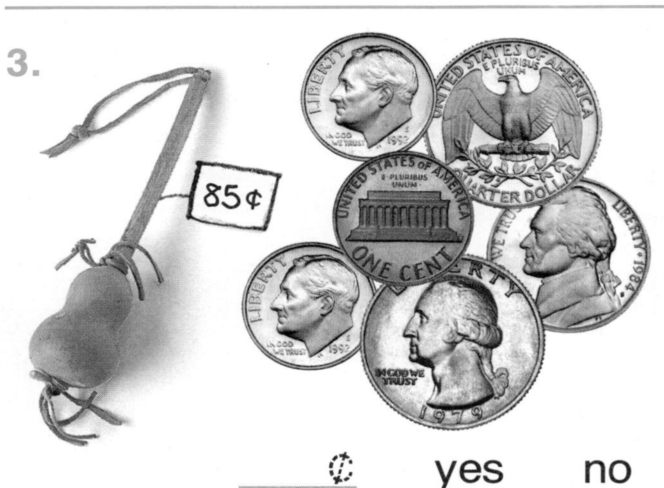

____¢ yes no

4.

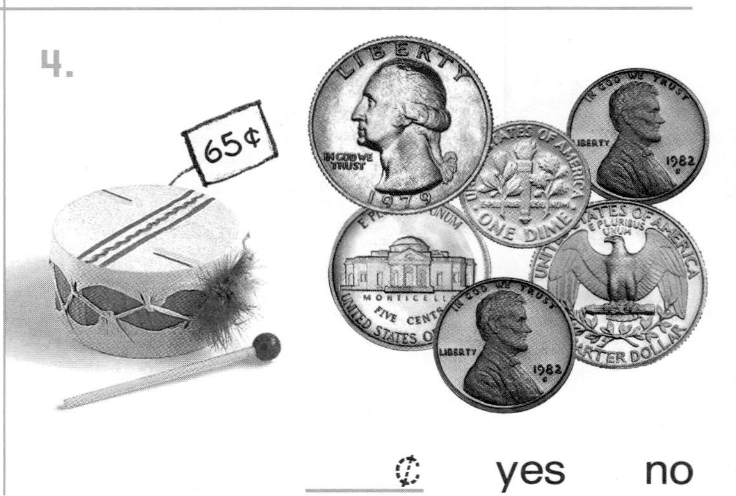

____¢ yes no

Critical Thinking Corner

Number Sense

5. Circle the coins you would use to make 75¢.

Name________________________________ **Comparing Sets of Coins**

Who earned more money?

Write each amount.
Circle the greater amount.

1.

____ ¢

____ ¢

2.

____ ¢

____ ¢

3.

____ ¢

____ ¢

Home Connection Your child has been comparing sets of coins. Show your child two groups of coins. Have him or her tell which group has the greater amount.

Write each amount.
Circle the greater amount.

1.

_____ ¢

_____ ¢

2.

_____ ¢

_____ ¢

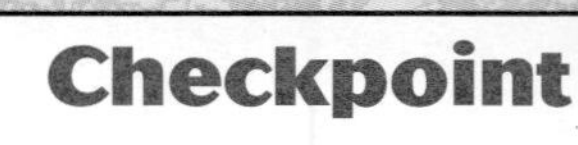

1. Count on to find the total amount.

_____ ¢ _____ ¢ _____ ¢ _____ ¢ _____ ¢ _____ ¢ _____ ¢ total

2. Draw or trace coins to make 25¢.

Name____________________

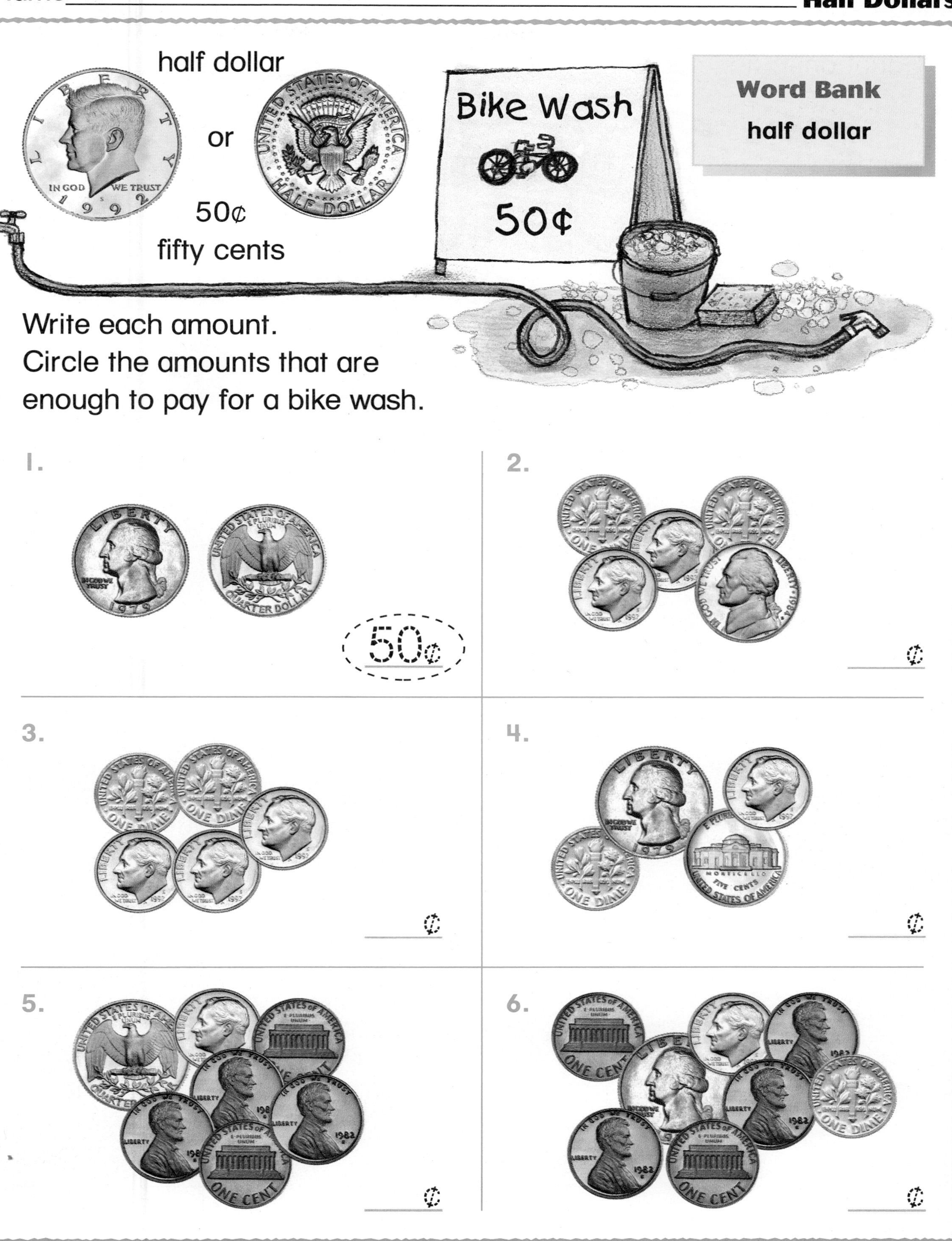

Word Bank
half dollar

Write each amount.
Circle the amounts that are enough to pay for a bike wash.

1. 50¢

2. ____¢

3. ____¢

4. ____¢

5. ____¢

6. ____¢

Home Connection Your child is learning the value of a half dollar. Ask your child to make a group of coins that equals a half dollar. Remind him or her to begin with the coin of greatest value.

Count on to find each amount.

1.    

 50¢ 75¢ 80¢ 81¢  81¢ total

2.     

____¢ ____¢ ____¢ ____¢ ____¢ ____¢ total

3.    

____¢ ____¢ ____¢ ____¢ ____¢ total

4.     

____¢ ____¢ ____¢ ____¢ ____¢ ____¢ total

5.    

____¢ ____¢ ____¢ ____¢ ____¢ ____¢ total

Name______________________________

What coins could you use to pay?

I could use 3 quarters.
I could use 2 quarters, 2 dimes,and 1 nickel.
I could use 1 half dollar and 1 quarter.
Pet Sitting 75¢

Use coins to show the amounts in different ways.
Draw or trace coins to show one way.

1. 37¢

2. 66¢

Home Connection Your child is learning how to show the same amount of money in different ways. Challenge your child to show you how many ways he or she can show 75¢.

Use coins to show each amount in different ways.
Use tally marks to record the coins you use.

1.

Ways to show 58¢				
half dollars	**quarters**	**dimes**	**nickels**	**pennies**
		𝍸	𝍷	𝍷𝍷𝍷

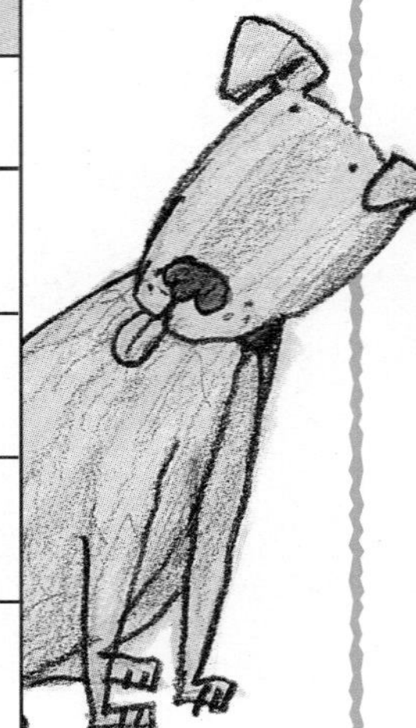

2.

Ways to show 86¢				
half dollars	**quarters**	**dimes**	**nickels**	**pennies**

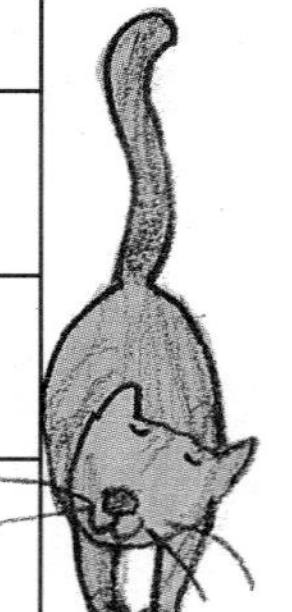

What Do You Think?

I can show 61¢ in 3 ways.
How many ways can you show 61¢?

Name______________________________ **Exploring Dollars**

100¢
one dollar
$1.00

Word Bank
dollar

Draw or trace more coins to make one dollar.
Write the number of coins.
Write each amount in cents.

1. Use quarters.

4 quarters

100¢

$1.00

2. Use dimes.

_____ dimes

_____¢

$1.00

3. Use nickels.

_____ nickels

_____¢

$1.00

Home Connection Your child is learning amounts of money equivalent to $1.00. Have your child use coins to show ways to make $1.00.

Write each amount in cents.
Circle the amounts that make one dollar.

1.

2.

_____ ¢

3.

_____ ¢

4.

_____ ¢

5. Draw or trace coins to make $1.00 another way.

Name________________________________

Use the picture to find the price.
Is there enough money? Write **yes** or **no**.

You want to buy	You have	Do you have enough money?
1.		yes
2.		______
3.		______
4.		______

Home Connection Your child is learning to estimate the amount of money needed to buy something costing less than $1.00. You can have your child practice while you shop together.

Use the picture to find the price.
Is there enough money? Write **yes** or **no**.

You want to buy	You have	Do you have enough money?
1.		______
2.		______
3.		______
4.		______
5.		______

Name______________________________ **Making Change**

Use pennies.
Count up from the price.
Write how much change.

Price	You pay	Your change
1. 18¢		2¢
2. 26¢		___¢
3. 32¢		___¢

Home Connection Your child is learning to count up to make change. Play store to help your child practice making change.

Use pennies.
Count up from the price.
Write how much change.

Price	You pay	Your change
1. 27¢	LIBERTY IN GOD WE TRUST; LIBERTY IN GOD WE TRUST; UNITED STATES OF AMERICA ONE DIME	____ ¢
2. 31¢	LIBERTY IN GOD WE TRUST 1979; UNITED STATES OF AMERICA ONE DIME	____ ¢
3. 48¢	LIBERTY IN GOD WE TRUST 1992	____ ¢
4. 74¢	UNITED STATES OF AMERICA E PLURIBUS UNUM QUARTER DOLLAR; LIBERTY 1979; UNITED STATES OF AMERICA E PLURIBUS UNUM QUARTER DOLLAR	____ ¢
5. 98¢	FEDERAL RESERVE NOTE THE UNITED STATES OF AMERICA B 92223879 J ONE DOLLAR	____ ¢

Name______________________________ **Checkpoint** 

1. Count on to find the total amount.

____ ¢ ____ ¢ ____ ¢ ____ ¢ ____ ¢ ____ ¢
total

---

2. Write each amount.
Circle the greater amount.

____ ¢

____ ¢

---

3. Draw or trace coins to make 78¢.

---

4. Write each amount.
Circle the amount that makes $1.00.

____ ¢

____ ¢

Name________________________________ **Extra Practice**

Use coins to solve each problem.

1. You have 6 coins that total 67¢.
   Circle the coins you could have.

2. Match coins to the circles.
   Write the amount on each circle.
   Write the total amount.

______ ¢

Name________________________________ **Chapter Test**

1. Draw or trace more coins to make 25¢.

   = 

2. Count on to find the total amount.

____¢ ____¢ ____¢ ____¢ ____¢ ____¢
total

Write each amount.
Is there enough to buy the toy?
Circle **yes** or **no**.

3.

____¢ yes no

4.

____¢ yes no

5. Count up from the price to find your change.
Write how much change.

Price	You pay	Your change
12¢		____¢

Name______________________________ **Performance Assessment**

What You Need

penny nickel dime quarter

Write an amount of money more than 50¢.
Draw or trace coins to show the amount in 2 ways.

Ways to show _____¢

1.

2.

What if your friend gave you 9¢ more.
Draw or trace coins to show how much you have now.

3.

Name ________________________

$2.00 $2.25 $2.35 $2.40 $2.40 total

First count the bills, then the coins.
Count on to find the total amount.

1.    

$. ____ $. ____ $. ____ $. ____ $. ____ total

2.    

$. ____ $. ____ $. ____ $. ____ $. ____ total

3.    

$. ____ $. ____ $. ____ $. ____ $. ____ total

4.    

$. ____ $. ____ $. ____ $. ____ $. ____ total

Name________________________

Money and the MathProcessor™

You can use the MathProcessor to find change.

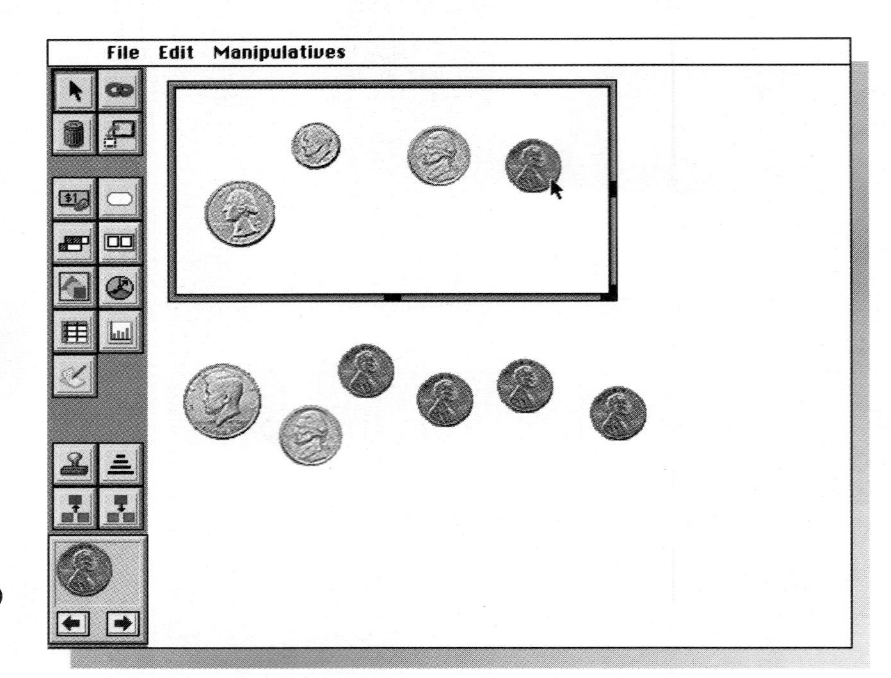

Use the MathProcessor to complete the chart below.

1 Show the money you have.

Click on the **money button** to show a workspace.

Click on the **arrow** to pick a coin or bill.

Click on the **coin** or **bill** to show it.

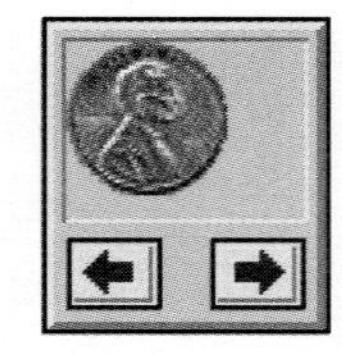

2 Show the money you spend.

Drag money out of the workspace to show what you spend.

Click on a **trade button** if you need to trade.

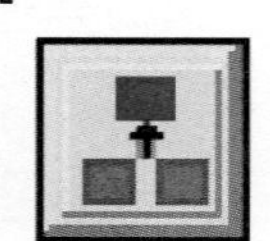

	you have	you spend	your change
1.	$1.00	59¢	41¢
2.	$1.00	36¢	
3.	$1.00	89¢	
4.	$1.00	43¢	

CHAPTER 5
Adding Two-Digit Numbers
The Life of a Can
written by Geoff Johnson
illustrated by Nathan Jarvis
This Math Storybook
belongs to
A

Hi! I'm a can. I started out in a can factory just like the cans you see here.
15 cans are up above. 25 cans are down below. Not counting me, how many cans do you see?
B

First, the cans are filled with food. Next, they are sealed and labeled. Then, they are sent to the grocery store. Not counting me, how many cans do you see?

When someone takes them home, the cans sit on a shelf. They keep food fresh for a long time. Look at the 12 cans on the top. Look at the 16 cans on the bottom. Not counting me, how many cans do you see?

Remember, when a can is empty, please don't throw it away. It can be used again. Look at the 14 cans in the bin. Look at the 10 others. Not counting me, how many cans do you see?

When cans are recycled, they go back to the can factory. There they get ready to be used again. There are 50 cans in the truck. The children have 25 cans. Not counting me, how many cans will there be?
50 CANS
25 CANS
F

Draw more cans to fill the top shelf.
Now draw more cans on the bottom shelf.
How many cans are there?

A Note to the Family

Here are some learning ideas you can share with your child.

Enjoy *The Life of a Can* Together

- Read the story aloud with your child. Talk about what happens to a can after it leaves the can factory. Help your child add the numbers on each page to find out how many cans there are. Talk about how your child added.
- Look at the last page. Ask your child to draw more cans to fill the two shelves. Talk about what your child might draw on the labels to show what food is inside.

At-Home Activities

- During a trip to the grocery store, point out the wide variety of cans on the shelves. At home, ask your child to help you put away cans. He or she can then count and add to find out how many cans are on your shelves.
- As a family, try sorting your recyclables for one week. Have one bag for cans, one for glass, one for plastic, and one for paper. At the end of the week, bring the bags to a recycling center.

Read More About It!

Here are some books you might enjoy sharing with your child. Look for them in your library or bookstore.

- *Earth Book* by Linda Schwartz (The Learning Works, 1990)
- *One to One Hundred* by Teri Sloat (Dutton Children's Books, 1990)

Visit Our Web Site!

www.sbgmath.com

Name________________________________ **Adding Tens**

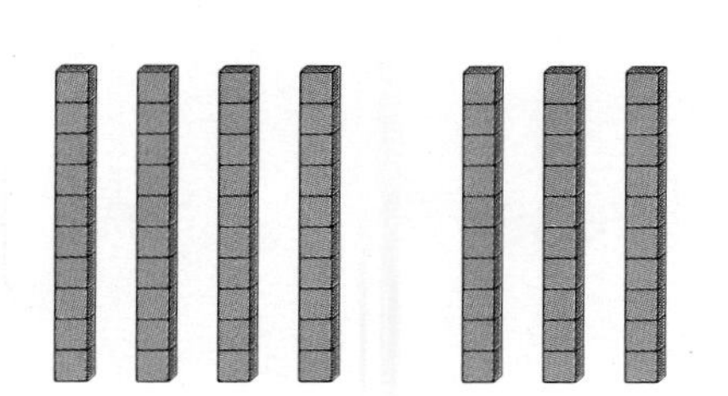

4 tens + 3 tens = 7 tens

40 + 30 = 70

Find each sum.
Use tens models if you like.

1. 2 tens + 4 tens = ____ tens
   20 + 40 = ____

2. 8 tens + 1 ten = ____ tens
   80 + 10 = ____

3. 3 tens + 4 tens = ____ tens
   30 + 40 = ____

4. 6 tens + 2 tens = ____ tens
   60 + 20 = ____

5. 3 tens + 5 tens = ____ tens
   30 + 50 = ____

6. 2 tens + 3 tens = ____ tens
   20 + 30 = ____

7. 7 tens + 2 tens = ____ tens
   70 + 20 = ____

8. 5 tens + 2 tens = ____ tens
   50 + 20 = ____

9. 1 ten + 3 tens = ____ tens
   10 + 30 = ____

10. 3 tens + 6 tens = ____ tens
    30 + 60 = ____

11. 7 tens + 1 ten = ____ tens
    70 + 10 = ____

12. 3 tens + 3 tens = ____ tens
    30 + 30 = ____

Home Connection Children can use basic facts to help them add tens. Ask your child to add numbers like these.

Find each sum. Write the missing numbers.
Use tens models if you like.

1. 1 ten + 4 tens = 5 tens
   10 + 40 = 50

2. 4 tens + 4 tens = ____ tens
   ____ + ____ = ____

3. 5 tens + 1 ten = ____ tens
   ____ + ____ = ____

4. 2 tens + 6 tens = ____ tens
   ____ + ____ = ____

5. 1 ten + 8 tens = ____ tens
   ____ + ____ = ____

6. 2 tens + 2 tens = ____ tens
   ____ + ____ = ____

7. 3 tens + 4 tens = ____ tens
   ____ + ____ = ____

8. 2 tens + 1 ten = ____ tens
   ____ + ____ = ____

9. 4 tens + 5 tens = ____ tens
   ____ + ____ = ____

10. 1 ten + 6 tens = ____ tens
    ____ + ____ = ____

Critical Thinking Corner

Number Sense

Write **yes** or **no**.

11. The school is having a used toy sale. Jesse has 4 dimes. Kristen has 3 dimes. If they add their money together, do they have enough to buy a ball? ________
    Tell how you know.

Name________________________

You can count on by tens to add.

27 + 20 = 47

Start at 27.
Count on 2 tens.
27, 37, 47

0	1	2	3	4	5	6	7	8	9
10	11	12	13	14	15	16	17	18	19
20	21	22	23	24	25	26	27	28	29
30	31	32	33	34	35	36	37	38	39
40	41	42	43	44	45	46	47	48	49

Use the chart or Workmat 5.
Count on by tens to add.

1. 14 + 30 = 44   20 + 10 = ____   26 + 20 = ____

2. 24 + 20 = ____   10 + 18 = ____   20 + 21 = ____

3. 10 + 30 = ____   5 + 20 = ____   20 + 29 = ____

4. 20 + 16 = ____   10 + 33 = ____   10 + 7 = ____

5. 15 + 20 = ____   12 + 30 = ____   18 + 20 = ____

6. 40 + 7 = ____   14 + 10 = ____   17 + 20 = ____

Home Connection Counting on by tens can help children add. Choose a number from the chart above. Ask your child to add 10, 20, or 30 to that number.

Count on by tens to add.
Use Workmat 5 if you like.

1.	66 + 10 = 76	54 + 30 = ____	20 + 22 = ____
2.	10 + 84 = ____	37 + 20 = ____	32 + 30 = ____
3.	30 + 56 = ____	72 + 10 = ____	39 + 20 = ____
4.	35 + 20 = ____	30 + 35 = ____	43 + 10 = ____
5.	52 + 20 = ____	11 + 10 = ____	30 + 13 = ____
6.	64 + 30 = ____	10 + 34 = ____	77 + 20 = ____
7.	26 + 10 = ____	45 + 30 = ____	64 + 10 = ____
8.	20 + 34 = ____	41 + 10 = ____	57 + 20 = ____

Critical Thinking Corner

Mental Math

9. Circle the row of numbers that shows counting on to find 48 + 30. Tell how you know.

49, 50, 51

58, 68, 78

Name____

You can use tens to estimate sums.

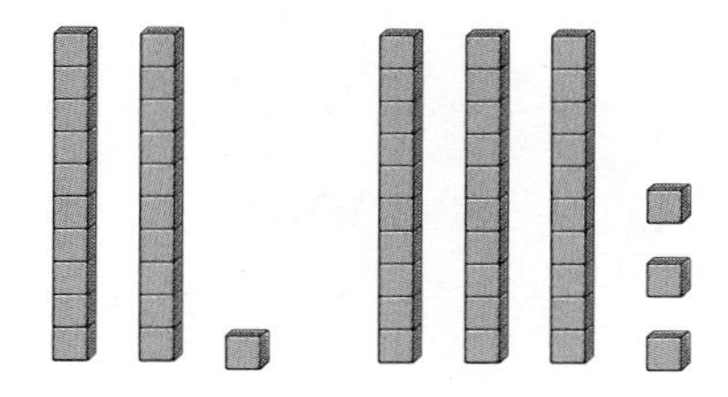

21 + 33 is about 50

Circle the best estimate.

1. 19 + 23 is about

10

20

40 (circled)

2. 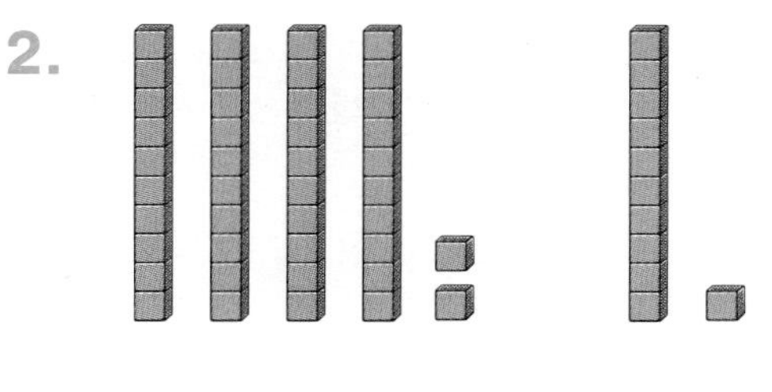

42 + 11 is about

20

50

90

3. 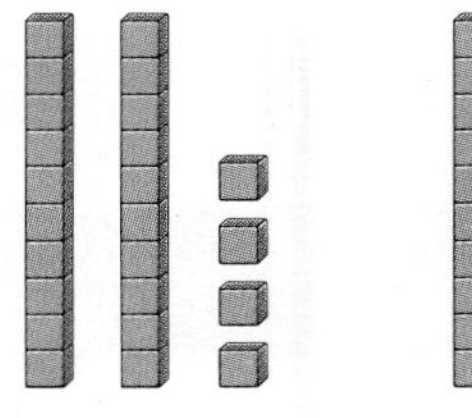

24 + 39 is about

20

30

60

4. 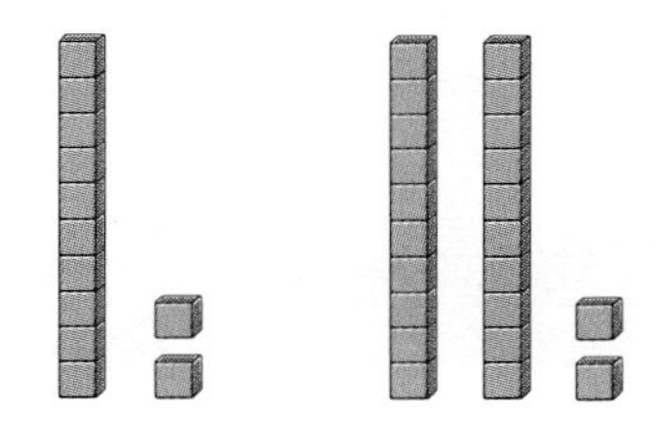

12 + 22 is about

30

50

70

5. 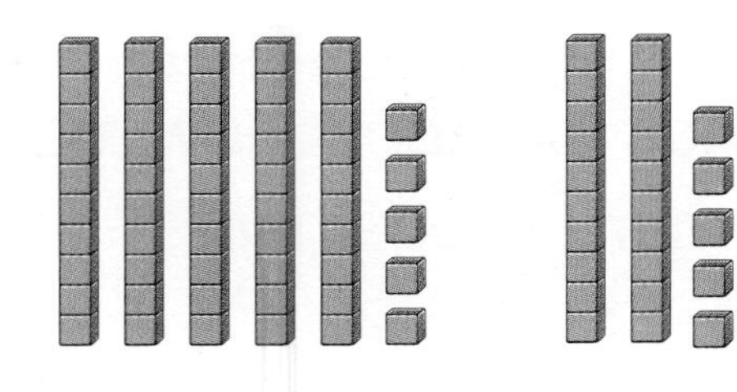

55 + 27 is about

40

80

100

6. 33 + 29 is about

20

40

60

Home Connection Use pennies and dimes to estimate amounts with your child. Show your child an amount like 29¢. Ask if 29¢ is closer to 20¢ or 30¢ and why.

Circle the best estimate. Use models if you like.

1. 28 + 57 is about 30 / 60 / 90

2. 37 + 44 is about 50 / 80 / 100

3. 51 + 33 is about 60 / 80 / 100

4. 19 + 38 is about 20 / 30 / 60

5. 9 + 49 is about 20 / 40 / 60

6. 18 + 27 is about 50 / 90 / 100

7. 69 + 21 is about 20 / 60 / 90

8. 28 + 27 is about 30 / 60 / 90

Problem Solving

Use models. Circle the better estimate.

9. Dillon collected 33 cans on Monday. On Tuesday, he collected 31 cans. About how many cans did he collect in all?

less than 60 more than 60

10. There are 25 cans in one recycling bin. There are 19 in another. About how many are there altogether?

less than 40 more than 40

Name______________________________

You have 3 tens and 4 ones.
How do you add 8 ones?

Sometimes you need to regroup.

1. Show 3 tens 4 ones.

Tens	Ones

2. Add 8 ones.

Tens	Ones

3. Regroup 10 ones as one ten.

Tens	Ones

4 tens 2 ones

Word Bank
regroup

Use tens and ones models and Workmat 3.
Complete the chart.

	Do you need to regroup?	**How many in all?**
1. Show 2 tens 7 ones. Add 6 ones.	(yes) no	3 tens 3 ones
2. Show 5 tens 2 ones. Add 9 ones.	yes no	____ tens ____ one
3. Show 4 tens 7 ones. Add 2 ones.	yes no	____ tens ____ ones
4. Show 3 tens 8 ones. Add 4 ones.	yes no	____ tens ____ ones
5. Show 6 tens 5 ones. Add 5 ones.	yes no	____ tens ____ ones

Home Connection Children need to recognize when it is necessary to regroup 10 ones as 1 ten. Ask your child to explain his or her decision about regrouping in each example on this page.

Use tens and ones models and Workmat 3.
Complete the chart.

	Do you need to regroup?	How many in all?
1. Show 5 tens 7 ones. Add 5 ones.	(yes) no	6 tens 2 ones
2. Show 4 tens 2 ones. Add 8 ones.	yes no	___ tens ___ ones
3. Show 7 tens 4 ones. Add 3 ones.	yes no	___ tens ___ ones
4. Show 3 tens 9 ones. Add 6 ones.	yes no	___ tens ___ ones
5. Show 1 ten 7 ones. Add 6 ones.	yes no	___ tens ___ ones
6. Show 4 tens 6 ones. Add 2 ones.	yes no	___ tens ___ ones
7. Show 2 tens 8 ones. Add 5 ones.	yes no	___ tens ___ ones

PROBLEM SOLVING

Problem Solving

Solve.

8. Raul has 3 dimes and 5 pennies.
His grandmother gives him
a nickel and a penny.
How much money does he have?

Name____

How many bottles are there?

① Add the ones.
Regroup 10 ones as 1 ten.

	Tens	Ones
	1	
	2	5
+	3	7
		2

② Add the tens.

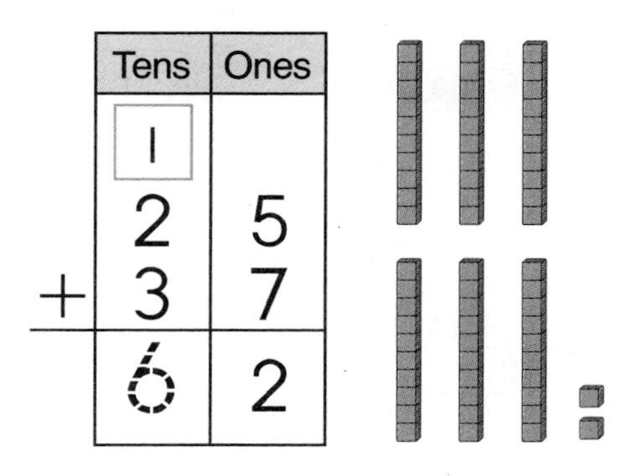

	Tens	Ones
	1	
	2	5
+	3	7
	6	2

There are 62 bottles.

Add. Use tens and ones models and Workmat 3.

1.

	Tens	Ones
	☐	
	4	8
+		6

	Tens	Ones
	☐	
	5	9
+	2	4

	Tens	Ones
	☐	
	1	4
+	7	2

	Tens	Ones
	☐	
	2	9
+		5

2.

	Tens	Ones
	☐	
	5	4
+	2	3

	Tens	Ones
	☐	
		4
+	1	8

	Tens	Ones
	☐	
	1	4
+	2	8

	Tens	Ones
	☐	
	5	2
+		9

Home Connection Your child is learning how to add two-digit numbers. Ask him or her to explain how he or she knows that regrouping is necessary.

Use tens and ones models and Workmat 3.
Find each sum.

1.

	Tens	Ones
	1	
	6	3
+		7
	7	0

	Tens	Ones
		9
+	7	6

	Tens	Ones
	4	7
+	2	6

	Tens	Ones
	3	0
+	3	9

2.

	Tens	Ones
	2	1
+	1	8

	Tens	Ones
	5	4
+	3	7

	Tens	Ones
	4	2
+	5	3

	Tens	Ones
		8
+	8	8

3.

	Tens	Ones
	2	4
+	3	4

	Tens	Ones
	3	3
+		7

	Tens	Ones
	7	1
+	1	9

	Tens	Ones
	3	6
+		5

Critical Thinking Corner

Visual Thinking

Look for a pattern. Draw the next number.

4.

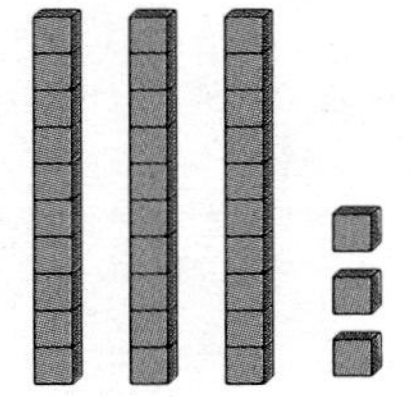

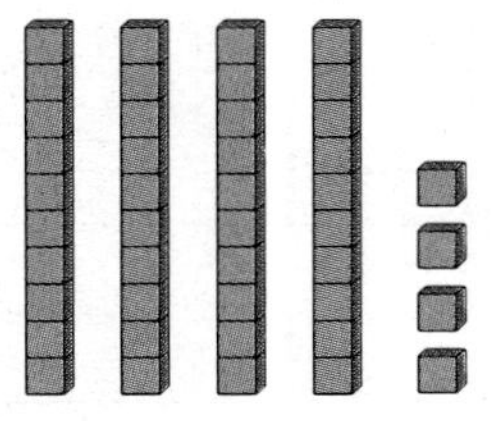

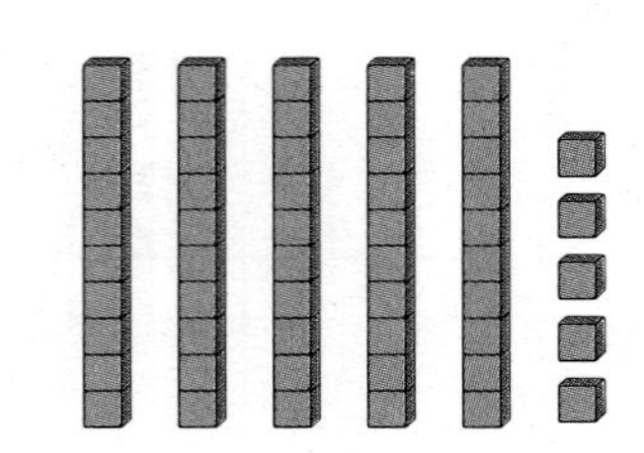

Name______________________________________ **Modeling Addition**

There are 24 cans of peppers and 19 cans of beans. How many cans are there altogether?

43 cans

	Tens	Ones
	1	
	2	4
+	1	9
	4	3

Use tens and ones models and Workmat 3.
Find each sum.

1.

	Tens	Ones
	3	5
+	1	6

	Tens	Ones
	4	7
+		8

	Tens	Ones
	8	3
+	1	1

	Tens	Ones
	5	2
+	2	6

2.

	Tens	Ones
		3
+	1	7

	Tens	Ones
	1	2
+	3	7

	Tens	Ones
	5	4
+	2	8

	Tens	Ones
		4
+	6	1

3.

	Tens	Ones
	4	8
+		9

	Tens	Ones
		4
+	1	8

	Tens	Ones
	1	3
+	2	4

	Tens	Ones
	5	2
+		9

Home Connection Have your child show you the exercises on this page that required regrouping 10 ones as 1 ten.

Use tens and ones models and Workmat 3.
Find each sum.

1.

	Tens	Ones
	7	0
+	2	0
	9	0

	Tens	Ones
	3	5
+	4	6

	Tens	Ones
	1	1
+	8	2

	Tens	Ones
	2	4
+	3	7

2.

	Tens	Ones
	1	0
+	7	8

	Tens	Ones
		2
+	3	9

	Tens	Ones
	6	5
+		3

	Tens	Ones
	1	9
+	1	2

3.

	Tens	Ones
	3	5
+	3	9

	Tens	Ones
	7	4
+	1	4

	Tens	Ones
	5	5
+	1	5

	Tens	Ones
	1	3
+	7	9

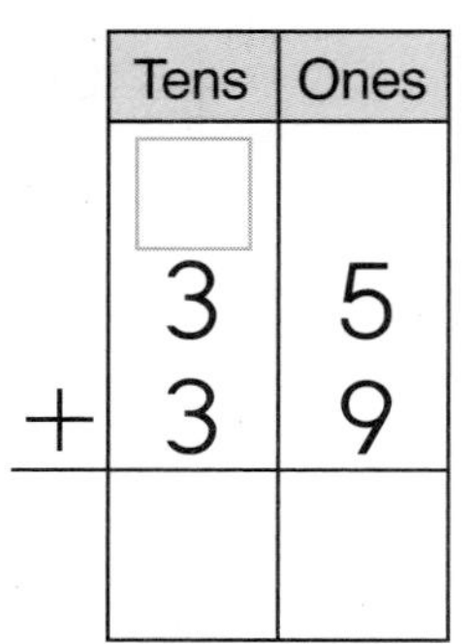

Problem Solving

Which two boxes will make each total?
Write the numbers.

4. Total of 53 books _____ and _____

5. Total of 44 books _____ and _____

6. Greatest total _____ and _____

Name ______________________

Use pictures of tens and ones to find 34 + 18.

1. Add the ones. Regroup.

	Tens	Ones
	1	
	3	4
+	1	8
		2

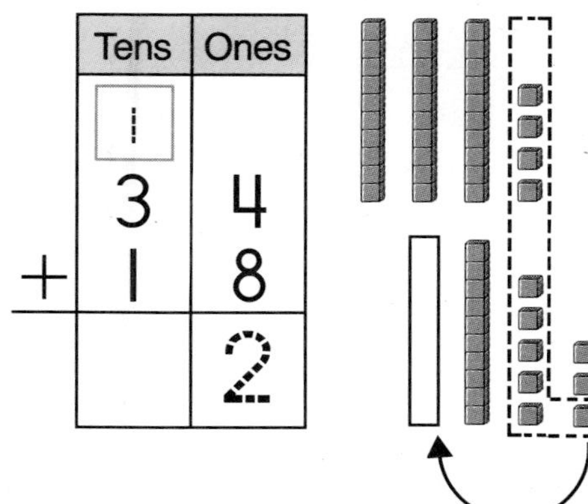

2. Add the tens.

	Tens	Ones
	1	
	3	4
+	1	8
	5	2

Regroup 10 ones for 1 ten.

Find each sum.
Regroup. Circle 10 ones when you can.

1.

	Tens	Ones
	4	9
+	2	5

2.

	Tens	Ones
	3	4
+	3	6

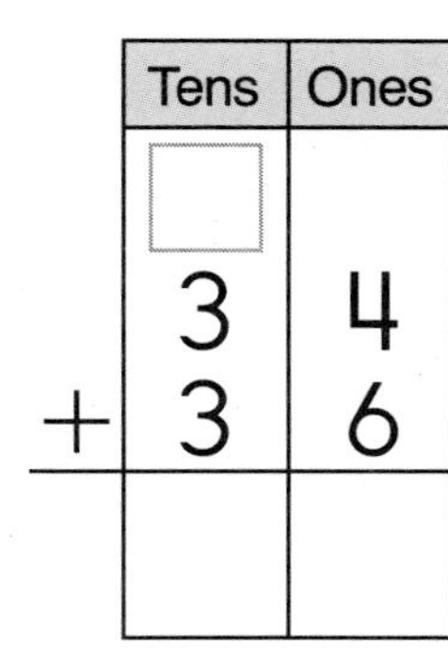

3.

	Tens	Ones
	3	7
+	5	2

4.

	Tens	Ones
	2	8
+	3	5

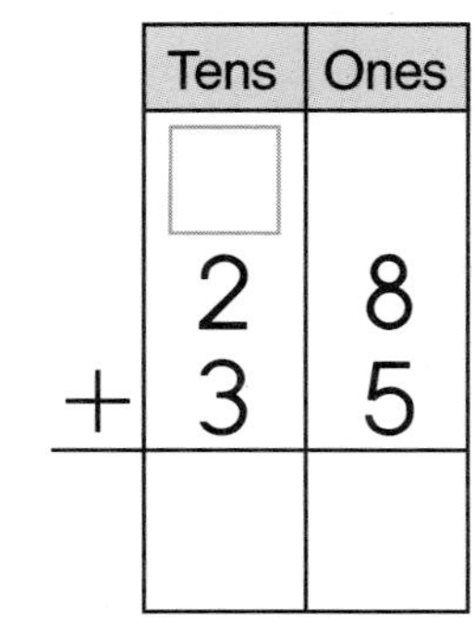

Home Connection Using pictures of tens and ones can help children understand two-digit addition. Ask your child to explain how he or she found each sum.

Find each sum.
Regroup. Circle 10 ones when you can.

1.

	Tens	Ones
	1	
	5	8
+	3	7
	9	5

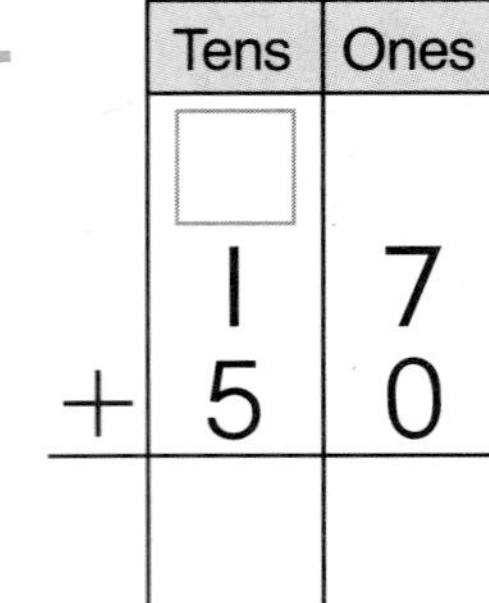

2.

	Tens	Ones
	1	7
+	5	0

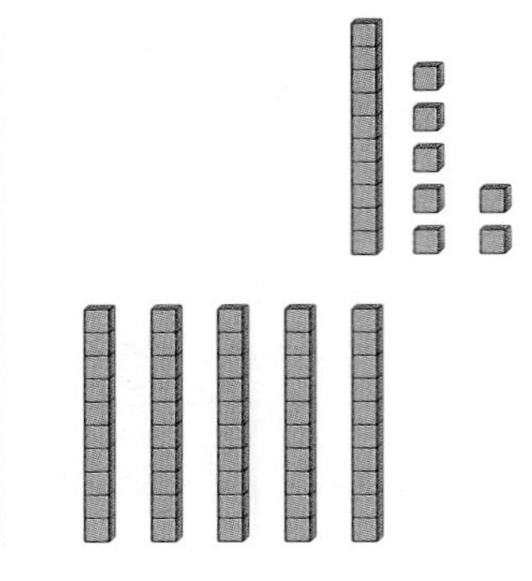

3.

	Tens	Ones
	4	1
+	3	8

4.

	Tens	Ones
	4	9
+	4	3

5.

	Tens	Ones
	2	1
+	6	8

6.

	Tens	Ones
	3	7
+	2	3

7.

	Tens	Ones
	4	4
+		9

8.

	Tens	Ones
	1	8
+	2	3

Name________________________________

Cans Collected	
Class	**Number of cans**
Mr. Carrera	58
Mrs. Earl	36

How many cans did the classes collect altogether?

① Add the ones. Regroup.

	Tens	Ones
	1	
	5	8
+	3	6
		4

② Add the tens.

	Tens	Ones
	1	
	5	8
+	3	6
	9	4

94 cans

Add. Use tens and ones models if you like.

1. $\begin{array}{r} {}^{1}34 \\ +29 \\ \hline 63 \end{array}$ $\begin{array}{r} 54 \\ +\ 7 \\ \hline \end{array}$ $\begin{array}{r} 68 \\ +12 \\ \hline \end{array}$ $\begin{array}{r} 45 \\ +43 \\ \hline \end{array}$ $\begin{array}{r} 18 \\ +59 \\ \hline \end{array}$ $\begin{array}{r} 20 \\ +34 \\ \hline \end{array}$

2. $\begin{array}{r} 21 \\ +36 \\ \hline \end{array}$ $\begin{array}{r} 27 \\ +63 \\ \hline \end{array}$ $\begin{array}{r} 42 \\ +30 \\ \hline \end{array}$ $\begin{array}{r} 8 \\ +84 \\ \hline \end{array}$ $\begin{array}{r} 26 \\ +16 \\ \hline \end{array}$ $\begin{array}{r} 13 \\ +25 \\ \hline \end{array}$

3. $\begin{array}{r} 24 \\ +\ 9 \\ \hline \end{array}$ $\begin{array}{r} 52 \\ +25 \\ \hline \end{array}$ $\begin{array}{r} 39 \\ +37 \\ \hline \end{array}$ $\begin{array}{r} 16 \\ +16 \\ \hline \end{array}$ $\begin{array}{r} 19 \\ +11 \\ \hline \end{array}$ $\begin{array}{r} 64 \\ +15 \\ \hline \end{array}$

4. $\begin{array}{r} 36 \\ +45 \\ \hline \end{array}$ $\begin{array}{r} 28 \\ +14 \\ \hline \end{array}$ $\begin{array}{r} 15 \\ +58 \\ \hline \end{array}$ $\begin{array}{r} 87 \\ +11 \\ \hline \end{array}$ $\begin{array}{r} 18 \\ +38 \\ \hline \end{array}$ $\begin{array}{r} 48 \\ +19 \\ \hline \end{array}$

Home Connection Write two-digit addition problems like the ones on this page for your child to solve. Ask your child to explain how to find each sum.

Add. Use tens and ones models if you like.

1. $\begin{array}{r} 34 \\ +24 \\ \hline 58 \end{array}$ $\quad$ $\begin{array}{r} 19 \\ +45 \\ \hline \end{array}$ $\quad$ $\begin{array}{r} 23 \\ +62 \\ \hline \end{array}$ $\quad$ $\begin{array}{r} 34 \\ +56 \\ \hline \end{array}$ $\quad$ $\begin{array}{r} 70 \\ +18 \\ \hline \end{array}$ $\quad$ $\begin{array}{r} 53 \\ +29 \\ \hline \end{array}$

2. $\begin{array}{r} 25 \\ +25 \\ \hline \end{array}$ $\quad$ $\begin{array}{r} 47 \\ +40 \\ \hline \end{array}$ $\quad$ $\begin{array}{r} 38 \\ +27 \\ \hline \end{array}$ $\quad$ $\begin{array}{r} 20 \\ +60 \\ \hline \end{array}$ $\quad$ $\begin{array}{r} 84 \\ +\ 7 \\ \hline \end{array}$ $\quad$ $\begin{array}{r} 63 \\ +27 \\ \hline \end{array}$

3. $\begin{array}{r} 28 \\ +58 \\ \hline \end{array}$ $\quad$ $\begin{array}{r} 32 \\ +49 \\ \hline \end{array}$ $\quad$ $\begin{array}{r} 48 \\ +12 \\ \hline \end{array}$ $\quad$ $\begin{array}{r} 9 \\ +36 \\ \hline \end{array}$ $\quad$ $\begin{array}{r} 17 \\ +35 \\ \hline \end{array}$ $\quad$ $\begin{array}{r} 24 \\ +56 \\ \hline \end{array}$

4. $\begin{array}{r} 32 \\ +26 \\ \hline \end{array}$ $\quad$ $\begin{array}{r} 46 \\ +35 \\ \hline \end{array}$ $\quad$ $\begin{array}{r} 42 \\ +39 \\ \hline \end{array}$ $\quad$ $\begin{array}{r} 26 \\ +\ 8 \\ \hline \end{array}$ $\quad$ $\begin{array}{r} 50 \\ +14 \\ \hline \end{array}$ $\quad$ $\begin{array}{r} 77 \\ +13 \\ \hline \end{array}$

Checkpoint

Find each sum.
Use tens and ones models if you like.

1. $30 + 60 =$ ____ $\quad$ $10 + 50 =$ ____ $\quad$ $20 + 30 =$ ____

2. $40 + 36 =$ ____ $\quad$ $12 + 80 =$ ____ $\quad$ $50 + 21 =$ ____

3.

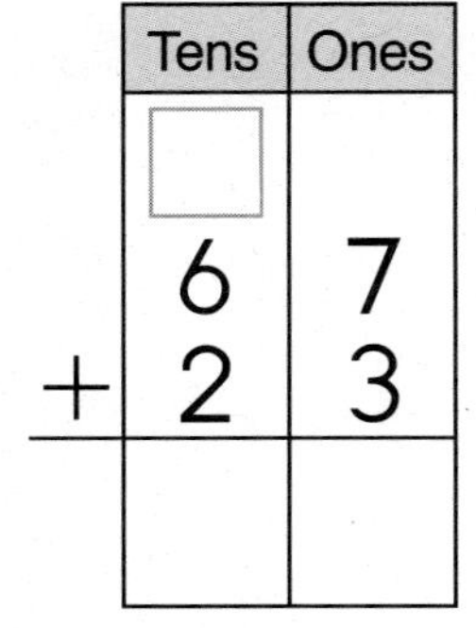

	Tens	Ones
	6	7
+	2	3

	Tens	Ones
		8
+	5	5

	Tens	Ones
	3	7
+	2	2

	Tens	Ones
	4	3
+	1	8

Name______________________________

Add. Use tens and ones models if you like.

1.

	Tens	Ones
	1	
	2	1
+	4	9
	7	0

	Tens	Ones
	8	0
+	1	9

	Tens	Ones
		8
+	4	6

	Tens	Ones
	2	8
+	4	3

2. $\begin{array}{r} 48 \\ +12 \\ \hline \end{array}$ $\begin{array}{r} 57 \\ +36 \\ \hline \end{array}$ $\begin{array}{r} 66 \\ +33 \\ \hline \end{array}$ $\begin{array}{r} 10 \\ +39 \\ \hline \end{array}$ $\begin{array}{r} 44 \\ +18 \\ \hline \end{array}$ $\begin{array}{r} 18 \\ +12 \\ \hline \end{array}$

3. $\begin{array}{r} 63 \\ +15 \\ \hline \end{array}$ $\begin{array}{r} 45 \\ +20 \\ \hline \end{array}$ $\begin{array}{r} 47 \\ +47 \\ \hline \end{array}$ $\begin{array}{r} 30 \\ +10 \\ \hline \end{array}$ $\begin{array}{r} 16 \\ +39 \\ \hline \end{array}$ $\begin{array}{r} 34 \\ +\ 7 \\ \hline \end{array}$

4. $\begin{array}{r} 45 \\ +14 \\ \hline \end{array}$ $\begin{array}{r} 94 \\ +\ 3 \\ \hline \end{array}$ $\begin{array}{r} 76 \\ +22 \\ \hline \end{array}$ $\begin{array}{r} 50 \\ +\ 7 \\ \hline \end{array}$ $\begin{array}{r} 19 \\ +26 \\ \hline \end{array}$ $\begin{array}{r} 82 \\ +\ 8 \\ \hline \end{array}$

5. $\begin{array}{r} 16 \\ +30 \\ \hline \end{array}$ $\begin{array}{r} 55 \\ +\ 6 \\ \hline \end{array}$ $\begin{array}{r} 44 \\ +28 \\ \hline \end{array}$ $\begin{array}{r} 10 \\ +77 \\ \hline \end{array}$ $\begin{array}{r} 21 \\ +12 \\ \hline \end{array}$ $\begin{array}{r} 14 \\ +78 \\ \hline \end{array}$

6. $\begin{array}{r} 27 \\ +53 \\ \hline \end{array}$ $\begin{array}{r} 46 \\ +26 \\ \hline \end{array}$ $\begin{array}{r} 14 \\ +15 \\ \hline \end{array}$ $\begin{array}{r} 33 \\ +59 \\ \hline \end{array}$ $\begin{array}{r} 32 \\ +26 \\ \hline \end{array}$ $\begin{array}{r} 56 \\ +15 \\ \hline \end{array}$

Home Connection Make up two-digit addition story problems for your child to solve.

Rewrite the numbers. Then add.

1. 35 + 19

	Tens	Ones
	1	
	3	5
+	1	9
	5	4

94 + 5

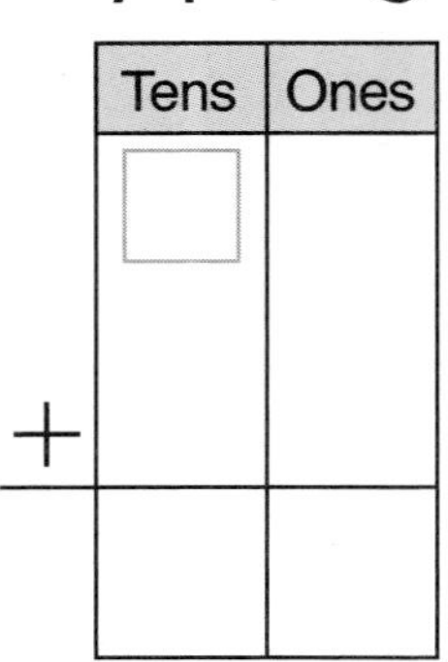

42 + 19

37 + 54

2. 64 + 28

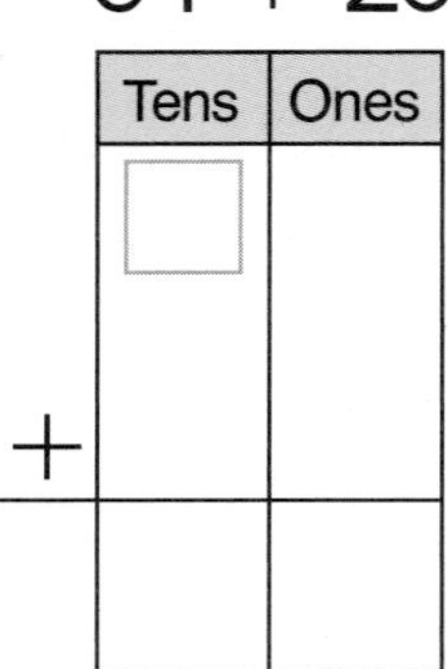

29 + 10

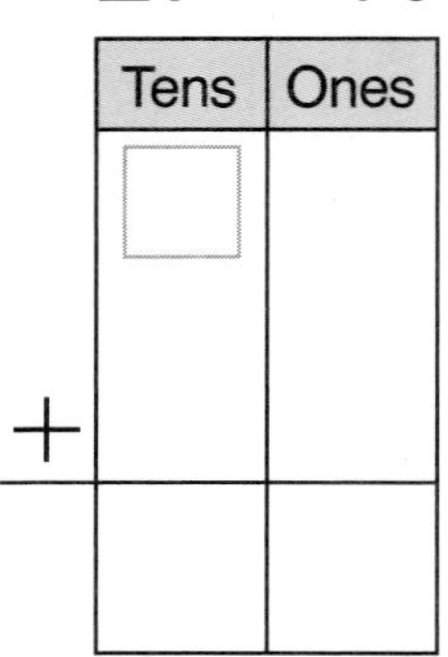

18 + 49

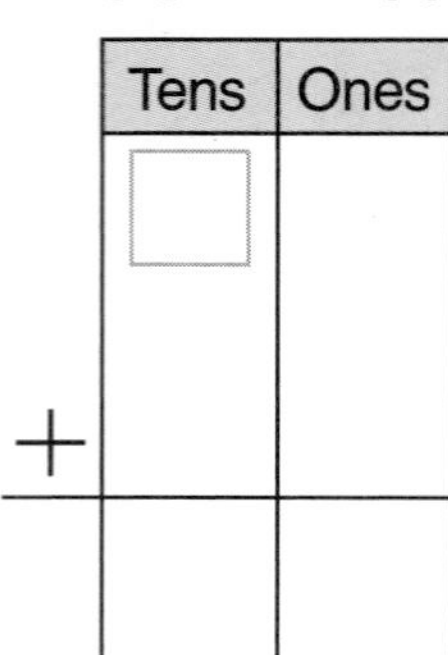

13 + 16

3. 15 + 20

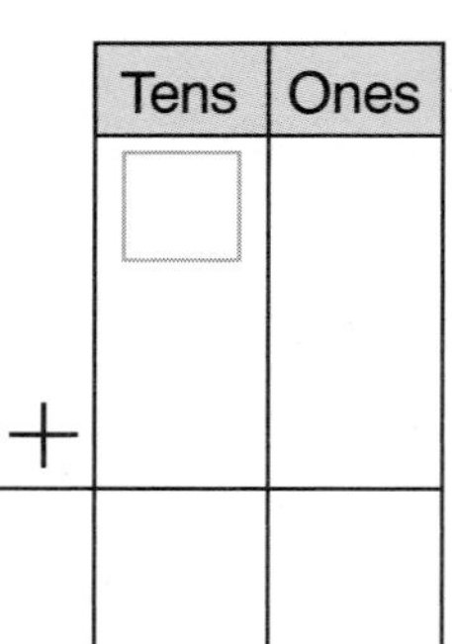

82 + 9

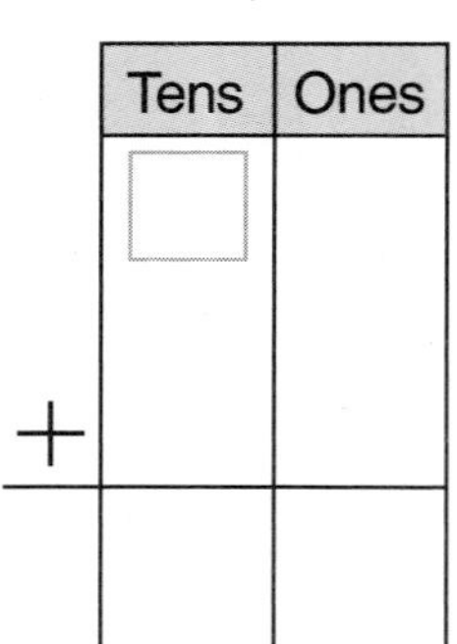

16 + 67

63 + 14

Problem Solving

Solve.

4. One box has 39 jars and 20 bottles.
The other box has 52 jars.
How many jars are there altogether?

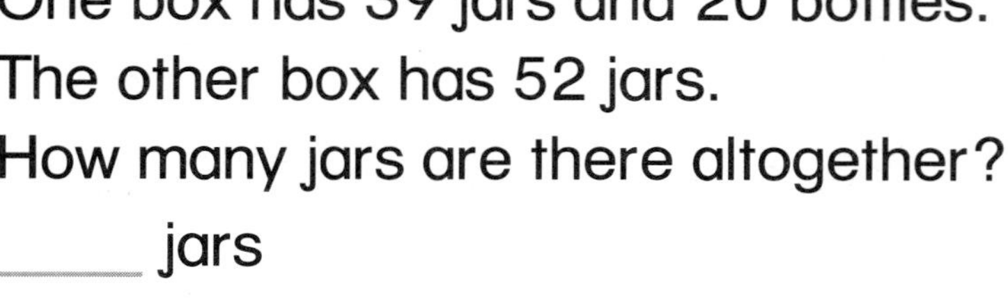

_____ jars

Name ______________________________

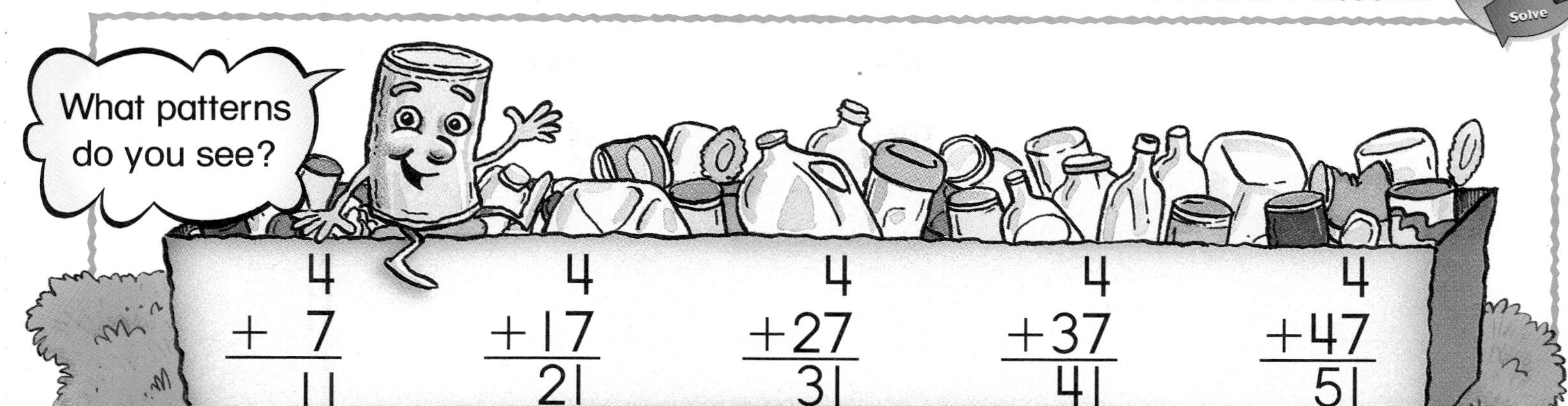

Add. Continue the pattern.
Use tens and ones models if you like.

1. $17 + 6 = 23$ $\quad 17 + 16 \quad 17 + 26 \quad 17 + 36 \quad 17 + 46 \quad + \_\_\_$

2. $10 + 9 \quad 10 + 19 \quad 10 + 29 \quad 10 + 39 \quad + \_\_\_ \quad + \_\_\_$

3. $2 + 8 \quad 12 + 8 \quad 22 + 8 \quad 32 + 8 \quad + \_\_\_ \quad + \_\_\_$

4. $22 + 60 \quad 22 + 50 \quad 22 + 40 \quad 22 + 30 \quad + \_\_\_ \quad + \_\_\_$

Home Connection Recognizing number patterns can help children add. Ask your child to explain the different patterns in each row above.

Add. Continue the pattern.
Use tens and ones models if you like.

1. $\begin{array}{r} 30 \\ +\ 6 \\ \hline 36 \end{array}$ $\begin{array}{r} 30 \\ +16 \\ \hline \end{array}$ $\begin{array}{r} 30 \\ +26 \\ \hline \end{array}$ $\begin{array}{r} 30 \\ +36 \\ \hline \end{array}$ $\begin{array}{r} \\ + \quad \\ \hline \end{array}$ $\begin{array}{r} \\ + \quad \\ \hline \end{array}$

2. $\begin{array}{r} 8 \\ +\ 4 \\ \hline \end{array}$ $\begin{array}{r} 8 \\ +14 \\ \hline \end{array}$ $\begin{array}{r} 8 \\ +24 \\ \hline \end{array}$ $\begin{array}{r} 8 \\ +34 \\ \hline \end{array}$ $\begin{array}{r} \\ + \quad \\ \hline \end{array}$ $\begin{array}{r} \\ + \quad \\ \hline \end{array}$

3. $\begin{array}{r} 42 \\ +56 \\ \hline \end{array}$ $\begin{array}{r} 42 \\ +46 \\ \hline \end{array}$ $\begin{array}{r} 42 \\ +36 \\ \hline \end{array}$ $\begin{array}{r} 42 \\ +26 \\ \hline \end{array}$ $\begin{array}{r} \\ + \quad \\ \hline \end{array}$ $\begin{array}{r} \\ + \quad \\ \hline \end{array}$

4. $\begin{array}{r} 9 \\ +40 \\ \hline \end{array}$ $\begin{array}{r} 19 \\ +40 \\ \hline \end{array}$ $\begin{array}{r} 29 \\ +40 \\ \hline \end{array}$ $\begin{array}{r} 39 \\ +40 \\ \hline \end{array}$ $\begin{array}{r} \\ + \quad \\ \hline \end{array}$ $\begin{array}{r} \\ + \quad \\ \hline \end{array}$

5. Write your own addition pattern.

$\begin{array}{r} \\ + \quad \\ \hline \end{array}$ $\begin{array}{r} \\ + \quad \\ \hline \end{array}$ $\begin{array}{r} \\ + \quad \\ \hline \end{array}$ $\begin{array}{r} \\ + \quad \\ \hline \end{array}$ $\begin{array}{r} \\ + \quad \\ \hline \end{array}$ $\begin{array}{r} \\ + \quad \\ \hline \end{array}$

Name ______________________ **Ways to Add**

How would you solve this problem?

You have 20 large cans and 27 small cans. How many cans do you have?

I would use paper and pencil.

I would use mental math... 27, 37, 47.

I would use a hundred chart.

I would use tens and ones models.

Find each sum.
Use models or paper and pencil.

1.	13 + 39 = 52	58 + 6	36 + 44	17 + 52	7 + 29	45 + 26
2.	54 + 29	23 + 68	72 + 8	36 + 36	63 + 18	16 + 7

Use a hundred chart or mental math.

3. 15 + 20 = ____ 19 + 30 = ____ 76 + 10 = ____
4. 44 + 30 = ____ 57 + 10 = ____ 38 + 20 = ____
5. 26 + 10 = ____ 72 + 20 = ____ 35 + 30 = ____

Home Connection Encourage your child to explain the different ways to add two-digit numbers. What are different ways to find 19 + 22?

Sometimes one way is easier than another.

Look at each problem.
Choose one of the ways to solve it.
Circle your choice. Then solve.

1. $\begin{array}{r} 26 \\ +16 \\ \hline \end{array}$
   a. tens and ones
   b. hundred chart
   c. paper and pencil
   d. mental math

2. $\begin{array}{r} 53 \\ +30 \\ \hline \end{array}$
   a. tens and ones
   b. hundred chart
   c. paper and pencil
   d. mental math

3. $\begin{array}{r} 18 \\ +\ \ 3 \\ \hline \end{array}$
   a. tens and ones
   b. hundred chart
   c. paper and pencil
   d. mental math

4. $\begin{array}{r} 17 \\ +30 \\ \hline \end{array}$
   a. tens and ones
   b. hundred chart
   c. paper and pencil
   d. mental math

5. $\begin{array}{r} 40 \\ +50 \\ \hline \end{array}$
   a. tens and ones
   b. hundred chart
   c. paper and pencil
   d. mental math

6. $\begin{array}{r} 18 \\ +65 \\ \hline \end{array}$
   a. tens and ones
   b. hundred chart
   c. paper and pencil
   d. mental math

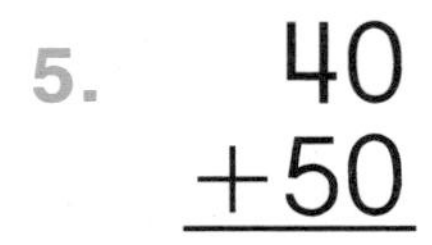
PROBLEM SOLVING

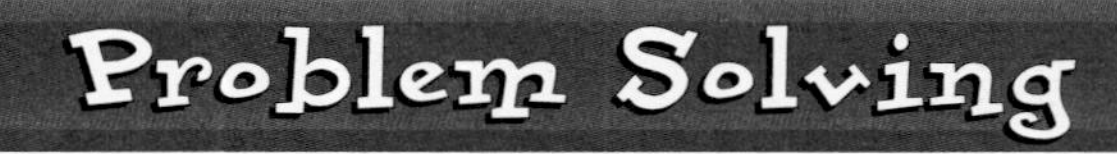
Problem Solving

Solve.

7. Bobby collected 25 newspapers on Monday. What if he collects 10 more newspapers every day for 4 days? How many would he have on Tuesday? _____
   Wednesday? _____
   Thursday? _____
   Friday? _____

Name________________________

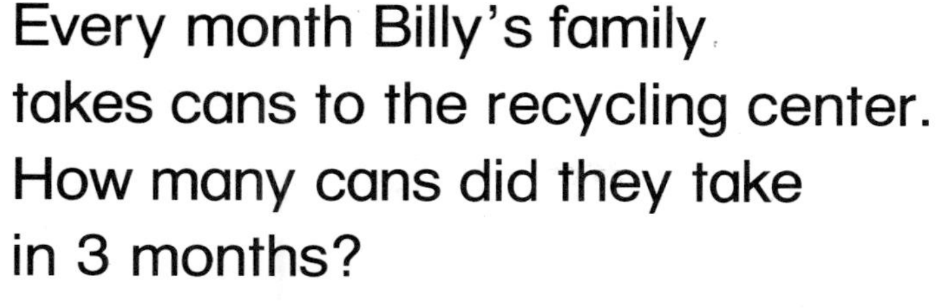

Every month Billy's family takes cans to the recycling center. How many cans did they take in 3 months?

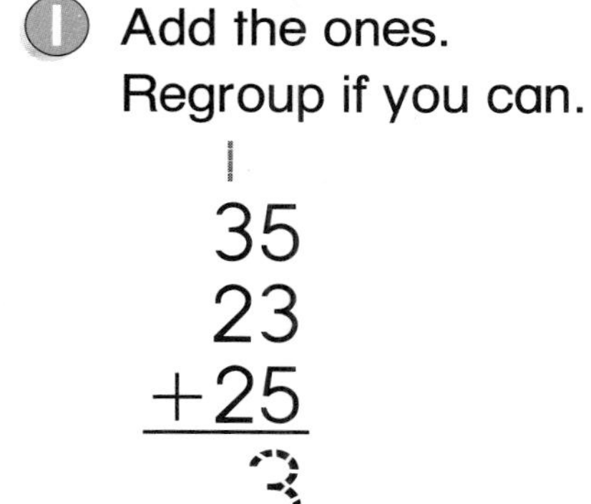

1. Add the ones. Regroup if you can.

$$\begin{array}{r} ^{1}\\ 35\\ 23\\ +25\\ \hline 3 \end{array}$$

2. Add the tens.

$$\begin{array}{r} ^{1}\\ 35\\ 23\\ +25\\ \hline 83 \end{array}$$

Add. Use tens and ones models if you like.

1.

42	16	3	25	34	44
33	7	40	25	6	15
+19	+54	+25	+25	+11	+27

2.

34	26	42	13	64	56
21	6	15	7	14	11
+24	+57	+25	+23	+ 5	+ 3

3.

17	35	8	22	39	34
45	25	36	17	20	45
+23	+14	+12	+40	+31	+10

Home Connection Once children understand addition of two numbers, they should be able to add three numbers. Discuss with your child how he or she added the numbers above.

Find each sum.

1.	26 13 + 4 43	32 37 +13	29 6 +40	45 13 +25	30 16 + 6	12 29 +15
2.	53 8 +24	9 25 +41	13 42 +25	20 30 +18	35 18 +25	22 12 +62
3.	43 27 +16	34 12 +44	13 38 +42	12 52 +32	7 20 +37	25 12 +40
4.	19 21 +20	37 12 + 5	61 16 +14	42 3 +34	6 21 +19	24 34 + 9

What Do You Think?

Is it easy for you to add these numbers in your head? Think of a way. Explain how.

$20 + 31 + 10 =$ ____

Name________________________________

Problem-Solving Application
Getting Data From a Table

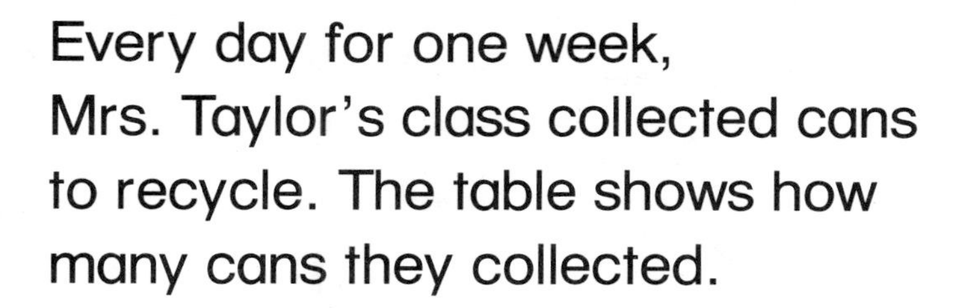

Every day for one week, Mrs. Taylor's class collected cans to recycle. The table shows how many cans they collected.

Cans Collected					
Day	Mon.	Tues.	Wed.	Thurs.	Fri.
Number of cans	9	14	20	17	24

Use the table to solve each problem. Show your work.

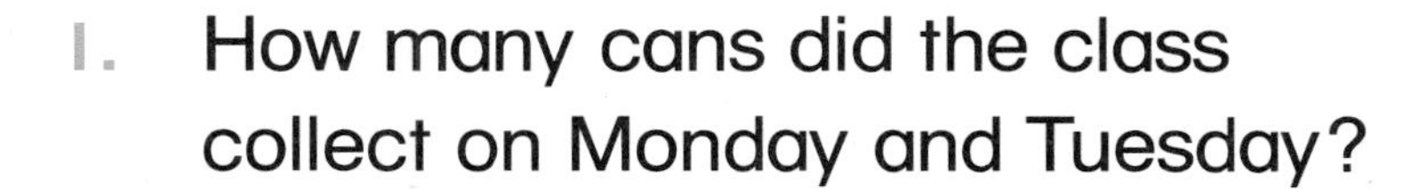

1. How many cans did the class collect on Monday and Tuesday?

   23 cans

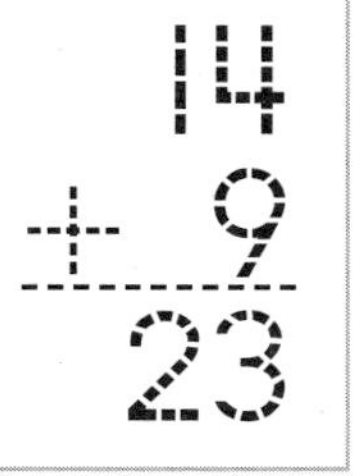

$$\begin{array}{r} 14 \\ +\ 9 \\ \hline 23 \end{array}$$

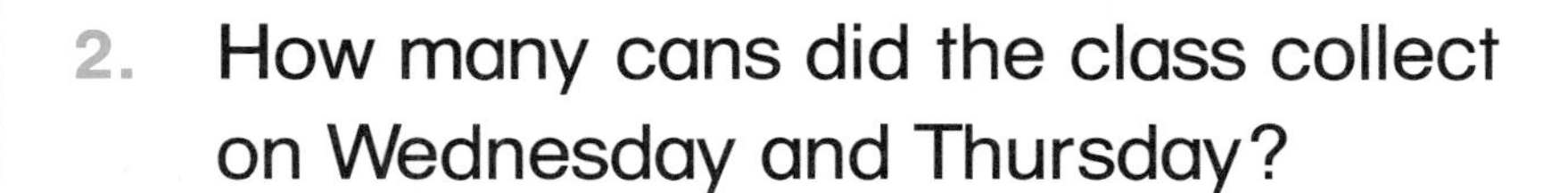

2. How many cans did the class collect on Wednesday and Thursday?

   _____ cans

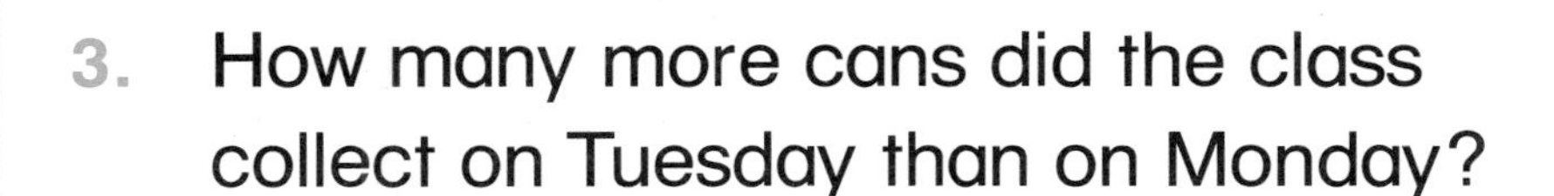

3. How many more cans did the class collect on Tuesday than on Monday?

   _____ cans

4. How many cans did the class collect on Monday, Tuesday, and Wednesday?

   _____ cans

Home Connection Using a table can help children organize data. Ask your child to make a table that shows what has been recycled in your home during a week.

Do you know that each person in the United States creates about 4 pounds of trash every day?

Wow! That's a lot!

4 pounds

The children collected cans for six weeks. The table shows how many pounds of cans they collected to recycle.

Pounds Collected						
Week	1	2	3	4	5	6
Pounds	9	16	7	13	11	18

Use the table to solve each problem. Show your work.

1. During which two weeks did the class collect the most pounds?

   Week _____ and Week _____

   How many pounds did they collect those weeks?

   _____ pounds

2. How many more pounds were collected during Week 6 than during Week 1?

   _____ pounds

Circle the answer that makes sense.

3. About how many pounds did the children collect in all?

   about 30 pounds

   about 70 pounds

Name ____________________ **Checkpoint**

Add.

1. $48 + 12$ $63 + 21$ $37 + 46$ $59 + 7$ $71 + 19$ $32 + 28$

Rewrite the numbers. Then add.

2. $16 + 28$ $46 + 19$ $55 + 34$ $66 + 25$

Tens	Ones
+	

Tens	Ones
+	

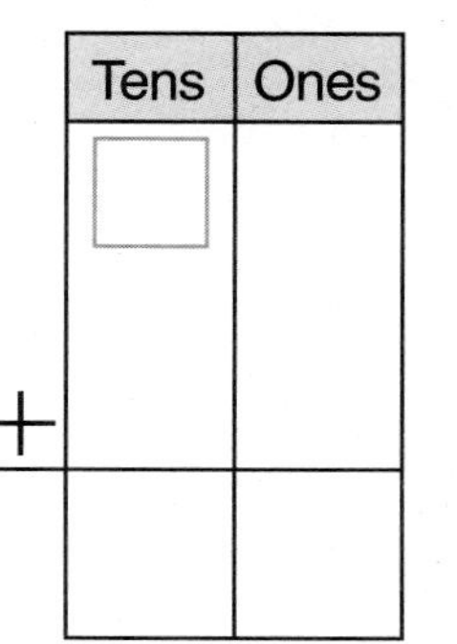

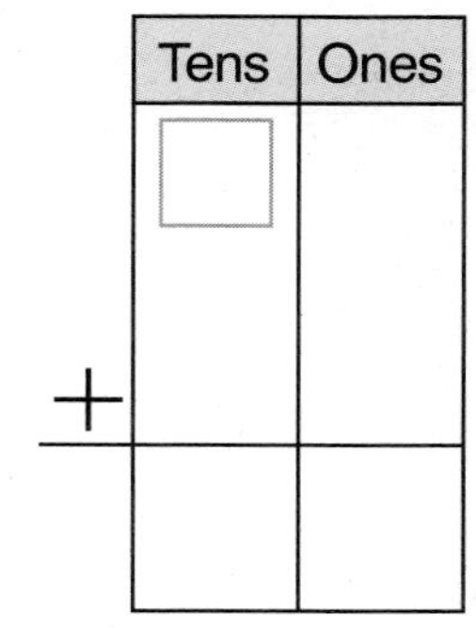

Add. Continue the pattern.

3. $10 + 16$ $20 + 16$ $30 + 16$ $40 + 16$ + ___   + ___

4. $17 + 8$ $27 + 8$ $37 + 8$ $47 + 8$ + ___   + ___

Add. Use tens and ones models if you like.

5. $41 + 16 + 24$ $38 + 21 + 35$ $32 + 7 + 25$ $14 + 24 + 34$ $26 + 9 + 12$ $10 + 50 + 30$

Name______________________________________ **Extra Practice**

Find each sum.

Color sums less than 40 red.

Color sums between 40 and 60 blue.

Color sums greater than 60 yellow.

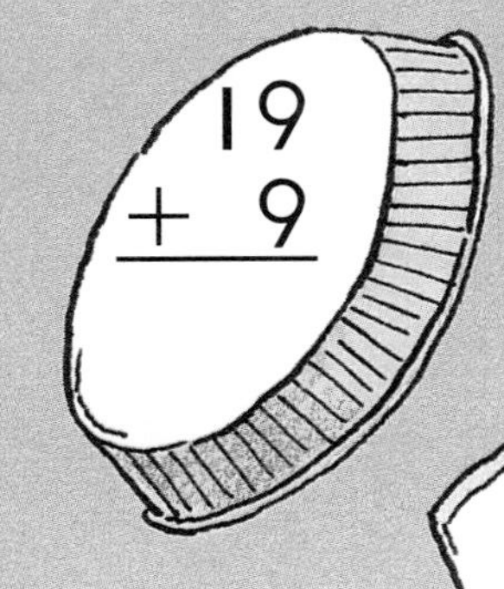

$$\begin{array}{r} 19 \\ +\ 9 \\ \hline \end{array}$$

$$\begin{array}{r} 33 \\ +15 \\ \hline \end{array}$$

$$\begin{array}{r} 70 \\ +\ 5 \\ \hline \end{array}$$

$$\begin{array}{r} 23 \\ +15 \\ \hline \end{array}$$

$$\begin{array}{r} 29 \\ +22 \\ \hline \end{array}$$

$$\begin{array}{r} 57 \\ +34 \\ \hline \end{array}$$

$$\begin{array}{r} 29 \\ +\ 7 \\ \hline \end{array}$$

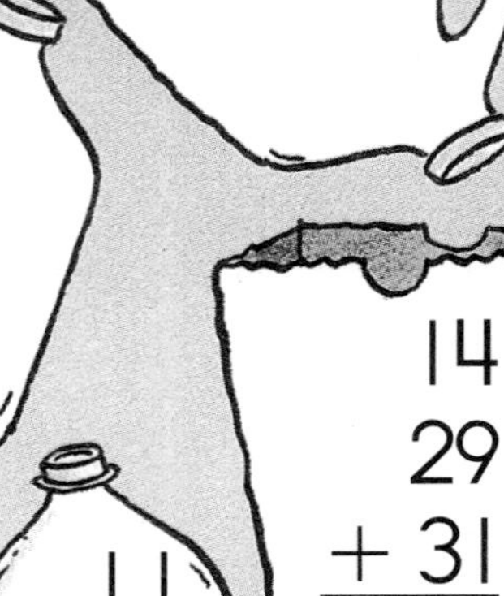

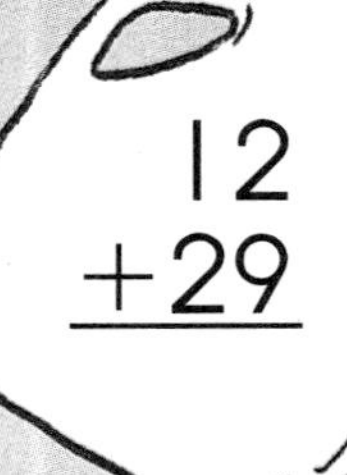

$$\begin{array}{r} 12 \\ +29 \\ \hline \end{array}$$

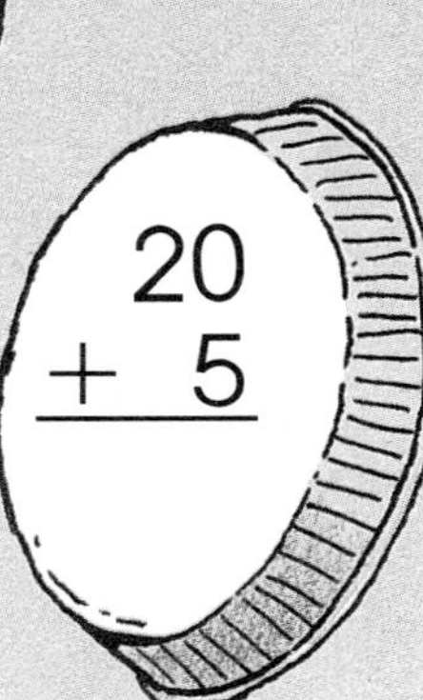

$$\begin{array}{r} 20 \\ +\ 5 \\ \hline \end{array}$$

$$\begin{array}{r} 14 \\ 29 \\ +31 \\ \hline \end{array}$$

$$\begin{array}{r} 16 \\ +82 \\ \hline \end{array}$$

$$\begin{array}{r} 11 \\ +39 \\ \hline \end{array}$$

$$\begin{array}{r} 20 \\ +14 \\ \hline \end{array}$$

$$\begin{array}{r} 26 \\ 18 \\ +10 \\ \hline \end{array}$$

$$\begin{array}{r} 32 \\ 33 \\ +15 \\ \hline \end{array}$$

Count on by tens to add.

1. 64 + 30 = ____ 20 + 77 = ____ 39 + 20 = ____

2. 40 + 58 = ____ 35 + 30 = ____ 12 + 10 = ____

Circle the best estimate.

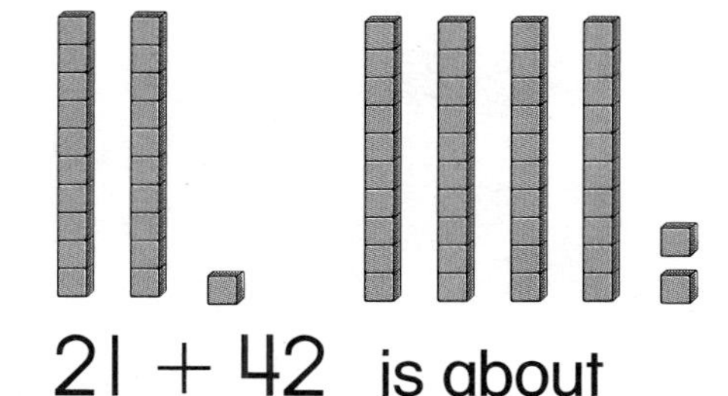

21 + 42 is about 20 40 60

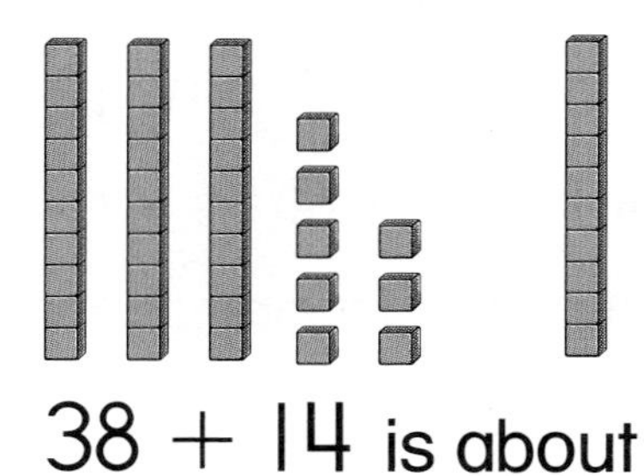

38 + 14 is about 30 50 90

Find each sum.

5.

	Tens	Ones
	5	4
+	1	9

	Tens	Ones
	5	8
+	2	6

	Tens	Ones
	3	7
+	2	1

	Tens	Ones
	8	9
+		2

Add.

6. 37 + 13 26 + 37 10 + 79 28 + 4 63 + 30 14 + 27

Use the table to solve. Show your work.

7. Which group collected the most cans?

	Cans Collected		
	Group 1	**Group 2**	**Group 3**
Day 1	25	17	26
Day 2	23	34	18

Group ____

Name ____________________ **Performance Assessment** 

What You Need

2 number cubes

1. Roll both number cubes. Use the numbers to write a two-digit number.
2. Roll again. Write another two-digit number.
3. Use your numbers to write an addition problem. Find the sum.

---

1. 1st number _____

   2nd number _____

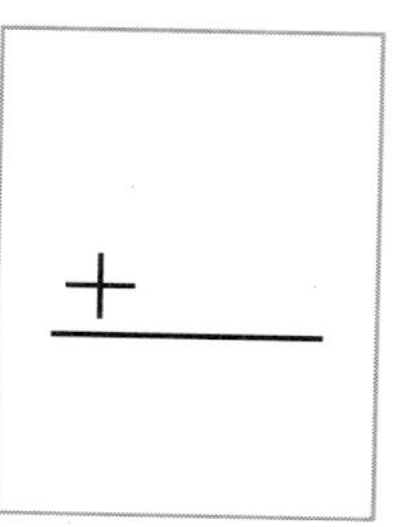

2. 1st number _____

   2nd number _____

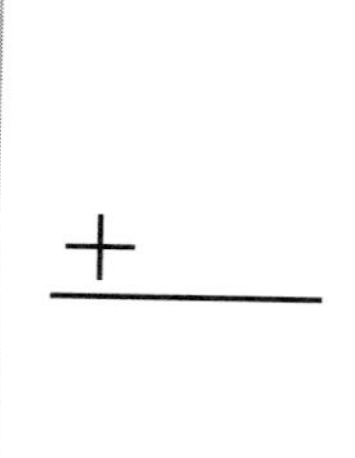

3. 1st number _____

   2nd number _____

   + _____

4. 1st number _____

   2nd number _____

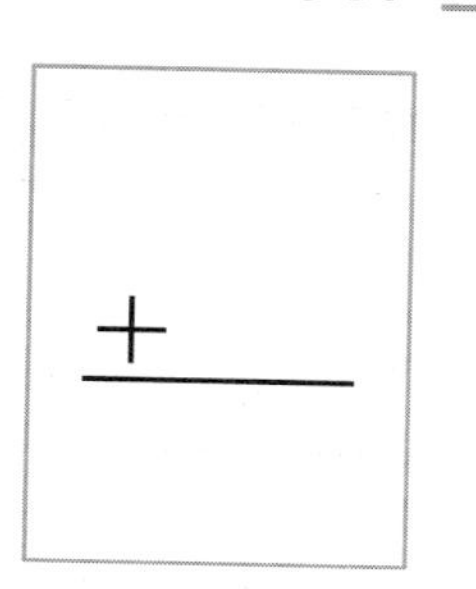

5. 1st number _____

   2nd number _____

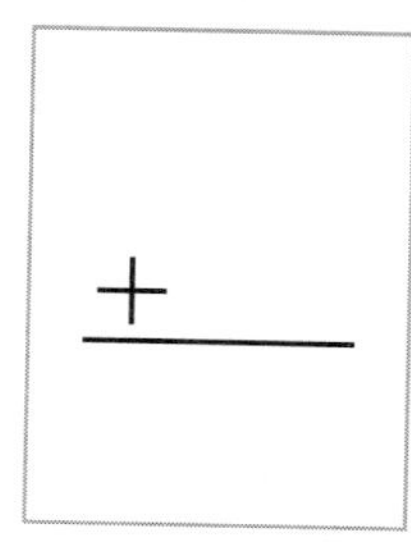

6. 1st number _____

   2nd number _____

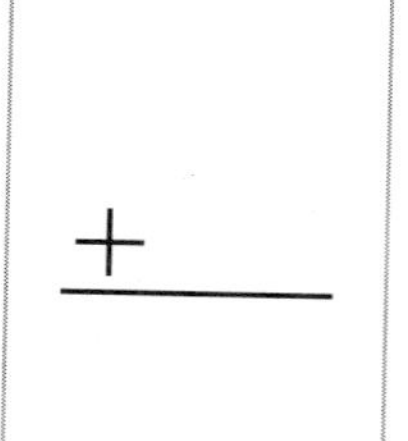

Look at your work.
Did you need to regroup? Tell why or why not.

Name____________________________________

Use the numbers to make addends.
Find the greatest sum.

1.

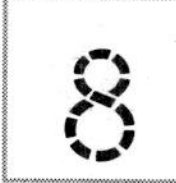

+ 2

86

6
5 1

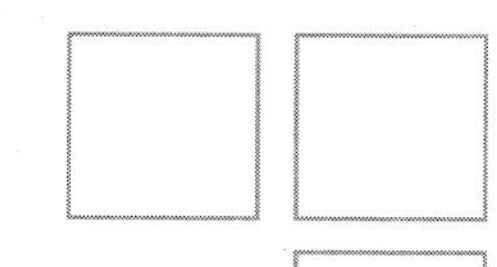

+

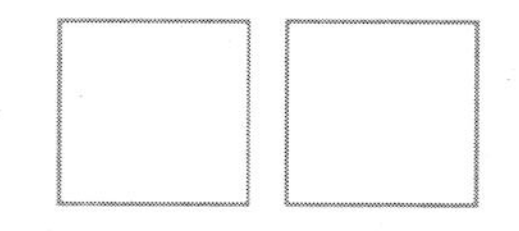

+

2.

+

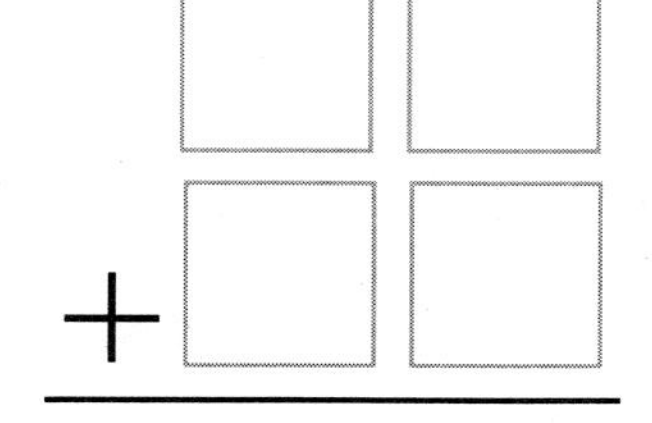

+

2
3 5
4

+

Use the numbers to make addends.
Find the least sum.

3.

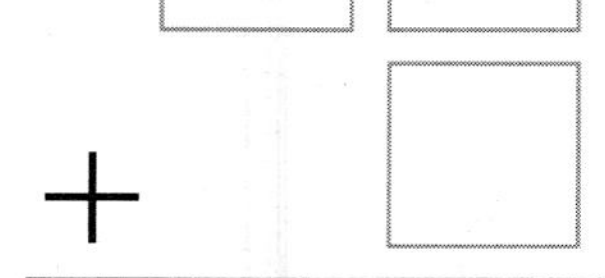

+

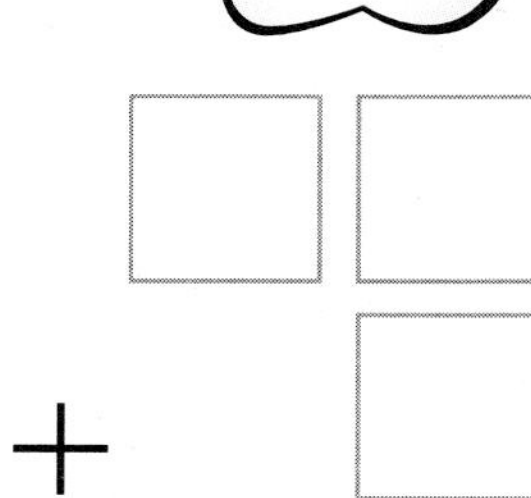

+

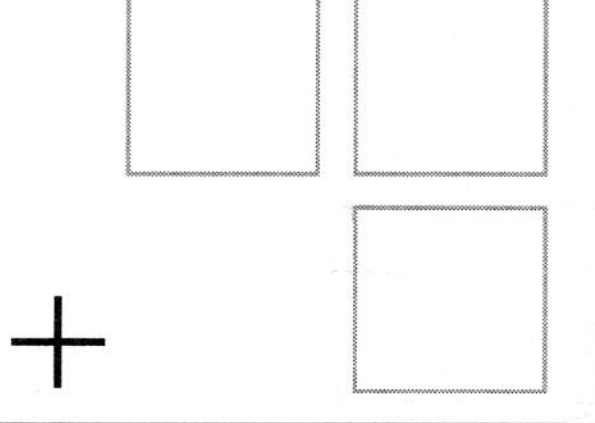

+

Name ____________________

Use a calculator to find which two addends make each sum.
Write the numbers.

Addends **Sums**

1. 29 51 25 — ON/C 2 9 + 5 1 = 8 0

2. 23 19 24 — ON/C ___ ___ + ___ ___ = 4 7

 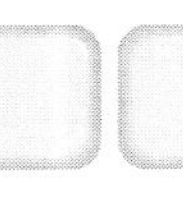   

3. 54 26 18 — ON/C ___ ___ + ___ ___ = 7 2

4. 39 19 29 — ON/C ___ ___ + ___ ___ = 5 8

5. 44 55 36 — ON/C ___ ___ + ___ ___ = 9 1

6. 27 29 36 — ON/C ___ ___ + ___ ___ = 6 3

7. 36 49 28 — ON/C ___ ___ + ___ ___ = 7 7

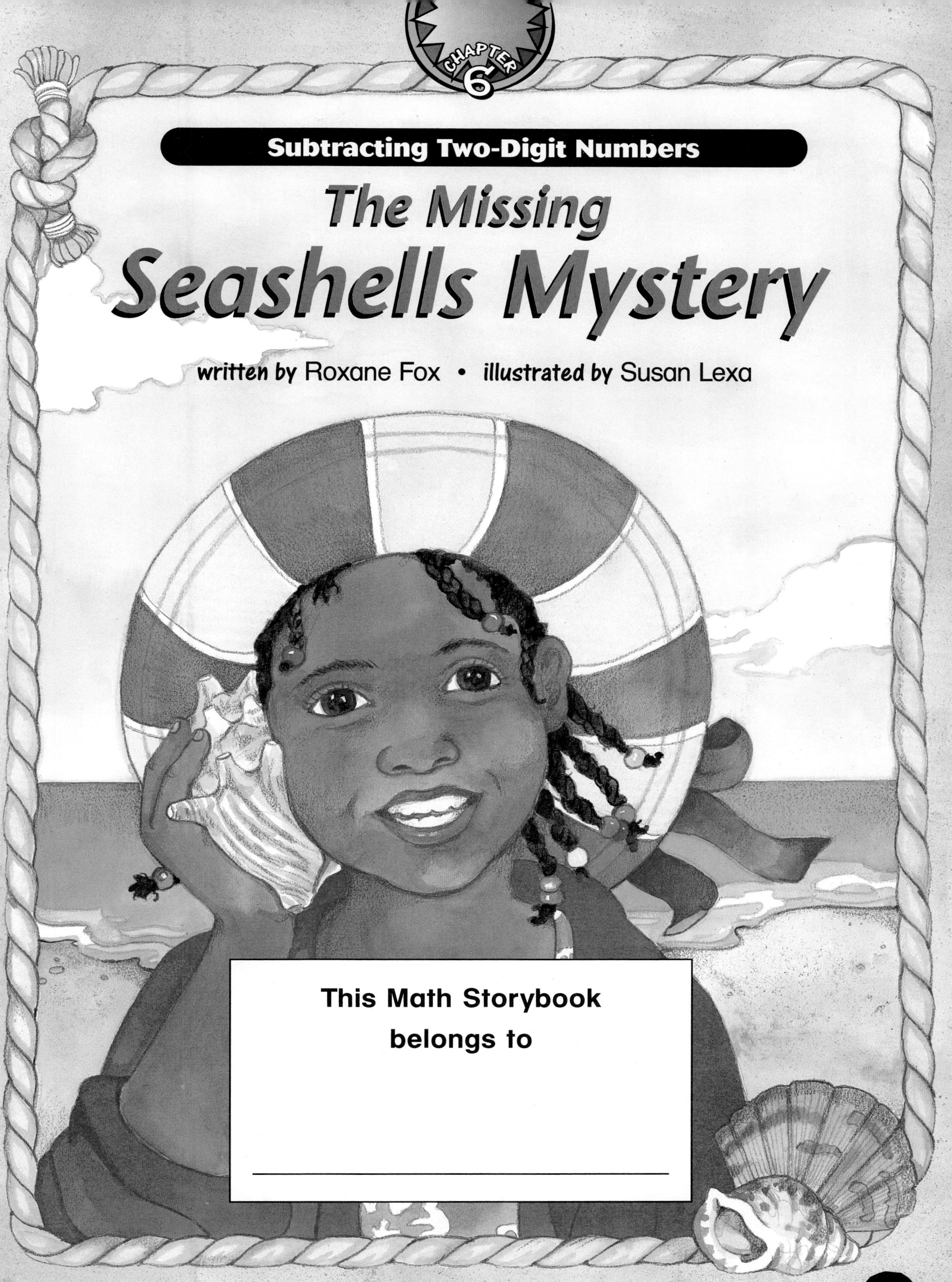
CHAPTER 6
Subtracting Two-Digit Numbers
The Missing Seashells Mystery
written by Roxane Fox • illustrated by Susan Lexa
This Math Storybook belongs to
A

One morning, Cheryl finds 31 seashells. She puts them down and walks along the beach. When she returns, there are shells missing. What happened?
B

Cheryl looks for more shells but
doesn't find any. When she returns,
there are more shells missing.
What happened?
c

Cheryl wonders why her shells are missing. She walks along the beach and looks for them. When she returns, she finds that only 10 shells are left.
D

Cheryl decides to stay close by and watch her shells. Suddenly 2 of them move. They move all by themselves!
E

Cheryl picks up one of the shells.
Inside she sees a hermit crab.
No wonder the shells are moving! Next time I think I'll collect rocks.
F

Here are 25 shells of your
very own. Color some of them.
How many did you color?
How many are not colored?
www.sbgmath.com
G

A Note to the Family

Here are some learning ideas you can share with your child.

Enjoy *The Missing Seashells Mystery* Together

- Read the story with your child. After each page, ask what happens to the number of shells Cheryl has. Encourage your child to tell a subtraction story to show how many are left. For example, there were 31 shells. Two are missing; 29 are left. $31 - 2 = 29$.
- Have your child show you the shells he or she colored on the last page of the story. Ask your child to explain how he or she figured out how many shells were left.

At-Home Activity

- Your child might enjoy going on a button hunt. (If buttons are not readily available, you can use beads, pennies, pasta, or other small objects.) When your child has collected about 25 items, take turns removing some and figuring out how many are left.

Read More About It!

To read more stories about subtraction with your child, look for the following books in your local library.

- *Mike's Kite* by Elizabeth MacDonald (Orchard Books, 1990)
- *Wake Up, City!* by Alvin Tresselt (Lothrop, 1989)

Visit Our Web Site!

www.sbgmath.com

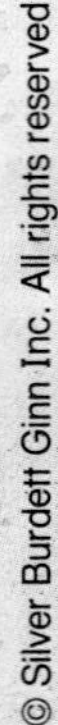

Name______________________________

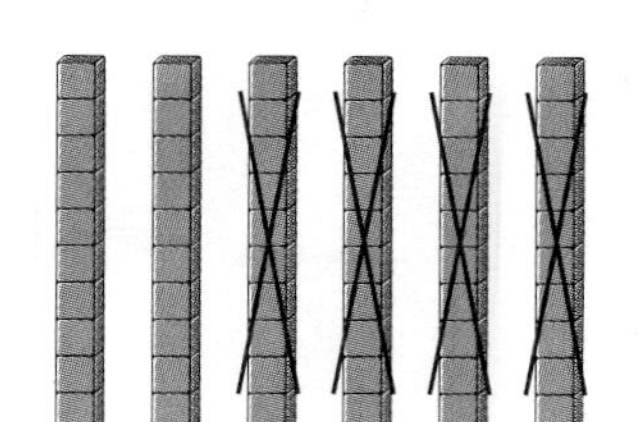

6 tens − 4 tens = 2 tens

60 − 40 = 20

Think 6 − 4 = 2.

Find each difference.
Use tens models if you like.

1. 7 tens − 3 tens = ____ tens
   70 − 30 = ____

2. 9 tens − 6 tens = ____ tens
   90 − 60 = ____

3. 8 tens − 5 tens = ____ tens
   80 − 50 = ____

4. 6 tens − 1 ten = ____ tens
   60 − 10 = ____

5. 5 tens − 4 tens = ____ ten
   50 − 40 = ____

6. 9 tens − 5 tens = ____ tens
   90 − 50 = ____

7. 8 tens − 2 tens = ____ tens
   80 − 20 = ____

8. 7 tens − 5 tens = ____ tens
   70 − 50 = ____

9. 6 tens − 3 tens = ____ tens
   60 − 30 = ____

10. 4 tens − 3 tens = ____ ten
    40 − 30 = ____

Home Connection Children can use basic facts to help them subtract tens. Ask your child to subtract numbers like the ones on this page.

Find each difference. Write the missing numbers.
Use tens models if you like.

1. 5 tens − 3 tens = 2 tens
50 − 30 = 20

2. 9 tens − 2 tens = ____ tens
____ − ____ = ____

3. 8 tens − 4 tens = ____ tens
____ − ____ = ____

4. 6 tens − 5 tens = ____ ten
____ − ____ = ____

5. 6 tens − 2 tens = ____ tens
____ − ____ = ____

6. 5 tens − 2 tens = ____ tens
____ − ____ = ____

7. 8 tens − 7 tens = ____ ten
____ − ____ = ____

8. 7 tens − 4 tens = ____ tens
____ − ____ = ____

9. 9 tens − 3 tens = ____ tens
____ − ____ = ____

10. 3 tens − 2 tens = ____ ten
____ − ____ = ____

Critical Thinking Corner

Number Sense

11. Write the numbers.

5 dimes − 2 dimes = ____ dimes

____¢ − ____¢ = ____¢

Name______________________

You can count back by tens to subtract.

$35 - 20 = \underline{15}$

Start at 35.
Count back 2 tens.
35, 25, 15

0	1	2	3	4	5	6	7	8	9
10	11	12	13	14	15	16	17	18	19
20	21	22	23	24	25	26	27	28	29
30	31	32	33	34	35	36	37	38	39
40	41	42	43	44	45	46	47	48	49

Use the chart or Workmat 5.
Count back by tens to subtract.

1. $48 - 30 =$ ____ $42 - 20 =$ ____ $33 - 10 =$ ____

2. $40 - 30 =$ ____ $27 - 10 =$ ____ $31 - 30 =$ ____

3. $43 - 20 =$ ____ $37 - 20 =$ ____ $41 - 10 =$ ____

4. $22 - 10 =$ ____ $47 - 20 =$ ____ $49 - 10 =$ ____

5. $35 - 30 =$ ____ $34 - 20 =$ ____ $29 - 20 =$ ____

Home Connection Counting back by tens can help children subtract. Choose a number from the chart above. Ask your child to subtract 10, 20, or 30 from that number.

Count back by tens to subtract.
Use Workmat 5 if you like.

1. 86 − 30 = 56 | 43 − 30 = ____ | 82 − 10 = ____

2. 40 − 20 = ____ | 75 − 20 = ____ | 32 − 30 = ____

3. 95 − 20 = ____ | 91 − 30 = ____ | 67 − 20 = ____

4. 53 − 30 = ____ | 72 − 10 = ____ | 84 − 30 = ____

5. 62 − 20 = ____ | 56 − 30 = ____ | 76 − 10 = ____

6. 26 − 10 = ____ | 45 − 20 = ____ | 74 − 30 = ____

7. 85 − 20 = ____ | 58 − 30 = ____ | 39 − 20 = ____

8. 98 − 10 = ____ | 29 − 10 = ____ | 64 − 30 = ____

PROBLEM SOLVING

Problem Solving

Solve.

9. 38 fish are in the cove. 20 fish swim out of the cove. How many fish are still in the cove?

____ fish

10. 65 dolphins are in the bay. 30 dolphins are outside the bay. How many more dolphins are in the bay?

____ dolphins

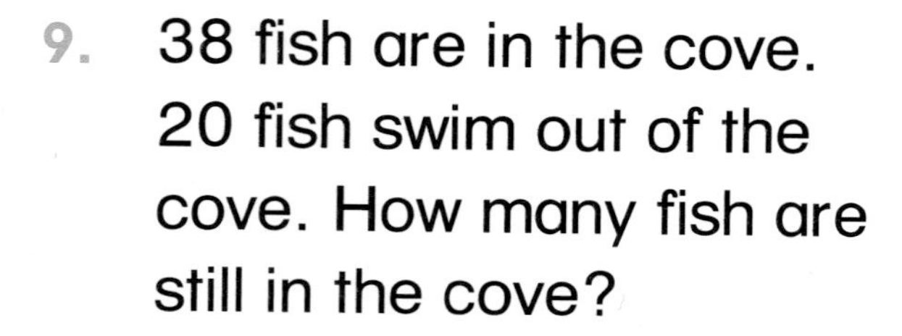

Name____________________________________ **Deciding When to Regroup**

You have 3 tens and 2 ones.
How can you subtract 7 ones?

Word Bank
regroup

Sometimes you need to regroup.

1. Show 3 tens 2 ones.

Tens	Ones
3 tens	2 ones

2. Regroup 1 ten as 10 ones.

Tens	Ones
2 tens	12 ones

3. Subtract 7 ones.

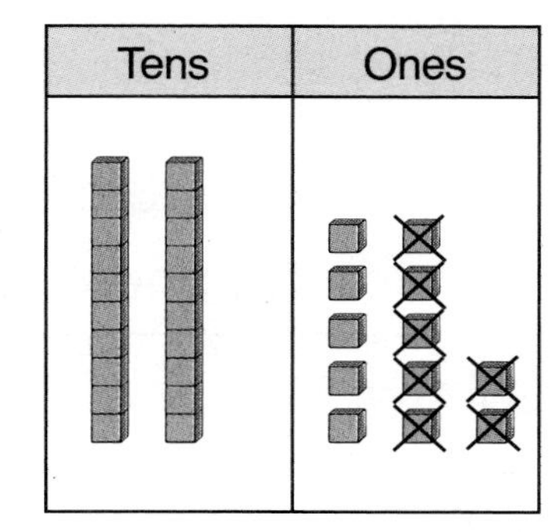

2 tens 5 ones are left.

Use tens and ones models and Workmat 3.
Complete the chart.

	Do you need to regroup?	How many are left?
1. Show 3 tens 6 ones. Subtract 8 ones.	(yes) no	2 tens 8 ones
2. Show 2 tens 5 ones. Subtract 7 ones.	yes no	___ ten ___ ones
3. Show 4 tens 8 ones. Subtract 5 ones.	yes no	___ tens ___ ones
4. Show 5 tens 1 one. Subtract 3 ones.	yes no	___ tens ___ ones
5. Show 6 tens 2 ones. Subtract 5 ones.	yes no	___ tens ___ ones

Home Connection Children use tens and ones models to learn when regrouping is necessary in order to subtract. Ask your child to explain what he or she did in each problem.

Use tens and ones models and Workmat 3.
Complete the chart.

	Do you need to regroup?	How many are left?
1. Show 2 tens 3 ones. Subtract 6 ones.	(yes) no	1 ten 7 ones
2. Show 1 ten 9 ones. Subtract 7 ones.	yes no	____ ten ____ ones
3. Show 4 tens 6 ones. Subtract 8 ones.	yes no	____ tens ____ ones
4. Show 3 tens 2 ones. Subtract 9 ones.	yes no	____ tens ____ ones
5. Show 4 tens 2 ones. Subtract 6 ones.	yes no	____ tens ____ ones

Problem Solving

Solve.

6. You have 2 dimes and 2 pennies.
You want to give 5 pennies to a friend.
What would you do?

____

____

Name________________________________ **Using Models to Subtract**

There are 35 angelfish on the coral reef.
19 leave to search for food.
How many angelfish are left?

1. Show 35. Do you need to regroup?

	Tens	Ones
	3	5
−	1	9

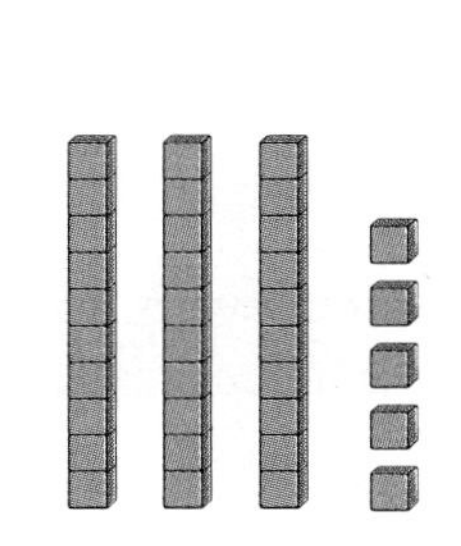

2. Regroup 1 ten as 10 ones.

	Tens	Ones
	2	15
	~~3~~	~~5~~
−	1	9

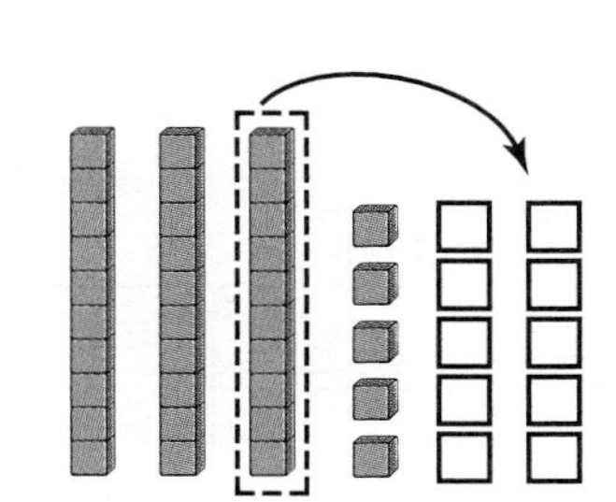

3. Subtract the ones.

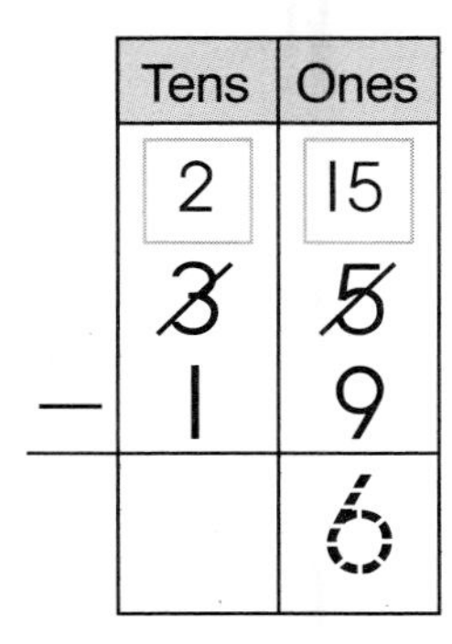

	Tens	Ones
	2	15
	~~3~~	~~5~~
−	1	9
		6

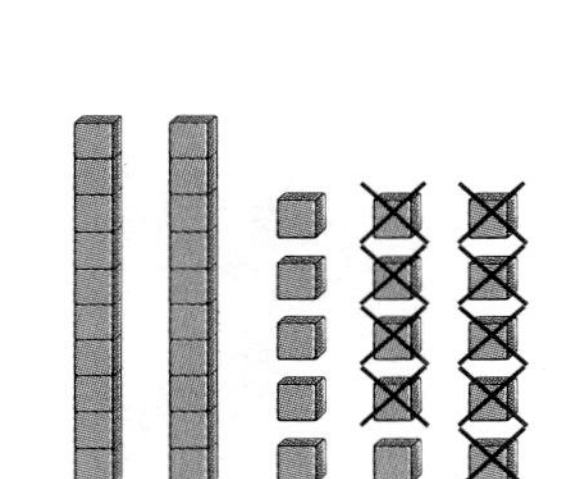

4. Subtract the ten.

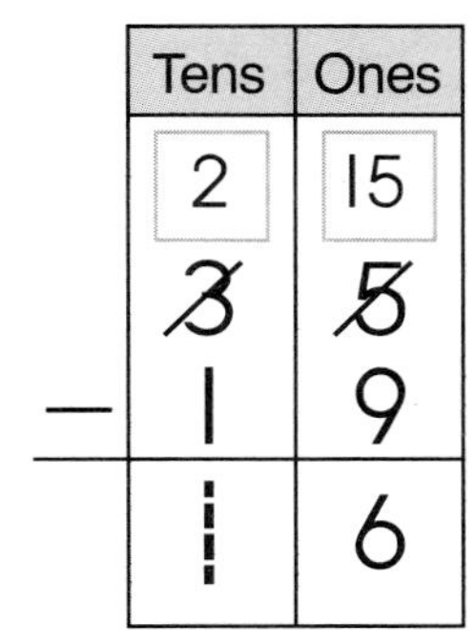

	Tens	Ones
	2	15
	~~3~~	~~5~~
−	1	9
	1	6

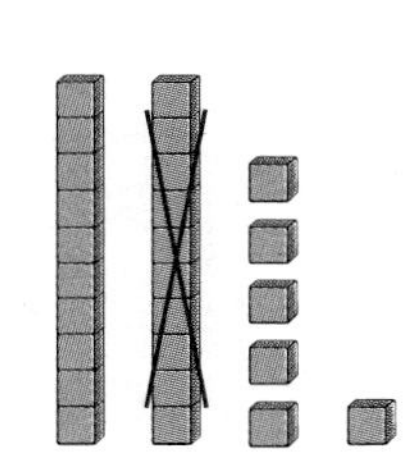

16 angelfish are left.

Use tens and ones models and Workmat 3.
Decide if you need to regroup. Then subtract.

1.

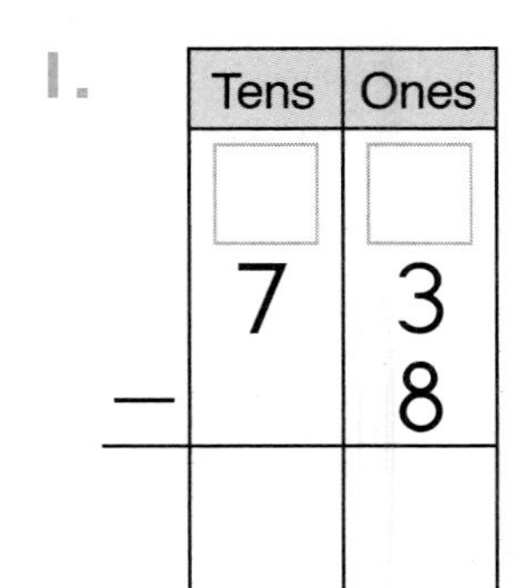

	Tens	Ones
	7	3
−		8

	Tens	Ones
	5	5
−		7

	Tens	Ones
	4	8
−	2	8

	Tens	Ones
	3	5
−	2	6

Home Connection Your child is learning how to subtract two-digit numbers. Ask your child to explain how he or she would solve a problem like 29 − 4.

Use tens and ones models and Workmat 3.
Decide if you need to regroup. Then subtract.

1.

	Tens	Ones
	2	12
	~~3~~	~~2~~
−		8
	2	4

	Tens	Ones
	6	5
−	2	5

	Tens	Ones
	7	0
−		6

	Tens	Ones
	6	7
−	2	8

2.

	Tens	Ones
	5	4
−	2	6

	Tens	Ones
	2	7
−		9

	Tens	Ones
	8	5
−		6

	Tens	Ones
	7	4
−		3

3.

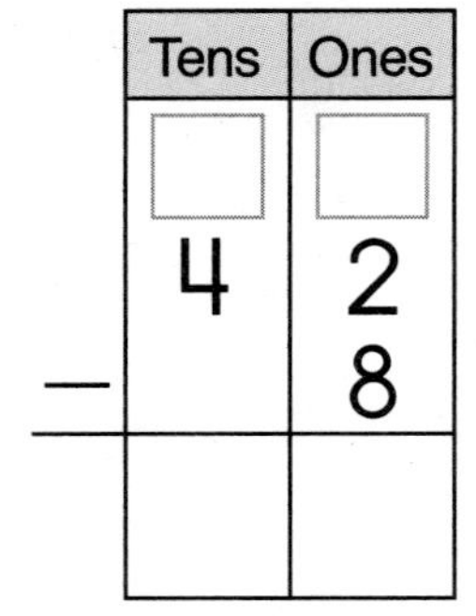

	Tens	Ones
	4	2
−		8

	Tens	Ones
	9	5
−	4	2

	Tens	Ones
	2	3
−		7

	Tens	Ones
	5	5
−	3	7

Critical Thinking Corner

Number Sense

4. Put an X on the wrong way to show 42 − 9. Tell why it is wrong.

$$\begin{array}{r} 42 \\ -\ \ 9 \\ \hline \end{array} \qquad \begin{array}{r} 42 \\ -9\ \ \\ \hline \end{array}$$

Name________________________________ **Modeling Subtraction**

There are 54 sea gulls on the rocks. 15 fly away. How many are left?

39 sea gulls

Tens	Ones
4	14
~~5~~	~~4~~
− 1	5
3	9

Use tens and ones models and Workmat 3.
Decide if you need to regroup. Then subtract.

1.

Tens	Ones
5	8
− 2	7

Tens	Ones
3	2
− 1	8

Tens	Ones
4	8
−	9

Tens	Ones
6	0
− 3	6

2.

Tens	Ones
8	9
− 2	6

Tens	Ones
7	1
− 1	2

Tens	Ones
8	5
− 6	8

Tens	Ones
3	0
−	7

3.

Tens	Ones
9	5
− 3	8

Tens	Ones
4	7
− 1	8

Tens	Ones
5	3
−	8

Tens	Ones
7	6
− 5	6

Home Connection Your child is learning when to regroup in order to subtract two-digit numbers. Ask your child to explain why he or she needed to regroup to solve one of the exercises above.

Use tens and ones models and Workmat 3.
Decide if you need to regroup. Then subtract.

1.

	Tens	Ones
	5	13
	~~6~~	~~3~~
−		9
	5	4

	Tens	Ones
	5	6
−	3	4

	Tens	Ones
	4	2
−	1	6

	Tens	Ones
	5	7
−	3	9

2.

	Tens	Ones
	3	5
−		8

	Tens	Ones
	3	7
−	1	8

	Tens	Ones
	8	0
−	5	2

	Tens	Ones
	8	6
−	2	6

3.

	Tens	Ones
	4	4
−	2	5

	Tens	Ones
	7	1
−	3	7

	Tens	Ones
	3	0
−	1	7

	Tens	Ones
	9	6
−		9

Problem Solving

Solve.

4. 35 terns fly over the ocean. 9 terns dive into the water. Then 7 more dive. How many terns keep flying?

____ terns

Use pictures of tens and ones to find 43 − 27.

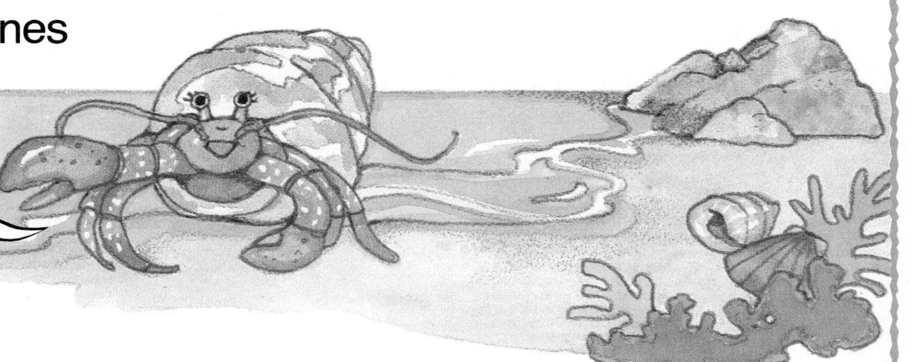

You need to regroup 1 ten as 10 ones.

1 Look at the picture. Does it show regrouping?

	Tens	Ones
	3	13
	~~4~~	~~3~~
−	2	7

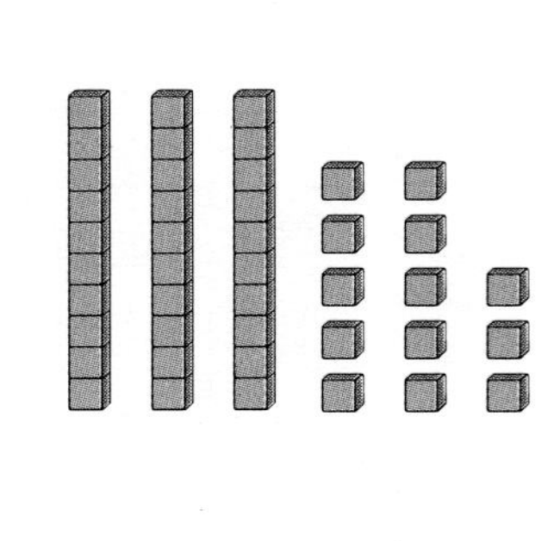

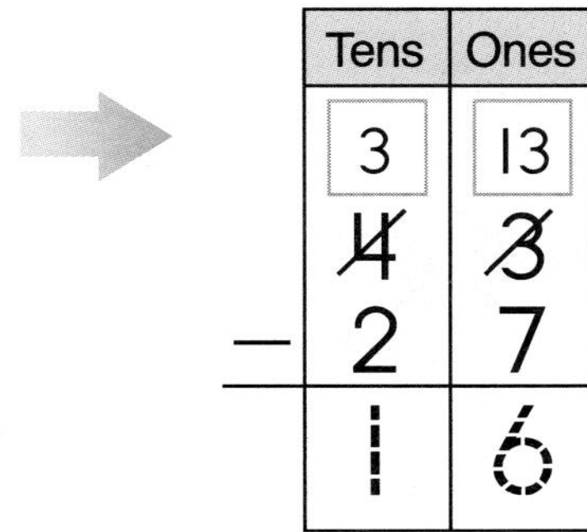

2 Cross out ones and tens to subtract. Write the difference.

	Tens	Ones
	3	13
	~~4~~	~~3~~
−	2	7
	1	6

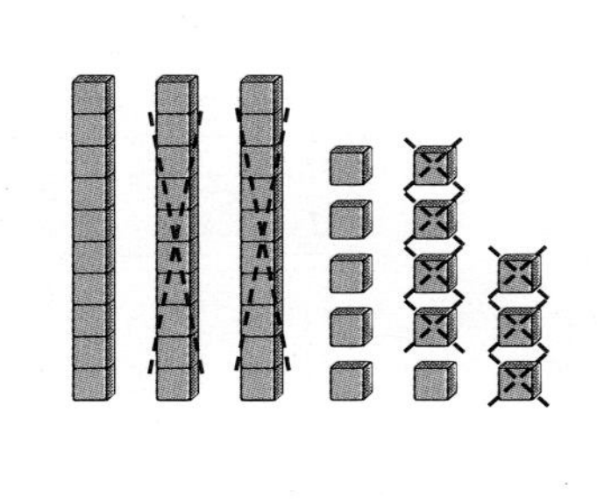

Find each difference.
Cross out to subtract.

1.

	Tens	Ones
	4	11
	~~5~~	~~1~~
−	3	4

2.

	Tens	Ones
	2	14
	~~3~~	~~4~~
−	1	6

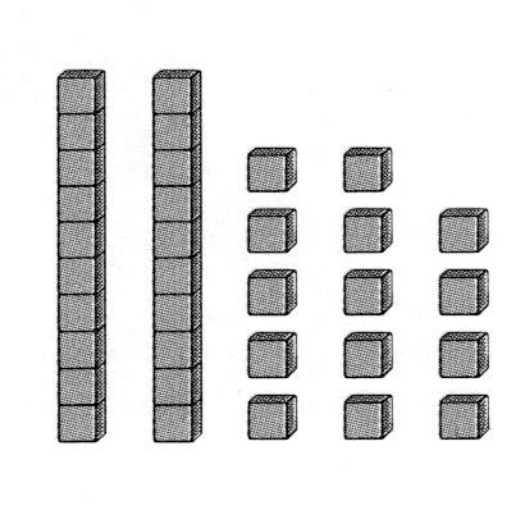

3.

	Tens	Ones
	6	5
−	3	5

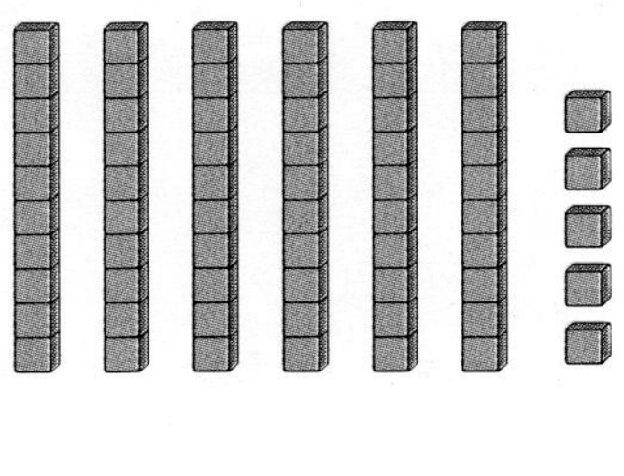

4.

	Tens	Ones
	3	15
	~~4~~	~~5~~
−	3	6

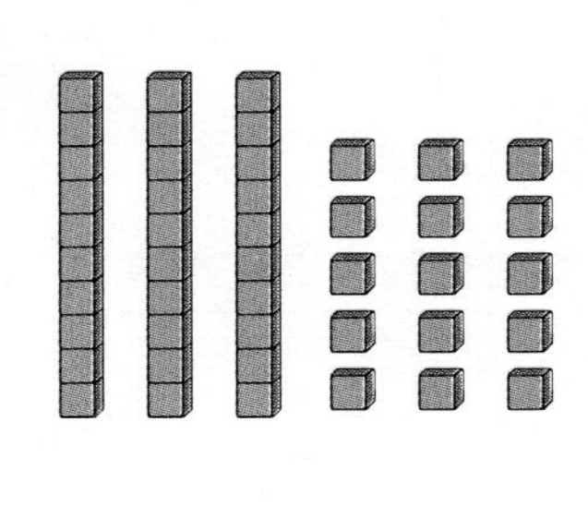

Home Connection Using pictures of tens and ones can help children understand two-digit subtraction. Ask your child to explain how he or she completed each of the exercises on this page.

Find each difference.
Cross out to subtract.

1.

	Tens	Ones
	1	15
	~~2~~	~~5~~
−		7
	1	8

2.

	Tens	Ones
	4	12
	~~5~~	~~2~~
−	2	8

3.

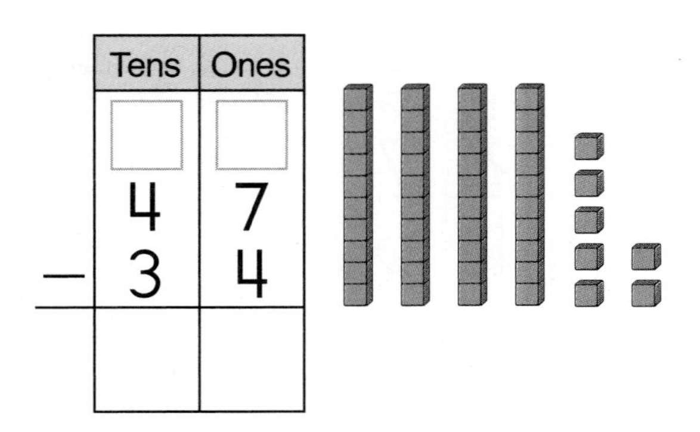

	Tens	Ones
	4	7
−	3	4

4.

	Tens	Ones
	3	10
	~~4~~	~~0~~
−	2	1

5.

	Tens	Ones
	2	13
	~~3~~	~~3~~
−		6

6.

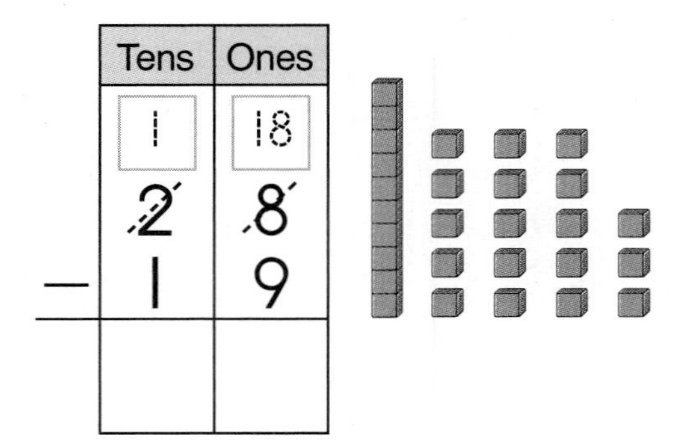

	Tens	Ones
	1	18
	~~2~~	~~8~~
−	1	9

Critical Thinking Corner

Mental Math

Using Algebra

Write a number that makes each number sentence true.

7. $50 - 30 < 50 -$ ____ 8. $80 - 20 > 80 -$ ____

Name________________________________

Harborside Aquarium rescued 72 seals last year. It released 54 seals.
How many seals are still at the aquarium?

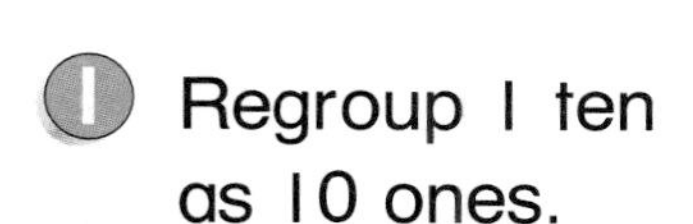

1. Regroup 1 ten as 10 ones.

	Tens	Ones
	6	12
	~~7~~	~~2~~
−	5	4

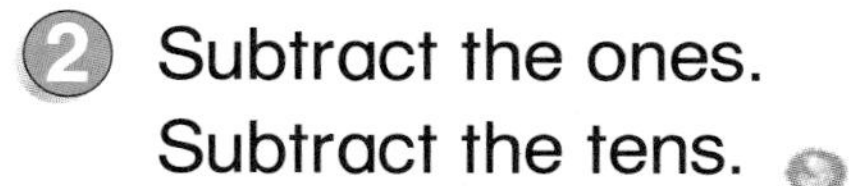

2. Subtract the ones. Subtract the tens.

	Tens	Ones
	6	12
	~~7~~	~~2~~
−	5	4
	1	8

18 seals

Subtract. Use tens and ones models if you like.

1.	3 13 ~~43~~ − 15 28	65 − 48	36 − 24	50 − 32	74 − 9	47 − 25
2.	64 − 59	28 − 10	62 − 19	41 − 24	90 − 27	53 − 33
3.	80 − 46	54 − 28	61 − 40	77 − 69	80 − 8	36 − 17

Home Connection Write two or three subtraction problems like the ones on this page. Ask your child to find each difference.

Subtract. Use tens and ones models if you like.

1.	5 16 66 − 8 58	37 −19	75 −15	40 −23	84 −37	53 −21
2.	58 −39	90 −56	27 − 9	89 −38	60 −25	35 −27
3.	70 −25	48 − 9	83 −61	47 −18	94 − 5	28 − 9

Checkpoint

Find each difference.
Use tens and ones models or Workmat 5 if you like.

1. $80 - 50 =$ ____ $60 - 20 =$ ____ $90 - 20 =$ ____

2. $46 - 10 =$ ____ $72 - 20 =$ ____ $35 - 20 =$ ____

3.

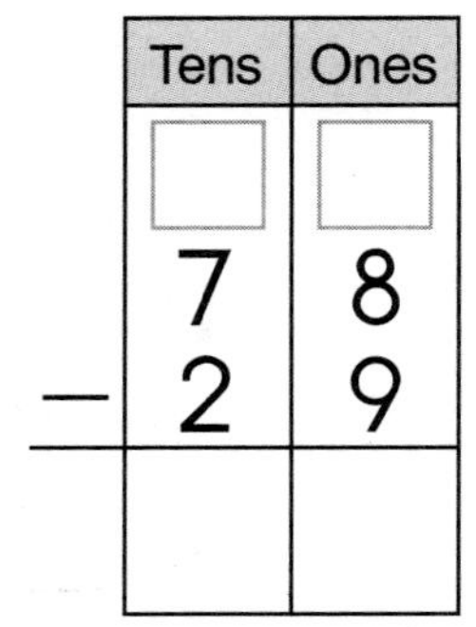

	Tens	Ones
	☐	☐
	7	8
−	2	9

	Tens	Ones
	☐	☐
	5	0
−		6

	Tens	Ones
	☐	☐
	6	7
−	3	4

	Tens	Ones
	☐	☐
	3	6
−	1	7

Name________________________________ **Practicing Subtraction**

Subtract. Use tens and ones models if you like.

1.

Tens	Ones
6	16
~~7~~	~~6~~
− 4	9
2	7

Tens	Ones
5	3
− 2	8

Tens	Ones
4	6
− 1	3

Tens	Ones
8	0
− 2	1

2. $98 - 25$ $\quad 60 - 35$ $\quad 83 - 51$ $\quad 35 - 17$ $\quad 60 - 6$ $\quad 37 - 18$

3. $63 - 15$ $\quad 45 - 20$ $\quad 77 - 28$ $\quad 36 - 19$ $\quad 90 - 30$ $\quad 76 - 47$

4. $27 - 19$ $\quad 82 - 46$ $\quad 55 - 17$ $\quad 50 - 7$ $\quad 75 - 46$ $\quad 96 - 34$

5. $30 - 16$ $\quad 99 - 39$ $\quad 85 - 9$ $\quad 44 - 28$ $\quad 66 - 10$ $\quad 51 - 48$

6. $62 - 25$ $\quad 81 - 19$ $\quad 45 - 22$ $\quad 73 - 35$ $\quad 51 - 35$ $\quad 28 - 15$

Home Connection Write two or three subtraction problems like those on this page. Ask your child to find each difference and tell if he or she needs to regroup.

Rewrite the numbers in the boxes below.
Then subtract.

1. 64 − 17

Tens	Ones
5	14
~~6~~	~~4~~
− 1	7
4	7

45 − 8

Tens	Ones
−	

70 − 21

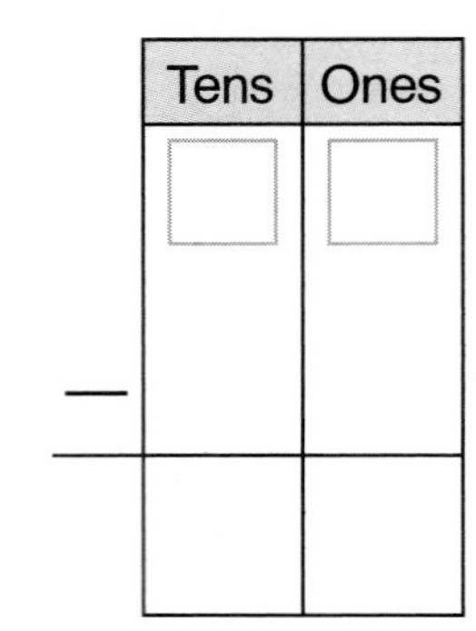

Tens	Ones
−	

32 − 10

Tens	Ones
−	

2. 80 − 28

Tens	Ones
−	

40 − 26

Tens	Ones
−	

95 − 45

Tens	Ones
−	

36 − 8

Tens	Ones
−	

Problem Solving

Solve.

3. Jed found 33 shells at the beach. He gave 16 shells to his sister. How many did he have then?

_____ shells

4. Austin found 47 shells at Sand Beach. He found 63 shells at Long Beach. How many more shells did he find at Long Beach?

_____ shells

Name ____________________

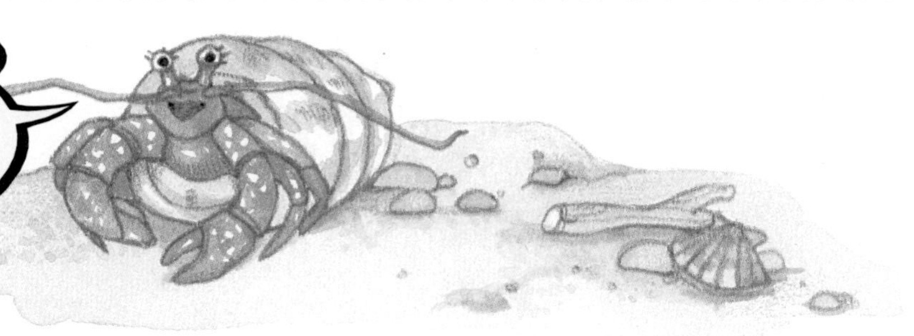
What number patterns do you see?

52	52	52	52	52
− 8	− 18	− 28	− 38	− 48
44	34	24	14	4

Subtract. Continue the pattern.
Use tens and ones models if you like.

1.	65 − 6 = 59 (5 15)	65 − 16	65 − 26	65 − 36	65 − 46	−
2.	58 − 3	58 − 13	58 − 23	58 − 33	−	−
3.	60 − 2	60 − 12	60 − 22	60 − 32	−	−
4.	76 − 10	76 − 20	76 − 30	76 − 40	−	−

Home Connection Recognizing number patterns can help children subtract. Ask your child to describe some of the patterns on this page.

Subtract. Continue the pattern.
Use tens and ones models if you like.

1. $\begin{array}{r} \overset{7\,12}{\cancel{8}\cancel{2}} \\ -\ 7 \\ \hline 75 \end{array}$ $\quad \begin{array}{r} 82 \\ -17 \\ \hline \end{array}$ $\quad \begin{array}{r} 82 \\ -27 \\ \hline \end{array}$ $\quad \begin{array}{r} 82 \\ -37 \\ \hline \end{array}$ $\quad \begin{array}{r} \\ - \quad \\ \hline \end{array}$ $\quad \begin{array}{r} \\ - \quad \\ \hline \end{array}$

2. $\begin{array}{r} 95 \\ -\ 5 \\ \hline \end{array}$ $\quad \begin{array}{r} 95 \\ -15 \\ \hline \end{array}$ $\quad \begin{array}{r} 95 \\ -25 \\ \hline \end{array}$ $\quad \begin{array}{r} 95 \\ -35 \\ \hline \end{array}$ $\quad \begin{array}{r} \\ - \quad \\ \hline \end{array}$ $\quad \begin{array}{r} \\ - \quad \\ \hline \end{array}$

3. $\begin{array}{r} 71 \\ -\ 2 \\ \hline \end{array}$ $\quad \begin{array}{r} 71 \\ -12 \\ \hline \end{array}$ $\quad \begin{array}{r} 71 \\ -22 \\ \hline \end{array}$ $\quad \begin{array}{r} 71 \\ -32 \\ \hline \end{array}$ $\quad \begin{array}{r} \\ - \quad \\ \hline \end{array}$ $\quad \begin{array}{r} \\ - \quad \\ \hline \end{array}$

4. Write your own subtraction pattern.

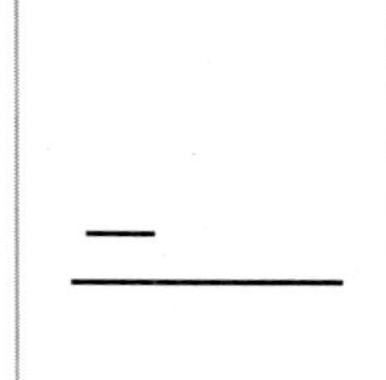
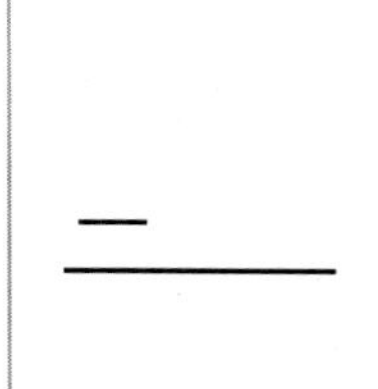
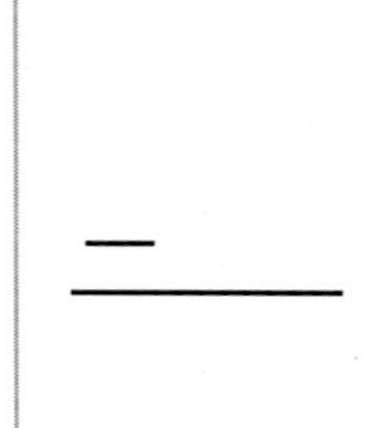

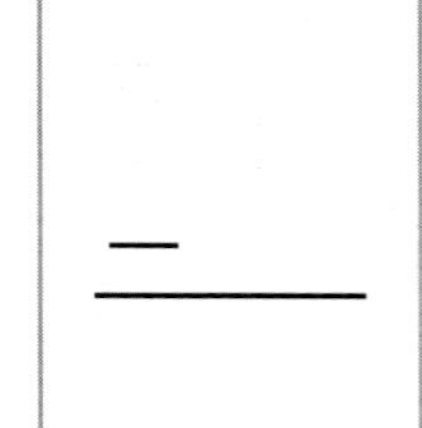

Critical Thinking Corner

Number Sense

5. Look for a pattern. Write the missing numbers.

$\begin{array}{r} 62 \\ -\ \boxed{9} \\ \hline 53 \end{array}$ $\quad \begin{array}{r} 62 \\ -\ \boxed{19} \\ \hline 43 \end{array}$ $\quad \begin{array}{r} 62 \\ -\ \boxed{} \\ \hline 33 \end{array}$ $\quad \begin{array}{r} \boxed{} \\ -\ 39 \\ \hline 23 \end{array}$ $\quad \begin{array}{r} 62 \\ -\ \boxed{} \\ \hline 13 \end{array}$

Name ______________________ **Ways to Subtract** THERE'S ALWAYS A WAY!

How would you solve this problem?
47 puffins were swimming.
20 puffins left to rest on rocks.
How many puffins kept swimming?

I would use mental math....47, 37, 27.

I would use paper and pencil.

47
−20
27
27 puffins

I would use tens and ones models.

I would use a hundred chart.

Find each difference.
Use tens and ones models or paper and pencil.

1. $\begin{array}{r} 53 \\ -23 \\ \hline 30 \end{array}$ $\begin{array}{r} 45 \\ -\ 8 \\ \hline \end{array}$ $\begin{array}{r} 70 \\ -45 \\ \hline \end{array}$ $\begin{array}{r} 72 \\ -14 \\ \hline \end{array}$ $\begin{array}{r} 23 \\ -18 \\ \hline \end{array}$ $\begin{array}{r} 93 \\ -48 \\ \hline \end{array}$

2. $\begin{array}{r} 85 \\ -49 \\ \hline \end{array}$ $\begin{array}{r} 50 \\ -22 \\ \hline \end{array}$ $\begin{array}{r} 34 \\ -\ 9 \\ \hline \end{array}$ $\begin{array}{r} 91 \\ -29 \\ \hline \end{array}$ $\begin{array}{r} 88 \\ -77 \\ \hline \end{array}$ $\begin{array}{r} 76 \\ -29 \\ \hline \end{array}$

Use a hundred chart or mental math.

3. $90 - 30 =$ ____ $73 - 20 =$ ____ $38 - 30 =$ ____

4. $56 - 10 =$ ____ $80 - 10 =$ ____ $41 - 20 =$ ____

5. $67 - 20 =$ ____ $29 - 10 =$ ____ $70 - 30 =$ ____

Home Connection Ask your child to tell you about different ways to subtract. Ask if she or he has a favorite way.

Look at each problem.
Circle one of the ways to solve it.
Then solve.

Sometimes one way is easier than another.

1. $\begin{array}{r} 42 \\ -16 \\ \hline \end{array}$
   a. tens and ones
   b. hundred chart
   c. paper and pencil
   d. mental math

2. $\begin{array}{r} 63 \\ -20 \\ \hline \end{array}$
   a. tens and ones
   b. hundred chart
   c. paper and pencil
   d. mental math

3. $\begin{array}{r} 82 \\ -\ 3 \\ \hline \end{array}$
   a. tens and ones
   b. hundred chart
   c. paper and pencil
   d. mental math

4. $\begin{array}{r} 50 \\ -33 \\ \hline \end{array}$
   a. tens and ones
   b. hundred chart
   c. paper and pencil
   d. mental math

5. $\begin{array}{r} 80 \\ -30 \\ \hline \end{array}$
   a. tens and ones
   b. hundred chart
   c. paper and pencil
   d. mental math

6. $\begin{array}{r} 34 \\ -19 \\ \hline \end{array}$
   a. tens and ones
   b. hundred chart
   c. paper and pencil
   d. mental math

PROBLEM SOLVING

Problem Solving

Does the answer make sense? Write **yes** or **no**.
Explain your choice.

7. Miguel found 53 shells on the beach. He kept 36. How many shells did he leave on the beach?

   89 shells ______________________

   ____

Name________________________________

Keiko has 52 shells.
34 are scallop shells.
The rest are conch shells.
How many are conch shells?

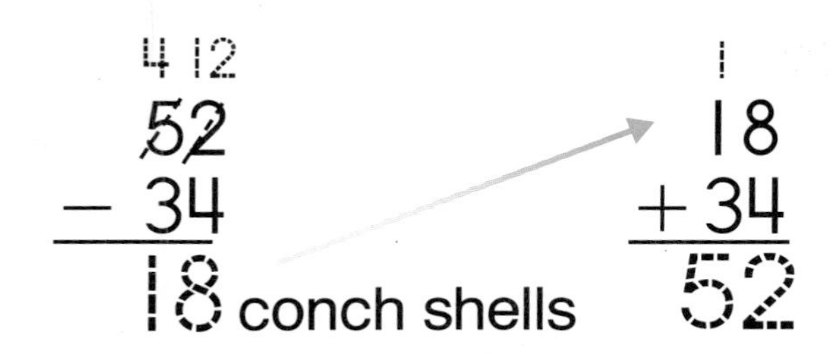

$$\begin{array}{r} \scriptstyle 4\ 12 \\ \not{5}\not{2} \\ -\ 34 \\ \hline 18 \end{array}$$ conch shells

$$\begin{array}{r} \scriptstyle 1 \\ 18 \\ +\ 34 \\ \hline 52 \end{array}$$

Start with the difference. Add 34.
Why should the sum be 52?

Subtract. Check by adding.
Use tens and ones models if you like.

1. $\begin{array}{r} \scriptstyle 2\ 15 \\ \not{3}\not{5} \\ -\ 17 \\ \hline 18 \end{array}$ $\begin{array}{r} 18 \\ +\ 17 \\ \hline 35 \end{array}$

2. $\begin{array}{r} 86 \\ -41 \\ \hline \end{array}$ $+\underline{\quad}$

3. $\begin{array}{r} 40 \\ -25 \\ \hline \end{array}$ $+\underline{\quad}$

4. $\begin{array}{r} 63 \\ -23 \\ \hline \end{array}$ $+\underline{\quad}$

5. $\begin{array}{r} 50 \\ -27 \\ \hline \end{array}$ $+\underline{\quad}$

6. $\begin{array}{r} 91 \\ -\ 6 \\ \hline \end{array}$ $+\underline{\quad}$

7. $\begin{array}{r} 37 \\ -25 \\ \hline \end{array}$ $+\underline{\quad}$

8. $\begin{array}{r} 72 \\ -34 \\ \hline \end{array}$ $+\underline{\quad}$

Home Connection Write two or three subtraction problems and ask your child to solve and check them. Ask your child to explain why adding is a good way to check.

Subtract. Check by adding.
Use tens and ones models if you like.

1. $\begin{array}{r} 35 \\ -23 \\ \hline 12 \end{array}$ $\begin{array}{r} 12 \\ +23 \\ \hline 35 \end{array}$

2. $\begin{array}{r} 53 \\ -28 \\ \hline \end{array}$ $\begin{array}{r} \\ + \\ \hline \end{array}$

3. $\begin{array}{r} 82 \\ -26 \\ \hline \end{array}$ $\begin{array}{r} \\ + \\ \hline \end{array}$

4. $\begin{array}{r} 70 \\ -18 \\ \hline \end{array}$ $\begin{array}{r} \\ + \\ \hline \end{array}$

5. $\begin{array}{r} 38 \\ -9 \\ \hline \end{array}$ $\begin{array}{r} \\ + \\ \hline \end{array}$

6. $\begin{array}{r} 96 \\ -10 \\ \hline \end{array}$ $\begin{array}{r} \\ + \\ \hline \end{array}$

7. $\begin{array}{r} 62 \\ -39 \\ \hline \end{array}$ $\begin{array}{r} \\ + \\ \hline \end{array}$

8. $\begin{array}{r} 85 \\ -8 \\ \hline \end{array}$ $\begin{array}{r} \\ + \\ \hline \end{array}$

What Do You Think?

I think checking is important because it helps you catch your mistakes. Everybody makes mistakes sometimes.

Do you think checking is important? Tell why or why not.

Adding and subtracting money is just like adding and subtracting two-digit numbers.

$$\begin{array}{r} {}^{1} \\ 29¢ \\ +\ 38¢ \\ \hline 67¢ \end{array} \qquad \begin{array}{r} {}^{6\,15} \\ \not{7}\not{5}¢ \\ -\ 67¢ \\ \hline 8¢ \end{array}$$

Add or subtract.
Use dimes and pennies if you like.

1.	36¢ + 28¢	90¢ + 8¢	50¢ − 26¢	77¢ − 27¢	83¢ − 37¢
2.	60¢ − 41¢	15¢ + 45¢	45¢ − 20¢	57¢ + 29¢	63¢ + 27¢
3.	54¢ − 11¢	95¢ − 36¢	70¢ − 7¢	33¢ + 28¢	65¢ + 15¢
4.	43¢ − 26¢	94¢ − 20¢	56¢ + 34¢	70¢ − 32¢	18¢ + 56¢

Home Connection Your child is learning that adding and subtracting money is like adding and subtracting whole numbers. Ask your child to add and subtract money while playing store.

Add or subtract.
Use dimes and pennies if you like.

1. $\begin{array}{r} \overset{3\ 13}{\cancel{4}\cancel{3}}¢ \\ -\ 18¢ \\ \hline 25¢ \end{array}$ $\begin{array}{r} 39¢ \\ +\ \ 7¢ \\ \hline \end{array}$ $\begin{array}{r} 54¢ \\ -30¢ \\ \hline \end{array}$ $\begin{array}{r} 62¢ \\ -28¢ \\ \hline \end{array}$ $\begin{array}{r} 41¢ \\ +36¢ \\ \hline \end{array}$

2. $\begin{array}{r} 87¢ \\ -42¢ \\ \hline \end{array}$ $\begin{array}{r} 60¢ \\ +35¢ \\ \hline \end{array}$ $\begin{array}{r} 28¢ \\ +\ \ 9¢ \\ \hline \end{array}$ $\begin{array}{r} 13¢ \\ +63¢ \\ \hline \end{array}$ $\begin{array}{r} 53¢ \\ -25¢ \\ \hline \end{array}$

Rewrite the numbers in the boxes below.
Then add or subtract.

3. 18¢ + 32¢

	Tens	Ones
	1	
	1	8¢
+	3	2¢
	5	0¢

90¢ − 45¢

	Tens	Ones
−		

44¢ + 27¢

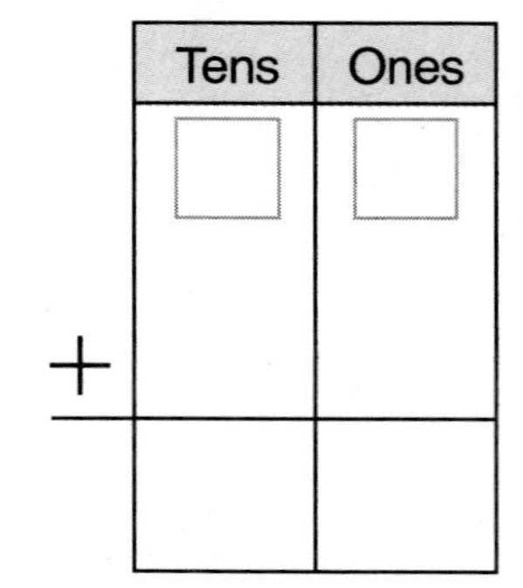

	Tens	Ones
+		

Problem Solving

Solve.

4. Nell saves 57¢ for a new shell for her hermit crab. Her dad gives her a quarter. How much money does she have now? ______

5. Nell buys a shell for 69¢. She gives the store clerk 8 dimes. How much change should she get? ______

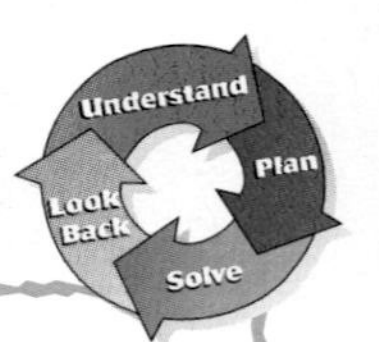

Name ______________________________

Natalia has 36 shells. She uses 28 shells to make a necklace. How many shells does she have left?

Do you add or subtract?

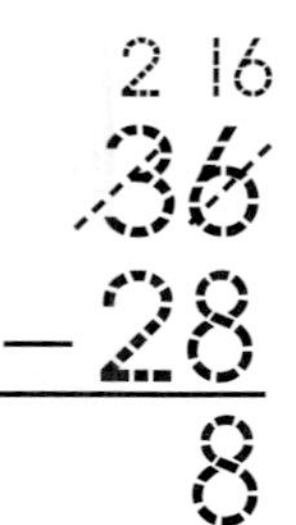

8 shells

Circle **add** or **subtract**. Solve.

1. Tor has 42 shells. He buys 19 more shells. How many shells does he have now?

   add subtract ____ shells

2. Jessie has 51 shells. Mike has 28 shells. How many more shells does Jessie have than Mike?

   add subtract ____ shells

3. Ben has 64 shells. He uses 18 shells to make a bracelet. How many shells does he have now?

   add subtract ____ shells

Home Connection Ask your child to explain how he or she decided whether to add or subtract to solve one of the problems in this lesson.

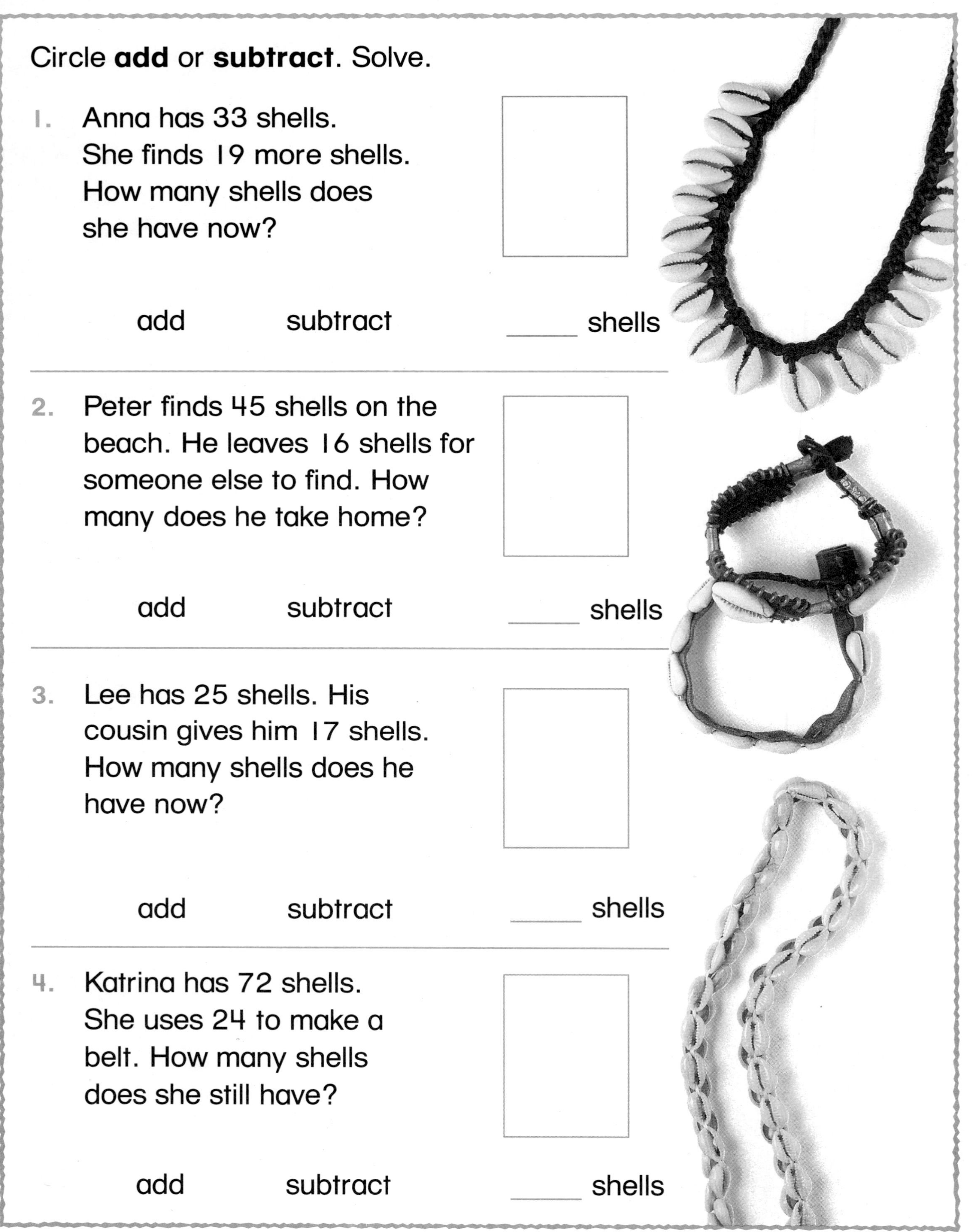

Circle **add** or **subtract**. Solve.

1. Anna has 33 shells.
   She finds 19 more shells.
   How many shells does
   she have now?

   add   subtract   ____ shells

2. Peter finds 45 shells on the beach. He leaves 16 shells for someone else to find. How many does he take home?

   add   subtract   ____ shells

3. Lee has 25 shells. His cousin gives him 17 shells. How many shells does he have now?

   add   subtract   ____ shells

4. Katrina has 72 shells. She uses 24 to make a belt. How many shells does she still have?

   add   subtract   ____ shells

Name______________________________________ **Checkpoint** 

1. Rewrite the numbers in the boxes below.
Then subtract.

84 − 36

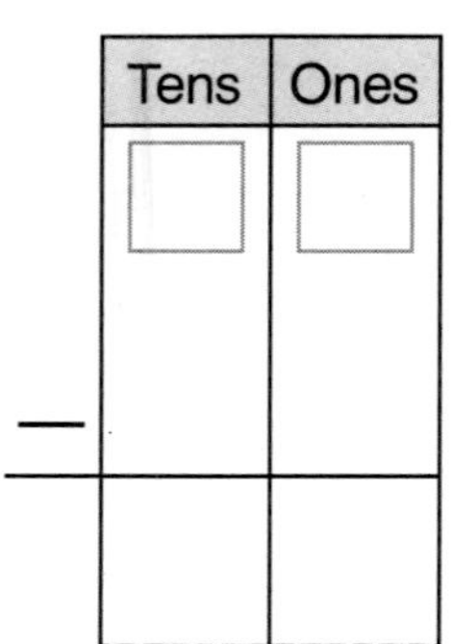

45 − 9

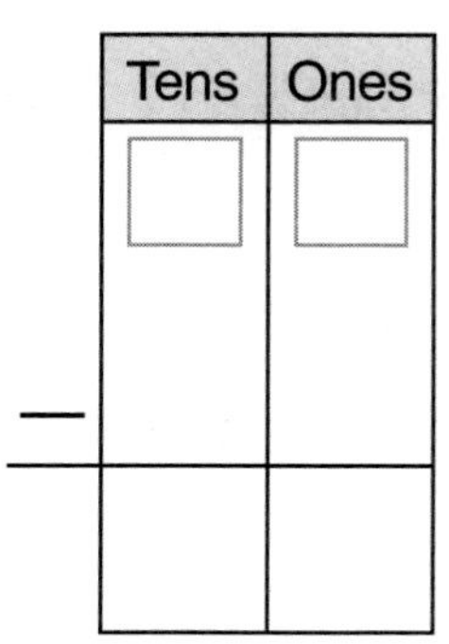

90 − 46

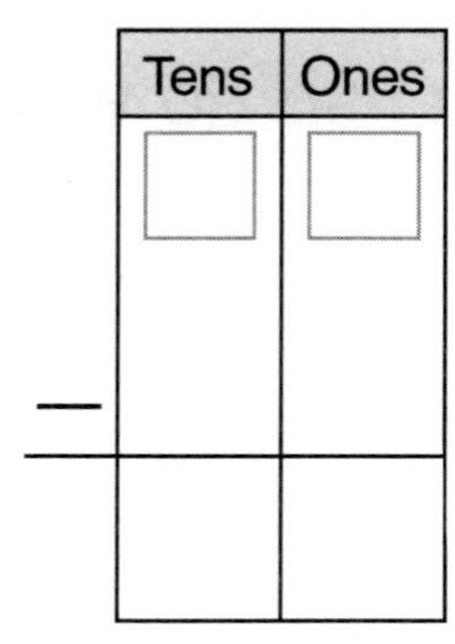

66 − 26

Tens	Ones

---

2. Subtract. Continue the pattern.
Use tens and ones models if you like.

$$\begin{array}{r} 73 \\ -\ 6 \\ \hline \end{array} \quad \begin{array}{r} 73 \\ -16 \\ \hline \end{array} \quad \begin{array}{r} 73 \\ -26 \\ \hline \end{array} \quad \begin{array}{r} 73 \\ -36 \\ \hline \end{array} \quad \begin{array}{r} \\ -\quad \\ \hline \end{array} \quad \begin{array}{r} \\ -\quad \\ \hline \end{array}$$

---

3. Subtract. Check by adding.
Use tens and ones models if you like.

$$\begin{array}{r} 32 \\ -19 \\ \hline \end{array} \quad \begin{array}{r} \\ +\quad \\ \hline \end{array} \qquad \begin{array}{r} 40 \\ -21 \\ \hline \end{array} \quad \begin{array}{r} \\ +\quad \\ \hline \end{array} \qquad \begin{array}{r} 65 \\ -26 \\ \hline \end{array} \quad \begin{array}{r} \\ +\quad \\ \hline \end{array}$$

---

4. Add or subtract.

$$\begin{array}{r} 16¢ \\ +37¢ \\ \hline \end{array} \quad \begin{array}{r} 59¢ \\ -11¢ \\ \hline \end{array} \quad \begin{array}{r} 70¢ \\ -59¢ \\ \hline \end{array} \quad \begin{array}{r} 46¢ \\ +36¢ \\ \hline \end{array} \quad \begin{array}{r} 83¢ \\ -47¢ \\ \hline \end{array}$$

Name______________________________ **Extra Practice**

Subtract.
Use the code to solve the riddle.
Write the letter for each difference.

What does a clown fish do when it grows up?

Code

12	15	17	20	21	24	27	32	41	46	53
E	O	N	S	C	H	J	I	T	U	R

$81 - 49 = 32$ I

$77 - 36 =$ ☐

$74 - 47 =$ ☐

$45 - 30 =$ ☐

$60 - 28 =$ ☐

$83 - 66 =$ ☐

$43 - 23 =$ ☐

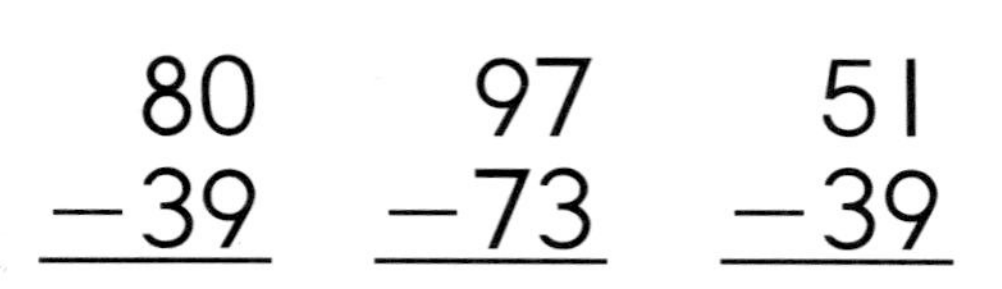

$80 - 39 =$ ☐

$97 - 73 =$ ☐

$51 - 39 =$ ☐

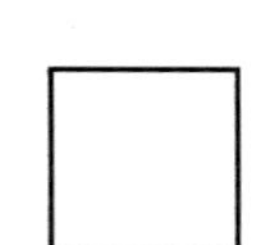

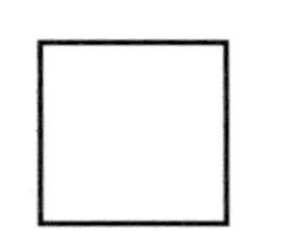

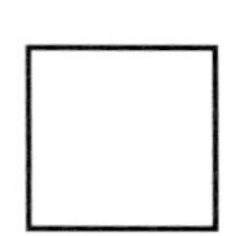

$60 - 39 =$ ☐

$70 - 38 =$ ☐

$72 - 19 =$ ☐

$42 - 21 =$ ☐

$83 - 37 =$ ☐

$50 - 30 =$ ☐

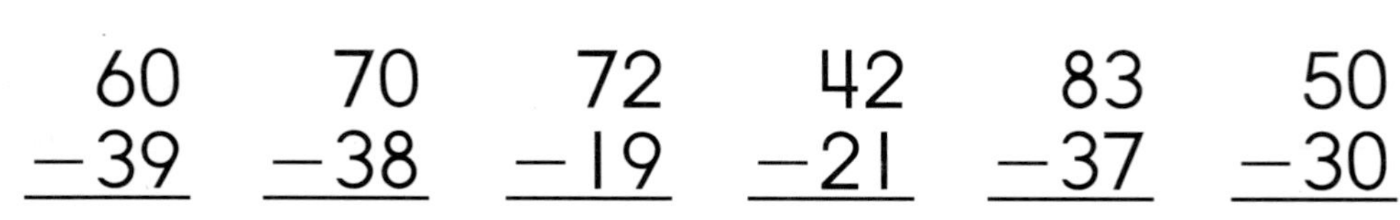

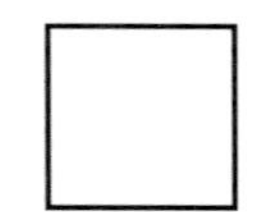

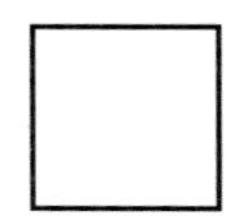

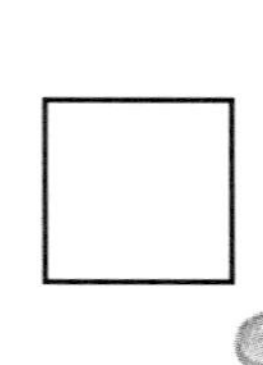

Name ______________________________ **Chapter Test** 

1. Subtract.

$\begin{array}{r} 50 \\ -30 \\ \hline \end{array}$ $\begin{array}{r} 63 \\ -35 \\ \hline \end{array}$ $\begin{array}{r} 37 \\ -20 \\ \hline \end{array}$ $\begin{array}{r} 44 \\ -\ 8 \\ \hline \end{array}$ $\begin{array}{r} 77 \\ -48 \\ \hline \end{array}$ $\begin{array}{r} 88 \\ -18 \\ \hline \end{array}$

2. Subtract. Check by adding.

$\begin{array}{r} 74 \\ -38 \\ \hline \end{array}$ $+$ ____ $\begin{array}{r} 40 \\ -23 \\ \hline \end{array}$ $+$ ____ $\begin{array}{r} 85 \\ -56 \\ \hline \end{array}$ $+$ ____

3. Add or subtract.

$\begin{array}{r} 93¢ \\ -38¢ \\ \hline \end{array}$ $\begin{array}{r} 20¢ \\ +69¢ \\ \hline \end{array}$ $\begin{array}{r} 50¢ \\ -35¢ \\ \hline \end{array}$ $\begin{array}{r} 65¢ \\ -15¢ \\ \hline \end{array}$ $\begin{array}{r} 37¢ \\ +53¢ \\ \hline \end{array}$

Circle **add** or **subtract**.
Then solve.

4. Jen has 37 shells. Her friend Alexi has 63 shells. How many more shells does Alexi have than Jen?

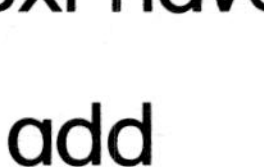

add subtract

____ shells

5. Luis found 16 shells on Sunday. On Monday, he found 45 more. How many shells did he find altogether?

add subtract

____ shells

Name_______________________________ **Performance Assessment** 

What You Need

 2 number cubes

1. Roll both number cubes. Use the numbers to write a two-digit number.
2. Roll again. Write another two-digit number.
3. Compare the numbers. Subtract the lesser number from the greater number.

---

1. 1st number _____

   2nd number _____

   − ______

2. 1st number _____

   2nd number _____

   − ______

3. 1st number _____

   2nd number _____

   − ______

---

4. 1st number _____

   2nd number _____

   − ______

5. 1st number _____

   2nd number _____

   − ______

6. 1st number _____

   2nd number _____

   − ______

Look at your work. Did you need to regroup? Tell why or why not.

Name______________________________

Choose the two numbers that make each difference.
Write the numbers. Check by adding.

1. 50 90 30

Tens	Ones
9	0
− 5	0
4	0

$$\begin{array}{r} 40 \\ +\ 50 \\ \hline 90 \end{array}$$

2. 88 60 68

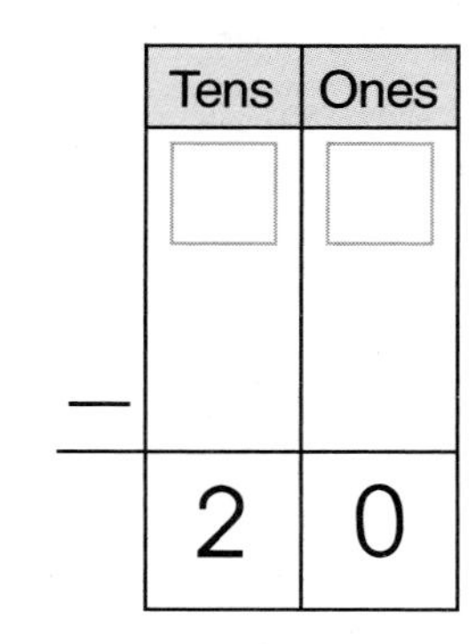

$+$ ____

3. 12 56 40

Tens	Ones
−	
2	8

$+$ ____

4. 43 93 23

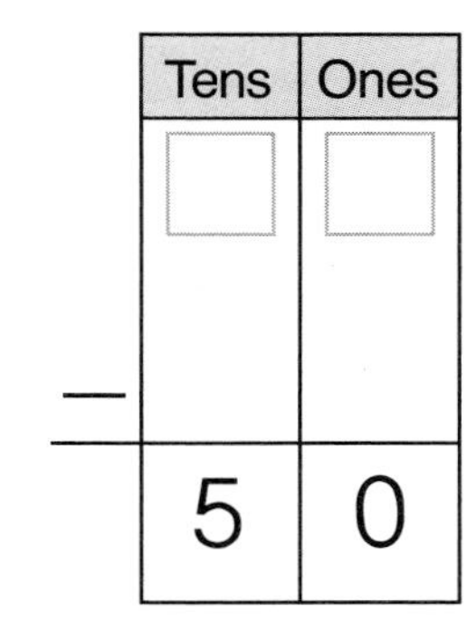

$+$ ____

5. 30 63 47

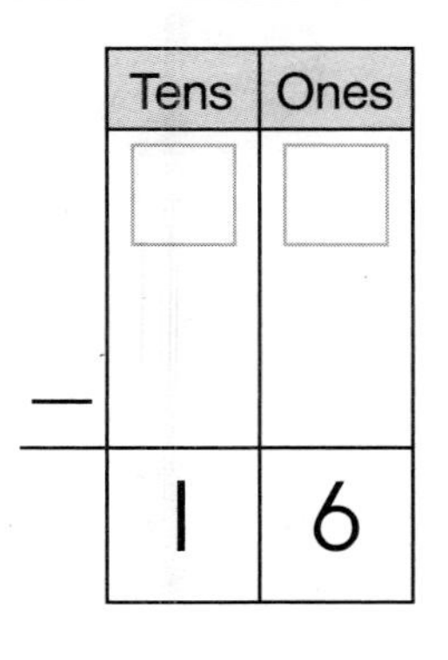

$+$ ____

6. 71 24 18

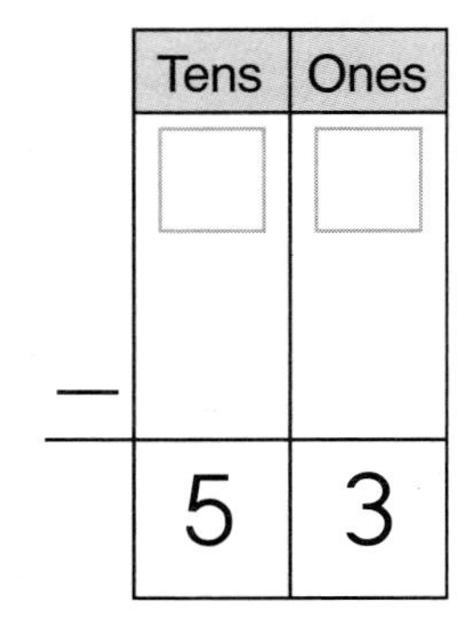

$+$ ____

Name________________________________

You can use tens to estimate differences.

Think about subtracting tens.
Think 50 − 30 = 20.

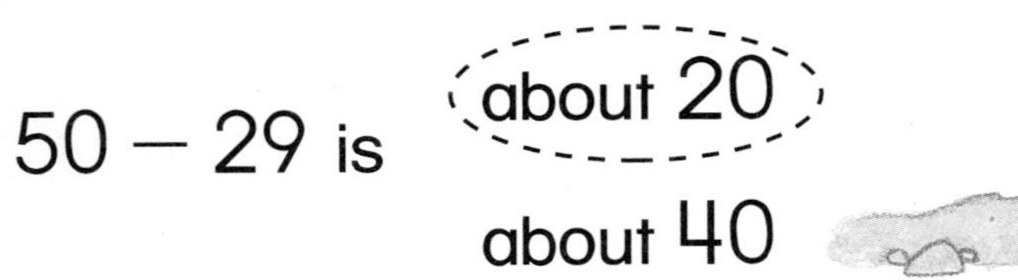

50 − 29 is (about 20) about 40

Then use a calculator to find the exact difference.

Press 

21

Circle the better estimate for each difference.
Then use a calculator to find the exact difference.
Write the numbers.
Was your estimate the better choice?

1. 60 − 31 about 10 about 30

Press 

 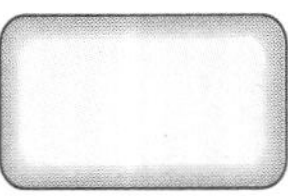 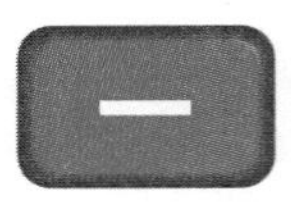

____

---

2. 50 − 19 about 30 about 50

Press 

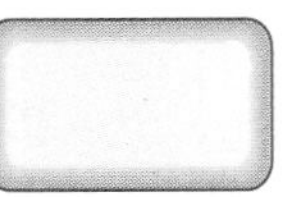 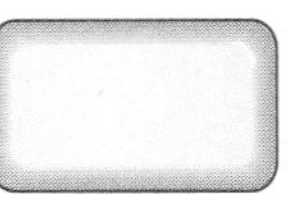 

____

---

3. 80 − 38 about 20 about 40

Press 

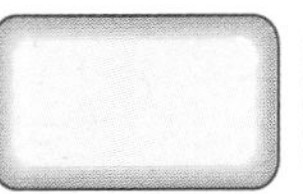  

____

---

4. 90 − 58 about 30 about 50

Press 

____

Fill in the ⬭ for the correct answer.

Add or subtract.

1. $\begin{array}{r} 7 \\ +8 \\ \hline \end{array}$

   ⬭ 15 ⬭ 16 ⬭ 17 ⬭ 18

2. $\begin{array}{r} 11 \\ -4 \\ \hline \end{array}$

   ⬭ 6 ⬭ 7 ⬭ 8 ⬭ 9

3. $\begin{array}{r} 5 \\ 3 \\ +7 \\ \hline \end{array}$

   ⬭ 9 ⬭ 11 ⬭ 13 ⬭ 15

4. $14 - 5 =$ ____

   ⬭ 8 ⬭ 9 ⬭ 10

5. $9 + 9 =$ ____

   ⬭ 16 ⬭ 17 ⬭ 18

6. $16 - 8 =$ ____

   ⬭ 6 ⬭ 7 ⬭ 8

Find the related fact.

7. $\begin{array}{r} 6 \\ +9 \\ \hline \end{array}$

   ⬭ $14 - 7 = 7$
   ⬭ $15 - 9 = 6$
   ⬭ $15 - 7 = 8$

8. $\begin{array}{r} 5 \\ +8 \\ \hline \end{array}$

   ⬭ $11 - 4 = 7$
   ⬭ $13 - 4 = 9$
   ⬭ $13 - 8 = 5$

Find the number shown.

9. 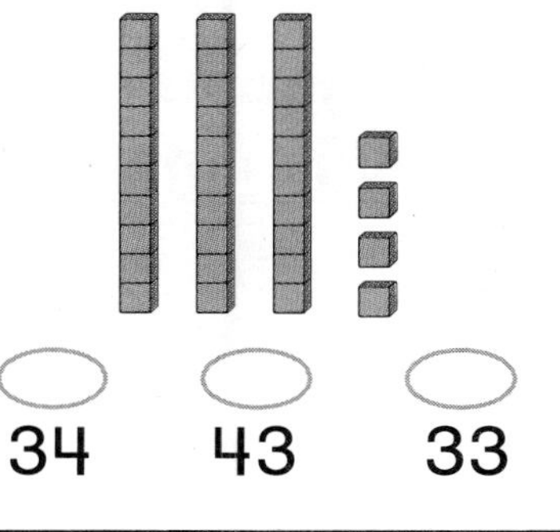

   ⬭ 34 ⬭ 43 ⬭ 33

10. 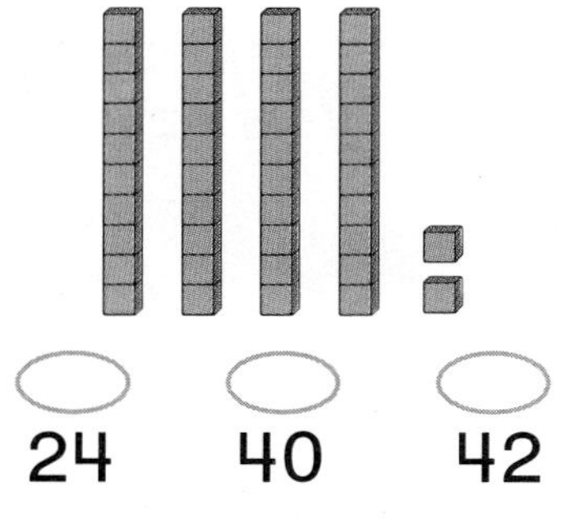

   ⬭ 24 ⬭ 40 ⬭ 42

11. 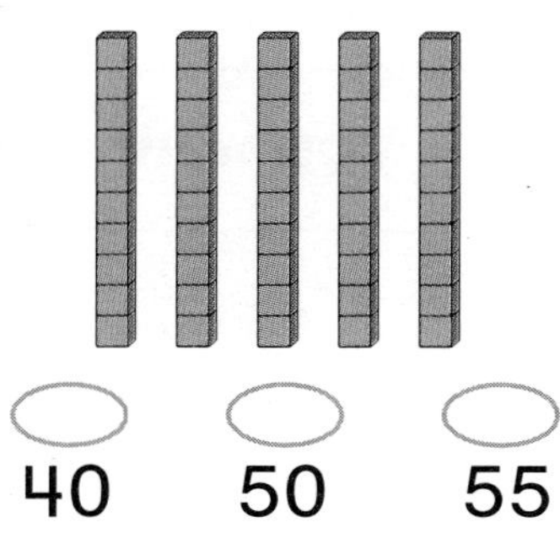

   ⬭ 40 ⬭ 50 ⬭ 55

Find the number that is less.

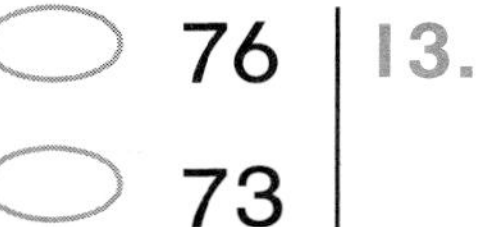

12. 63

   ⬭ 76 ⬭ 73 ⬭ 67 ⬭ 56

13. 38

   ⬭ 39 ⬭ 35 ⬭ 48 ⬭ 51

14. 46

   ⬭ 42 ⬭ 47 ⬭ 50 ⬭ 52

Find the total amount.

15. 

- ◯ 36¢
- ◯ 41¢
- ◯ 46¢
- ◯ 28¢

16. 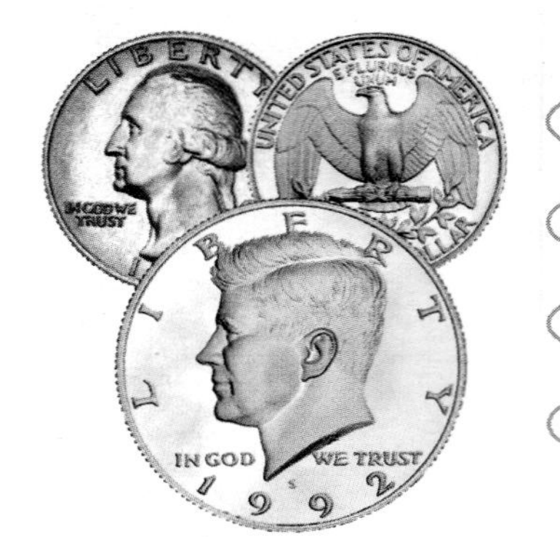

- ◯ 75¢
- ◯ 50¢
- ◯ $1.00
- ◯ 85¢

Add or subtract.

17. $\begin{array}{r} 58 \\ +17 \\ \hline \end{array}$

- ◯ 65
- ◯ 55
- ◯ 75
- ◯ 60

18. $\begin{array}{r} 63 \\ -47 \\ \hline \end{array}$

- ◯ 26
- ◯ 20
- ◯ 16
- ◯ 11

19. $\begin{array}{r} 23¢ \\ +46¢ \\ \hline \end{array}$

- ◯ 49¢
- ◯ 69¢
- ◯ 60¢
- ◯ 66¢

20. $\begin{array}{r} 90¢ \\ -55¢ \\ \hline \end{array}$

- ◯ 40¢
- ◯ 45¢
- ◯ 25¢
- ◯ 35¢

21. $\begin{array}{r} 52 \\ -20 \\ \hline \end{array}$

- ◯ 30
- ◯ 18
- ◯ 32
- ◯ 72

22. $\begin{array}{r} 39¢ \\ +54¢ \\ \hline \end{array}$

- ◯ 90¢
- ◯ 83¢
- ◯ 43¢
- ◯ 93¢

Do you have enough money to buy the raisins?

23.

You want to buy	**You have**	**Do you have enough money?**
76¢		◯ yes ◯ no

Solve.

24. There are 55 fish swimming together. 29 swim away. How many are there now?

- ◯ 84
- ◯ 26
- ◯ 36

25. 42 puffins are on the rocks. 18 puffins join them. How many are there now?

- ◯ 26
- ◯ 50
- ◯ 60

Time

Larry Wins at Last

written by Janice Richardson
illustrated by Jackie Urbanovic

This Math Storybook belongs to

____

One early spring morning at 8 o'clock,
Larry's alarm clock sounded.
"It's time to wake up," said Mother Bear.
"Today is the day of the Animal Olympics."
"But I'm still tired," said Larry.

Larry walked to the field.
At 9 o'clock he was supposed to be
in the jump-rope contest.
But Larry fell asleep—and Rita won.

At 11:30, Larry was supposed to be in the 100-yard dash.
Larry was still asleep—and Cory won.

At 1 o'clock, Larry was supposed to be
in the long jump.
Larry was still asleep—and Janice won.

At 3:30, Larry was in the last contest.
It was a sleeping contest.
And guess what?
Larry won!

Larry wakes up at 8:00 in the morning.
What time do you wake up?
Draw hands on the clock to show the time.

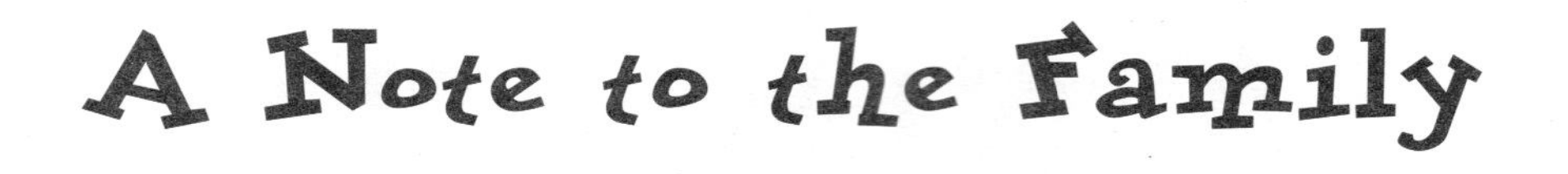

Here are some learning ideas you can share with your child.

Enjoy *Larry Wins at Last* Together

- Read the story aloud with your child. Find the clock on each page and ask your child to tell you the time shown. Then ask him or her to find the words in the story that say the time.
- Look at the last page of the story. Talk with your child about the time he or she showed on the clock. Help your child find out how many hours he or she sleeps. Talk about some other important times in your home schedule—for example, the time your child leaves for school or the time he or she has dinner.

At-Home Activity

- Work with your child to make a simple paper-plate clock. Together write the numbers on the clock face. Attach a long and a short hand with a paper fastener. Show some times to the hour, half-hour, or quarter-hour. Then ask your child to tell you the time.

Read More About It!

To read more about time, look for these books in your local library.

- *Big Book of Time* by William Edmonds (Readers Digest, 1994)
- *It's About Time* by Lee Bennett Hopkins (Simon & Schuster, 1993)
- *Time for School, Nathan* by Lulu Delacre (Scholastic, 1991)
- *The Wonderful Counting Clock* by Cooper Edens (Simon & Schuster, 1995)

Visit Our Web Site!

www.sbgmath.com

Name____

I think I can jump 60 times in 1 minute.
Word Bank
minute

How many can you do in one minute? Guess.
Then work with a partner to do each activity.

1. Touch your toes.

   guess ____

   count ____

2. Count to 10.

   guess ____

   count ____

3. Say the alphabet.

   guess ____

   count ____

4. Snap your fingers.

   guess ____

   count ____

5. Hop on one foot.

   guess ____

   count ____

6. Click your tongue.

   guess ____

   count ____

Home Connection Your child is learning to estimate one minute. Ask your child to name some things that he or she can do in about one minute.

Can you do the activity in a minute?
Circle **yes** or **no**.

1. Write your name.

yes no

2. Play soccer.

yes no

3. Eat breakfast.

yes no

4. Tie your shoes.

yes no

5. Do a puzzle.

yes no

6. Sharpen some pencils.

yes no

What Do You Think?

I can do 20 jumping jacks in a minute.
How many do you think you can do?

Name ______________________________

Problem-Solving Strategy
Use Logical Reasoning

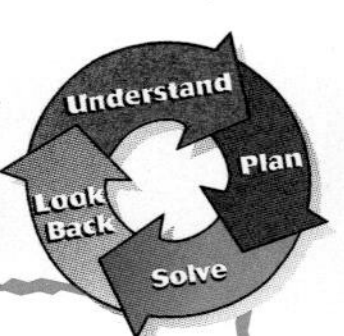

Take a trip.	Be at school.	Get dressed.

about 5 days	about 5 hours	about 5 minutes

Word Bank
hour

About how long does each take?
Circle the more reasonable answer.

1. Brush your teeth.

3 days
3 minutes

2. Bake a cake.

1 day
1 hour

3. Take a bath.

20 hours
20 minutes

4. Take a hike.

1 day
1 minute

5. Have a party.

2 days
2 hours

6. Sleep at night.

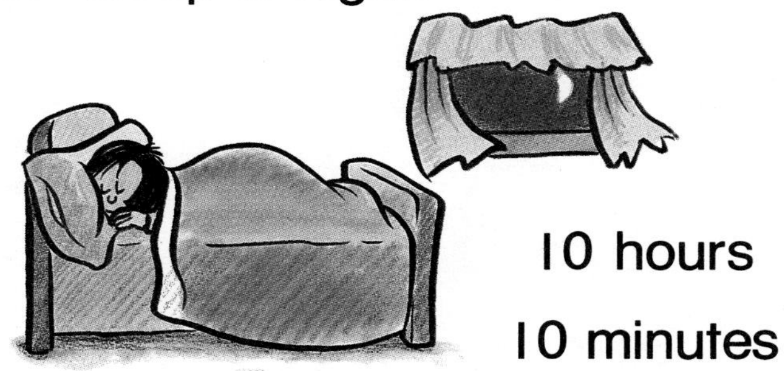

10 hours
10 minutes

Home Connection Your child is learning to compare how long different activities take. Talk with your child about activities that take about a day, an hour, or a minute.

Circle the activities that take about the same time.
Think minutes, hours, or days.

1.

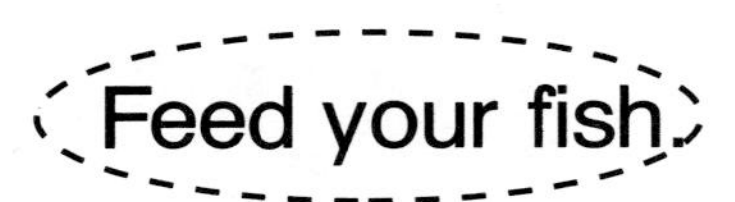

Paint a fence.

2.

Play soccer.

Watch a movie.

Paint a house.

3.

Rake leaves.

Blow up a balloon.

Open a gift.

4.

Eat an apple.

Visit the zoo.

Play at the beach.

Name________________________________ **Time to the Hour and Half-Hour**

The minute hand points to 12.

The hour hand points to 3.

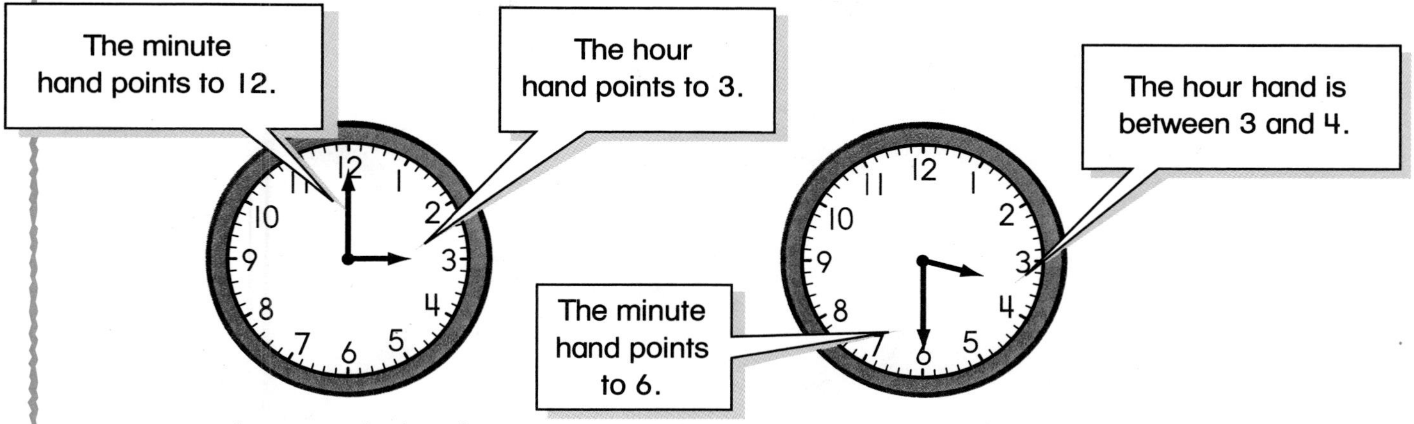

three o'clock

3:00

The hour hand is between 3 and 4.

The minute hand points to 6.

three-thirty

3:30

Word Bank

hour hand
minute hand

Write the time.

1. ___ : ___ ___ : ___

2. ___ : ___ ___ : ___

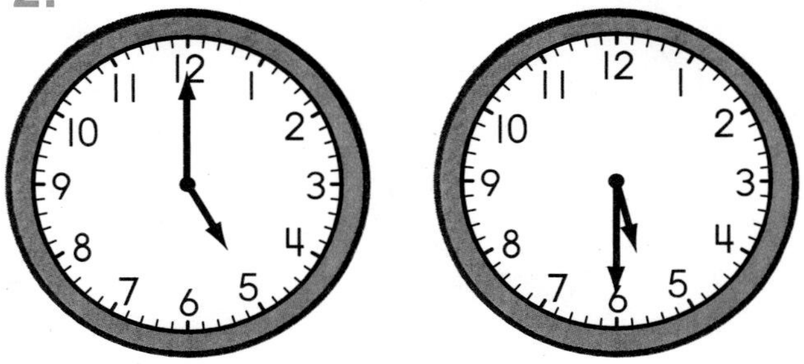

3. ___ : ___ ___ : ___

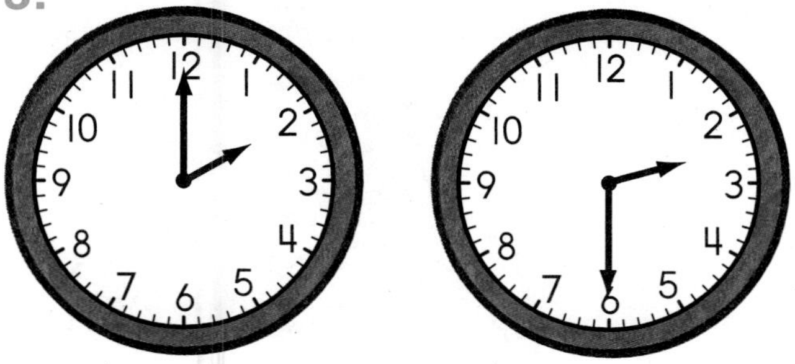

4. ___ : ___ ___ : ___

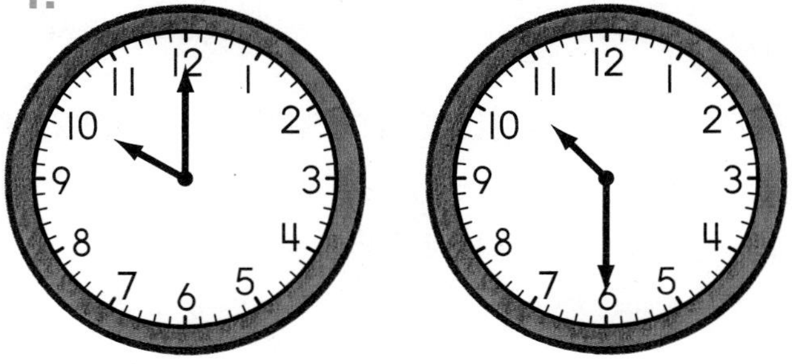

Home Connection Your child is telling and writing time to the hour and half-hour. Have your child tell you the times that are shown on the clocks above.

Draw the clock hands. Write the time.

1. four o'clock

4:00

seven-thirty

:

one o'clock

:

2. ten-thirty

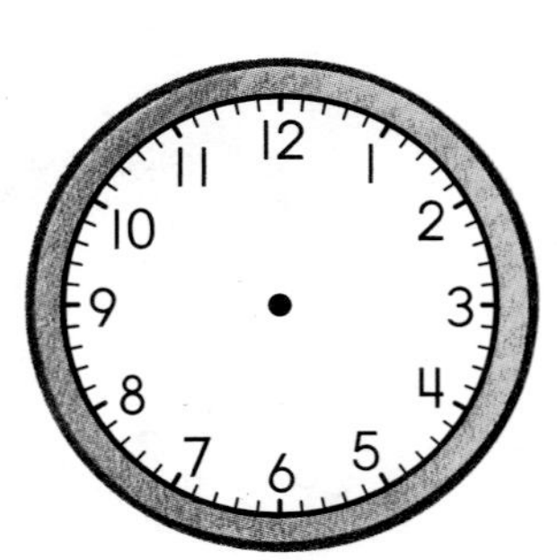

:

twelve o'clock

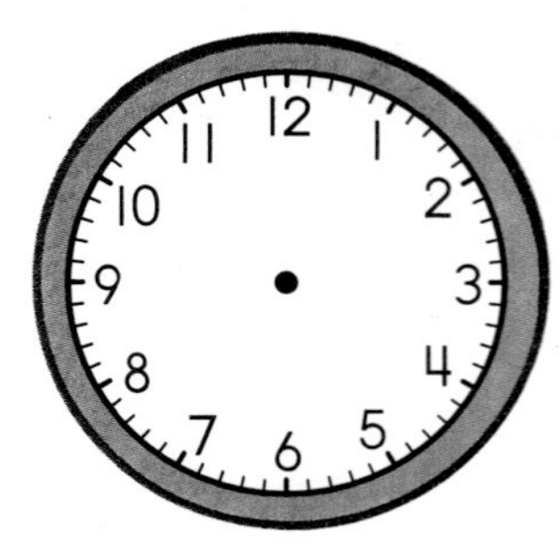

:

nine-thirty

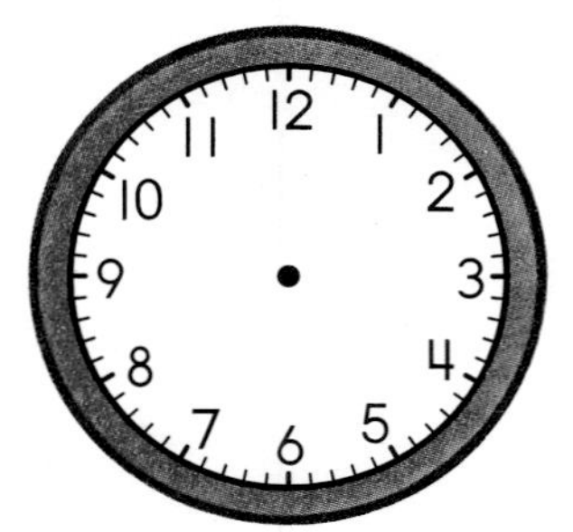

:

Problem Solving

Use the picture to solve. Write **early** or **late.**

3. Tanya arrived at 3:30.

Tanya was __________.

4. Marta arrived at 2:30.

Marta was __________.

Name____ **Time to Five Minutes**

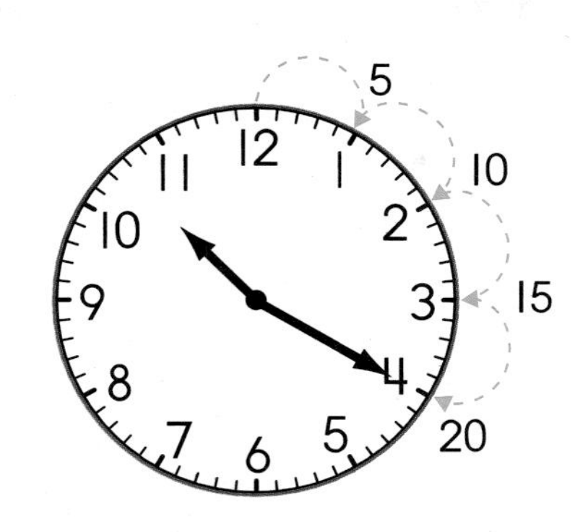

Count by 5s to find the minutes after the hour.

10:00

10:20

20 minutes after 10

Find the minutes after the hour.
Write the time.

1.

_____ minutes after _____

2.

_____ minutes after _____

3.

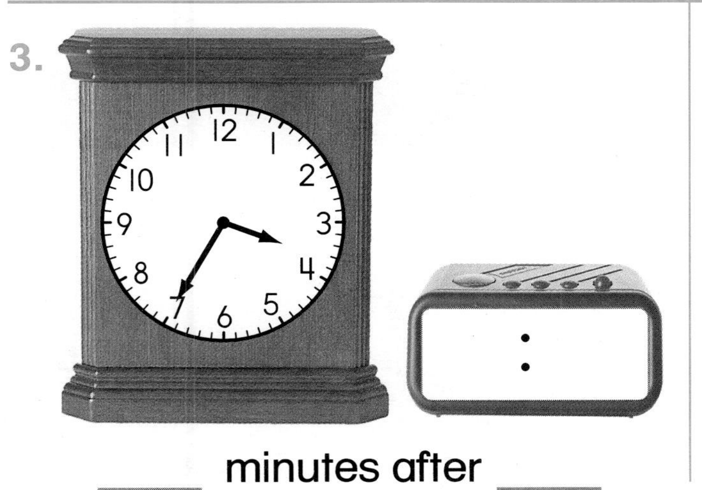

_____ minutes after _____

4.

_____ minutes after _____

Home Connection Your child is learning to tell time in five-minute intervals. Ask your child to tell time on different clocks around the house.

Draw the clock hands. Write the time.

1. 5 minutes after 8

2. 40 minutes after 5

3. 25 minutes after 12

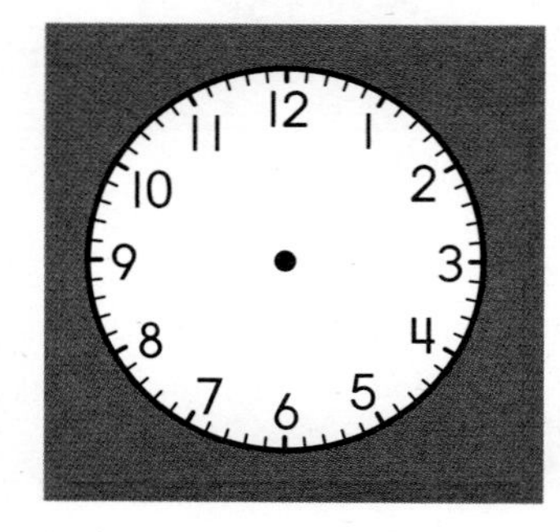

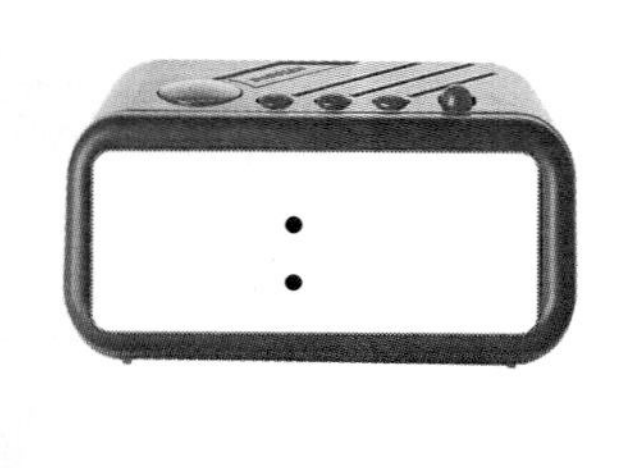

4. 20 minutes after 9

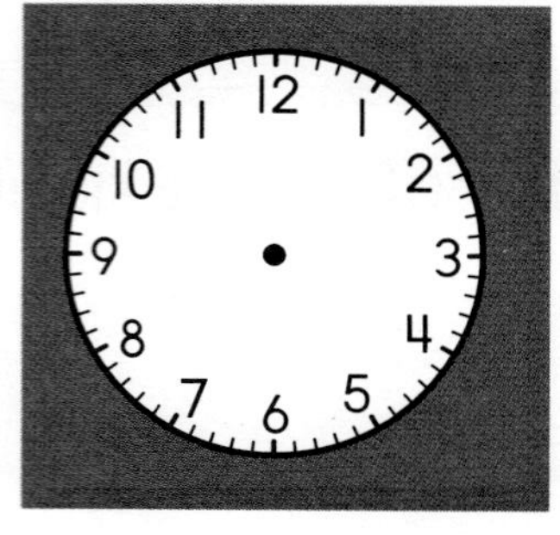

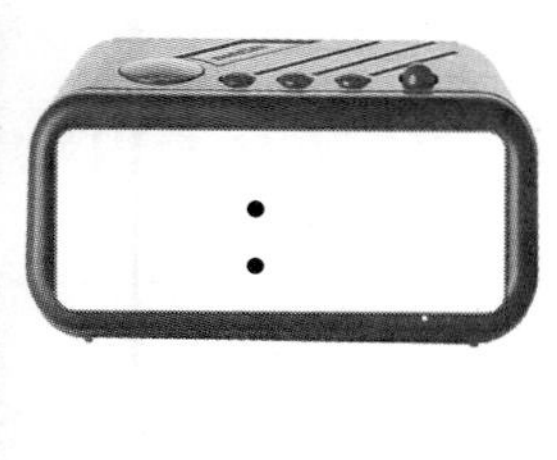

5. 55 minutes after 4

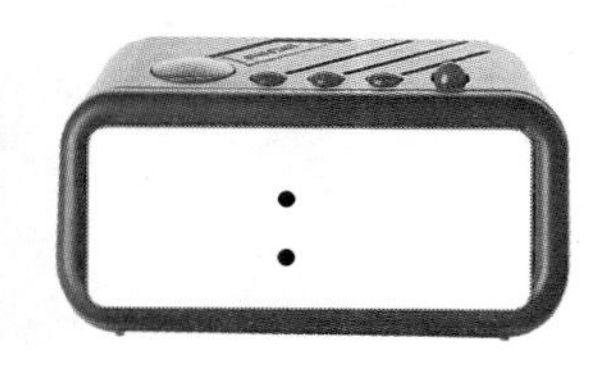

6. 35 minutes after 2

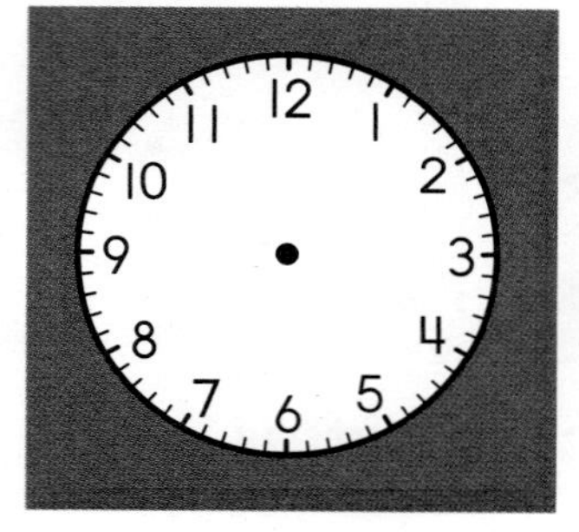

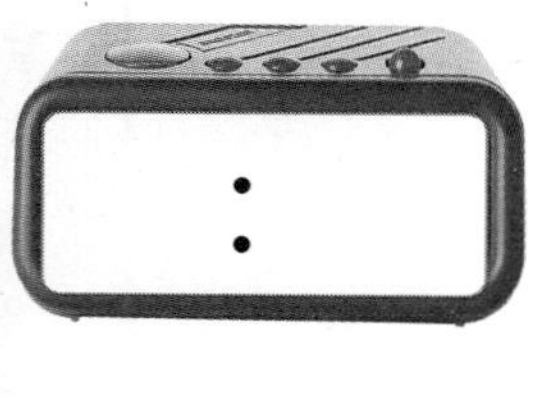

Problem Solving

About what time does each activity start?
Circle the better estimate. Use a clock if you like.

7. The relay race starts at 11:25.

about 11:00 about 11:30

8. The long jump starts at 1:55.

about 1:30 about 2:00

Name______________________________ **Time to the Quarter-Hour**

Races start every 15 minutes.

Draw the missing hands to complete each pattern.
Write each time. Use a clock if you like.

1.

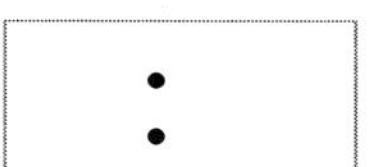

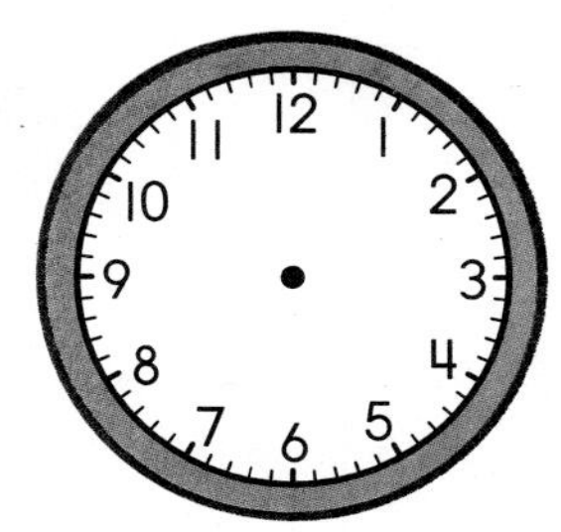

2.

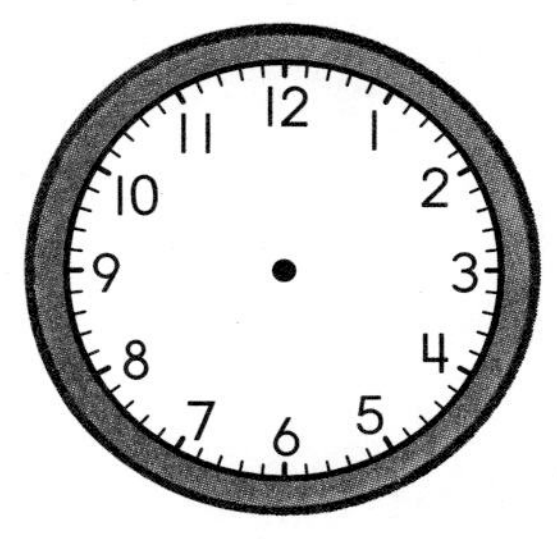

3.

Home Connection Your child is learning to tell time to the quarter-hour. Make up a pattern like the ones above. Challenge your child to complete the pattern.

Write the time. Look for a pattern.

1.

2.

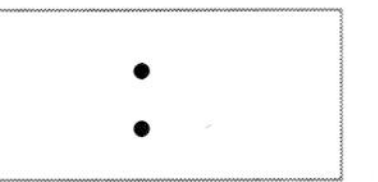 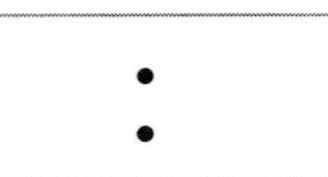

3.

Critical Thinking Corner

Visual Thinking

4. Look for a pattern. What time would the last clock show? Write the time and draw the hands.

   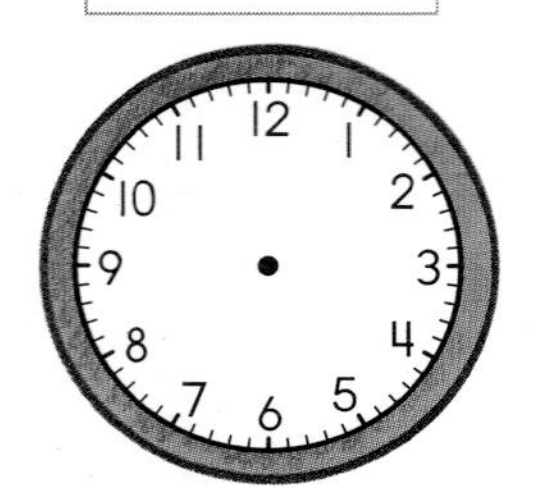

Name________________________________ **Telling Time**

Record the matching time.

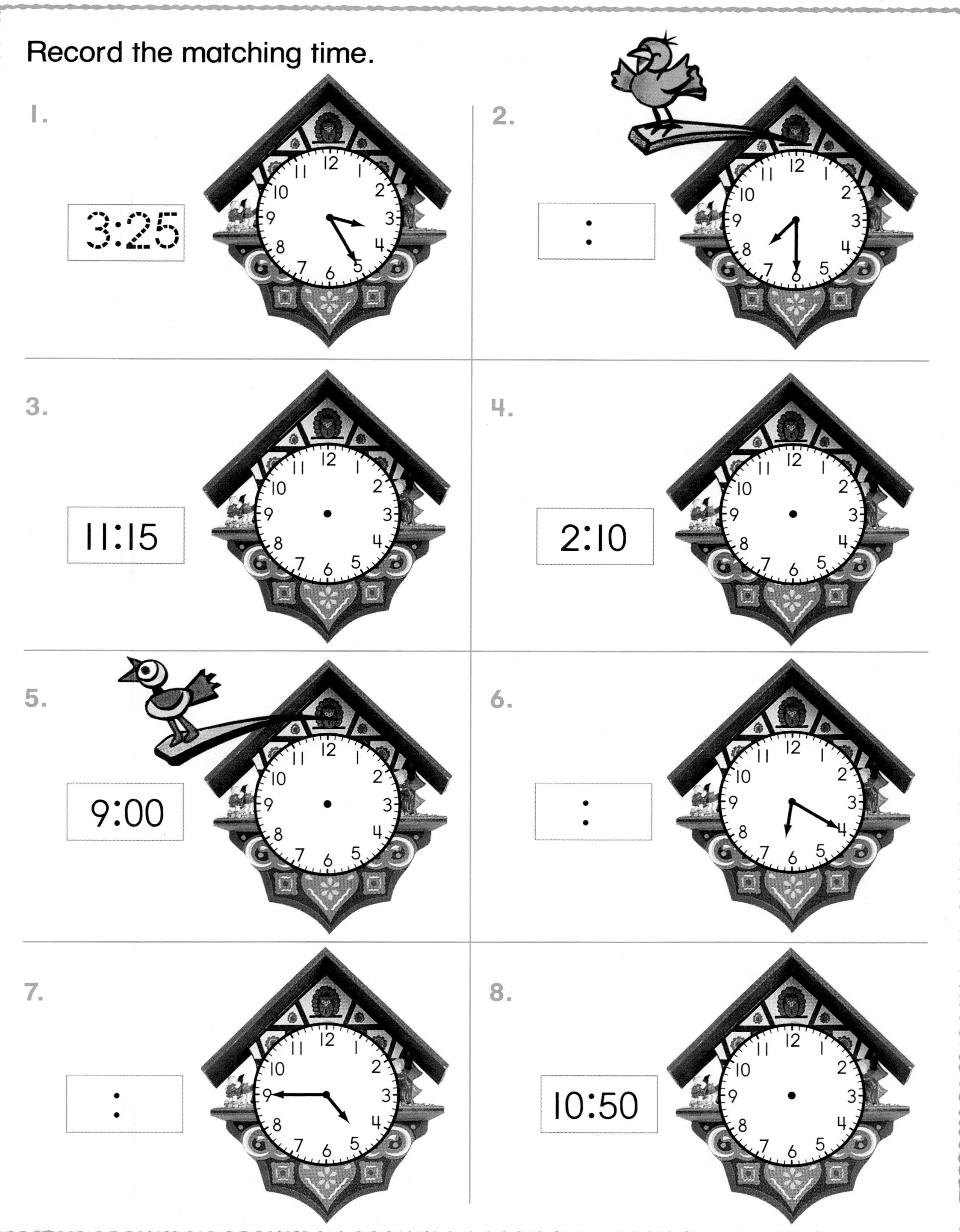

Home Connection Help your child practice telling time. Ask your child to tell the time at breakfast, dinner, or bedtime.

Record the matching time.

1.

2.

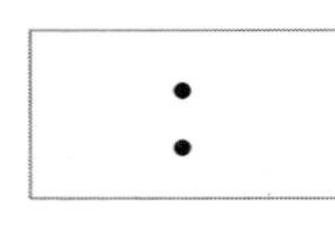

3.

4.

7:15

Checkpoint

1. Can you put on your socks in one minute? Circle **yes** or **no.**

yes no

2. Write the time.

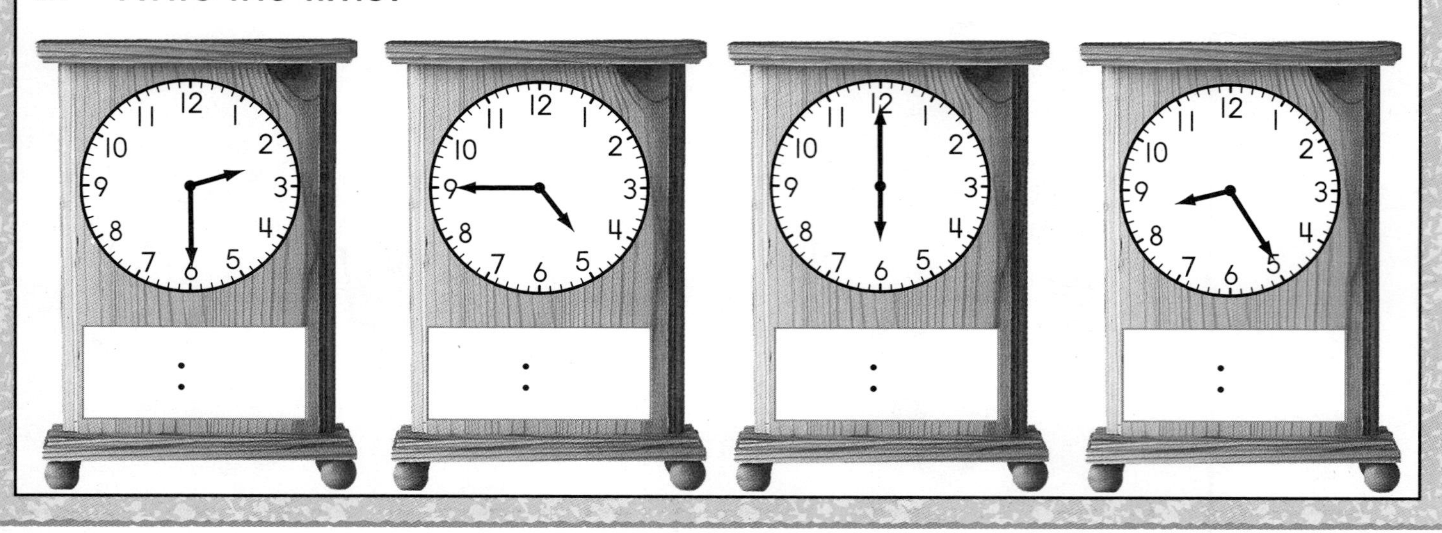

Name______________________________ **Elapsed Time**

The swim meet started at 10 o'clock. Now it is 12 o'clock. It took 2 hours.

10:00 12:00 2 hours

Write the start and end times.
Write how many hours passed.

1.

Watch a baseball game.

Start End

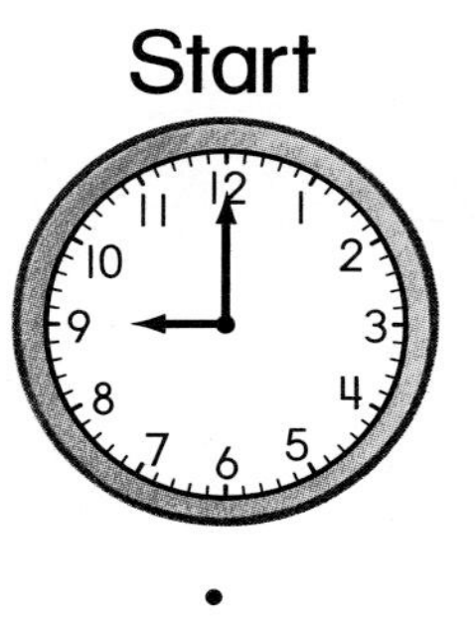

___:___ ___:___

____ hours

2.

Visit an amusement park.

Start End

___:___ ___:___

____ hours

3.

Go to the circus.

Start End

___:___ ___:___

____ hours

Home Connection You can help your child practice finding elapsed time by noting the time when he or she goes to bed and gets up.

Draw hands on each clock to show the later time.
Write the time. Use a clock if you like.

1. 

I hour and
30 minutes later

9:30

2. 

2 hours later

___:___

3. 

3 hours later

___:___

4. 

I hour and
30 minutes later

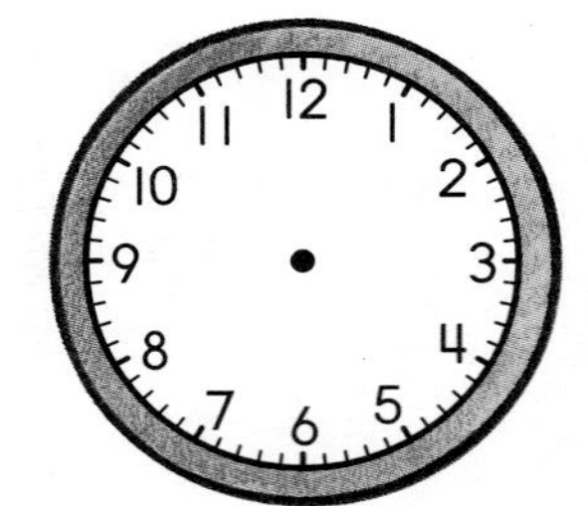

___:___

Problem Solving

Circle the correct time. Use a clock if you like.

5. School starts at 9:00.
It takes a half-hour to walk to school.
It takes I hour to get ready for school.
What time should I get up?

7:00 7:30 8:00

Name ______________________________

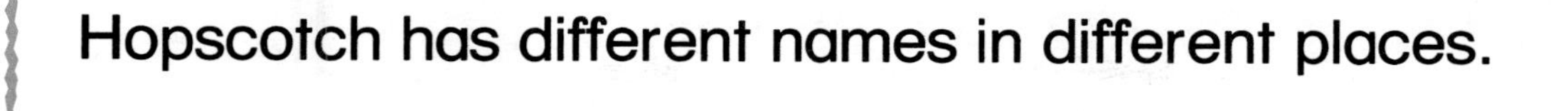

Hopscotch has different names in different places.

Hopscotch Festival

Game time	Name of the game	Country it is from
9:00 – 9:30	Gat Fei Gei	China
9:30 – 10:00	Chilly	India
10:00 – 10:30	La Thunkuña	Bolivia
10:30 – 11:00	Escargot	France
11:00 – 11:30	Ta Galagala	Nigeria

Use the schedule to complete each sentence.
Use a clock if you like.

1. Each game is ______ minutes long.
2. Hopscotch from China starts at _______.
3. Hopscotch from Nigeria ends at _______.
4. Hopscotch from India starts at _______.
5. From the start of the first game to the end of the second game is ______ hour.
6. The festival will last ______ hours and ______ minutes.

Home Connection Your child is learning to read a schedule. You can have your child practice by choosing a program from a TV schedule to watch together.

School Day Schedule	
Time	**Activity**
9:00 – 10:30	Reading
10:30 – 11:15	Language Arts
11:15 – 12:15	Math
12:15 – 1:00	Lunch
1:00 – 1:30	Music
1:30 – 2:15	Science
2:15 – 2:45	Art

Use the schedule.
Write the time and draw the clock hands.

1. Reading starts at

9:00

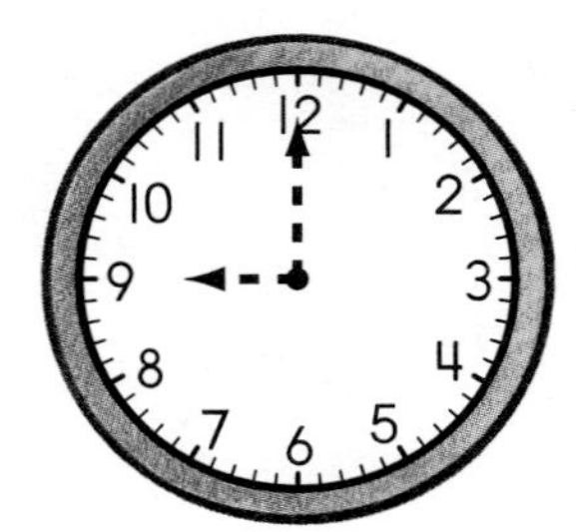

2. Math starts at

___ : ___

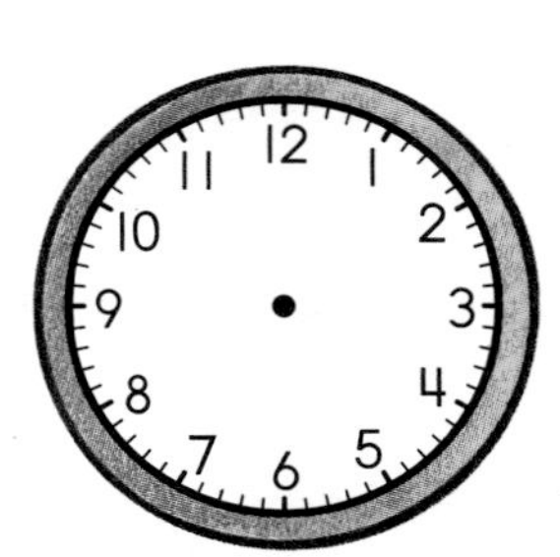

3. Science starts at

___ : ___

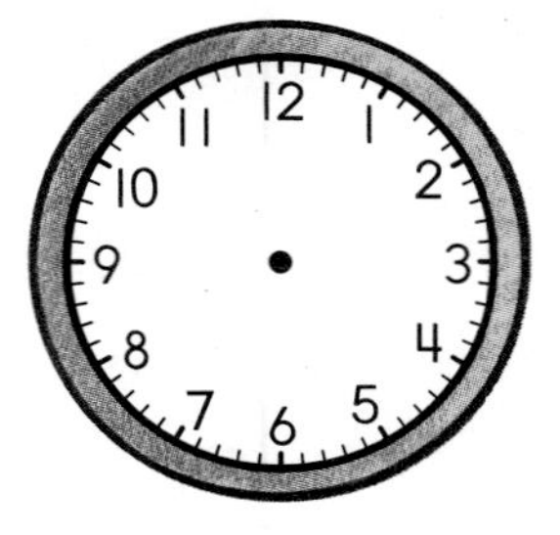

4. Art ends at

___ : ___

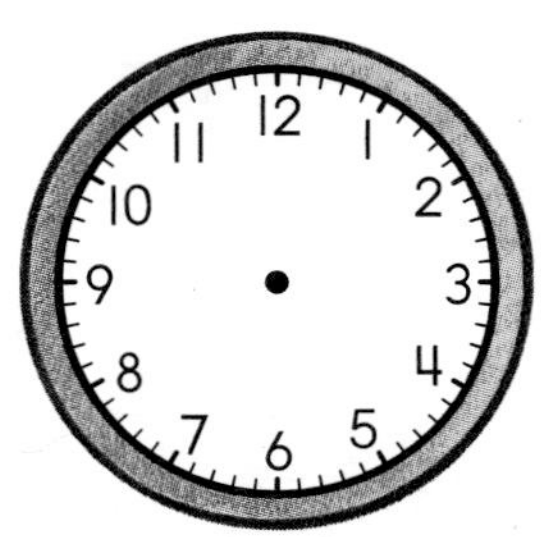

5. Lunch ends at

___ : ___

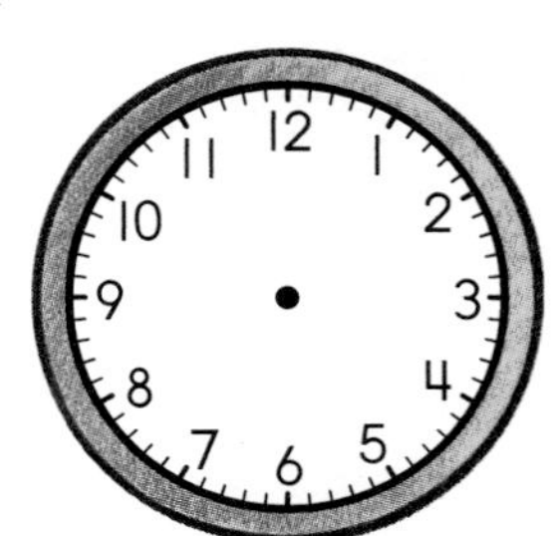

6. Math ends at

___ : ___

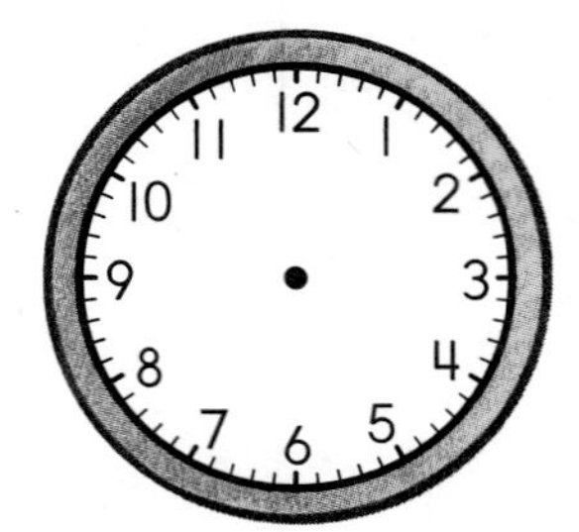

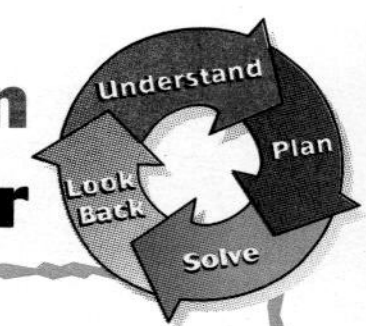

Name____

Complete the calendar for this month.

Word Bank
calendar

Month ________________ Year ______________

Sunday	Monday	Tuesday	Wednesday	Thursday	Friday	Saturday

Use the calendar to answer each question.

1. How many Sundays are in this month? ____________________
2. What is the date of the second Monday? ____________________
3. What day of the week is the 19th? ____________________
4. What is the date of the last Friday? ____________________
5. What day of the week is the 25th? ____________________
6. On what day of the week will the next month start? ____________
7. On what day of the week did last month end? ____________

Home Connection Look at a calendar with your child. Ask him or her to tell you today's date and what the date will be in three days. Have your child tell the date of any holidays or special occasions.

One Year

January

S	M	T	W	T	F	S
				1	2	3
4	5	6	7	8	9	10
11	12	13	14	15	16	17
18	19	20	21	22	23	24
25	26	27	28	29	30	31

February

S	M	T	W	T	F	S
1	2	3	4	5	6	7
8	9	10	11	12	13	14
15	16	17	18	19	20	21
22	23	24	25	26	27	28

March

S	M	T	W	T	F	S
1	2	3	4	5	6	7
8	9	10	11	12	13	14
15	16	17	18	19	20	21
22	23	24	25	26	27	28
29	30	31				

April

S	M	T	W	T	F	S
			1	2	3	4
5	6	7	8	9	10	11
12	13	14	15	16	17	18
19	20	21	22	23	24	25
26	27	28	29	30		

May

S	M	T	W	T	F	S
					1	2
3	4	5	6	7	8	9
10	11	12	13	14	15	16
17	18	19	20	21	22	23
24/31	25	26	27	28	29	30

June

S	M	T	W	T	F	S
	1	2	3	4	5	6
7	8	9	10	11	12	13
14	15	16	17	18	19	20
21	22	23	24	25	26	27
28	29	30				

July

S	M	T	W	T	F	S
			1	2	3	4
5	6	7	8	9	10	11
12	13	14	15	16	17	18
19	20	21	22	23	24	25
26	27	28	29	30	31	

August

S	M	T	W	T	F	S
						1
2	3	4	5	6	7	8
9	10	11	12	13	14	15
16	17	18	19	20	21	22
23/30	24/31	25	26	27	28	29

September

S	M	T	W	T	F	S
		1	2	3	4	5
6	7	8	9	10	11	12
13	14	15	16	17	18	19
20	21	22	23	24	25	26
27	28	29	30			

October

S	M	T	W	T	F	S
				1	2	3
4	5	6	7	8	9	10
11	12	13	14	15	16	17
18	19	20	21	22	23	24
25	26	27	28	29	30	31

November

S	M	T	W	T	F	S
1	2	3	4	5	6	7
8	9	10	11	12	13	14
15	16	17	18	19	20	21
22	23	24	25	26	27	28
29	30					

December

S	M	T	W	T	F	S
		1	2	3	4	5
6	7	8	9	10	11	12
13	14	15	16	17	18	19
20	21	22	23	24	25	26
27	28	29	30	31		

Use the calendar to complete each sentence.

1. The month right before June is ______________.
2. The month right after September is ______________.
3. Two months after July is ______________.
4. The fourth month of the year is ______________.

Critical Thinking Corner

Logical Thinking

5. Larry's birthday is in February.
   Rita's birthday is 2 months before Larry's.
   Rita's birthday is in ______________.

Name ______________________________ **Checkpoint**

About how long does each take?
Circle the more reasonable answer.

1. Brush your hair.

   5 minutes　　5 hours

2. Go shopping.

   2 hours　　2 days

Write the start and end times.
Write how many hours passed.

3. **Start**　　**End**

[:]　　[:]

_____ hours

4. **Start**　　**End**

[:]　　[:]

_____ hours

5. Draw hands on the clock to show the later time. Write the time.

   10:00　　2 hours and 30 minutes later

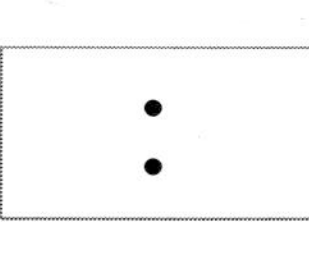

[:]

Use the schedule to solve. Write the time.

6. The nature walk starts at [:]

7. Story time ends at [:]

Camp Schedule	
Time	**Activity**
9:15–10:45	Arts and Crafts
10:45–11:30	Nature walk
11:30–12:00	Story time

Name________________________________ **Extra Practice**

Help Larry plan his morning.

Write the time for each activity.
Then write the numbers 1 to 5 to order the activities from earliest time to latest time.

Name________________________________ **Chapter Test**

Can you do the activity in one minute?
Circle **yes** or **no**.

1. Wash your hands.
   yes no

2. Rake leaves.
   yes no

Record the matching time.

3.

4.

5.

6.

Draw hands on the clock to show the later time. Write the time.

7.

4 hours later

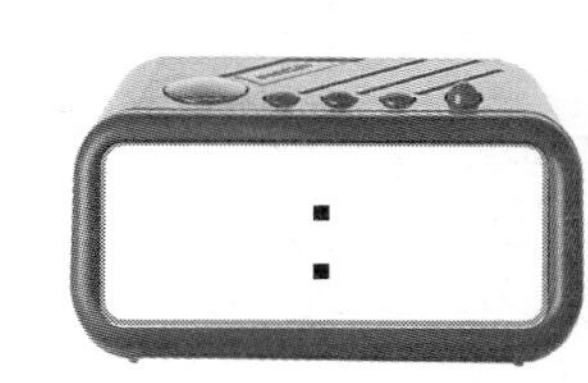

Use the calendar to answer the questions.

8. What is the date of the 4th Thursday?

____

9. What day of the week is the 13th?

____

March

S	M	T	W	T	F	S
			1	2	3	4
5	6	7	8	9	10	11
12	13	14	15	16	17	18
19	20	21	22	23	24	25
26	27	28	29	30	31	

Name______________________________ **Performance Assessment**

What You Need

spinner

1. Spin the spinner to find the hour.
2. Write the missing hour.
3. Then draw hands on the clock to show that time

---

1. ____:00

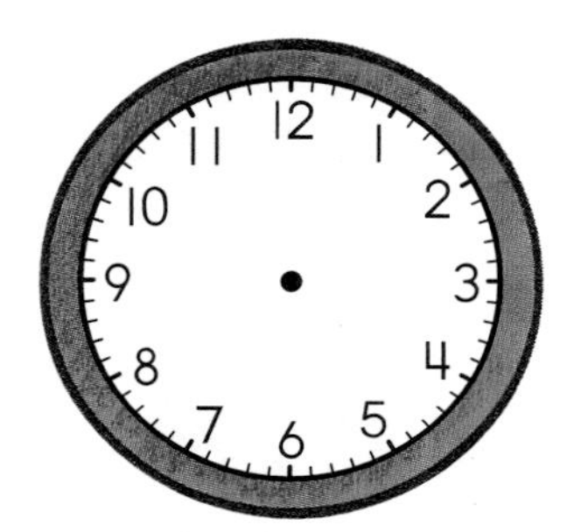

2. ____:15

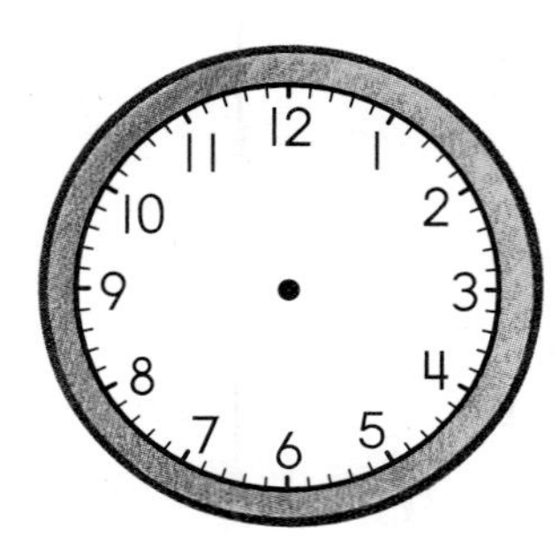

3. ____:10

4. ____:45

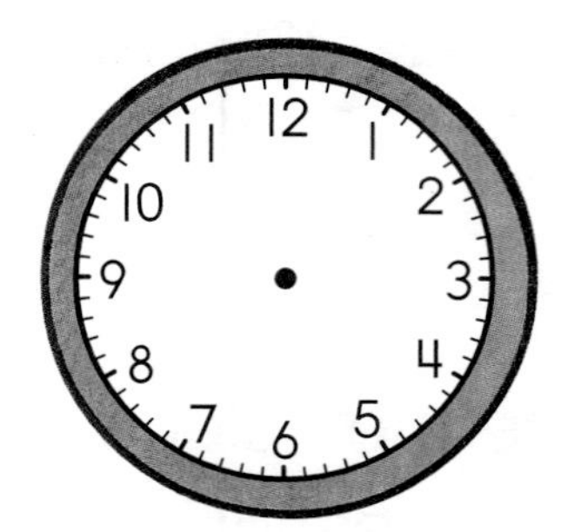

5. ____:25

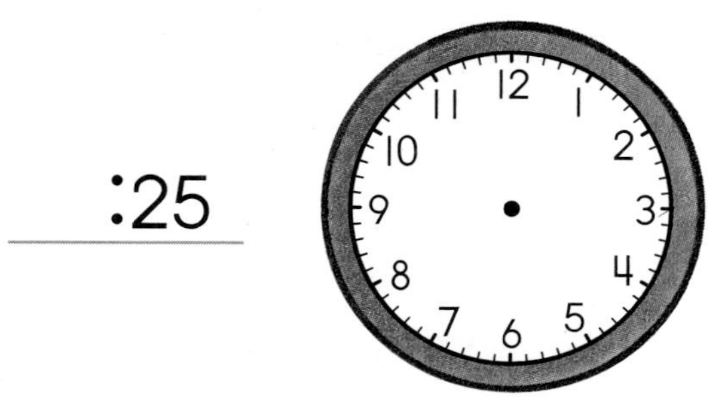

6. ____:30

Name____________________________

Roman Numerals	1	2	3	4	5	6	7	8	9	10	11	12
	I	II	III	IV	V	VI	VII	VIII	IX	X	XI	XII

10:00

10:00

Fill in the missing Roman numerals.
Write the time.

Name________________________________ **Time and the MathProcessor™**

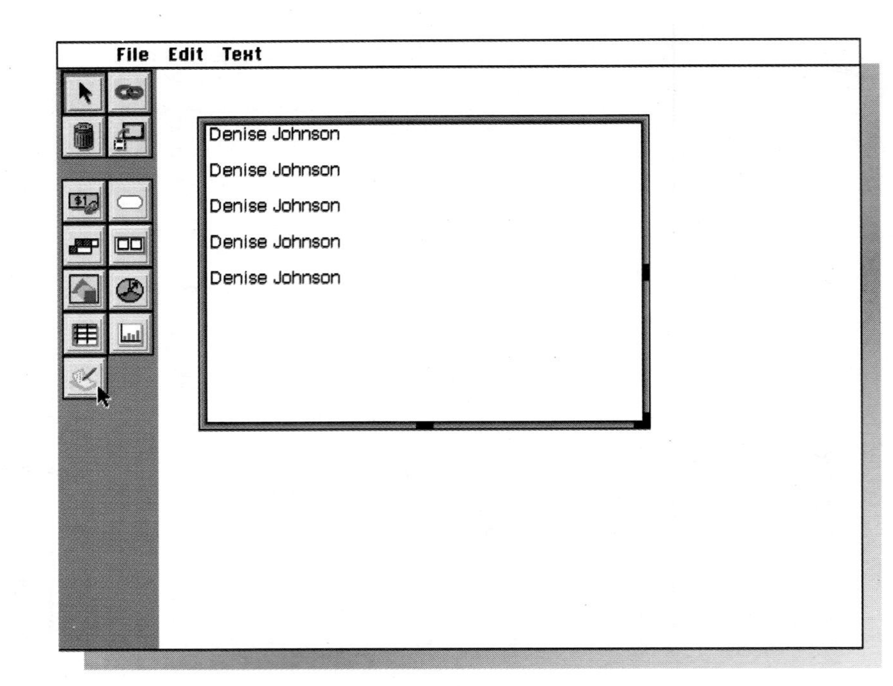

Use the MathProcessor.
Take turns with a partner.

1. Click on the **writing button** to get a writing space.

2. Click-and-drag the **writing space** to make it larger.

3. Look at the activities below.
Can you do each one in a minute?
Try to do each one as your partner counts to 60 slowly.

	Activities
1.	Type your name 5 times.
2.	Type the alphabet.
3.	Type the numbers 1 to 50.
	(Don't forget to put a space between each number.)
4.	Type the last sentence on this page.

Measurement

Chen's Dragon

written by Joyce Mallery

illustrated by Chi Chung • *photographs by* Mike Peters

This Math Storybook belongs to

____

Chen was excited to see Grandfather. He was also a little worried. Grandfather said he was giving Chen a dragon for his birthday.

One by one, Grandfather took many supplies out of the bag he brought—string, tape, scissors, markers, glue, paint, paper, and a ruler. Chen didn't see a dragon.

"What are we going to do with all of these things, Grandfather?" asked Chen.

"We're going to make something special for your birthday," said Grandfather.

Grandfather showed Chen how to use the ruler to measure the paper. They measured up, down, and across. They measured in inches. They measured in feet.

Chen thought that Grandfather had probably forgotten about the dragon.

Grandfather showed Chen how to cut the paper into strips that were nine inches wide. He asked Chen to tape the strips together.

Then Grandfather picked up the paint and began drawing. Chen wondered what Grandfather was doing now.

Finally, Grandfather was finished.

"You fooled me, Grandfather!" said Chen. "You really did give me a dragon for my birthday. It's a dragon kite with a very long tail."

"The tail is as long as you are old," said Grandfather. "Happy 8th birthday, Chen!"

Here is a dragon kite for you.
Talk about how to measure each side.
Then make a dragon face and color it.
www.sbgmath.com
G

A Note to the Family

Here are some learning ideas you can share with your child.

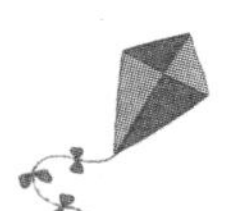

Enjoy *Chen's Dragon* Together

- Read the story with your child. Ask him or her to identify the measuring tool that was used. Talk about other things you could measure with a ruler. Encourage your child to think of other measuring tools around your home, such as a yardstick, a scale, or a measuring cup. Talk about what they are used for.
- Look at the last page of the story. Ask your child to show you how she or he could measure each side of the dragon kite. You may wish to give your child an inch ruler to measure each side.

At-Home Activities

- Parts of the human body were some of the earliest units of measure. Investigate using your feet as a unit of measure. Choose a room in your home to measure, such as the kitchen. Begin by making a guess of the length of the room, using your foot as the unit of measure. Then measure, using a heel-to-toe process. Ask your child to do the same, and talk about why the measurements are different.

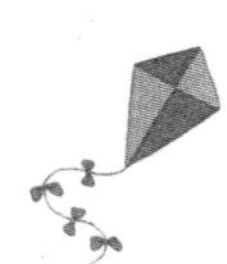

Read More About It!

To read more books about kites and measurement, look for the following books in your library.

- *Kites* by Susan Wardle (Price Stern Sloan, 1996)
- *Length* by Henry Pluckrose (Franklin Watts, 1988)
- *How Big Is a Foot?* by Rolf Myller (Dell, 1991)

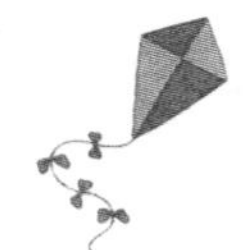

Visit Our Web Site!

www.sbgmath.com

Name________________________________

Word Bank
length
height

Find objects like the ones shown.
Estimate the length or height of each in cubes.
Then use cubes to measure.

	Estimate	Measure
1. scissors	about _____ cubes	about _____ cubes
2. pencil	about _____ cubes	about _____ cubes
3. book	about _____ cubes	about _____ cubes
4. eraser	about _____ cubes	about _____ cubes
5. crayon	about _____ cubes	about _____ cubes

Home Connection Your child is learning how to measure. Ask your child to use objects such as blocks or paper clips to measure the length or height of items around the home.

How many cubes long is each pencil? Estimate.
Then use cubes to measure.

1.

estimate: about _____ cubes measure: about _____ cubes

2.

estimate: about _____ cubes measure: about _____ cubes

3.

estimate: about _____ cubes measure: about _____ cubes

4.

estimate: about _____ cubes measure: about _____ cubes

5.

estimate: about _____ cubes measure: about _____ cubes

6.

estimate: about _____ cubes measure: about _____ cubes

Name______________________________ **Inches and Feet**

This paper clip is about 1 inch long.
There are 12 inches in 1 foot.

Word Bank

inch (in.)
foot (ft)

Find objects like the ones shown.
Work with a partner. Estimate.
Then use a ruler to measure.

	Estimate	**Measure**
1. crayon	about _____ inches	about _____ inches
2. eraser	about _____ inches	about _____ inches
3. marker	about _____ inches	about _____ inches
4. sneaker	about _____ inches	about _____ inches

Home Connection Your child is learning to measure in inches and feet. Help your child use a ruler to measure household items in either inches or feet.

About how many inches or feet would the real one be?
Circle the better estimate.

Remember,
12 in. = 1 ft

1.

man

2 feet tall

6 feet tall

2.

hammer

11 inches long

1 inch long

3.

nail

2 inches long

12 inches long

4.

workbench

50 feet long

5 feet long

5.

toolbox

2 feet long

20 feet long

6.

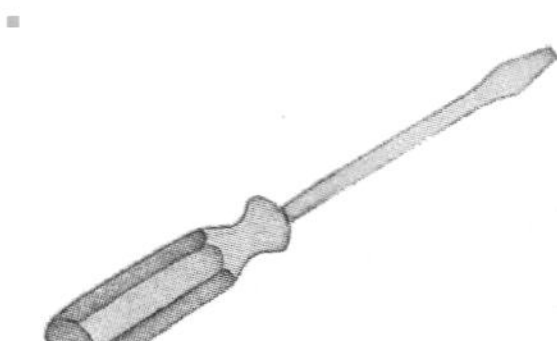

screwdriver

1 inch long

10 inches long

Problem Solving

Solve.

7. Patti had a stick one foot long. She cut off a piece five inches long for her birdhouse. How long is the stick now?

_____ inches

Name____ **Inches, Feet, and Yards**

The door is 3 feet wide. 3 feet is the same as 1 yard.

Word Bank
yard (yd)

Would you measure the real thing in inches, feet, or yards? Circle the best unit.

1. 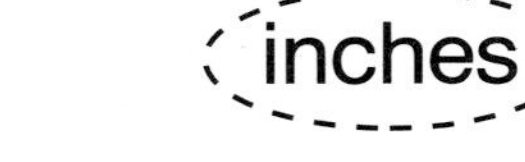
length of a tube
inches (circled)
feet
yards

2. 
height of a girl
inches
feet
yards

3. 
length of a paint box
inches
feet
yards

4. 
height of an easel
inches
feet
yards

5. 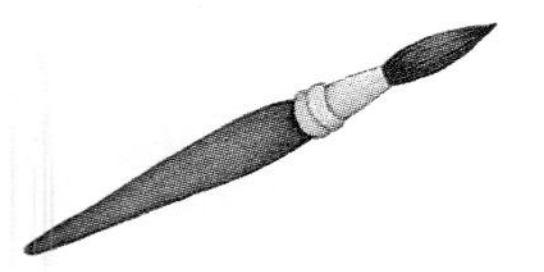
length of a brush
inches
feet
yards

6. 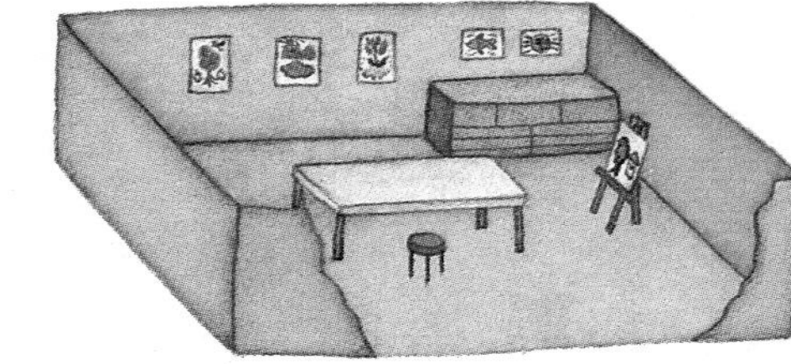
length of a room
inches
feet
yards

Home Connection Your child is learning to choose the best unit of measure. Point out things at home. Ask your child if it is easier to measure these things in inches, feet, or yards.

About how long or tall would the real object be?
Circle the best estimate.

1. height of a door

7 inches

7 feet

7 yards

2. length of a marker

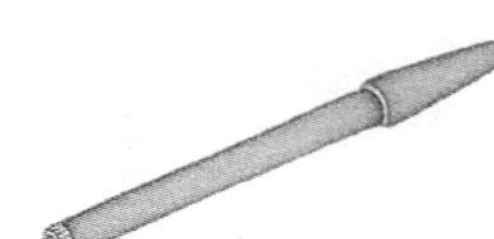

5 inches

5 feet

5 yards

3. length of a table

1 inch

1 foot

1 yard

4. height of a bookcase

6 inches

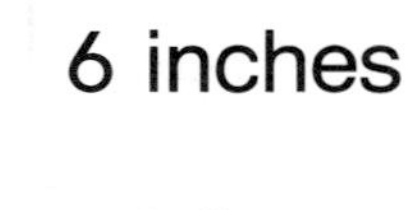

6 feet

6 yards

5. length of a large clip

2 inches

2 feet

2 yards

6. length of a bus

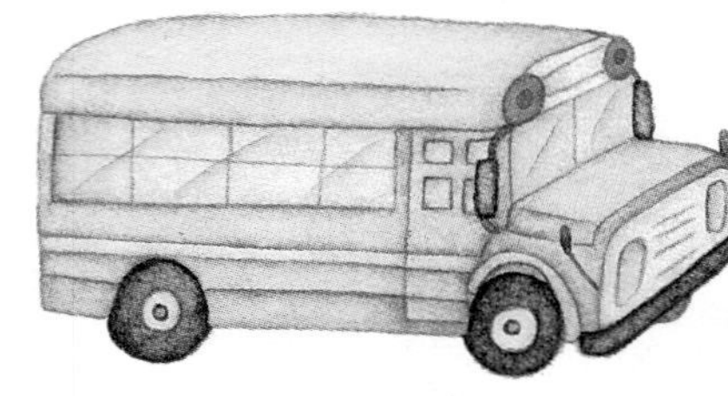

4 inches

4 feet

4 yards

Critical Thinking Corner

Number Sense

7. Cindy and Mike each measured the bookcase.
Cindy's measure was 2 yards.
Mike's measure was 6 feet.
Could they both be correct?
Tell why or why not.

Journal Idea

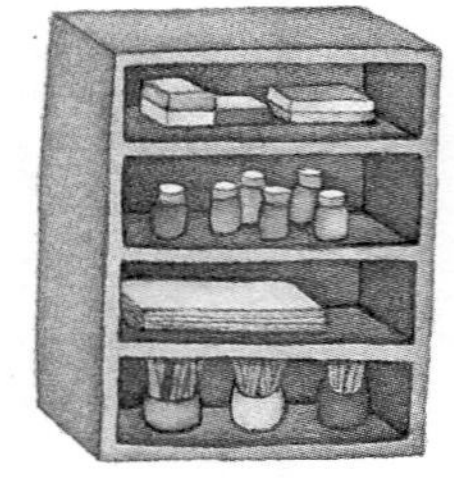

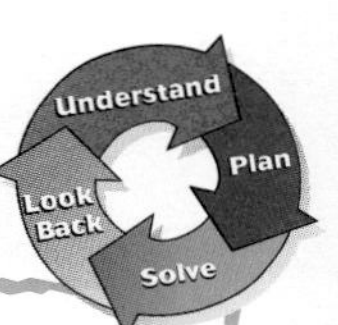

Name______________________________

How can you measure a path that is not straight?

You can measure each part with a ruler.

Then add the parts.

1 inch + 1 inch = 2 inches

You can measure with string.

Then measure the string with a ruler.

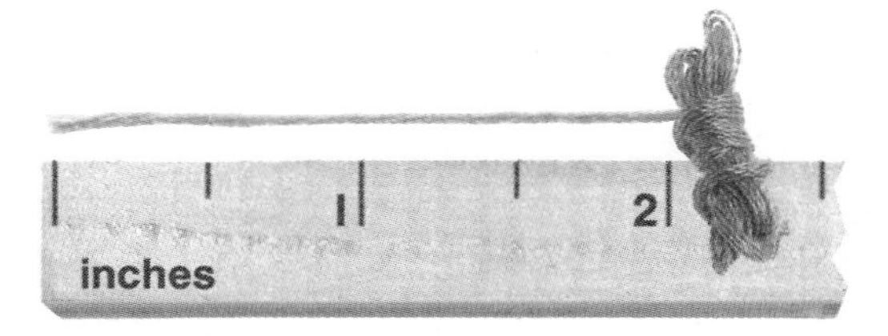

Estimate the length of each path.
Then measure.

1.

estimate: about _____ inches

measure: about _____ inches

2.

estimate: about _____ inches

measure: about _____ inches

3.

estimate: about _____ inches

measure: about _____ inches

Home Connection Your child is learning to estimate and measure a path that is not straight. Create a path at home and have your child estimate and measure to the nearest inch or foot.

Estimate the length of each path.
Then measure.

1.

estimate: about _____ inches

measure: about _____ inches

2.

estimate: about _____ inches

measure: about _____ inches

3.

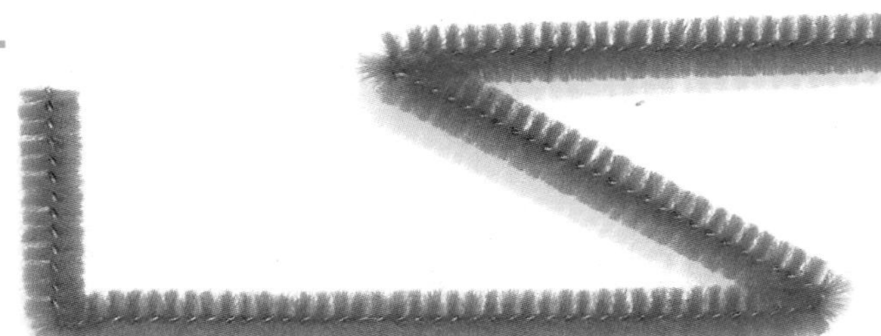

estimate: about _____ inches

measure: about _____ inches

Critical Thinking Corner

Visual Thinking

Which path is longer?

4. Estimate. Write **A** or **B**.

_____

5. Measure to check.

A _____ inches **B** _____ inches

A

B

Name________________________________

The glue stick is about 10 centimeters long. That's 1 decimeter.
The table is about 1 meter long.
100 centimeters = 1 meter

Word Bank
centimeter (cm)
decimeter (dm)
meter (m)

Find objects like the ones shown. Estimate. Then use a ruler to measure.

	Estimate	**Measure**
1. eraser	about ____ cm	about ____ cm
2. marker	about ____ cm	about ____ cm
3. chalk	about ____ cm	about ____ cm
4. chalkboard	about ____ m	about ____ m

Home Connection Your child is learning to measure length in centimeters. Ask your child to find things in your home that are about one centimeter long and about one meter long.

About how long or tall would the real object be? Circle the better estimate.

Remember,
cm = centimeters
m = meters

1. 

15 cm (circled)

15 m

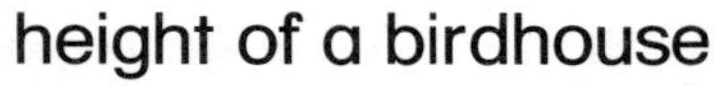

height of a birdhouse

2. 

2 cm

2 m

length of a picnic table

3. 

1 cm

1 m

height of a doghouse

4. 

40 cm

40 m

length of a swing seat

5. 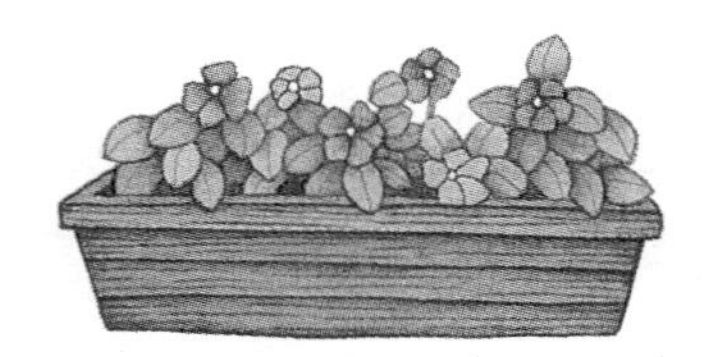

50 cm

50 m

length of a flower box

6. 

3 cm

3 m

length of a fence

Critical Thinking Corner

Estimation

7. Find objects that you think are about 1 decimeter long or tall. Use a ruler to check. Tell about what you find.

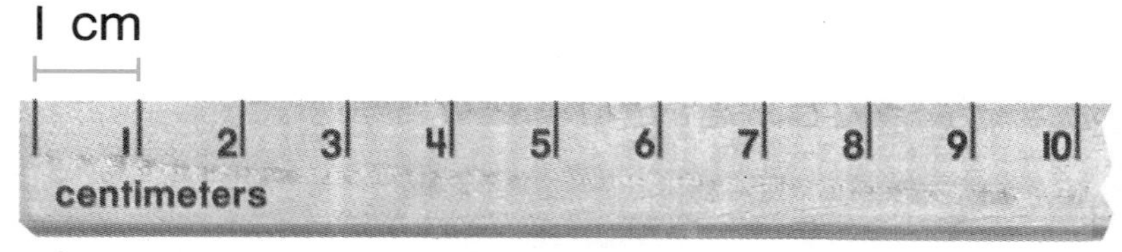

10 centimeters = 1 decimeter

Name______________________________________ **Understanding Weight**

The marker weighs less than 10 cubes.

Word Bank
weight

Find objects like the ones shown.
Does each object weigh **more** or **less** than 10 cubes?
Circle your estimate. Then use a scale to measure.

	Estimate	**Measure**
1. book	more less	more less
2. eraser	more less	more less
3. ruler	more less	more less
4. box of crayons	more less	more less

Home Connection Your child is learning about weight. Hand your child a small object and then challenge him or her to find other things that are heavier, lighter, and about the same weight.

What object would make the scale look like this? Circle the best choice.

1.

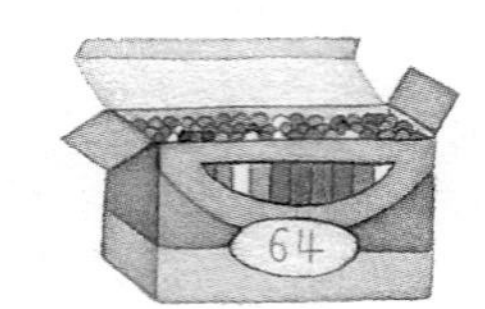

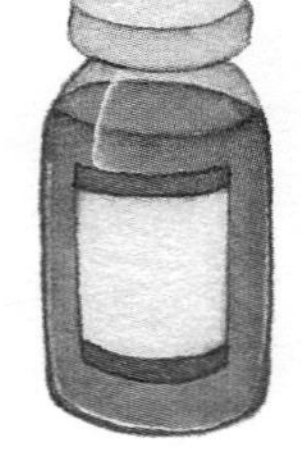

2.

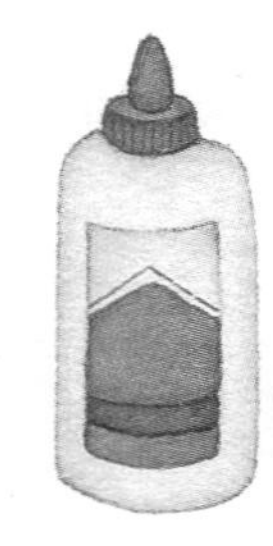

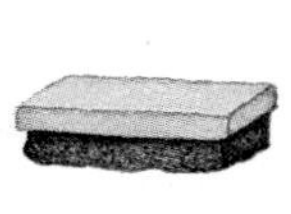

3.

Problem Solving

4. What is wrong with this picture? Draw or write to show how the scale should look.

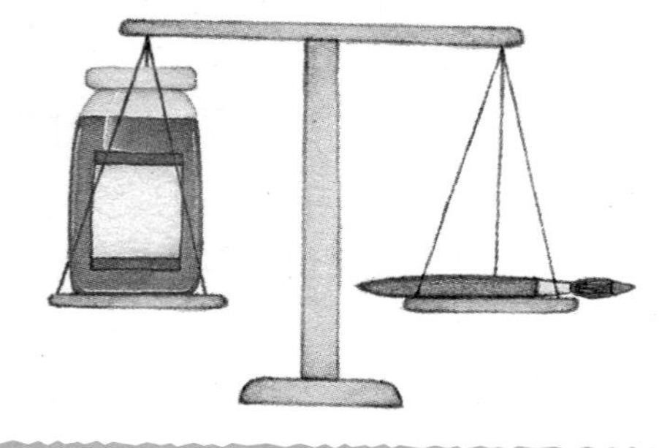

Name______________________________________ **Pounds**

less than 1 pound

about 1 pound

more than 1 pound

Word Bank
pound (lb)

Does it weigh more or less than 1 pound?
Write **more** or **less.**

1.

less

2.
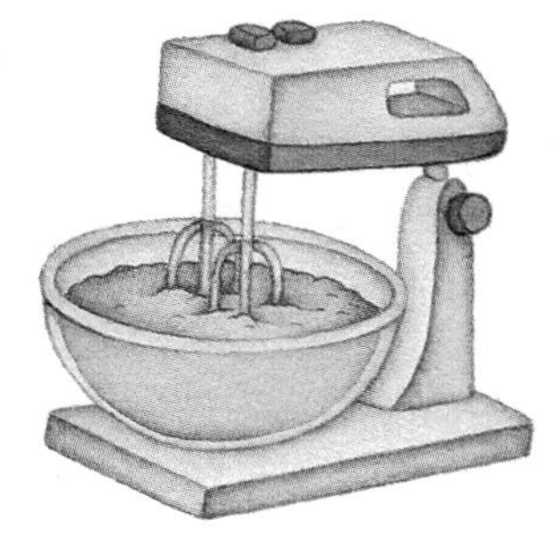
____

3.

____

4.
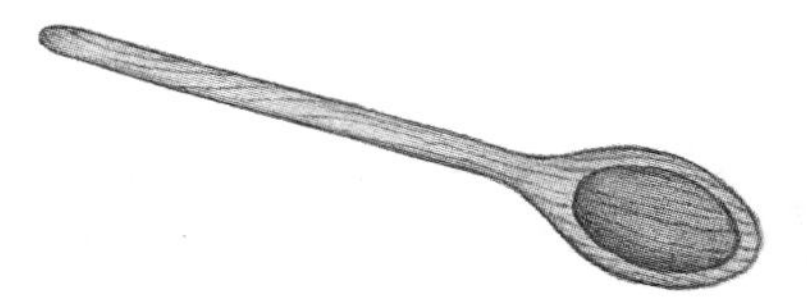
____

5.

____

6.

____

Home Connection Your child is learning to measure in pounds. Help your child identify objects in the kitchen that are more than, less than, or about 1 pound.

Read each scale to find the weight.
Write the weight to the nearest pound.

1. 

2 pounds

2. 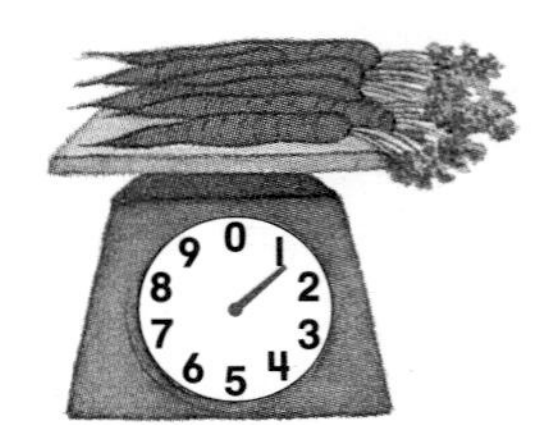

_____ pound

3. 

_____ pounds

4. 

_____ pounds

5. 

_____ pounds

6. 

_____ pounds

7. 

_____ pounds

8. 

_____ pounds

9. 

_____ pounds

10. Draw something that weighs about 1 pound.

Name______________________________________

A sheet of paper weighs about 1 gram.

less than
I kilogram

about
I kilogram

more than
I kilogram

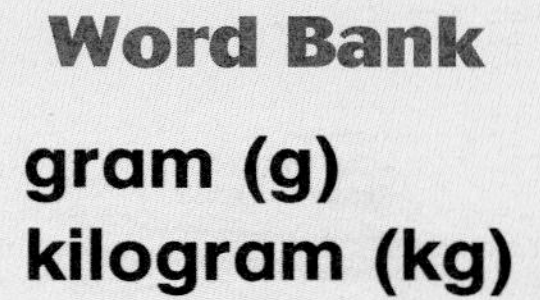
Word Bank
gram (g)
kilogram (kg)

Does each weigh more or less than I kilogram?
Write **more** or **less**.

1.

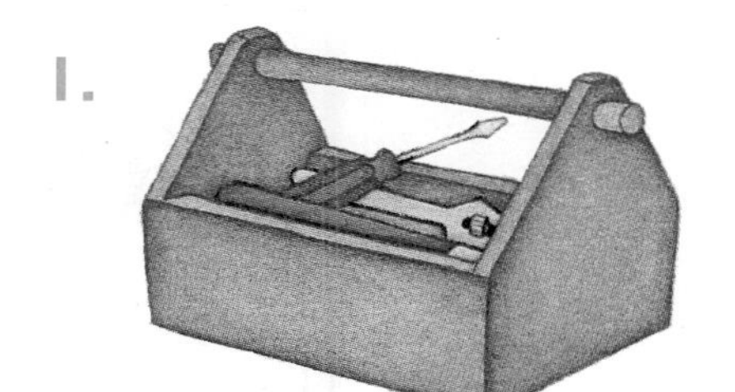

2.

____

3.

____

4.

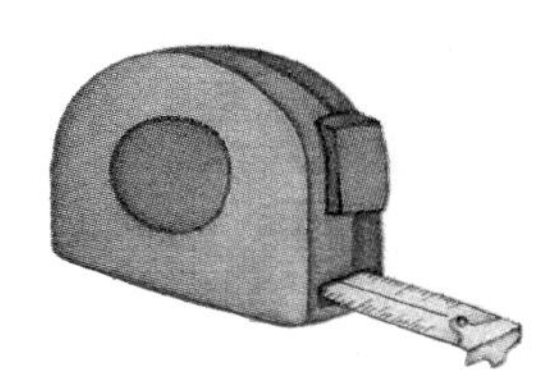

____

5.

____

6.

____

Home Connection Your child is learning to measure in grams and kilograms. Ask your child to find objects at home that weigh more than, less than, or about I kilogram.

About how much would the real object weigh?
Circle the better estimate.

1. 

(7 grams)

7 kilograms

2. 

30 grams

30 kilograms

3. 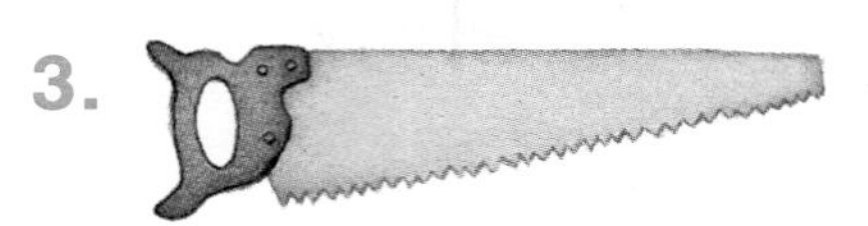

50 grams

50 kilograms

4. 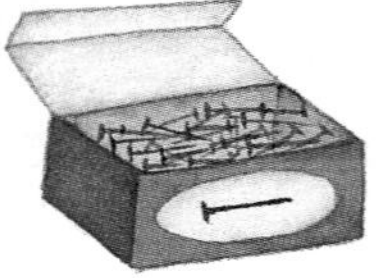

1 gram

1 kilogram

5. 

20 grams

20 kilograms

6. 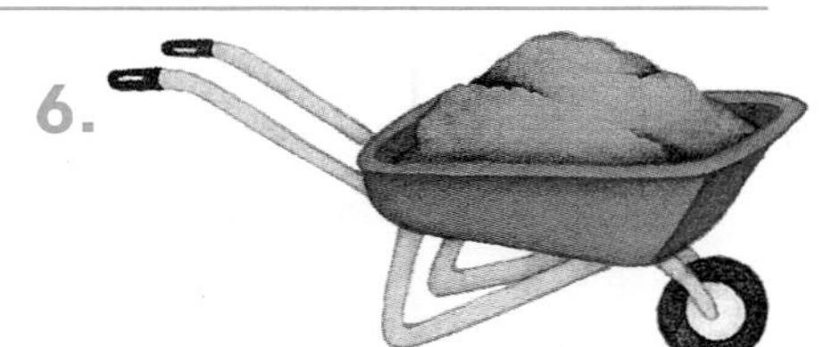

50 grams

50 kilograms

Checkpoint

About how long or tall would the real object be?
Circle the better estimate.

1. 

4 inches

4 feet

4 yards

2. 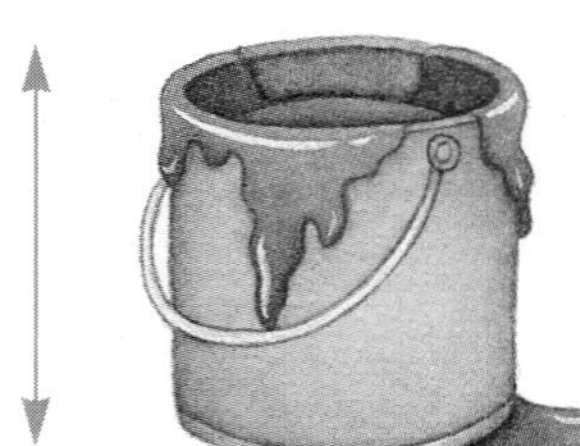

10 inches

10 feet

10 yards

3. 

6 cm

6 m

4. 

10 cm

10 m

Name________________________________

Find objects like the ones shown.
Does each object hold **more** or **less** than a paper cup?
Circle your estimate. Then use a cup and beans to measure.

	Estimate	Measure
1. jar	more less	more less
2 wastebasket	more less	more less
3. milk carton	more less	more less
4. can	more less	more less
5. Draw your own.	more less	more less

Home Connection Your child is learning about capacity. Give your child two containers of different sizes and shapes. Help him or her determine which holds more by pouring water or rice from one to the other.

Circle the objects that hold about the same.

1.

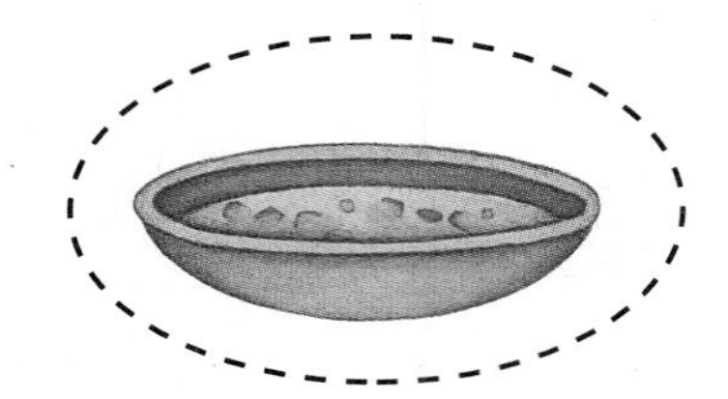

2.

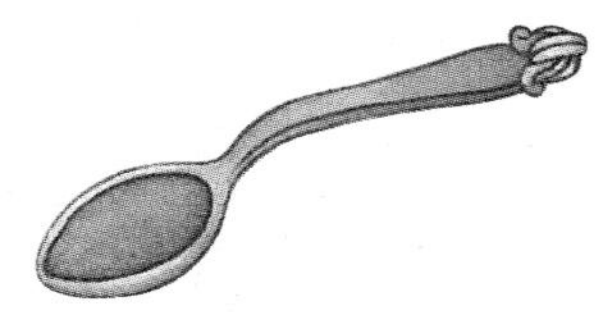

3.

4.

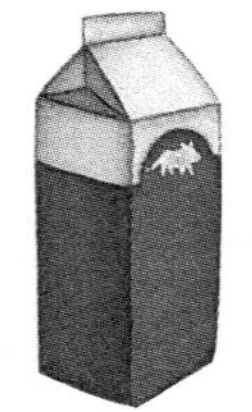
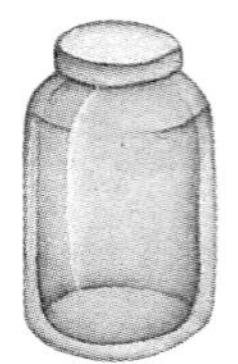

5.

Problem Solving

6. How many cubes are there in all?
Use cubes if you like.

_____ cubes

Name______________________________

2 cups fill 1 pint.

4 cups or 2 pints fill 1 quart.

Word Bank

cup (c)
pint (pt)
quart (qt)

Circle the containers you can fill.

1.

1 pint

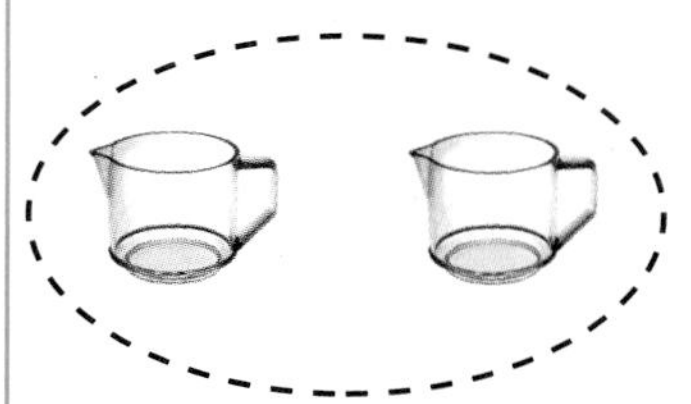

2.

1 quart

3.

1 quart

4.

2 quarts

Home Connection Your child is learning to recognize the relative sizes of cups, pints, and quarts. Ask your child to compare cup, pint, and quart containers in your home or at the grocery store.

Complete the chart.
Write how many cups, pints, or quarts.

	Cups	Pints	Quarts
1.	4	2	1
2.	____	____	2
3.	12	____	____
4.	____	8	____
5.	____	____	5

Problem Solving

=

2 quarts fill a half gallon.

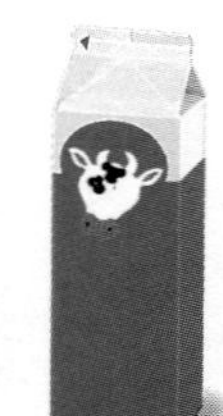

=

4 quarts fill a gallon.

Use the pictures to solve. Write **more** or **less**.

6. 5 quarts is __________ than 1 gallon.

7. 3 quarts is __________ than 1 gallon.

8. 3 quarts is __________ than a half gallon.

Name____

less than 1 liter

about 1 liter

more than 1 liter

Word Bank
liter (L)

Does it hold more or less than 1 liter?
Write **more** or **less**.

1.

less

2.

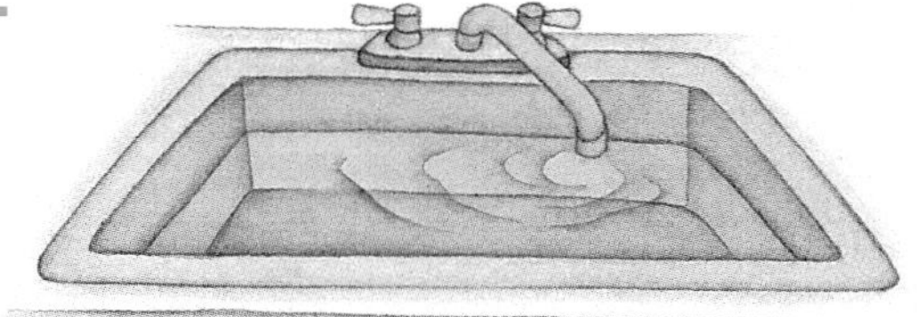

____

3.

____

4.

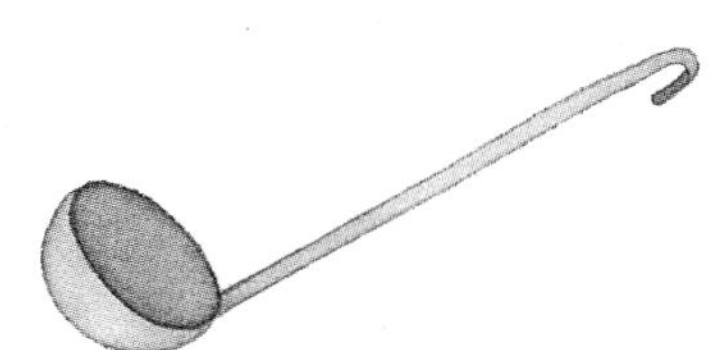

____

5.

____

6.

____

Home Connection Your child is learning about liters. Ask your child to find containers that hold more than, less than, or about 1 liter.

About how many liters does it hold?
Circle the better estimate.

1.

30 liters

2.

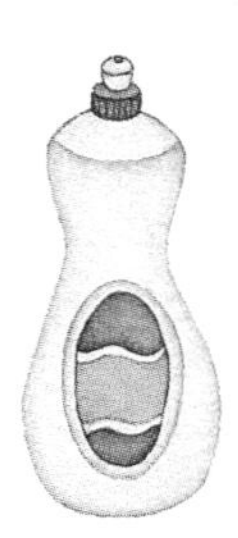

1 liter

60 liters

3.

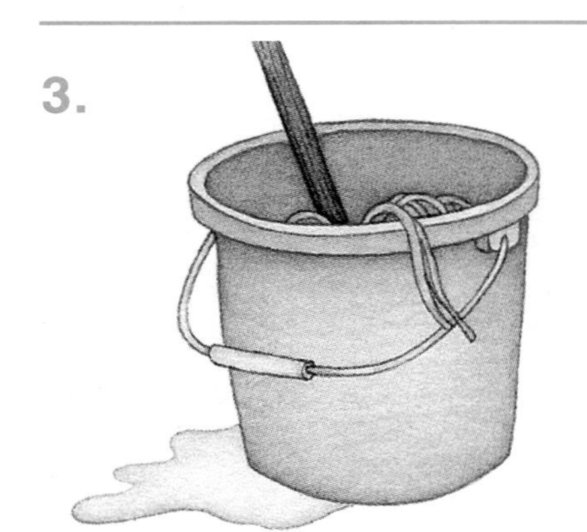

1 liter

10 liters

4.

5 liters

50 liters

5.

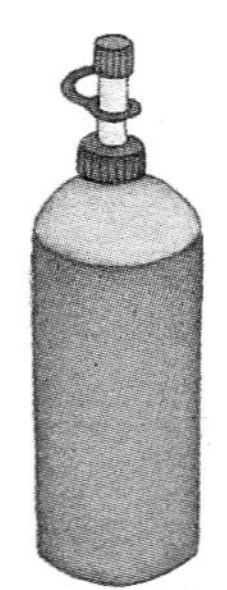

1 liter

40 liters

6.

1 liter

20 liters

What Do You Think?

I drink about 2 liters of water a day.
How many liters of water do you think
you drink in one day?

Name________________________________

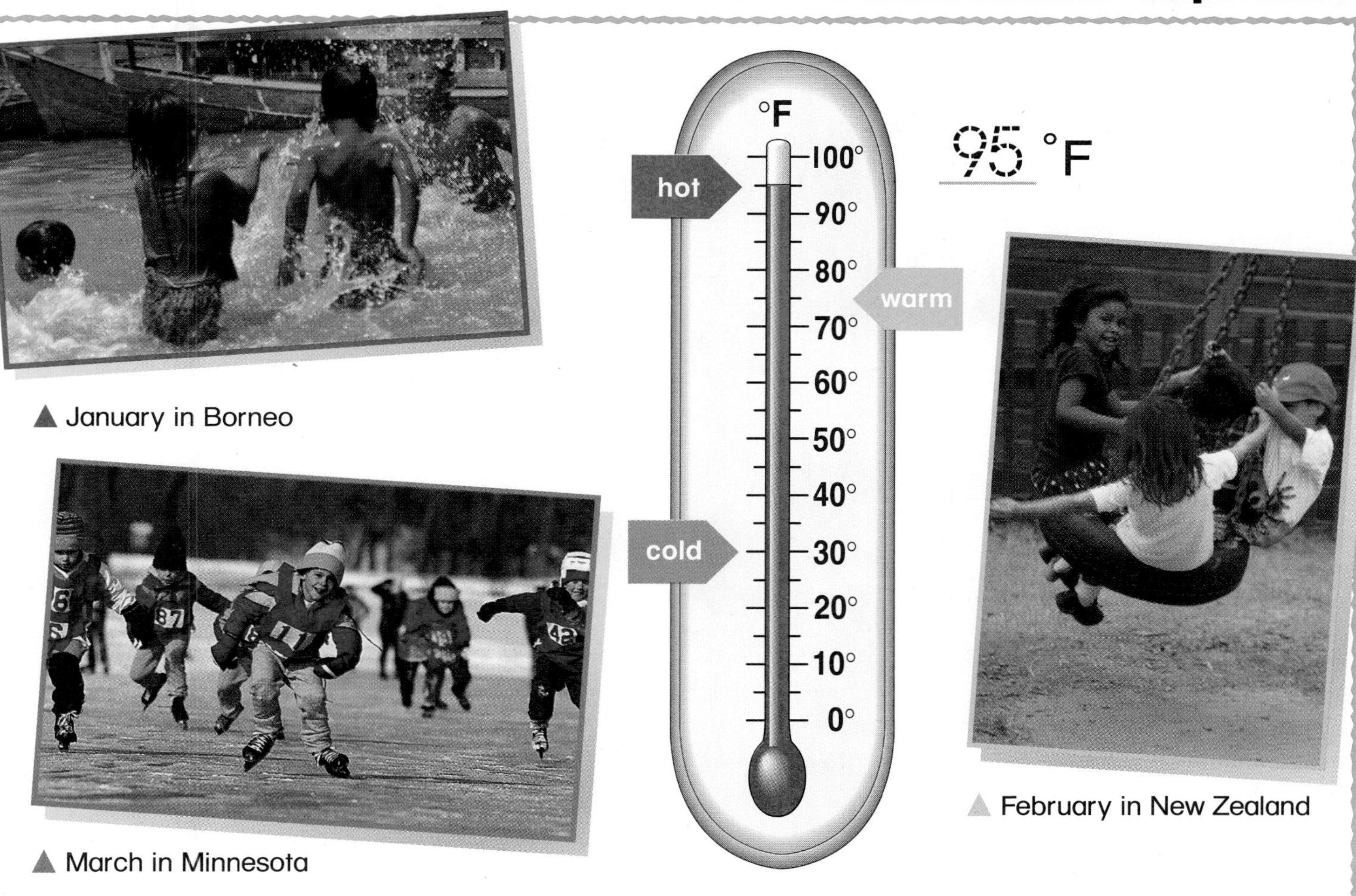

▲ January in Borneo

▲ March in Minnesota

▲ February in New Zealand

Write each temperature.
Circle the hottest temperature in red.
Circle the coldest temperature in blue.

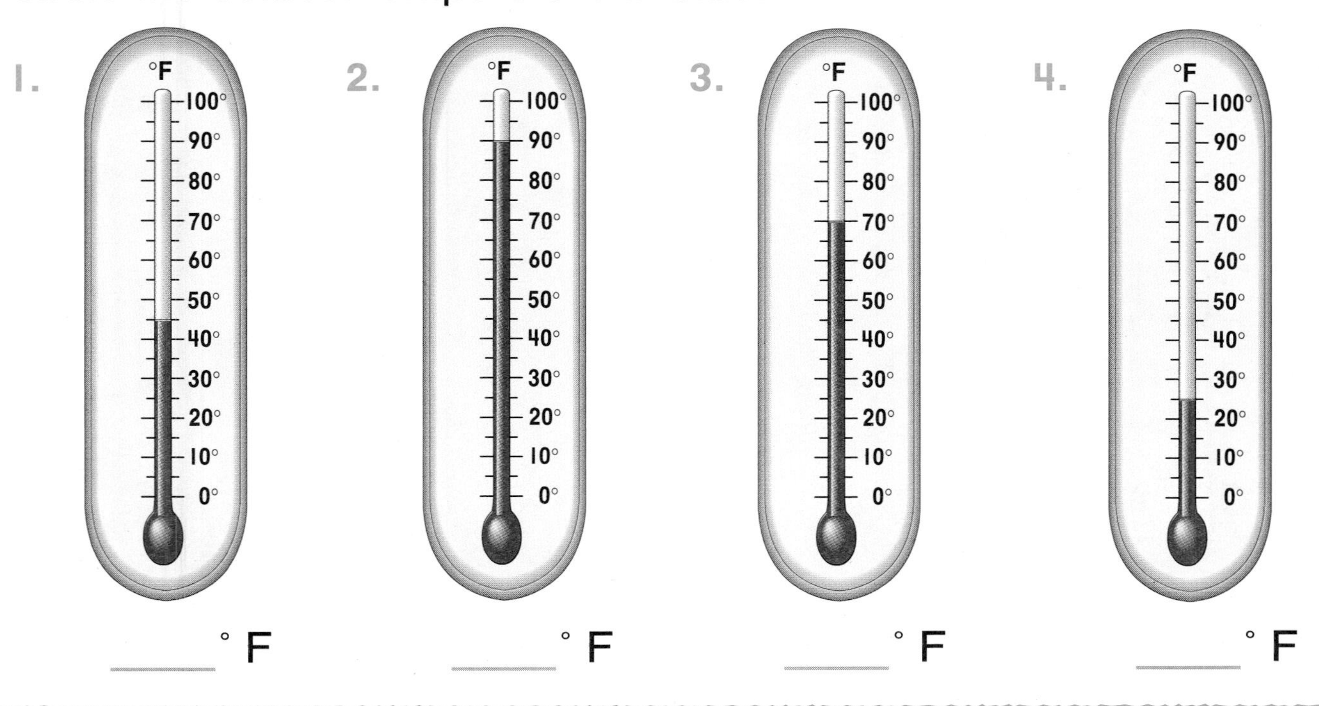

1. ____ °F
2. ____ °F
3. ____ °F
4. ____ °F

Home Connection Your child is learning to read temperature on Fahrenheit and Celsius thermometers. Talk about the temperature each day and what kind of clothing is appropriate.

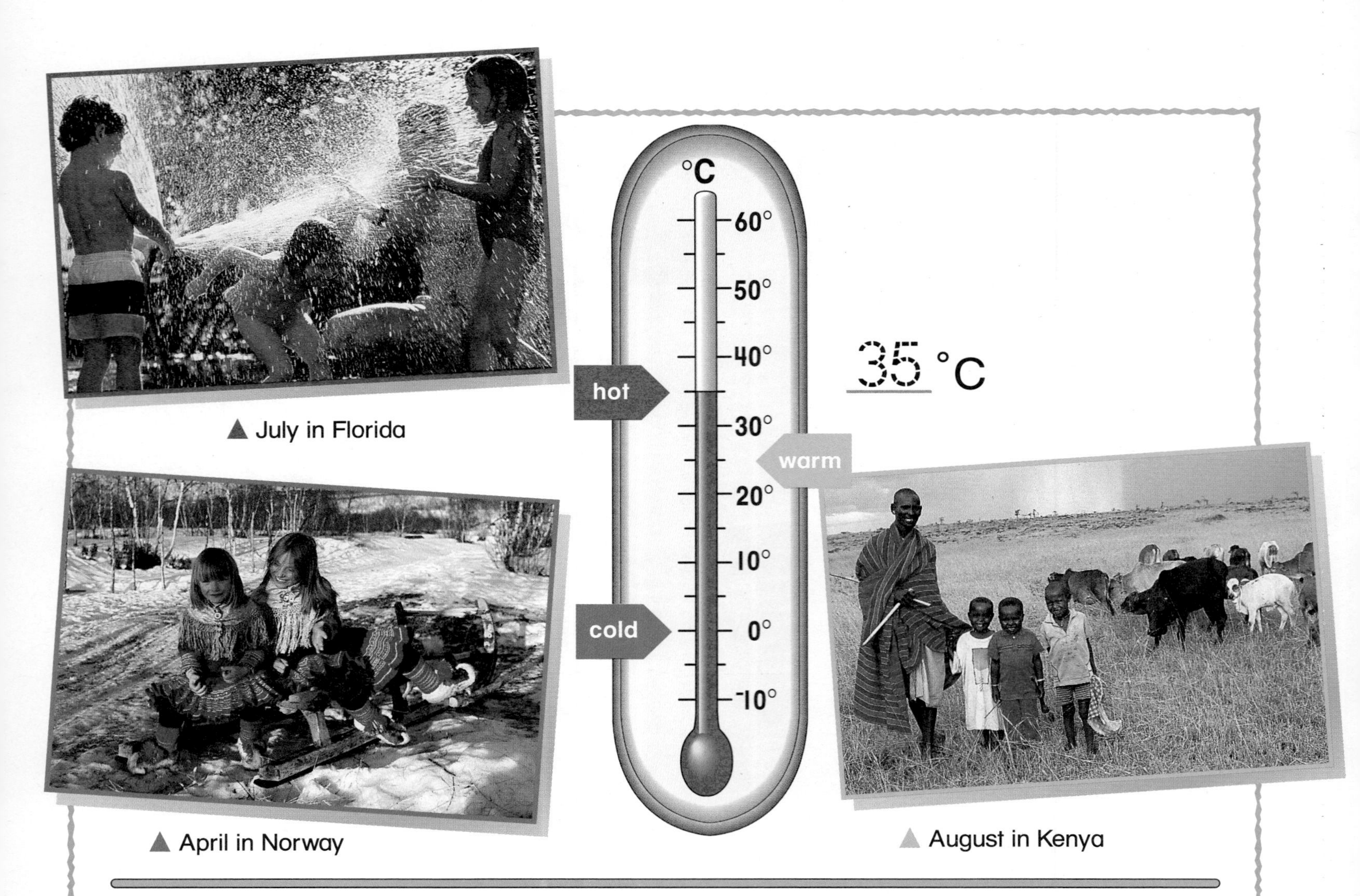

▲ July in Florida

▲ April in Norway

▲ August in Kenya

Write each temperature.
Circle the hottest temperature in red.
Circle the coldest temperature in blue.

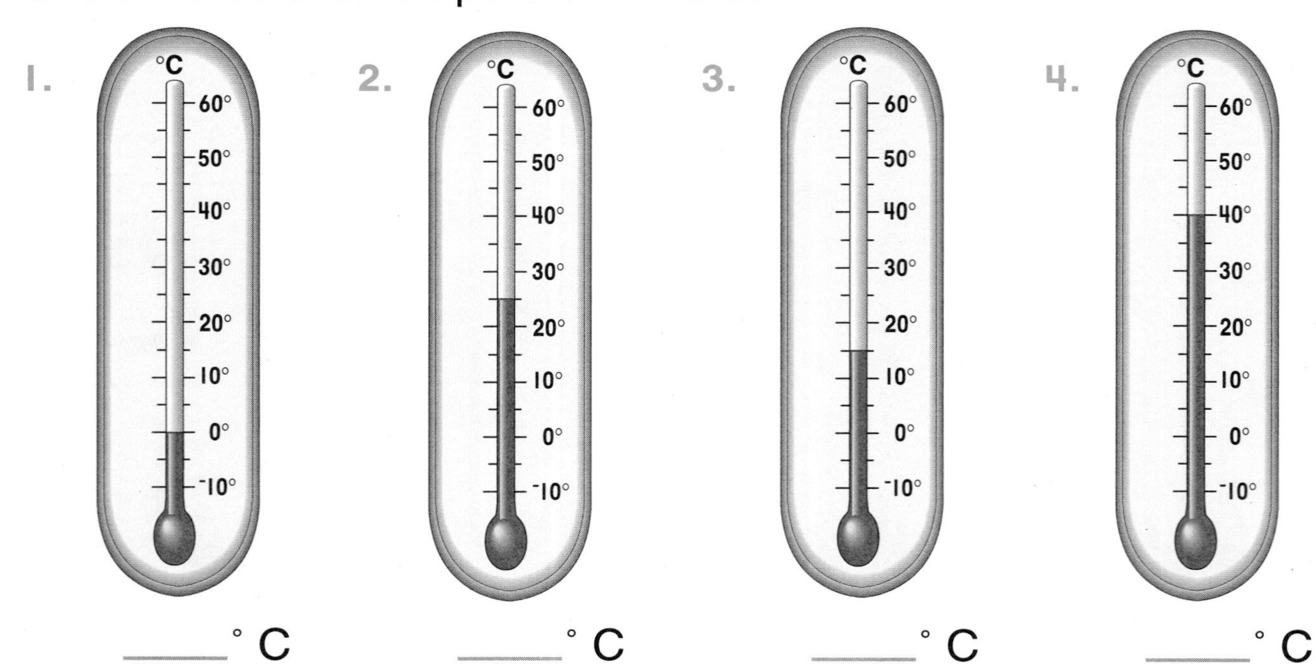

1. ____ °C
2. ____ °C
3. ____ °C
4. ____ °C

Name________________________________

Circle the tool you would use to answer each question.

1. How long is it?

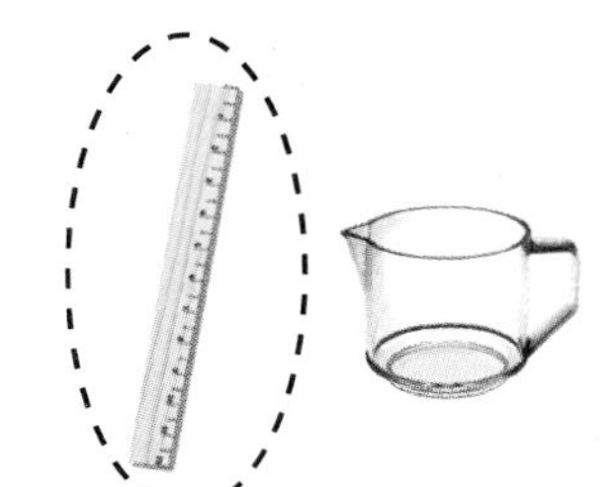
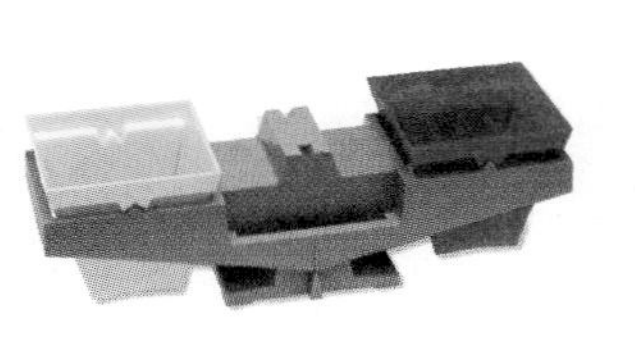
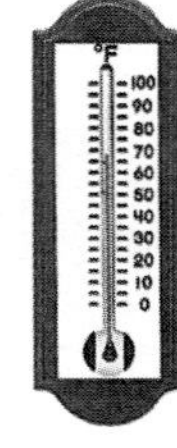

2. How much does it hold?

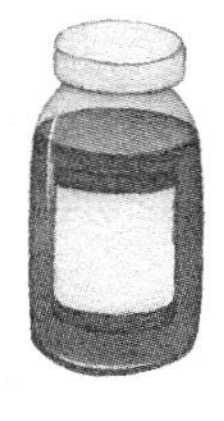

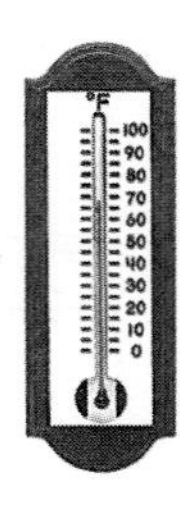

3. Which object is heavier?

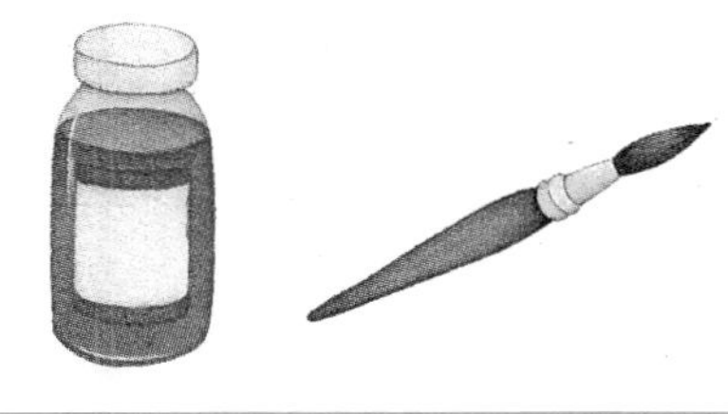

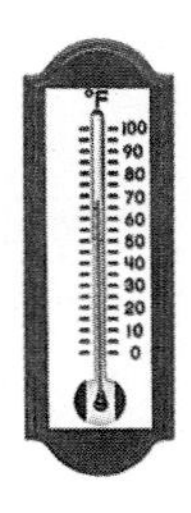

4. How cold is it?

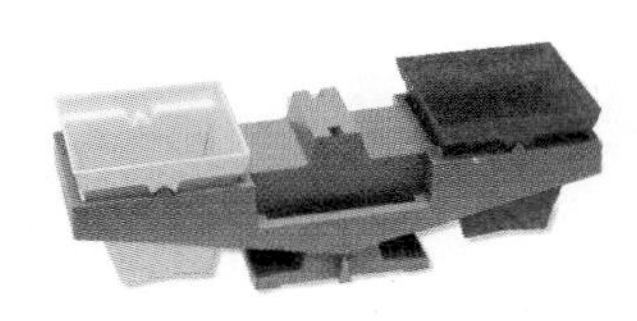
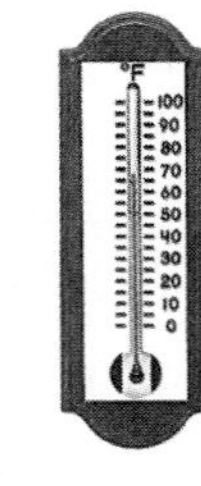

Home Connection Your child is learning to use the appropriate measurement tools. Have your child identify things at home that can be measured with a ruler, scale, measuring cup, or thermometer.

Circle the correct unit of measure to answer each question.

1. How heavy is it?

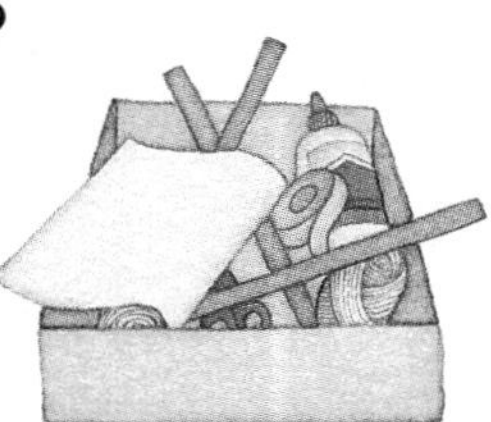

inches	pounds 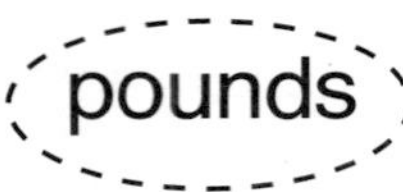
cups	°F

2. How long is it?

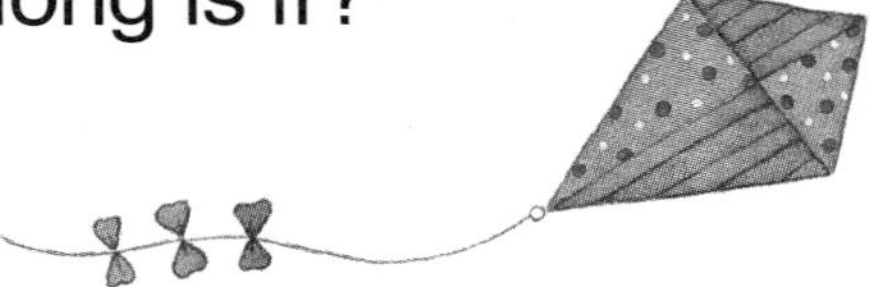

inches	pounds
pints	°F

3. How tall is it?

feet	pounds
quarts	°F

4. How much does it hold?

centimeter	grams
liter	°C

5. How hot is it?

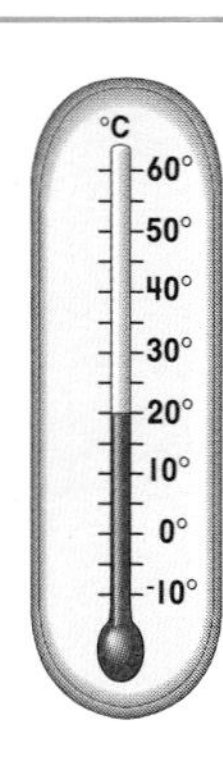

centimeters	kilograms
liters	°C

Name______________________________ **Checkpoint** 

About how much does it weigh?
Circle the better estimate.

1. 

1 pound

10 pounds

2. 

40 grams

40 kilograms

Circle the two that hold about the same.

3.  

4.  

5. 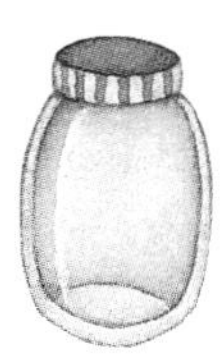 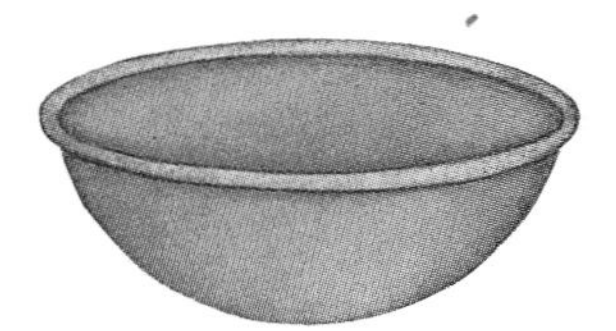 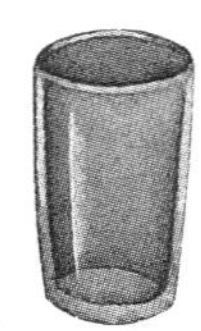

Write each temperature.

6. 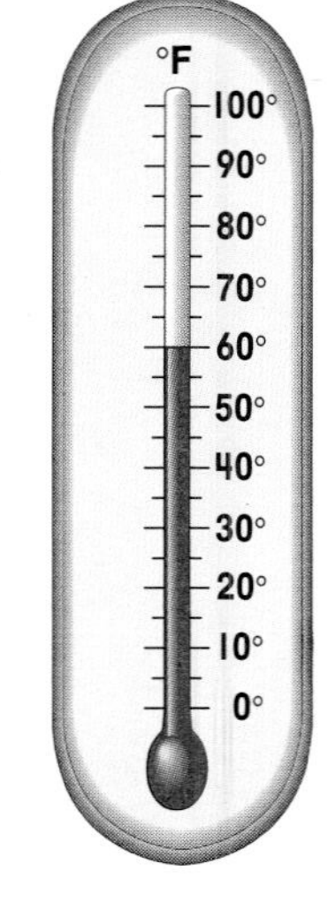

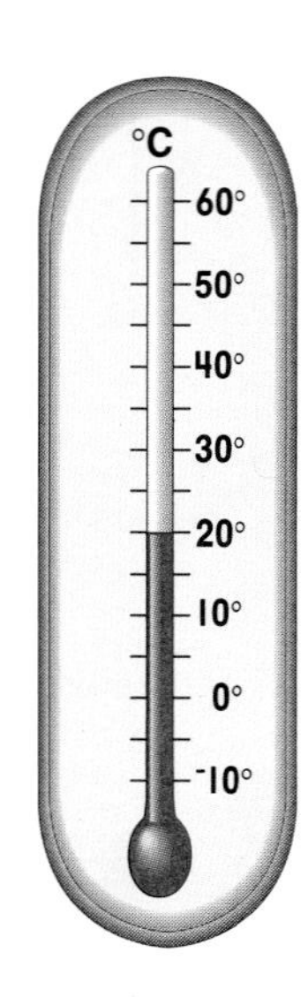

_____ °F _____ °C

Estimate the length.
Then measure.

7. 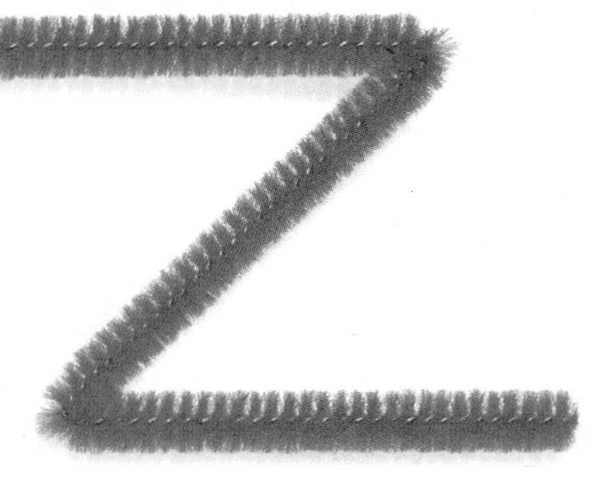

estimate: about _____ inches

measure: about _____ inches

Name________________________________ **Extra Practice**

Use a ruler.
Draw lines to connect the dots.

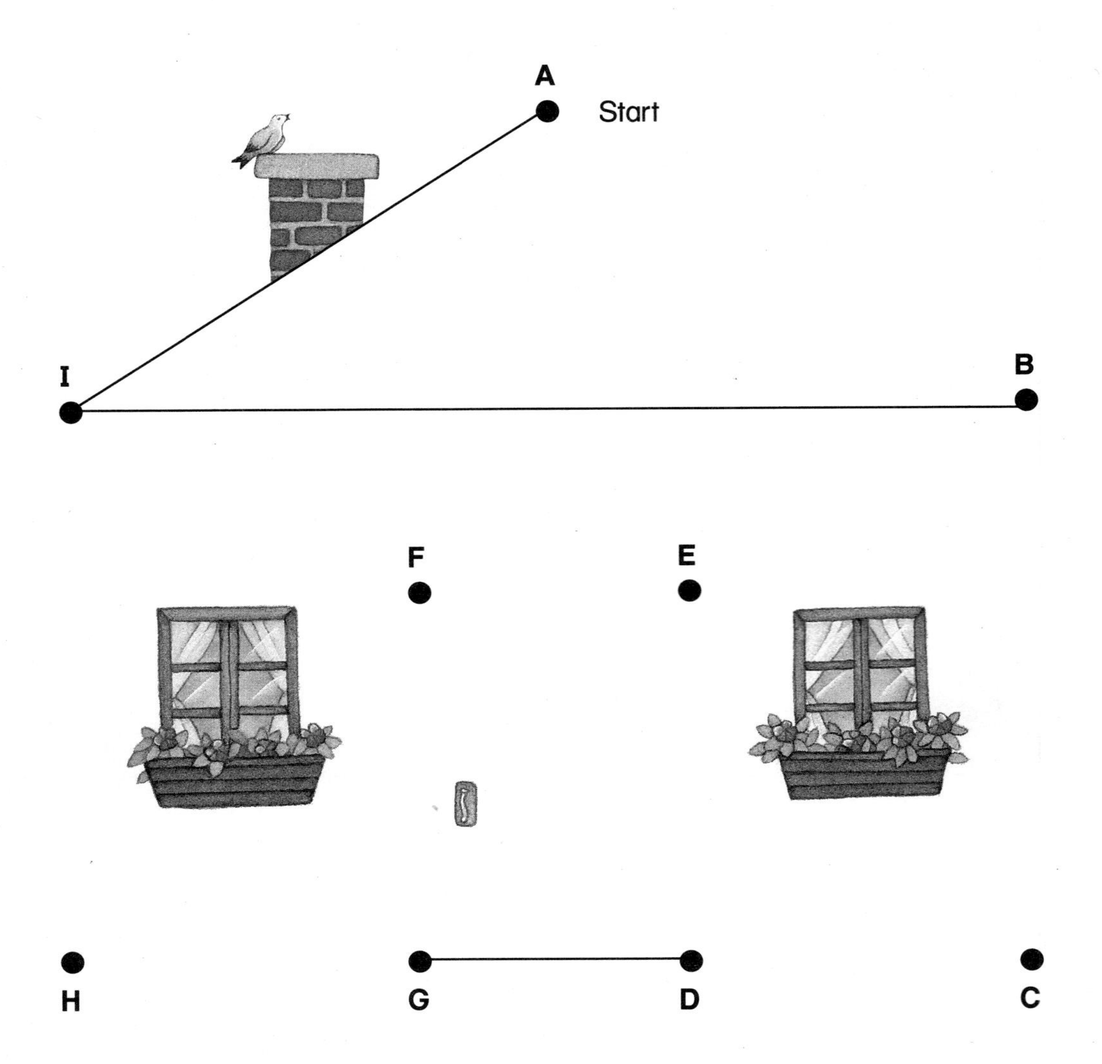

Use a ruler to measure.
Complete each sentence.

1. From **A** to **B** is about __3__ inches.
2. From **D** to **E** is about _____ inches.
3. From **H** to **I** is about _____ inches.
4. From _____ to _____ is about 5 inches.
5. From **B** to **C** is about the same length as from _____ to _____.

Name________________________________ **Chapter Test** 

Circle the better estimate.

About how long is each object?

1. 3 inches 6 inches

2. 1 cm 5 cm

About how long would the real object be?

3. 2 inches / 2 feet

4. 7 cm / 7 m

About how much would the real object weigh?

5. 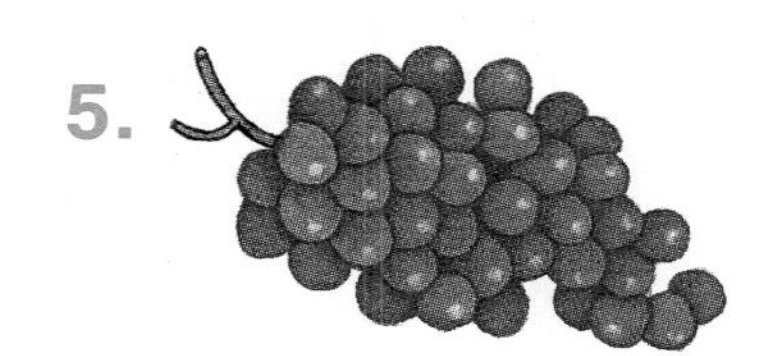 1 pound / 10 pounds

6. 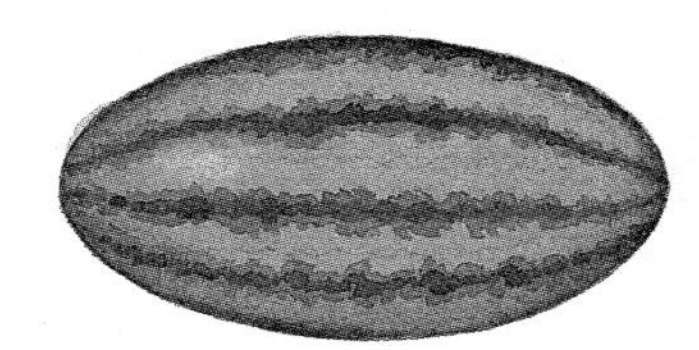 6 grams / 6 kilograms

About how much would the real object hold?

7.  more than 1 cup / less than 1 cup

8.  more than 1 liter / less than 1 liter

Circle the tool you would use to answer each question.

9. How long is it? 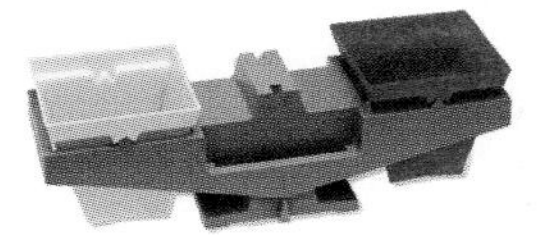 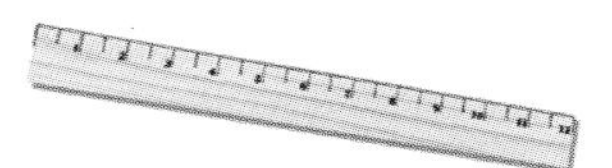

10. Which object is heavier?  

11. How much does it hold? 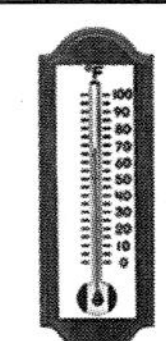 

Name ______________________________ **Performance Assessment**

What You Need

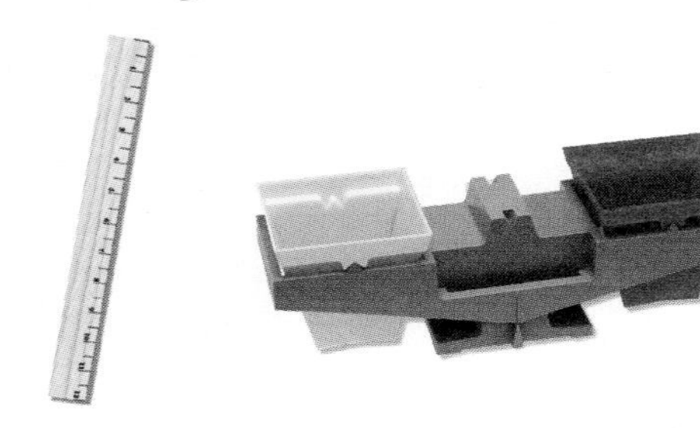

ruler scale cup

1. Find objects to measure to answer each question.
2. Draw or write to show the object.
3. Measure and record.

	Measure	Object
1.	How tall is it? about _____ inches	
2.	How wide is it? about _____ inches	
3.	How long is it? about _____ feet	
4.	How much will it hold? about _____ cups	
5.	How heavy is it? about _____ pounds	

Name____

You can measure to the nearest half inch.

The yarn is about 4 and $\frac{1}{2}$ inches long.

About how long is each object?
Circle the best estimate.

1.

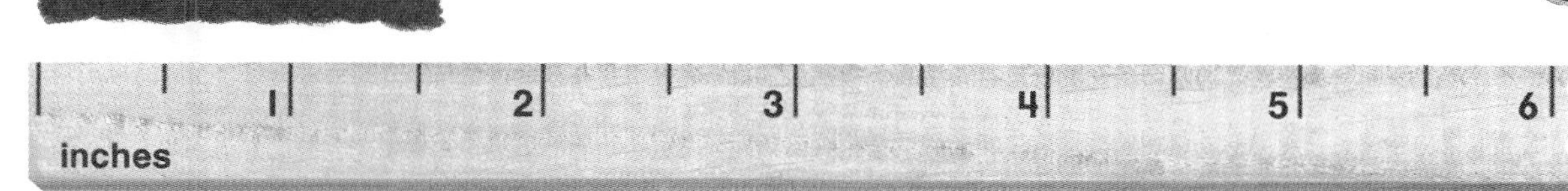

1 inch	1 and $\frac{1}{2}$ inches	2 inches

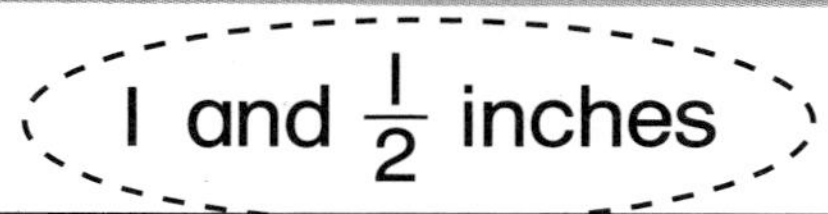

2.

5 inches	5 and $\frac{1}{2}$ inches	6 inches

3.

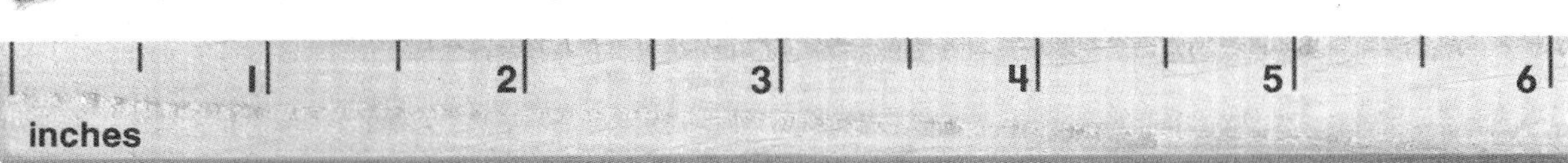

2 inches	2 and $\frac{1}{2}$ inches	3 inches

4.

3 inches	3 and $\frac{1}{2}$ inches	4 inches

5.

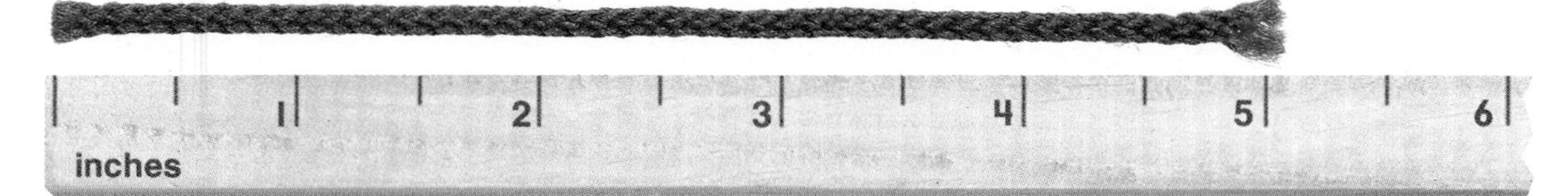

4 inches	4 and $\frac{1}{2}$ inches	5 inches

Name________________________________

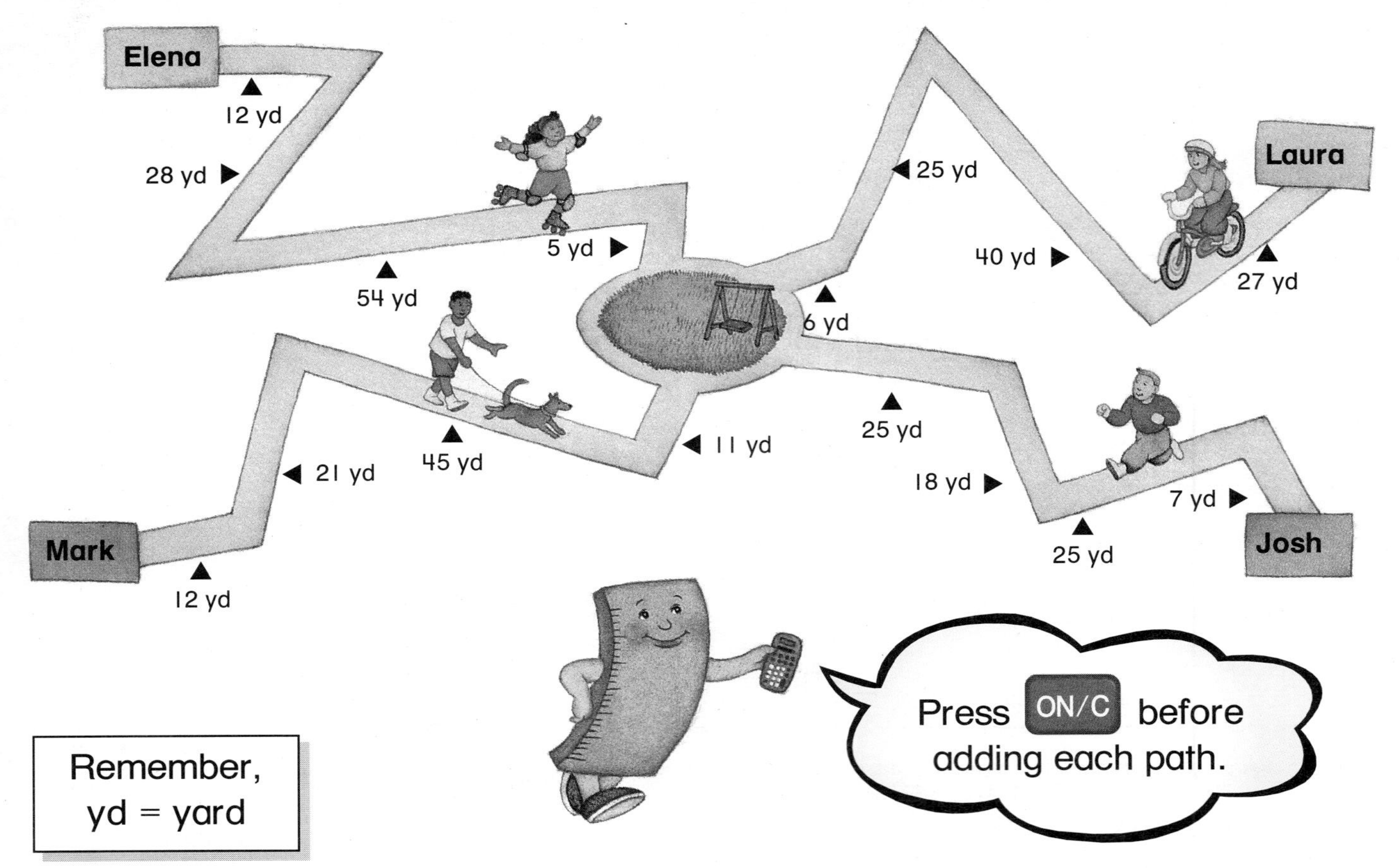

Press ON/C before adding each path.

Remember,
yd = yard

Write the numbers to find the length of each path.
Then use a calculator to add.

1. Elena 12 + 28 + 54 + 5 = 99 yards

2. Mark ____ + ____ + ____ + ____ = ____ yards

3. Laura ____ + ____ + ____ + ____ = ____ yards

4. Josh ____ + ____ + ____ + ____ = ____ yards

Who has the shortest walk to the park? ____________

CHAPTER 9
Patterns and Numbers to 1,000
Carl's Collections
written by Shereen Gertel Rutman
illustrated by Amy Wummer
This Math Storybook
belongs to
A

Carl loved to collect things.
He collected pennies.
He saved 360 cents.
That's 300 pennies and 60 more.

Carl collected stones.
He had colored stones, smooth stones,
and stones that sparkled.
He filled his room with 441 stones.
That's 400, 40, and 1 more.

Carl collected trading cards.
He stacked cards on the bed and the floor.
There were 595 cards.
That's 500, 90, and 5 more.

That night, Carl fell asleep and began to dream.
In his dream, everything spilled all over the floor.
There were piles taller than Carl.
There were hundreds and hundreds of things.

Carl woke up and jumped out of bed.
He put away his pennies, stones, and cards.
Then he picked up a red car and a blue car.
Oh no! Here he goes again.

What if Carl collected these cars?
How many cars would he have?

_____ cars

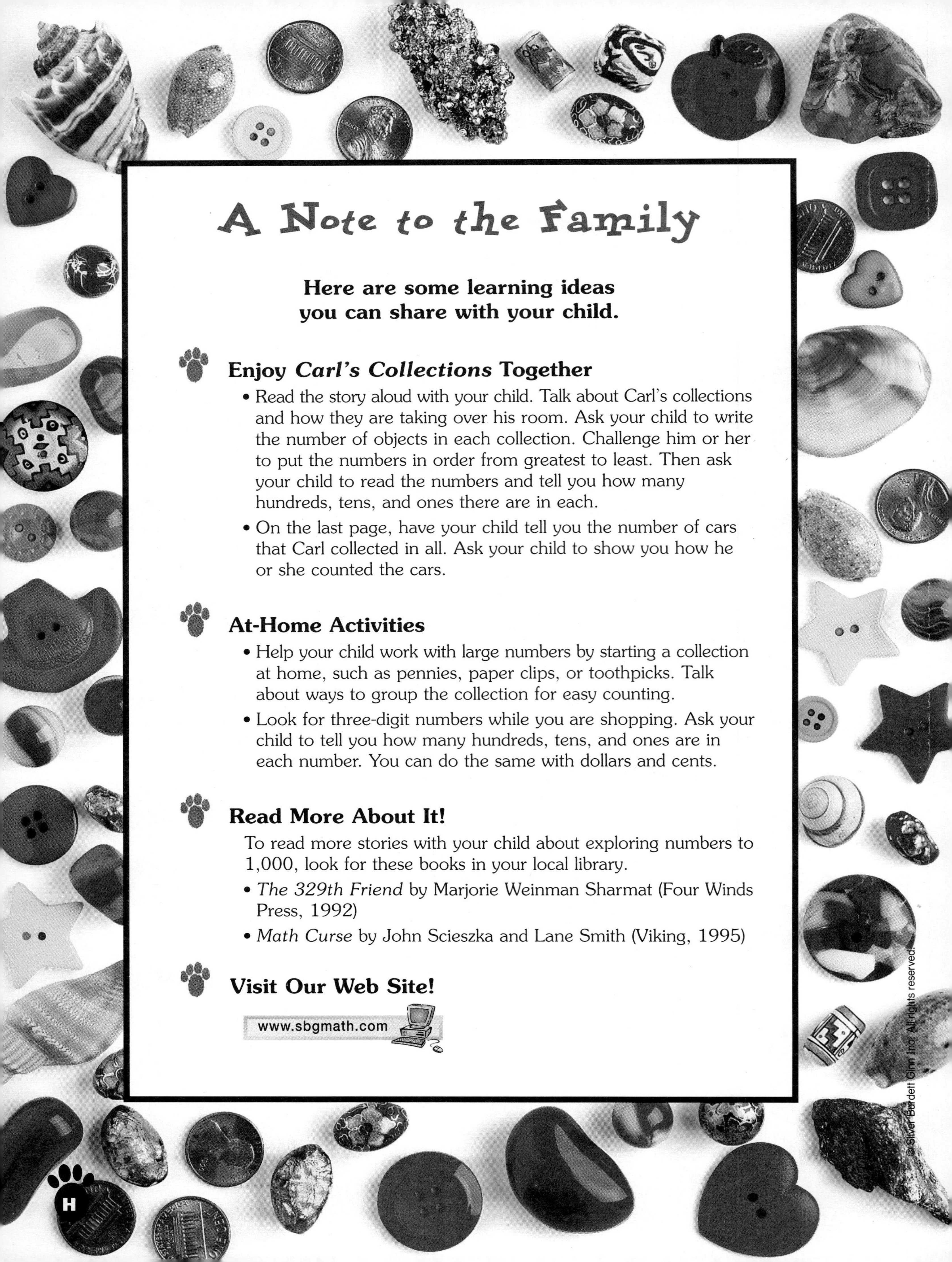

A Note to the Family

Here are some learning ideas you can share with your child.

Enjoy *Carl's Collections* Together

- Read the story aloud with your child. Talk about Carl's collections and how they are taking over his room. Ask your child to write the number of objects in each collection. Challenge him or her to put the numbers in order from greatest to least. Then ask your child to read the numbers and tell you how many hundreds, tens, and ones there are in each.
- On the last page, have your child tell you the number of cars that Carl collected in all. Ask your child to show you how he or she counted the cars.

At-Home Activities

- Help your child work with large numbers by starting a collection at home, such as pennies, paper clips, or toothpicks. Talk about ways to group the collection for easy counting.
- Look for three-digit numbers while you are shopping. Ask your child to tell you how many hundreds, tens, and ones are in each number. You can do the same with dollars and cents.

Read More About It!

To read more stories with your child about exploring numbers to 1,000, look for these books in your local library.

- *The 329th Friend* by Marjorie Weinman Sharmat (Four Winds Press, 1992)
- *Math Curse* by John Scieszka and Lane Smith (Viking, 1995)

Visit Our Web Site!

www.sbgmath.com

Name____________________

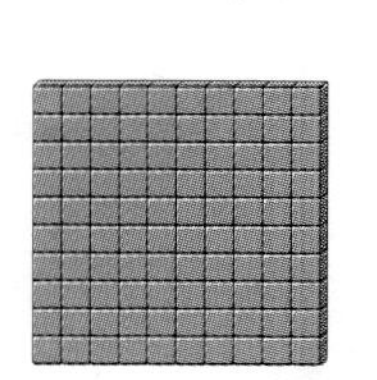
1 hundred
100

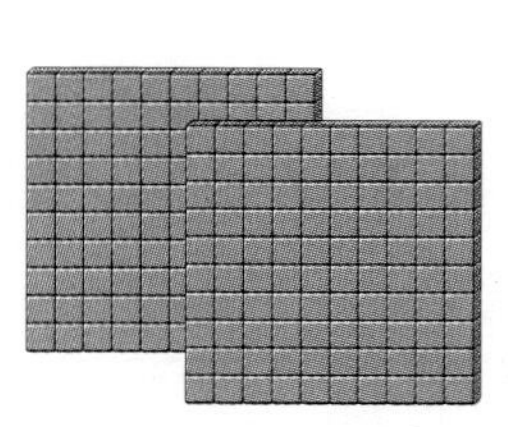
2 hundreds
200

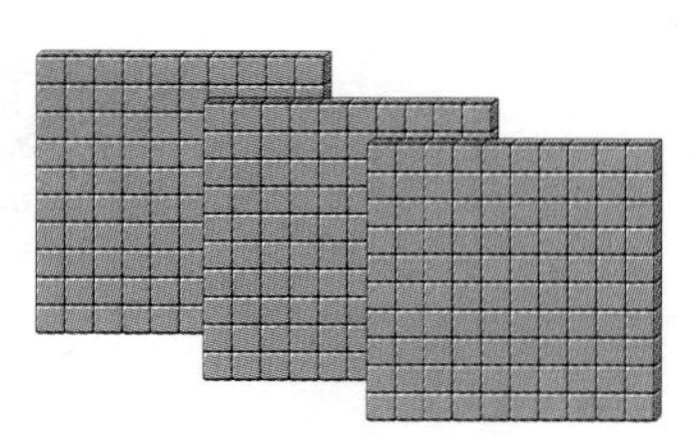
3 hundreds
300

Word Bank
hundreds

Count by hundreds. Write the numbers.
Use models if you like.

1. 1 hundred

Hundreds	Tens	Ones
1	0	0

100

2. 2 hundreds

Hundreds	Tens	Ones

____

3. 3 hundreds

Hundreds	Tens	Ones

____

4. 4 hundreds

Hundreds	Tens	Ones

____

5. 5 hundreds

Hundreds	Tens	Ones

____

6. 6 hundreds

Hundreds	Tens	Ones

____

7. 7 hundreds

Hundreds	Tens	Ones

____

8. 8 hundreds

Hundreds	Tens	Ones

____

9. 9 hundreds

Hundreds	Tens	Ones

____

10. 10 hundreds

Hundreds	Tens	Ones

____

Home Connection Your child is learning to build and count hundreds. Give your child some small objects, such as dried beans, to group and count by hundreds.

Count by hundreds. Write the numbers.

1.

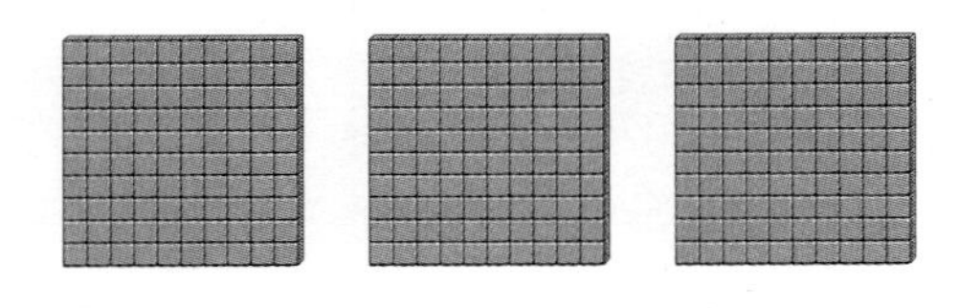

Hundreds	Tens	Ones

______

2.

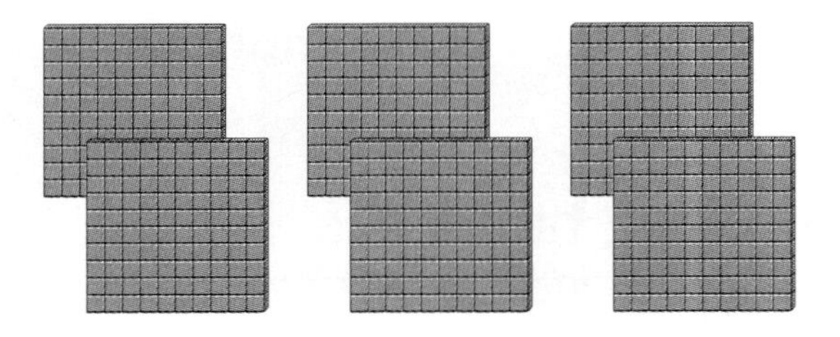

Hundreds	Tens	Ones

______

3.

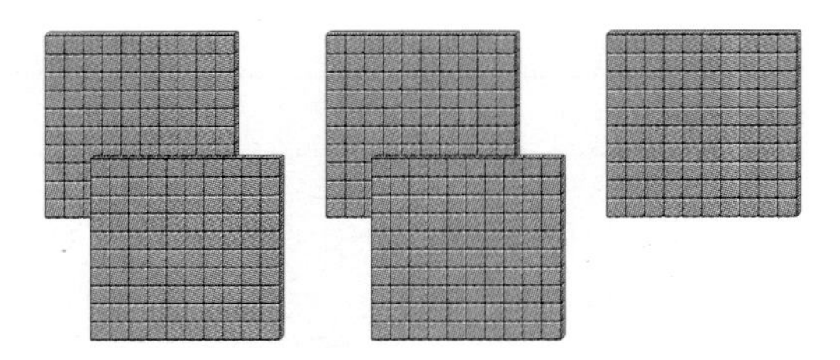

Hundreds	Tens	Ones

______

4.

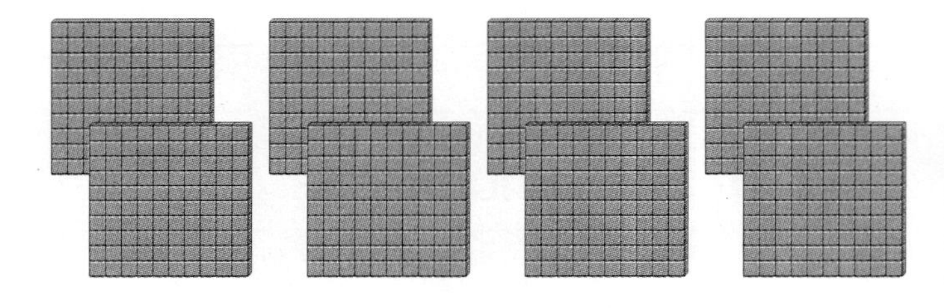

Hundreds	Tens	Ones

______

5.

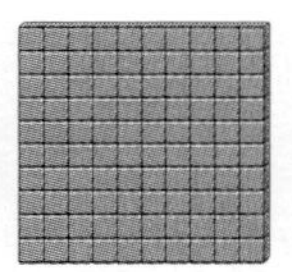

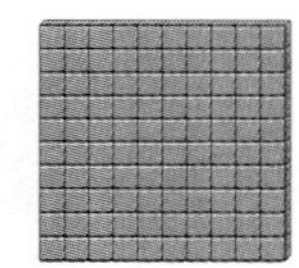

Hundreds	Tens	Ones

______

What Do You Think?

I think that counting by hundreds is as easy as counting by ones. Do you agree? Tell why.

Name________________________

What You Need

models

spinner

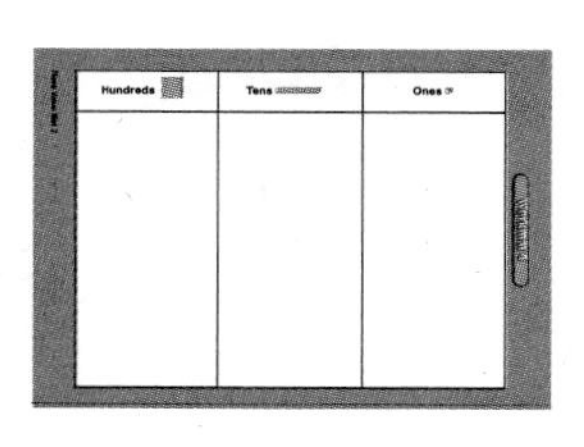

Workmat 4

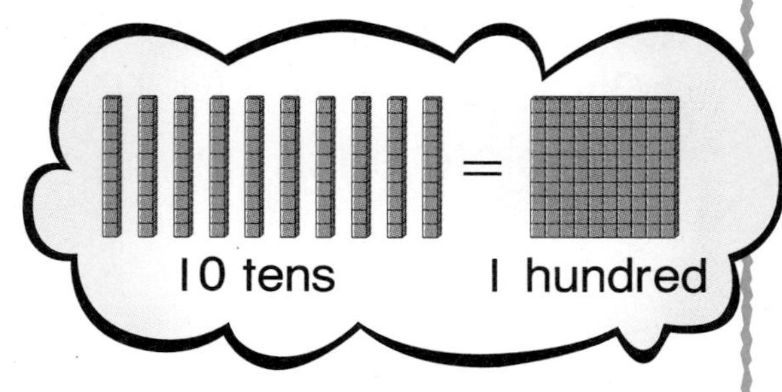

1. Spin the spinner 2 times. Record each spin.
2. Take that many tens. Regroup 10 tens as 1 hundred if you can.
3. Write how many hundreds, tens, and ones.
4. Write the number.

1. 1st spin_____ 2nd spin_____

Hundreds	Tens	Ones

_____

2. 1st spin_____ 2nd spin_____

Hundreds	Tens	Ones

_____

3. 1st spin_____ 2nd spin_____

Hundreds	Tens	Ones

_____

4. 1st spin_____ 2nd spin_____

Hundreds	Tens	Ones

_____

5. 1st spin_____ 2nd spin_____

Hundreds	Tens	Ones

_____

6. 1st spin_____ 2nd spin_____

Hundreds	Tens	Ones

_____

Home Connection Your child is learning to build three-digit numbers. Have your child tell you how he or she built the numbers on this page.

Use models to build each number.
Follow the rule. Regroup if you can.
Complete each chart.

1. Add 1.

Hundreds	Tens	Ones
2	0	0
2	0	1

Hundreds	Tens	Ones
3	1	5

Hundreds	Tens	Ones
4	3	8

2. Add 10.

Hundreds	Tens	Ones
1	9	0
2	0	0

Hundreds	Tens	Ones
3	0	6

Hundreds	Tens	Ones
2	7	4

Name_______________ **Understanding Three-Digit Numbers**

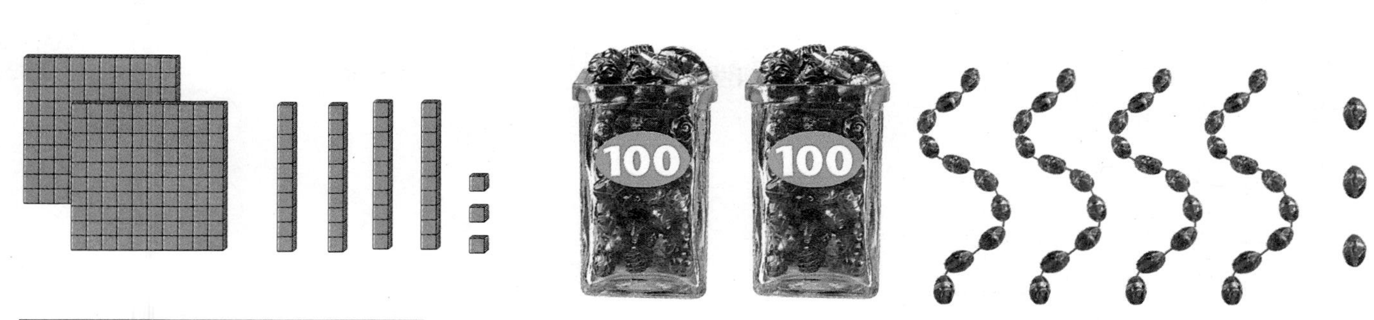

Hundreds	Tens	Ones
2	4	3

243

Write how many hundreds, tens, and ones.
Write the number.

1.

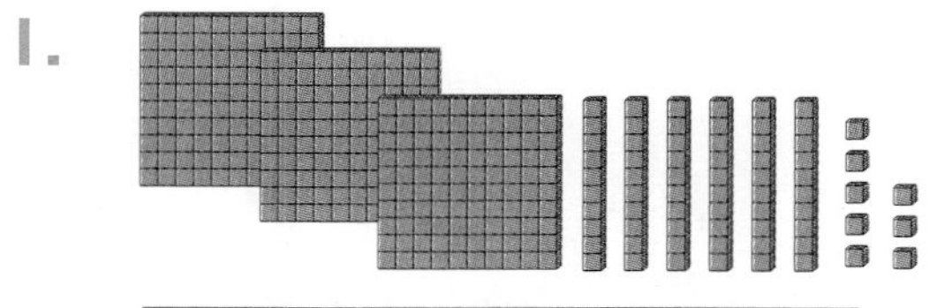

Hundreds	Tens	Ones

____

2.

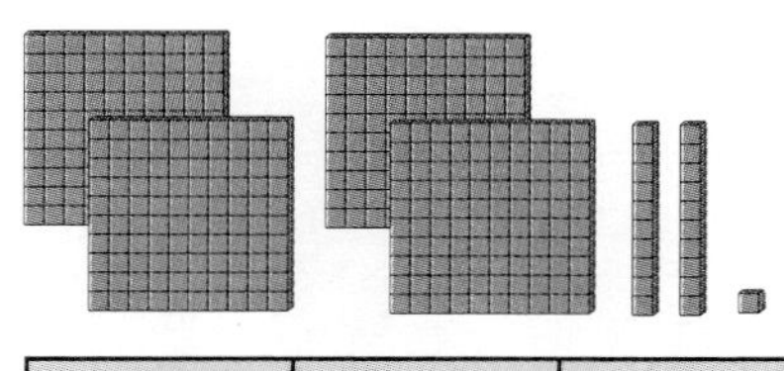

Hundreds	Tens	Ones

____

3.

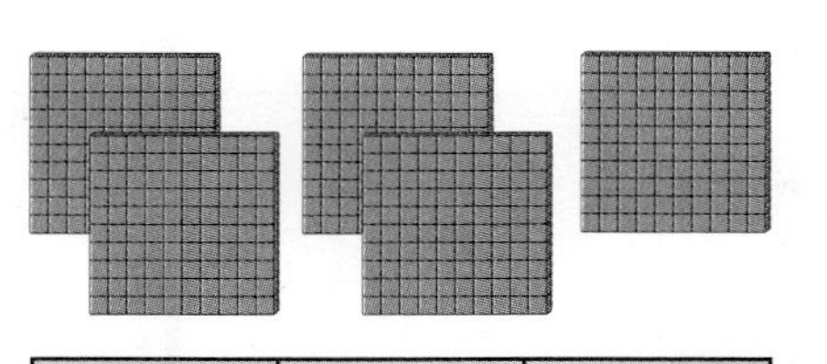

Hundreds	Tens	Ones

____

4.

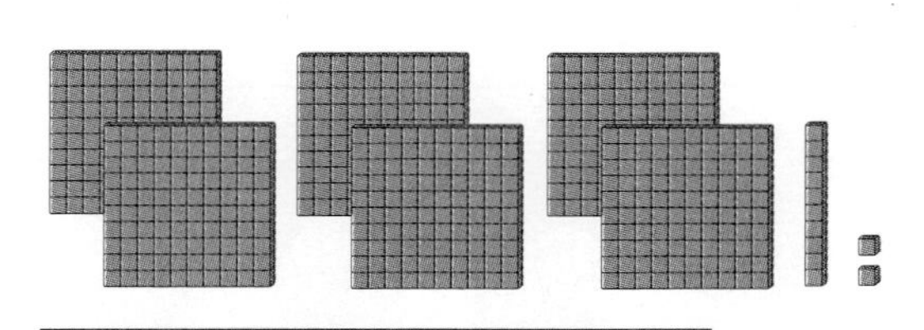

Hundreds	Tens	Ones

____

5.

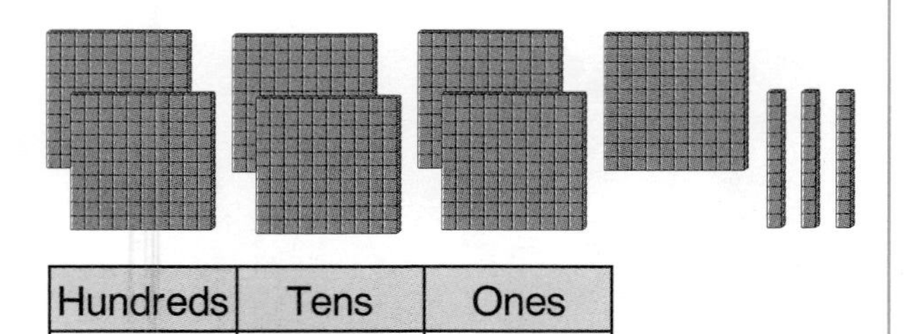

Hundreds	Tens	Ones

____

6.

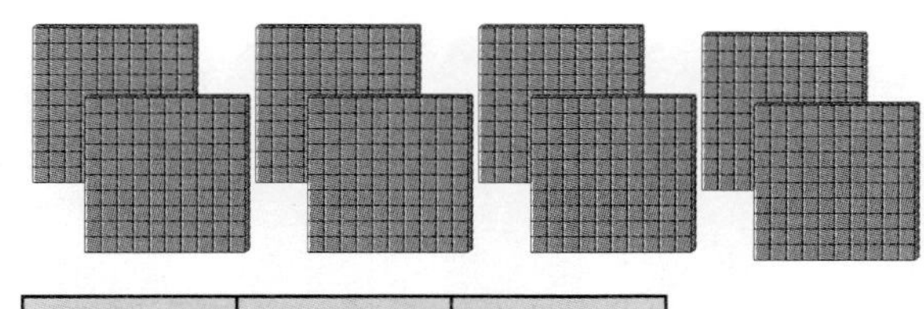

Hundreds	Tens	Ones

____

Home Connection Your child is learning that three-digit numbers are composed of hundreds, tens, and ones. Say or write numbers like 425. Have your child tell the number of hundreds, tens, and ones.

Write how many hundreds, tens, and ones.
Write the number.

1.    

3 hundreds 7 tens 5 ones 375

2.     

____ hundreds ____ ten ____ ones ____

3.       

____ hundreds ____ tens ____ ones ____

4.        

____ hundreds ____ tens ____ ones ____

5.       

____ hundreds ____ tens ____ one ____

Name________________________________ **Ways to Show Numbers**

In what other way can you show the number one hundred forty-five?
I can use models.
I can write hundreds, tens, and ones.
I can write the number.
1 hundred 4 tens 5 ones
145

Show each number in a different way.

1. 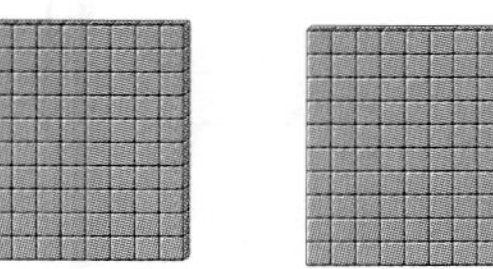

____ hundreds ____ tens ____ ones

2. 965 ____ hundreds ____ tens ____ ones

3. 782 ____ hundreds ____ tens ____ ones

Write each number.

4. 4 hundreds 1 ten 6 ones

____

5. 6 hundreds 0 tens 9 ones

____

6. five hundred twenty-four

____

7. three hundred sixteen

____

Home Connection Your child is learning different ways to show the same number. Ask your child to show each number on this page in another way.

Circle another way to show each number.

1. 

235 253 532

2. 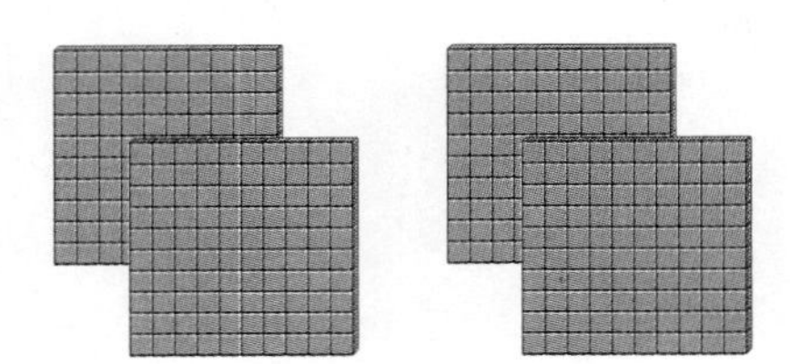

445 454 544

3. seven hundred fifty-two

752 725 527

4. five hundred eighty

805 508 580

5. 3 hundreds 4 tens 8 ones

438 384 348

6. 6 hundreds 3 tens 2 ones

236 632 623

Problem Solving

Circle the collections that show the same number of beads. Tell another way to show this number.

7.

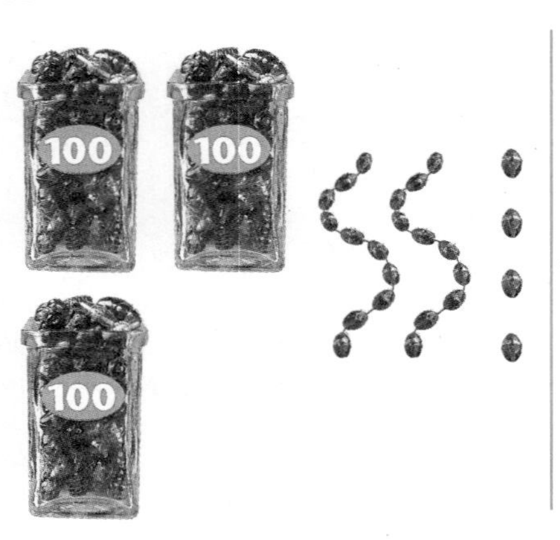

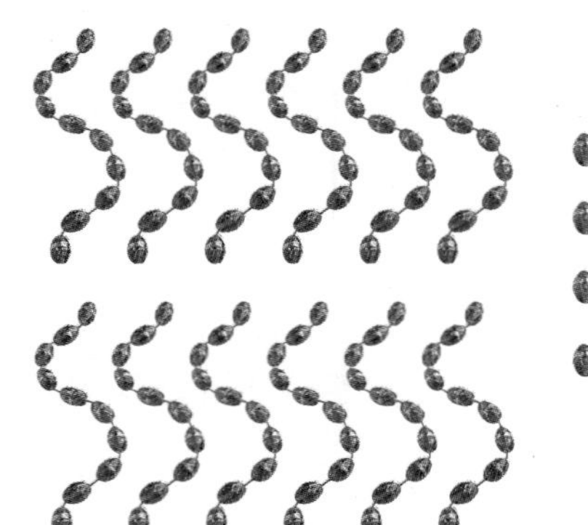

Name______________________________ **Understanding Place Value**

Write the value of the red digit.

1. 204 200	2. 936 ____	3. 319 ____
4. 562 ____	5. 638 ____	6. 154 ____
7. 825 ____	8. 741 ____	9. 498 ____
10. 370 ____	11. 947 ____	12. 583 ____
13. 416 ____	14. 672 ____	15. 805 ____

Home Connection Your child is learning the value of each digit in a three-digit number. Have your child tell you the value of the digits in various three-digit numbers that you say.

Circle the matching number.

1. $300 + 60 + 1$

(361) 316

2. $500 + 30 + 6$

563 536

3. $700 + 20 + 9$

729 792

4. $600 + 10 + 0$

610 601

5. $3 + 70 + 100$

173 371

6. $4 + 80 + 200$

482 284

Checkpoint

1. Count by hundreds. Write the missing numbers.

100, ____, 300, ____, ____, 600, 700, ____, ____

Write the numbers.

2.

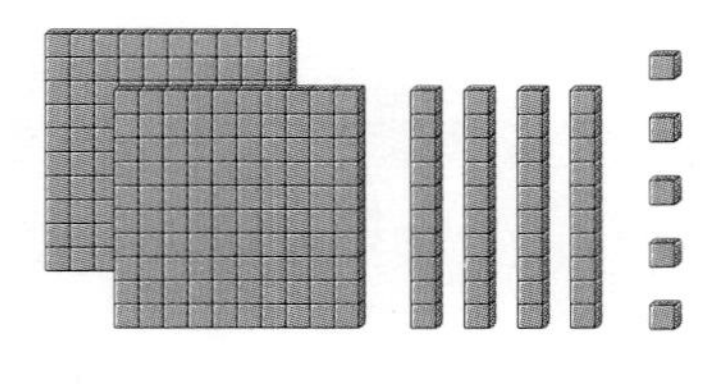

Hundreds	Tens	Ones

____

3.

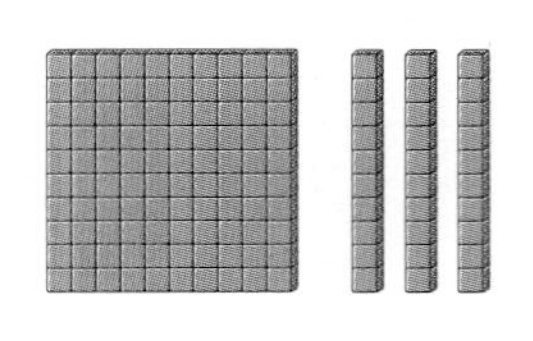

Hundreds	Tens	Ones

____

4.

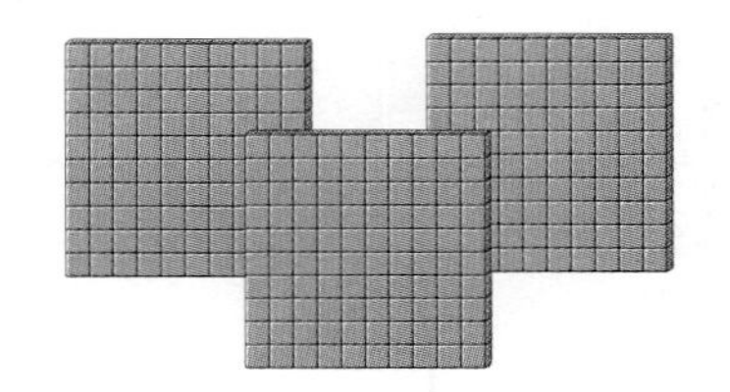

Hundreds	Tens	Ones

____

Name____

1. Write the missing numbers.

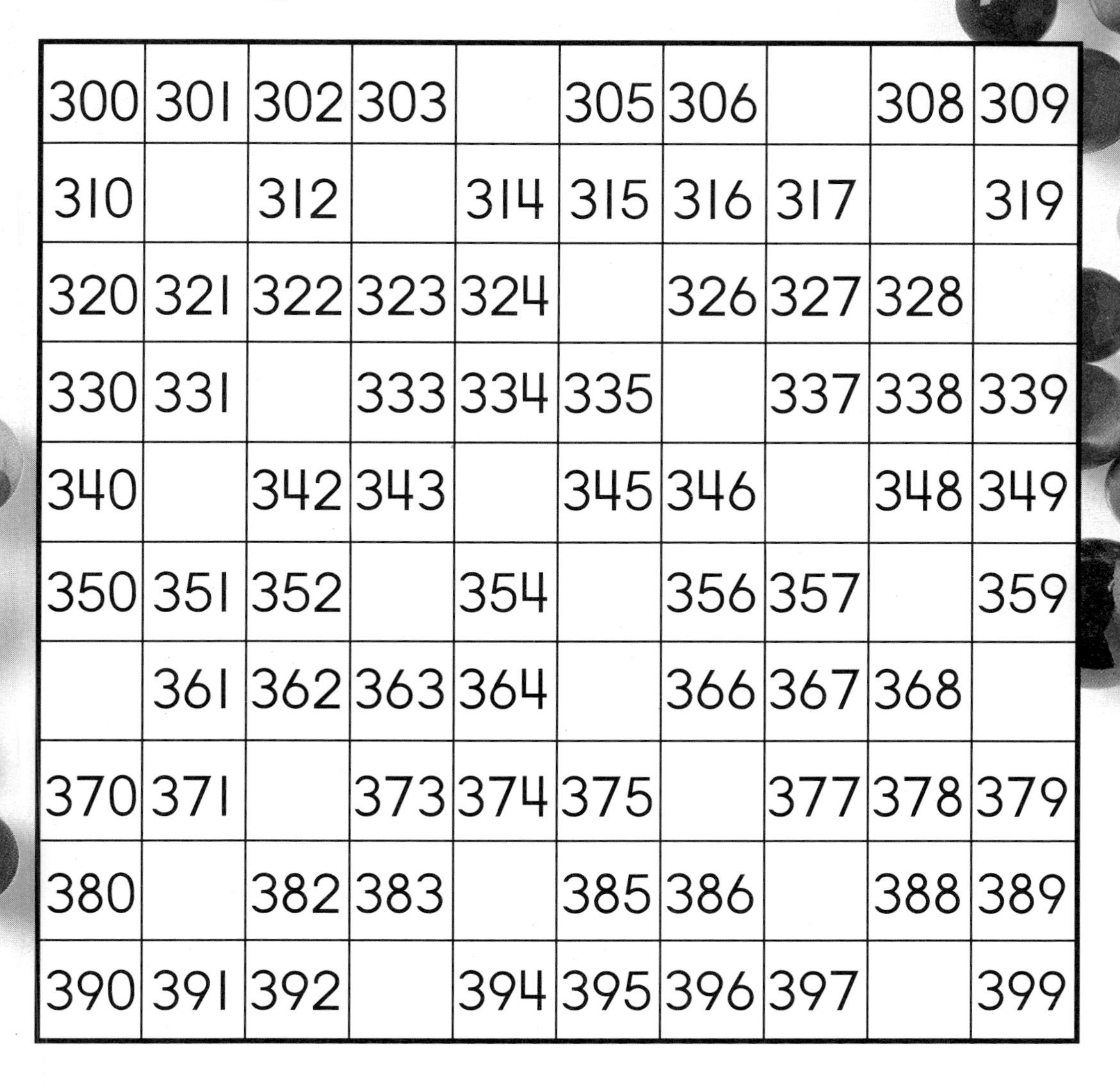

300	301	302	303		305	306		308	309
310		312		314	315	316	317		319
320	321	322	323	324		326	327	328	
330	331		333	334	335		337	338	339
340		342	343		345	346		348	349
350	351	352		354		356	357		359
	361	362	363	364		366	367	368	
370	371		373	374	375		377	378	379
380		382	383		385	386		388	389
390	391	392		394	395	396	397		399

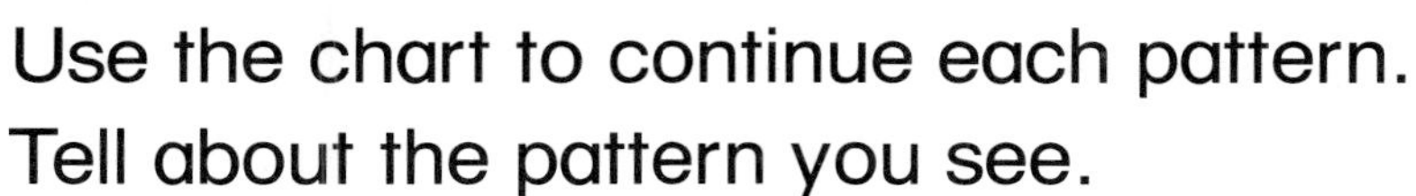

Use the chart to continue each pattern.
Tell about the pattern you see.

2. 300, 310, 320, _____, _____, _____, _____, _____

3. 325, 335, 345, _____, _____, _____, _____, _____

4. 382, 372, 362, _____, _____, _____, _____, _____

5. 320, 331, 342, _____, _____, _____, _____, _____

Home Connection Ask your child to find patterns in the chart. Encourage your child to find patterns that go across, up and down, and diagonally.

1. Write the missing numbers.

900	901								909
	911							918	
920		922							929
				934					
							947		
			953						
					965				
						976			
								988	

Use the chart to continue each pattern.
Tell about the pattern you see.

2. 989, 988, 987, 986, ____, ____, ____, ____

3. 922, 932, 942, ____, ____, ____, ____, ____

4. 909, 918, 927, ____, ____, ____, ____, ____

Make Your Own

Use the chart to make your own pattern.

5. ____, ____, ____, ____, ____, ____, ____

Name________________________________ **Dollars and Cents**

Count $1.00, $2.00, $2.10, $2.20, $2.25, $2.26.

total

First count the dollar bills. Then count the coins.
Count on to find the total amount.

1.

$ ___ . ___
total

2.

$ ___ . ___
total

3.

$ ___ . ___
total

4.

$ ___ . ___
total

Home Connection Your child is learning to count and write dollars and cents. Give your child some one-dollar bills and coins to count. Ask him or her to write each amount.

Circle the money you need to buy each item.
Use bills and coins if you like.

1. $1.15

2. $2.36

3. $2.41

Critical Thinking Corner

Mental Math

4. Count the bills and coins to find the total amount.

$ ____ . ____ total

First compare the hundreds.

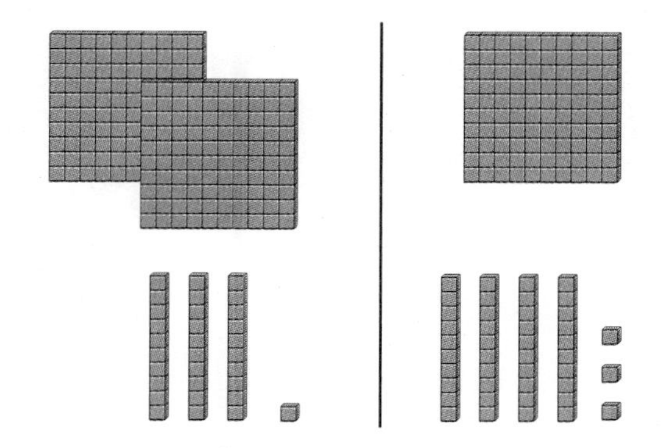

231 is **greater than** 143.

231 > 143

If the hundreds are the same, compare the tens.

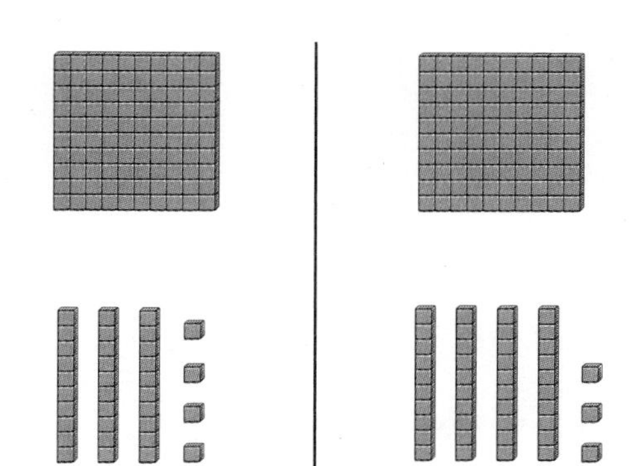

134 is **less than** 143.

134 < 143

What do you do if the tens are the same?

Circle **greater than** or **less than**.
Then write < or >. Use models if you like.

1. 325 is greater than / less than 251
   325 ◯ 251

2. 425 is greater than / less than 446
   425 ◯ 446

3. 237 is greater than / less than 437
   237 ◯ 437

4. 583 is greater than / less than 581
   583 ◯ 581

5. 698 is greater than / less than 700
   698 ◯ 700

6. 820 is greater than / less than 802
   820 ◯ 802

Home Connection Your child is comparing numbers to 1,000. Show your child a three-digit number. Ask him or her to write one number that is greater than and another that is less than your number.

Compare. Write $>$ or $<$.
Use models if you like.

1.	267 $<$ 276	829 ◯ 819	300 ◯ 299
2.	742 ◯ 724	351 ◯ 352	409 ◯ 421
3.	698 ◯ 800	572 ◯ 527	200 ◯ 201
4.	186 ◯ 168	660 ◯ 460	716 ◯ 761
5.	950 ◯ 850	437 ◯ 347	513 ◯ 517
6.	333 ◯ 233	699 ◯ 700	811 ◯ 788
7.	472 ◯ 473	105 ◯ 150	602 ◯ 502
8.	589 ◯ 598	265 ◯ 264	999 ◯ 998

Problem Solving

Use the clues to find each number.

9. It is greater than 498.
   It is less than 501.
   It has a 9 in the tens place.

   The number is _____.

10. It is greater than 621.
    It is less than 629.
    It has a 6 in the ones place.

    The number is _____.

Name________________________________ **Ordering Numbers to 1,000**

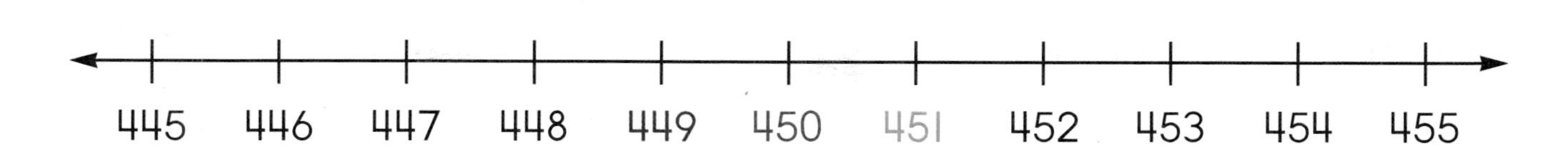

449 is **after** 448.

450 is **before** 451.

451 is **between** 450 and 452.

Write the number that comes **after**.

1. 106, 107   614, ____   548, ____
2. 329, ____   263, ____   409, ____
3. 777, ____   950, ____   899, ____

Write the number that comes **before**.

4. 417, 418   ____, 221   ____, 776
5. ____, 802   ____, 163   ____, 689
6. ____, 320   ____, 919   ____, 500

Write the number that comes **between**.

7. 333, 334, 335   558, ____, 560
8. 205, ____, 207   997, ____, 999
9. 499, ____, 501   809, ____, 811

Home Connection Your child is learning to order three-digit numbers. Name a three-digit number and have your child identify the numbers that come before and after your number.

Write the missing numbers.

1. 316, 317, 318, ____, ____, ____, 322, ____

2. 431, 432, ____, ____, 435, ____, ____, 438

3. ____, 568, ____, ____, ____, 572, ____, ____

4. 650, ____, ____, ____, 654, ____, ____, ____

5. ____, 729, ____, ____, ____, ____, ____, 735

6. 897, ____, ____, ____, ____, 902, ____, ____

7. ____, 995, ____, ____, ____, 999, 1,000

Critical Thinking Corner

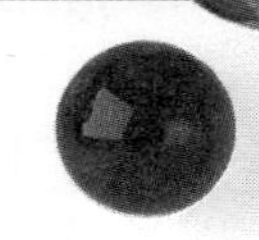

Logical Thinking

Match the marbles to the correct person.

8. Pete has more marbles than Bea.
Bob has fewer marbles than Pete.
Bea has more marbles than Bob.

Bob	252 marbles
Bea	136 marbles
Pete	140 marbles

Name____________________

140
240
340
440
540
640
740
To count back by 100s, think of one less hundred each time.
To count on by 100s, think of one more hundred each time.

Count on and back by 100s. Look for patterns.
Use models if you like.

1. 125, 225, 325, 425, 525, 625, 725
2. ____, ____, ____, 560, ____, ____, ____
3. ____, ____, ____, 699, ____, ____, ____
4. ____, ____, ____, 507, ____, ____, ____
5. ____, ____, ____, 310, ____, ____, ____

Count on and back by 10s. Look for patterns.

6. 110, 120, 130, 140, 150, 160, 170
7. ____, ____, ____, 352, ____, ____, ____
8. ____, ____, ____, 664, ____, ____, ____
9. ____, ____, ____, 932, ____, ____, ____
10. ____, ____, ____, 580, ____, ____, ____

Home Connection Help your child practice using number patterns. Write a number such as 436. Ask your child to count on or back by 100s or 10s from the number.

Use models if you like.

1. Write the number that is 2 **hundreds more**.

367	441	230	673
567	______	______	______

2. Write the number that is 2 **hundreds less**.

781	513	949	803
______	______	______	______

3. Write the number that is 2 **tens more**.

415	720	945	570
______	______	______	______

4. Write the number that is 2 **tens less**.

330	225	714	501
______	______	______	______

Critical Thinking Corner

Number Sense

5. If $25 + 10 = 35$, then $250 + 100 =$ ______

6. If $48 + 10 = 58$, then $480 + 100 =$ ______

Name______________________________

Fill in the ◯ for the correct answer.

Add or subtract.

1. $\begin{array}{r} 9 \\ +7 \\ \hline \end{array}$

◯ 14
◯ 15
◯ 16
◯ 17

2. $\begin{array}{r} 14 \\ -\ 9 \\ \hline \end{array}$

◯ 5
◯ 6
◯ 7
◯ 8

3. $\begin{array}{r} 6 \\ 2 \\ +\ 8 \\ \hline \end{array}$

◯ 14
◯ 15
◯ 16
◯ 17

4. $\begin{array}{r} 35 \\ +29 \\ \hline \end{array}$

◯ 54
◯ 64
◯ 65
◯ 55

5. $\begin{array}{r} 64 \\ -17 \\ \hline \end{array}$

◯ 47
◯ 57
◯ 81
◯ 71

6. $\begin{array}{r} 56 \\ +31 \\ \hline \end{array}$

◯ 25
◯ 97
◯ 15
◯ 87

7. $\begin{array}{r} 70 \\ -43 \\ \hline \end{array}$

◯ 27
◯ 33
◯ 37
◯ 36

8. $\begin{array}{r} 28 \\ +52 \\ \hline \end{array}$

◯ 36
◯ 81
◯ 70
◯ 80

9. $\begin{array}{r} 97 \\ -80 \\ \hline \end{array}$

◯ 10
◯ 17
◯ 27
◯ 70

Find the total amount.

10. 

◯ 65¢
◯ 60¢
◯ 45¢
◯ 29¢

11. 
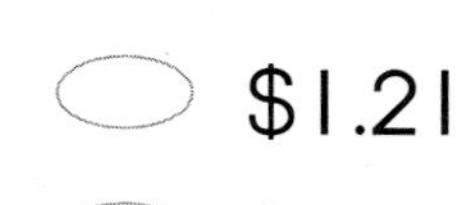

◯ $1.21
◯ $2.30
◯ $2.21
◯ $2.15

Choose the correct number.

12. 3 tens 6 ones

◯ 63 ◯ 36 ◯ 33 ◯ 66

13. 4 hundreds 7 tens 9 ones

◯ 794 ◯ 497 ◯ 749 ◯ 479

Match the time.

14. 

- ◯ 5:40
- ◯ 8:25
- ◯ 5:45
- ◯ 8:35

15. 

- ◯ 9:10
- ◯ 2:45
- ◯ 1:45
- ◯ 1:15

Estimate the length of each object.

16.

- ◯ 1 foot
- ◯ 2 feet
- ◯ 2 inches
- ◯ 1 inch

17. 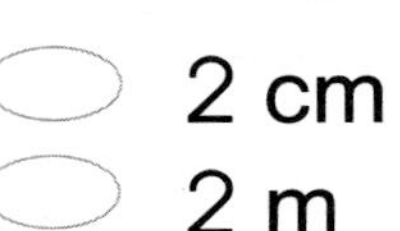

- ◯ 2 cm
- ◯ 7 cm
- ◯ 2 m
- ◯ 7 m

Find the value of the red digit.

18. 346

- ◯ 400
- ◯ 40
- ◯ 4

19. 621 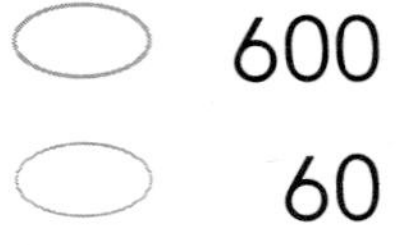

- ◯ 600
- ◯ 60
- ◯ 6

20. 511

- ◯ 100
- ◯ 10
- ◯ 1

Complete each pattern.

21. 665, 765, 865, ____

◯ 866 ◯ 965 ◯ 875 ◯ 975

22. 261, 271, 281, ____

◯ 391 ◯ 282 ◯ 381 ◯ 291

Choose the correct unit of measure to answer each question.

23. How long is it?

◯ pounds ◯ cups ◯ inches ◯ °F

24. How heavy is it?

◯ grams ◯ cm ◯ liters ◯ °C

Use the calendar to answer the question.

25. What is the date of the third Monday?

◯ 3 ◯ 21 ◯ 14 ◯ 30

S	M	T	W	T	F	S
		1	2	3	4	5
6	7	8	9	10	11	12
13	14	15	16	17	18	19
20	21	22	23	24	25	26
27	28	29	30			

CHAPTER 10
Geometry, Fractions, and Probability
Shapes Around Us
written by Becky Manfredini
NEW YORK YANKEES
Atlanta BRAVES
NEW YORK KNICKS
This Math Storybook belongs to
A

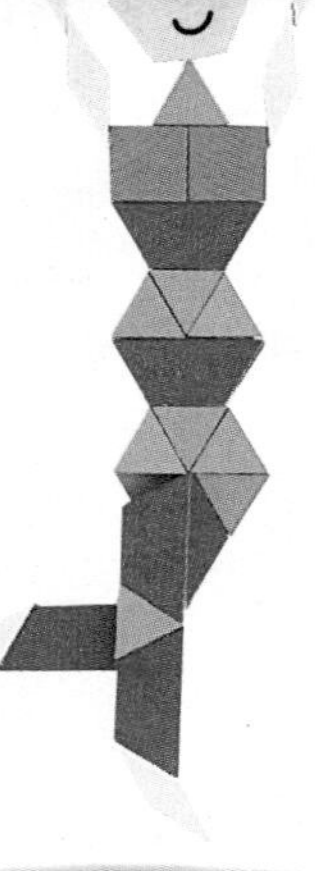

Shapes are all around us.
They're found most everywhere.
Can you find a **triangle**,
a **circle**, and a **square**?

Now I spy a **rectangle**
and on it I will write.
On the shelf I spy a **sphere**
that spins from left to right.

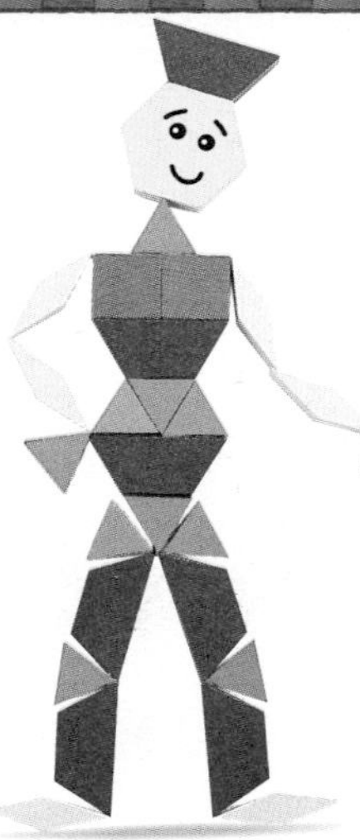

Now I spy two **circles**
that are standing side by side.
And I spy a **cylinder**
to crawl into and hide.

Now I spy some tasty **spheres**
with sugar **cones** below.
I could eat each one of them.
They're lined up in a row!

Now I spy a **rectangle**
I pass through every day.
It's how I get inside
to eat and sleep and play.

www.sbgmath.com

Shapes are all around us.
They're found most anywhere.
Draw some things with **circles,**
triangles, and **squares**.

A Note to the Family

Here are some learning ideas you can share with your child.

Enjoy *Shapes Around Us* Together

- Read the story aloud with your child. After reading each page, have your child find and identify the shapes that are pictured. Talk about the attributes of each shape and why certain objects have particular shapes. For example, point out that an ice-cream cone is wider at the top to hold ice cream and narrows to a point to make it easier to hold.
- On the last page, have your child describe what he or she has drawn. Ask your child to name the shapes he or she used.

At-Home Activities

- Provide your child with several different shapes of various sizes cut out from cardboard or paper. Allow your child to arrange the shapes in different ways to make a new shape. Talk about what the new shape might be.
- Look for different shapes in buildings and objects around you. For example, look for windows that are shaped like rectangles, squares, and circles. Point out that windows are often divided into equal parts.

Read More About It!

To read more about geometry and fractions, look for these books in your local library.

- *The Amazing Book of Shapes* by Lydia Sharman (Dorling Kindersley, 1994)
- *The Greedy Triangle* by Marilyn Burns (Scholastic, 1995)
- *Shape Space* by Cathryn Falwell (Clarion Books, 1992)

Visit Our Web Site!

www.sbgmath.com

Name______________________________

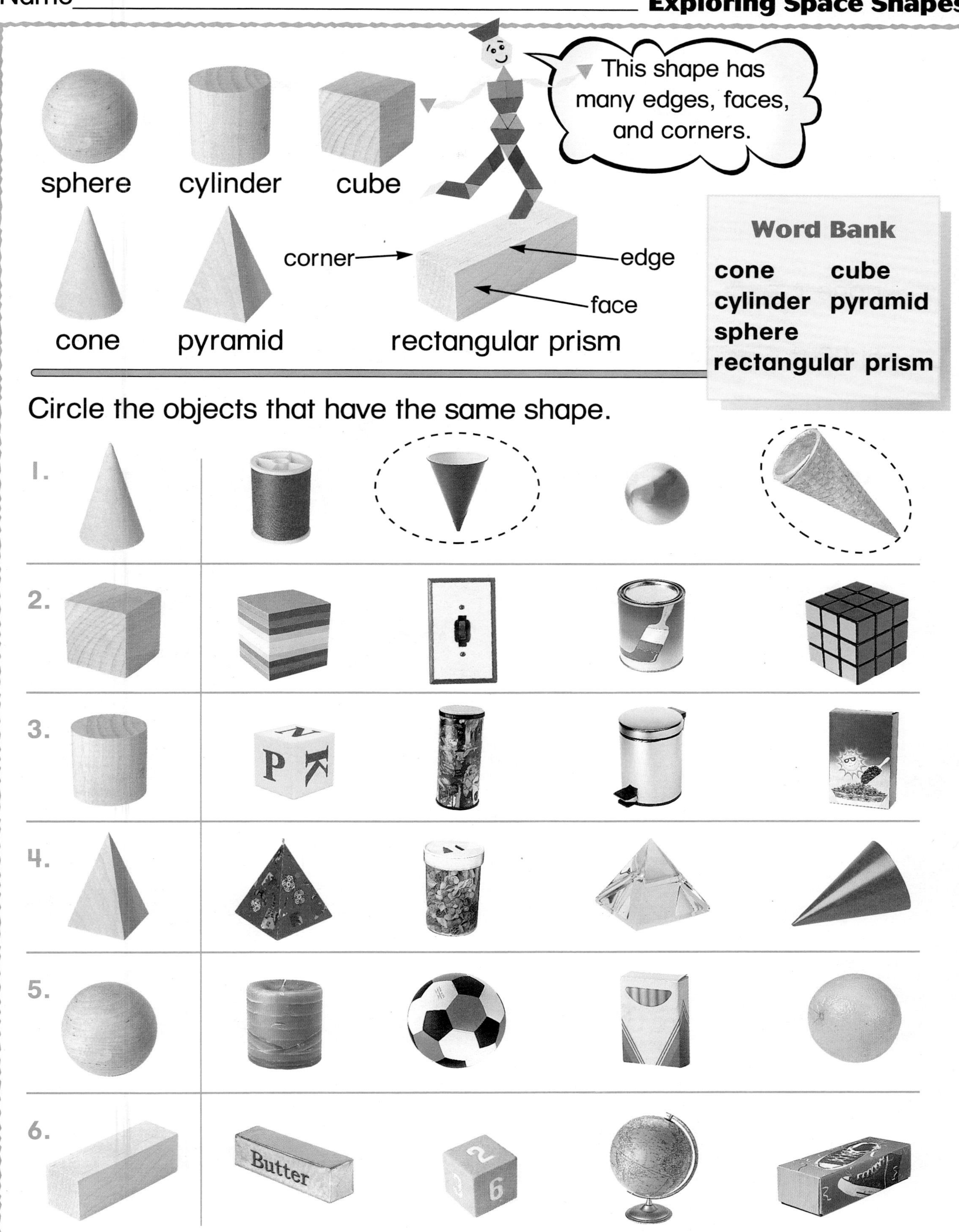

Home Connection Your child is learning to identify the shape of common objects. Ask him or her to find some objects in your home that have the shapes shown above.

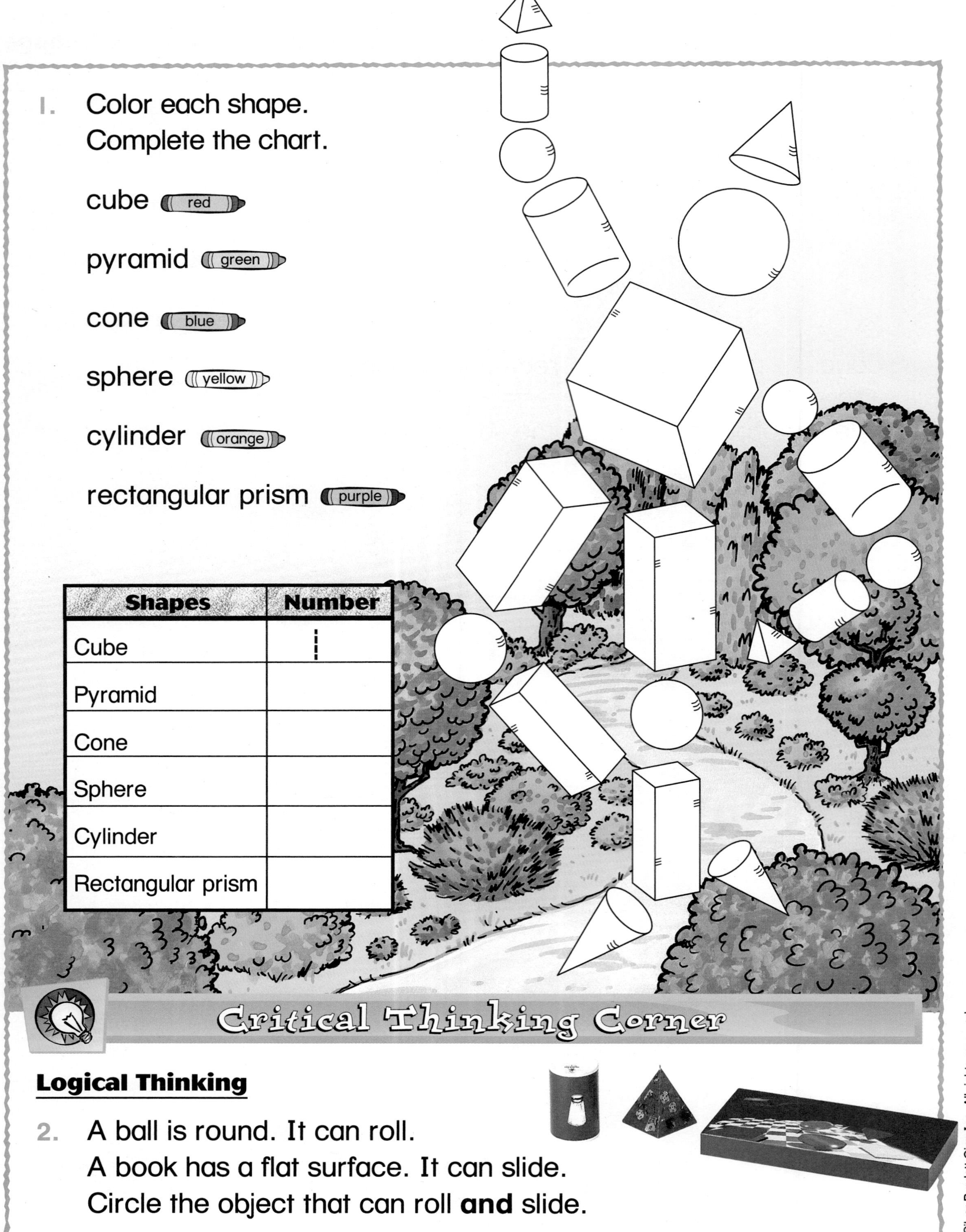

1. Color each shape.
Complete the chart.

cube red

pyramid green

cone blue

sphere yellow

cylinder orange

rectangular prism purple

Shapes	Number
Cube	
Pyramid	
Cone	
Sphere	
Cylinder	
Rectangular prism	

Critical Thinking Corner

Logical Thinking

2. A ball is round. It can roll.
A book has a flat surface. It can slide.
Circle the object that can roll **and** slide.

Name____________________

You can use a space shape to draw a plane shape.

If I draw around the face of a cone, what shape will I make?

Word Bank
- circle
- square
- rectangle
- triangle

Circle the space shape you could use to draw each plane shape.

1. 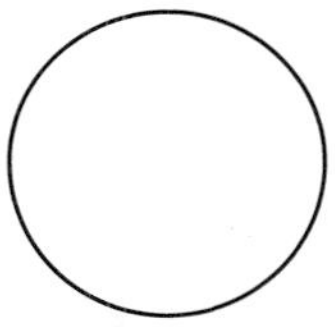 circle 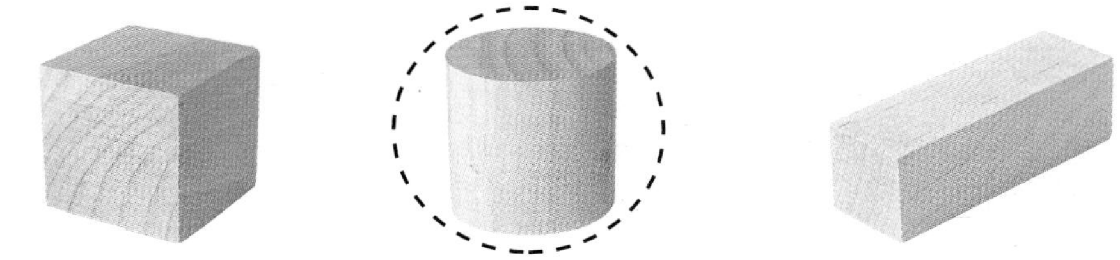
2. square 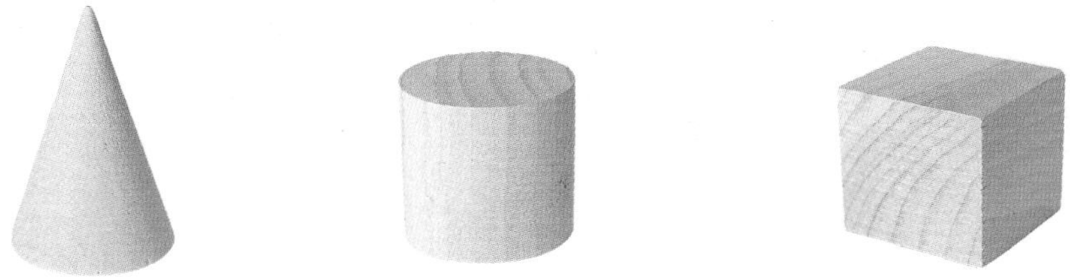
3. 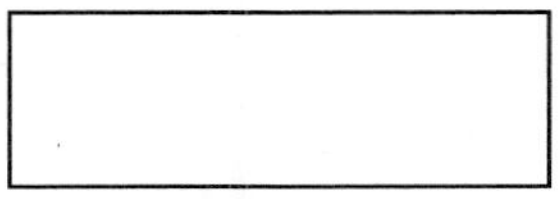 rectangle 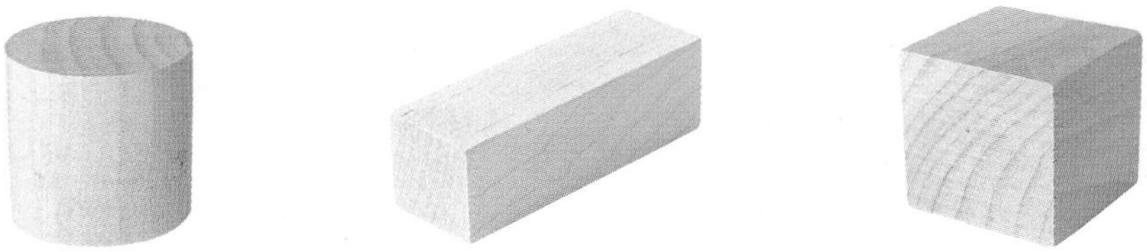
4. 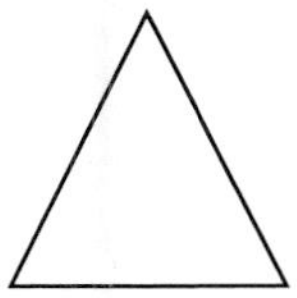 triangle 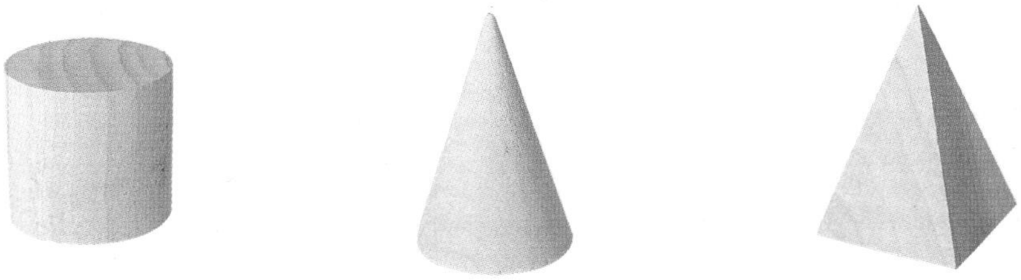
5. 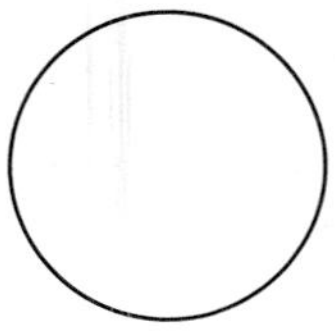 circle

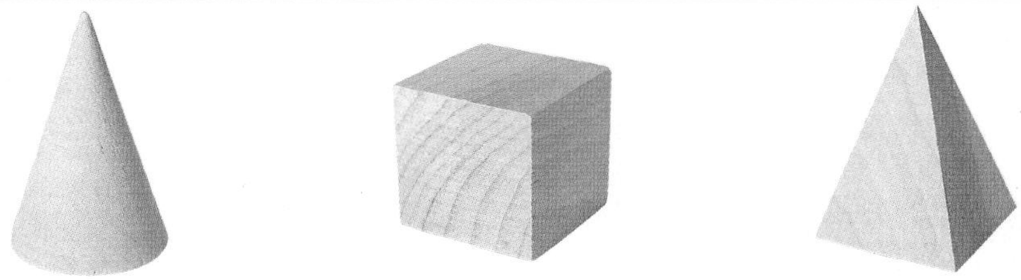

Home Connection Your child is learning to identify the faces of three-dimensional objects. Ask him or her to draw around an object, such as a cereal box, and tell what shape is made.

What if you drew around the face of each object?
Circle the shape you would make.

1.  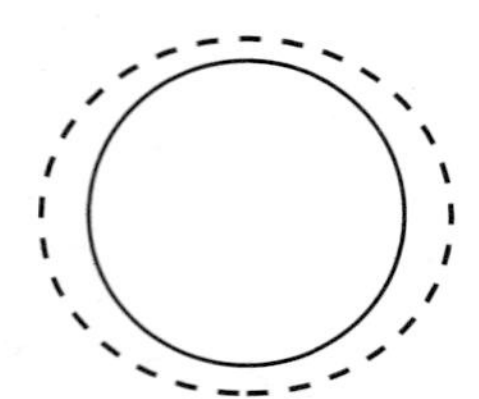 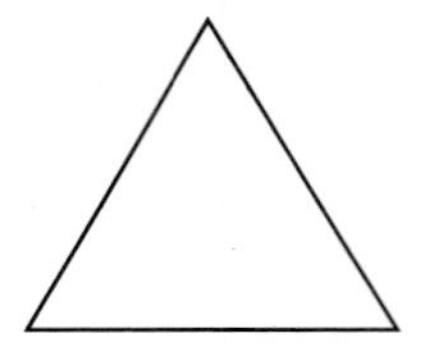

2.  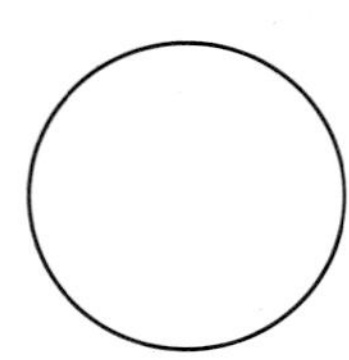 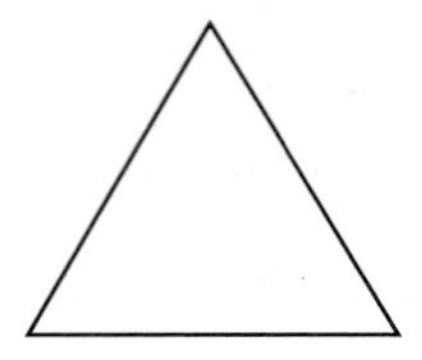 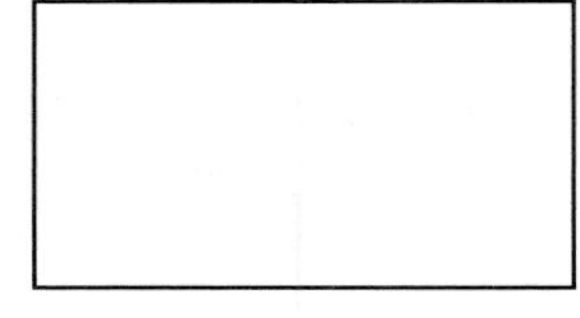

3. 

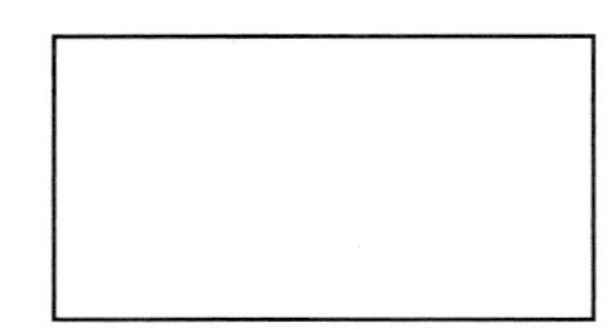 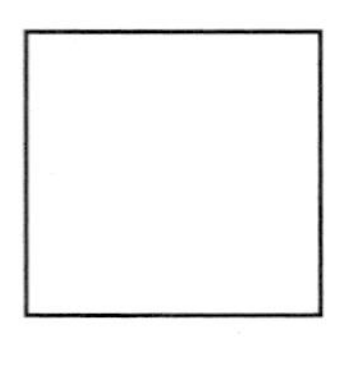 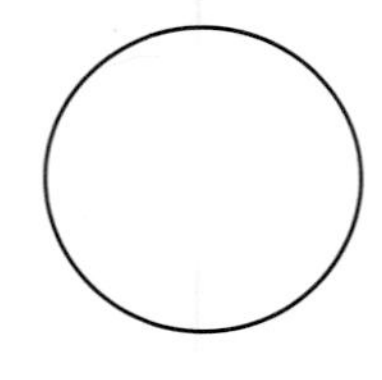

4.  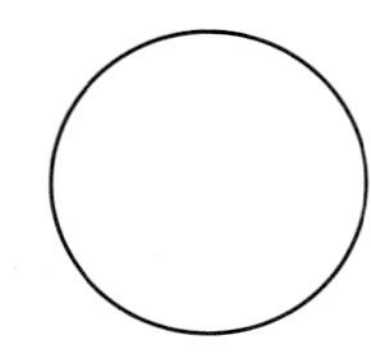 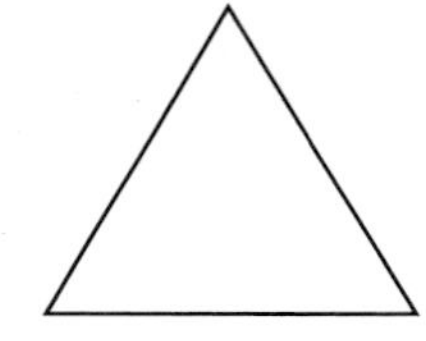 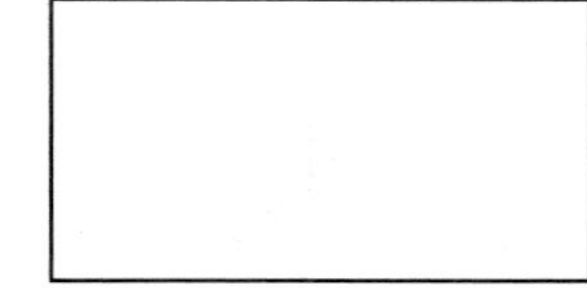

Problem Solving

Solve.

5. How many faces does each shape have?

sphere _____

cylinder _____

cube _____

rectangular prism _____

Name________________________________ **Making New Shapes**

You can make new shapes from shapes you know.

This new shape looks like a duck!

Use pattern blocks.
Try different ways to make each shape.
Color to show one way.

1.

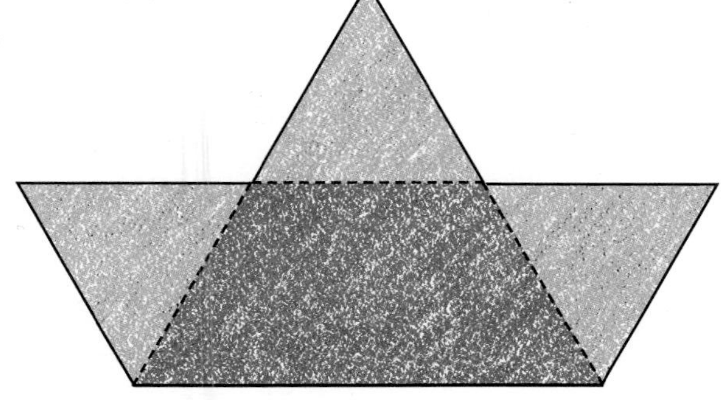

2.

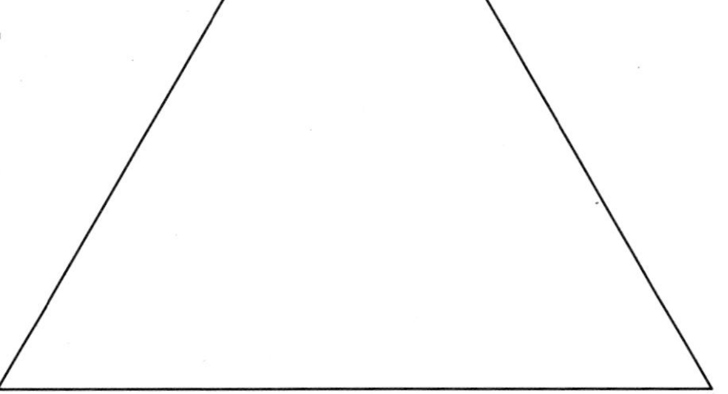

3.

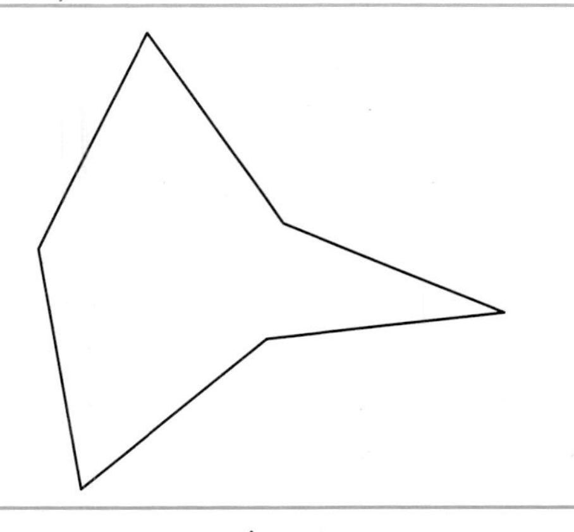

4.

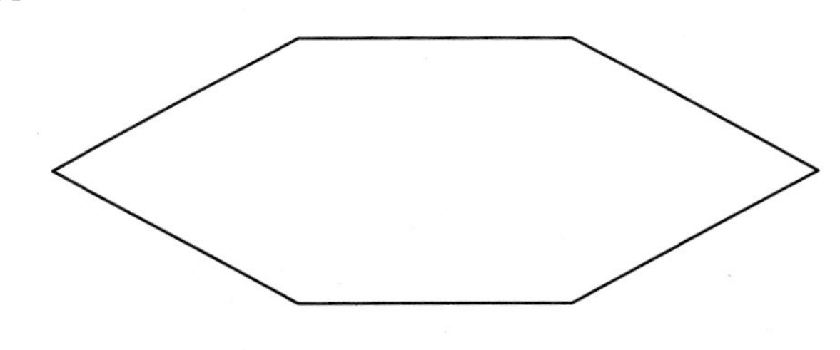

5.

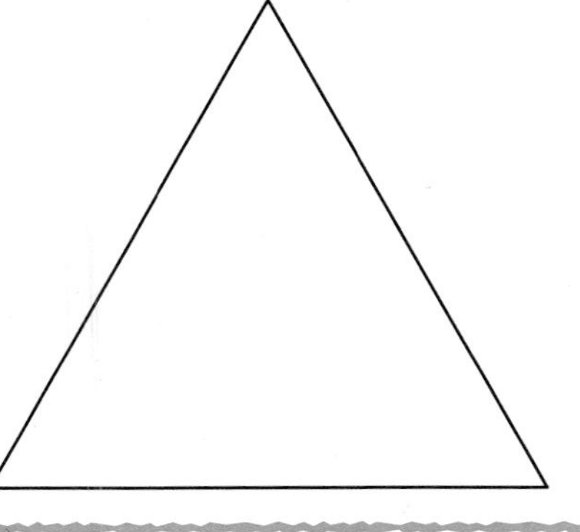

6.

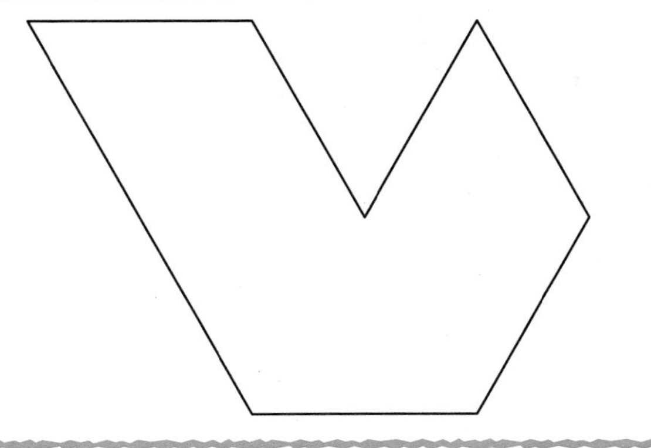

Home Connection Your child is learning how to use pattern blocks to make shapes. Invite him or her to draw a shape made of two or more shapes.

Use pattern blocks.
Try different ways to make each shape.
Color to show one way.

1.

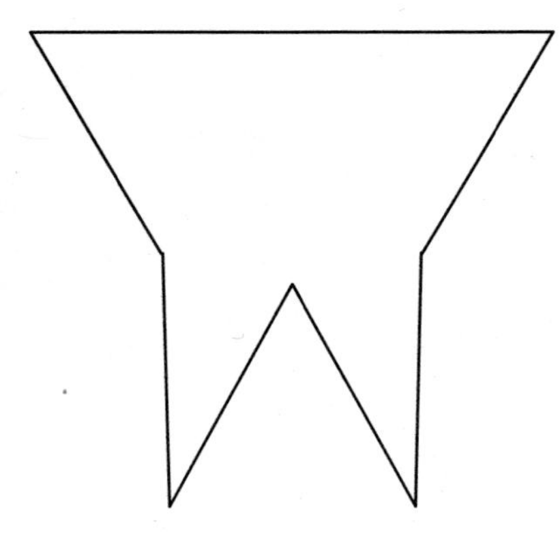

2.

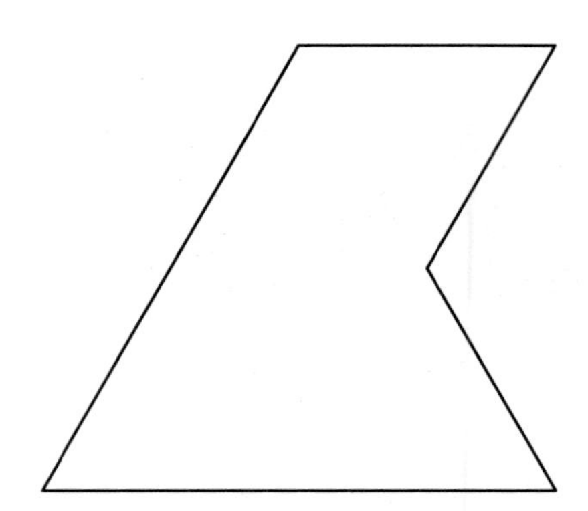

3. Make your own shape. Trace around pattern blocks.
Color to show the blocks you used.

Critical Thinking Corner

Visual Thinking

4. Use and to make the shape below.
Make a pattern with the blocks.
Color to show the pattern.

Name____

How many corners and sides does a square have?

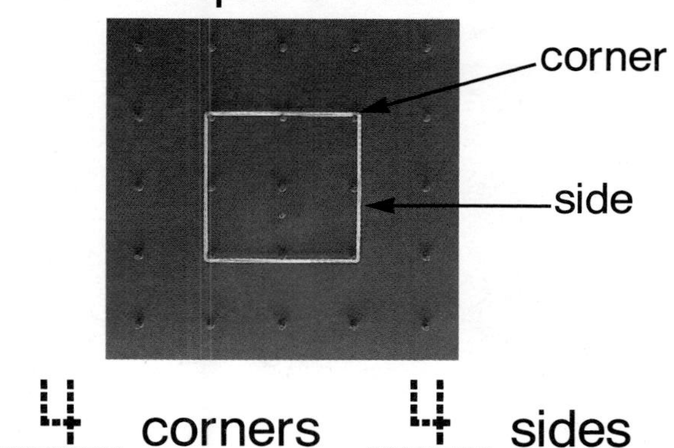

4 corners 4 sides

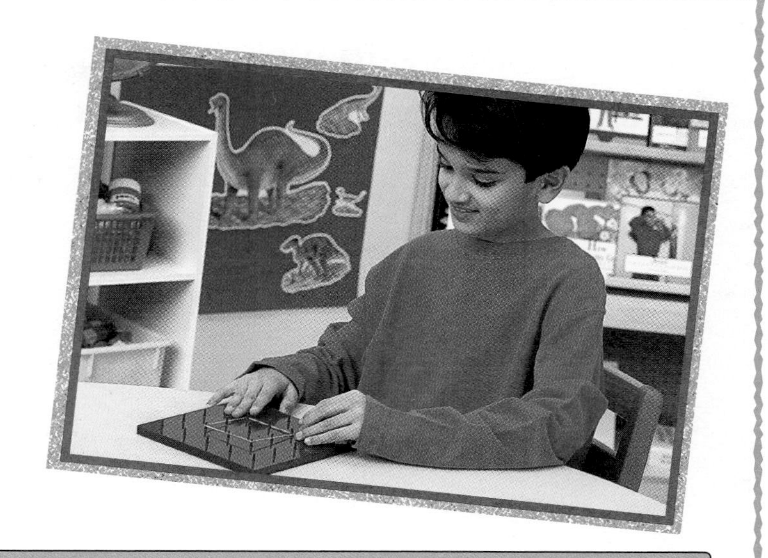

Use a geoboard to make each shape.
Draw the shape. Write the number of corners and sides.

1. large square

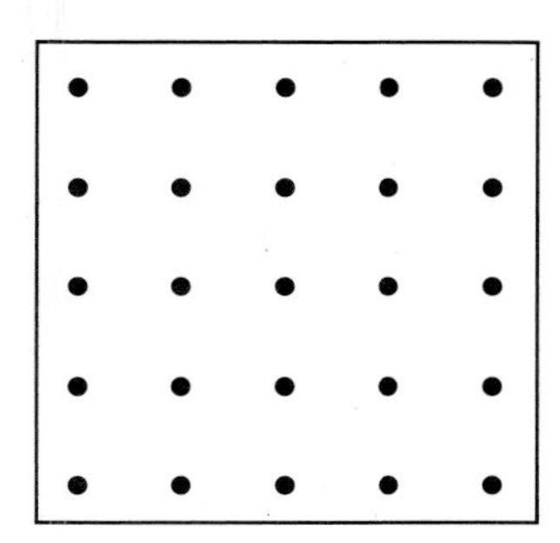

____ corners ____ sides

2. triangle

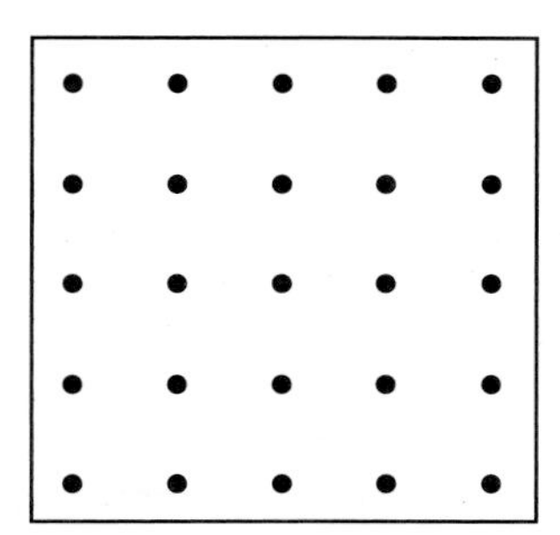

____ corners ____ sides

3. small rectangle

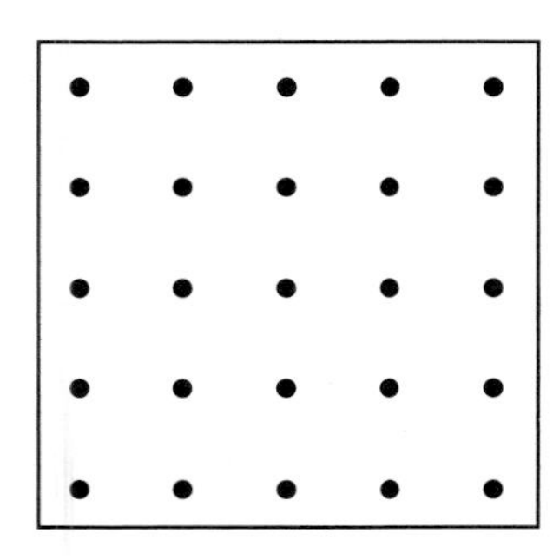

____ corners ____ sides

4. large rectangle

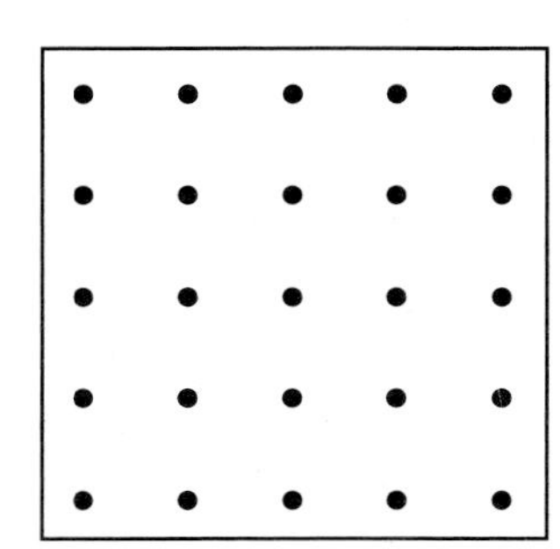

____ corners ____ sides

Home Connection Your child is learning how to identify and count corners and sides on shapes. Ask him or her to draw a plane shape and tell how many corners and sides it has.

Use a geoboard to make each shape.
Write the number of corners and sides.

1.

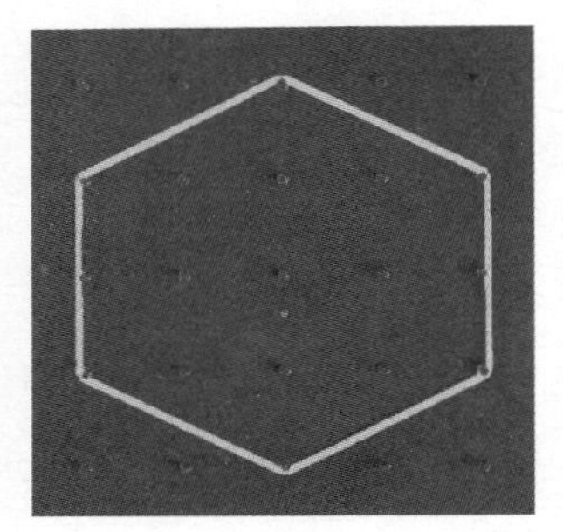

_____ corners _____ sides

2.

_____ corners _____ sides

Use a geoboard to make your own shapes.
Draw the shapes. Write the number of corners and sides.

3.

_____ corners _____ sides

4.

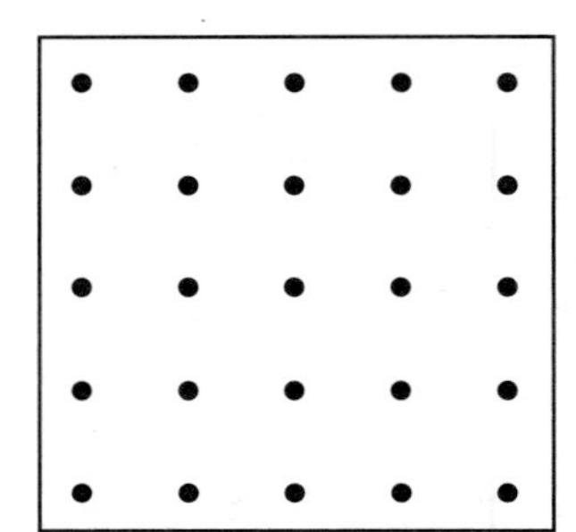

_____ corners _____ sides

Problem Solving

Solve.

5. Jon drew a plane shape with 3 corners and 3 sides. What shape did he draw?

____

6. Aidan drew a plane shape with 4 corners and 4 equal sides. What shape did she draw?

____

Name____

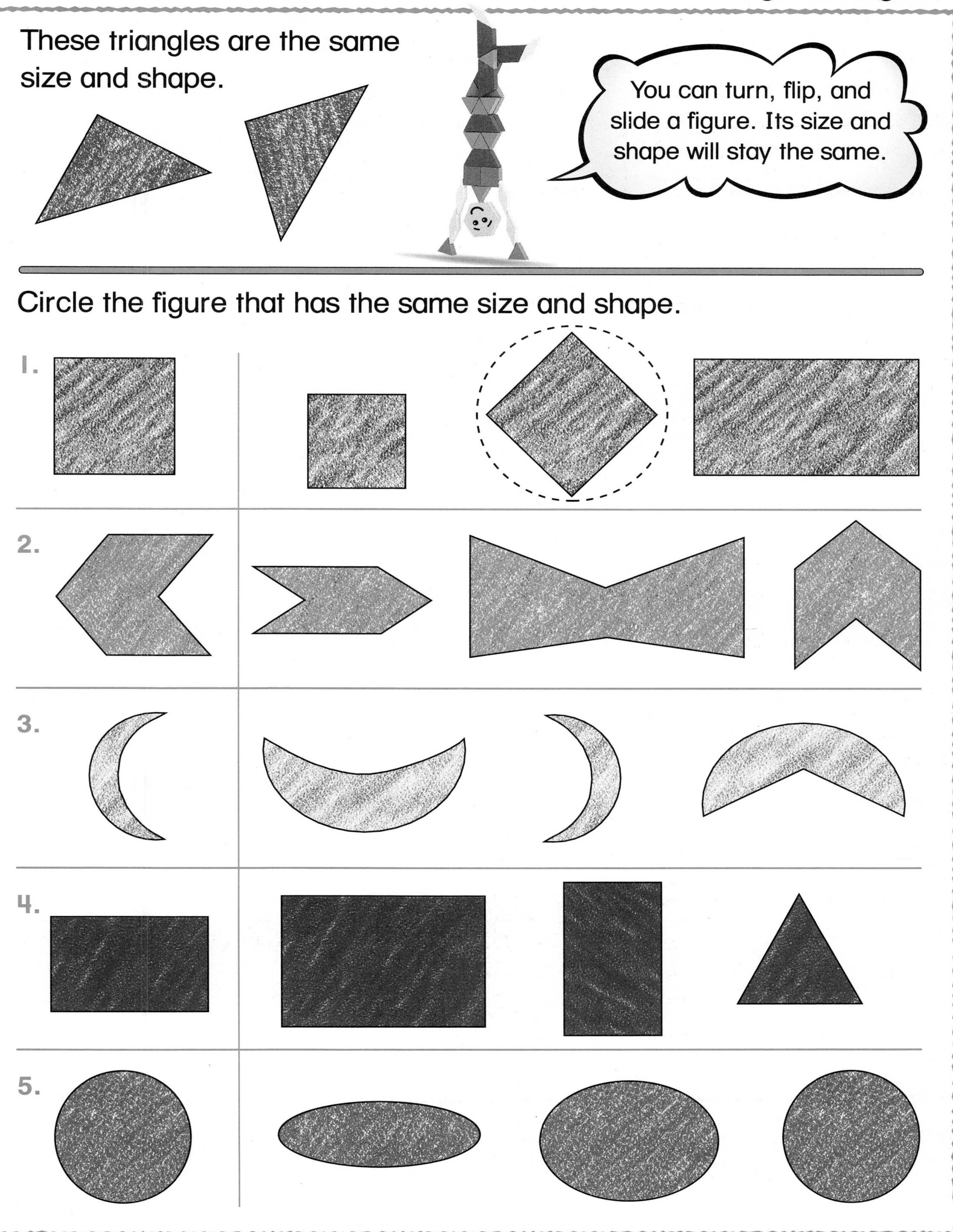

You can turn, flip, and slide a figure. Its size and shape will stay the same.

These triangles are the same size and shape.

Circle the figure that has the same size and shape.

1.

2.

3.

4.

5.

Home Connection Your child is learning to recognize figures that are the same size and shape. Ask your child to explain how he or she found the matching figures in the exercises on this page.

Draw a figure that is the same size and shape.
Write the number of corners and sides.

1.

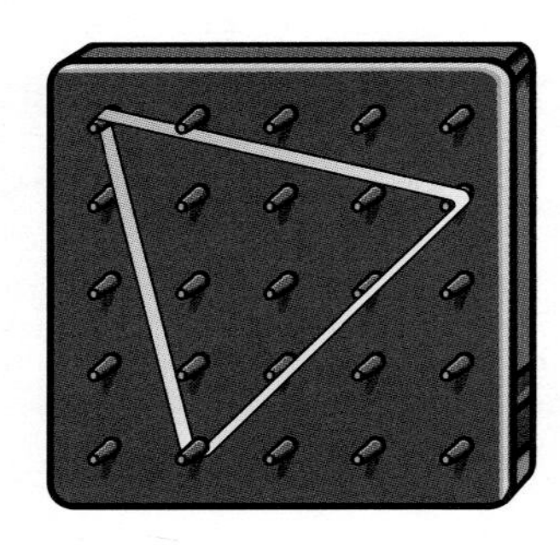

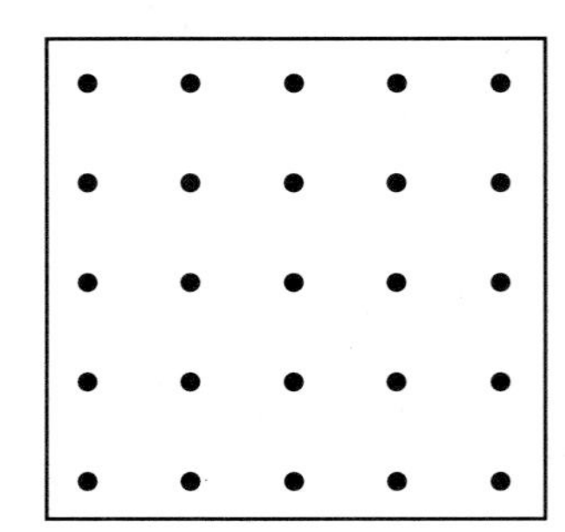

_____ corners

_____ sides

2.

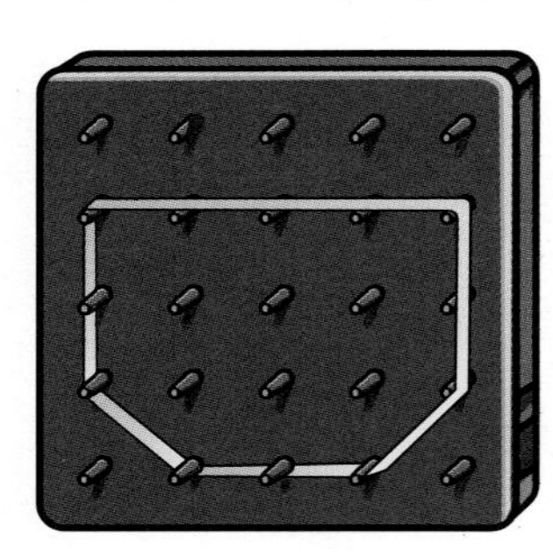

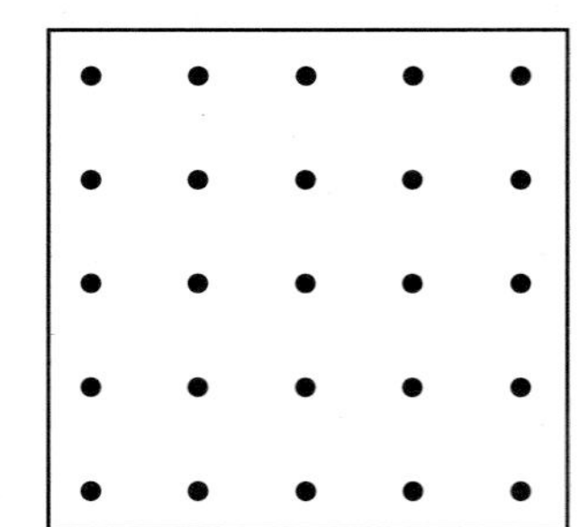

_____ corners

_____ sides

3.

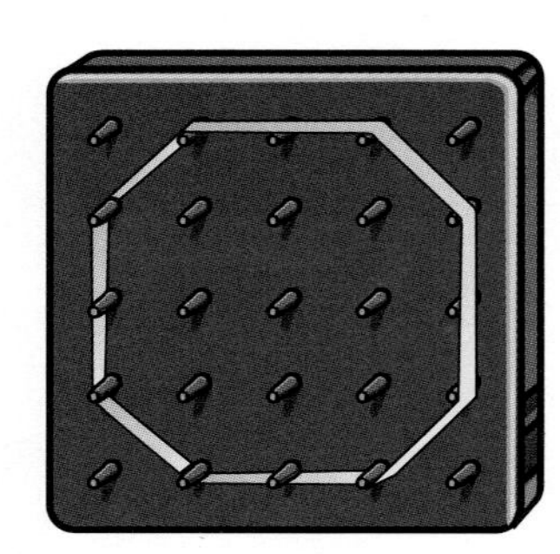

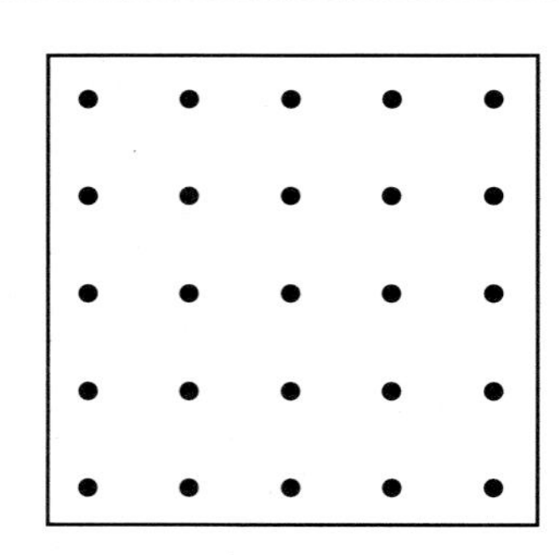

_____ corners

_____ sides

Critical Thinking Corner

Visual Thinking

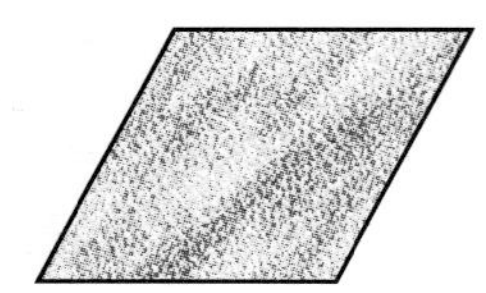

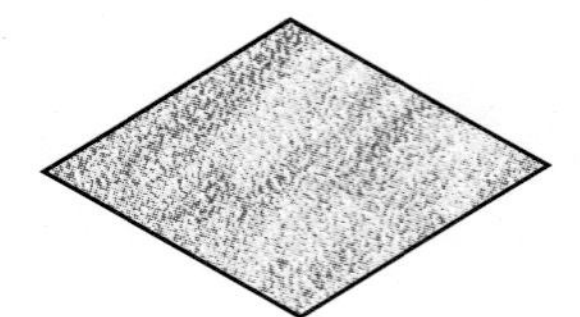

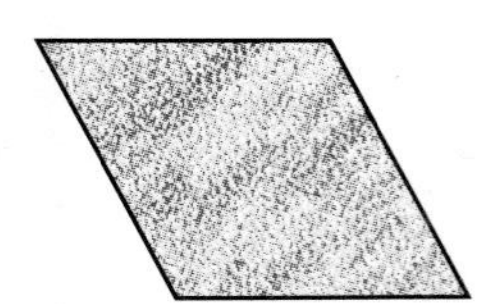

4. Are all three figures the same size and shape?
Write **yes** or **no**. Explain your answer.

____

____

Name________________________________

What is the distance around the rectangle?
Count the number of inches around to find out.

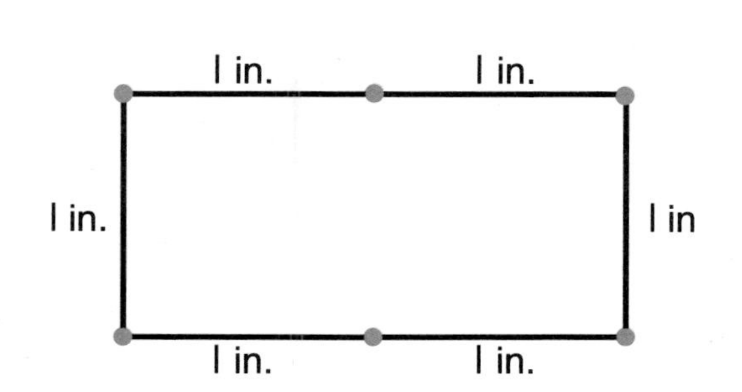

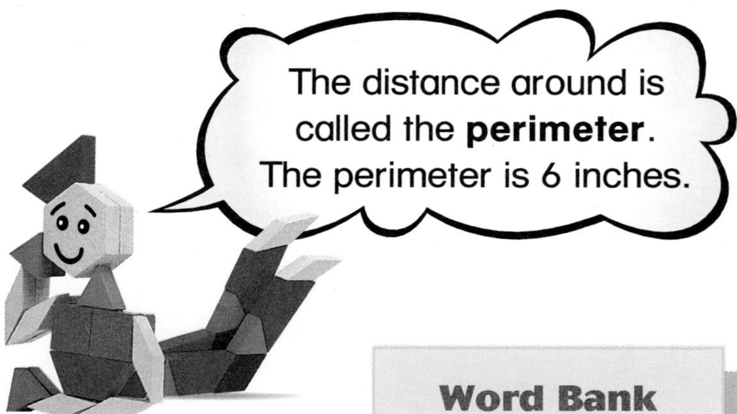

The distance around is called the **perimeter**. The perimeter is 6 inches.

Word Bank
perimeter

Find the perimeter of each shape.
Count the number of inches around.

1.

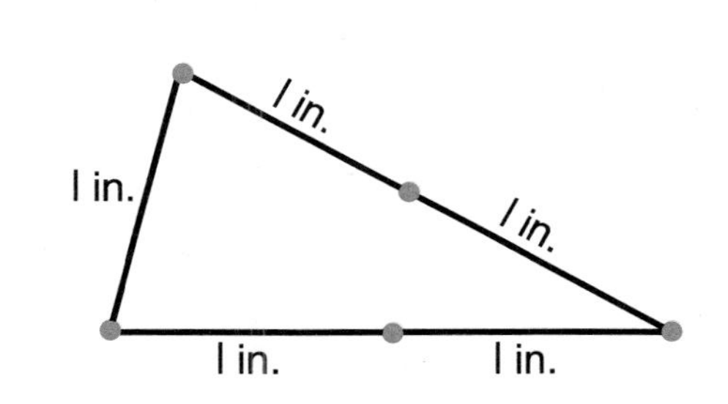

____ in.

2.

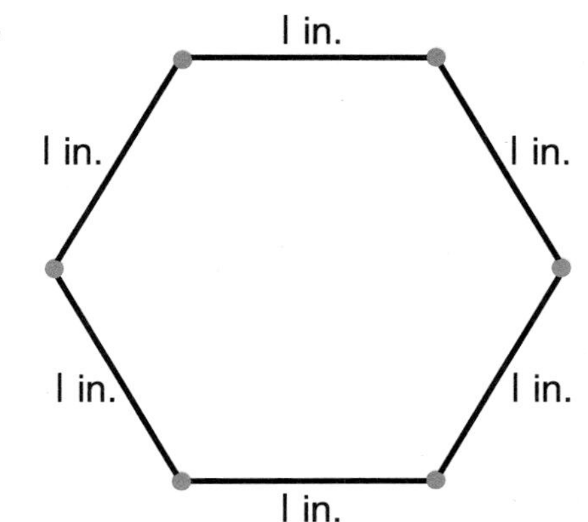

____ in.

3.

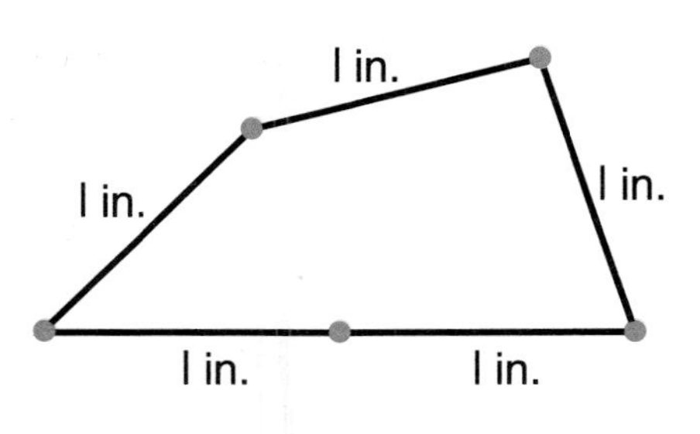

____ in.

4.

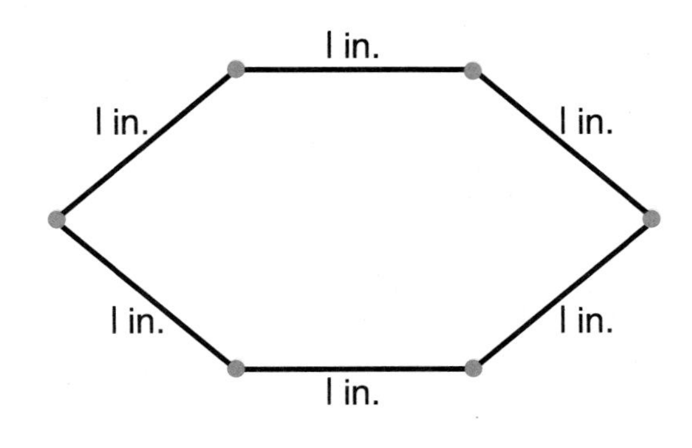

____ in.

Home Connection Your child is learning to find perimeter. Draw a triangle, square, or rectangle with sides that are 1, 2, or 3 inches in length. Ask your child to find the perimeter.

1. Use the grid to draw a square and a rectangle.
Make each side of the shapes 1, 2, or 3 inches long.
Write the perimeter.

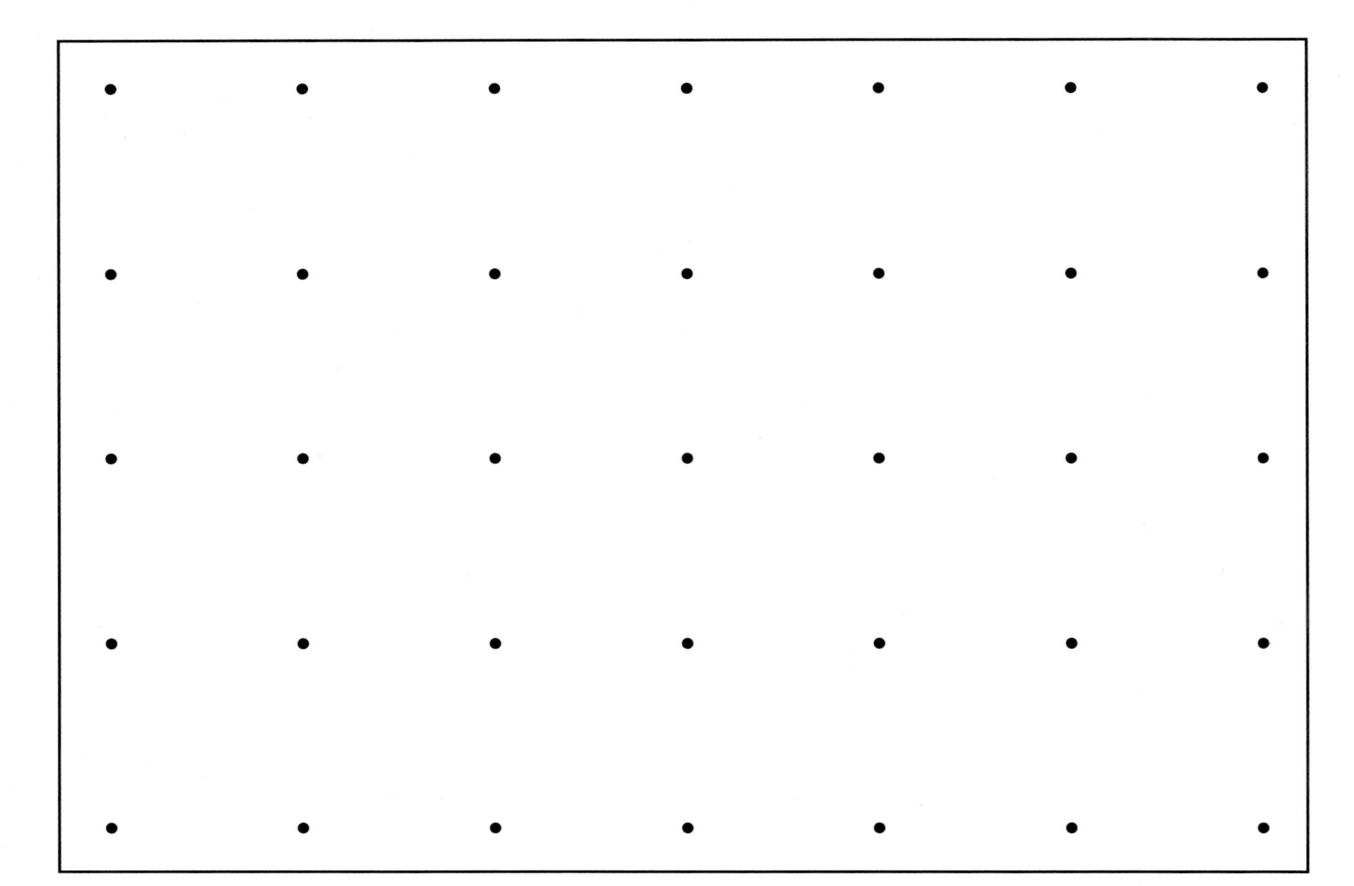

perimeter of square _____ in.   perimeter of rectangle _____ in.

Problem Solving

How many square units cover each shape? 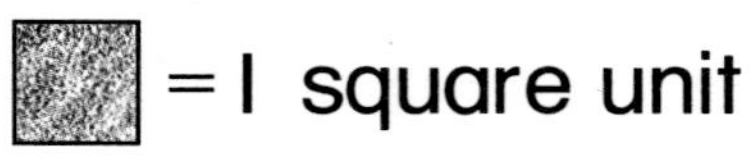

2. 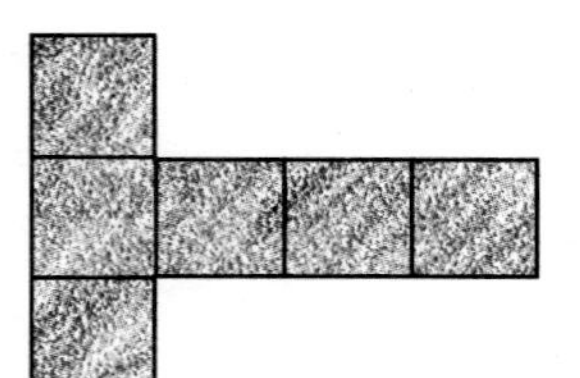 _____ square units

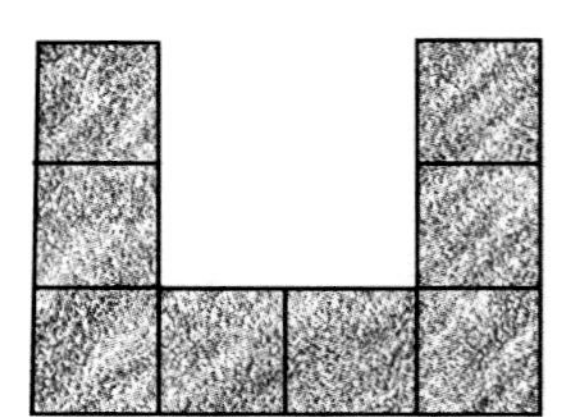 _____ square units

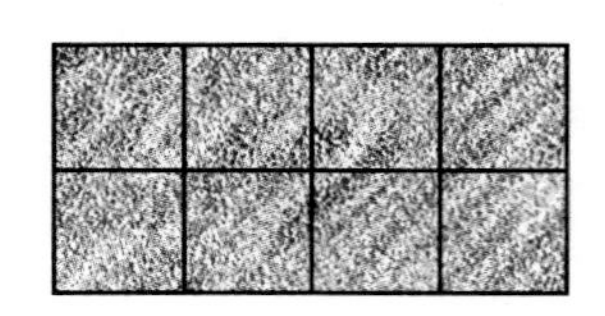 _____ square units

Name______________________________

You can make a bar graph to show how many squares of each color are in the quilt.

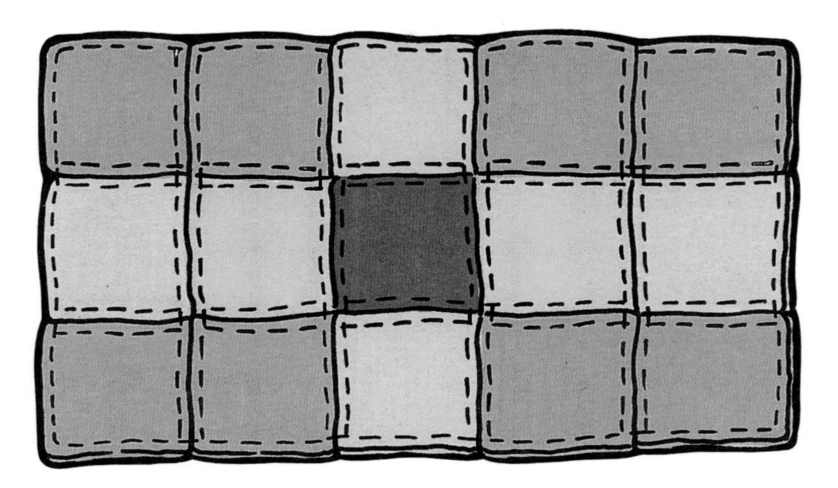

Color one box for each quilt square.
Use the graph to answer each question.

1. How many blue squares are there? _____ blue squares
2. How many more blue squares are there than yellow squares? _____ blue squares
3. Which color squares are used most often? __________
4. How many squares are in the quilt? _____ squares
5. How many boxes are colored in the graph? _____ boxes

Quilt Squares

8
7
6
5
4
3
2
1
0

Make a bar graph.
Color 1 box for each quilt square.

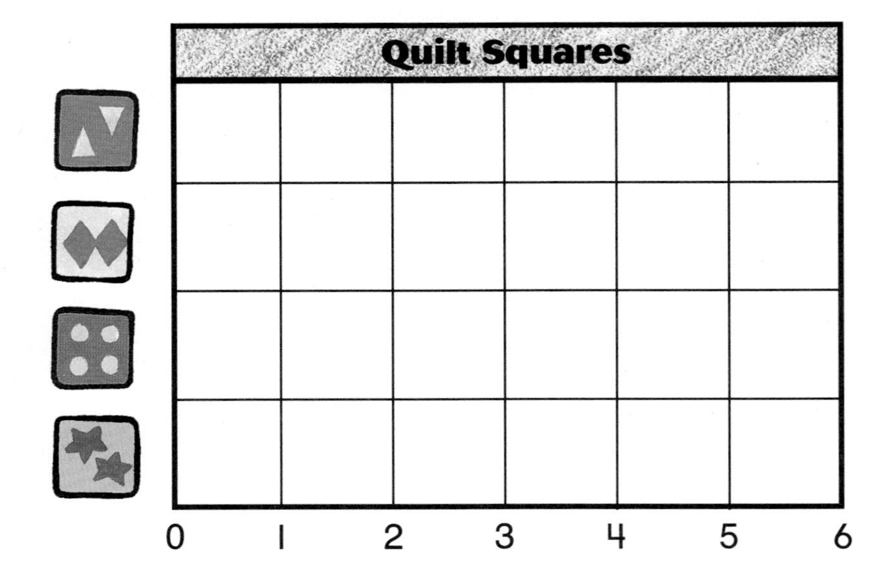

1. Circle the quilt squares that are used an equal number of times.

2. Look at the top row of the quilt.
What if you added another row that is the same?
How would the graph change?

____

____

Critical Thinking Corner

Visual Thinking

3. Pat made this quilt square out of small pieces of cloth. Put an X on the numbered piece that does not belong.

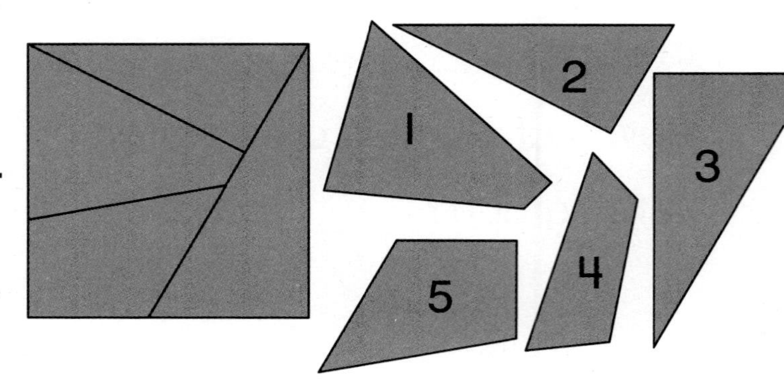

Name____ **Symmetry**

Objects with a line of symmetry have matching parts.

Word Bank
line of symmetry

line of symmetry

matching parts

line of symmetry

matching parts

not a line of symmetry

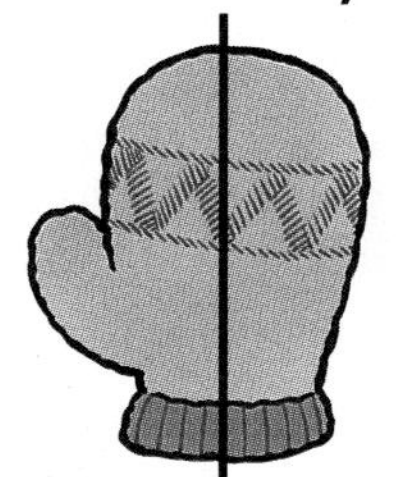

no matching parts

Does each picture have a line of symmetry?
Circle **yes** or **no**. If **yes**, draw a line of symmetry.

1.

yes

no

2.

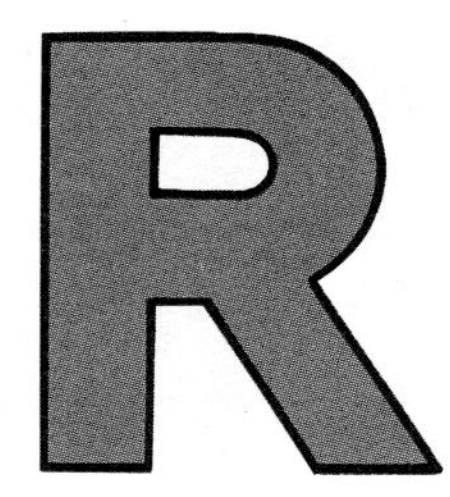

yes

no

3.

yes

no

4.

yes

no

5.

yes

no

6.

yes

no

Home Connection Your child is learning to recognize symmetrical figures. Ask him or her to find 2 or 3 household objects that have a line of symmetry.

Draw a line of symmetry if you can.

1.

2.

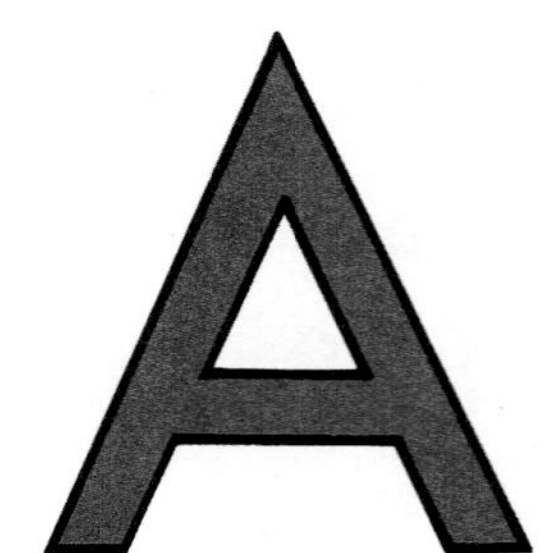

1. Circle the objects that have the same shape.

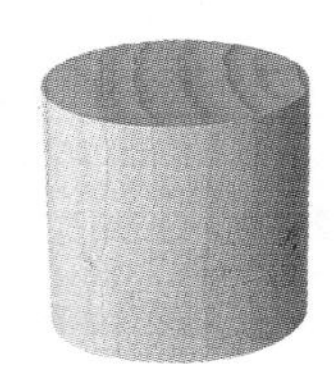

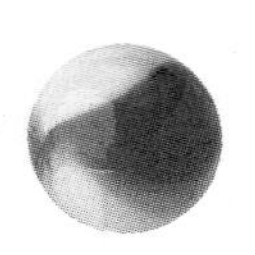

2. Write the number of corners and sides.

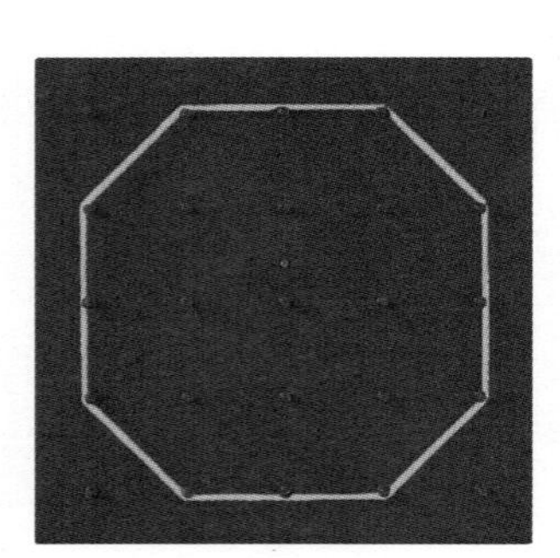

_____ corners

_____ sides

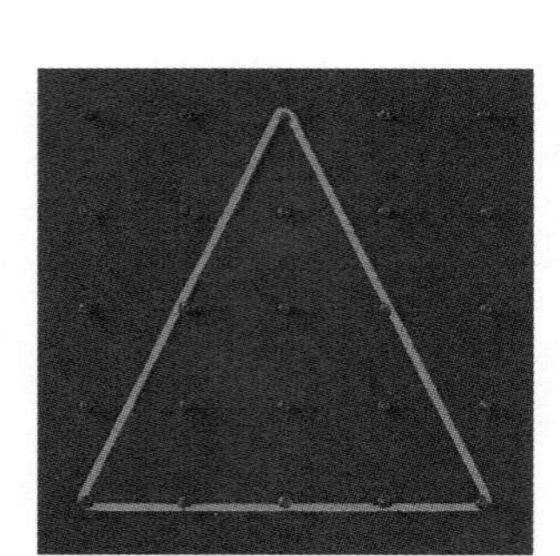

_____ corners

_____ sides

Name______________________________ **Equal Parts**

Each shape shows equal parts.

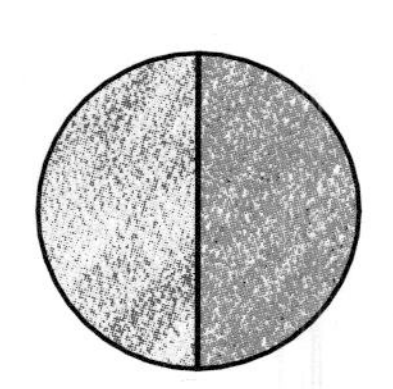

halves
2 equal parts

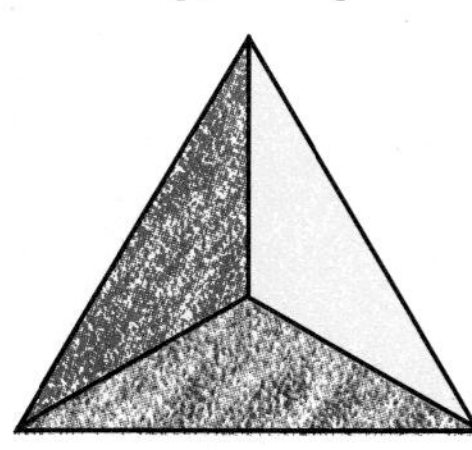

thirds
3 equal parts

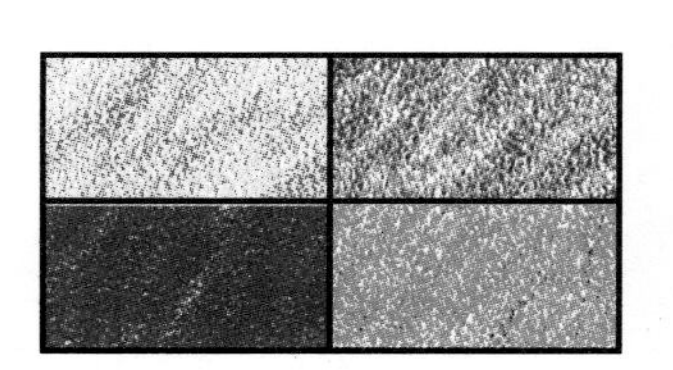

fourths
4 equal parts

Word Bank

halves
thirds
fourths

Write the number of parts.
Circle **equal** or **not equal**.

1. 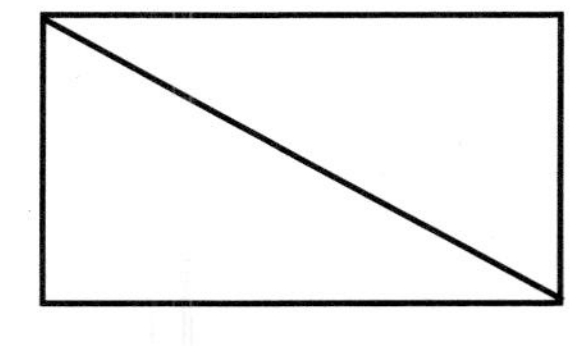

2 parts

equal

not equal

2. 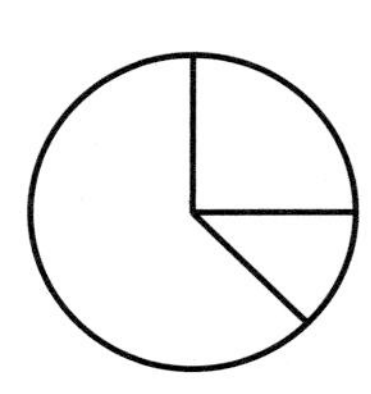

____ parts

equal

not equal

3. 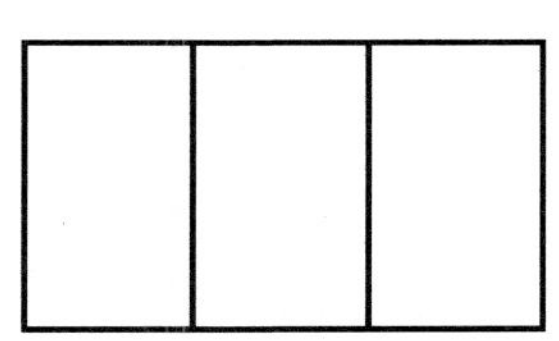

____ parts

equal

not equal

4. 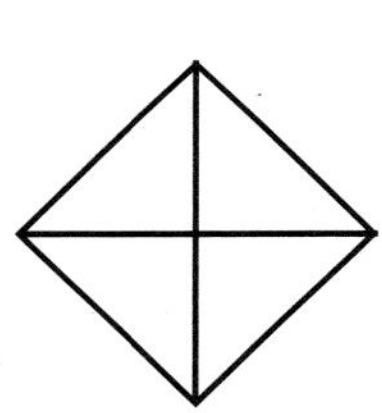

____ parts

equal

not equal

5. ____ parts

equal

not equal

6. 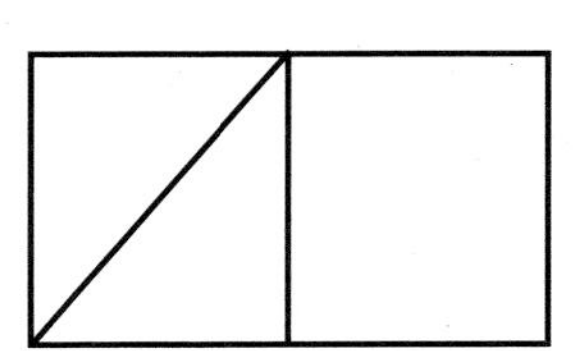

____ parts

equal

not equal

7. ____ parts

equal

not equal

8. 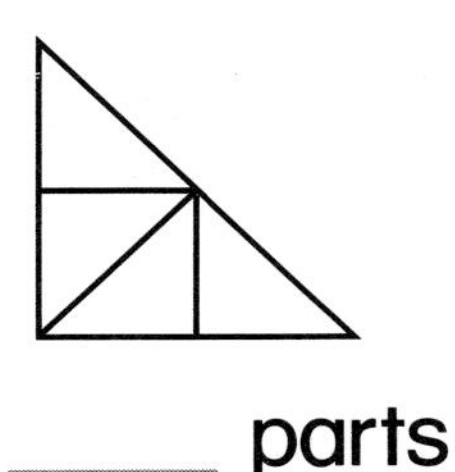

____ parts

equal

not equal

Home Connection Your child is learning to identify equal and unequal parts of shapes. Have your child make equal parts of a shape by folding a piece of paper into 2, 4, and 8 equal parts.

Draw to show equal parts.

1. halves

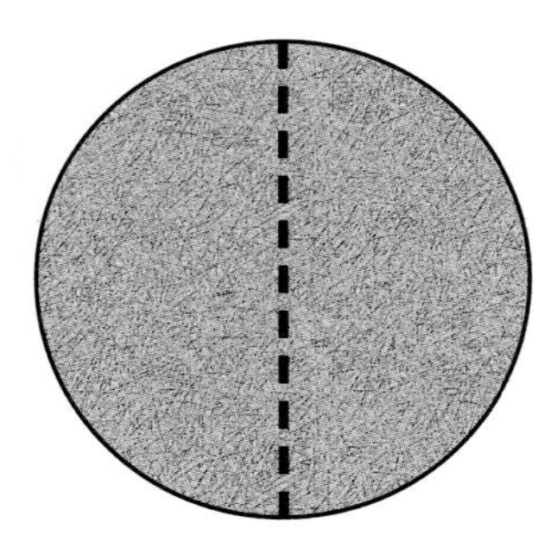

2. fourths

3. fourths

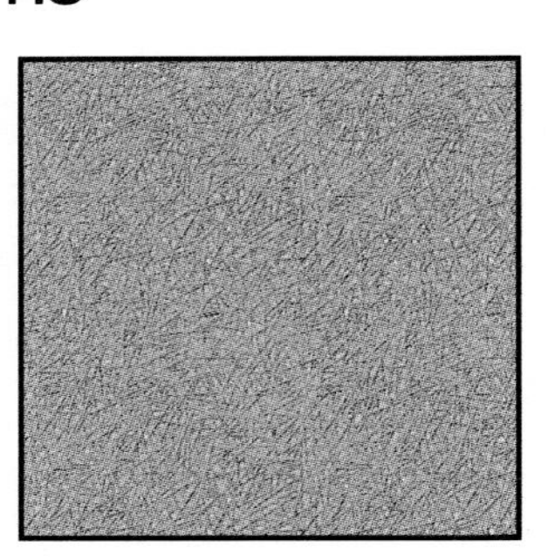

4. halves

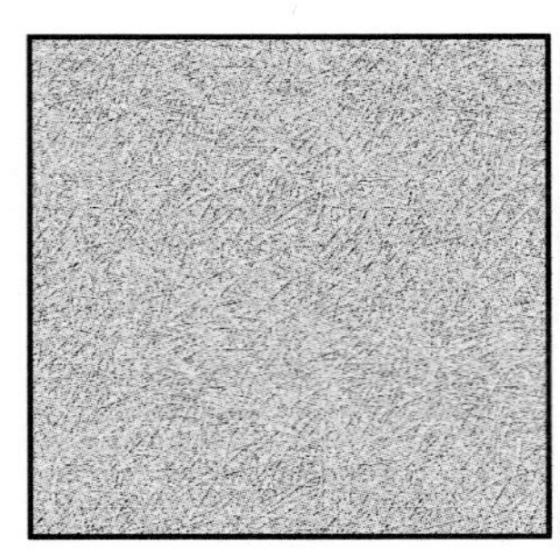

5. thirds

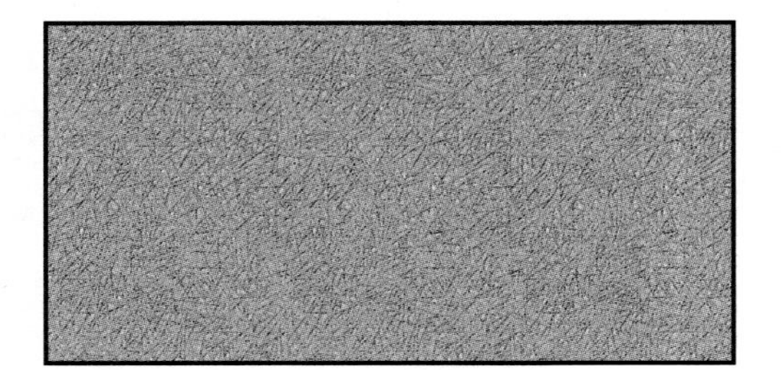

6. fourths

Problem Solving

Solve.

7. Sam and Lydia want to fold a piece of paper into fourths. Draw 2 different ways they could fold the paper. Can you think of other ways?

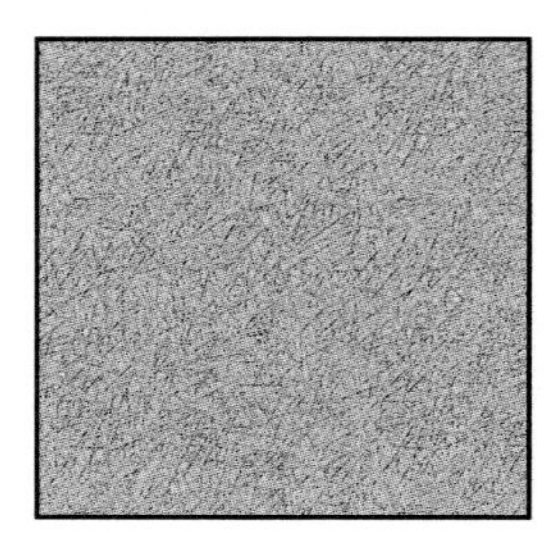

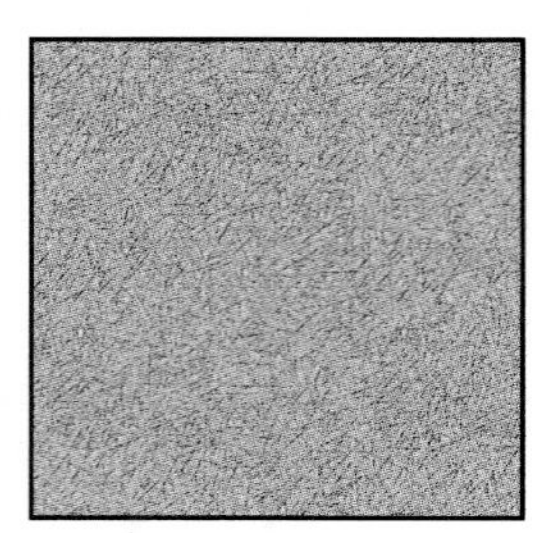

Name____

A fraction can name one equal part.

1 of 2 equal parts	1 of 3 equal parts	1 of 4 equal parts
$\frac{1}{2}$ 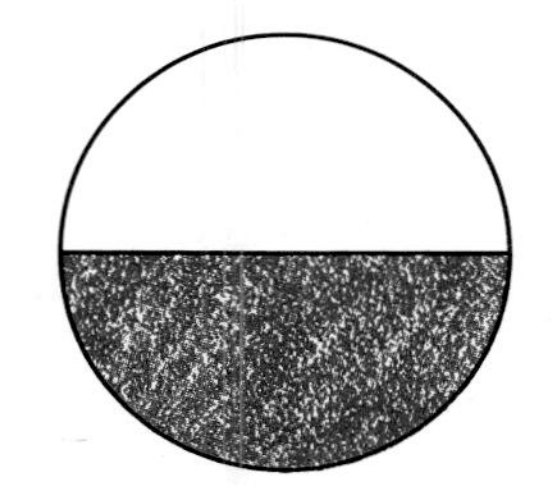	$\frac{1}{3}$ 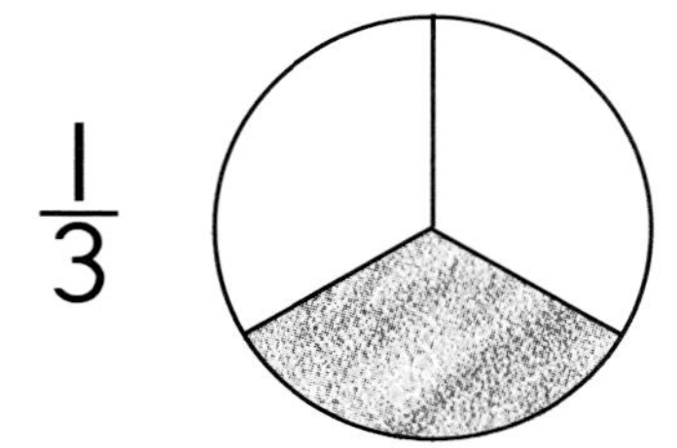	$\frac{1}{4}$ 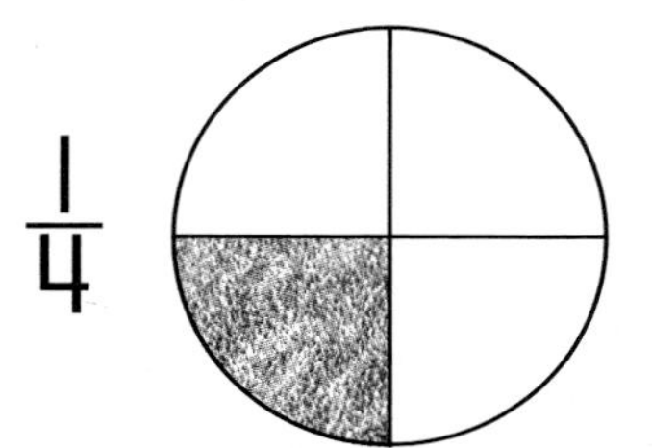
one half	one third	one fourth

Write the fraction for the shaded part.

1. 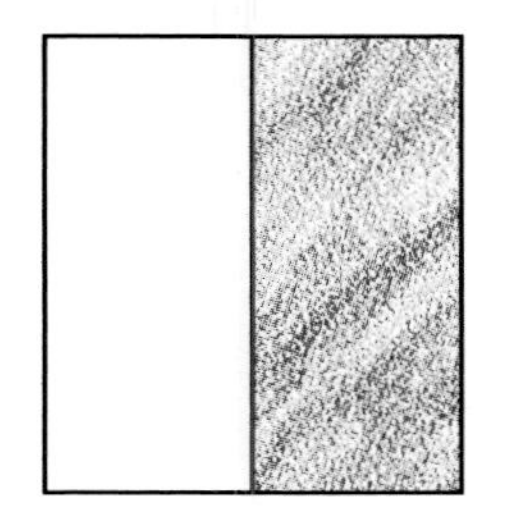 $\frac{1}{2}$

2. 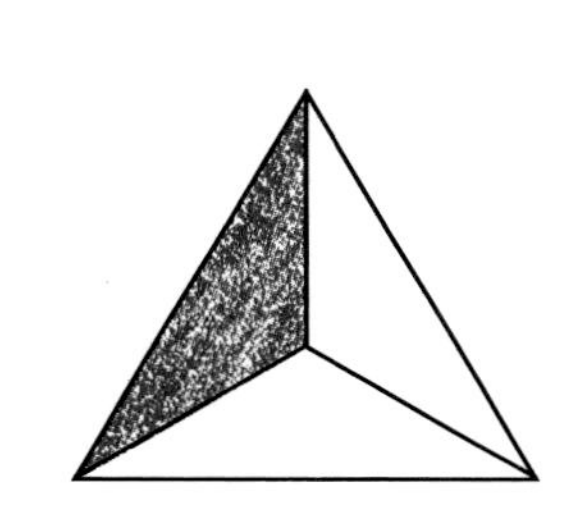 ____

3. 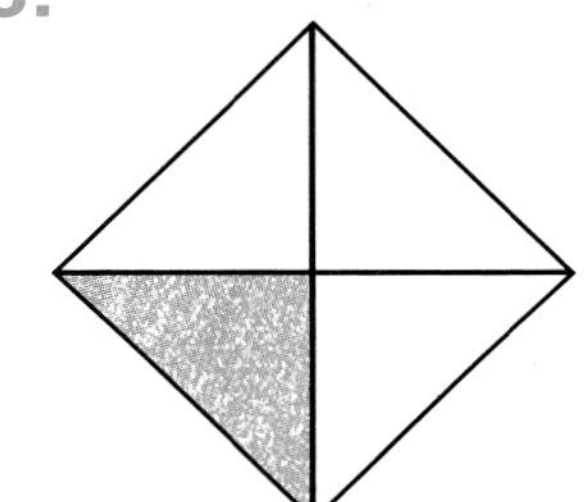 ____

4. 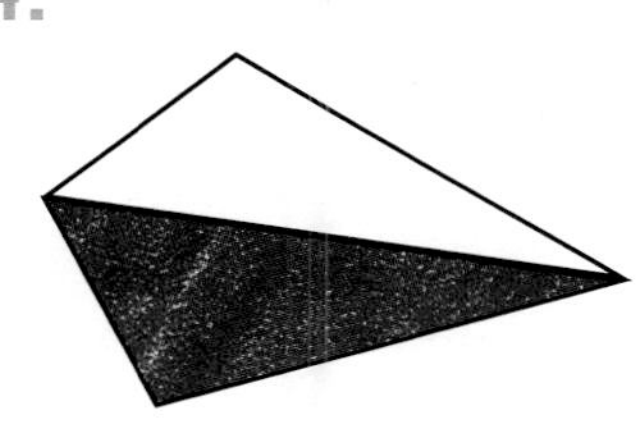 ____

5. 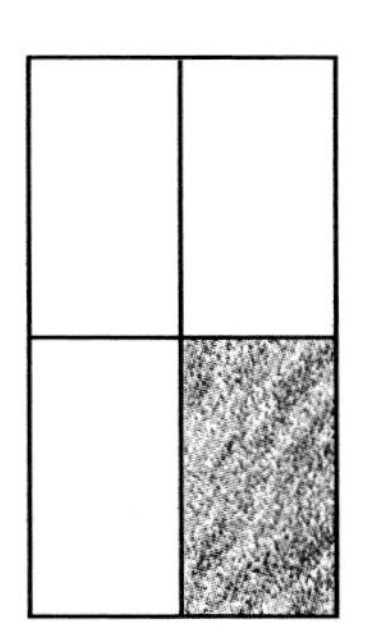 ____

6. 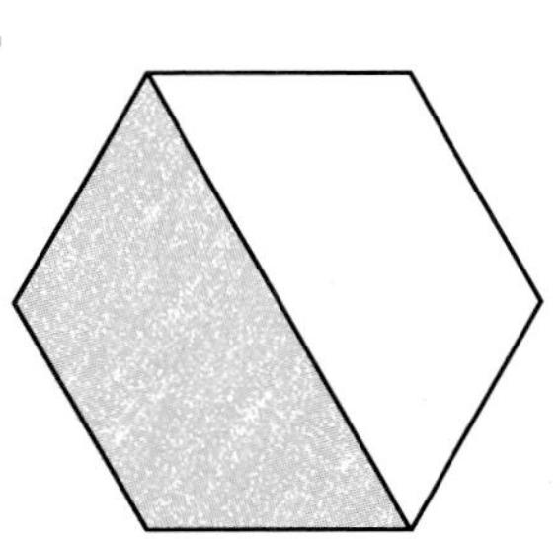 ____

7. 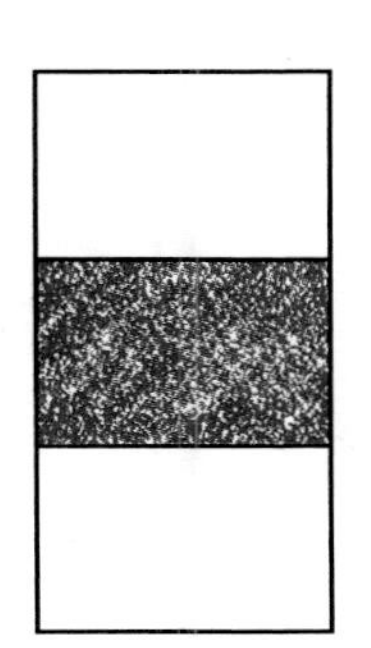 ____

8. 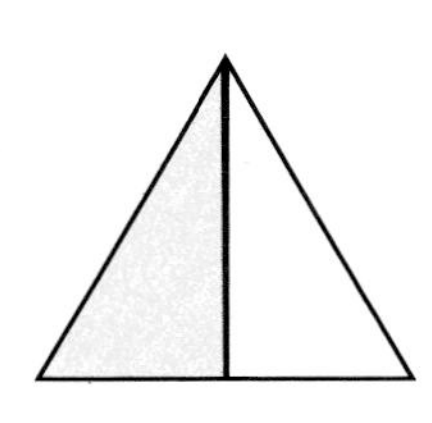 ____

9. 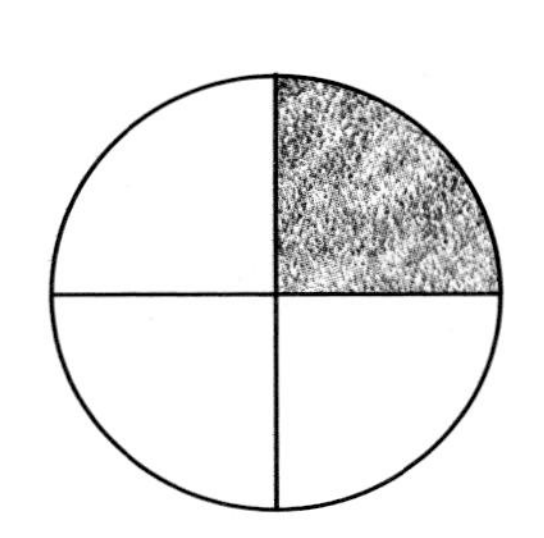 ____

Home Connection Your child is learning about fractions. Ask your child to make pictures showing $\frac{1}{2}$, $\frac{1}{3}$, and $\frac{1}{4}$.

Color to show the fraction.

1. $\frac{1}{2}$

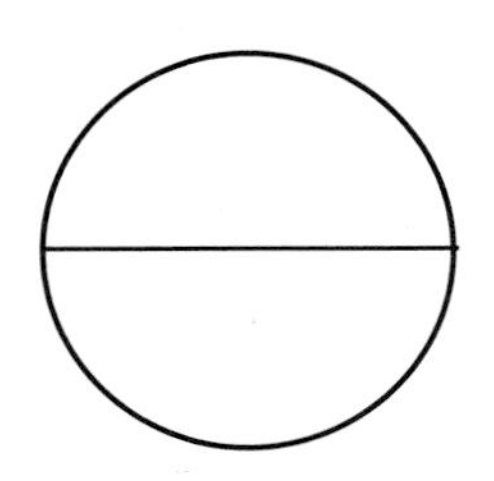

2. $\frac{1}{3}$

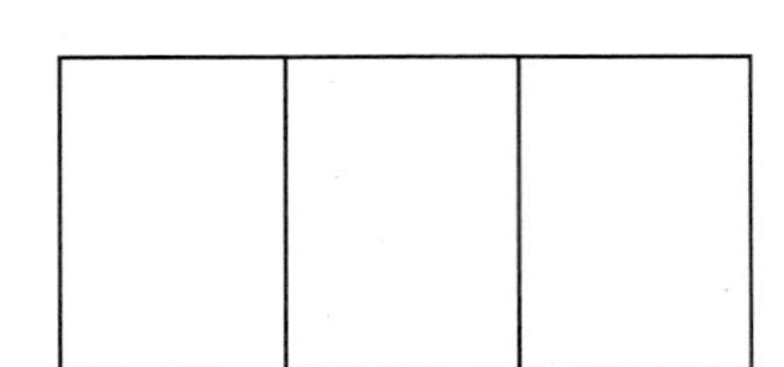

3. $\frac{1}{4}$

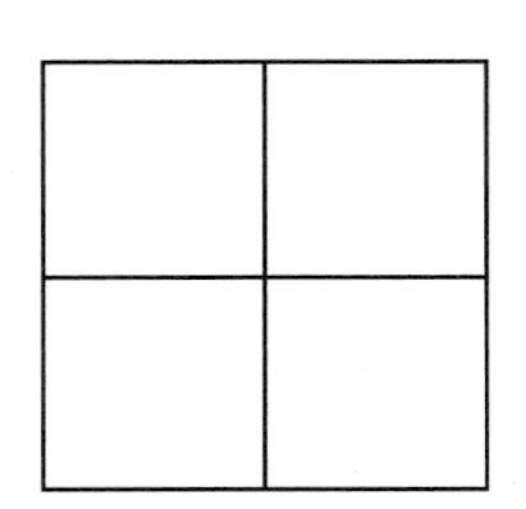

4. $\frac{1}{3}$

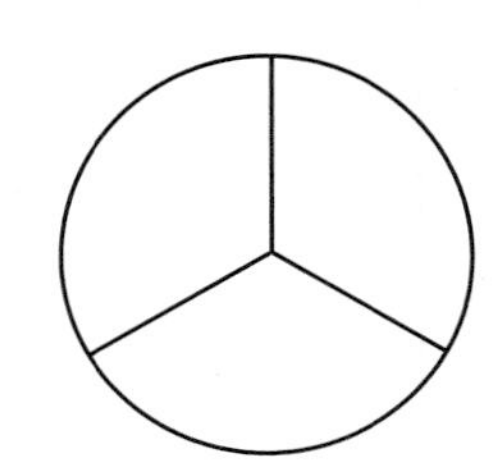

5. $\frac{1}{2}$

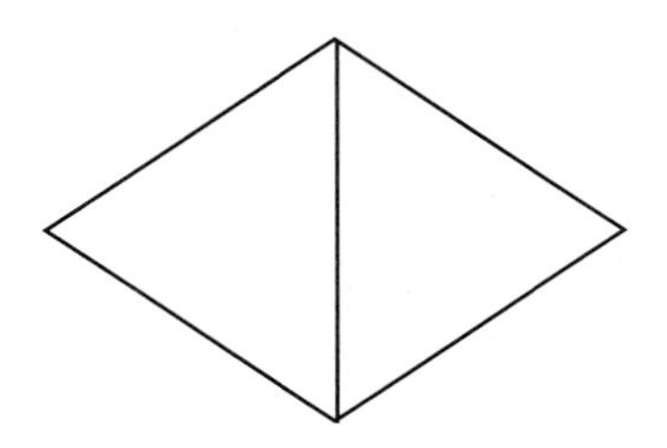

6. $\frac{1}{4}$

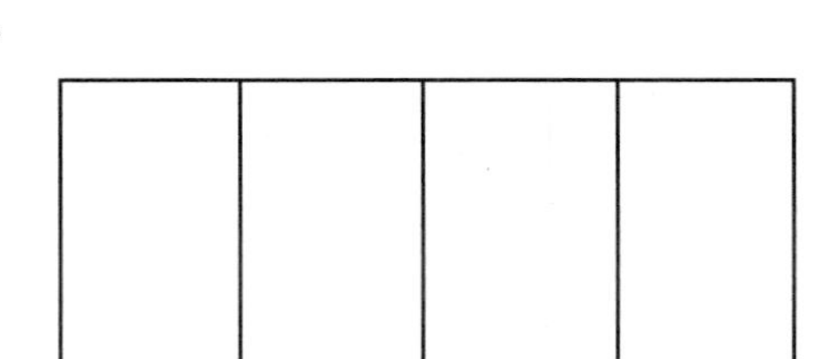

7. $\frac{1}{4}$

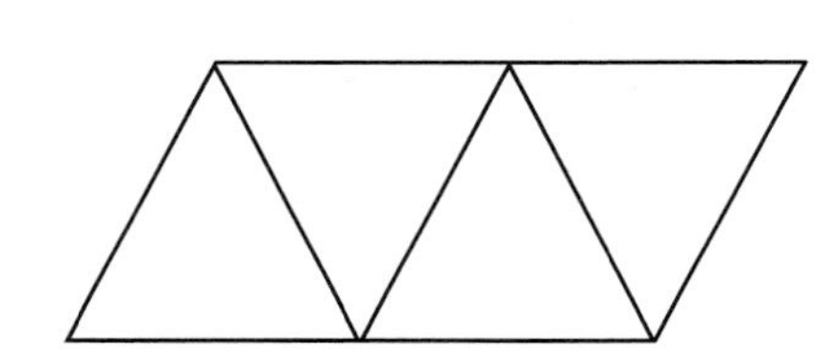

8. $\frac{1}{2}$

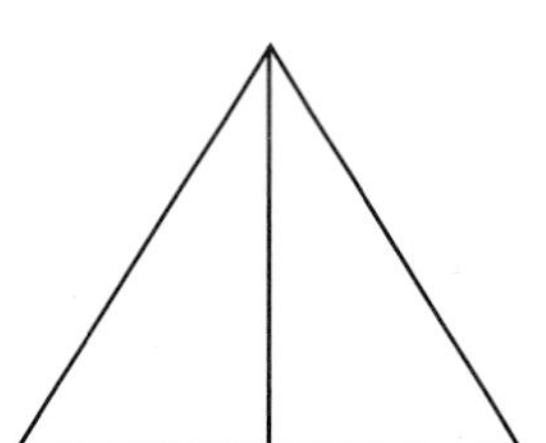

What Do You Think?

I would rather have $\frac{1}{2}$ of a bag of popcorn than $\frac{1}{3}$.
Would you rather have $\frac{1}{2}$ or $\frac{1}{3}$? Tell why.

Name________________________________

A fraction can name more than one equal part.

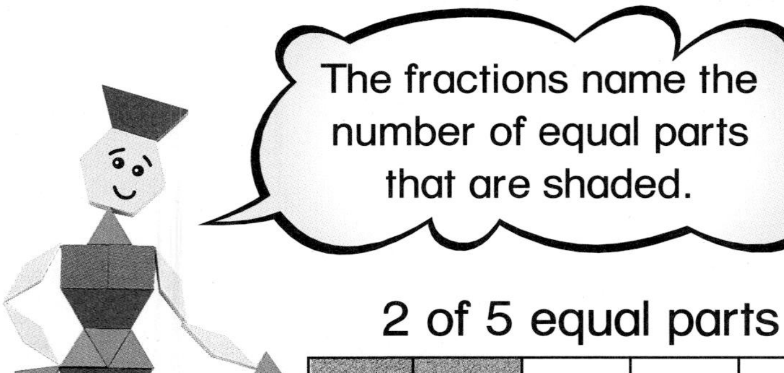

The fractions name the number of equal parts that are shaded.

2 of 5 equal parts

$\frac{2}{5}$ 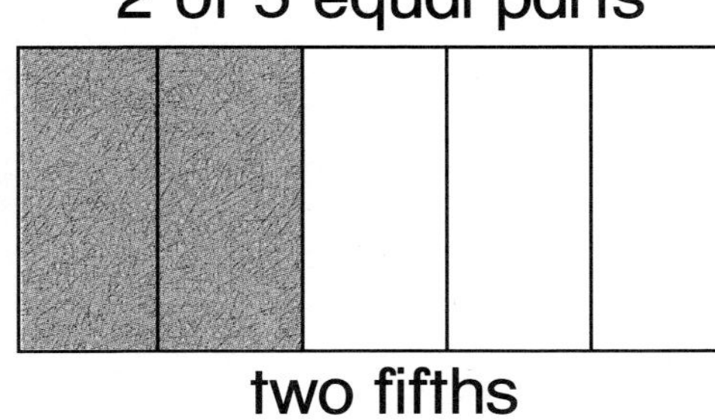

two fifths

3 of 6 equal parts

$\frac{3}{6}$ 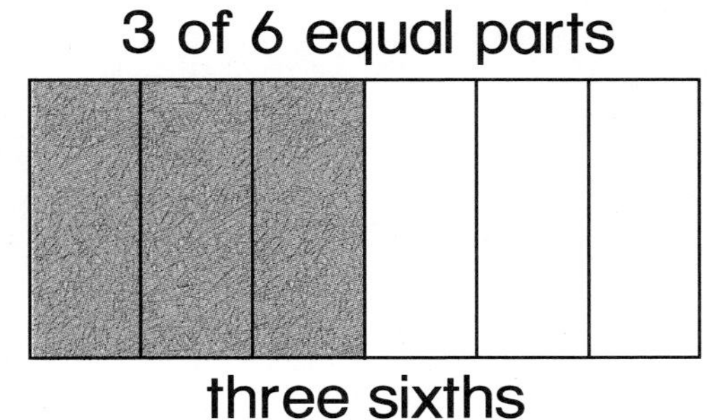

three sixths

Circle the fraction that names the shaded parts.

1. 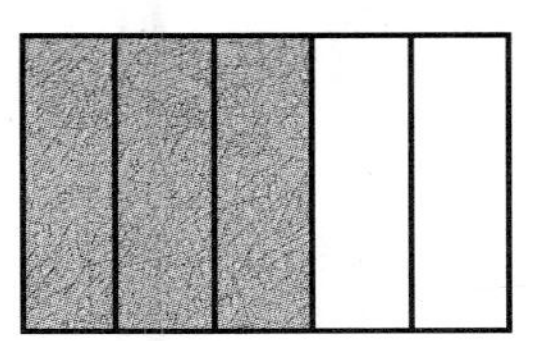

$\frac{2}{5}$  $\frac{3}{5}$ $\frac{4}{6}$

2. 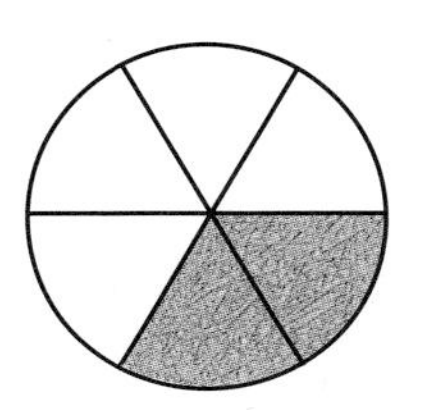

$\frac{2}{6}$ $\frac{2}{8}$ $\frac{3}{6}$

3. 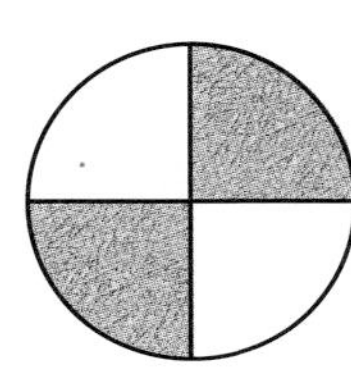

$\frac{2}{3}$ $\frac{1}{4}$ 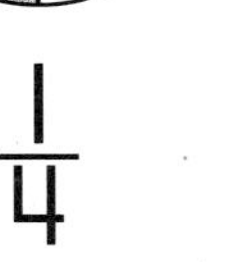 $\frac{2}{4}$

4. 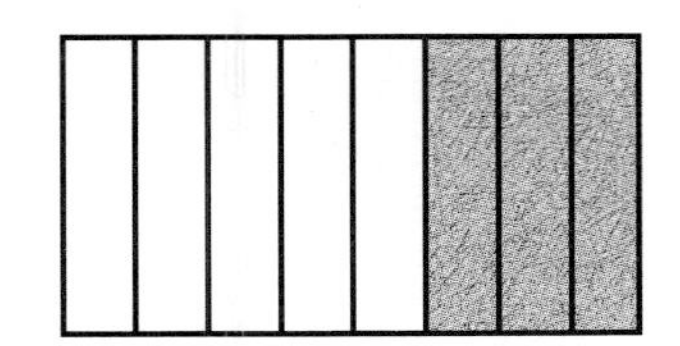

$\frac{5}{8}$ $\frac{3}{6}$ $\frac{3}{8}$

5. 

$\frac{2}{5}$ $\frac{4}{5}$ $\frac{2}{6}$

6. 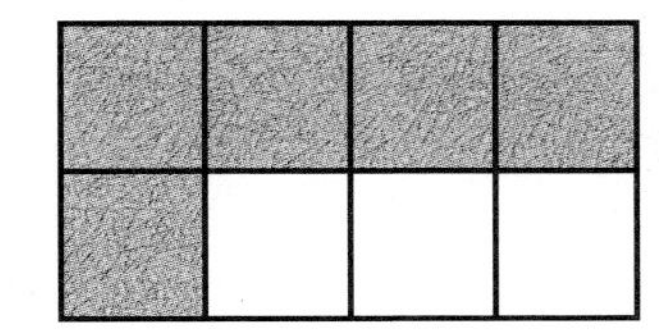

$\frac{5}{6}$ $\frac{5}{8}$ $\frac{6}{8}$

7. 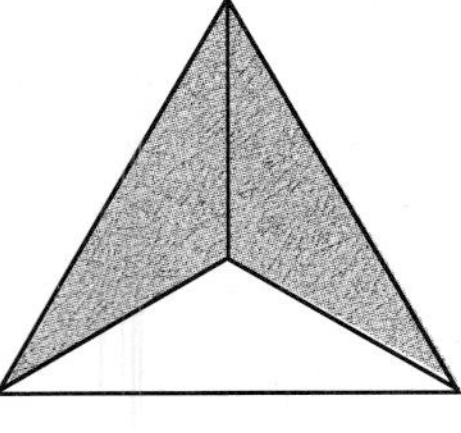

$\frac{1}{2}$ $\frac{2}{3}$ $\frac{3}{3}$

8. 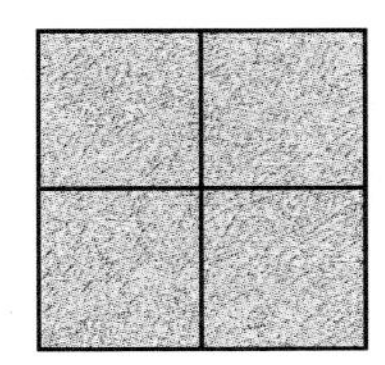

$\frac{3}{4}$ $\frac{3}{5}$ $\frac{4}{4}$

9. 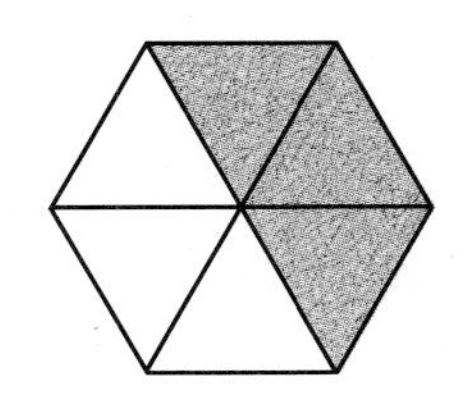

$\frac{3}{6}$ $\frac{4}{6}$ $\frac{3}{8}$

Home Connection Your child is learning more about fractions. Draw a simple shape, divide it into thirds or fourths, and shade more than one part. Ask your child to identify the fraction that names the shaded parts.

Color to show the number of shaded parts.
Write the fraction that names the shaded parts.

1. 2 shaded parts

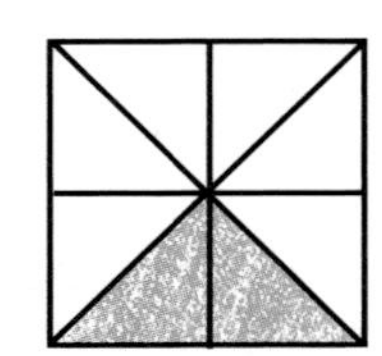

2. 4 shaded parts

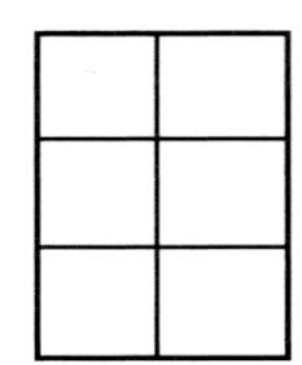

3. 2 shaded parts

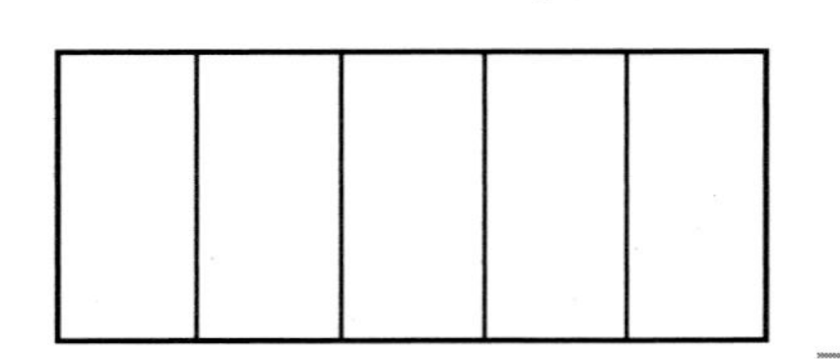

4. 3 shaded parts

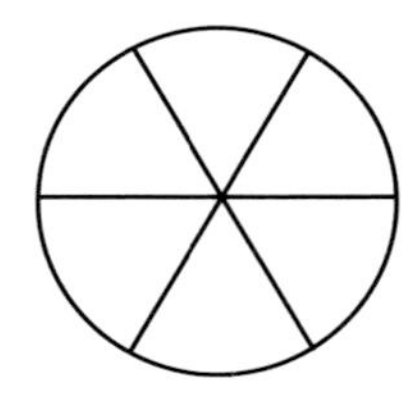

5. 2 shaded parts

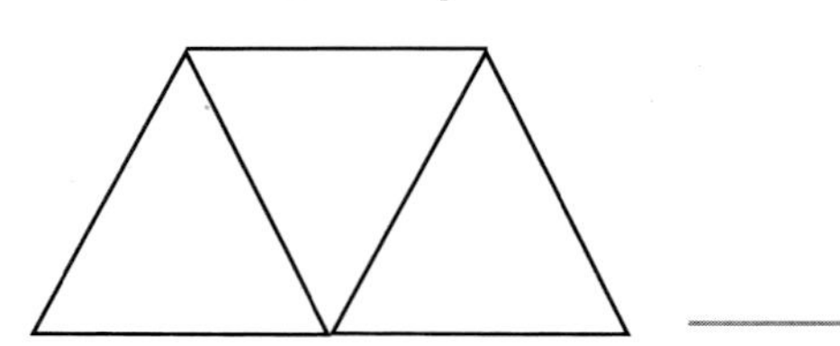

6. 5 shaded parts

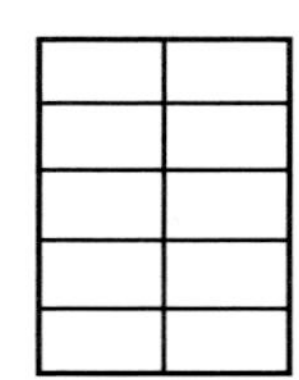

7. 7 shaded parts

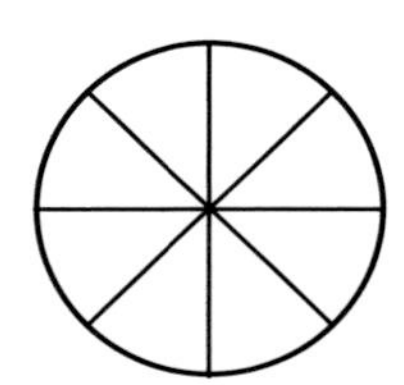

8. 3 shaded parts

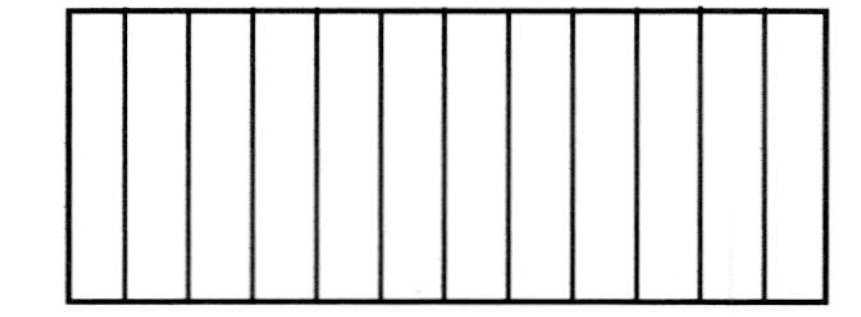

Critical Thinking Corner

Visual Thinking

9. Color each square to show the fraction. Circle the fractions that show the same amount of colored space.

$\frac{1}{2}$ 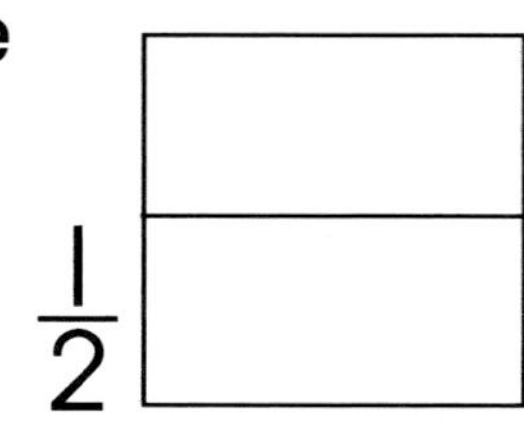 $\frac{1}{3}$ $\frac{2}{4}$

Name_______________________________________ **Fractions of a Group**

What You Need

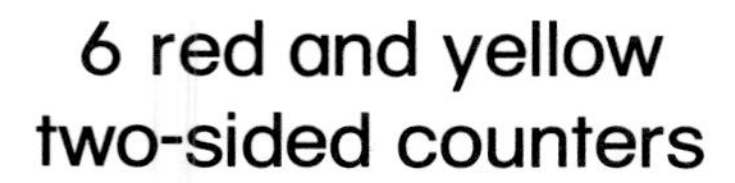

6 red and yellow two-sided counters

cup

1. Put counters in the cup and shake.
2. Spill them out. Color to show how the counters landed.
3. Write the fractions.

1. Use 4 counters.

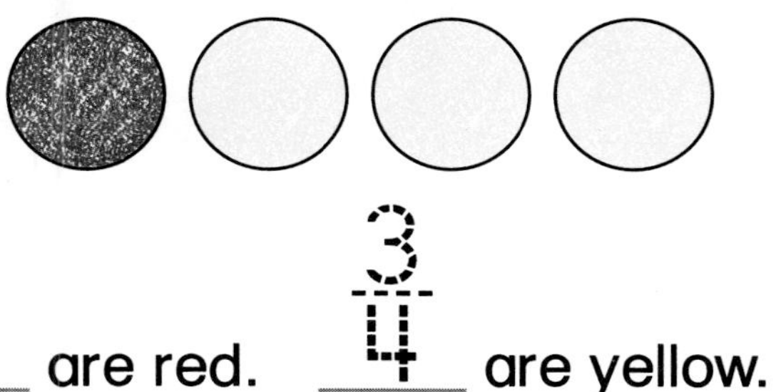

$\frac{1}{4}$ are red. $\frac{3}{4}$ are yellow.

2. Use 4 counters.

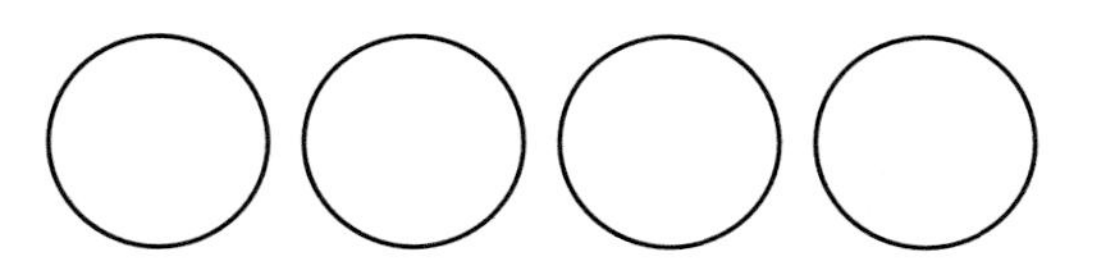

_____ are red. _____ are yellow.

3. Use 5 counters.

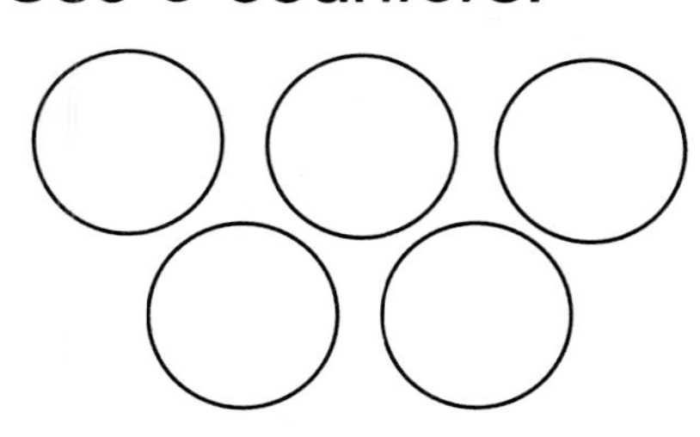

_____ are red. _____ are yellow.

4. Use 5 counters.

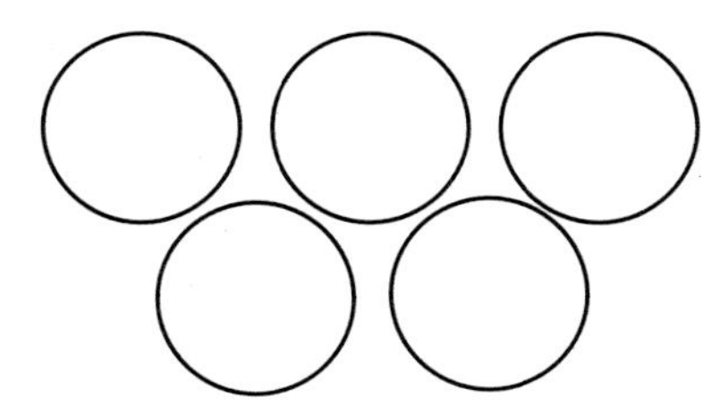

_____ are red. _____ are yellow.

5. Use 6 counters.

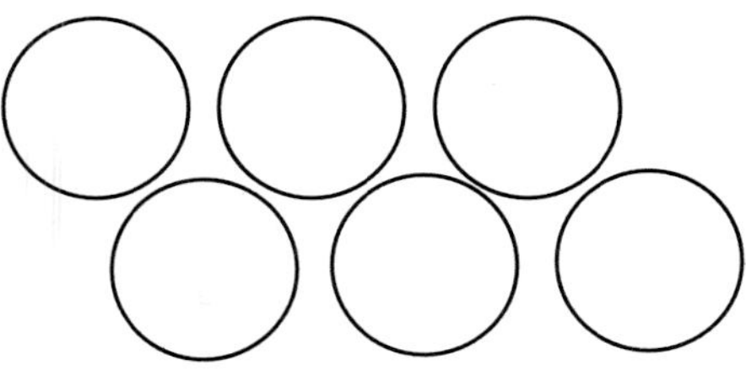

_____ are red. _____ are yellow.

6. Use 6 counters.

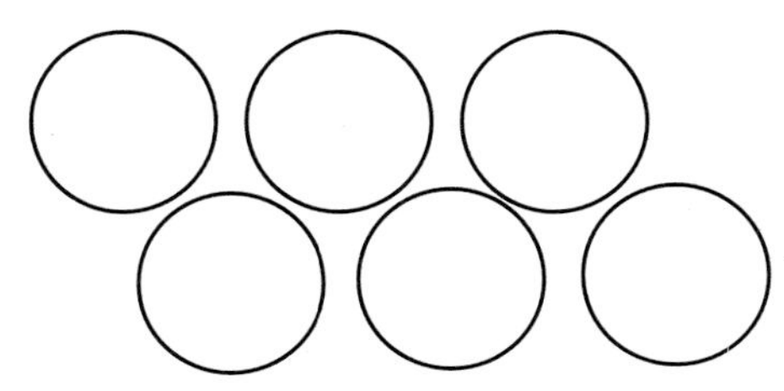

_____ are red. _____ are yellow.

Home Connection Your child is learning to identify fractions of a group. Show him or her 6 pennies, some placed heads up and others tails up. Ask your child what fraction names the pennies that are heads up.

Circle part of each group to show the fraction.

1. $\frac{2}{3}$

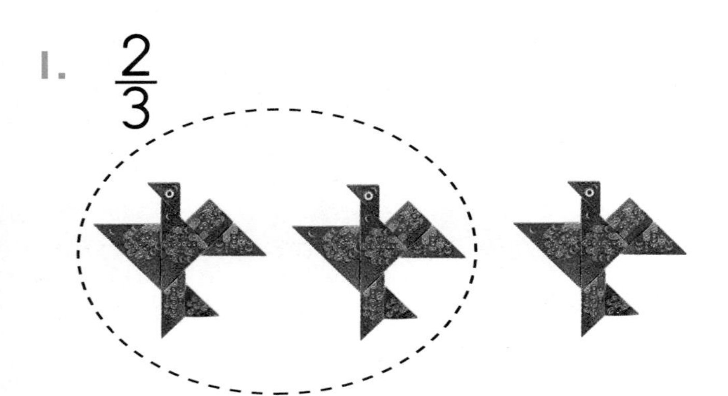

2. $\frac{3}{4}$

3. $\frac{4}{5}$

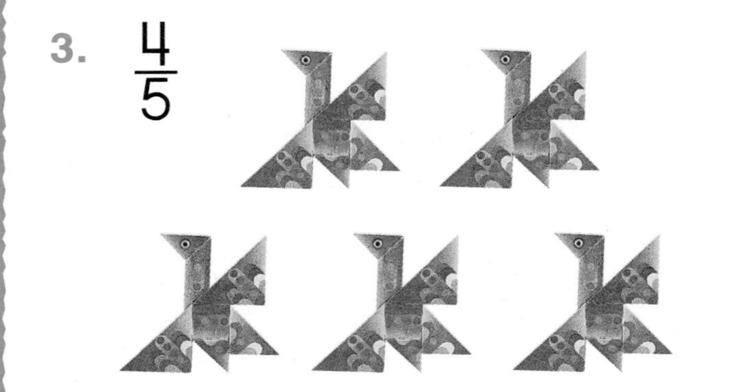

4. $\frac{1}{2}$

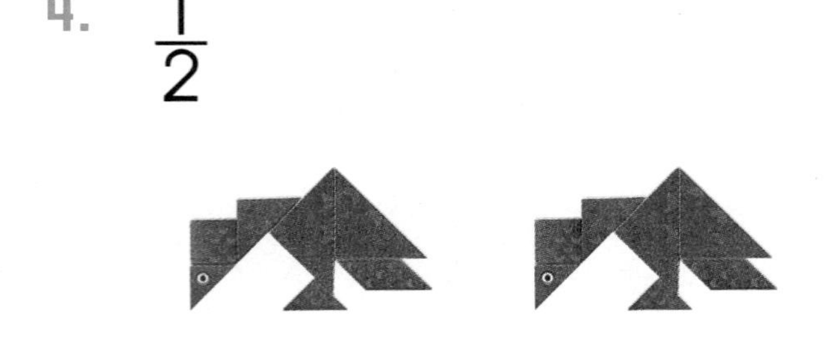

5. $\frac{3}{6}$

6. $\frac{2}{5}$

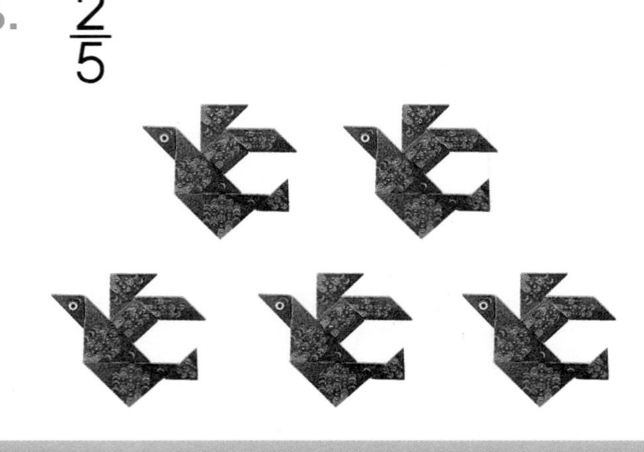

Critical Thinking Corner

Estimation

7. Circle the glass that shows about $\frac{1}{2}$.

Name______________________________

Take a survey. Ask 10 classmates to choose the indoor activity they like best. Make a tally mark for each answer. Then write the total.

Favorite Indoor Activities		
Activity	**Tally**	**Total**
Playing board games		
Doing arts and crafts		
Reading stories		
Playing computer games		

Use the chart to answer each question.

1. Which activity was chosen the most?

____

2. Which activity was chosen the least?

____

3. Suppose you asked all your classmates. Which activity do you think would be chosen the most? Why?

____

____

4. Which activity do you like best?

____

Home Connection Your child is learning how to record and use data from a survey. Ask your child to explain how he or she collected information and what he or she learned.

Terry took a survey. He asked children in his neighborhood to choose the activity they liked best.

1. Complete the chart to show what Terry found out.

Favorite Outdoor Activities		
Activity	Tally	Total
Bike riding	𝍸 ||	7
Jumping rope	||	
In-line skating	||||	
Playing hide-and-seek	𝍸	

2. Make a bar graph. Color one box for each time an activity was chosen.

	Favorite Outdoor Activities							
Bike riding								
Jumping rope								
In-line skating								
Playing hide-and-seek								
	0 – 1	1 – 2	2 – 3	3 – 4	4 – 5	5 – 6	6 – 7	7 – 8

Use the graph to answer each question.

3. Which activity was chosen the most? ____________

4. Which activity was chosen the least? ____________

5. How many more children liked bike riding better than in-line skating? ____________

6. How many children did Terry survey? ____________

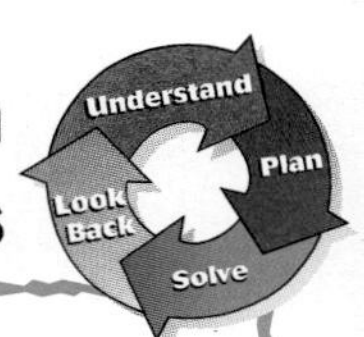

Name______________________________

Put red and blue cubes in a bag.
Predict how many times you will pick each color.
Pick 1 cube without looking.
Color a box to show your pick.
Put the cube back.
Repeat 9 more times.

1. Put 5 red and 5 blue cubes in the bag.

prediction _____ red _____ blue

Pick	1	2	3	4	5	6	7	8	9	10
Color										

2. Put 2 red and 8 blue cubes in the bag.

prediction _____ red _____ blue

Pick	1	2	3	4	5	6	7	8	9	10
Color										

3. Put 1 red and 9 blue cubes in the bag.

prediction _____ red _____ blue

Pick	1	2	3	4	5	6	7	8	9	10
Color										

Home Connection Your child is learning how to predict the outcome of a simple experiment. Try repeating the experiment with your child, using a paper bag and small paper squares in two different colors.

Write **red** or **blue** to tell which color you think you are more likely to pick. Pick a cube and then color a box to show your pick. Write the totals.

1. Put 7 red and 3 blue cubes in the bag.

more likely to pick ______

Pick	1	2	3	4	5	6	7	8	9	10
Color										

total _____ red _____ blue

2. Put 3 red and 7 blue cubes in the bag.

more likely to pick ______

Pick	1	2	3	4	5	6	7	8	9	10
Color										

total _____ red _____ blue

Problem Solving

Solve.

3. You have 20 red and 80 blue marbles in a bag. Circle what you think is most likely to happen.
   - Red is more likely to be picked.
   - Blue is more likely to be picked.
   - Red and blue are equally likely to be picked.

Name ______________________________ **Checkpoint**

Write the number of parts.
Circle **equal** or **not equal**.

1. 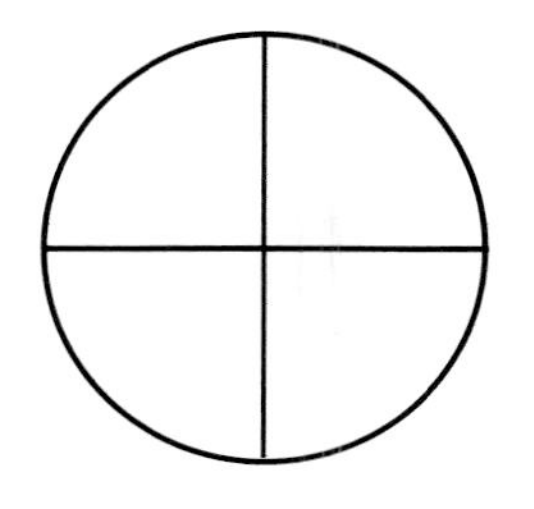

equal

not equal

____ parts

2. 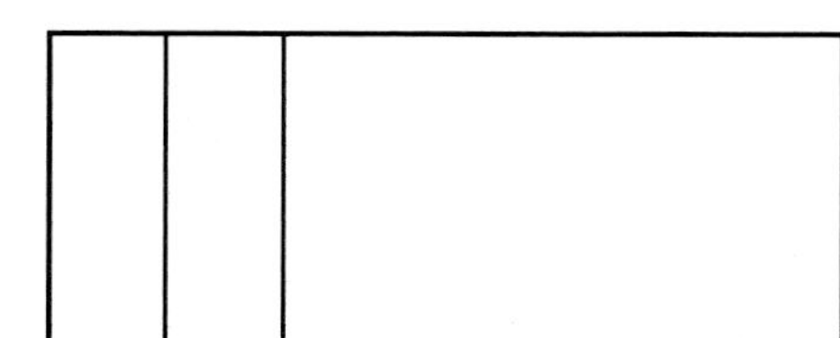

equal

not equal

____ parts

Write the fraction that names the shaded parts.

3. 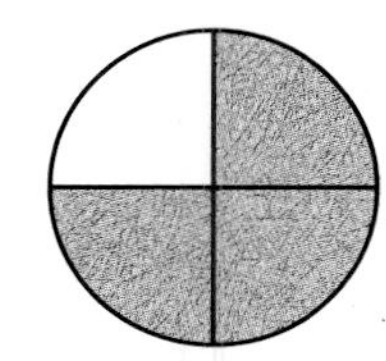

____

4. 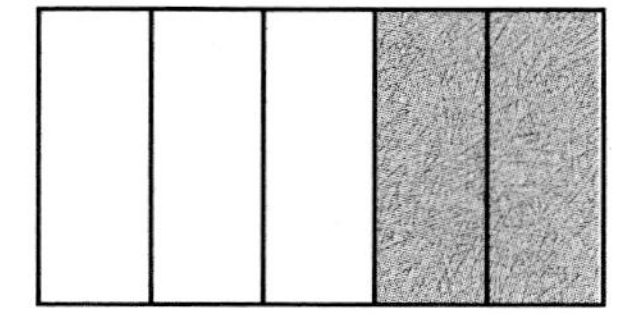

____

5. 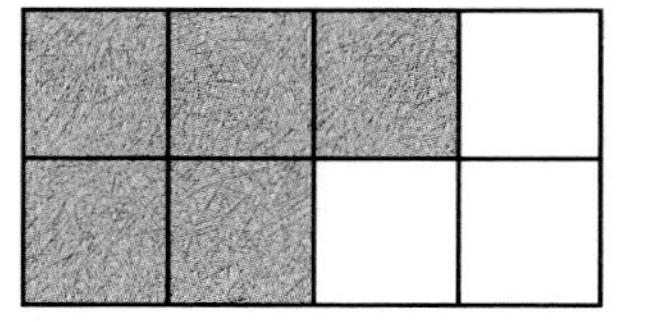

____

Circle part of each group to show the fraction.

6. $\frac{2}{6}$  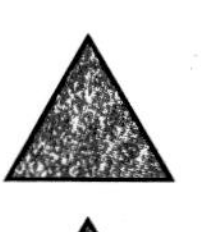

7. $\frac{3}{4}$ 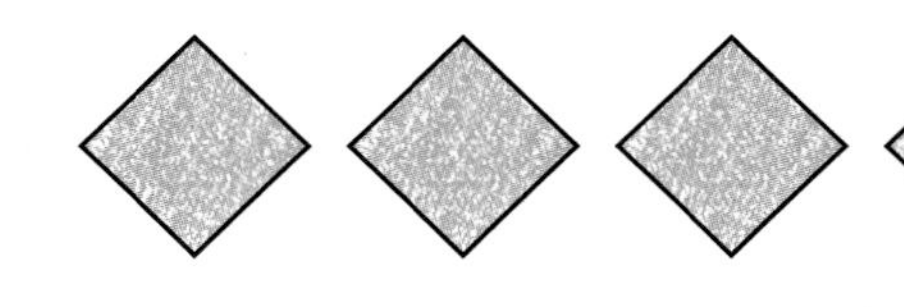

Use the picture to make a graph.
Color a box for each shape.

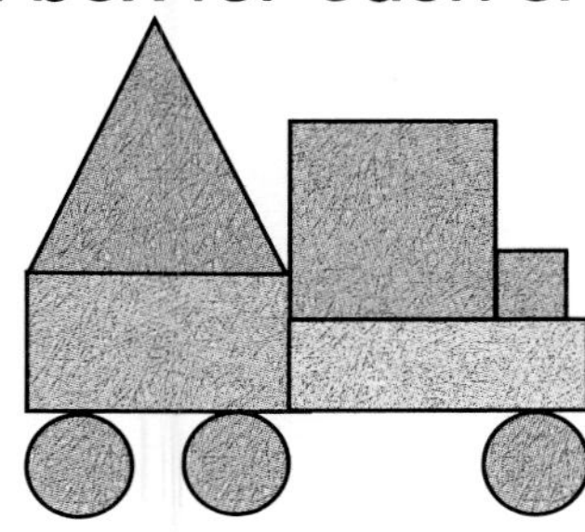

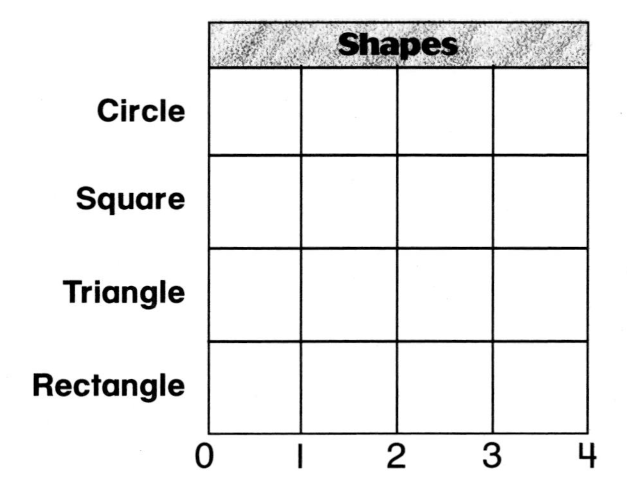

8. Which shape was used most often? ______________

Name____ **Extra Practice**

1. Draw shapes to decorate the gift.
   Draw 3 triangles, 6 squares, 5 circles, and 4 rectangles.

2. Color 2 of the triangles (green).
   Color 5 of the squares (blue).
   Color 3 of the circles (red).
   Color 4 of the rectangles (yellow).

3. Write fractions to name the number of each shape that is colored.

____	____	____	____
triangles	squares	circles	rectangles

Name______________________________ **Chapter Test** 

1. What if you drew around the face of the object? Circle the shape you would make.

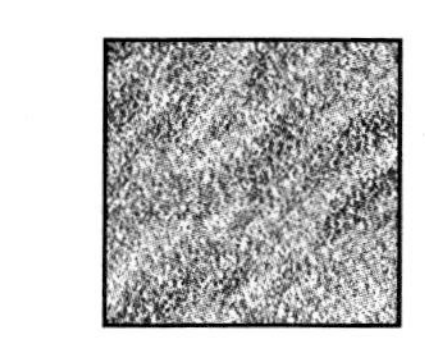 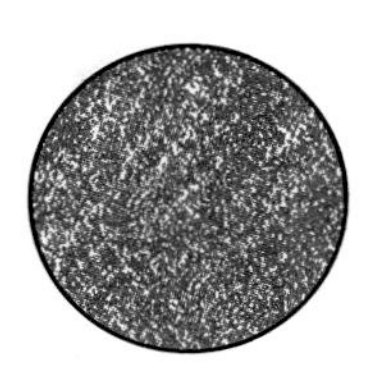 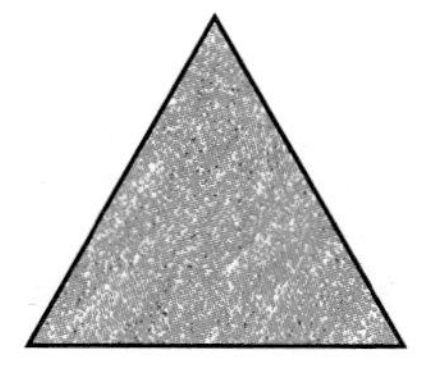

---

2. Draw a line of symmetry if you can.

B M  L I 

---

3. Circle the figure that has the same size and shape.

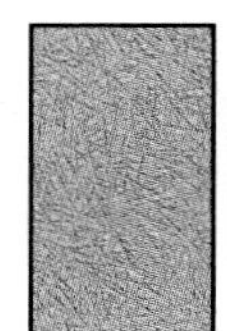

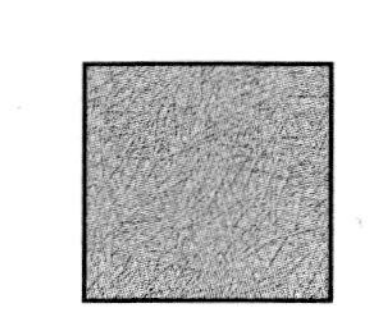  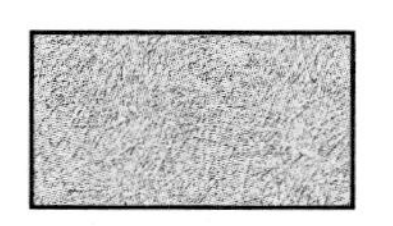

---

4. Write the fraction for the shaded parts.

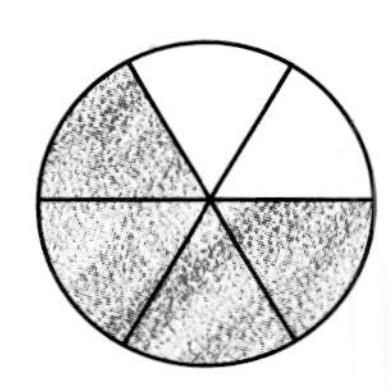 ____  ____ 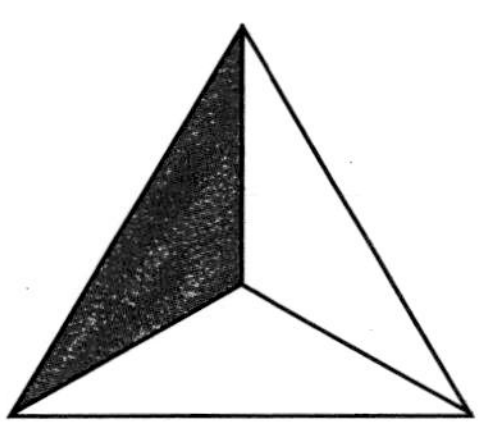 ____

---

5. Look at the chart. Make a bar graph.
Color one box for each time a sport was chosen.

Favorite Sports	
Sport	**Tally**
Baseball	𝍸
Tennis	I
Soccer	IIII
Swimming	III

	Favorite Sports				
Baseball					
Tennis					
Soccer					
Swimming					
	0 1	2	3	4	5

Name________________________________ **Performance Assessment**

You Will Need

geoboard and rubber bands

1. Make each shape on the geoboard. Use rubber bands to show equal parts.
2. Draw the shape you made.
3. Write a fraction that names one or more parts.

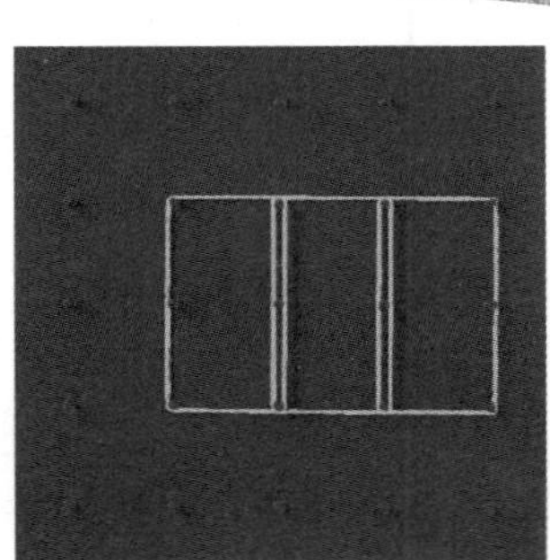

---

1. triangle with 2 equal parts

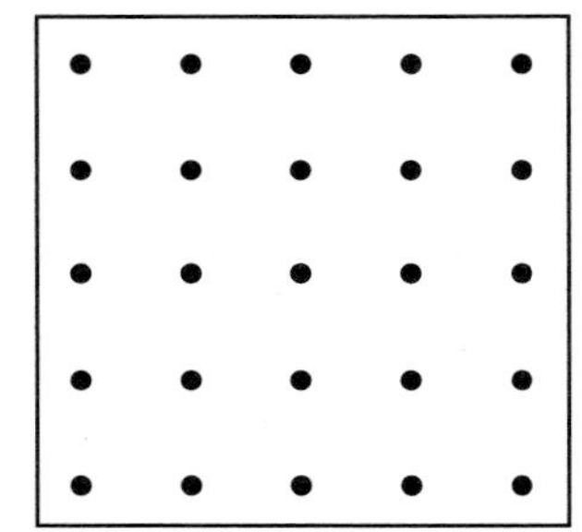

I part is _____.

2. rectangle with 4 equal parts

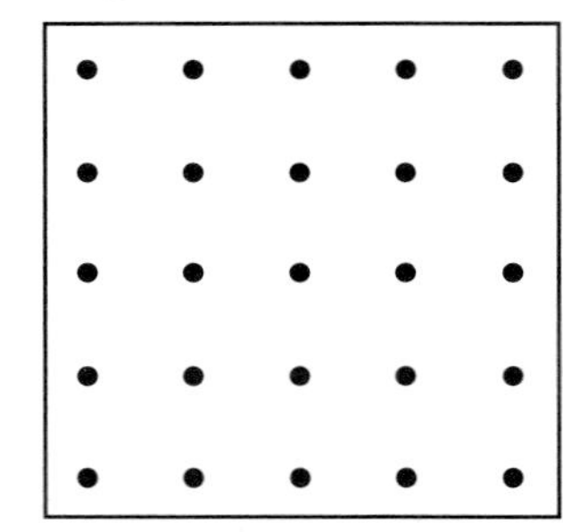

2 parts are _____.

3. square with 8 equal parts

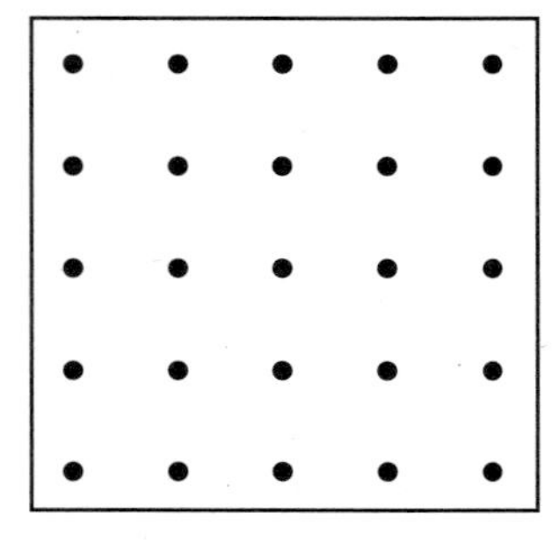

3 parts are _____.

4. rectangle with 6 equal parts

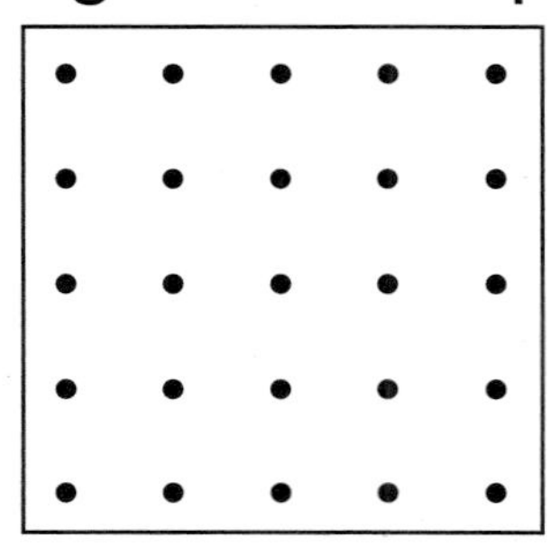

4 parts are _____.

Name________________________________

You can use pairs of numbers to find a place on a grid.
To find 2 1, start at 0.
Go across 2.
Then go up 1.

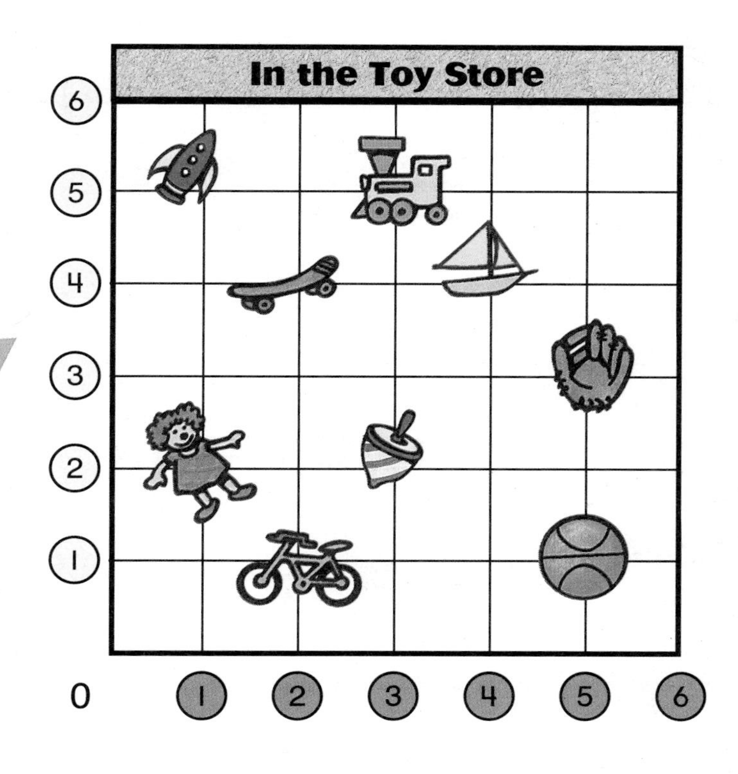

Circle the toy you find at each place.
First go across. Then go up.

1.    

2. 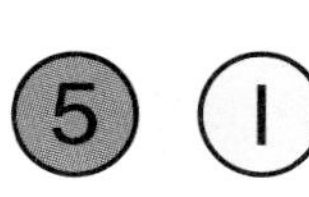  

3.    

4. 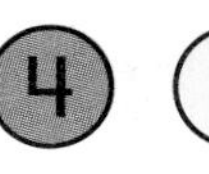  

5. 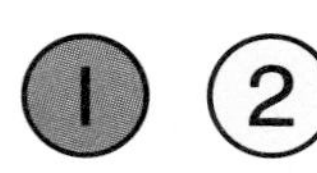  

6.   

7.    

8.   

Name________________________________

Area and the MathProcessor™

Look at the screen.
How many cubes cover each workspace?

36 cubes cover each workspace. The area of each shape is 36 cubes.

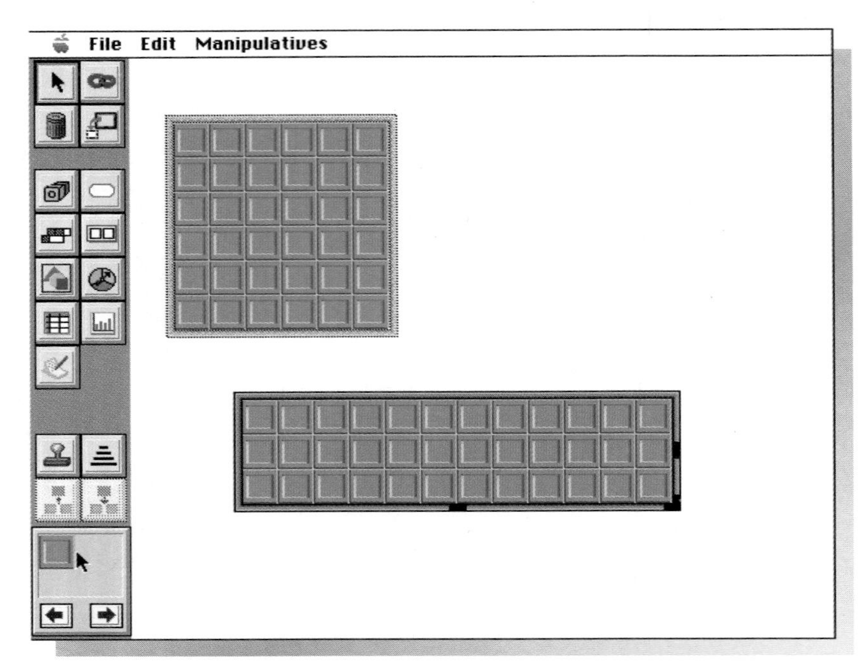

Take turns with a partner.

1. Click on the **cube button** to show a workspace.

2. Click on the **cube** again and again to cover the workspace. What is the area?

3. Show another workspace. Click-and-drag the sides to change its shape. Try to make the area the same as the first workspace.

4. Click on the **cube** to cover the new workspace. Is the area the same as the first workspace? If not, try again.

Make other workspaces.
Try to make some shapes with the same area.

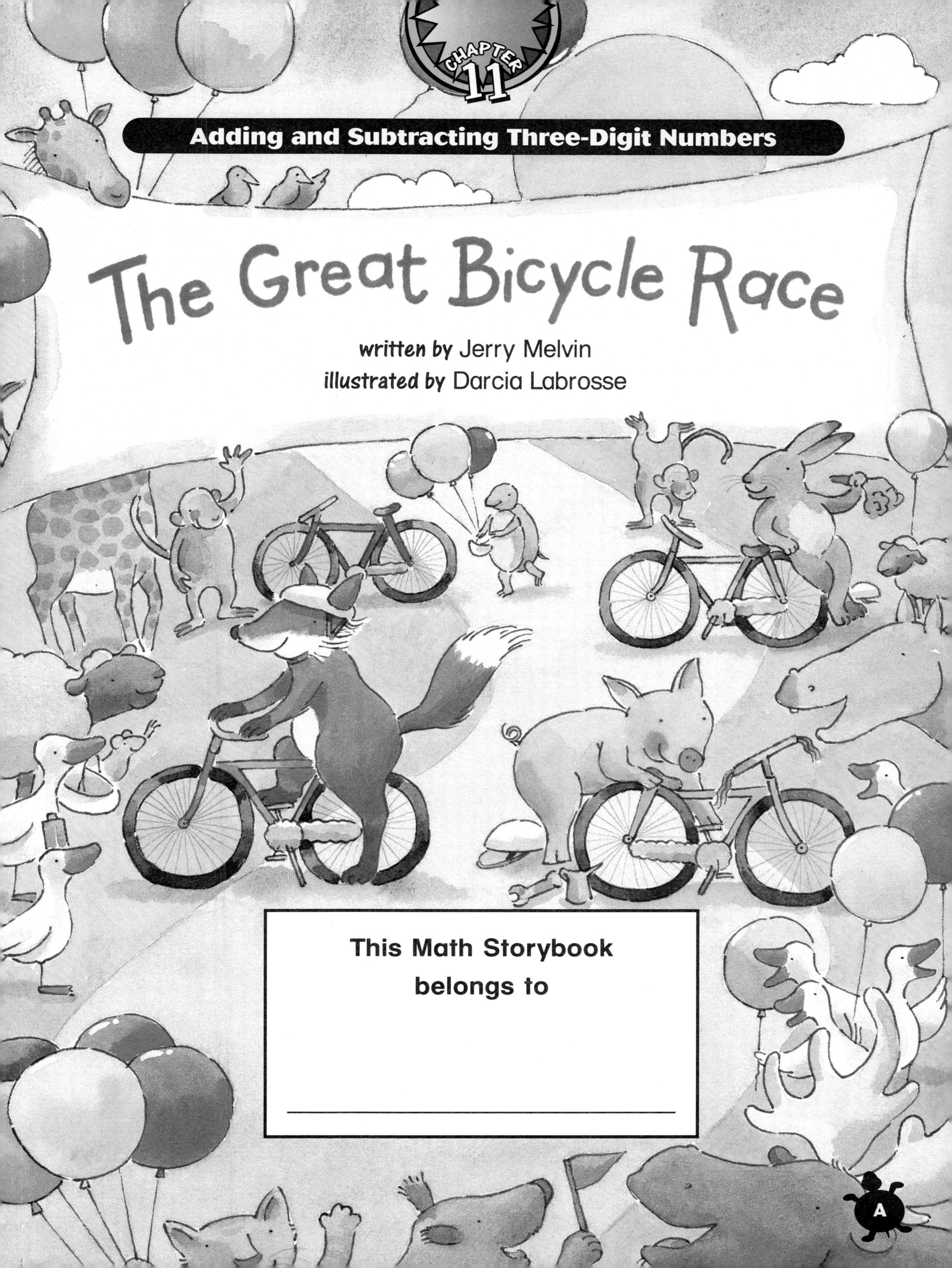
CHAPTER
11
Adding and Subtracting Three-Digit Numbers
The Great Bicycle Race
written by Jerry Melvin
illustrated by Darcia Labrosse
This Math Storybook
belongs to
A

Today is the day of the bicycle race!
It's 500 miles at quite a fast pace.
The racers line up in one narrow row.
Bear begins shouting, "Ready, set, go!"

After 100 miles, Fox takes the lead.
400 to go — he could win it, indeed!

At 200 miles, Hare quickens her pace.
With 300 more, she might win the race!

At 300 miles, Pig stops to rest.
With 200 more, he is trying his best!

With 100 left in the bicycle race,
Turtle speeds up to win her first race!

Here are scenes from the bicycle race
that you can follow from place to place.

Pick any place to end and start.
How many miles are the places apart?

A Note to the Family

Here are some learning ideas you can share with your child.

Enjoy *The Great Bicycle Race* Together

- Read each page with your child. Ask him or her to tell an addition or subtraction story about pages C, D, and E.
- Using the scenes on page G, make up an addition problem for your child to solve, for example, how far is it from the first place to the last place?

At-Home Activity

- Make up addition and subtraction problems for your child to solve. For example, say, “On the first day you travel 200 miles and on the second day you travel 300 miles. How many miles do you travel in all?”

Read More About It!

To read more about adding and subtracting large numbers, look for these books in your local library.

- *Arthur's Funny Money* by Lillian Hoban (HarperCollins, 1981)
- *Four Dollars and Fifty Cents* by Eric Kimmel (Holiday House, 1989)

Visit Our Web Site!

www.sbgmath.com

Name____________________________________

How far is it from Springfield to Cincinnati?

Springfield — 200 miles — Indianapolis — 100 miles — Cincinnati

To add 200 + 100, think 2 + 1 = 3.

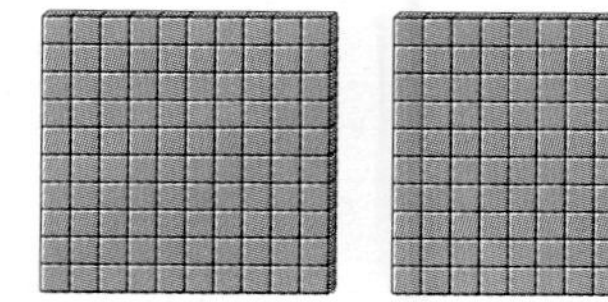

2 hundreds + 1 hundred 3 hundreds	200 + 100 300 miles

Find each sum.
Use models if you like.

1. 2 hundreds + 3 hundreds = ____ hundreds   200 + 300

2. 3 hundreds + 3 hundreds = ____ hundreds   300 + 300

3. 5 hundreds + 2 hundreds = ____ hundreds   500 + 200

4. 2 hundreds + 4 hundreds = ____ hundreds   200 + 400

5. 3 hundreds + 1 hundred = ____ hundreds   300 + 100

6. 1 hundred + 2 hundreds = ____ hundreds   100 + 200

7. 2 hundreds + 2 hundreds = ____ hundreds   200 + 200

8. 1 hundred + 4 hundreds = ____ hundreds   100 + 400

Home Connection Your child is using basic facts to add hundreds. Give your child two numbers to add, such as 400 + 300. Talk about how knowing 4 + 3 can help.

Add. Look for a pattern.

1.	2 + 6 = 8	20 + 60 = 80	200 + 600 = 800	2.	4 + 5	40 + 50	400 + 500
3.	1 + 3	10 + 30	100 + 300	4.	6 + 1	60 + 10	600 + 100
5.	4 + 1	40 + 10	400 + 100	6.	1 + 5	10 + 50	100 + 500
7.	3 + 5	30 + 50	300 + 500	8.	7 + 2	70 + 20	700 + 200
9.	4 + 4	40 + 40	400 + 400	10.	3 + 4	30 + 40	300 + 400

What Do You Think?

I think I can solve these problems much faster in my head than with a calculator.

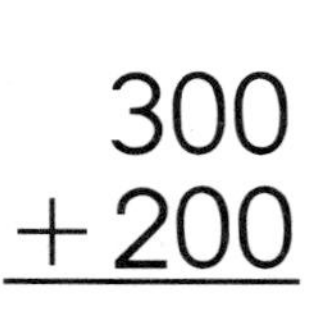

300 + 200	20 + 20	500 + 100

Which way do you think is faster? Tell why. Solve.

Name________________________________ **Exploring Three-Digit Addition**

What You Need

models

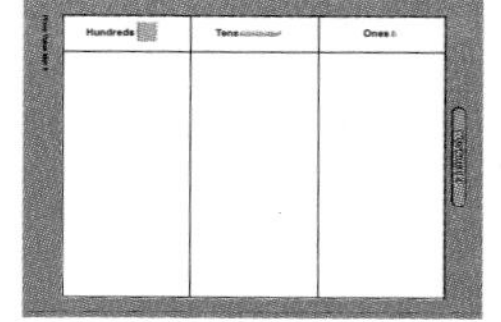
Workmat 4

spinner

1. Build the number.
2. Spin the spinner twice to make a two-digit number to add.
3. Record and build that number.
4. Add. Regroup if you need to.

	Number	Number to Add	Sum
1.	245		
2.	436		
3.	521		
4.	382		
5.	459		
6.	174		
7.	397		
8.	269		

Home Connection Your child is building and adding two- and three-digit numbers. Write a problem such as 374 + 608. Ask your child to tell the number of hundreds, tens, and ones in each number.

Use models and Workmat 4.
Show each number.
Find the sum. Regroup if you need to.

1.

6 hundreds	1 ten	4 ones
+ 1 hundred	7 tens	8 ones
7 hundreds	9 tens	2 ones

3 hundreds	5 tens	0 ones
+ 2 hundreds	9 tens	7 ones
___ hundreds	___ tens	___ ones

2.

4 hundreds	8 tens	6 ones
+ 2 hundreds	0 tens	7 ones
___ hundreds	___ tens	___ ones

2 hundreds	4 tens	4 ones
+ 2 hundreds	7 tens	3 ones
___ hundreds	___ ten	___ ones

3.

2 hundreds	2 tens	3 ones
+	9 tens	0 ones
___ hundreds	___ ten	___ ones

5 hundreds	8 tens	6 ones
+	6 tens	2 ones
___ hundreds	___ tens	___ ones

4.

1 hundred	8 tens	5 ones
+ 3 hundreds	7 tens	2 ones
___ hundreds	___ tens	___ ones

1 hundred	3 tens	6 ones
+ 4 hundreds	1 ten	6 ones
___ hundreds	___ tens	___ ones

5.

Make Your Own

___ hundreds	___ tens	___ ones
+ ___ hundreds	___ tens	___ ones
___ hundreds	___ tens	___ ones

Name________________________________ **Adding Three-Digit Numbers**

Sunshine Grove has 162 orange trees and 253 grapefruit trees. How many trees are there in all?

1. Add the ones. Regroup if you need to.

H	T	O
1	6	2
+ 2	5	3
		5

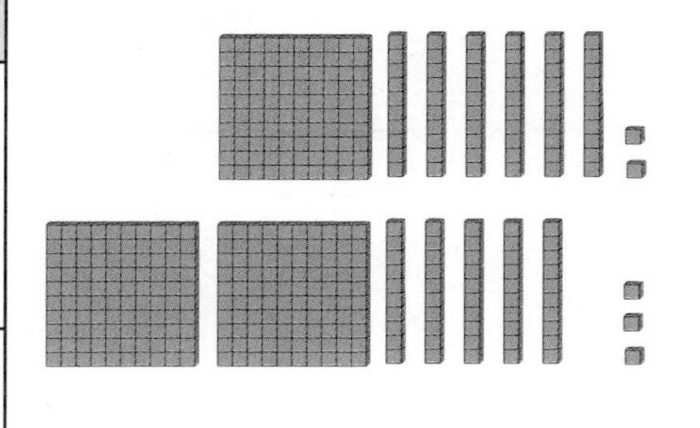

2. Add the tens. Regroup if you need to.

H	T	O
1		
1	6	2
+ 2	5	3
	1	5

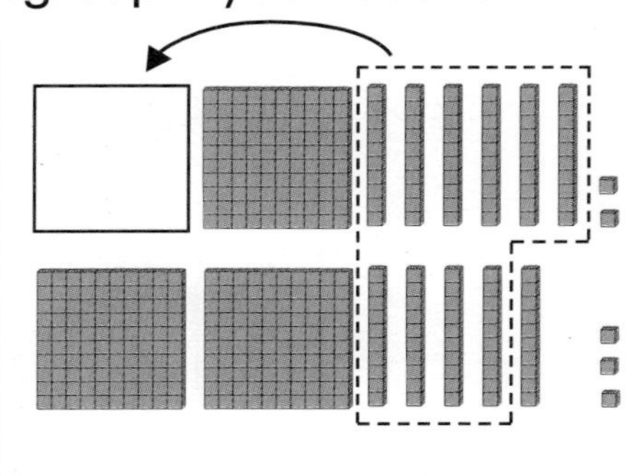

3. Add the hundreds.

H	T	O
1		
1	6	2
+ 2	5	3
4	1	5

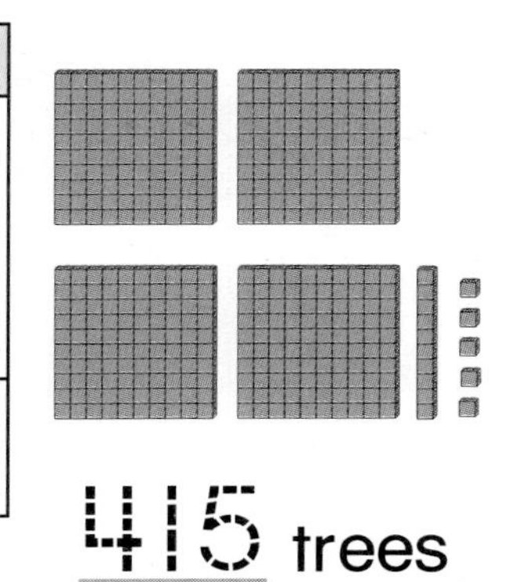

415 trees

Use models and Workmat 4. Add.

1.

H	T	O
4	8	6
+ 2	0	7

2.

H	T	O
1	4	4
+ 2	7	3

3.

H	T	O
3	5	2
+ 1	9	6

Home Connection Your child is learning to add three-digit numbers. Ask him or her to explain what regrouping is and how it works.

Use models and Workmat 4.
Find each sum.

1.

	H	T	O
	1		
	3	6	4
+	2	8	1
	6	4	5

	H	T	O
	6	3	8
+	1	4	0

	H	T	O
	5	4	8
+		2	6

2.

	H	T	O
	7	8	0
+	1	3	6

	H	T	O
	2	0	9
+	2	2	7

	H	T	O
	1	8	3
+	6	5	5

3.

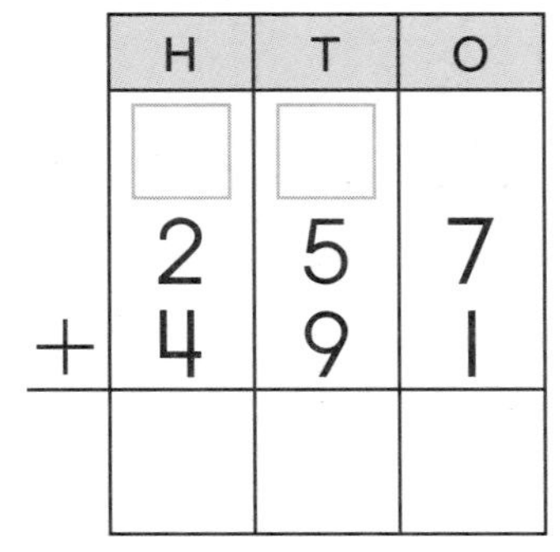

	H	T	O
	2	5	7
+	4	9	1

	H	T	O
	3	0	0
+	3	5	9

	H	T	O
	6	7	4
+	2	5	1

PROBLEM SOLVING

Problem Solving

Niagara Falls

Solve. Show your work.

4. One morning, 248 people rode the steamer for a close look at the falls. Later, 190 people rode the steamer. How many people rode in all?

_____ people

Name______________________________ **Practicing Addition**

How can you find out how many cattle there are altogether?

Lone Star
Texas Ranch
236 Herefords
318 Angus

1. Add the ones. Regroup if you need to.

	H	T	O
		1	
	2	3	6
+	3	1	8
			4

2. Add the tens. Regroup if you need to.

	H	T	O
		1	
	2	3	6
+	3	1	8
		5	4

3. Add the hundreds.

	H	T	O
		1	
	2	3	6
+	3	1	8
	5	5	4

554 cattle

Add. Use models if you like.

1. $\begin{array}{r} \scriptstyle 1 \\ 274 \\ +183 \\ \hline 457 \end{array}$ $\quad \begin{array}{r} 623 \\ +105 \\ \hline \end{array}$ $\quad \begin{array}{r} 539 \\ +\ 84 \\ \hline \end{array}$ $\quad \begin{array}{r} 417 \\ +268 \\ \hline \end{array}$ $\quad \begin{array}{r} 305 \\ +629 \\ \hline \end{array}$

2. $\begin{array}{r} 720 \\ +196 \\ \hline \end{array}$ $\quad \begin{array}{r} 865 \\ +\ \ 9 \\ \hline \end{array}$ $\quad \begin{array}{r} 155 \\ +380 \\ \hline \end{array}$ $\quad \begin{array}{r} 247 \\ +391 \\ \hline \end{array}$ $\quad \begin{array}{r} 582 \\ +\ 60 \\ \hline \end{array}$

3. $\begin{array}{r} 604 \\ +137 \\ \hline \end{array}$ $\quad \begin{array}{r} 271 \\ +319 \\ \hline \end{array}$ $\quad \begin{array}{r} 516 \\ +235 \\ \hline \end{array}$ $\quad \begin{array}{r} 442 \\ +\ 46 \\ \hline \end{array}$ $\quad \begin{array}{r} 353 \\ +150 \\ \hline \end{array}$

Home Connection Have your child identify the exercises on this page that required regrouping.

Add. Use models if you like.

1. $\begin{array}{r} \overset{1}{4}67 \\ +262 \\ \hline 729 \end{array}$ $\begin{array}{r} 308 \\ +528 \\ \hline \end{array}$ $\begin{array}{r} 124 \\ +159 \\ \hline \end{array}$ $\begin{array}{r} 731 \\ +196 \\ \hline \end{array}$ $\begin{array}{r} 349 \\ +464 \\ \hline \end{array}$

Write in vertical form. Then add.

2. 581 + 173 229 + 430 675 + 93 386 + 8

$\begin{array}{r} 581 \\ +173 \\ \hline 754 \end{array}$

Checkpoint

Find each sum.

1.

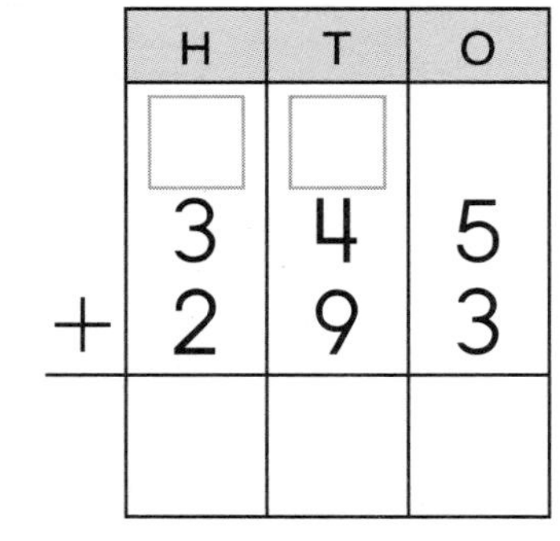

	H	T	O
	☐	☐	
	3	4	5
+	2	9	3

	H	T	O
	☐	☐	
	4	0	6
+	1	3	7

	H	T	O
	☐	☐	
	6	5	2
+	2	7	4

2. $\begin{array}{r} 428 \\ +233 \\ \hline \end{array}$ $\begin{array}{r} 90 \\ +438 \\ \hline \end{array}$ $\begin{array}{r} 572 \\ +245 \\ \hline \end{array}$ $\begin{array}{r} 300 \\ +400 \\ \hline \end{array}$ $\begin{array}{r} 285 \\ +350 \\ \hline \end{array}$

Name____

It is 600 miles from Denver to Kansas City. How far is it from Hays to Kansas City?

To subtract 600 − 300, think 6 − 3 = 3.

Denver

Hays

Kansas City

300 miles

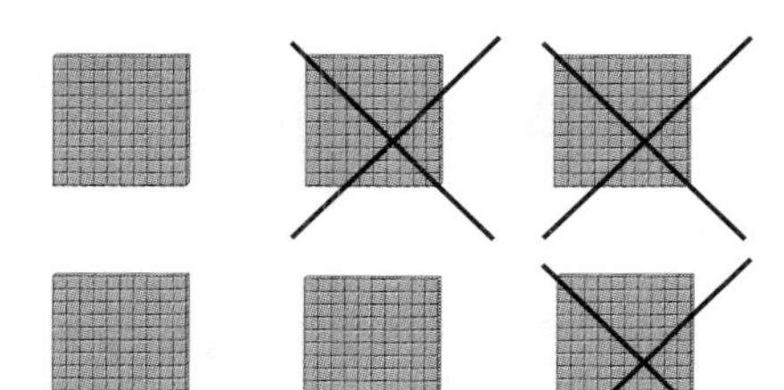

6 hundreds	600
− 3 hundreds	− 300
3 hundreds	300 miles

Find each difference. Use models if you like.

1.
4 hundreds	400
− 1 hundred	− 100
___ hundreds	

2.
7 hundreds	700
− 5 hundreds	− 500
___ hundreds	

3.
5 hundreds	500
− 3 hundreds	− 300
___ hundreds	

4.
5 hundreds	500
− 4 hundreds	− 400
___ hundred	

5.
3 hundreds	300
− 2 hundreds	− 200
___ hundred	

6.
4 hundreds	400
− 2 hundreds	− 200
___ hundreds	

7.
7 hundreds	700
− 3 hundreds	− 300
___ hundreds	

8.
5 hundreds	500
− 1 hundred	− 100
___ hundreds	

Home Connection Your child is using basic facts to subtract hundreds. Give your child two numbers to subtract, such as 600−400. Talk about how knowing 6−4 can help.

Subtract. Look for a pattern.

1. $9 - 4 = 5$ $\quad 90 - 40 = 50$ $\quad 900 - 400 = 500$

2. $4 - 3$ $\quad 40 - 30$ $\quad 400 - 300$

3. $5 - 3$ $\quad 50 - 30$ $\quad 500 - 300$

4. $7 - 4$ $\quad 70 - 40$ $\quad 700 - 400$

5. $8 - 3$ $\quad 80 - 30$ $\quad 800 - 300$

6. $6 - 2$ $\quad 60 - 20$ $\quad 600 - 200$

7. $9 - 6$ $\quad 90 - 60$ $\quad 900 - 600$

8. $8 - 4$ $\quad 80 - 40$ $\quad 800 - 400$

9. $6 - 1$ $\quad 60 - 10$ $\quad 600 - 100$

10. $7 - 5$ $\quad 70 - 50$ $\quad 700 - 500$

Critical Thinking Corner

Number Sense

Subtract. Continue the pattern.
Tell about the patterns you see.

11. $500 - 400$ $\quad 600 - 400$ $\quad 700 - 400$ $\quad 800 - 400$ $\quad$ – ______

Name________________________________ **Exploring Three-Digit Subtraction**

What You Need

models

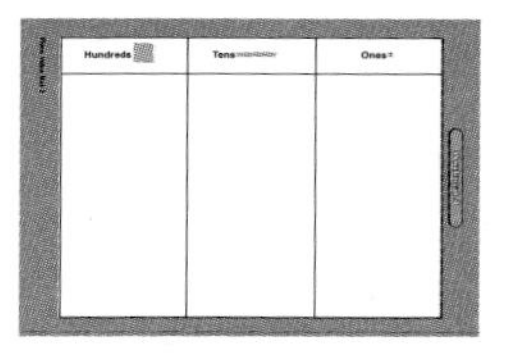

Workmat 4

spinner

1. Build the number.

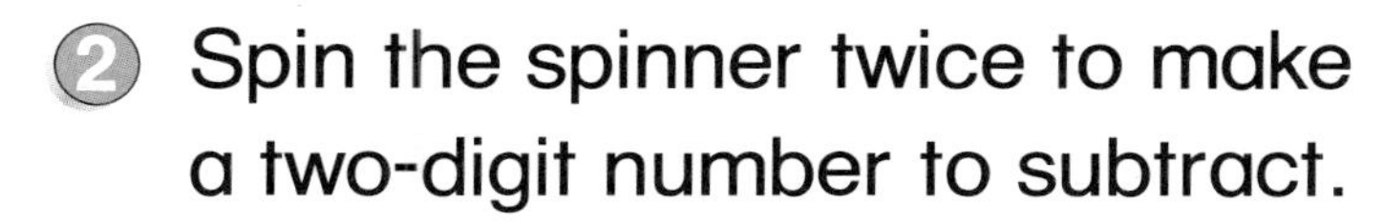

2. Spin the spinner twice to make a two-digit number to subtract.
3. Record that number.
4. Subtract. Regroup if you need to.

	Number	Number to Subtract	Difference
1.	682		
2.	427		
3.	561		
4.	354		
5.	439		
6.	670		
7.	392		
8.	518		

Home Connection Your child is learning to subtract two- and three-digit numbers. Write a problem such as 567−239. Have your child explain subtraction with regrouping.

Use models and Workmat 4.
Show each number.
Find the difference. Regroup if you need to.

1.

	6 hundreds	3 tens	5 ones
−	2 hundreds	7 tens	4 ones
	3 hundreds	6 tens	1 one

	3 hundreds	2 tens	8 ones
−	1 hundred	4 tens	3 ones
	___ hundred	___ tens	___ ones

2.

	4 hundreds	7 tens	3 ones
−	2 hundreds	5 tens	8 ones
	___ hundreds	___ ten	___ ones

	3 hundreds	5 tens	4 ones
−	1 hundred	6 tens	8 ones
	___ hundred	___ tens	___ ones

3.

	5 hundreds	2 tens	9 ones
−	2 hundreds	0 tens	7 ones
	___ hundreds	___ tens	___ ones

	6 hundreds	2 tens	1 one
−	3 hundreds	3 tens	1 one
	___ hundreds	___ tens	___ ones

4.

	5 hundreds	8 tens	3 ones
−	2 hundreds	9 tens	0 ones
	___ hundreds	___ tens	___ ones

	3 hundreds	0 tens	5 ones
−		8 tens	2 ones
	___ hundreds	___ tens	___ ones

5.

	_____ hundreds	_____ tens	_____ ones
−	_____ hundreds	_____ tens	_____ ones
	_____ hundreds	_____ tens	_____ ones

Name________________________ **Subtracting Three-Digit Numbers**

123 people hiked into the Grand Canyon. 315 people rode mules. How many fewer people hiked than rode mules?

1. Subtract the ones. Regroup if you need to.

H	T	O
3	1	5
− 1	2	3
		2

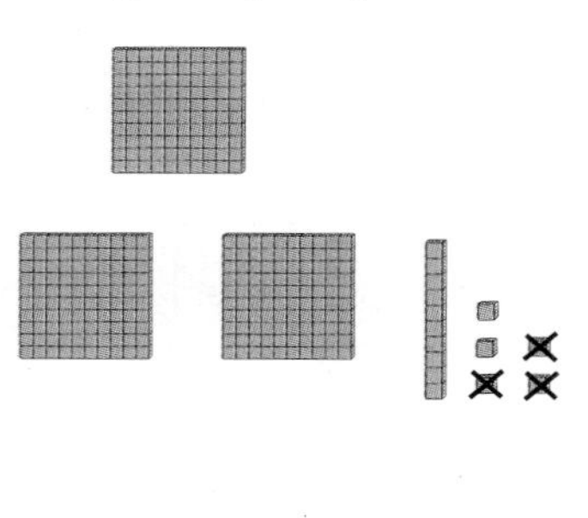

2. Subtract the tens. Regroup if you need to.

H	T	O
2	11	
3	1	5
− 1	2	3
	9	2

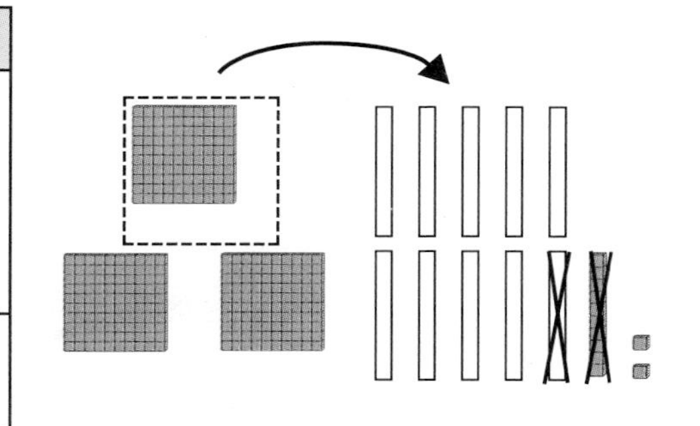

3. Subtract the hundreds.

H	T	O
2	11	
3	1	5
− 1	2	3
1	9	2

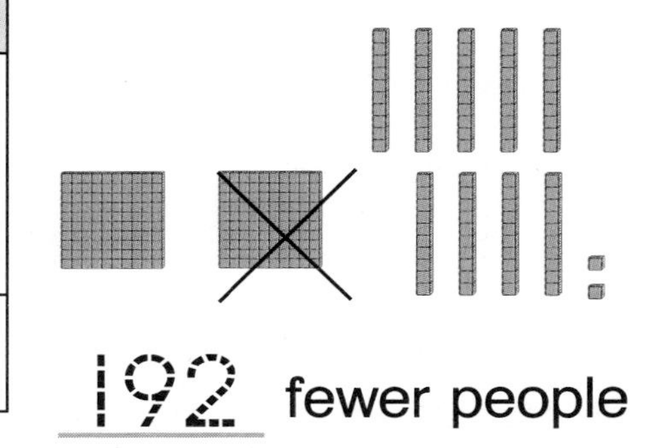

192 fewer people

Use models and Workmat 4. Subtract.

1.

H	T	O
4	5	3
− 2	1	7

2.

H	T	O
3	2	7
− 1	5	4

3.

H	T	O
5	0	6
− 3	4	2

Home Connection Your child is subtracting three-digit numbers. Ask your child to tell you how he or she knows when it is necessary to regroup.

Use models and Workmat 4. Subtract.

1.

	H	T	O
		2	14
	2	3	4
−	1	2	6
	1	0	8

	H	T	O
	6	2	0
−	3	0	8

	H	T	O
	4	6	7
−	1	8	4

2.

	H	T	O
	2	8	5
−	1	4	0

	H	T	O
	3	4	5
−	1	8	2

	H	T	O
	7	3	6
−	4	4	2

3.

	H	T	O
	5	7	3
−	2	4	8

	H	T	O
	8	2	1
−	5	0	0

	H	T	O
	6	8	5
−	2	9	4

Problem Solving

Which two numbers will make each sum or difference?
Write the numbers.

4. Difference of 126 ______ and ______

5. Difference of 342 ______ and ______

6. Sum of 537 ______ and ______

Name ____ **Practicing Subtraction**

346 adults and 182 children visited the Gateway Arch. How many more adults visited the arch?

Gateway Arch ▶

1 Subtract the ones. Regroup if you need to.

	H	T	O
	3	4	6
−	1	8	2
			4

2 Subtract the tens. Regroup if you need to.

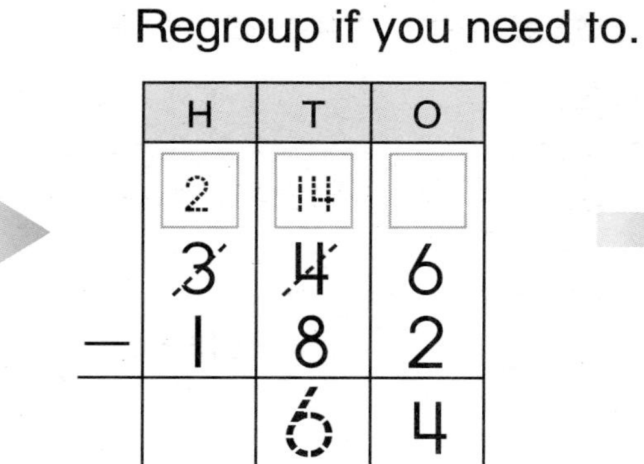

	H	T	O
	2	14	
	~~3~~	~~4~~	6
−	1	8	2
		6	4

3 Subtract the hundreds.

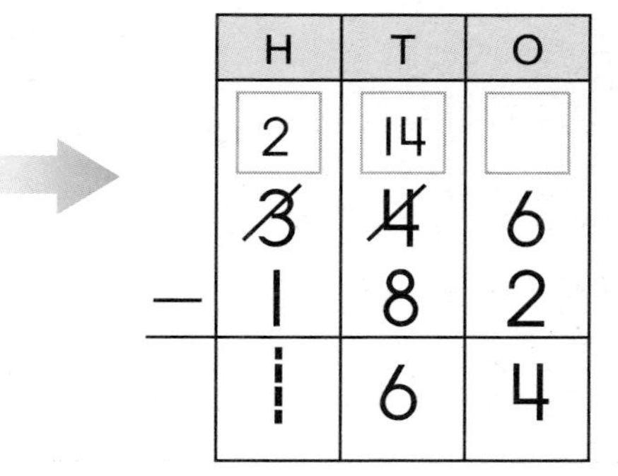

	H	T	O
	2	14	
	~~3~~	~~4~~	6
−	1	8	2
	1	6	4

164 more adults

Subtract. Use models if you like.

1. $536 - 270$ $952 - 618$ $470 - 9$ $715 - 225$ $429 - 374$

2. $391 - 166$ $865 - 634$ $529 - 273$ $463 - 436$ $308 - 126$

3. $783 - 577$ $672 - 345$ $819 - 596$ $568 - 50$ $608 - 45$

Home Connection Have your child show you exercises on this page that require regrouping 1 ten as 10 ones and exercises that require regrouping 1 hundred as 10 tens.

Write in vertical form. Subtract.

1. 426 − 118   923 − 561   861 − 307   409 − 45

$$\begin{array}{r} {\scriptstyle 1\ 16} \\ 426 \\ -\ 118 \\ \hline 308 \end{array}$$

2. 438 − 215   647 − 9   533 − 218   464 − 146

Critical Thinking Corner

Estimation

Circle the most reasonable answer.
Explain your thinking.

3. 472 − 68 is about _____.

200

400

800

4. 236 − 87 is _____.

greater than 200

about 200

less than 200

Name ____________________

What would you buy?
Use coins and bills to act it out.
Write what you spend.
Find out how much is left.

$1.45 $5.25

	You have	You spend	Amount left
1.		$3.72	$0.28
2.		___.___	___.___
3.		___.___	___.___
4.		___.___	___.___

Home Connection Your child is learning what a given amount of money will buy. Play "store" with your child to have him or her practice making purchases.

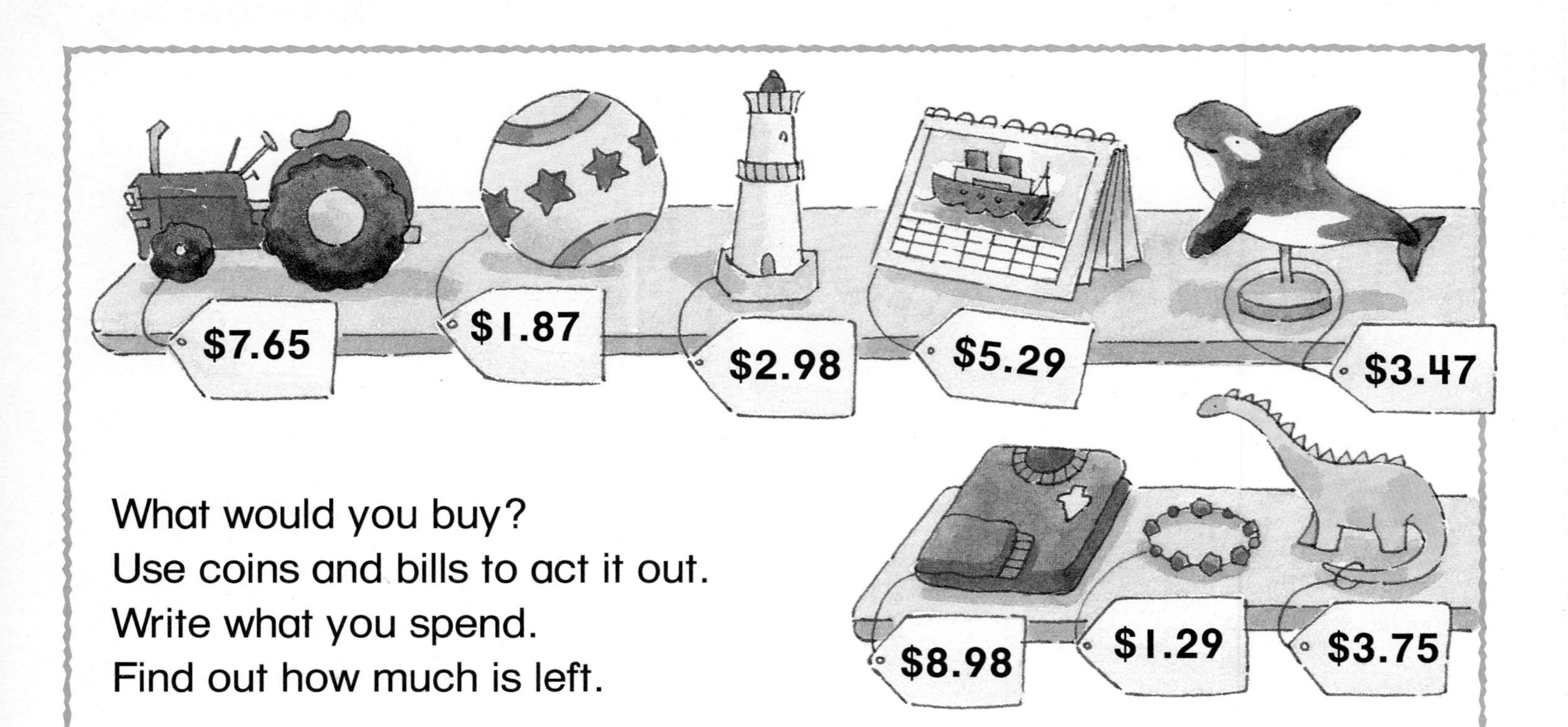

What would you buy?
Use coins and bills to act it out.
Write what you spend.
Find out how much is left.

	You have	You spend	Amount left
1.		___.___	___.___
2.		___.___	___.___
3.		___.___	___.___
4.		___.___	___.___

I had \$6.00. I bought a puzzle for \$2.67 and postcards for \$1.23.

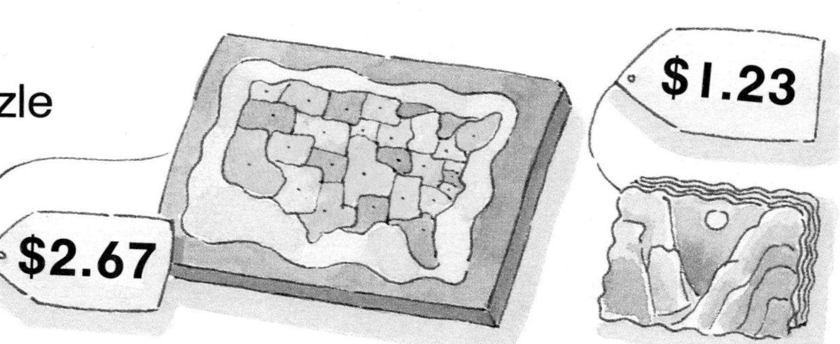

How much did I spend? Add.	How much do I have left? Subtract.
$\begin{array}{r} \scriptstyle 1 \\ \$2.67 \\ +\ 1.23 \\ \hline \$3.90 \end{array}$	$\begin{array}{r} \scriptstyle 5\ 10 \\ \$\not{6}.\not{0}0 \\ -\ 3.90 \\ \hline \$2.10 \end{array}$

Add or subtract.

1.	$\begin{array}{r} \$3.48 \\ +\ 2.45 \\ \hline \end{array}$	$\begin{array}{r} \$2.05 \\ -\ 0.15 \\ \hline \end{array}$	$\begin{array}{r} \$6.00 \\ +\ 2.35 \\ \hline \end{array}$	$\begin{array}{r} \$7.50 \\ -\ 2.25 \\ \hline \end{array}$	$\begin{array}{r} \$9.41 \\ -\ 6.26 \\ \hline \end{array}$
2.	$\begin{array}{r} \$5.94 \\ +\ 0.75 \\ \hline \end{array}$	$\begin{array}{r} \$4.65 \\ +\ 2.19 \\ \hline \end{array}$	$\begin{array}{r} \$9.25 \\ -\ 7.80 \\ \hline \end{array}$	$\begin{array}{r} \$5.26 \\ -\ 2.08 \\ \hline \end{array}$	$\begin{array}{r} \$3.42 \\ +\ 1.08 \\ \hline \end{array}$
3.	$\begin{array}{r} \$8.14 \\ -\ 5.62 \\ \hline \end{array}$	$\begin{array}{r} \$7.04 \\ +\ 0.89 \\ \hline \end{array}$	$\begin{array}{r} \$4.25 \\ -\ 1.08 \\ \hline \end{array}$	$\begin{array}{r} \$6.56 \\ +\ 1.93 \\ \hline \end{array}$	$\begin{array}{r} \$8.78 \\ -\ 5.83 \\ \hline \end{array}$
4.	$\begin{array}{r} \$6.23 \\ -\ 1.61 \\ \hline \end{array}$	$\begin{array}{r} \$8.28 \\ -\ 3.25 \\ \hline \end{array}$	$\begin{array}{r} \$2.52 \\ +\ 4.18 \\ \hline \end{array}$	$\begin{array}{r} \$4.44 \\ +\ 1.82 \\ \hline \end{array}$	$\begin{array}{r} \$6.45 \\ -\ 3.63 \\ \hline \end{array}$

Home Connection Your child is learning real-life applications for addition and subtraction. Help him or her practice adding and subtracting money.

Add or subtract.

1.

$7.48 − 1.19 $6.29	$1.26 + 2.66	$3.56 − 1.81	$4.54 + 1.28	$5.23 − 2.61

2.

$3.29 + 4.64	$2.48 + 6.03	$8.17 − 3.42	$7.73 − 2.56	$0.83 + 3.45

3.

$8.47 − 5.93	$6.08 − 3.64	$2.71 + 0.78	$1.57 + 4.83	$6.00 − 4.30

Problem Solving

Solve. Show your work.

4. Pam buys stickers for $3.22 and a poster for $2.48. She gives the clerk $6.00. How much change does she get?

_______ change

5. Ken buys a ball for $1.56 and a cap for $5.34. He gives the clerk $7.00. How much change does he get?

_______ change

Name________________________ **Choosing a Computation Method**

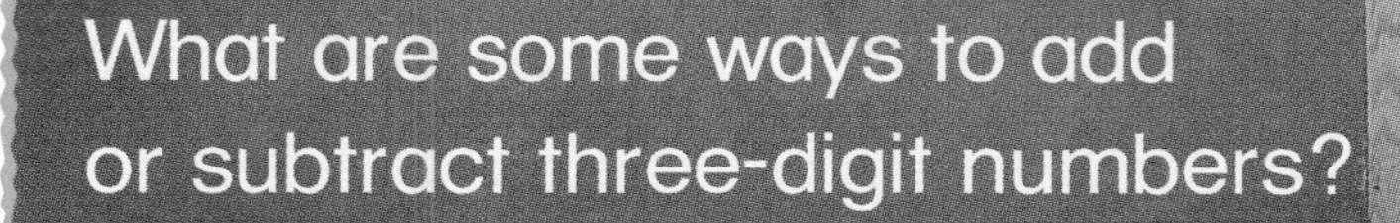

What are some ways to add
or subtract three-digit numbers?

Sometimes I use a calculator.

If it looks easy, I use mental math.

I like to use paper and pencil.

Sometimes I use models.

Add or subtract.
Choose your own method. Tell why.

1. $\begin{array}{r} 473 \\ +282 \\ \hline 755 \end{array}$ $\quad \begin{array}{r} 525 \\ -361 \\ \hline \end{array}$ $\quad \begin{array}{r} 673 \\ +251 \\ \hline \end{array}$ $\quad \begin{array}{r} 136 \\ +218 \\ \hline \end{array}$ $\quad \begin{array}{r} 394 \\ -237 \\ \hline \end{array}$

2. $\begin{array}{r} 607 \\ -362 \\ \hline \end{array}$ $\quad \begin{array}{r} 284 \\ +509 \\ \hline \end{array}$ $\quad \begin{array}{r} 413 \\ +165 \\ \hline \end{array}$ $\quad \begin{array}{r} 726 \\ -432 \\ \hline \end{array}$ $\quad \begin{array}{r} 845 \\ -630 \\ \hline \end{array}$

3. $\begin{array}{r} 289 \\ +603 \\ \hline \end{array}$ $\quad \begin{array}{r} 574 \\ -436 \\ \hline \end{array}$ $\quad \begin{array}{r} 850 \\ +\ 65 \\ \hline \end{array}$ $\quad \begin{array}{r} 443 \\ -281 \\ \hline \end{array}$ $\quad \begin{array}{r} 939 \\ -644 \\ \hline \end{array}$

4. $100 + 400 =$ ____ $\qquad 327 + 10 =$ ____

5. $600 - 200 =$ ____ $\qquad 457 - 100 =$ ____

Home Connection Encourage your child to explain the different ways to add three-digit numbers such as 371 + 254.

Sometimes one way is easier than another.

Choose a way to solve each problem.
Circle your choice. Then solve.

1. $\begin{array}{r} 428 \\ +236 \\ \hline \end{array}$

a. models
b. paper and pencil
c. mental math
d. calculator

2. $\begin{array}{r} 649 \\ -100 \\ \hline \end{array}$

a. models
b. paper and pencil
c. mental math
d. calculator

3. $\begin{array}{r} 186 \\ +280 \\ \hline \end{array}$

a. models
b. paper and pencil
c. mental math
d. calculator

4. $\begin{array}{r} 591 \\ -258 \\ \hline \end{array}$

a. models
b. paper and pencil
c. mental math
d. calculator

5. $\begin{array}{r} 354 \\ +200 \\ \hline \end{array}$

a. models
b. paper and pencil
c. mental math
d. calculator

6. $\begin{array}{r} 706 \\ -544 \\ \hline \end{array}$

a. models
b. paper and pencil
c. mental math
d. calculator

7. $\begin{array}{r} 385 \\ +263 \\ \hline \end{array}$

a. models
b. paper and pencil
c. mental math
d. calculator

8. $\begin{array}{r} 879 \\ -300 \\ \hline \end{array}$

a. models
b. paper and pencil
c. mental math
d. calculator

9. $\begin{array}{r} 733 \\ +148 \\ \hline \end{array}$

a. models
b. paper and pencil
c. mental math
d. calculator

10. $\begin{array}{r} 924 \\ -205 \\ \hline \end{array}$

a. models
b. paper and pencil
c. mental math
d. calculator

Name ____________________

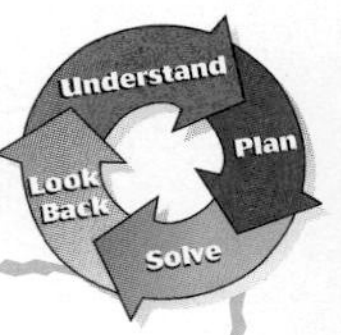

Some information might not help you solve a problem.

The Empire State Building is 381 m tall.
~~It has 102 floors.~~
The World Trade Center is 417 m tall.
Which building is taller? How much tall

$$\begin{array}{r} \overset{3\ 11}{\cancel{4}\cancel{1}7} \\ -\ 381 \\ \hline 36 \end{array}$$

The World Trade Center is 36 m taller.

Empire State Building ▲

▲ World Trade Center

Cross out the information you do not need. Solve.

1. The General Sherman Tree is 275 ft tall. Its lowest branch is 130 ft above the ground. The tree is 103 ft around. How many ft is it from the lowest branch to the top of the tree?

▲ General Sherman Tree

_____ ft

2. The Space Needle is 607 ft tall. 273 people visited the building in the morning. 346 people visited in the afternoon. How many people visited in all?

▲ Space Needle

_____ people

Home Connection Your child is learning to identify the facts needed to solve problems. Have your child explain why he or she eliminated some facts in the problems above.

Cross out the information you do not need. Solve.

1. At the fair, 207 adults and 463 children rode the Ferris wheel. 350 children rode the merry-go-round. How many people rode the Ferris wheel?

▲ Western Idaho Fair

_____ people

2. The Astrodome is 208 ft high. At an Astros ballgame, 693 people ate hot dogs. 426 adults ate hot dogs. How many children ate hot dogs?

▲ The Houston Astrodome

_____ children

Critical Thinking Corner

Number Sense

What information do you need to solve the problem?

Sometimes you do not have enough information to solve a problem.

3. The Clark family drove to the Smoky Mountains in 2 days. They drove 200 miles on Day 1. How many miles did they drive on Day 2?

Name________________________________ **Checkpoint**

Find each difference.

1.

H	T	O
☐	☐	☐
3	5	2
− 1	9	1

H	T	O
☐	☐	☐
4	7	5
− 2	6	3

H	T	O
☐	☐	☐
6	4	2
− 3	2	7

2. $\begin{array}{r} 600 \\ -400 \\ \hline \end{array}$ $\begin{array}{r} 763 \\ -327 \\ \hline \end{array}$ $\begin{array}{r} 435 \\ -253 \\ \hline \end{array}$ $\begin{array}{r} 546 \\ -190 \\ \hline \end{array}$ $\begin{array}{r} 874 \\ -\ \ 32 \\ \hline \end{array}$

Add or subtract.

3. $\begin{array}{r} \$3.25 \\ +2.17 \\ \hline \end{array}$ $\begin{array}{r} \$5.63 \\ +3.74 \\ \hline \end{array}$ $\begin{array}{r} \$6.80 \\ -3.23 \\ \hline \end{array}$ $\begin{array}{r} \$7.52 \\ -0.60 \\ \hline \end{array}$ $\begin{array}{r} \$2.45 \\ +1.32 \\ \hline \end{array}$

4. $\begin{array}{r} 300 \\ +\ \ \ 7 \\ \hline \end{array}$ $\begin{array}{r} 293 \\ -124 \\ \hline \end{array}$ $\begin{array}{r} 582 \\ -166 \\ \hline \end{array}$ $\begin{array}{r} 706 \\ -253 \\ \hline \end{array}$ $\begin{array}{r} 454 \\ +271 \\ \hline \end{array}$

What would you buy?
Use coins and bills to act it out.
Complete the chart.

5.

You have	You spend	Amount left
(one-dollar bill)	$ ___.___	$ ___.___

Name______________________________ **Extra Practice**

Use the numbers on the signs.
Write 2 addition problems and 2 subtraction problems.
Find each sum and difference.

1.

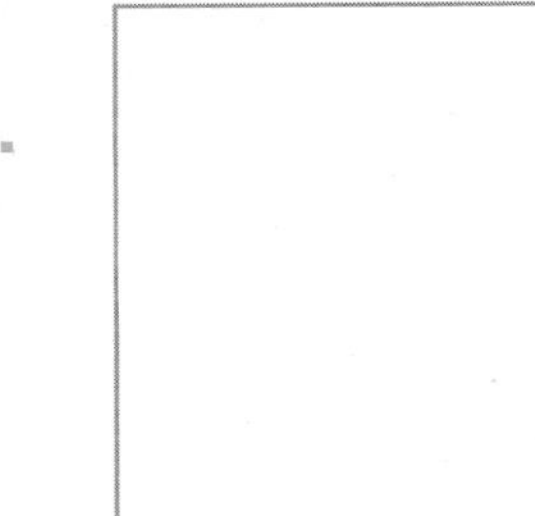

Write the missing digits to complete each problem.

2.

2 4 □	3 7 2	1 6 4	4 8 3
+ 3 0 6	+ 4 □ 6	+ 2 2 □	+ □ 6 2
5 5 2	8 1 8	3 9 2	8 4 5

3.

4 □ 3	□ 4 6	6 3 7	5 6 □
− 2 4 1	− 1 6 4	− 2 □ 0	− 3 0 6
2 2 2	1 8 2	3 8 7	2 5 6

4.

3 2 7	1 3 4	7 2 6	6 5 9
+ 1 5 4	+ 2 6 5	− 3 4 0	− 4 7
4 8 □	3 □ 9	□ 8 6	6 1 □

Name______________________________ **Chapter Test** 

Add.

1.

400	370	$2.56	529	643
+ 300	+ 47	+ 3.36	+ 7	+ 232

2.

$4.08	791	359	272	586
+ 2.63	+ 144	+ 135	+ 460	+ 333

Subtract.

3.

800	$5.73	906	647	758
− 500	− 4.65	− 551	− 86	− 224

4.

348	480	$6.34	228	554
− 262	− 163	− 3.52	− 9	− 462

Cross out the information you do not need. Solve.

5. The Jackson family has to drive 650 miles to visit Mount Rushmore. The faces of 4 presidents are carved in the mountain. The Jacksons have gone 335 miles. How many more miles do they have to go?

_____ miles

Mount Rushmore

Name______________________________ **Performance Assessment**

Write in vertical form.
Add or subtract.
Do you need to regroup?
Tell how you know.

1. $326 + 428$ $286 + 103$ $473 + 355$ $542 + 173$

2. $516 - 209$ $326 - 140$ $476 - 245$ $638 - 264$

Add or subtract.
Tell how you found each answer.

3. $432 + 200 =$ ____ $799 - 799 =$ ____

4. $629 - 20 =$ ____ $500 + 8 =$ ____

Name______________________________

The farmer sold 212 ears of corn on Monday and 386 ears of corn on Tuesday. About how many did she sell in all?

You can estimate sums and differences.

212 is about 200.

386 is about 400.

212 + 386 is about 600.

Write the nearest hundred.
Estimate each sum or difference.

1. 303 is about ____.
   189 is about ____.
   303 + 189 is about ____.

2. 230 is about ____.
   483 is about ____.
   230 + 483 is about ____.

3. 621 is about ____.
   378 is about ____.
   621 − 378 is about ____.

4. 582 is about ____.
   273 is about ____.
   582 − 273 is about ____.

5. 425 is about ____.
   192 is about ____.
   425 + 192 is about ____.

6. 798 is about ____.
   327 is about ____.
   798 − 327 is about ____.

Name ______________________________

Time for Technology
Adding and Subtracting Money

Use a calculator to add or subtract.
Record the keys you press.

Press 

each time you begin.

Remember to press the decimal point.

1. $2.78 + $3.61 = $6.39

2 . 7 8 + 3 . 6 1 =

2. $4.65 − $2.23 = ______

−   =

3. $1.19 + $6.47 = ______

+   =

4. $7.80 − $4.36 = ______

−   =

---

5. $5.67 + $1.04 = ______

 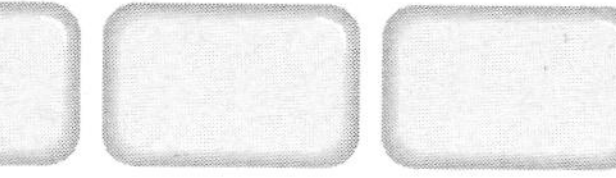     

+   =

CHAPTER 12

Exploring Multiplication and Division

Pepper's Problem

written by Joyce Mallery

illustrated by Paul Yalowitz

MAP

This Math Storybook belongs to

____

A

I'm a bird named Pepper.
I love to count all day.
I count so much that now I'm lost
and cannot find my way.
B

I know that I am lost.
I know I'm in a fix.
Oh, look! I see 3 groups of 2.
3 groups of 2 make 6.

I'm looking for my friends
and flying by some trees.
When I stop to look at them,
I see 12 in groups of 3.
D

I fly around to find my friends.
I know that I am late.
I see 2 groups of 4 balloons.
2 groups of 4 make 8.

Suddenly I find my friends.
They're flying in the sky.
Now we're in 3 groups of 5.
15 in all fly by.
F

www.sbgmath.com
Draw some birds in groups of 3.
How many birds do you see?
G

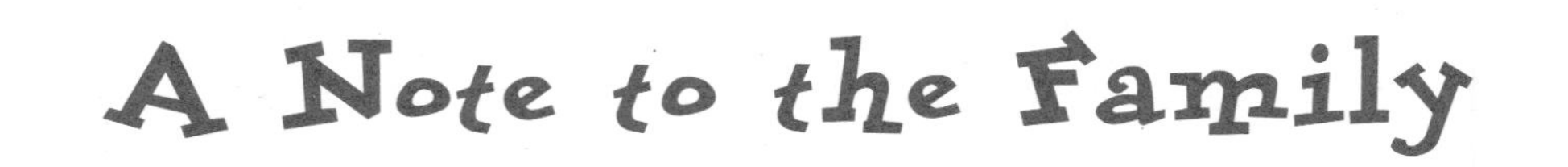

A Note to the Family

Here are some learning ideas you can share with your child.

Enjoy *Pepper's Problem* Together

- Read the story aloud with your child. On each page, ask him or her to find the groups of objects that Pepper is counting. You may wish to help your child write multiplication sentences to show the total number of objects.
- Talk about the groups of birds that your child drew on the last page of the book and find the total number.

At-Home Activity

- Explore the concepts of multiplication and division by playing "leftovers" with your child. Use 15 small objects, such as pennies or buttons. Ask your child to make groups of 2. Before he or she makes the groups, ask your child to guess if any objects will be left over. Then make the groups, say the number of groups, and check the guess. If your child was correct, he or she scores a point. Take turns and continue making groups of 3, 4, and 5.

Read More About It!

To read more stories about multiplication and division with your child, look for the following books in your local library.

- *Each Orange Had Eight Slices: A Counting Book* by Paul Giganti, Jr. (Morrow, 1992)
- *Momotaro, the Peach Boy* by Hiroko C. Quackenbush (Kodansha, 1993)
- *One Hundred Hungry Ants* by Eleanor J. Pinczes (Houghton Mifflin Company, 1993)

Visit Our Web Site!

www.sbgmath.com

H

Name________________________

What You Need

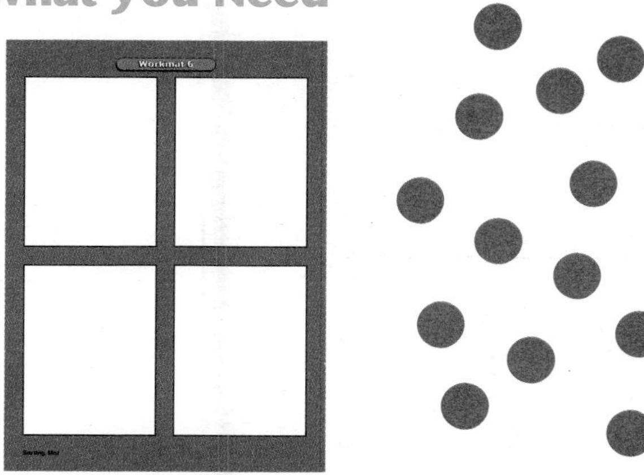
Workmat 6 and counters

3 groups of 4...
that's 12 in all.

Put counters in equal groups.
Complete the chart.

	Number of Groups	Number in Each Group	Number in All
1.	3	4	12
2.	3	5	
3.	2	3	
4.	4	3	
5.	2	2	
6.	4	1	
7.	3	2	
8.	2	5	
9.	1	4	
10.	4	2	

Home Connection Your child is developing a basic understanding of multiplication. Have your child use pennies to form equal groups and then find how many in all.

Draw to show equal groups.
Write how many in all.

1. Make 3 groups of 2.

6 in all

2. Make 2 groups of 4.

____ in all

3. Make 4 groups of 4.

____ in all

4. Make 2 groups of 5.

____ in all

5. Make 3 groups of 4.

____ in all

6. Make 3 groups of 1.

____ in all

7. Make ____ groups of ____.

Make Your Own

____ in all

Name______________________________

How many are there in all?

3 groups of 2

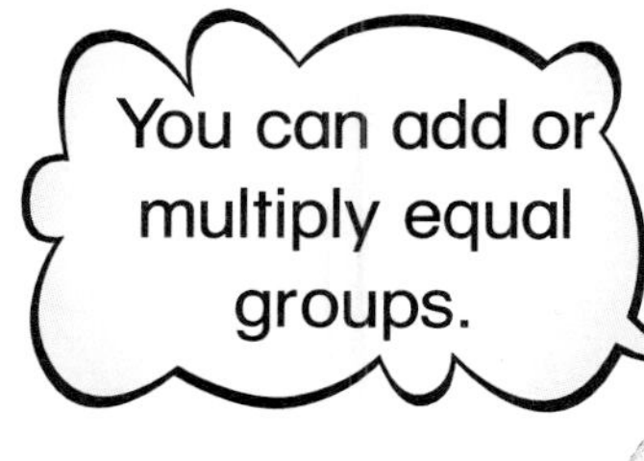

$2 + 2 + 2 = \underline{6}$

$3 \times 2 = \underline{6}$

times   product

Word Bank

times
product
multiply

Add. Then multiply.
Use counters if you like.

1.

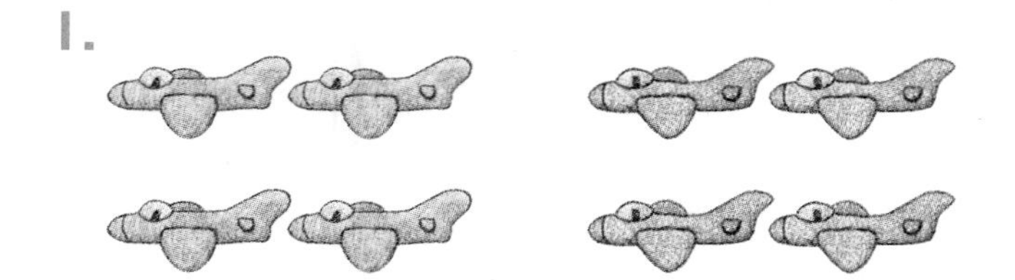

$4 + 4 = \_\_\_\_$

$2 \times 4 = \_\_\_\_$

2.

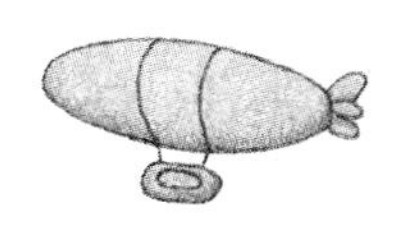

$1 + 1 = \_\_\_\_$

$2 \times 1 = \_\_\_\_$

3.

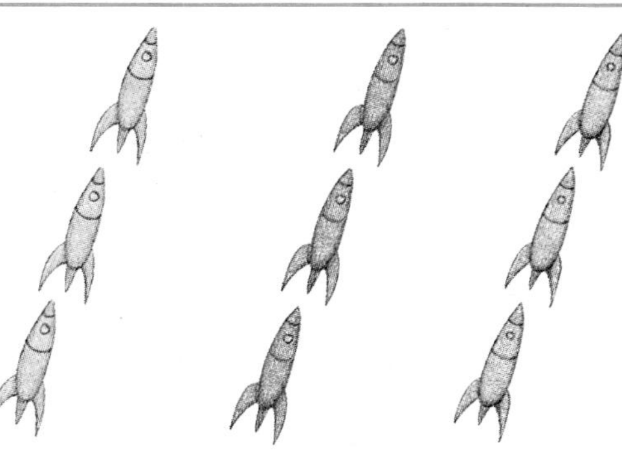

$3 + 3 + 3 = \_\_\_\_$

$3 \times 3 = \_\_\_\_$

4.

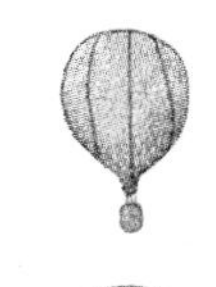

$2 + 2 + 2 + 2 = \_\_\_\_$

$4 \times 2 = \_\_\_\_$

Home Connection Your child is learning that 2 + 2 + 2 is the same as 3 x 2. Ask your child to write addition and multiplication sentences about equal groups, such as 5 groups of 2.

Add. Then multiply.
Use counters if you like.

1.

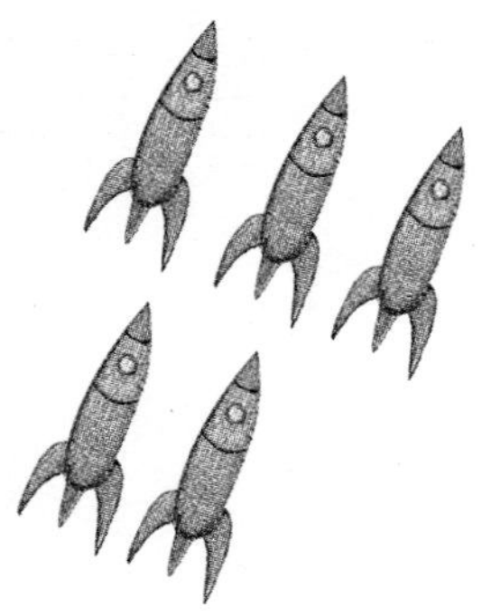

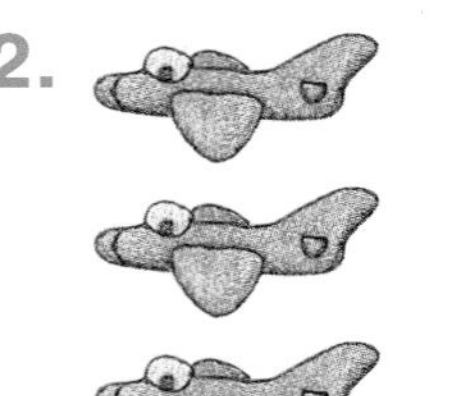

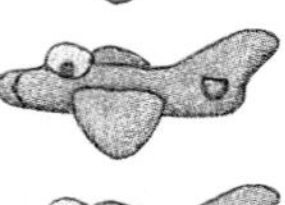

$5 + 5 =$ ____

$2 \times 5 =$ ____

2.

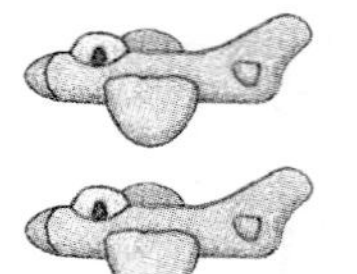

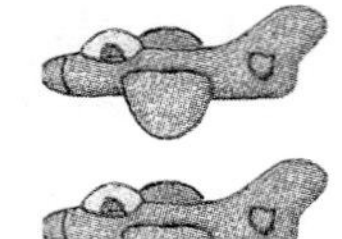

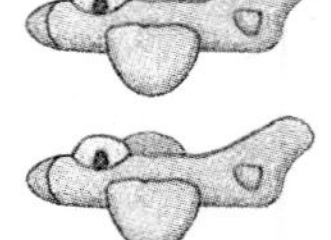

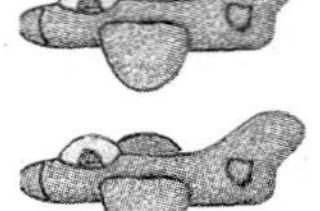

$4 + 4 + 4 =$ ____

$3 \times 4 =$ ____

3.

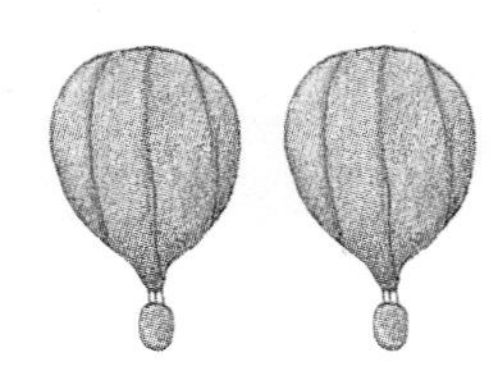

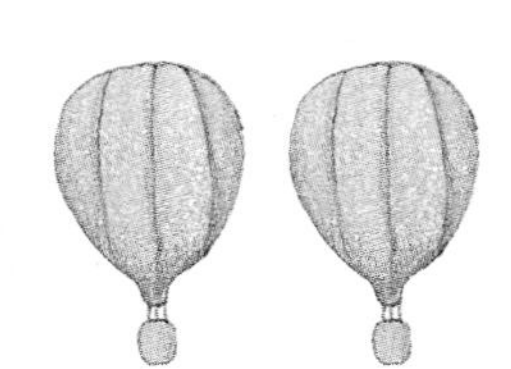

$2 + 2 =$ ____

$2 \times 2 =$ ____

4.

$5 + 5 + 5 =$ ____

$3 \times 5 =$ ____

Critical Thinking Corner

Visual Thinking

5. Look at the picture.
Complete each number sentence.

____ + ____ = ____

____ × ____ = ____

Name______________________________ **Exploring Arrays**

There are 4 rows. There are 2 in each row.

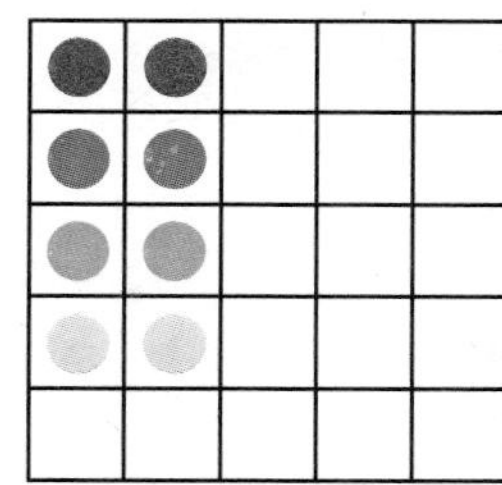

4 × 2 = 8

rows | in each row | in all

Use counters and the grid to show each fact.

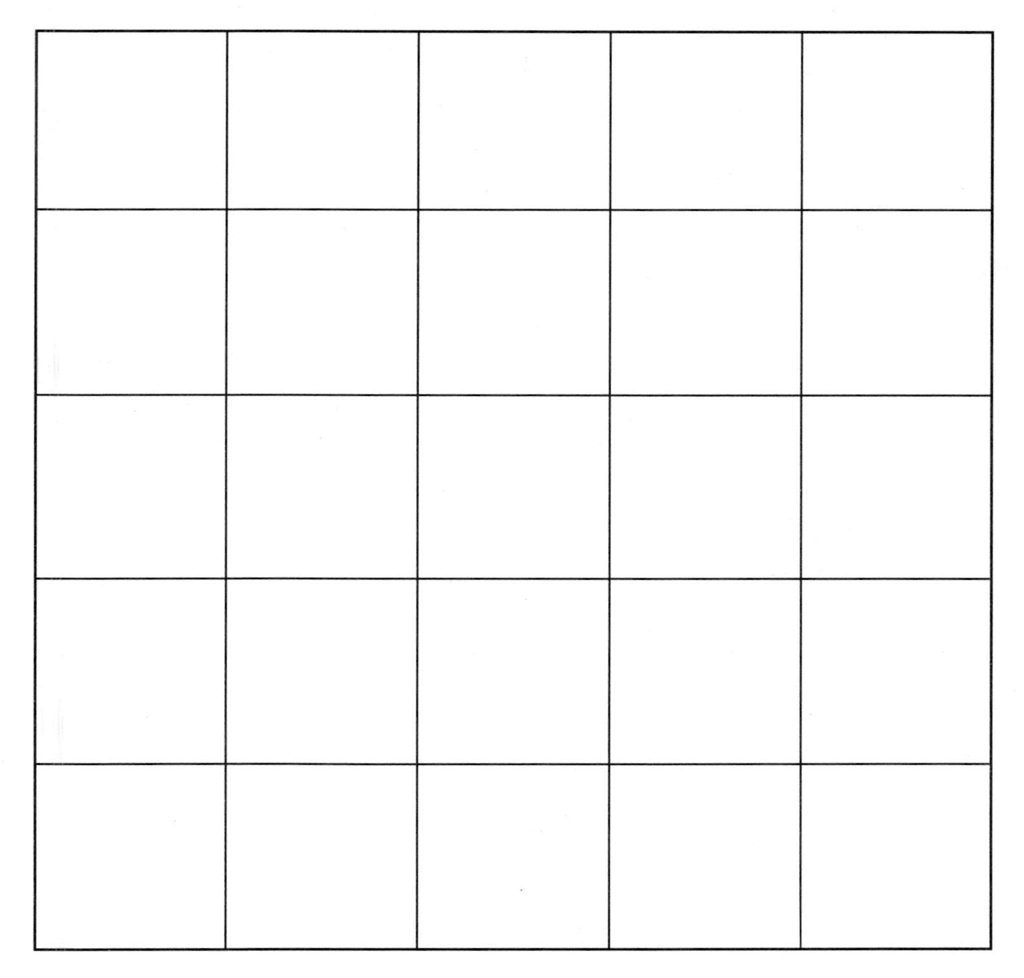

1. 3 × 2 = ____
   rows | in each row | in all

2. 3 × 3 = ____
   rows | in each row | in all

3. 2 × 5 = ____
   rows | in each row | in all

4. 4 × 5 = ____
   rows | in each row | in all

Home Connection Your child is learning to multiply by placing counters in rows and columns. Have her or him place pennies on the grid on this page to multiply numbers like 2 x 3 and 3 x 4.

Write each multiplication fact.

1. 

3 × 5 = 15

rows, in each row, in all

2. 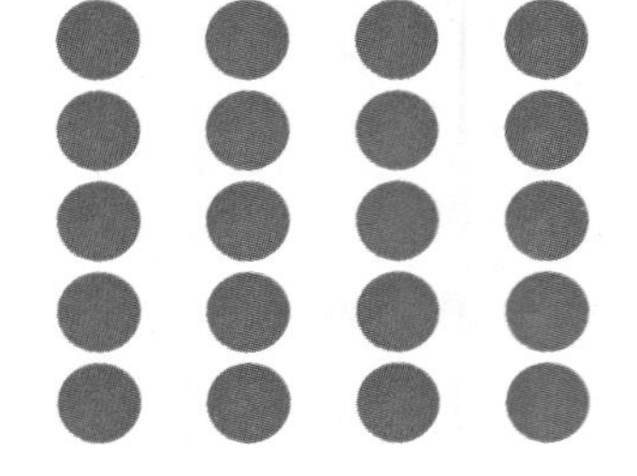

___ × ___ = ___

rows, in each row, in all

3. 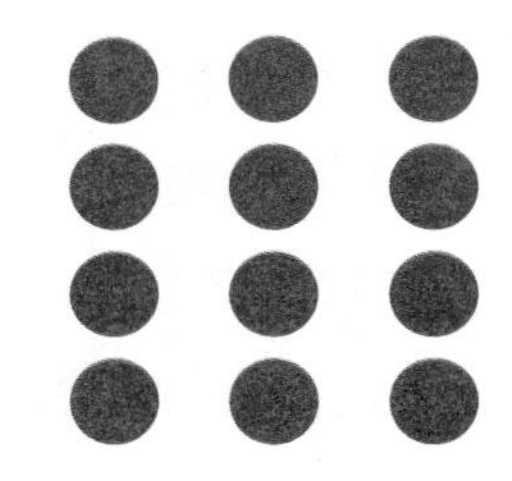

___ × ___ = ___

rows, in each row, in all

4. 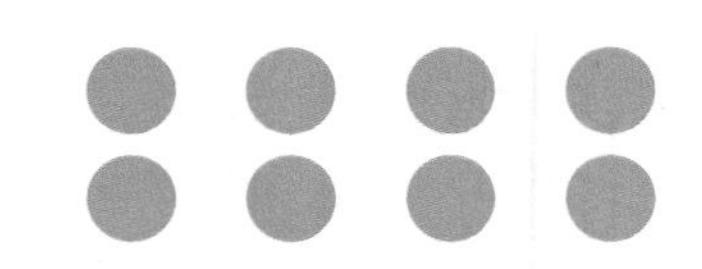

___ × ___ = ___

rows, in each row, in all

5. 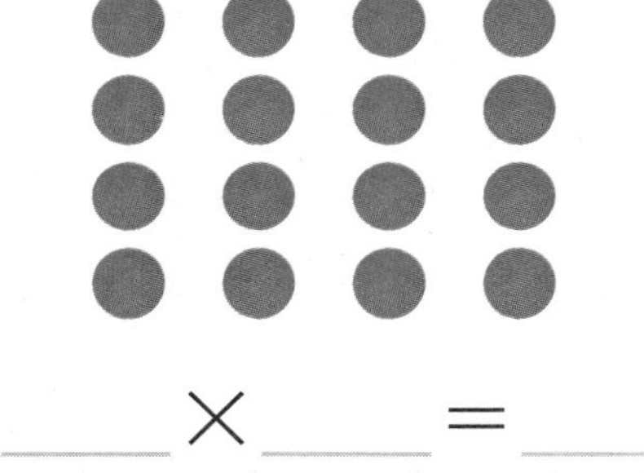

___ × ___ = ___

rows, in each row, in all

6. 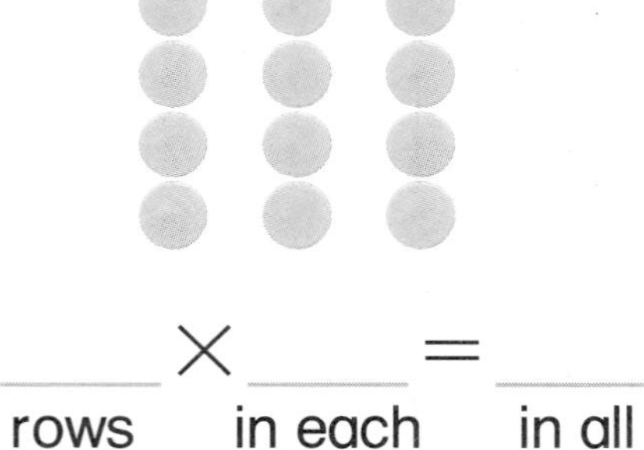

___ × ___ = ___

rows, in each row, in all

Critical Thinking Corner

Visual Thinking

7. Put an X on the picture that does not show a multiplication fact. Explain your answer.

Name________________________

Multiplying Across and Down

You can multiply across or down.

2 groups of kites

5 kites in each group

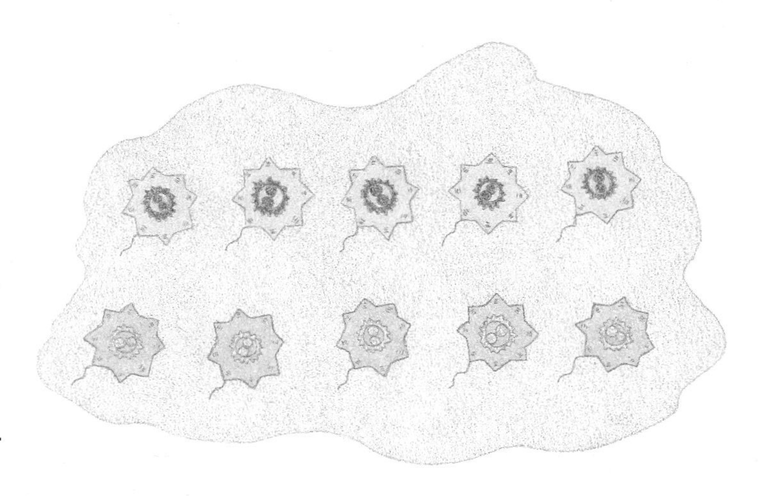

$2 \times 5 = \underline{10}$

$$\begin{array}{r} 5 \\ \times 2 \\ \hline 10 \end{array}$$

Find each product.

1. 4 groups of 2

$4 \times 2 = \_\_\_\_$

$$\begin{array}{r} 2 \\ \times 4 \\ \hline \end{array}$$

2. 1 group of 4

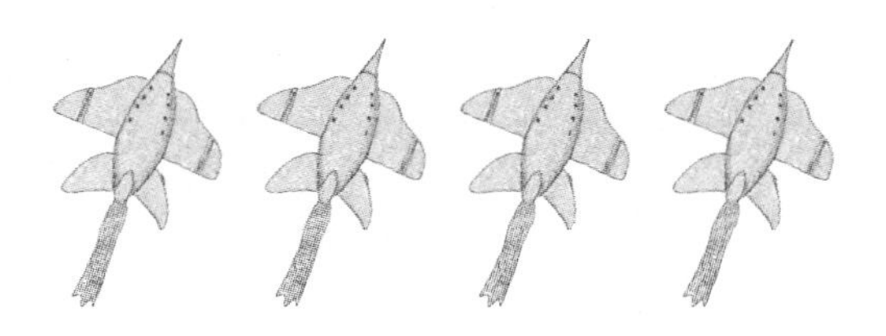

$1 \times 4 = \_\_\_\_$

$$\begin{array}{r} 4 \\ \times 1 \\ \hline \end{array}$$

3. 2 groups of 2

$2 \times 2 = \_\_\_\_$

$$\begin{array}{r} 2 \\ \times 2 \\ \hline \end{array}$$

4. 5 groups of 3

$5 \times 3 = \_\_\_\_$

$$\begin{array}{r} 3 \\ \times 5 \\ \hline \end{array}$$

Home Connection Your child is learning to multiply vertically and horizontally. Show your child 3 groups of 5 pennies. Ask him or her to write the multiplication fact both vertically and horizontally.

Multiply across and down. Write the numbers.

1.

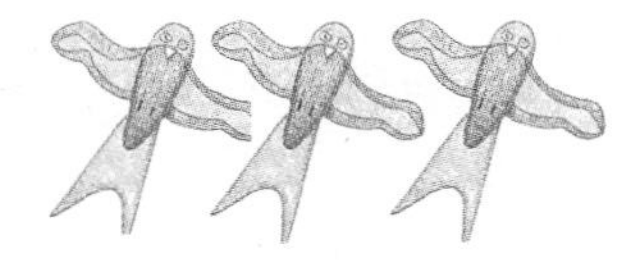

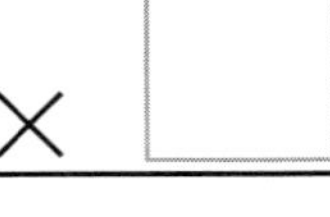

$$\begin{array}{r} 3 \\ \times\ 2 \\ \hline 6 \end{array}$$

2 × 3 = 6

2.

$$\begin{array}{r} \square \\ \times\ \square \\ \hline \end{array}$$

____ × ____ = ____

3.

$$\begin{array}{r} \square \\ \times\ \square \\ \hline \end{array}$$

____ × ____ = ____

4.

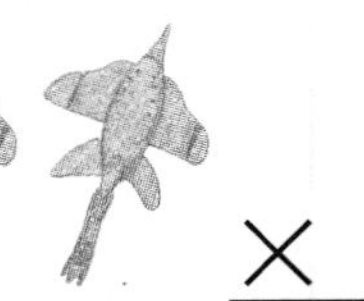
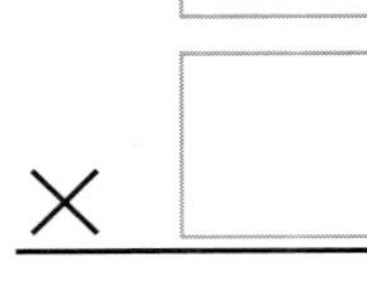

$$\begin{array}{r} \square \\ \times\ \square \\ \hline \end{array}$$

____ × ____ = ____

5.

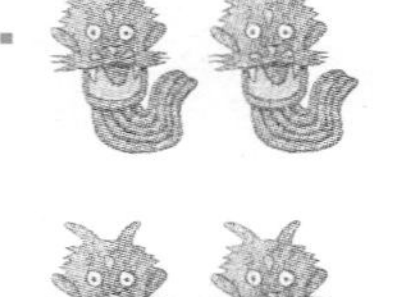

$$\begin{array}{r} \square \\ \times\ \square \\ \hline \end{array}$$

____ × ____ = ____

6.

$$\begin{array}{r} \square \\ \times\ \square \\ \hline \end{array}$$

____ × ____ = ____

Problem Solving

Write the number sentence to solve.

7. There are 3 groups of kites. There are 2 kites in each group. How many kites are there in all?

____ ◯ ____ = ____

8. There are 3 kites in one group. There are 2 kites in the other group. How many kites are there in all?

____ ◯ ____ = ____

Name________________________________ **Multiplying in Any Order**

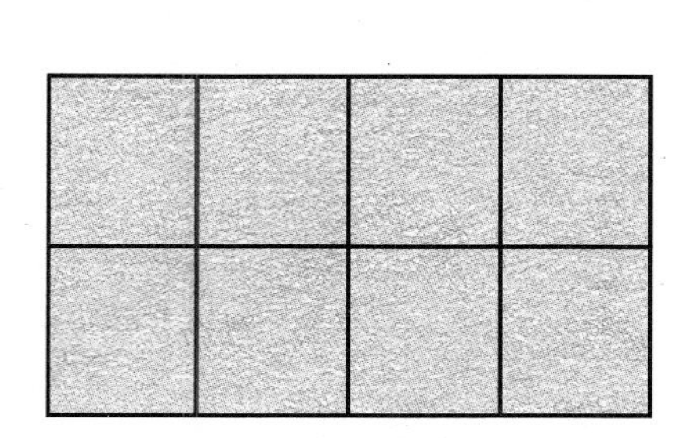

2 rows of 4

$2 \times 4 =$ 8

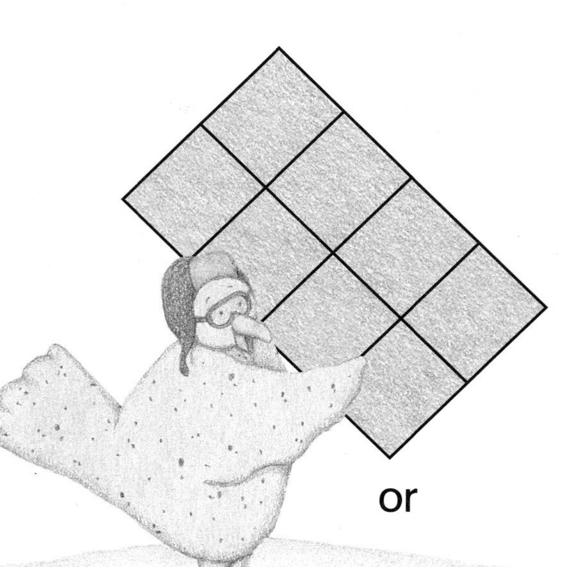

or

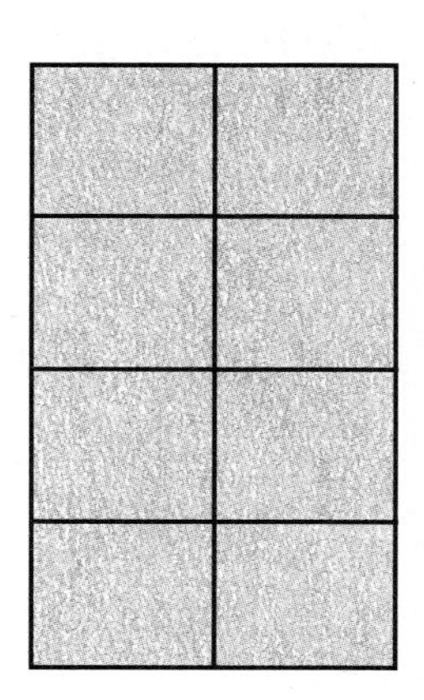

4 rows of 2

$4 \times 2 =$ 8

Word Bank

multiplication sentence

Use grid paper.
Color to show the number in each row.
Then turn the grid.
Write the multiplication sentences.

1. 5 rows of 2 or 2 rows of 5

   ____ $\times$ ____ = ____ ____ $\times$ ____ = ____

2. 4 rows of 3 or 3 rows of 4

   ____ $\times$ ____ = ____ ____ $\times$ ____ = ____

3. 1 row of 4 or 4 rows of 1

   ____ $\times$ ____ = ____ ____ $\times$ ____ = ____

4. 0 rows of 5 or 5 rows of 0

   ____ $\times$ ____ = ____ ____ $\times$ ____ = ____

Home Connection Your child is learning that numbers can be multiplied in any order. Ask your child to draw rows to show that order does not change the product of 2 x 4.

Write the missing numbers. Multiply.

1. 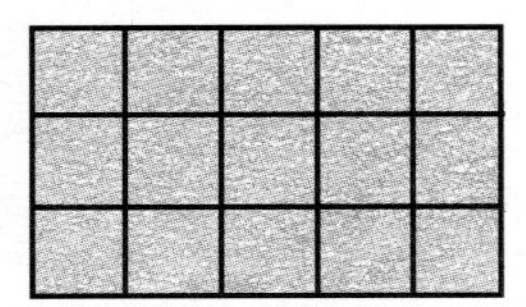 ___ rows of ___

$3 \times 5 =$ ___

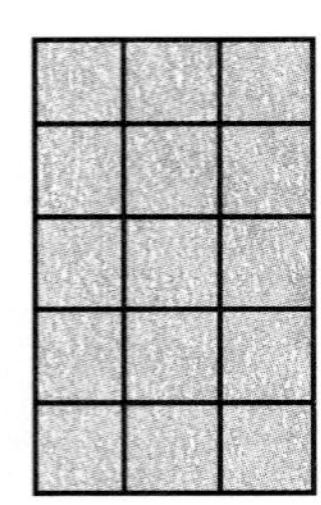 ___ rows of ___

$5 \times 3 =$ ___

2.  ___ rows of ___

$2 \times 3 =$ ___

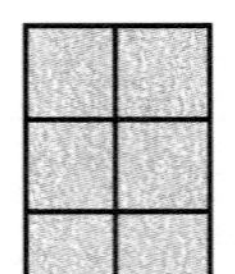 ___ rows of ___

$3 \times 2 =$ ___

3. 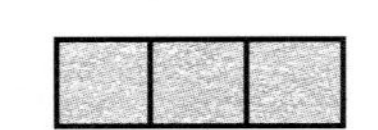 ___ row of ___

$1 \times 3 =$ ___

 ___ rows of ___

$3 \times 1 =$ ___

Add or multiply.

Checkpoint 

1. 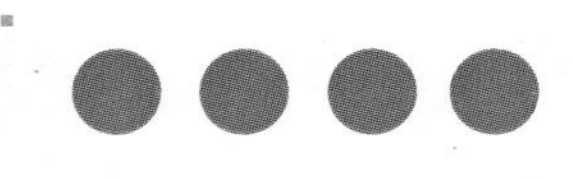 

$4 + 4 =$ ___

$2 \times 4 =$ ___

2. 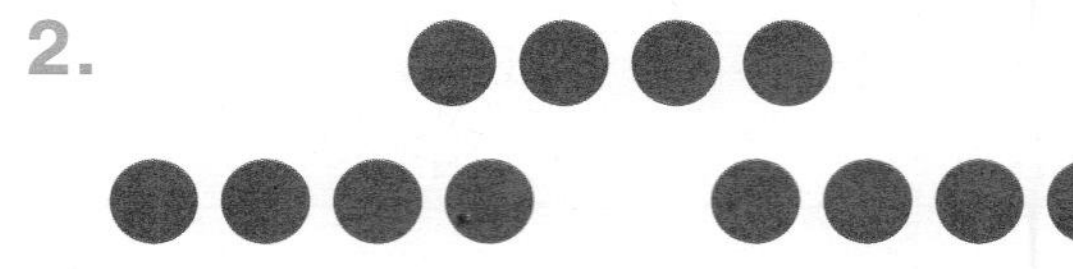

$4 + 4 + 4 =$ ___

$3 \times 4 =$ ___

3.  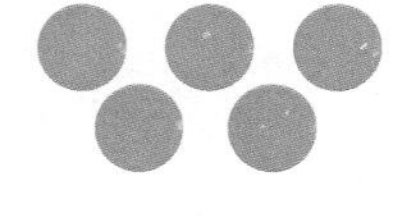  

$\begin{array}{r} 5 \\ \times 4 \\ \hline \end{array}$

$4 \times 5 =$ ___

4. 

$\begin{array}{r} 2 \\ \times 3 \\ \hline \end{array}$

$3 \times 2 =$ ___

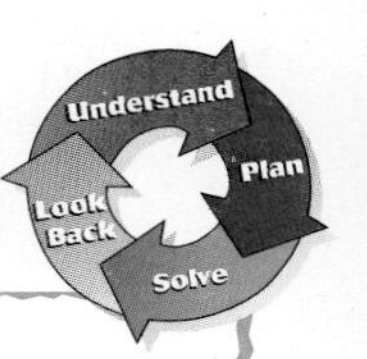

Name____

There are 3 leaves. There are 3 bugs on each leaf. How many bugs are there in all?

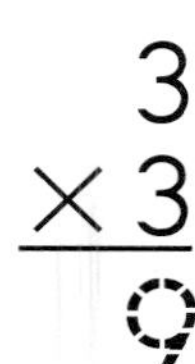

 bugs

Draw pictures to solve each problem. Write the answer.

1. There are 4 flowers. Each flower has 2 leaves. How many leaves are there?

_____ leaves

2. There are 4 cats and 2 ducks. How many legs are there on all the animals?

_____ legs

3. Becky has 8 eggs. She needs 2 eggs to make 1 cake. How many cakes can she make?

_____ cakes

Home Connection Your child is learning to solve problems by drawing pictures. Ask your child to explain the picture he or she drew to solve each of the problems on this page.

Draw a picture to solve each problem.
Circle each correct answer.

1. Are there more legs on 2 horses or 3 ducks?

2. Are there more legs on 3 mice or 2 spiders?

3 mice   2 spiders

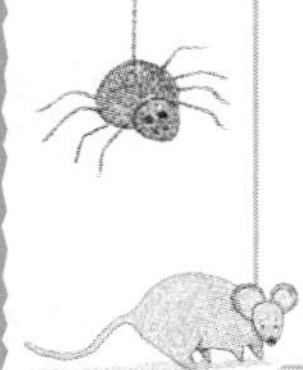

3. Ann has 8 apples. She cuts each apple in half. How many halves does she have?

4 halves   16 halves

4. Paul gave 2 cookies to each of his 5 friends.
He kept 3 cookies for himself.
How many cookies did he start with?

10 cookies   13 cookies

Name________________________________ **Ways to Multiply**

Solve. Draw or write to show how.

1. There are 4 branches with 3 birds on each branch. How many birds are there in all? _____ birds

2. There are 5 posts with 2 birds on each post. How many birds are there in all? _____ birds

3. There are 3 puddles with 1 bird in each puddle. How many birds are there in all? _____ birds

Home Connection Encourage your child to show you different ways to multiply. Ask how he or she would solve 5 x 4.

Choose a way to find each product.
Draw or write to show your choice.

Use addition.

Use counters.

Draw a picture.

1. $4 \times 2 =$ ____

2. $5 \times 4 =$ ____

3. $5 \times 5 =$ ____

What Do You Think?

I think multiplying by 0 or 1 is easy.
What do you think? Tell why.

Name______________________________

Three children are making 12 paper airplanes. They want to share the work equally. How many airplanes should each child make?
There are 3 children. Each child should make 4 airplanes.

Use counters and Workmat 6.
Use the chart to make equal groups.
Write the number in each group.

	Number in All	Number of Groups	Number in Each Group
1.	12	3	4
2.	8	4	
3.	15	3	
4.	20	4	
5.	9	3	
6.	10	2	
7.	16	4	

Home Connection Your child is learning to divide a group of objects into equal groups. Give your child 12 objects, such as pennies or markers. Have him or her make 2, 3, or 4 equal groups.

Circle equal groups.
Write the number in each group.

1\. 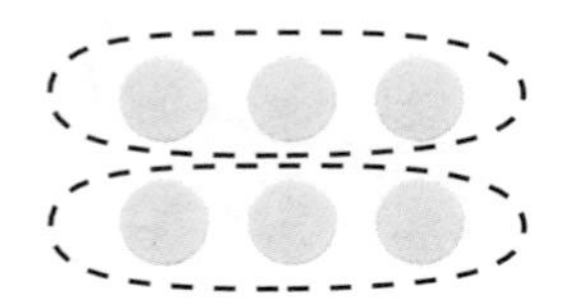

2 groups of 

2\. 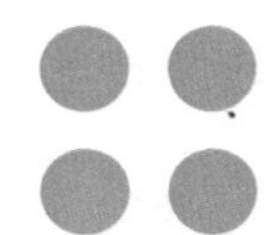

2 groups of ____

3\. 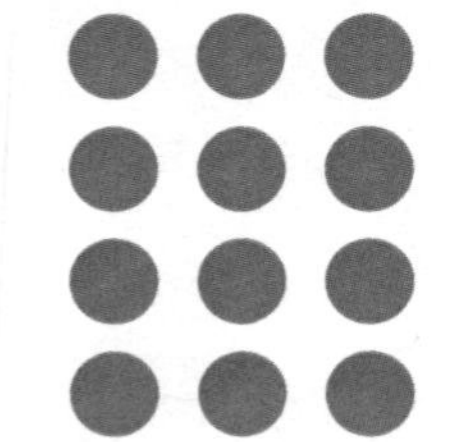

4 groups of ____

4\. 

4 groups of ____

5\. 

3 groups of ____

6\. 

4 groups of ____

Problem Solving

Solve. Use counters if you like.

7\. You have 9 paper airplanes. You want to give an equal number to each of your 3 friends. How many airplanes should you give to each friend?

____ airplanes

8\. You have 14 airplanes. Can you give an equal number to each of your 3 friends? Tell why or why not.

____

____

Name______________________________

2 groups of 3...
that's 6 in all.
3 groups of 2...
that's 6 in all.
Tengo
seis
años

Use counters.
Make equal groups in different ways.
Record each way.

1. **8 counters in all**

____ groups of 1

____ groups of 2

____ groups of 4

____ group of 8

2. **10 counters in all**

____ groups of 1

____ groups of 2

____ groups of 5

____ group of 10

3. **12 counters in all**

____ groups of 1

____ groups of 2

____ groups of 3

____ groups of 4

____ groups of 6

____ group of 12

4. **16 counters in all**

____ groups of 1

____ groups of 2

____ groups of 4

____ groups of 8

____ group of 16

Home Connection Your child is learning to divide quantities into equal groups. Ask your child to use 6 objects to make equal groups in different ways—such as 2 groups of 3 or 3 groups of 2.

Circle equal groups.
Write the numbers.

1. 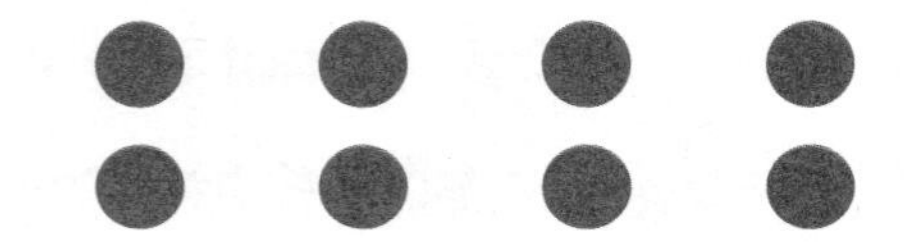

8 in all

_____ groups of _____

2. 

6 in all

_____ groups of _____

3. 

10 in all

_____ groups of _____

4. 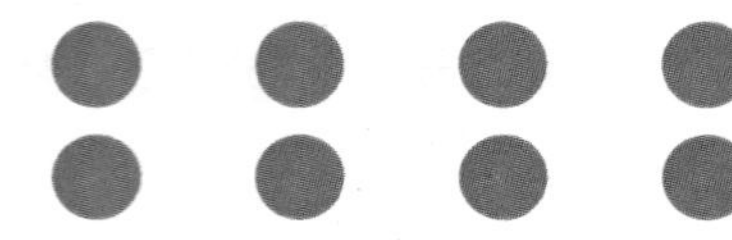

12 in all

_____ groups of _____

5.     

16 in all

_____ groups of _____

Problem Solving

Use counters to solve.

6. Travis has 10 slices of bread. He needs 2 slices to make a sandwich. How many sandwiches can he make?

_____ sandwiches

7. Maggie has 9 slices of bread. She needs 2 slices to make a sandwich. She wants to make 6 sandwiches. How many more slices does Maggie need?

_____ slices

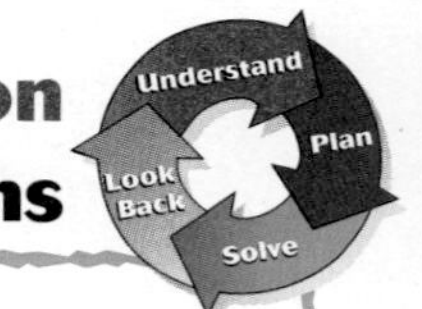

Name______________________________

Mrs. Brown asked the children in her class to pick their favorite kites. The pictograph shows how many children picked each kite.

Favorite Kites	(stick figure) = 2 children
Diamond	🧍 🧍 🧍 🧍 🧍
Delta	🧍 🧍 🧍
Box	🧍 🧍 🧍 🧍
Dragon	🧍

Use the graph to answer each question.

1. How many children picked each kite?

   _____ diamond kite　　_____ box kite

   _____ delta kite　　_____ dragon kite

2. How many more children picked the diamond kite than the box kite? _____ children

3. How many children picked the delta kite and the dragon kite? _____ children

4. How many children are in Mrs. Brown's class?

   _____ children

Home Connection Your child is learning to read and interpret a pictograph. Have your child explain the graph on this page.

Jason's class went on a class picnic. The chart shows the number of children who did each activity.

Children Doing Activities			
Flew kites	Ran races	Went hiking	Played soccer
4	8	6	10

1. Use the chart to make a pictograph.
   Draw 1 ☺ to show 2 children.

Children Doing Activities	☺ = 2 children
Flew kites	
Ran races	
Went hiking	
Played soccer	

Use the pictograph to answer each question.

2. How many more children played soccer than went hiking? _____ children

3. Suppose 12 children ran races.
   How many ☺ would you draw in all? _____

Critical Thinking Corner

Number Sense

Use the graph you made above.

4. What if 1 ☺ = 3 children?
   How many children flew kites? _____ children

Name________________________________ **Checkpoint**

Find each product.

1. 

$3 \times 2 =$ ____

2. 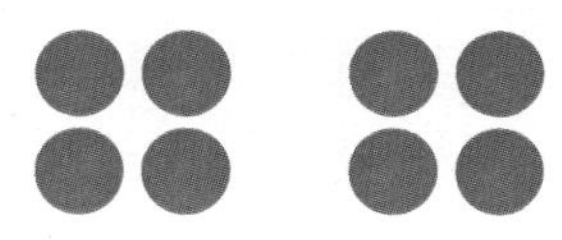

$4 \times 4 =$ ____

Write the missing numbers. Multiply.

3. 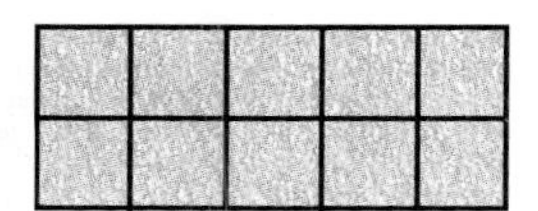

____ rows of ____

$2 \times 5 =$ ____

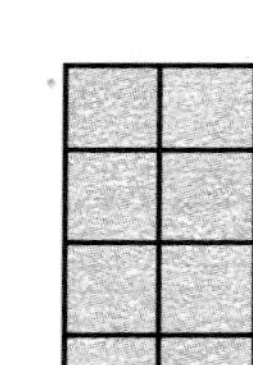

____ rows of ____

$5 \times 2 =$ ____

Draw circles to make equal groups.
Write the numbers.

4. 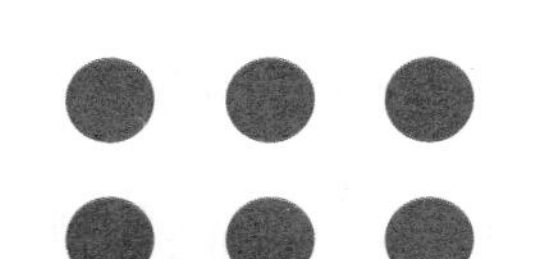

6 in all

____ groups of ____

5. 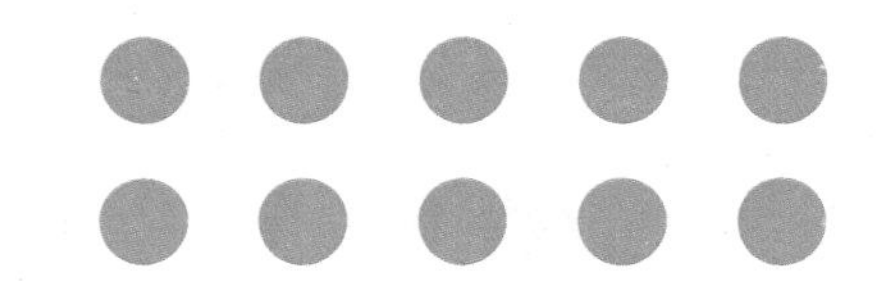

10 in all

____ groups of ____

Draw a picture to solve.
Write the answer.

6. There are 3 nests.
Each nest holds 3 birds.
How many birds are there?

____ birds

Name______________________________ **Extra Practice**

Pepper takes a flight over the city.
Find each product below.
Then draw to show what Pepper sees.

I need some help multiplying!

$3 \times 2 =$ ____ trees

$5 \times 3 =$ ____ flowers

$0 \times 5 =$ ____ bikes

$2 \times 6 =$ ____ cars

$4 \times 2 =$ ____ kites

$3 \times 1 =$ ____ people

Name________________________________ **Chapter Test**

Add. Then multiply.

1.

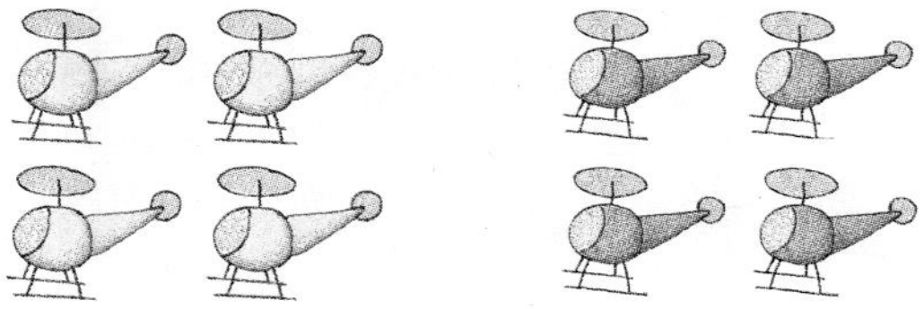

$4 + 4 =$ ____

$2 \times 4 =$ ____

2.

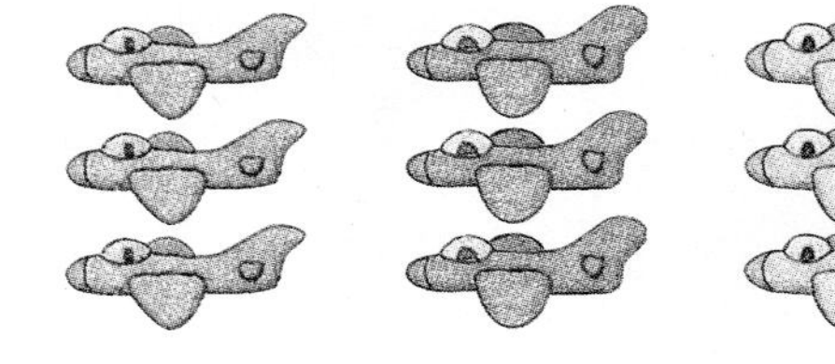

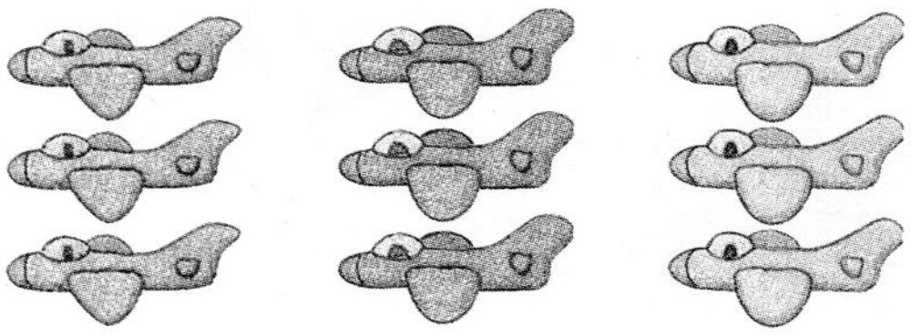

$3 + 3 + 3 =$ ____

$3 \times 3 =$ ____

Multiply across and down. Write the numbers.

3.

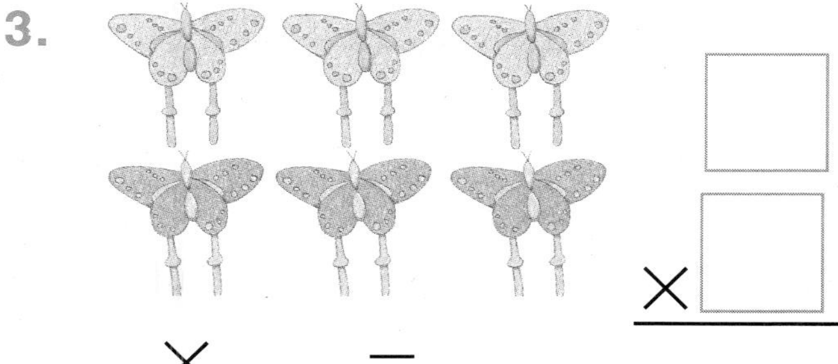

____ × ____ = ____

4.

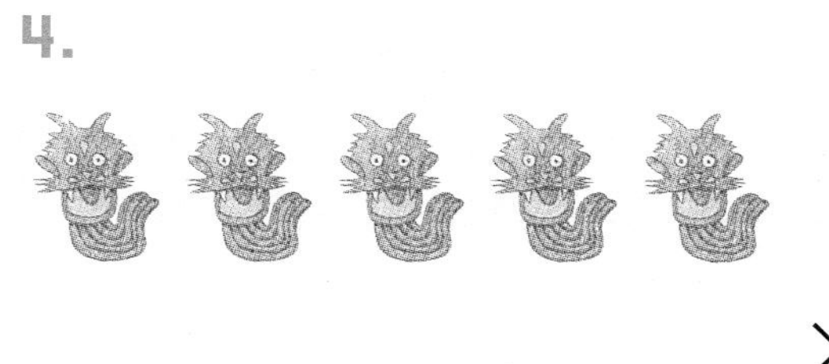

____ × ____ = ____

Circle equal groups.
Write the number in each group.

5.

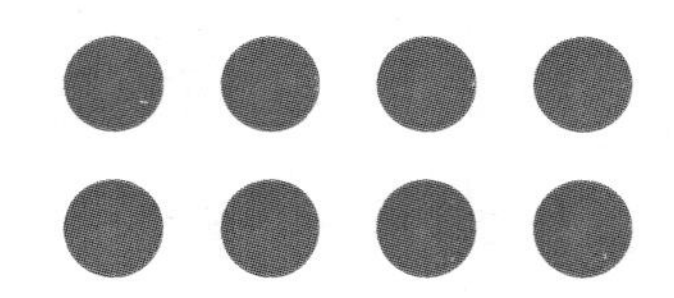

4 groups of ____

6.

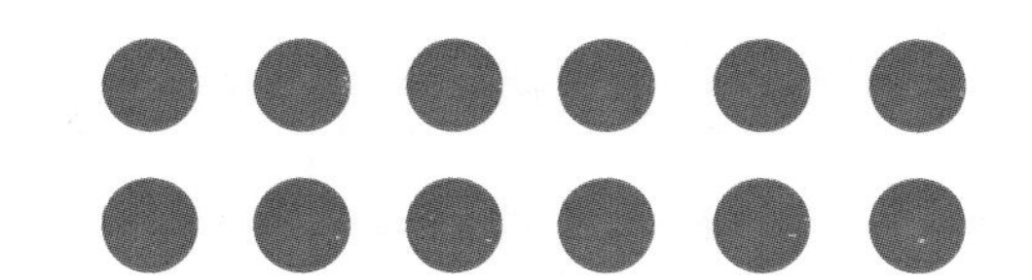

3 groups of ____

Use the graph to answer each question.

Helicopter Rides (1 helicopter = 2)	
Tina	 3 helicopters
Casey	 4 helicopters
Allen	 1 helicopter

7. How many helicopter rides did each child take?

Tina____ Casey____ Allen____

8. How many more rides did Casey have than Allen?

____rides

Name______________________________ **Performance Assessment**

What You Need

spinner

Workmat 6

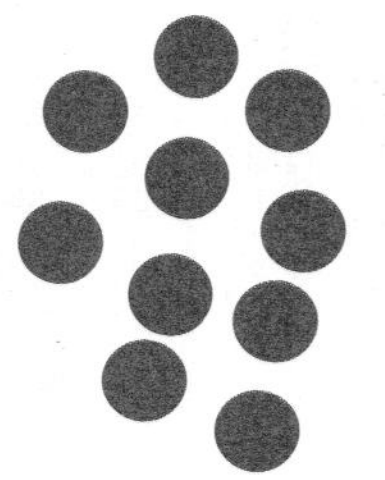

counters

1. Spin the spinner to find the number of groups. Record the number.
2. Spin again to find the number in each group. Record again.
3. Use counters to show the numbers.
4. Write the multiplication sentence.

	Number of Groups	Number in Each Group	Multiplication Sentence
1.			____ × ____ = ____
2.			____ × ____ = ____
3.			____ × ____ = ____
4.			____ × ____ = ____
5.			____ × ____ = ____
6.			____ × ____ = ____

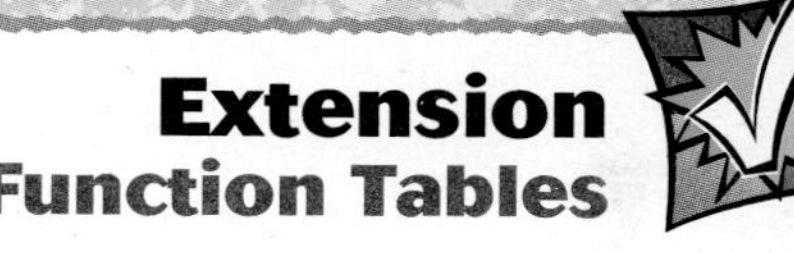

Name____

There are 2 wings on 1 airplane.

There are 14 wings on 7 airplanes.

Airplanes	1	2	3	4	5	6	7
Wings	2	4	6	8	10	12	14

Complete each chart.

1. There are 3 landing wheels on 1 plane.

Airplanes	1	2	3	4	5	6	7	8
Landing wheels	3							

2. There are 4 blades on 1 helicopter.

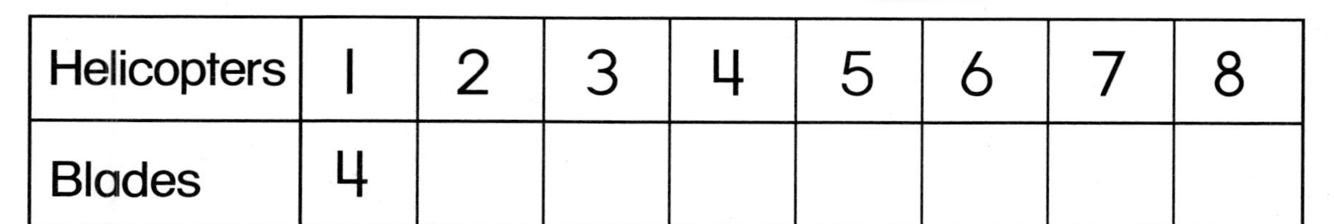

Helicopters	1	2	3	4	5	6	7	8
Blades	4							

3. One very light plane holds 5 gallons of fuel.

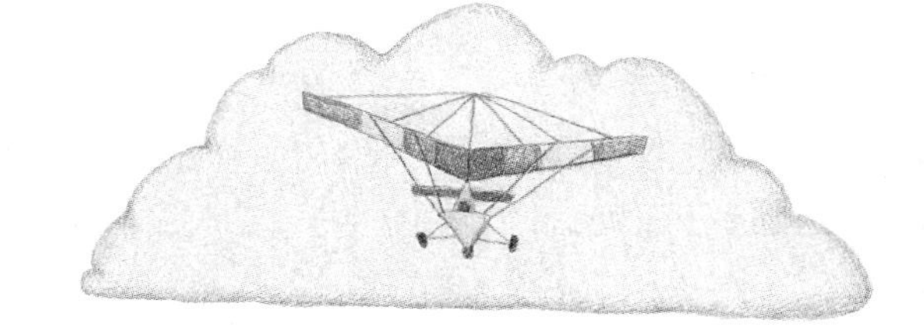

Very light planes	1	2	3	4	5	6	7	8
Gallons of fuel	5							

Name____________________

You can use the MathProcessor to multiply.

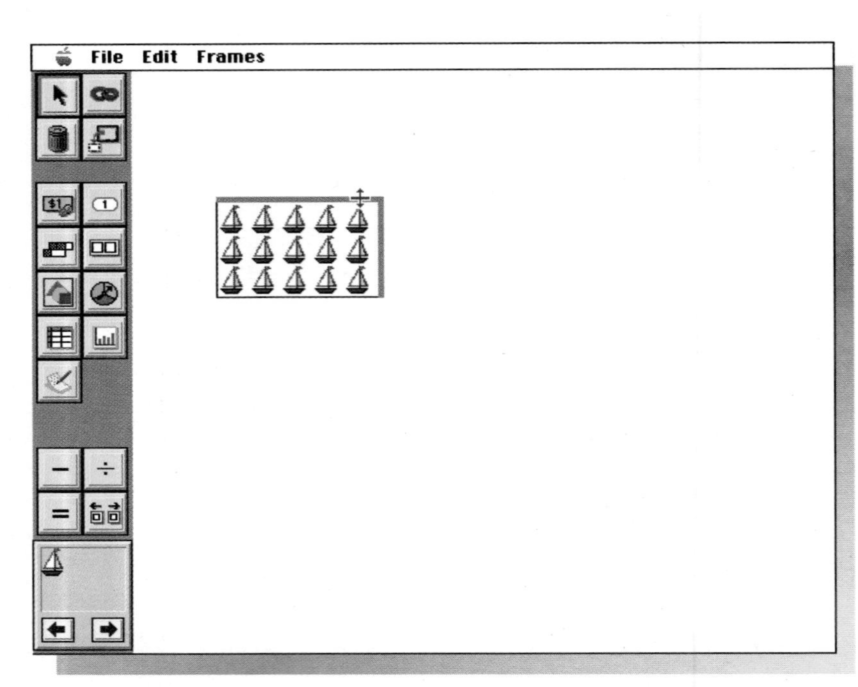

Work with a partner.

1. Click on the **frame button** to show a frame.

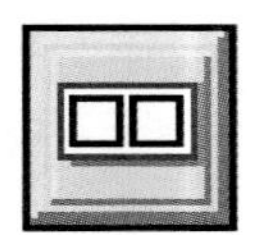

2. Click on the **arrow** to pick a picture. Then click on the **picture.**

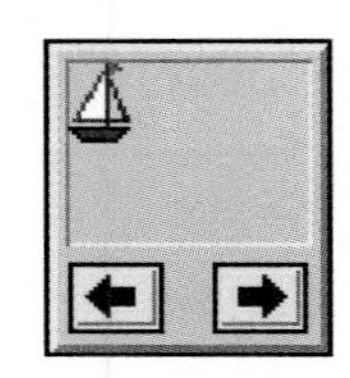

3. Click-and-drag the **right side of the frame** to make a row of 5.

4. Click-and-drag the **top of the frame** to make a column of 3. Find the product.

Use the MathProcessor to find each product.

1. $4 \times 5 =$ ____ $5 \times 2 =$ ____ $2 \times 1 =$ ____

2. $3 \times 3 =$ ____ $1 \times 5 =$ ____ $4 \times 3 =$ ____

Name______________________________

Fill in the ⬭ for the correct answer.

Add or subtract.

1. $8 + 9$
   - ⬭ 15
   - ⬭ 12
   - ⬭ 18
   - ⬭ 17

2. $15 - 7$
   - ⬭ 6
   - ⬭ 8
   - ⬭ 9
   - ⬭ 5

3. $32 + 41 + 5$
   - ⬭ 62
   - ⬭ 65
   - ⬭ 78
   - ⬭ 80

4. $63 + 19$
   - ⬭ 72
   - ⬭ 74
   - ⬭ 82
   - ⬭ 84

5. 55¢ − 24¢
   - ⬭ 21¢
   - ⬭ 29¢
   - ⬭ 30¢
   - ⬭ 31¢

6. 80¢ − 59¢
   - ⬭ 21¢
   - ⬭ 30¢
   - ⬭ 31¢
   - ⬭ 39¢

Use the clues to find the number.

7. • It is less than 70.
   • It is greater than 56.
   • It is odd.
   - ⬭ 76
   - ⬭ 59
   - ⬭ 48
   - ⬭ 64

Find the total amount.

8. 
   - ⬭ 51¢
   - ⬭ 60¢
   - ⬭ 71¢
   - ⬭ 76¢

9. 
   - ⬭ 80¢
   - ⬭ 75¢
   - ⬭ $1.00
   - ⬭ 60¢

Find the matching time.

10. 
   - ⬭ 2:30
   - ⬭ 2:35
   - ⬭ 3:35
   - ⬭ 7:10

How tall would the real object be?

11. 
   - ⬭ 3 inches
   - ⬭ 3 feet
   - ⬭ 3 yards

Find the number of corners and sides.

12. 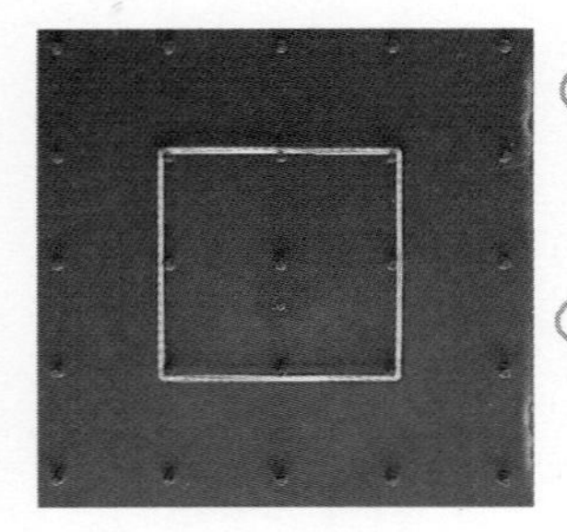

- ◯ 4 corners, 4 sides
- ◯ 4 corners, 2 sides

13. 

- ◯ 4 corners, 4 sides
- ◯ 5 corners, 5 sides

Find the fraction that names the shaded part or parts.

14. 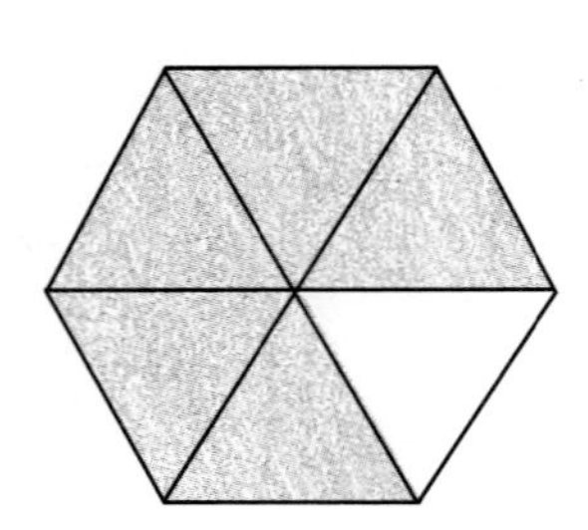

- ◯ $\frac{5}{6}$
- ◯ $\frac{4}{6}$
- ◯ $\frac{4}{5}$

15. 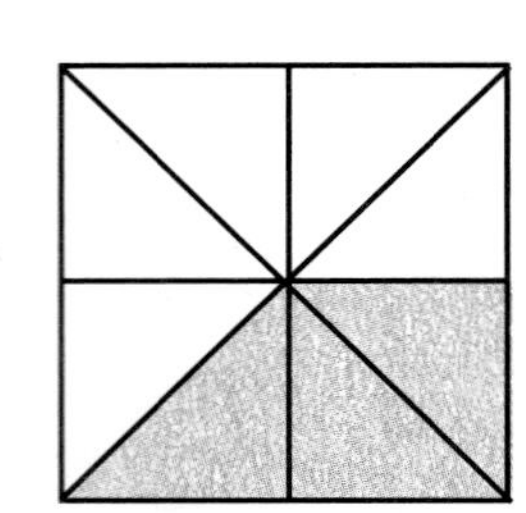

- ◯ $\frac{3}{6}$
- ◯ $\frac{3}{8}$
- ◯ $\frac{2}{8}$

Find the sum or difference.

16. $520 + 96$

- ◯ 516
- ◯ 616
- ◯ 636
- ◯ 708

17. $817 - 208$

- ◯ 609
- ◯ 619
- ◯ 625
- ◯ 715

18. $368 - 157$

- ◯ 161
- ◯ 201
- ◯ 211
- ◯ 261

Multiply.

19.   

$4 \times 5 =$ ____

- ◯ 12
- ◯ 15
- ◯ 16
- ◯ 20

Use the pictograph to find the answer.

Airplane Trips	✈ = 2
Matt	✈ ✈ ✈ ✈
Chris	✈ ✈ ✈

20. How many more airplane trips did Matt take than Chris?

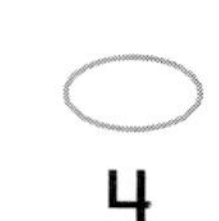

◯ 1 ◯ 2 ◯ 4 ◯ 7

Name____________________

add

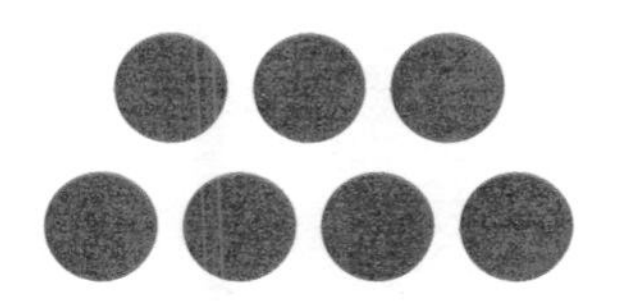

$7 + 2 = 9$

between

20, 21, 22

21 is between 20 and 22.

addend

$4 + 3 = 7$

addends

calendar

October						
S	M	T	W	T	F	S
			1	2	3	4
5	6	7	8	9	10	11
12	13	14	15	16	17	18
19	20	21	22	23	24	25
26	27	28	29	30	31	

addition sentence

$7 + 3 = 10$

cent

or

1¢ 1 cent

after

21, 22

22 is after 21.

centimeter (cm)

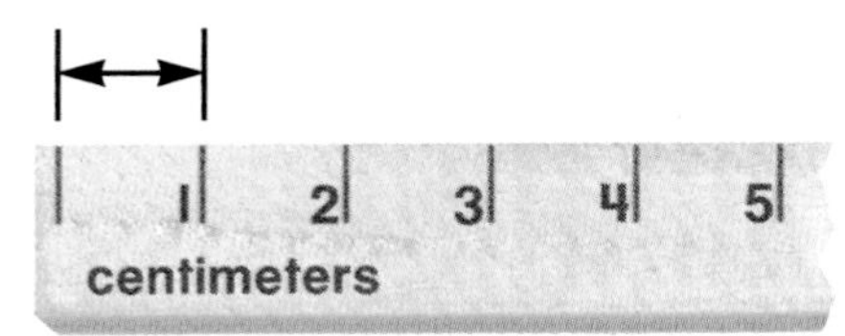

before

20, 21

20 is before 21.

circle

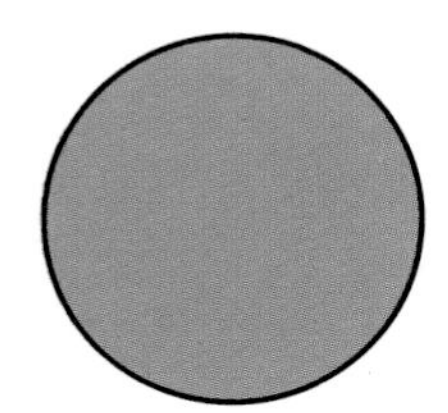

cone

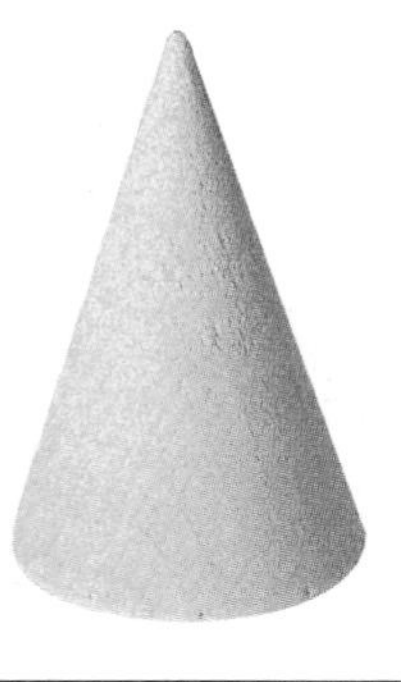

count back

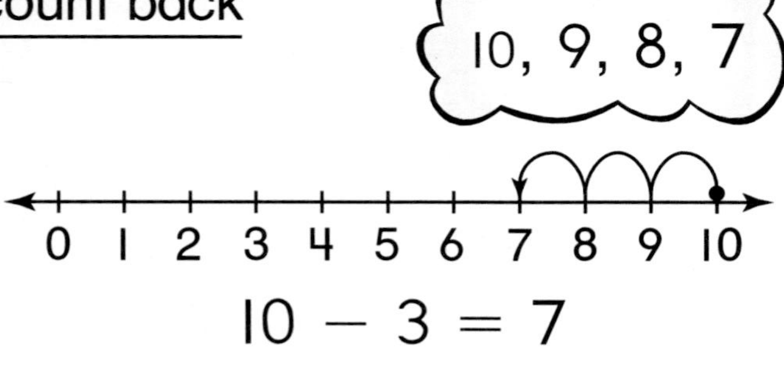

$10 - 3 = 7$

count on

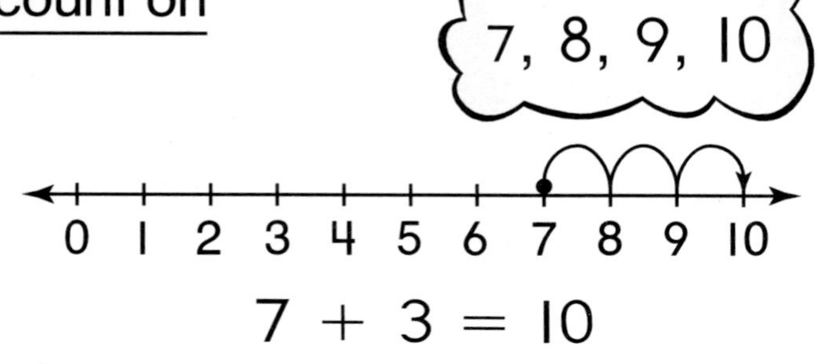

$7 + 3 = 10$

cube

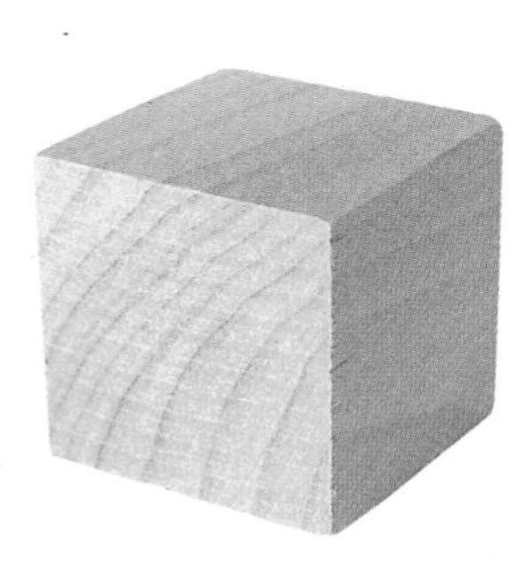

cup (c)

cylinder

decimeter (dm)

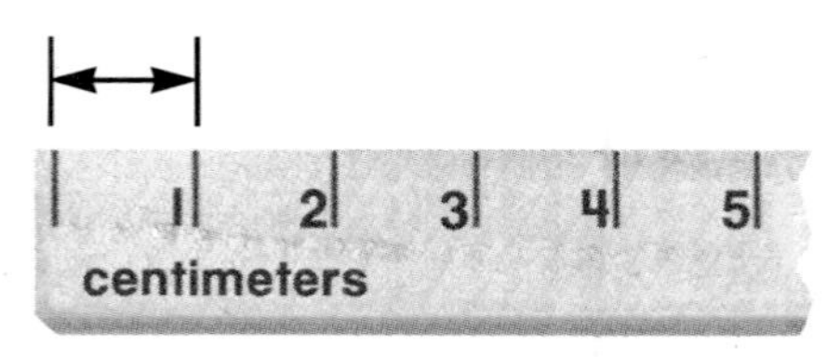

10 centimeters = 1 decimeter

difference

$8 - 3 = 5$

$$\begin{array}{r} 8 \\ -\ 3 \\ \hline 5 \end{array}$$

difference (5)

digit

digit ↓ 32 ↑ digit

32 has two digits.

dime

 or 

10¢ 10 cents

dollar

$100¢$ or $\$1.00$

double

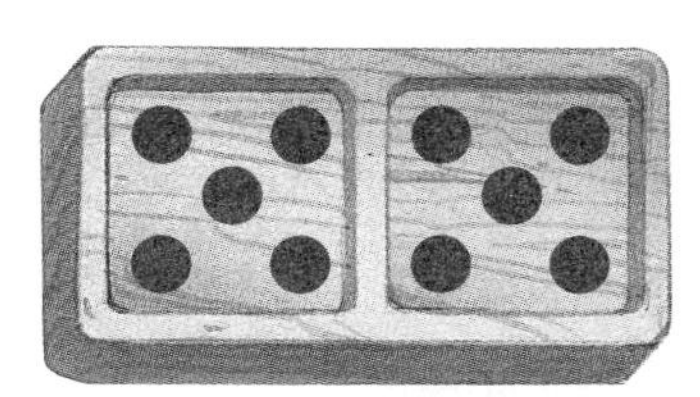

$5 + 5 = 10$

equals

$7 + 2 \overset{\downarrow}{=} 9$

estimate

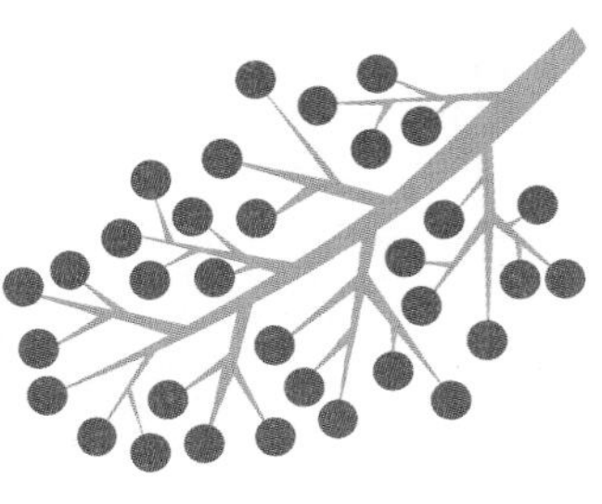

about 30 berries

even

2 4 6

fact family

$9 + 1 = 10$ $10 - 9 = 1$

$1 + 9 = 10$ $10 - 1 = 9$

foot (ft)

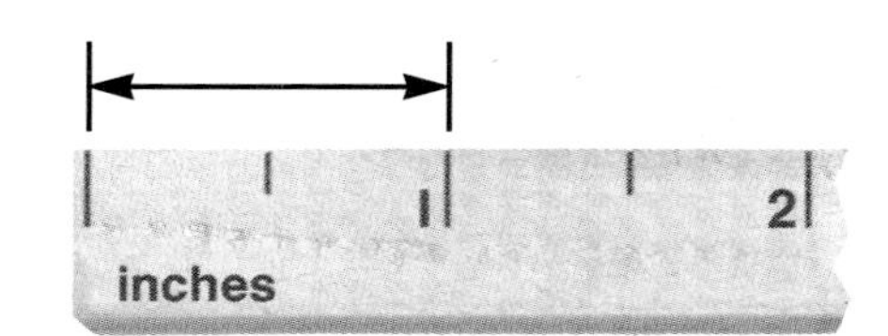

12 inches = 1 foot

fourths

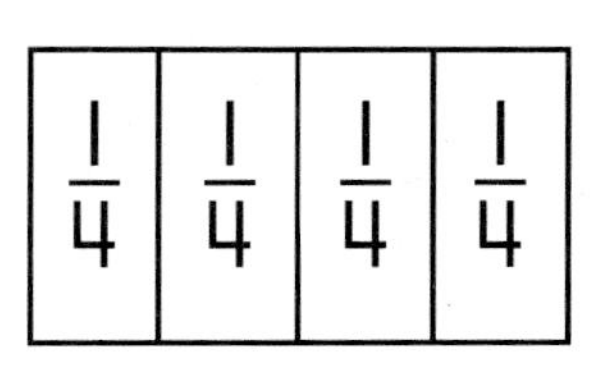

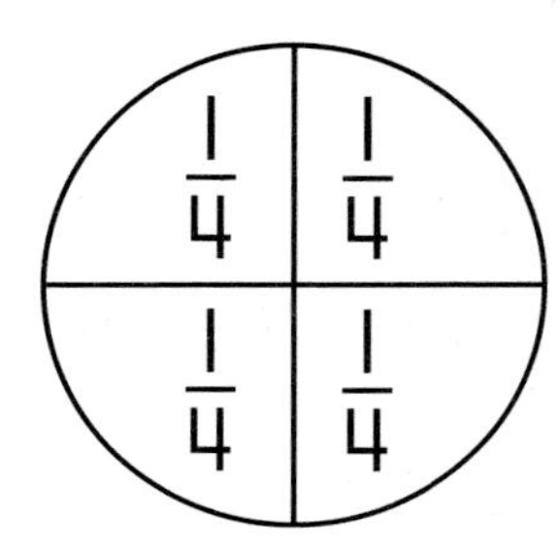

fraction

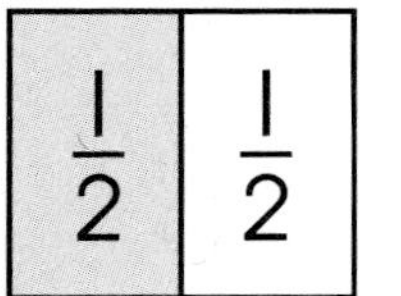

$\frac{1}{3}$ $\frac{1}{3}$ $\frac{1}{3}$

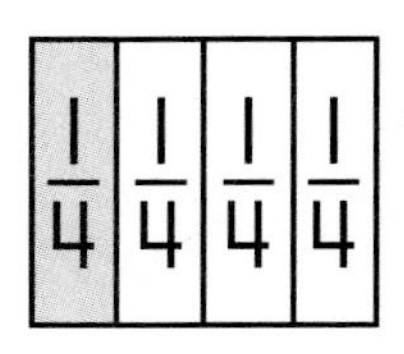

one half one third one fourth

gram (g)

A sheet of paper weighs about 1 gram.

greater than

52 > 48

52 is greater than 48.

half dollar

50¢ or 50 cents

halves

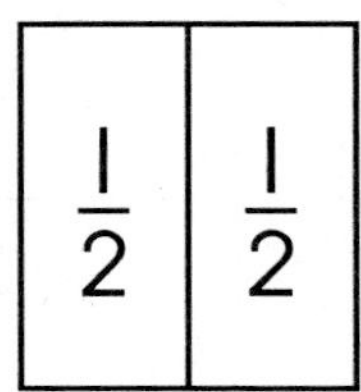

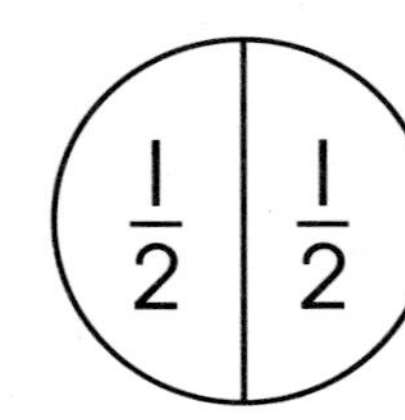

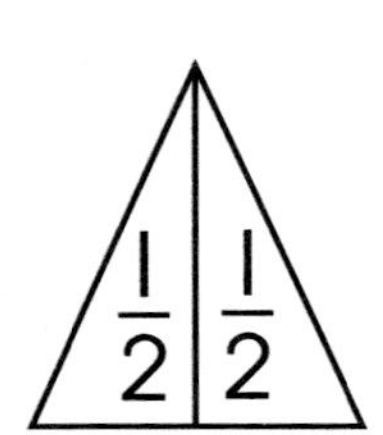

height

hour

It takes about an hour.

hour hand

hour hand

hundreds

2 hundreds

inch (in.)

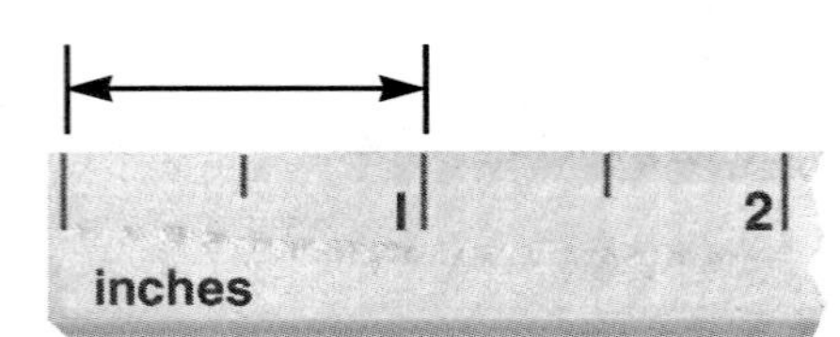

kilogram (kg)

It weighs about 1 kilogram.

length

less than

$47 < 48$

47 is less than 48.

line of symmetry

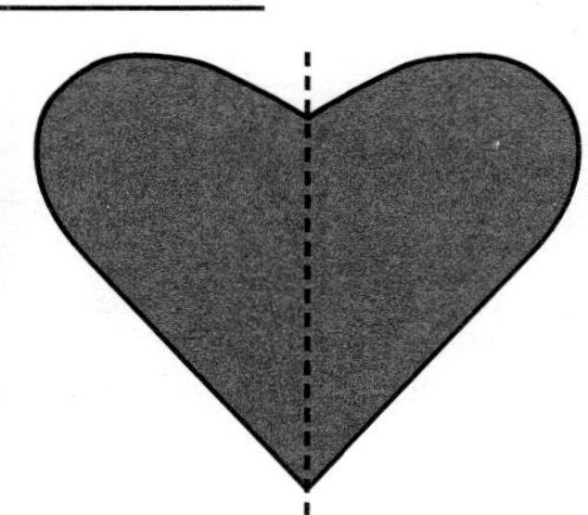

liter (L)

meter (m)

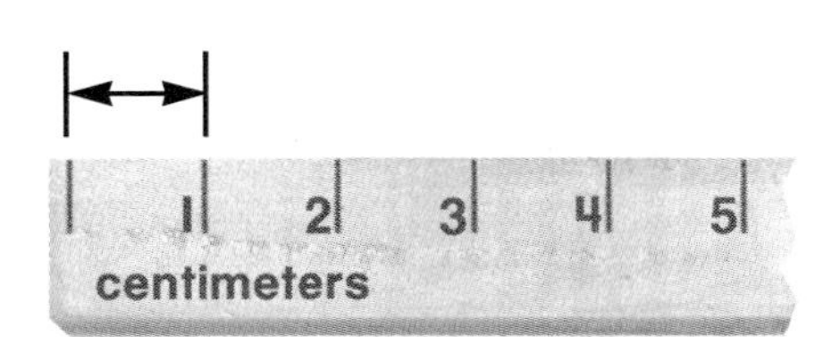

100 centimeters = 1 meter

minus

$10 - 2 = 8$

minute

It takes about a minute.

minute hand

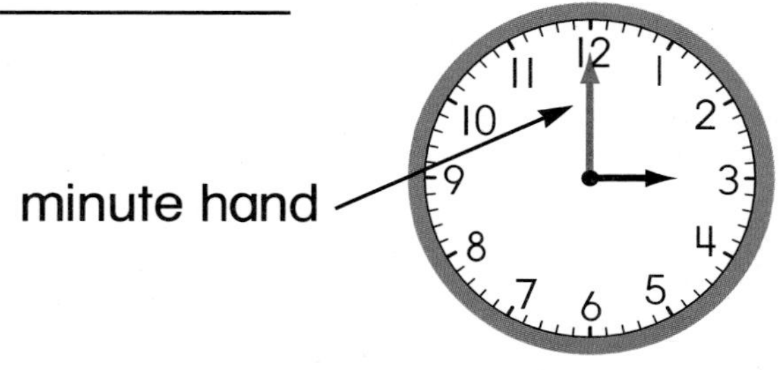

multiplication sentence

$4 \times 3 = 12$

multiply

$3 \times 2 = 6$

nickel

or

5¢ 5 cents

number line

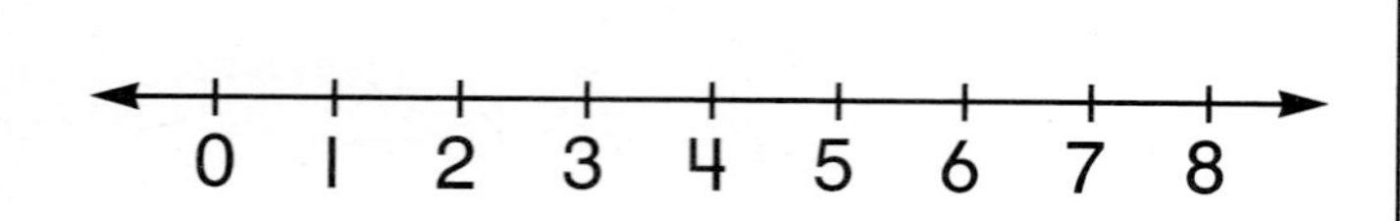

perimeter

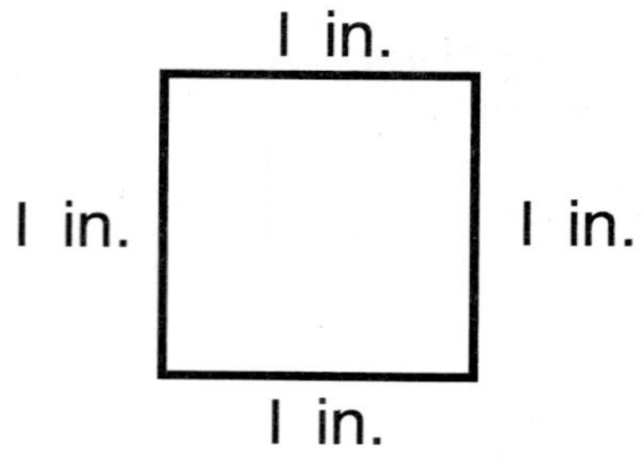

perimeter = 4 inches

odd

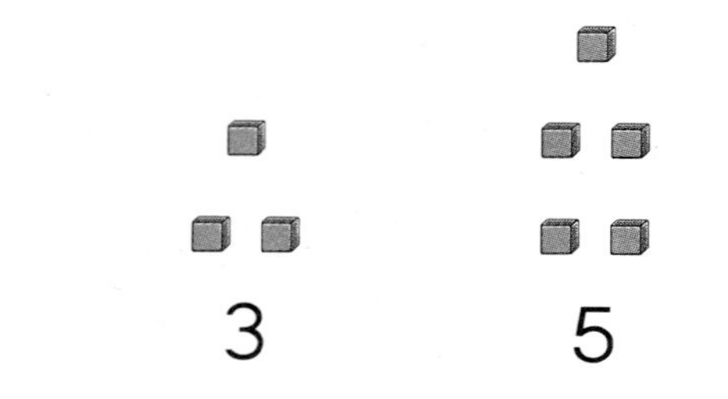

1 3 5

pint (pt)

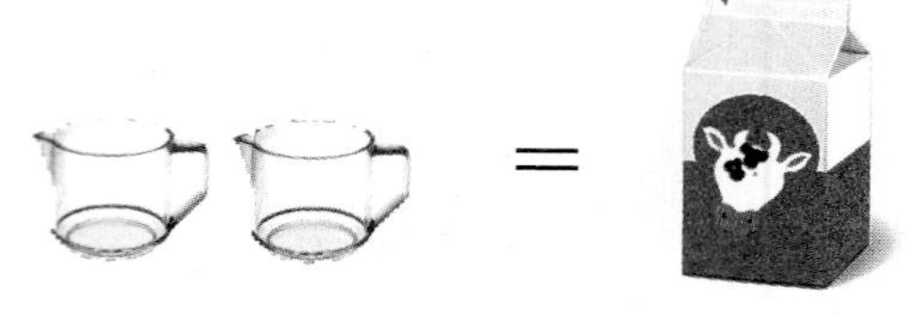

ones

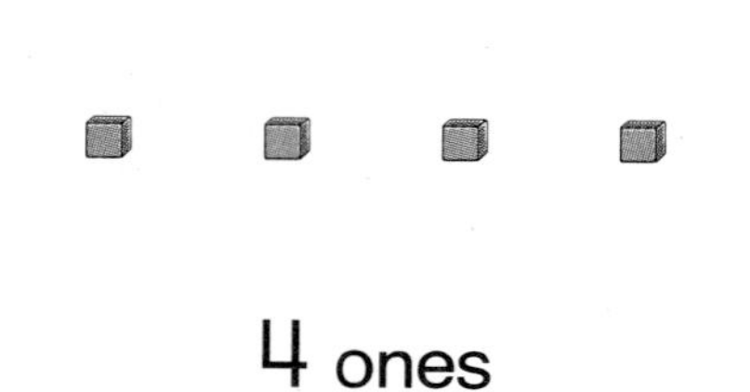

4 ones

plus

$$8 + 1 = 9$$

pattern

pound (lb)

The butter weighs about 1 pound.

penny

or

1¢ 1 cent

product

$$3 \times 2 = 6$$

$$\begin{array}{r} 3 \\ \times\ 2 \\ \hline 6 \end{array}$$

product

Name ____________________

pyramid

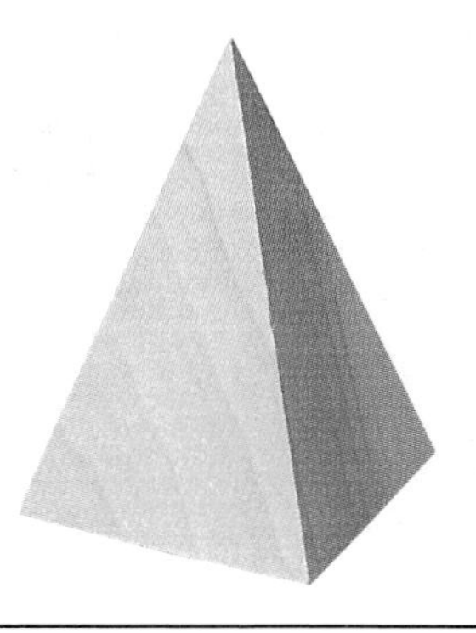

regroup

10 ones = 1 ten

quart (qt)

  = 

related facts

7 + 5 = 12

12 − 5 = 7

quarter

or

25¢ 25 cents

skip count

2 4 6 8 10

rectangle

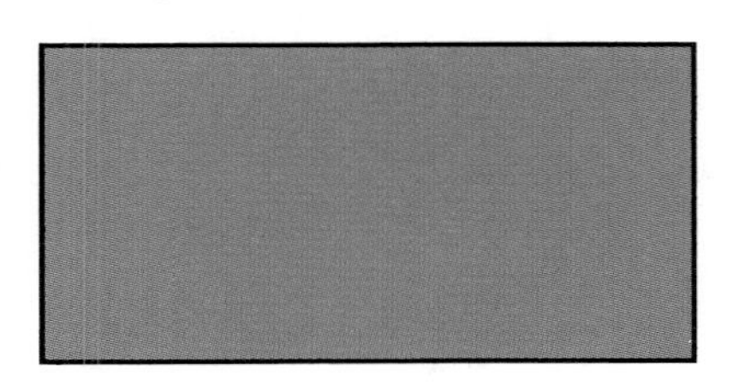

sphere

rectangular prism

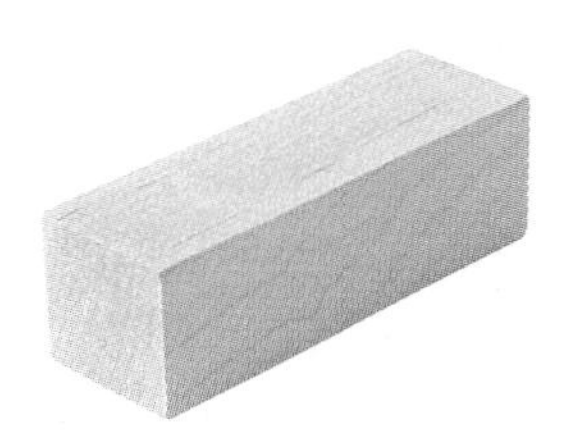

square

subtract

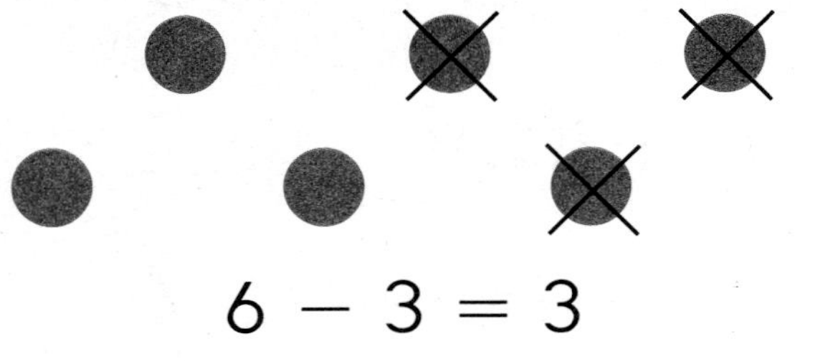

$6 - 3 = 3$

subtraction sentence

$12 - 6 = 6$

sum

$10 + 3 = 13$

$$\begin{array}{r} 10 \\ +\ 3 \\ \hline 13 \end{array}$$

sum

ten-frame

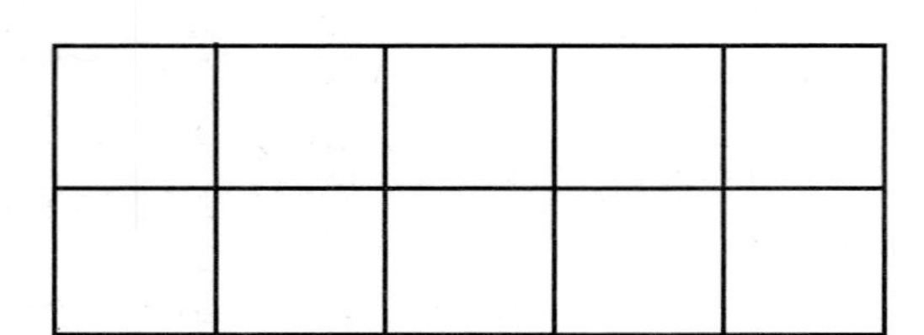

tens

3 tens

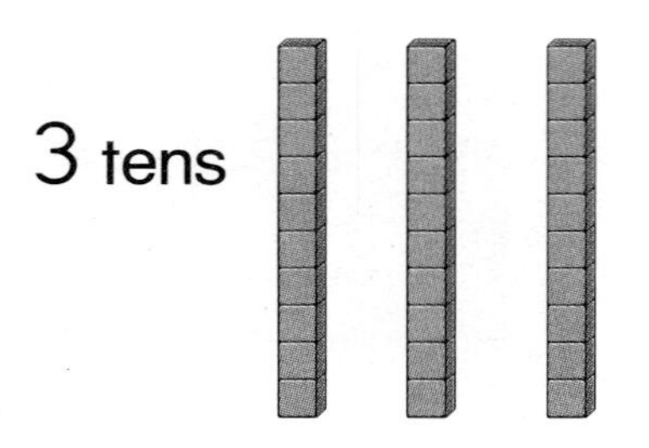

thirds

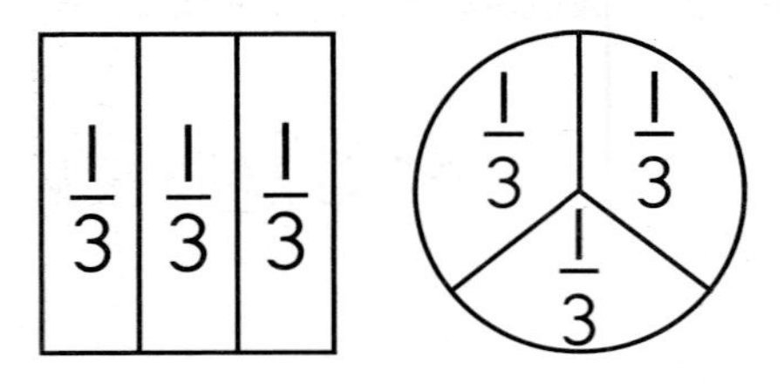

times

$2 \times 5 = 10$

triangle

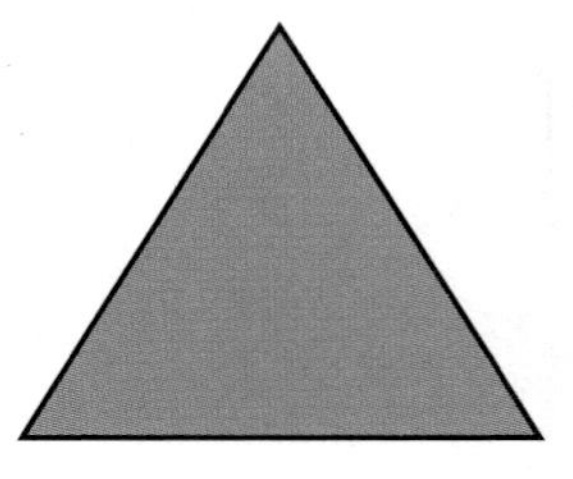

weight

yard (yd)

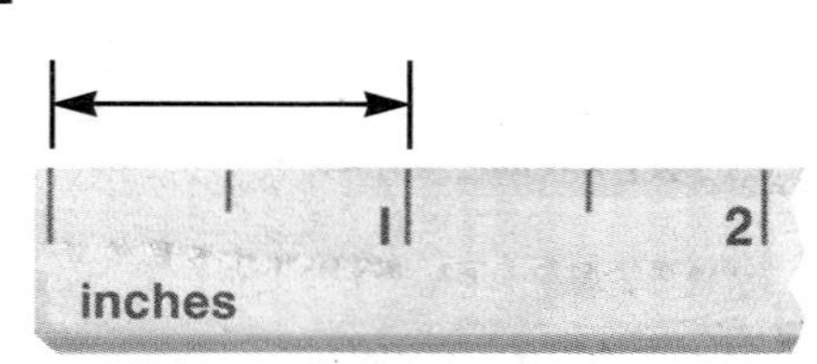

36 inches = 1 yard